Lecture Notes in Computer Science 16423

Founding Editors

Gerhard Goos
Juris Hartmanis

Editorial Board Members

Elisa Bertino, *Purdue University, West Lafayette, IN, USA*
Wen Gao, *Peking University, Beijing, China*
Bernhard Steffen, *TU Dortmund University, Dortmund, Germany*
Moti Yung, *Columbia University, New York, NY, USA*

The series Lecture Notes in Computer Science (LNCS), including its subseries Lecture Notes in Artificial Intelligence (LNAI) and Lecture Notes in Bioinformatics (LNBI), has established itself as a medium for the publication of new developments in computer science and information technology research, teaching, and education.

LNCS enjoys close cooperation with the computer science R & D community, the series counts many renowned academics among its volume editors and paper authors, and collaborates with prestigious societies. Its mission is to serve this international community by providing an invaluable service, mainly focused on the publication of conference and workshop proceedings and postproceedings. LNCS commenced publication in 1973.

Christos Zaroliagis · Dinabandhu Bhandari ·
Prosenjit Gupta · Swagatam Das
Editors

Applied Algorithms

Third International Conference, ICAA 2026
Kolkata, India, January 7–9, 2026
Proceedings

 Springer

Editors
Christos Zaroliagis
University of Patras
Patras, Greece

Prosenjit Gupta
Heritage Institute of Technology
Kolkata, West Bengal, India

Dinabandhu Bhandari
Heritage Institute of Technology
Kolkata, West Bengal, India

Swagatam Das
Indian Statistical Institute
Kolkata, West Bengal, India

ISSN 0302-9743   ISSN 1611-3349 (electronic)
Lecture Notes in Computer Science
ISBN 978-3-032-15620-4   ISBN 978-3-032-15621-1 (eBook)
https://doi.org/10.1007/978-3-032-15621-1

This Springer imprint is published by the registered company Springer Nature Switzerland AG
The registered company address is: Gewerbestrasse 11, 6330 Cham, Switzerland

If disposing of this product, please recycle the paper.

Preface

This volume contains papers accepted for presentation at the International Conference on Applied Algorithms (ICAA 2026), held at the Heritage Institute of Technology, Kolkata, India from January 7 to January 9, 2026. Additionally, it includes abstracts of 7 invited lectures given by Partha Bhowmick (Indian Institute of Technology, Kharagpur, India), Samarjit Chakrabarty (University of North Carolina at Chapel Hill, USA), Gautam Das (University of Texas at Arlington, USA), Swagatam Das (Indian Statistical Institute, Kolkata, India), John Iacono (Université libre de Bruxelles, Belgium), Subhamoy Maitra (Indian Statistical Institute, Kolkata, India), and Kurt Mehlhorn (Max Planck Institute for Informatics, Germany).

ICAA strives to offer a forum for researchers in applied algorithms. The conference welcomes original work on the design, analysis, implementation, and experimental evaluation of efficient algorithms and data structures aimed at solving practical, real-world problems. Submissions may highlight novel algorithmic strategies, computational techniques, innovative real-world applications, or case studies demonstrating how algorithms effectively address complex challenges. Papers were sought in two tracks: Discrete Algorithms and Applications (Track A), and AI and Machine Learning (Track B).

In response to the call for papers, 92 submissions were received from authors in 9 countries. The Program Committee, consisting of 77 members from 15 countries, selected 33 full papers for presentation. The Program Committee was assisted by 49 external reviewers in arriving at their decisions. Each paper was reviewed in a single-blind process by an average of 3 reviewers.

We would like to thank all those who submitted papers to ICAA 2026, and the program committee members and the external reviewers for their support in the process. Also thanks to all the invited speakers for readily agreeing to deliver their talks and helping us put together a quality program. Special thanks to the Steering Committee members for their valuable guidance and suggestions. We would like to especially thank the management of Heritage Institute of Technology and Kalyan Bharathi Trust for their generous support and precious advice in hosting the conference. Last but not least, the entire Organizing Committee at Heritage Institute of Technology provided continuous support in all spheres to make the conference a success.

Christos Zaroliagis
Dinabandhu Bhandari
Prosenjit Gupta
Swagatam Das

Organization

Advisors

H. K. Chaudhary (Chairman)	Kalyan Bharati Trust, Kolkata, India
P. R. Agarwala (Chairman, Board of Governors)	Heritage Institute of Technology, Kolkata, India
P. K. Agarwal (CEO)	Kalyan Bharati Trust, Kolkata, India
Basab Chaudhuri (Principal)	Heritage Institute of Technology, Kolkata, India
Sujit K. Barua (Registrar)	Heritage Institute of Technology, Kolkata, India
Souvik Bhattacharyya (Principal Advisor, Higher Education)	Kalyan Bharati Trust, Kolkata, India
Amitava Bagchi (Former Professor)	Heritage Institute of Technology, Kolkata, India

Steering Committee Chairs

Bhargab B. Bhattacharya	Indian Statistical Institute, Kolkata, India
Sandeep Sen	Ashoka University, India

General Chair

Subhashis Majumder	Heritage Institute of Technology, Kolkata, India

Program Committee Co-chairs

Christos Zaroliagis	University of Patras, Greece
Dinabandhu Bhandari	Heritage Institute of Technology, Kolkata, India
Prosenjit Gupta	Heritage Institute of Technology, Kolkata, India
Swagatam Das	Indian Statistical Institute, Kolkata, India

Organizing Chair

Diganta Sengupta	Heritage Institute of Technology, Kolkata, India

Finance Chair

Manoj Saraogi — Kalyan Bharati Trust, Kolkata, India

Publicity Chairs

Nilanjana G. Basu — Heritage Institute of Technology, Kolkata, India
Sabyasachee Banerjee — Heritage Institute of Technology, Kolkata, India

Registration Chairs

Poulami Das — Heritage Institute of Technology, Kolkata, India
Pratyusa Dash — Heritage Institute of Technology, Kolkata, India

Program Committee

Track A: Discrete Algorithms and Applications

Akash Agrawal — Meta, Menlo Park, USA
Amitava Mukherjee — BITS Pilani Dubai, UAE
Ananda S. Das — Alcon Solutions, India
Aniruddha Dasgupta — Bluebell Research, Australia
Anup K. Sen — Heritage Institute of Technology, Kolkata, India
Arijit Bishnu — ISI Kolkata, India
Arijit Karati — National Sun Yat-sen University, Taiwan
Bhaskar Dasgupta — University of Illinois Chicago, USA
Bruhadeshwar Bezawada — South Arkansas University, USA
Christos Zaroliagis (Co-chair) — University of Patras, Greece
Daniele Frigioni — University of L'Aquila, Italy
Debasish Jana — Heritage Institute of Technology, India
Deeksha Arya — University of Tokyo, Japan
Deepika Prakash — JK Lakshmipat University, India
Elisavet Konstantinou — University of the Aegean, Greece
G. B. Mund — KIIT Bhubaneswar, India
Gautam Das — University of Texas, Arlington, USA
Ioannis Chatzigiannakis — Sapienza University of Rome, Italy
Md. Anul Haq — Majmaah University, Saudi Arabia
Michiel Smid — Carleton University, Canada

Nilanjana G. Basu	Heritage Institute of Technology, India
Othon Michail	University of Liverpool, UK
Partha Bhowmick	IIT Kharagpur
Prosenjit Gupta (Co-chair)	Heritage Institute of Technology, India
Ravi Janardan	University of Minnesota, USA
S. K. Venkatesan	CQRL Bits LLP, India
Sabyasachee Banerjee	Heritage Institute of Technology, India
Saladi Rahul	IISc Bangalore, India
Samarjit Chakrabarty	University of North Carolina at Chapel Hill, USA
Sharath Raghvendra	North Carolina State University, USA
Spyros Kontogiannis	University of Patras, Greece
Subhajit Datta	Heritage Institute of Technology, Kolkata, India
Subhamoy Maitra	ISI Kolkata, India
Subhas C. Nandy	ISI Kolkata, India
Subhashis Majumder	Heritage Institute of Technology, Kolkata, India
Suman Sanyal	Goa Institute of Management, India
Trupil Limbasiya	Desay SV Automotive, Singapore
Uros Cibej	University of Ljubljana, Slovenia
Wing-Kai Hon	National Tsing Hua University, Taiwan

Track B: AI and Machine Learning

Anagha Joshi	University of Bergen, Norway
Anindya Halder	North-Eastern Hill University, India
Anirban Dasgupta	IIT Guwahati
Anupam Ghosh	Netaji Subhash Engineering College, India
Anurina Tarafdar	Heritage Institute of Technology, Kolkata, India
Arkajyoti Saha	University of California, Irvine, USA
B. K. Panigrahi	IIT Delhi
B. Uma Shankar	ISI, Kolkata
Carlos A. Coello Coello	Cinvestav, Mexico
Deba Prasad Mandal	ISI, Kolkata, India
Debashis Sen	IIT, Kharagpur
Debranjan Sarkar	Heritage Institute of Technology, India
Diganta Sengupta	Heritage Institute of Technolog, India
Haider Banka	IIT, Dhanbad
Hisao Ishibuchi	Southern University of Science and Technology, China
Ivan Zelinka	VSB TU Ostrava, Czech Republic
Jugal Kalita	University of Colorado, Colorado Springs, USA
Mandar Mitra	ISI, Kolkata
Nabendu Chaki	Calcutta University

Nikhil R. Pal	ISI Kolkata, India
Nishchal Verma	IIT Kanpur, India
Paramartha Dutta	Visvabharati University, India
Partha Basuchowdhuri	IACS Kolkata, India
Poulami Das	Heritage Institute of Technology, Kolkata, India
Pradipta Maji	ISI Kolkata, India
Rajat K. De	ISI Kolkata, India
Rammohan Mallipeddi	Kyungpook National University, South Korea
Rituparna Chaki	Calcutta University, India
Roman Šenkeřík	Thomas Bata University, Czech Republic
Sanjay Saha	Jadavpur University, India
Sankha S. Mullick	Dolby, India
Somdatta Chakraborty	Maulana Abul Kalam Azad University of Technology, India
Subhrajit Roy	Google DeepMind, India
Sujay Saha	Heritage Institute of Technology, Kolkata, India
Suman Kundu	IIT, Jodhpur, India
Swarup K. Roy	Tezpur University, India
Tanmay Basu	Indian Institute of Science Education and Research Bhopal, India
Tom Luk R. Michoel	University of Bergen, Norway
Utpal Roy	Visvabharati University, India

Additional Reviewers

Abdullah Almethen	Qassim University, Saudi Arabia
Abhijit Dasgupta	SRM-AP University, India
Adrija Bhattacharya	Vellore Institute of Technology, India
Amritendu Dhar	IISc Bangalore, India
Anil Bag	Heritage Institute of Technology, Kolkata, India
Anindita Kundu	Vellore Institute of Technology, India
Anindya Sen	Heritage Institute of Technology, Kolkata, India
Anirban Sengupta	Sujosu Technology, India
Anish Chakrabarty	Indian Statistical Institute, Kolkata, India
Apratim Chakraborty	TCG Crest, Kolkata, India
Arghya Pratidar	Indian Statistical Institute, Kolkata, India
Arkaprabha Basu	Indian Statistical Institute, Kolkata, India
Arpita Talukdar	Heritage Institute of Technology, Kolkata, India
Bhaskar Pramanik	Indian Statistical Institute, Kolkata, India
Biswajit Sarkar	Variable Energy Cyclotron Centre, India
Chandreyee Chowdhury	Jadavpur University, India

Debamita Acharjya	Indian Statistical Institute, Kolkata, India
Debanjan Dutta	Indian Statistical Institute, Kolkata, India
Deblina Chowdhuri	Heritage Institute of Technology, Kolkata, India
Dipankar Kundu	SRM-AP University, India
Duncan Adamson	University of St. Andrews, UK
Indranil Ojha	Indian Statistical Institute, Kolkata, India
Jhalak Dutta	Heritage Institute of Technology, Kolkata, India
Joydeep Das	Heritage Academy, India
Kartick Chandra Mondal	Jadavpur University, India
Kushal Bose	Indian Statistical Institute, Kolkata, India
Minakshi Banerjee	RCC Institute of Information Technology, India
Nilina Bera	Heritage Institute of Technology, Kolkata, India
Partha Pratim Roy	IIT Dhanbad, India
Piyali Datta	Institute of Engineering & Management, Kolkata, India
Prasun Dutta	SRM-AP University, India
Pratyusha Dash	Heritage Institute of Technology, Kolkata, India
Priyobrata Mondal	Indian Statistical Institute, Kolkata, India
Rajarshi Pal	Bandhan Bank, India
Reshma Roychoudhuri	Heritage Institute of Technology, Kolkata, India
Rituparna Sinha	Heritage Institute of Technology, Kolkata, India
Sabyasachi Chatterjee	Heritage Institute of Technology, Kolkata, India
Saikat Bandopadhyay	Netaji Subhas Engineering College, India
Sandip Samaddar	Heritage Institute of Technology, Kolkata, India
Sanjoy Chowdhuri	University of Maryland, College Park, USA
Satabdi Barman	Heritage Institute of Technology, Kolkata, India
Shilpi Saha	Heritage Institute of Technology, Kolkata, India
Smritikona Barai	Heritage Institute of Technology, Kolkata, India
Soumya Sen	Calcutta University, India
Suman Saha	Jaypee University Anoopshahr, India
Sumon Ghosh	Heritage Institute of Technology, Kolkata, India
Sunirmal Khatua	Calcutta University, India
Surojit Saha	University of Utah, USA
Swarup Chattopadhyay	XIM University, India

Organizing Committee

(From Heritage Institute of Technology, Kolkata, India)
Amitabha Acharya
Anup Kumar Sen
Anurina Tarafdar

Arindam Chatterjee
Aritra Saha
Debasish Jana
Debranjan Sarkar
Jhalak Dutta
Kamal Podder
Reshma Roychoudhuri
Sandip Samaddar
Saswati Naskar
Satabdi Barman
Shilpi Saha
Smritikona Barai
Somak Sen
Somenath Sengupta
Susobhan Baidya
Abhijit Sinha
Anirban Manna
Ankur Roy
Avijit Dutta
Debalina Sengupta
Debasish Sarkar
Deepsikha Chaudhury
Sanchayita Sarkar
Sudipta Chakrabarty
Sujoy Kumar Dasgupta
Surajit Acharya
Tarak Nath Bhowmick
Viswayani Chowdhury

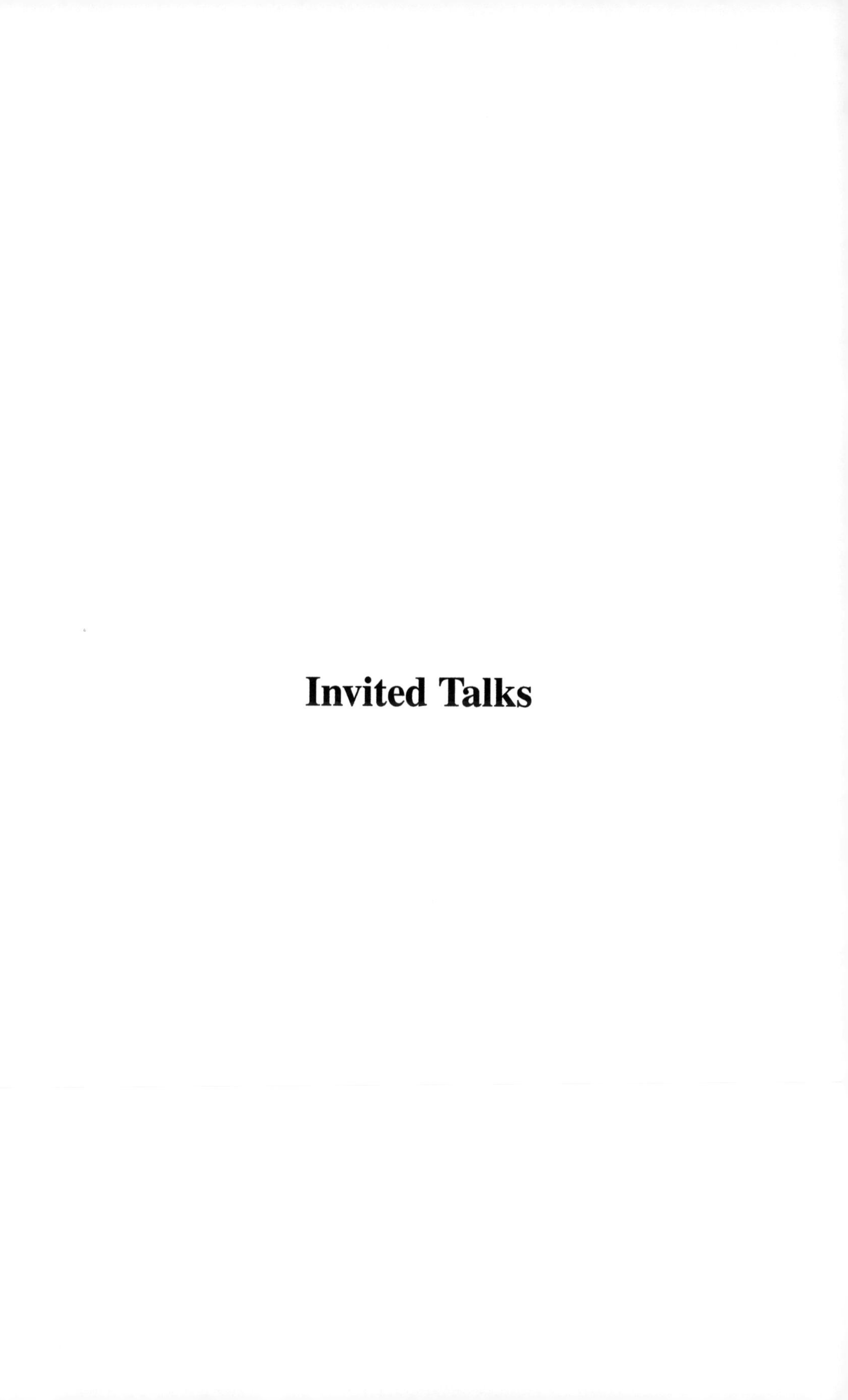

Invited Talks

Algorithmic Art: A Lost Glory and its Digital Renaissance

Partha Bhowmick

IIT Kharagpur
pb@cse.iitkgp.ac.in
https://cse.iitkgp.ac.in/~pb/

Abstract. Algorithmic art transcends time and geography. It is a universal rhythm that has quietly pulsed through human creativity for millennia. From the precise geometry of Vedic altars and the sacred mandalas of the Upanishads to the patterned mosaics of ancient Europe, every civilization once celebrated the harmony between mathematics and art. India – known worldwide as a cradle of art and culture, with its boundless artistic and spiritual heritage was once a luminous center of this tradition. But alas, the land that birthed algorithmic imagination seems to have let its glory fade amid modern abstraction. Across the world, however, the pulse continues – revived through TSP art, Voronoi patterns, Digital Circlism, Generative Mandalas, and beyond. This talk journeys through that continuum – from Vedic algorithms to digital pixels, revealing how ancient intelligence finds new life in today's computational creativity, reuniting logic and beauty, machine and mind, tradition and tomorrow.

Perfectly Imperfect Autonomy and Machine Learning

Samarjit Chakraborty[1,2]

[1] The University of North Carolina at Chapel Hill, USA
[2] TU Munich Institute for Advanced Study, Germany

In this talk we argue that in contrast to prevalent practice, autonomous systems [1, 6] should not be engineered by insisting every component (schedulers, controllers, machine learning modules, sensors, etc.) behave "*perfectly.*" Instead, designers should start from a system-level safety specification that includes an explicit tolerance margin—a "*safety pipe*"—around the ideal behavior of the system. Such ideal behaviors may be modeled by the desired dynamics or the closed-loop trajectory of the autonomous system (plant + controller) in a chosen state space. As long as the actual trajectory stays within this safety pipe, components are allowed (and can even be designed) to be imperfect—missing occasional deadlines, making approximate inferences, or sensing noisily—thereby saving cost and resources without compromising safety.

To operationalize this idea, we will discuss how to derive allowable component behaviors in an autonomous cyber-physical system—consisting of controllers [10], machine learning components, real-time components, schedulers and various sensors—and from a specified system-level safety pipe [14]. Towards this, we will provide multiple examples. For timing [12, 11, 21], we will encode patterns of allowed deadline hits/misses as regular languages over an alphabet $\{0, 1\}$, where 0 denotes a control task missing its deadline or where a control input is purposely not computed and instead an old control input is applied to save computational resources, and 1 denotes that a control input is computed in a timely fashion [8]. We use approximate reachability analysis to check that all closed-loop trajectories under a chosen regular language of deadline hit/miss pattern remain inside the safety pipe. Accepted patterns are accumulated into a regular language, captured as an automaton, and used to synthesize multi-controller schedules [25–27] that intentionally miss deadlines to save computation, yet guarantee specified system-level safety [9, 30].

Next, we will discuss safety-driven approaches to *sizing* deep neural networks (DNNs). The goal is to purposely design small, imperfect DNNs, used for state estimation inside autonomous systems, in contrast to the prevailing practice of maximizing each model's inference accuracy in isolation. Such small but imperfect DNNs can fit inside resource-constrained graphics processing units (GPUs) available in autonomous systems or edge devices like cars, robots or drones [28]. We again start from the closed-loop dynamics of the autonomous system $\dot{x} = f(x, g(\hat{x}))$ and define safety as a bound on the deviation between the "ideal" trajectory (with perfect state x) and the realized trajectory (with estimated state $\hat{x}$). Here, f captures the continuous-time nonlinear dynamics of the system being controlled (the "plant") and $g(x)$ is the control policy or feedback controller, which maps the system's current state to an actuation command. The system is unsafe if $\|\hat{\xi}(t) - \xi(t)\| > d$ for a chosen threshold d, where $\xi(t)$ denotes the trajectory of the ideal closed-loop system, in which the controller has access to the true state x and $\hat{\xi}(t)$ represents the trajectory of the actual system, when the controller relies on estimated states $\hat{x}$ (e.g., inferred by DNNs) rather than true states that may be returned by perfect DNNs.

To allocate a fixed GPU budget across multiple perception DNNs in the autonomous system, where each DNN is responsible for estimating a different component of the state, we linearize the dynamics by expanding $f(x, g(x + \delta x))$ and obtain $\dot{x} = (A + B\delta x)x$, where δx represents the estimation error (or uncertainty) in the state perceived by the system—that is, the difference between the estimated state (produced by a DNN) and the true physical state. We then rank state components by sensitivity via the change in the largest singular value of $A + B\delta x_i$, where the x_is are the different components of the state, each being estimated using a different DNN. The design rule is to give larger (more accurate) DNNs only to the most safety-critical state components, and accept smaller, less accurate models elsewhere—so the aggregate system remains safe while saving compute and memory [34]. This reframes machine learning design as co-design with control under system-level safety, rather than a race for per-model accuracy. The key takeaway is that carefully designed small DNNs, placed where they matter most, keep the whole autonomy stack safe while reducing GPU footprint and energy, offering a novel, system-first lens for machine learning (ML) design in autonomous systems.

Finally, we will discuss a problem in distributed DNN implementations on edge/cloud platforms [2]. Today, it represents a core challenge in ML-enabled autonomy: perception DNNs face a latency-accuracy trade-off that can make "edge-only" (fast but error-prone) or "cloud-only" (accurate but delayed) designs unsafe [31]. To address this, we will discuss a controller and edge/cloud DNN co-design [33] that intentionally combines two imperfect DNN models—a small, low-latency edge DNN and a higher-latency, more accurate cloud DNN—so the controller [7] first applies an early control based on the edge estimate and then refines it when the cloud estimate arrives (or blends them with a weighted hybrid), with system-level safety as the objective (distance from an ideal trajectory as in the GPU partitioning problem, or the size of the reachable set being a measure of safety). This *split-computing* [4, 3] controller can be shown to reduce the reachable set of the closed-loop system—and thus improve safety—relative to edge-only or cloud-only baselines. This problem of joint sizing/allocation of edge and cloud DNNs may be formulated as an optimization problem over system-safety, and not as conventional per-model DNN inference accuracy optimization.

In summary, our proposal is to begin with a quantifiable [15] and relaxed [13, 29] notion of system-level safety [18], allocate imperfection across the system's components, and design timing analysis [19, 22], scheduling [5, 16, 20] and resource management schemes [24, 23] to achieve robust, cost-effective autonomous and ML systems. This approach may be extended to other system components too, such security protocols [17, 32], where potential attacks under limited protection might impact performance but not violate safety.

Acknowledgments. This work has been done with multiple research collaborators and students and is supported by the US National Science Foundation award

#2038960. Chakraborty's research is additionally supported by a Dieter Schwarz Courageous Research Grant from Germany, where he is a Fellow of the TUM IAS in addition to his regular appointment at UNC Chapel Hill.

References

1. Bordoloi, U.D., et al.: Autonomy-driven emerging directions in software-defined vehicles. In: Design, Automation and Test in Europe Conference (DATE) (2023)
2. Capogrosso, L., et al.: Learning-enabled CPS for edge-cloud computing. In: International Symposium on Industrial Embedded Systems (SIES) (2024)
3. Capogrosso, L., et al.: MTL-split: multi-task learning for edge devices using split computing. In: Design Automation Conference (DAC) (2024)
4. Capogrosso, L., et al.: LO-SC: local-only split computing for accurate deep learning on edge devices. In: International Conference on VLSI Design (VLSID) (2025)
5. Chakraborty, S., Erlebach, T., Thiele, L.: On the complexity of scheduling conditional real-time code. In: Dehne, F., Sack, JR., Tamassia, R. (eds) Algorithms and Data Structures. WADS 2001. LNCS, vol 2125, pp. 38–49. Springer, Heidelberg (2001). https://doi.org/10.1007/3-540-44634-6_5
6. Chakraborty, S., et al.: Automotive cyber-physical systems: a tutorial introduction. IEEE Design. Test 33(4), 92–108 (2016)
7. Ganguli, P., et al.: Trading delays with uncertainty: controller design for DNN-based perception processing on edge-cloud platforms. In: 33rd International Conference on Real-Time Networks and Systems (RTNS) (2025)
8. Ghosh, B., et al.: Statistical hypothesis testing of controller implementations under timing uncertainties. In: IEEE 28th International Conference on Embedded and Real-Time Computing Systems and Applications (RTCSA) (2022)
9. Ghosh, B., et al.: Statistical verification of autonomous system controllers under timing uncertainties. Real-Time Syst. 60(1), 108–149 (2024)
10. Goswami, D., Schneider, R., Chakraborty, S.: Co-design of cyber-physical systems via controllers with flexible delay constraints. In: Asia and South Pacific Design Automation Conference (ASP-DAC) (2011)
11. Goswami, D., Schneider, R., Chakraborty, S.: Re-engineering cyber-physical control applications for hybrid communication protocols. In: Design, Automation and Test in Europe Conference (DATE) (2011)
12. Goswami, D., Schneider, R., Chakraborty, S.: Relaxing signal delay constraints in distributed embedded controllers. IEEE Trans. Control Syst. Technol. 22(6), 2337–2345 (2014)
13. Goswami, D., et al.: Relaxing Signal Delay Constraints in Distributed Embedded Controllers. IEEE Trans. Control Syst. Technol. 22(6), 2337–2345 (2014)
14. Hobbs, C., et al.: Safety analysis of embedded controllers under implementation platform timing uncertainties. IEEE Trans. Comput.-Aided Design Integr. Circuit Syst. 41(11), 4016–4027 (2022)
15. Hobbs, C., et al.: Quantitative safety-driven co-synthesis of cyber-physical system implementations. In: Intertional Conference on Cyber-Physical Systems (ICCPS) (2024)

16. Maxiaguine, A., et al.: Rate analysis for streaming applications with on-chip buffer constraints. In: Asia & South Pacific Design Automation Conference (ASP-DAC) (2004)
17. Mundhenk, P., et al.: Security analysis of automotive architectures using probabilistic model checking. In: Design Automation Conference (DAC) (2015)
18. Oetjens, J.H., et al.: Safety evaluation of automotive electronics using virtual prototypes: State of the art and research challenges. In: Design Automation Conference (DAC) (2014)
19. Phan, L.T.X., et al.: Modeling buffers with data refresh semantics in automotive architectures. In: International Conference on Embedded Software (EMSOFT) (2010)
20. Roy, D., et al.: GoodSpread: criticality-aware static scheduling of CPS with multi-QoS resources. In: IEEE Real-Time Systems Symposium (RTSS) (2020)
21. Roy, D., et al.: Timing debugging for cyber-physical systems. In: Design, Automation and Test in Europe Conference (DATE) (2021)
22. Roy, D., et al.: Timing Debugging for Cyber-Physical Systems. In: Design, Automation and Test in Europe Conference Exhibition (DATE) (2021)
23. Sagstetter, F., et al.: Schedule integration framework for time-triggered automotive architectures. In: Design Automation Conference (DAC) (2014)
24. Schneider, R., Goswami, D., Zafar, S., Lukasiewycz, M., Chakraborty, S.: Constraint-driven synthesis and tool-support for flexray-based automotive control systems. In: International Conference on Hardware/Software Codesign and System Synthesis (CODES+ISSS) (2011)
25. Xu, S., et al.: Safety-aware flexible schedule synthesis for cyber-physical systems using weakly-hard constraints. In: Asia and South Pacific Design Automation Conference (ASP-DAC) (2023)
26. Xu, S., et al.: Safety-aware implementation of control tasks via scheduling with period boosting and compressing. In: International Conference on Embedded and Real-Time Computing Systems and Applications (RTCSA) (2023)
27. Xu, S., et al.: Statistical approach to efficient and deterministic schedule synthesis for cyber-physical systems. In: International Symposium on Automated Technology for Verification and Analysis (ATVA) (2023)
28. Xu, S., et al.: GPU partitioning & neural architecture sizing for safety-driven sensing in autonomous systems. In: International Conference on Autonomous Agents (ICAA) (2024)
29. Yeolekar, A., et al.: Checking scheduling-induced violations of control safety properties. In: Automated Technology for Verification and Analysis (ATVA) (2022)
30. Yeolekar, A., et al.: Repairing control safety violations via scheduler patch synthesis. In: ACM 16th International Conference on Cyber-Physical Systems (ICCPS) (2025)
31. Zhang, L., et al.: Schedule management framework for cloud-based future automotive software systems. In: International Conference on Embedded and Real-Time Computing Systems and Applications (RTCSA) (2016)
32. Zhao, Q., et al.: CAN bus intrusion detection based on auxiliary classifier gan and out-of-distribution detection. ACM Trans. Embed. Comput. Syst. **21**(4), 45:1–45:30 (2022)

33. Zhu, T., et al.: Controllers for edge-cloud cyber-physical systems. In: International Conference on Communication Systems and Networks (COMSNETS) (2025)
34. Zhu, T., et al.: Safety-driven DNN sizing for vehicular CPS. IEEE Embed. Syst. Lett. (2025). https://doi.org/10.1109/LES.2025.3595839

Anytime Algorithms for Approximate Functional Dependencies

Gautam Das

The University of Texas at Arlington
gdas@uta.edu
https://ranger.uta.edu/~gdas/

Abstract. We propose a computational framework for identifying approximate functional dependencies (AFDs) in a relation, leveraging the frequency distribution information of individual attributes. This framework operates without requiring access to the full database, processing records one at a time as necessary. Our approach generalizes existing measures for quantifying errors in perfect dependencies and formalizes two primary problems: finding top-k AFDs and identifying all AFDs within a specified error threshold, ε. Our proposed framework provides anytime solutions, meaning it returns results after processing each record. A key innovation of our work lies in effectively estimating error bounds of the candidate AFDs, which allows to produce anytime solutions. We present an exact algorithm that delivers precise solutions when possible. We also develop an algorithm that always returns a solution albeit with some imprecision in the output. We demonstrate the applicability of these algorithms under various data organization strategies, such as indexing by key or key-like attributes. Our experimental results, based on both real-world and synthetic datasets, validate the effectiveness of our approach and show that it outperforms state-of-the-art solutions.

Beyond Connectivity: Designing Fair, Expressive, and Trustworthy Graph Neural Networks through Statistical Foundations of Message Passing

Swagatam Das

Indian Statistical Institute, Kolkata
swagatam.das@isical.ac.in
https://www.isical.ac.in/~swagatam.das/

Abstract. Graph Neural Networks (GNNs) have rapidly evolved as powerful tools for learning from relational data, yet their performance often falters under the intertwined challenges of oversmoothing, oversquashing, heterophily, and algorithmic bias. In this keynote, we explore a unified perspective that connects these problems to the statistical principles of message passing and probabilistic dependence across graph structures. We discuss recent advances in rethinking graph learning beyond local homophily, through randomized path exploration, label-guided graph rewiring, asynchronous message propagation, and hyperbolic positional encoding, which collectively enhance the expressive power and stability of GNNs. Building on this foundation, the talk introduces *FairSplit-GNN*, a sensitivity-aware edge partitioning framework that explicitly separates homophilic and heterophilic relations to achieve fairness without compromising predictive performance. Together, these developments outline a new direction where machine learning, probability, and statistical reasoning converge to create GNNs that are not only deeper and more interpretable but also equitable and trustworthy for high-stakes decision-making.

Optimality

John Iacono

Université libre de Bruxelles
john@johniacono.com
https://john.iacono.web.ulb.be/

Abstract. What does it mean for a data structure or an algorithm to be optimal? In this talk we will explore many different notions of optimality. This will take us on a journey through beyond-worst-case analysis from older notions such as the dynamic optimality conjecture of binary search trees and optimal sorting under partial information, to newer ideas of optimality such as instance-based optimality and universal optimality.

Nonlinearity of Boolean Functions - Combinatorial Results with Cryptographic Significance

Subhamoy Maitra

Indian Statistical Institute, Kolkata

`maitra.subhamoy@gmail.com`

https://www.isical.ac.in/~subho/

Abstract. Boolean functions are one of the most important primitives in the design of symmetric cipher, and it is expected that the functions should have very high nonlinearity. The problem is mostly combinatorial in nature and it has relations to coding theory as well. In this presentation, we will briefly explain several state of the art results related to very high nonlinearity and also discuss some open problems.

Gabow's $O(\sqrt{n}m)$ Maximum Cardinality Matching Algorithm, Revisited Extended Abstract

Kurt Mehlhorn[1] and Romina Nobahari[2]

[1] Max Planck Institute for Informatics, Saarbrücken, Germany
[2] Sharif University, Tehran, Iran

Abstract. We revisit Gabow's $O(\sqrt{n}m)$ maximum cardinality matching algorithm (The Weighted Matching Approach to Maximum Cardinality Matching, Fundamenta Informaticae, 2017). Gabow's algorithm works iteratively. In each iteration, it constructs a maximal number of edge-disjoint shortest augmenting paths with respect to the current matching and augments them. It is well-known that $O(\sqrt{n})$ iterations suffice. Each iteration consists of three parts. In the first part, the length of the shortest augmenting path is computed. In the second part, an auxiliary graph H is constructed with the property that shortest augmenting paths in G correspond to augmenting paths in H. In the third part, a maximal set of edge-disjoint augmenting paths in H is determined, and the paths are lifted and augmented to G. We give a new algorithm for the first part. Gabow's algorithm for the first part is derived from Edmonds' primal-dual algorithm for weighted matching. We believe that our approach is more direct and will be easier to teach. The algorithm has been implemented, and the implementation is available at the companion webpage (https://people.mpi-inf.mpg.de/~mehlhorn/CompanionPag eGenMatchingImplementation.html).

1 Introduction

The maximum matching problem is one of the basic problems in graph theory and graph algorithms. Given an undirected graph, the goal is to find a matching, i.e., a set of edges no two of which share an endpoint, of maximum cardinality. Edmonds gave a polynomial time algorithm as early as 1965 [Edm65]. The running time of the algorithm was improved over time, culminating in the $O(nm\alpha(n))$ algorithm of Gabow [Gab76]] and the $O(nm)$ algorithm of Gabow and Tarjan [GT85]. An implementation of the former algorithm is available in LEDA [LED,MN99]. Kececioglu and Pecqueur [KP98] give heuristic improvements that often lead to considerably smaller running times. Algorithms with running time $O(\sqrt{n}m)$ were given in [MV80,Vaz94,Vaz12,Vaz20,Vaz24,GK04,GT91,Gab17]. Mattingly and Ritchey [MR91] and Huang and Stein [HS17] discuss implementations of the Micali-Vazirani algorithm, and Ansaripour, Danaei, and Mehlhorn [ADM24] give an implementation of Gabow's algorithm.

Gabow's $O(\sqrt{n}m)$ algorithm works iteratively, and so do the other $O(\sqrt{n}m)$ algorithms. In each iteration, it constructs a maximal number of edge-disjoint shortest augmenting paths with respect to the current matching and augments them. It is well-known that $O(\sqrt{n})$ phases suffice. Each iteration consists of three parts. The first part determines the length of the shortest augmenting paths. The second part constructs an auxiliary graph H with the property that shortest augmenting paths in G correspond to augmenting paths in H. The third part determines a maximal set of edge-disjoint augmenting paths in H, lifts the paths to G, and finally augments them to G. *We give a new algorithm for the first part.* Gabow's algorithm for the first part is derived from Edmonds' primal-dual algorithm for weighted matching. We believe that our approach is more direct and will be easier to teach.

In Section 2, we describe how to find a shortest augmenting path. This section is our main contribution. We do not describe the construction of H, the search for a maximal set of augmenting paths and their lifting to G in this extended abstract. The construction of H is an adaptation of Gabow's approach to our changes in the first part. The search for a maximal set of augmenting paths and their lifting to G is as in [Gab17]. The implementation is available on the companion webpage (https://people.mpi-inf.mpg.de/~mehlhorn/CompanionPageGenMatchingImplementation.html).

2 The New Algorithm for Part I: Finding a Shortest Augmenting Path

Let $G = (V, E)$ be the input graph, and let M be the current matching. A *blossom* in G with respect to M consists of a *stem* and a *cycle*. The cycle is an alternating path of odd length with the first and the last edge non-matching. The common endpoint of the first and the last edge is called the *base* of the blossom. The stem is an alternating path of even length starting at a free vertex and ending in the base. Stem and cycle are simple paths and vertex-disjoint except for the base. We refer to the cycle as *blossom-cycle* of the blossom. Contraction of the blossom-cycle into the base yields a contracted graph G/C. It is well-known [Edm65] that there is an augmenting path in G iff there is an augmenting path in G/C. Blossoms can be nested in the following sense. Assume there is a blossom in G/C whose blossom-cycle involves the base of a previously contracted blossom. Contraction of the blossom then results in a blossom in which the previously contracted blossom is nested.

In order to find a shortest augmenting path with respect to M, we grow a collection S of search structures, contractions of subgraphs of G, one for each free vertex of G. Each search structure is an alternating tree, i.e., along any root to leaf path, the edges alternate between matching and non-matching, the edge incident to the root being non-matching. We use "node" for the vertices of the search structures and "vertex" for the vertices of G. The growth is structured into phases 0, 1, ...; we use Δ for the number of the current phase. In phase zero, we initialize S with the free vertices. In later phases, we grow alternating trees rooted at the free nodes. Each node of S is labeled *even* or *odd*, depending on the parity of its depth; roots have depth zero and are therefore even. The nodes of S correspond to sets of vertices of G with odd cardinality. Odd nodes represent single vertices, whereas even nodes may correspond to larger subsets and then have internal structure. Even nodes are contractions of blossom-cycles, maybe nested. We refer to an even node of S as a *blossom*. Even nodes of cardinality one are trivial blossoms. Consider a tree with free vertex[1] f and a vertex v inside a blossom of the tree. Then there will be a unique shortest even-length alternating path in S from v to f. For this reason, the nodes inside a blossom are also called even. For the odd nodes of S, there will be a unique shortest odd-length alternating path in S from v to f. We refer to this path as the *canonical path* of the node. Canonical paths will be defined in the next section.

For a matching edge, either both endpoints belong to S or none does. Vertices not belonging to S are *unlabeled*. The unlabeled vertices come in pairs of vertices matched to each other. Note that S is initialized with the free nodes. For a matched vertex v, let *mate*(v) denote its matching partner. When a vertex is added to S, it is added either as an even or as an odd node. We also say it was born even or odd. A vertex born odd may become even at a later time, namely when it becomes part of a non-trivial blossom. A node born even stays even.

We compute two values for each vertex of G. For a vertex v, $lcp(v)$, the *length of the canonical path*, is (intended to be) the length of a shortest even length alternating path in S from a free node to v (if any), and, for a node born odd, $lcp_{odd}(v)$ is (intended to be) the length of a shortest odd-length alternating path in S from a free node to v. The level of a node is either $lcp(v)$ or $lcp_{odd}(v)$ depending on whether it is born even or odd. Free nodes are born even and have level zero.

2.1 The Growth of the Search Structure

We use two operations for growing S: Growth-steps and bridge-steps. Growth-steps are only performed in even phases. In phase Δ, we perform growth-steps at even nodes at level $\Delta - 2$ (if Δ is even), and we perform bridge-steps at non-matching edges $uv \in E$ with even endpoints and lcp-sum $2\Delta - 2$, i.e., $lcp(u) + lcp(v) = 2\Delta - 2$. The choice of the parameters $\Delta - 2$ and $2\Delta - 2$ will become clear below.

Grow-Steps: A grow-step adds two nodes to S. Let u be an even vertex with $lcp(u) = \Delta - 2$, and let $e = uv$ be an edge with v unlabeled. Then *mate*(v) is also unlabeled. We extend S by making v a child of the node containing u and *mate*(v) a child of v and set $lcp_{odd}(v) = lcp(u) + 1$ and $lcp(mate(v)) = lcp(u) + 2$. The canonical paths to v and *mate*(v) are the canonical path to u extended by the edge uv and by the edges uv and $v\,mate(v)$, respectively.

Bridge-Steps: We consider even-even non-matching edges uv with $lcp(u) + lcp(v) = 2\Delta - 2$ and u and v belonging to different blossoms.

u **and** v **belong to distinct trees:** We have found an augmenting path of length $lcp(u) + lcp(v) + 1 = 2\Delta - 1$, and Part I ends.

u **and** v **belong to the same tree:** We have found a blossom. Let B_u and B_v be the blossoms containing u and v, respectively, and let B be the lowest (= furthest from the root) common ancestor of B_u and B_v in S. If one of B_u or B_v is an ancestor of the other,

---

[1] The root of the tree is a blossom containing the free vertex.

then B is equal to this node and hence even. Otherwise, B_u and B_v are in different subtrees with respect to B and hence B is an even node, as odd nodes have only a single child. Note that, the child of an odd node is a blossom containing the mate of the odd node. We add the edge uv to S. The edge uv together with the paths from B_u and B_v to B form a cycle. All odd nodes on both paths become even.

Consider an odd node z on the path from B_v to B. The canonical path to z consists of the canonical path to u followed by the edge uv followed by the reversal of a suffix of the canonical path to u. It is the suffix starting in z. Then

$$lcp(z) = lcp(u) + 1 + lcp(v) - lcp_{odd}(z).$$

The *newly formed blossom* comprises the following nodes: All nodes contained in any of the blossoms on both paths plus the odd nodes on both paths. Note that the even nodes in a blossom may be blossoms shrunken earlier. A blossom comprises an odd number of nodes. This is obvious for trivial blossoms. A non-trivial blossom is formed by an odd-length cycle, and any vertex of the cycle stands for an odd number of nodes of G; the sum of an odd number of odd numbers is odd. For all but one node of a blossom, the mate also belongs to the blossom. The single node that is not mated inside the blossom is the base of the blossom; it is either a free node or has its mate outside the blossom. The canonical paths to all nodes in a blossom pass through the base of the blossom. We shrink the blossom into a supernode. The supernode has an even level in S.

The following lemma is well-known.

Lemma 1. *Consider a blossom B with base b and a node v of B. Then there is a unique even-length alternating path inside the blossom connecting v and b. This path is a suffix of the canonical path of v.*

Proof. Consider the blossom-cycle C of B, and let B_b and B_v be the nodes of C containing b and v, respectively. The even length path p from B_v to B_b either goes through the bridge of the blossom (if v was odd before forming the blossom) or straight to the base (if v was even before forming the blossom). Assume now that p passes through or ends in a nested blossom B'; in the latter case, B' contains b. Then p uses a non-matching edge incident to some vertex v' of B' and, if B' does not contain b, a matching edge incident to B'. Since the base of a blossom is the only vertex of a blossom that is not matched inside the blossom, the matching edge is incident to the base of B'. We now recurse to connect v' and the base of B'.

Synchronization between Grow-Steps and Bridge-Steps: The parameters $\Delta - 2$ for grow-steps and $2\Delta - 2$ for bridge-steps are chosen for proper synchronization of grow- and bridge-steps. We present the intuition now and defer the detailed justification to the next section. Recall that we want to find a shortest augmenting path. We find an augmenting path when we encounter a bridge connecting two different trees. This suggests processing bridge-steps in order of increasing lcp-sum. Similarly, we should grow the trees breadth-first, i.e., perform growth-steps out of nodes in increasing order of their lcp-values. When we grow out of a node at level $\Delta - 2$, we create new even nodes at level Δ that may form bridges with existing nodes at level $\Delta - 2$ (not smaller !!!) and hence we should perform bridge-steps with combined value $2\Delta - 2$ not before growth steps out of nodes at level $\Delta - 2$. When we process a bridge with lcp-sum $2\Delta - 2$, we may create new even nodes at level Δ (not smaller !!!) and hence we may perform growth-steps out of nodes with lcp-value Δ after processing bridge-steps with lcp-sum $2\Delta - 2$. So we use the order: For even Δ, growth-steps out of nodes with lcp-value $\Delta - 2$. Then bridge-steps with lcp-sum $2\Delta - 2$. Then bridge-steps with lcp-sum 2Δ. Increase Δ by two and repeat.

We summarize: In phase zero, we initialize the search structure with the free nodes. Each free node becomes the root of an alternating tree. In phase Δ, $\Delta \geq 1$, the following additions to the search structure take place:

Delta is even, growth-steps: We grow out of nodes v with $lcp(v) = \Delta - 2$. As long as there is a node v with $lcp(v) = \Delta - 2$ with an unlabeled neighbor, say x, we add x and $mate(x)$ to S, x at level $\Delta - 1$ with parent v, and $mate(x)$ at level Δ with parent x.

Delta is even or odd, bridge-steps: We add even-even edges xy with x and y belonging to different blossoms and $lcp(x) + lcp(y) = 2\Delta - 2$. This may make some odd nodes even. They have lcp-value larger than Δ. If x and y belong to different trees, we have found an augmenting path; if they belong to the same tree, we have found a blossom.

Figure 2 illustrates an execution of the algorithm. The pseudo-code is shown in Fig. 1.

```
function PART1                                    ▷ Returns True if an augmenting path exists and False otherwise
    Initialize search structures to empty structures;
    for (Δ = 0, Δ = Δ + 1, Δ ≤ n + 1) do                                        ▷ Phase Δ
        if Δ is even then
            grow the search structures to level Δ by either adding all free nodes (Δ = 0)
            or for Δ ≥ 2 by growing out of nodes v with lcp(v) = Δ − 2 as follows:
            while there is an edge vx with lcp(v) = Δ − 2 and x unlabeled do
                make x a child of v and mate(x) a child of x, label x odd and mate(x) even, and set
                lcp_odd(x) ← Δ − 1 and lcp(mate(x)) ← Δ;
            end while
        end if
        while ∃ even-even edge xy with lcp(x) + lcp(y) = 2Δ − 2 connecting different blossoms do
            if x and y belong to the same search structure then                 ▷ blossom
                add the edge to the search structure; let b be the base of the blossom formed and make all
                odd nodes on the paths from x and y to b even. For an odd node z in the newly formed
                blossom, set lcp(z) = lcp(x) + 1 + lcp(y) − lcp_odd(z).
            else                                                                ▷ sap, set up H
                Construct the contracted graph H;
                return true;
            end if
        end while
    end for
    return false;
end function
```

Fig. 1. Part I of the Matching Algorithm. Augmenting paths are only found for $\Delta \leq n/2$. The remaining phases are needed for the correct construction of the witness of optimality.

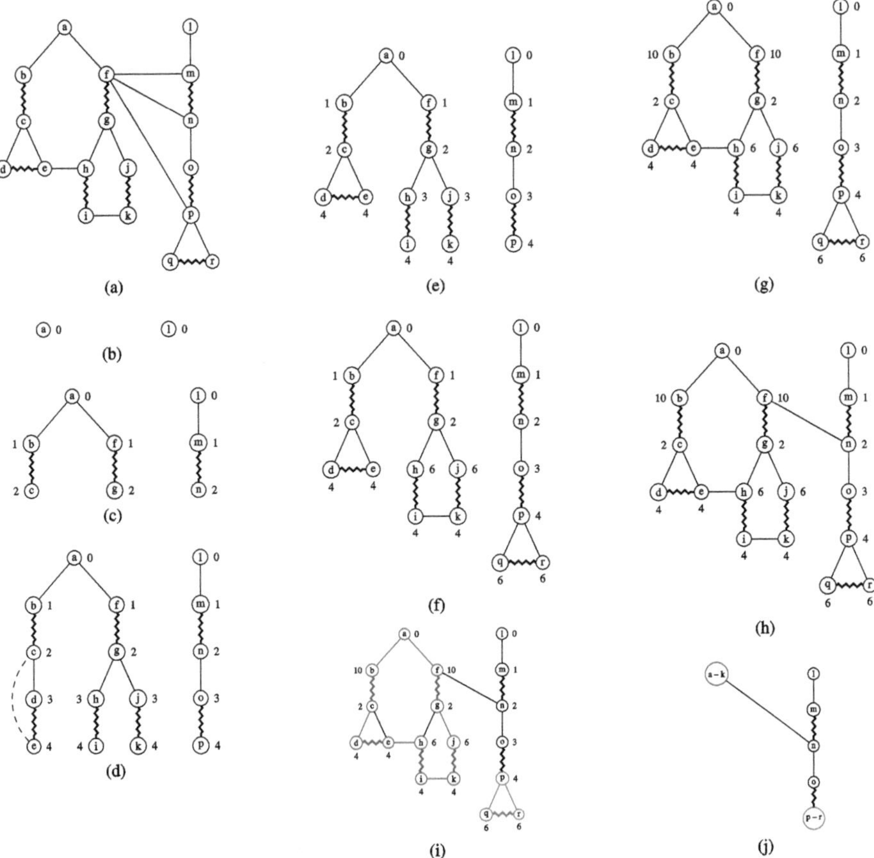

Fig. 2. The execution of part I on the example given in [Gab17]: (a) Shows the input graph. (b) At the end of phase 0, S consists of the two free nodes a and l. (c) At the end of phase 2, we have grown S to level 2. (d) After the growth-step in phase 4, S has grown to level 4. There is an even-even edge ce with $lcp(c)+lcp(e) = 2+4 = 2\cdot4-2$. (e) After the bridge-steps in phase 4, d is now even with $lcp(d) = 4$. (f) In phase 5, we add the bridge ik with $lcp(i)+lcp(k) = 4+4 = 2\cdot5-2$. The vertices h and j become even with lcp-value equal to 6. (g) In phase 6, we grow the tree and add node r at level 5 and node q at level 6. Then we process the bridge pq with $lcp(p)+lcp(q) = 4+6 = 2\cdot6-2$, r becomes even with $lcp(r) = 6$. We also add the bridge eh with $lcp(e)+lcp(h) = 4+6 = 2\cdot6-2$. Vertices b and f become even with lcp-value equal to 10. (h) Finally, in phase 7, we add the bridge fn with $lcp(f) + lcp(n) = 10 + 2 = 2 \cdot 7 - 2$. We have found an augmenting path of length 13, and Part I ends. (j) The contracted graph: Vertices a to k are contracted into the red supernode, and vertices p to r into the green supernode. Edges mf and pf are discarded. (i) also shows the structure inside the supernodes.

References

[ADM24]   Ansaripour, M., Danaei, A., Mehlhorn, K.: Gabow's cardinality matching algorithm in general graphs: implementation and experiments. CoRR, abs/2409.14849 (2024)

[Edm65]   Edmonds, J.: Maximum matching and a polyhedron with 0,1 - vertices. J. Res. Natl. Bur. Stan. **69**B, 125–130 (1965)

[Gab76]   Gabow, H.N.: An efficient implementation of Edmonds' algorithm for maximum matching on graphs. J. ACM **23**, 221–234 (1976)

[Gab17]   Gabow, H.: The weighted matching approach to maximum cardinality matching. Fundamenta Informaticae **154**, 109–130 (2017)

[GK04]   Goldberg, A.V., Karzanov, A.V.: Maximum skew-symmetric flows and matchings. Math. Program. Series A, **100**, 537–568 (2004)

[GT85]   Gabow, H.N., Tarjan, R.E.: A linear-time algorithm for a special case of disjoint set union. J. Comput. Syst. Sci. **30**(2), 209–221 (1985)

[GT91]   Gabow, H.N., Tarjan, R.E.: Faster scaling algorithms for general graph-matching problems. J. ACM **38**(4), 815–853 (1991)

[HK73]   Hopcroft, J.E., Karp, R.M.: An $n^{5/2}$ algorithm for maximum matchings in bipartite graphs. SIAM J. Comput. **2**(4), 225–231 (1973)

[HS17]   Huang, M., Stein, C.: Extending search phases in the Micali-Vazirani algorithm. In: 16th Symposium on Experimental Algorithmics (SEA), LIPIcs, pp. 10:1–10:19 (2017)

[KP98]   Kececioglu, J.D., Pecqueur, J.: Computing maximum-cardinality matchings in sparse general graphs. In: Proceedings of the 2nd Workshop on Algorithm Engineering (WAE'98), pp. 121–132. Max-Planck-Institut für Informatik (1998)

[LED]   LEDA (Library of Efficient Data Types and Algorithms). leda.uni-trier.de.

[MN99]   Mehlhorn, K., Näher, S.: The LEDA Platform for Combinatorial and Geometric Computing. Cambridge University Press, Cambridge (1999)

[MR91]   Mattingly, R.B., Ritchey, N.P.: Implementing an $O\sqrt{NM}$ cardinality matching algorithm. In: Johnson, D.S., McGeoch, C.C. (eds.) Network Flows and Matching, Proceedings of a DIMACS Workshop, DIMACS Series in Discrete Mathematics and Theoretical Computer Science. vol. 12, pp. 539–556 (1991)

[MV80]   Micali, S., Vazirani, V.: An $O(\sqrt{|V|}.|E|)$ algorithm for finding maximum matching in general graphs. In: Proceedings of the 21st IEEE Symposium on Foundations of Computer Science (FOCS), pp. 17–27 (1980)

[Vaz94]   Vazirani, V.V.: A theory of alternating paths and blossoms for proving correctness of the $O(\sqrt{V}E)$ general graph maximum matching algorithm. Combinatorica **14**(1), 71–109 (1994)

[Vaz12]   Vazirani, V.V.: An improved definition of blossoms and a simpler proof of the MV matching algorithm. CoRR, abs/1210.4594 (2012)

[Vaz20]   Vazirani, V.V: A proof of the MV matching algorithm. CoRR, abs/2012.03582 (2020)

[Vaz24]   Vazirani, V.V: A theory of alternating paths and blossoms from the perspective of minimum length. Math. Oper. Res. **49**(3), 2009–2047 (2024)

Contents

Track B

Track A

The Curious Case of Complexities: Discovering Causal Influences on Software Defects

Reshmi Maulik[1]([✉]) [iD] and Subhajit Datta[2] [iD]

[1] Meghnad Saha Institute of Technology, Kolkata, India
reshmi.maulik@msit.edu.in
[2] Heritage Institute of Technology, Kolkata, India
subhajit.datta@acm.org

Abstract. Software complexity has been long recognized as a key determinant of quality in large scale software development. However, complexity is multi-faceted and understanding how it relates to the number of defects in a software system has its challenges. Empirical studies on software complexity are mostly correlational in nature. In this paper, we examine two different aspects of complexity from a causal perspective and examine their relation to defects using a causal discovery based approach. The discovered causal model is validated using a large-scale development. Validation results, along with software engineering domain knowledge yield notable insights that are relevant for the design, development, and maintenance of robust and resilient software systems. To the best of our knowledge, our approach is among the pioneering studies that apply causal discovery techniques in understanding how code level complexity influences defect occurrence in real-world software development.

Keywords: causal inference · defects · GES · complexity · causal model

1 Introduction

Over time, as software systems address increasingly involved needs of varied stakeholders, internal structures of such systems become more complex. Understanding how the structural complexity of software affects its quality remains an enduring concern for researchers and practitioners. Since minimizing defects is a universal aim of software development, the association of complexity with defects have been studied from different perspectives. Given the practical limitations of running randomized controlled trials (RCTs) on real-world software systems, most existing studies on software complexity and defects are correlational in nature, whose results can not offer any causal insights.

In this paper, we analyze real-world software development data to determine whether different aspects of complexity have a *causal* impact on the number

C. Zaroliagis et al. (Eds.): ICAA 2026, LNCS 16423, pp. 3–14, 2026.
https://doi.org/10.1007/978-3-032-15621-1_1

of defects, after accounting for peripheral effects such as effort, difficulty etc. Instead of investigating whether the data conforms to a pre-conceived model of causal relationships, we use an approach where causal relationships are *discovered* from the data. The credibility, strength, and directionality of such discovered relationships are then examined in light of domain knowledge. Our study presents the following research contributions:(i) Establishing a causal relationship between complexity and defects using real-world software development data (ii) Discerning the varied nuances of the causal effects of different aspects of complexity. (iii) Offering insights for software designers and developers on the multiple factors that causally influence defects.

2   Related Work

The aim of scientific inquiry is to address the *why* question; any investigation of a phenomena seeks to understand the causal influences on the outcome of interest. Research in causality can be classified into two main areas: *causal discovery* and *causal inference* [19]. Causal discovery seeks to identify causal relationships from observational data without a pre-defined model or prior assumptions on how the variables relate to one another. On the other hand, causal inference is concerned with estimating the impact of changes in one variable on an outcome of interest, often using statistical techniques to account for confounding factors. In the interest of space, in this brief literature review, we will highlight existing results that relate to recent methods for understanding the influences on software defects, how causal analysis methods relate to the context of this study, and discuss *Greedy Equivalence Search (GES)*, a relatively recent causal discovery technique that we will use in this study. Long et al. had made a systematic literature review on the existing machine learning techniques being applied for bug report analysis [15]. They found that the bug report related evaluation metrics had yet not received sufficient attention and the majority of studies focus on general bug types rather then focusing on specific bug types. Kuccuk et al. proposed a software fault localization method—UniVal—that includes causal inference and machine learning to characterize and estimate the impact of program statements that cause the fault. Their method combines both the predicate outcomes and the variable values and transform predicates into assignment statements during fault localization. They have used Defects4J evaluation framework for their analysis [13]. He et al. had discovered a performance bug signature extraction tool for identifying the anomaly pattern and root cause function behind the performance bugs in cloud environment [10]. Pearl had used statistical technique to study causal relationships that exist among various variables in a system [20]. His work finds its application in multiple disciplines such as artificial intelligence, economics, philosophy, health, social sciences, software engineering, etc. In many software projects the availability of adequate and complete historical data for causal analysis can be challenging. Incomplete historical data can result in unreliable conclusions that will impact the causal models utilized [22]. The dynamic nature of software development, which comprises of continuous changes and updates, can further complicate the existence of a stable causal relationship [5]. Hasan and Gani introduce KGS: a new causal discovery algorithm that combines the Greedy Equivalency Search (GES) with prior knowledge. We discuss GES in detail in the next section. KGS facilitates search towards a causal graph through the incorporation of structural priors, or constraints in the form of known causal edges, along with observational data [9]. Ramsey et al. propose to enhance GES with parallelization and caching to arrive at a better approach, known as Fast Greedy Equivalence Search (fGES). This was evaluated on one million Gaussian variable fMRI dataset, to test its efficacy in high-dimensional cases [21]. Lu et al. point out the limitations of GES, which often produce suboptimal results when given finite data or when the causal faithfulness condition is violated. The authors propose a better score-based exhaustive search approach that is ideal [16]. The results reported in this paper complement these existing studies by applying causal discovery in general and GES in particular in a novel software engineering context. Some authors supports the argument that effect of object-oriented design metrics on defects may vary across different programming languages [4,23,27]. Subramanyam et al.'s findings on C++ and Java programming languages shows that an increased class size results in a greater number of defects. If class size is reduced then it may Influence the coupling between Objects (CBO) thereby increasing complexity which may in turn lead to a higher number of defects [27] .

3   Methodology

Our methodology consists of the following steps:

- Apply the Greedy Equivalence Search (GES) causal discovery method to find the influences on defects, based on the domain knowledge and the study setting (Sect. 3.1).
- Develop a causal model of the influences on defects, based on the outcome of the GES method and build the directed acyclic graph (DAG) (Sects. 3.3, 4.1).
- Apply standard causal inference techniques to validate causal model (Sect. 4.2).
- Make inferences based on the estimation of causal effects and model validation (Sect. 4.3).

3.1   Causal Discovery Using GES: An Outline

Causal discovery is considered an appropriate and often essential method when the goal is to understand why things happen, not just what happens. Causal discovery aids in the inference of structure from passive data in situations when randomized experiments are impractical. A known causal graph or model is necessary for causal inference. In such a graph, nodes or vertices represent variables of interest, and directed arrows between them denote causal relationships. If the graph is incorrect or incomplete, the estimated causal effect will not be reliable. That is why causal discovery is typically a prerequisite—it constructs the map before you start measuring the area. Causal discovery tells us which variables influence others, helping avoid misleading conclusions. For our study we have used GES causal discovery algorithm. GES seeks across Markov Equivalence Classes (MECs), groups of DAGs that capture the same conditional independencies, not individual DAGs [14].

This renders the method scalable to larger problems and vastly reduces the search space. GES can potentially recover the true causal graph as sample size goes up because it is proved to be consistent under conditions like faithfulness, Gaussian noise, and linearity. GES is a score-based method that optimizes a suitably defined score function in an attempt to determine the causal structure [6,11,14,28]. GES starts its search with an empty graph. The following stage is a forward search, in which the addition of edges between the nodes is intended to increase the Bayesian score. This procedure is done until no single edge addition improves the score [2,6]. A common instantiation of the Bayesian score in GES is the Bayesian Information Criterion (BIC), which balances model fit with complexity [24]. BIC is calculated using the following Eq. (1):

$$BIC = -2.ln(L) + k.ln(n) \tag{1}$$

Here, L is the likelihood of the data given the graph; k is the number of parameters; n is the sample size. Finally, it performs a backward search, deleting edges until no single edge can be removed to increase the score. The goal is to find a DAG that maximizes the score, representing the most plausible causal relationships. Multi-processing is not supported in this method [9].

3.2   Dataset Description

To explore the relationship between software complexity and defects, we use the KC1 dataset from PROMISE, a repository for real-world software projects from various sources [1]. The KC1 dataset is freely accessible and has been used in other studies [3,7,12,26]. The datasets in PROMISE come with a variety of static code measures, such as McCabe's complexity and Halstead's effort, both of which are important features when building software defect prediction models. A program's *essential complexity* is the amount of unstructuredness in it, indicating to what extent a program is away from the ideal of structured programming [17]. The software metric McCabe *design complexity*, often referred to as *cyclomatic complexity*, is used to quantify the intricate nature of a program's control flow and is critical for risk assessment, maintainability, and software testing [17]. A program's complexity, the amount of mental work needed to write or comprehend it, and even the cognitive challenge involved can all be measured using Halstead's derived metrics, which are *difficulty, effort,* and *intelligence* [8]. KC1, like the many of the datasets in PROMISE, provides a binary target variable to identify whether a unit of code is defective or not. *Our objective in this study is to discover the causal effects of essential complexity and design complexity on the number of defects, after accounting for other peripheral influences.*

The KC1 dataset contains 2109 rows and 22 columns[1]. Since we are trying to find out the effects of essential complexity and design complexity on the defects so we have considered the following seven variables of our interest based on our domain knowledge, and after removing other variables which are strongly correlated to one another:

- *Essential complexity* (ev_g): As defined above.
- *Design complexity* (iv_g): As defined above.
- *Halstead's measure of effort* (e): A high value of e indicates that writing or comprehending the code requires greater mental work.
- *Halstead's measure of difficulty* (d): A high value of d indicates that the code is intricate and possibly prone to errors.
- Halstead's measure of intelligence content (i): The code is more intelligent or efficient if 'i' is higher.
- The count of the number of lines that only contain executable code, not including blanks or comments (*loCode*).
- The number of defects in the software module is the outcome variable (*defects*).

3.3   Model Construction

Model 1 was developed to discover the causal effect (if any) of essential complexity *(ev_g)* on defects. With reference to the notation introduced in the previous section, the variables we have considered for Model 1 are *ev_g, e, d, i, loCode* and *defects*. On application of GES causal discovery algorithm, we obtained the causal relationships among variables as shown in Fig. 1.

Model 2 was developed to discover the causal effect (if any) of design complexity *(iv_g)* on defects. The variables we have considered for Model 2 are *iv_g, e, d, i, loCode* and *defects*, same as Model 1. On application of GES causal discovery algorithm, we obtained the causal relationships among variables as shown in Fig. 2.

4   Results and Discussion

4.1   DAG and Its Description

Figure 1 depicts the effect of essential complexity on defects based on the causal relationships obtained from the application GES alogithm on the KC1 dataset. As evident, the collection of nodes that represent the study's factors, such as difficulty, essential complexity, effort, etc., are represented as nodes in the DAG. Directed edges between nodes shows the causal influence of one variable on another or the conditional dependence between multiple variables. If there exists

---

[1] https://github.com/klainfo/NASADefectDataset.

a direct link between node A and node B then it implies that A has a direct causal impact on B. Here, we find that lines of executable code (*loCode*) have a direct causal impact on difficulty level(d), intelligence content(i), effort level (e), and essential complexity (*ev_g*), while essential complexity (*ev_g*) is directly affected by difficulty level, effort level, and intelligent content. *Essential complexity in turn has a direct causal impact upon the occurrence of defects.*

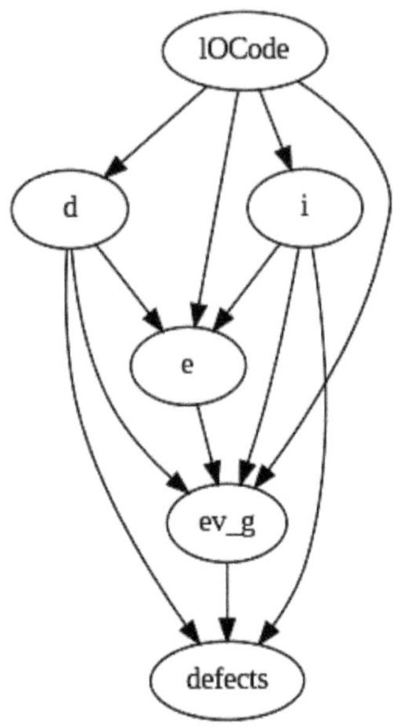

Fig. 1. Discovered Causal Model for Essential Complexity.

Figure 2 depicts the effect of design complexity on defects based on the causal relationships obtained from the application GES alogithm on the KC1 dataset. Here, we discover that the level of difficulty (d), intelligence content (i), effort level (e), and design complexity (*iv_g*) are all directly impacted causally by the lines of executable code (*loCode*), while design complexity (*iv_g*) is directly affected by difficulty, effort, and intelligent content. *However, defects are not found to be directly impacted causally by design complexity as there does not exist any edge between them in the DAG.*

4.2   Causal Inference

To give an analogy that is easy to relate to, causal discovery is like being given a map to find out the causal relationships among the variables whereas causal inference is about navigation the actual paths specified in the map. We require quantitative estimations of causal effects in order to make decisions regarding

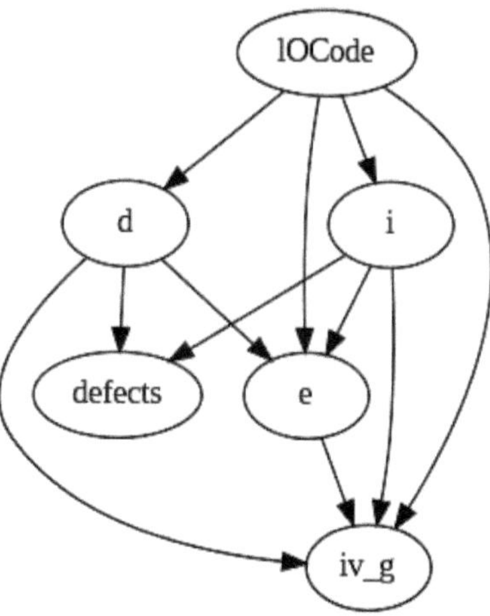

Fig. 2. Discovered Causal Model for Design Complexity.

the impact of one variable's interference with another. Discovery tells us who influences whom, but inference tells us how much and what happens if we execute the interventions.The application of statistical methods in determining if the evidence supports or refutes a statement is referred to as *statistical refutation*. It involves finding the probability that the given data conforms to the null hypothesis, or rejecting the null hypothesis in favor of the alternative hypothesis. By the process of refutation, the strength of the results are assessed for a model. When the p-value is below 0.05, the discrepancy between the new effect and estimated effect is statistically significant in refutation with a *random common cause* (RCC). The *data subset refuter* (DSR) technique is used in causal inference to evaluate the robustness of causal estimates by repeating the analysis on a random subset of the original data. By verifying if the causal influence observed is consistent across samples, this approach makes the results more reliable [18]. A *placebo treatment* (PT) is a technique used in causal inference to a subset of the data in which no real treatment was given. This increases the likelihood that the observed effect is due to the treatment itself rather than other factors that can lead to an erroneous understanding [25]. For a valid causal estimate PT should drop toward zero. Results of causal inference for Model 1 and Model 2 are summarized in the Tables 1 and 2 respectively.

In Table 1 we observe details of the causal inference analysis using the three refutation techniques mentioned earlier – namely RCC, DSR, and PT – to test the robustness of estimated treatment effects for four variables: ev_g, d, i, and e. We have 95% confidence interval $[-0.032, -0.014]$ for the significant causal effect of essential complexity (ev_g) on defects with a p-value of 0.000 when considered up to three decimal places. The estimated average effect is -0.02285. RCC and DSR values are nearly identical to the original estimate which implies that our causal estimate is robust. PT drops to -0.00042 which is very close to

Table 1. Results of Analysis for Essential Complexity (p-values in bold imply statistical significance)

Treatment var	Estimate		Refute		
	Mean	p-value	RCC	DSR	PT
ev_g	-0.02285	**0.0**	−0.02286	−0.02280	−0.00042
d	0.016427	**0.0**	0.016429	0.016479	−4.769297
i	0.003590	**0.0**	0.003591	0.003519	1.311119
e	−1.52067e-06	0.056	−1.52143e-06	−1.38663e-06	3.70350e-08

zero implying that our causal estimate is valid. We recall that essential complexity reflects how "unstructured" a program is. Our evidence indicates that higher levels of unstructuredness relates to fewer defects, and vice versa. A program becomes more structured as it matures. In a study setting as ours, advanced levels of maturity also indicate implementation of more involved functionality. Such functionality is more defect prone. It is most likely this dynamic is reflected in our results.

We have highly significant and positive causal effect of difficulty (d) on defects, with p-value 0.000 when considered up to three decimal places. The estimated average effect is 0.016427. The fact that the RCC and DSR values are almost the same as the initial estimate suggests that our causal estimate is reliable. A placebo treatment (-4.769297) raises the possibility of model misspecification or confounding. We have small but significant positive effect of the intelligence content (i) on defects with p-value 0.000 when considered up to three decimal places. The estimated average effect is 0.003590. We also discovered that a high difficulty level [11.008, 53.75] can increase the causal effect on defects to 0.004543. The reliability of our causal estimate is indicated by the RCC and DSR values being nearly identical to the initial estimate. Placebo treatment (1.31119) shows a strong effect where none should exist which implies that there is likely to be an existence of spurious relationship among variables. The measure of effort (e) has minor effect on defects, with the p-value of 0.056. RCC and DSR varies from initial estimate but still has low impact. PT drops to a value very close to zero, thus confirming lack of bias.

In Table 2 we observe details of the causal inference analysis using the three refutation techniques mentioned earlier – namely RCC, DSR, and PT – to test the robustness of estimated treatment effects for the four variables.

No causal effect of design complexity (iv_g) is discovered on defects. Similarly, effort (e) has no causal effect on defects. The causal estimate 0.016427 shows that difficulty (d) does have a significant impact on defects with p-value of 0.0, considering up to three decimal places. RCC is identical to initial causal estimate and DSR is very close to initial causal estimate, which implies that our causal estimate is robust. The fact that PT falls to 0.000251, which is quite near to zero, suggests that our causal estimate is correct. The causal estimate 0.003590 shows that 'intelligence content i does have a significant impact on defects at p-

Table 2. Results of Analysis for Design Complexity (p-values in bold imply statistical significance)

Treatment var	Estimate		Refute		
	Mean	p-value	RCC	DSR	PT
iv_g	No effect				
d	0.016427	**0.0**	0.016427	0.016631	0.000251
i	0.003590	**0.0**	0.003590	0.003592	−5.404159
e	No effect				

value of 0.0, considering up to three decimal places. Our causal estimate appears to be reliable because the RCC and DSR values are nearly identical to the initial estimate. A significant false impact (-5.404159) is revealed by PT which is not appropriate. This suggests that the initial estimate might be model-dependent.

4.3   Implications and Utility of the Results

In our study setting, we find evidence of a causal impact of essential complexity on the number of defects in a software module, whereas no such relation is found between design complexity and defects. Given that these two measures reflect on two different aspects of program complexity, our findings have notable implications in the design, development, and maintenance of quality software systems. With reference to the definitions of essential complexity and design complexity introduced earlier (see Sect. 3.2), we note that the former indicates how unstructured a program is, while the latter represents the level of intricacy in a program's control flow organization. Control flow structure of a program is a reflection of its internal logic; it is natural that the automation of complex real-world processes would engender complicated control flow. Enhanced design complexity is an essential characteristics of such systems, and may not necessarily lead to lower quality software (that is those with more defects); and the lack of causal connection between design complexity and defect count in our study corroborates this perspective. On the other hand, a lack of structure in a program makes its comprehension, maintenance, and enhancement difficult, which can lead to the introduction of inadvertent errors during these activities. The causal relationship between essential complexity and defect count that is discovered in this study is likely to be a manifestation of this dynamic. The causal effects of difficulty level, and intelligence content on defects as discovered in both of our models (Figs. 1 and 2) point to the impact of these factors on defects and the attention developers need to pay in addressing them upfront to ensure software quality. Our results offer actionable insights for different stakeholders. Developers can be benefited in the design of software systems by the clear causal connection established between essential complexity and defects, and the lack thereof between design complexity and defects. Testers can be informed in test case generation and execution by the causal effects of difficulty and intelligence content on quality. Managers can leverage our results to allow development teams the latitude to effectively manage *technical debt* such software is built for long term resilience and health.

5   Threats to Validity

- **Construct validity:** When a study is unable to quantify the theoretical notion, it purports to evaluate, it poses a threat to construct validity. Despite the data's apparent statistical soundness, this can result in conclusions that are deceptive. When the techniques, models, or measurements employed in causal discovery fall short of adequately capturing the actual causative relationships between variables, there is a threat to construct validity. All model variables were defined and computed with reference to Sect. 3.2, utilizing data gathered from peer-reviewed sources [3,7,12,26]. We have relied on a single GES algorithm or scoring method for identifying the causal relationships among the variables which may lead to limited construct coverage and reduced robustness. The GES algorithm makes the assumptions of causal sufficiency, Gaussian noise, or linearity. The results may be impacted if actual causal paths cannot be detected or if the causal direction is incorrectly identified. Violation of the assumptions of independence and faithfulness may lead to formation of incorrect graph structure. Latent confounders can influence both cause and effect. Since we have closely examined the context of the dataset, we believe such threats are not present to a notable extent in this study.
- **Internal validity:** Threats to internal validity in a study such as this one arises from factors that make it difficult to prove a real causal relationship between variables. Maturation effects, selection bias, historical impacts, and other problems can jeopardize the internal validity of a study's findings. We used historical data in this investigation. Therefore, neither selection bias nor maturation effects nor study duration pose a significant threat.
- **External validity:** Threats to external validity involve the difficulty in generalizing a study's findings outside of the particular context in which they were carried out. In the present study, we have analyzed data from a single system. Therefore, we make no claims on the generalizability of our findings. However, we employed the random control trial method to choose the population for our study and examined the impact of placebo treatment, to establish the robustness and correctness of the results.
- **Reliability:** Reliability relates to the repeatability, stability, and consistency of measurements or observations made in a study. The dataset that were analyzed in this study are publicly accessible, and hence our results can be replicated. Towards that end, we share the code used in our analysis[2].

---

[2] https://bit.ly/ICAA2026-RM.

6   Summary and Conclusions

Understanding the influence of code level complexity on defects in large-scale software systems has long been area of interest for researchers and practitioners. However, most of the studies in this area are correlational in nature. In this paper, we report results from applying Greedy Equivalence Search (GES) – a causal discovery technique – on a real-world dataset to understand how two different aspects of complexity – essential and design – causally affect the number of defects in software modules. The robustness and correctness of the GES outcomes are validated by the random common cause (RCC), data subset refuter (DSR), and placebo treatment (PT) approaches. After controlling for peripheral factors related to software modules such as lines of code, difficulty, effort, intelligence content, we find statistically significant evidence that essential complexity has causal impact on defect count, while design complexity does not. These results can inform design decisions, guide software development and testing, and influence managerial decision-making towards the production of higher quality software.

References

1. The promise repository of empirical software engineering data (2015)
2. Afrianto, N., et al.: Applying pc algorithm and ges to three clinical data sets: heart disease, diabetes, and hepatitis. In: IOP Conference Series: Materials Science and Engineering. vol. 1077, p. 012067. IOP Publishing (2021)
3. Aydin, Z.B.G., Samli, R.: Performance evaluation of some machine learning algorithms in nasa defect prediction data sets. In: 2020 5th International Conference on Computer Science and Engineering (UBMK), pp. 1–3. IEEE (2020)
4. Basili, V.R., Briand, L.C., Melo, W.L.: A validation of object-oriented design metrics as quality indicators. IEEE Trans. Softw. Eng. **22**(10), 751–761 (2002)
5. Bird, C., et al.: Fair and balanced? bias in bug-fix datasets. In: Proceedings of the 7th joint meeting of the European Software Engineering Conference and the ACM SIGSOFT Symposium on the Foundations of Software Engineering, pp. 121–130 (2009)
6. Chickering, D.M.: Optimal structure identification with greedy search. J. Mach. Learn. Res. **3**(Nov), 507–554 (2002)
7. Elish, K.O., Elish, M.O.: Predicting defect-prone software modules using support vector machines. J. Syst. Softw. **81**(5), 649–660 (2008)
8. Halstead, M.H.: Elements of Software Science (Operating and programming systems series). Elsevier Science Inc. (1977)
9. Hasan, U., Gani, M.O.: Kgs: Causal discovery using knowledge-guided greedy equivalence search. arXiv preprint arXiv:2304.05493 (2023)
10. He, J., Lin, Y., Gu, X., Yeh, C.C.M., Zhuang, Z.: Perfsig: extracting performance bug signatures via multi-modality causal analysis. In: Proceedings of the 44th International Conference on Software Engineering, pp. 1669–1680 (2022)
11. Huang, B., Zhang, K., Lin, Y., Schölkopf, B., Glymour, C.: Generalized score functions for causal discovery. In: Proceedings of the 24th ACM SIGKDD International Conference on Knowledge Discovery & Data Mining, pp. 1551–1560 (2018)

12. Iqbal, A., et al.: Performance analysis of machine learning techniques on software defect prediction using nasa datasets. Int. J. Adv. Comput. Sci. Appl. **10**(5) (2019)
13. Küçük, Y., Henderson, T.A., Podgurski, A.: Improving fault localization by integrating value and predicate based causal inference techniques. In: 2021 IEEE/ACM 43rd International Conference on Software Engineering (ICSE), pp. 649–660. IEEE (2021)
14. Li, L., et al.: On causal discovery in the presence of deterministic relations. Adv. Neural. Inf. Process. Syst. **37**, 130920–130952 (2024)
15. Long, G., Gong, J., Fang, H., Chen, T.: Learning software bug reports: a systematic literature review. ACM Trans. Softw. Eng. Methodol. (2025)
16. Lu, N.Y., Zhang, K., Yuan, C.: Improving causal discovery by optimal bayesian network learning. In: Proceedings of the AAAI Conference on Artificial Intelligence. vol. 35, pp. 8741–8748 (2021)
17. McCabe, T.J.: A complexity measure. IEEE Trans. Softw. Eng. **4**, 308–320 (1976)
18. Naser, M., Çiftçioğlu, A.Ö.: Causal discovery and inference for evaluating fire resistance of structural members through causal learning and domain knowledge. Struct. Concrete **24**(3), 3314–3328 (2023)
19. Nogueira, A.R., Pugnana, A., Ruggieri, S., Pedreschi, D., Gama, J.: Methods and tools for causal discovery and causal inference. WIREs Data Mining Knowl. Discov. **12**(2), e1449 (2022)
20. Pearl, J.: Causality. Cambridge university press (2009)
21. Ramsey, J., Glymour, M., Sanchez-Romero, R., Glymour, C.: A million variables and more: the fast greedy equivalence search algorithm for learning high-dimensional graphical causal models, with an application to functional magnetic resonance images. Int. J. Data Sci. Anal. **3**, 121–129 (2017)
22. Rathor, K., Kaur, J., Nayak, U.A., Kaliappan, S., Maranan, R., Kalpana, V.: Technological evaluation and software bug training using genetic algorithm and time convolution neural network (GA-TCN). In: 2023 Second International Conference on Augmented Intelligence and Sustainable Systems (ICAISS), pp. 7–12. IEEE (2023)
23. Ray, B., Posnett, D., Filkov, V., Devanbu, P.: A large scale study of programming languages and code quality in Github. In: Proceedings of the 22nd ACM SIGSOFT International Symposium on Foundations of Software Engineering. pp. 155–165 (2014)
24. Schwarz, G.: Estimating the dimension of a model. Ann. Stat. 461–464 (1978)
25. Sharma, A., Kiciman, E.: Dowhy: an end-to-end library for causal inference. arXiv preprint arXiv:2011.04216 (2020)
26. Siddiqui, T., Mustaqeem, M.: Performance evaluation of software defect prediction with NASA dataset using machine learning techniques. Int. J. Inf. Technol. **15**(8), 4131–4139 (2023)
27. Subramanyam, R., Krishnan, M.S.: Empirical analysis of CK metrics for object-oriented design complexity: implications for software defects. IEEE Trans. Softw. Eng. **29**(4), 297–310 (2003)
28. Wang, Y., Squires, C., Belyaeva, A., Uhler, C.: Direct estimation of differences in causal graphs. Adv. Neural Inf. Process. Syst. **31** (2018)

An Efficient Algorithm for Path Matrix Computation and Improved Path Energy Bounds

Amol P. Narke$^{(\boxtimes)}$ and Prashant P. Malavadkar

Dr. Vishwanath Karad MIT World Peace University, Pune 411038, India
{amol.narke,prashant.malavadkar}@mitwpu.edu.in

Abstract. The path matrix and path energy of a graph provide valuable insights into structural properties related to vertex-disjoint paths. In this paper, we present a new algorithm for computing the all-pairs path matrix of undirected graphs. The method employs Gomory-Hu trees with fast unit-capacity max-flow computations, achieving a time complexity of $O(|V|\,|E|\sqrt{|E|} + |V|^2)$. We further establish new bounds for the path energy in terms of the maximum degree and the Frobenius norm, which improve upon the existing bound of $2(n-1)^2$ and give sharper estimates for all non-complete graphs. In addition, we demonstrate a connection between classical graph energy and path energy, thereby contributing to the broader framework of spectral graph theory.

Keywords: Path matrix · Path energy · Vertex-connectivity · Gomory–Hu tree · Maximum flow · Spectral graph theory · Graph algorithms

1 Introduction

In this work, we primarily consider simple, undirected and finite graphs. A graph $G = (V, E)$ has order $n = |V|$ and size $m = |E|$. For $v \in V$, the degree of v is denoted $\deg(v)$, with minimum degree $\delta(G)$ and maximum degree $\Delta(G)$. The adjacency matrix $A(G)$ is the $n \times n$ $\{0, 1\}$-matrix that encodes the adjacencies of the vertices of G. The spectrum $\{\lambda_1, \ldots, \lambda_n\}$ of $A(G)$ constitutes a central object of study in classical spectral graph theory. One important spectral invariant is the *graph energy*, introduced by Gutman [2], defined as the sum of the absolute values of the eigenvalues of $A(G)$. Building on this spectral perspective, Patekar and Shikare [6] introduced the notion of the *path matrix* $P(G)$, where the (i, j)-entry gives the maximum number of internally vertex-disjoint paths between v_i and v_j. Path energy is defined analogously to graph energy. If $\beta_1, \beta_2, \ldots, \beta_n$ are the eigenvalues of $P(G)$, then the path energy of G is defined as $PE(G) = \sum_{i=1}^{n} |\beta_i|$. For more details, see [3–5].

In the Fig. 1, $A(G)$ denotes the adjacency matrix and $P(G)$ denotes the path matrix of the graph G. The spectrum of $A(G)$ is

$$\mathrm{Spec}(A(G)) = \{\, 1 + \sqrt{3},\ \sqrt{2},\ 0,\ 1 - \sqrt{3},\ -\sqrt{2},\ -2 \,\},$$

C. Zaroliagis et al. (Eds.): ICAA 2026, LNCS 16423, pp. 15–25, 2026.
https://doi.org/10.1007/978-3-032-15621-1_2

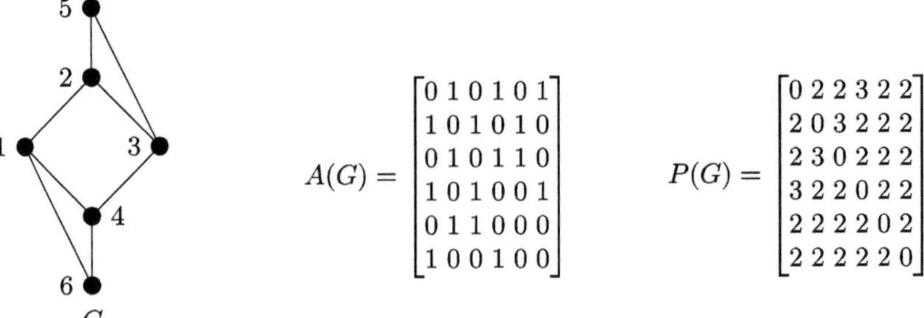

Fig. 1. Graph G with its adjacency matrix $A(G)$ and its path matrix $P(G)$.

and the spectrum of $P(G)$ is

$$\mathrm{Spec}(P(G)) = \{\, 10.6846,\ -1.0000,\ -1.6846,\ -2.0000,\ -3.0000,\ -3.0000 \,\}.$$

The path energy of the graph is

$$PE(G) = 21.369,$$

while the existing bound, $2(n-1)^2 = 50$, clearly demonstrates substantial scope for improvement.

To address this, it is essential to investigate the path spectral properties of graphs, which requires examining the path matrices of a broader class of graphs. By leveraging modern computational techniques, we develop a new algorithm with improved time complexity for computing path matrices, thereby enabling the establishment of sharper bounds for the path energy of graphs

2 An Efficient Computation of the Path Matrix for All-Pairs

In this section, we present a novel algorithm for computing the all-pairs path matrix of undirected graphs, significantly improving upon the $O(|E|\,|V|^3)$ complexity of the prior method by Ilić and Bašić [4]. Their approach relies on repeated Ford-Fulkerson calls for each vertex pair, which not only scales cubically with the number of vertices but also exhibits high computational cost on dense graphs. Our method overcomes these limitations using a Gomory-Hu tree [1] on the vertex-split network to efficiently compute all-pairs vertex connectivity via fast unit-capacity max-flow computations, achieving an overall time complexity of $O(|V|\,|E|\sqrt{|E|} + |V|^2)$. The algorithm proceeds as follows:

1. **Vertex-Split Reduction:** Transform the original graph into a unit-capacity network to model vertex connectivity. Each non-terminal vertex v is replaced by two nodes, v_{in} and v_{out}, connected by a directed edge of capacity 1. Each undirected edge (u, v) is replaced by two directed arcs of unit capacity, $(u_{\text{out}} \to v_{\text{in}})$ and $(v_{\text{out}} \to u_{\text{in}})$.

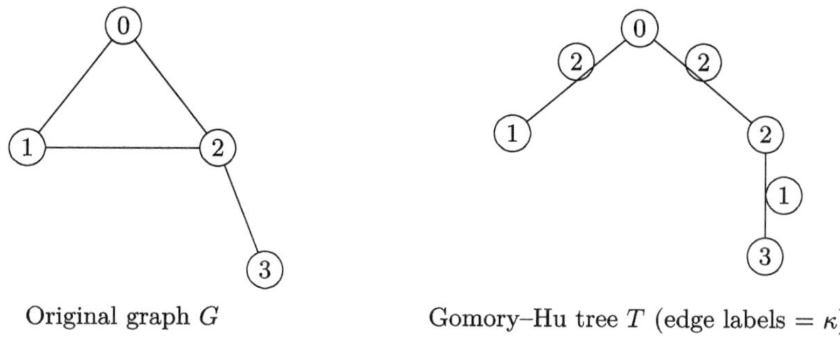

$$\kappa(0,1) = 2, \;\; \kappa(0,2) = 2, \;\; \kappa(0,3) = 1$$

Fig. 2. Graph G and the corresponding Gomory–Hu tree T. Edge labels denote vertex-connectivity values κ.

2. **Gomory–Hu Tree Construction:** Build a Gomory–Hu tree T using $|V| - 1$ unit-capacity max-flow computations. Each max-flow is computed via Dinic's algorithm in $O(|E|\sqrt{|E|})$ time, leading to a total complexity of $O(|V||E|\sqrt{|E|})$ for the tree construction.
3. **Preprocessing for Minimum-Edge Queries:** Preprocess the tree T to enable constant-time queries for the minimum-weight edge along any path. This step requires $O(|V|\log|V|)$ time.
4. **Path Matrix Extraction:** For every pair of vertices (i,j), the corresponding entry of the path matrix is obtained as

$$P_{ij} = \min\{w(e) : e \in \mathrm{path}_T(i,j)\},$$

which can be answered in $O(1)$ time per query. Assembling the full matrix P therefore requires $O(|V|^2)$ time.
5. **Overall complexity:**

$$O(|V| + |E|) + O(|V||E|\sqrt{|E|}) + O(|V|\log|V|) + O(|V|^2)$$
$$= O(|V||E|\sqrt{|E|} + |V|^2). \quad (1)$$

Overall, this approach reduces both the theoretical and practical complexity of computing all-pairs vertex-connectivity, providing a compact, reusable structure for efficient path matrix computation (Fig. 2).

Remark 1. (Why Endpoints Must Be Exempted). In the vertex-splitting reduction, internal vertices are capacity-1 to model internal-vertex usage. If the same capacity-1 is left on the *endpoints* during a given s–t max-flow, the endpoint itself may artificially limit flow and the computed s–t cut value will not equal the vertex-connectivity $\kappa(s,t)$. Setting s and t internal arcs to ∞ (or to a sufficiently large value) for the particular flow call removes this spurious bottleneck and yields the correct vertex min-cut.

The following theorem guarantees that the proposed algorithm correctly determines the number of vertex-disjoint paths between any pair of vertices.

Theorem 1. *The algorithm All-Pairs Vertex-Disjoint Paths via Corrected Gomory-Hu computes, for every pair $u, v \in V$, the vertex-connectivity $\kappa(u,v)$, i.e., the maximum number of internally vertex-disjoint u–v paths in the original graph G.*

Proof. The proof follows from three key observations:

1. **Vertex-splitting preserves connectivity**: By Menger's theorem [7], the maximum number of internally vertex-disjoint paths between u and v in G equals the maximum flow between u_{out} and v_{in} in the vertex-split network with u and v having infinite internal capacity.
2. **Gomory-Hu tree correctness**: The adapted Gomory-Hu construction on the vertex-split network correctly computes all-pairs maximum flows in that network [1].
3. **Cut correspondence**: Each minimum cut in the vertex-split network corresponds to a minimum vertex separator in the original graph, preserving the connectivity values.

Therefore, $\kappa(u,v) = \min\{w(e) : e \in \mathrm{path}_T(u,v)\}$ for all $u, v \in V$.

Using the proposed algorithms, we examined the path matrices and their spectra for ten different graphs, as illustrated in Fig. 3. These observations enable us to establish the new bounds for the path energy.

In the next section, we derive new bounds for the path energy of a graph in terms of its maximum degree and Frobenius norm, refining the best known bound $2(n-1)^2$ given by Shikare [5] and later proved by Ilić [4]. These bounds are particularly sharper when the graph is not complete.

3   New Bounds For Path Energy

We first establish two preliminary results which are useful in deriving Theorems 2 and 3. The following proposition provides an upper bound for the row sum of a path matrix in terms of the vertex degrees.

Proposition 1. *G be a graph on n vertices and $p_{i,j}$ is the total number of vertex disjoint paths from vertex i to vertex j then,*

$$\sum_{i \neq j=1}^{n} p_{i,j} \leq (n-1)deg(v_i),$$

for $i \neq j = 1, 2, \ldots, n.$

Algorithm 1: All-Pairs Vertex-Disjoint Paths via Corrected Gomory–Hu

---

Input: Undirected simple graph $G = (V, E)$

Output: Symmetric matrix $P \in Z_{\geq 0}^{|V| \times |V|}$ where P_{uv} is the maximum number of internally vertex-disjoint paths between u and v

Step 1: Vertex-split construction.

foreach $v \in V$ **do**
> create nodes v_{in} and v_{out};
> add directed edge $(v_{\text{in}} \to v_{\text{out}})$ with capacity 1;

foreach *edge* $\{u, v\} \in E$ **do**
> add directed edges $(u_{\text{out}} \to v_{\text{in}})$ and $(v_{\text{out}} \to u_{\text{in}})$ with capacity 1;

Note: For each max-flow query, endpoints internal capacity is set to ∞.

Step 2: Gomory–Hu tree construction.

Choose arbitrary root $r \in V$; initialize parent$[r] \leftarrow r$, and parent$[v] \leftarrow r$ for $v \neq r$;

Initialize empty tree T;

foreach $s \in V \setminus \{r\}$ **do**
> $t \leftarrow$ parent$[s]$;
> construct fresh vertex-split network;
> set capacities $(s_{\text{in}} \to s_{\text{out}}) \leftarrow \infty$ and $(t_{\text{in}} \to t_{\text{out}}) \leftarrow \infty$;
> $(f, C) \leftarrow$ MaxFlowMinCut(network, s_{out}, t_{in});
> add edge (s, t) to T with weight $w(s, t) \leftarrow f$;
> **foreach** *vertex* u *in cut* C *containing* s **do**
> > **if** parent$[u] = t$ **then**
> > > set parent$[u] \leftarrow s$

Step 3: Preprocessing.

Preprocess T in $O(|V| \log |V|)$ for min-edge queries on paths.

Step 4: Build path matrix P.

foreach $u, v \in V$ **do**
> **if** $u = v$ **then**
> > $P[u][v] \leftarrow 0$
>
> **else**
> > $P[u][v] \leftarrow \min\{w(e) : e \in \text{path}_T(u, v)\}$

return P.

Proof. We fixed i, $p_{i,j}$ is at most degree of v_i for all $i \neq j = 1, \ldots, n$ and for $i = j$ it is 0. That is, $p_{i,j} \leq deg(v_i)$ taking summation over j, we get

$$\sum_{j \neq i = 1}^{n} p_{i,j} \leq \sum_{j \neq i = 1}^{n} deg(v_i).$$

Lemma 1 provides the upper bound for the absolute eigenvalue of the path matrix in terms of the maximum vertex degree of a graph.

Lemma 1. *Let $P(G)$ denote the path matrix of a graph G on n vertices. If β is an eigenvalue of $P(G)$, then $|\beta| \leq (n-1)\Delta$.*

Proof. Let x be an eigenvector of $P(G)$ corresponding to eigenvalue β, then $Px = \beta x$. Write $x = (x_1, x_2, x_3, ..., x_n)^t$ where without loss of generality, $|x_1| = \max\limits_{1 \leq i \leq n} |x_i|$. $|\beta||x_1| = \sum\limits_{j \neq i = 1}^{n} p_{1,j} x_j \leq |x_1| \sum\limits_{j \neq i = 1}^{n} p_{1,j} \leq |x_1|(n-1)deg(v_i) \leq |x_1|(n-1)\Delta \leq |x_1|(n-1)\Delta.$

By using Lemma 1 we obsurved that, $\beta_i \leq (n-1)\Delta$, for all $i = 1, 2, \ldots, n$. Let M be a real symmetric matrix. The inertia of M is denoted by

$$\text{In}(M) = (n_+, n_-, n_0),$$

Where n_+, n_-, and n_0 represent the number of positive, negative, and zero eigenvalues of M, respectively. We define $\mu = \min\{n_+, n_-\}$ as the minimum of the number of positive and negative eigenvalues.

Theorem 2. *Let G be a graph with n vertices, and let $P(G)$ be its path matrix. Suppose the eigenvalues of $P(G)$ are denoted by $\beta_1 \geq \beta_2 \geq \cdots \geq \beta_n$ then*

$$PE(G) \leq 2\mu(n-1)\Delta.$$

Proof. The path energy is defined as the sum of the absolute values of the eigenvalues:

$$PE(G) = \sum_{i=1}^{n} |\beta_i|.$$

The trace of $P(G)$ is zero, thus we have:

$$\sum_{i=1}^{n} \beta_i = \sum_{n_+} \beta_i + \sum_{n_-} \beta_j = 0,$$

Which implies:

$$\sum_{n_+} \beta_j = -\sum_{n_-} \beta_i.$$

Therefore, without loss of generality, suppose $\mu = n_+$ then the path energy becomes:

$$PE(G) = \sum_{n_+} \beta_i - \sum_{n_-} \beta_j = 2\sum_{\mu} |\beta_i|.$$

Now, using Lemma 1, $|\beta_i| \leq (n-1)\Delta$ for each $i = 1, 2, \ldots, \mu$, it follows that:

$$\sum_{i=1}^{\mu} |\beta_i| \leq \mu(n-1)\Delta.$$

Multiplying both sides by 2 yields the desired bound:

$$PE(G) \leq 2\mu(n-1)\Delta.$$

This bound is sharper than the existing bound $2(n-1)^2$ when $\mu = 1$, and it attains its maximum possible value of $2(n-1)\Delta$. In practice, however, the actual path energy may be considerably smaller than $2\mu(n-1)\Delta$, depending on the structure of the graph. In the following theorem, we establish a tighter upper bound than $2\mu(n-1)\Delta$.

Theorem 3. *Let G be a graph with n vertices, and let $P(G)$ be its path matrix then*

$$PE(G) \le 2\sqrt{\mu} \cdot \left(\sum_{i=1}^{n} \beta_i^2 \right)^{1/2} = 2\sqrt{\mu} \cdot \|P\|_F,$$

where $\|P\|_F$ is the Frobenius norm of the path matrix $P(G)$, given by

$$\|P\|_F^2 = \sum_{i,j=1}^{n} P_{ij}^2.$$

Proof. Let the eigenvalues of $P(G)$ be $\beta_1, \beta_2, \ldots, \beta_n$. Since the trace of $P(G)$ is zero,

$$PE(G) = \sum_{i=1}^{n} |\beta_i| = \sum_{n_+} \beta_i - \sum_{n_-} \beta_i = 2 \sum_{n_+} |\beta_i|.$$

Now, applying the Cauchy–Schwarz inequality:

$$\sum_{\mu} |\beta_i| \le \sqrt{\mu} \cdot \left(\sum_{\mu} \beta_i^2 \right)^{1/2} \le \sqrt{\mu} \cdot \left(\sum_{i=1}^{n} \beta_i^2 \right)^{1/2}.$$

Hence,

$$PE(G) = 2 \sum_{\mu} |\beta_i| \le 2\sqrt{\mu} \cdot \left(\sum_{i=1}^{n} \beta_i^2 \right)^{1/2}.$$

As shown in [7], for any symmetric matrix representation of a graph, the sum of squares of eigenvalues equals the Frobenius norm squared, i.e.,

$$\sum_{i=1}^{n} \beta_i^2 = \|P\|_F^2 = \sum_{i,j=1}^{n} P_{ij}^2,$$

We obtain the final bound:

$$PE(G) \le 2\sqrt{\mu} \cdot \|P\|_F.$$

This bound is typically sharper than the upper bound $2\mu(n-1)\Delta$, especially when μ is small (in particular, for $\mu = 1$). The following corollary establishes a relation between the energy of a graph and its path energy.

Theorem 4. *Let G be a connected graph on n vertices then $E(G) \le \dfrac{n}{2} PE(G)$.*

Proof. Let G be a connected graph on n vertices. Ilic et al., in [4] proved the inequality $2(n-1) \le PE(G)$. Thus,

$$(n-1) \le \frac{PE(G)}{2} \tag{2}$$

Let $A(G)$ be an adjacency matrix of G. And x be an eigenvector of $A(G)$ corresponding to eigenvalue β' then,

$$Ax' = \beta' x'$$

Write $x' = (x_1', x_2', x_3', ..., x_n')^t$ where without loss of generality, $|x_1'| = \max\limits_{1 \le i \le n} |x_i'|$. Now,

$$|\beta'||x_i'| = \sum_{j=1}^{n} a_{1j} x_j' \le |x_1'| \sum_{j=1}^{n} a_{1j} \le |x_1'| deg(v_i) \le |x_1'| \Delta(v) \le |x_1'| \Delta(v).$$

Taking summation over $\beta' \in Spec\ A(G)$ we get, $E(G) \le n\Delta$. As G is simple connected graph, the maximum of Δ is $(n-1)$.
Thus,

$$E(G) \le n(n-1). \tag{3}$$

Combining Eqs. 2 and 3 we get, $E(G) \le \dfrac{n}{2} PE(G)$.

We next compare these bounds on a selection of connected graphs.

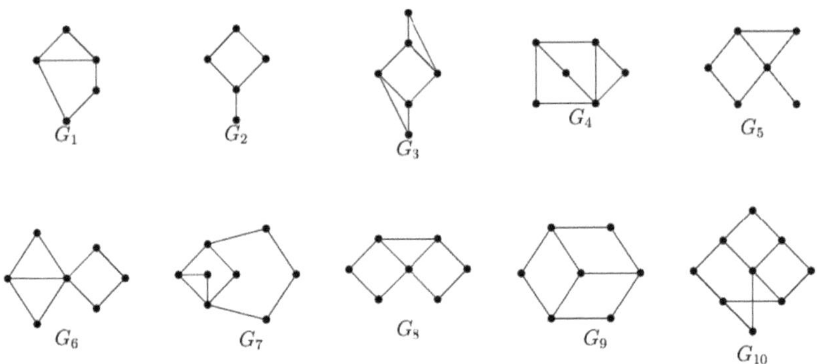

Fig. 3. Simple connected graphs on n vertices.

In the following table, the path matrices were computed using Algorithm 1, and their corresponding path energies are evaluated for the graphs depicted in Fig. 3. These energy values are then compared against three upper bounds: the classical bound $2(n-1)^2$, the spectral bound $2\mu(n-1)\Delta$ and the Frobenius norm-based bound $2\sqrt{\mu}\|P\|_F$ (Table 1).

Table 1. Summary of path eigenvalues and upper bounds for graphs G_1 to G_{10}.

Sr. No.	Graph	Path Eigenvalues	Path Energy	UB $2(n-1)^2$	UB $2\mu(n-1)\Delta$	UB $2\sqrt{\mu}\|P\|_F$
1	G_1	{8.424, -1.424, -2, -2, -3}	16.849	32	24	18.68
2	G_2	{6.606, -0.606, -2, -2, -2}	13.211	32	24	15.25
3	G_3	{10.685, -1, -1.685, -2, -3, -3}	21.369	50	30	22.58
4	G_4	{10.712, -1.321, -2, -2, -2, -3.391}	21.425	50	40	23.24
5	G_5	{8.980, -0.542, -1.438, -2, -2, -3}	17.960	50	40	19.62
6	G_6	{9.874, 1.030, -1.613, -2, -2, -2, -3.292}	21.809	72	120	32.36
7	G_7	{14.532, -1.134, -2, -2, -2, -2, -2, 3.397}	29.063	98	56	30.73
8	G_8	{12.610, -1.215, -2, -2, -2, -2, -3.395}	25.219	72	48	27.18
9	G_9	{13.865, -0.865, -2, -2, -3, -3, -3}	27.731	72	36	29.04
10	G_{10}	{18.434, -0.434, -2, -2, -2, -3, -3, -3, -3}	36.868	128	64	37.90

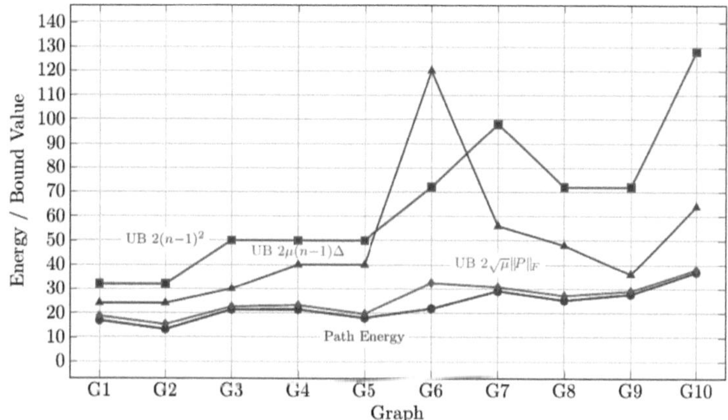

Fig. 4. Comparison of path energy and its upper bounds for graphs G_1–G_{10}.

The Fig. 4 illustrates a comparative line plot of the path energy and its three upper bounds for the graphs G_1 through G_{10} from Fig. 3. The blue line represents the actual path energy computed from the path eigenvalues of each graph. The red, green, and orange lines correspond to different upper bounds: the existing upper bound $2(n-1)^2$, the spectral bound $2\mu(n-1)\Delta$ and the Frobenius norm-based bound $2\sqrt{\mu}\|P\|_F$, respectively. This visual representation highlights how the actual path energy compares with theoretical upper bounds across different graph structures.

4   Motivation and Applications of Path Energy

The notion of path energy provides a quantitative measure of the structural tension distributed along a path in a graph. Intuitively, it captures how local vertex contributions accumulate to influence the robustness of a route. This type of metric has become relevant in several graph-theoretic settings.

First, path energy can be used as an indicator of *network reliability*: paths with high cumulative energy tend to pass through vertices with large spectral influence, which is correlated with criticality in connectivity analysis [2]. Consequently, energy-weighted shortest paths help identify vulnerable routing structures in communication and transportation systems [8].

Second, energy-based path scores naturally arise in *routing optimisation* on weighted and dynamic networks, where routing decisions incorporate both distance and vertex impact [9]. Such measures provide a more holistic view of routing cost than purely distance-based metrics.

Third, in spectral graph theory, path energy connects to the distribution of eigenvalues associated with induced subgraphs, enabling insights into dynamic processes such as information propagation and diffusion [10]. Models based on energy have been used to characterise spreading efficiency and bottleneck formation.

These examples highlight that path energy is not merely a theoretical construct but a practical descriptor of structural importance in real-world network analysis.

5   Conclusion

In this work, we first introduced a novel algorithmic framework for computing the all-pairs path matrix by combining vertex splitting with Gomory-Hu tree construction. This approach reduces the number of required maximum-flow computations from n^2 to $n - 1$, leading to an overall complexity of $O(|V||E|\sqrt{|E|} + |V|^2)$. In sparse graphs (i.e., $|E| = O(|V|)$, meaning the number of edges grows linearly with the number of vertices and the average degree remains $O(1)$), this yields a near-quadratic bound, while in dense graphs (i.e., $|E| = \Theta(|V|^2)$, meaning the number of edges grows quadratically with the number of vertices and the average degree is $\Theta(|V|)$), the runtime remains polynomial and competitive with state-of-the-art techniques. Compared to the $O(|E| \cdot n^3)$ complexity of the earlier algorithm of Ilić and Bašić (2019), our method achieves substantial improvements in scalability and efficiency, making it particularly well-suited for large-scale network applications.

Building on this computational foundation, we established new upper bounds for the path energy in terms of the Frobenius norm and the maximum degree. In particular, the Frobenius-based bound $2\sqrt{\mu}\,\|P\|_F$ provides a uniformly sharper estimate for all simply connected graphs except the complete graph, and it is especially tight when $\mu = 1$. For $\mu \geq 2$, the bound $2\mu(n - 1)\Delta$ often performs poorly in comparison with $2(n-1)^2$, whereas the Frobenius-based bound remains significantly stronger than both. These results underscore the effectiveness of spectral and norm-based techniques in graph energy analysis and align with the conjecture of Shikare et al. [5], later proved by Ilić [4].

In summary, this work advances the study of path matrices and their associated path energy by uniting algorithmic innovation with theoretical refinement, thereby laying a foundation for further exploration in both large-scale computational settings and structural graph theory.

Disclosure of Interests. The authors declare that they have no competing interests.

References

1. Gomory, R.E., Hu, T.C.: Multi-terminal network flows. J. Soc. Ind. Appl. Math. **9**(4), 551–570 (1961)
2. Gutman, I.: The energy of a graph. Ber. Math. Statist. Sekt. Forschungsz. Graz **103**, 1–22 (1978)
3. Akbari, S., Ghodrati, A.H., Gutman, I., Hosseinzadeh, M.A., Konstantinova, E.V.: On path energy of graphs. MATCH Commun. Math. Comput. Chem. **81**, 465–470 (2019)
4. Ilić, A., Bašić, M.: Path matrix and path energy of graphs. Appl. Math. Comput. **355**, 537–541 (2019)
5. Shikare, M.M., Malavadkar, P.P., Patekar, S.C., Gutman, I.: On path eigenvalues and path energy of graphs. MATCH Commun. Math. Comput. Chem. **79**, 387–398 (2018)
6. Patekar, S.C., Shikare, M.M.: On the path matrices of graphs and their properties. Adv. Appl. Discr. Math. **17**, 169–184 (2016)
7. Bapat, R.B.: Graphs and Matrices, 2nd edn. Springer, London (2014). https://doi.org/10.1007/978-1-4471-6569-9_9
8. Fiedler, M.: Algebraic connectivity of graphs. Czechoslov. Math. J. **23**(98), 298–305 (1973)
9. Estrada, E.: Structure of Complex Networks: Theory and Applications. Oxford University Press, Oxford (2012)
10. Nikiforov, V.: Graph eigenvalues and energy. Linear Algebra Appl. **422**, 111–129 (2007)

Small Uniquely Satisfiable Patterns

Uroš Čibej[(✉)]

University of Ljubljana, Faculty of Computer and Information Science,
Večna pot 113, 1000 Ljubljana, Slovenia
`uros.cibej@fri.uni-lj.si`

Abstract. Satisfiability (SAT) is a fundamental problem in computer science. This paper investigates a specific subclass of satisfiable expressions: those with a unique satisfying assignment (USAT). We introduce the concept of minimal USAT patterns — graph structures that represent USAT expressions which cease to be USAT if any clause is removed. We outline a method for identifying and cataloguing these patterns, present empirical findings from a database of them, and examine their practical applications. Finding these minimal patterns in larger SAT instances can serve multiple purposes, such as a preprocessing step to simplify the problem, a generalisation of a unit clause during the execution of a SAT solver, or as a distinctive feature in classifying SAT instances.

Keywords: Satisfiability · Uniquely Satisfiable · USAT · Minimal USAT · SMT

1 Introduction

The Boolean Satisfiability Problem (SAT) is a well-known NP-complete problem [5] that asks whether there exists an assignment of truth values to variables that makes a given Boolean formula true. While solvers for this problem have seen significant advancements, certain classes of formulas remain challenging. Our work focuses on the properties of a particular class: formulas with a single, unique satisfying assignment. Understanding the structural properties of such formulas could provide new insights into SAT solving.

We introduce the concept of a minimal uniquely satisfiable pattern (MUSAT pattern), which is a graph structure representing a class of uniquely satisfiable expressions that lose their unique satisfiability property if any clause is removed. We use the term pattern as a synonym for an undirected labelled graph, and we use it to abstract away variable names and negations. By building a database of these patterns, we aim to develop a new preprocessing technique for SAT solvers, as well as offering the possibility of dynamically identifying these patterns during the solving process. This paper provides a formal framework for defining minimal USAT patterns, describes a procedure for their systematic discovery, and presents preliminary empirical results on their prevalence and potential utility in real-world SAT instances.

The paper is structured as follows. The next section provides a brief overview of related concepts and work in the area of unique satisfiability. Section 3 presents the fundamental concepts and definitions. Section 4 describes the search methodology for the

C. Zaroliagis et al. (Eds.): ICAA 2026, LNCS 16423, pp. 26–37, 2026.
https://doi.org/10.1007/978-3-032-15621-1_3

USAT patterns, and Sect. 5 offers some empirical results and insights into the practical potential of the introduced concepts.

2   Related Work

The satisfiability (SAT) problem is a fundamental challenge in theoretical computer science, where it asks whether a given logical formula has a satisfying assignment. Its NP-completeness, proven by Cook and Levin [5,13], established its central role, both in theory and as a canonical problem for a wide range of practical applications, from hardware verification to logistics planning.

Progress in SAT solvers has been crucial in making SAT a practical tool. Early work, such as the Davis-Putnam-Logemann-Loveland (DPLL) algorithm [6], paved the way for modern solvers by using a systematic backtracking search. A key part of these algorithms is Unit Propagation (UP), a rule that simplifies a formula by recursively assigning values to literals in unit clauses (clauses with only one unassigned literal). This straightforward yet effective deduction technique is the backbone of modern SAT solvers. In fact, it has been empirically estimated that a state-of-the-art solver spends around 80% of its time performing unit propagation [7]. The DPLL framework was later transformed by the Conflict-Driven Clause Learning (CDCL) paradigm [14], which remains the most prevalent paradigm in state-of-the-art SAT solving.

Beyond the general SAT problem, the study of unique satisfiability (USAT) has gained significant attention. A formula is USAT if it has exactly one satisfying assignment. This problem is of high theoretical interest, as it belongs to the co-NP problems and is closely related to the more complex problem of counting satisfying assignments (#SAT) [18]. One of the main open theoretical questions is whether USAT is co-NP-complete and several attempts have been made to address this question [3,4]. While USAT is a challenging problem in its own right, recent research has focused on generating and studying specific classes of USAT formulas to create hard benchmarks and better understand their structure. For example, work by Haixia Jia et al. [12] explores techniques for generating hard, yet satisfiable, formulas by "hiding" solutions. Other efforts focus on generating USAT formulas with specific graph-theoretic properties [1,15].

Our work aims to uncover patterns that could serve as a useful tool for preprocessing. This is an area of research with a broad scope, as evidenced by the extensive work on preprocessing SAT formulas [2]. Many of these preprocessing steps rely focus on the goals of unit-propagation. Our aim is to extend these results to broader patterns that, like the unit clause, have unique assignments.

3   Definitions

Here's the most common description of the satisfiability problem: given a logical formula (with Boolean variables and standard logical operators), is it possible to assign values to the variables in such a way that the formula's value is 1? E.g., the formula $\phi = (x_1 \vee x_2) \implies (\neg x_1 \wedge x_2)$ is satisfiable since for $x_1 = 0, x_2 = 1$ the value of the expression is 1.

We will present a slightly different way to formulate this problem, which is equivalent but better suited to our description. Specifically, we use collections of sets instead of logical expressions.

First, we assume formulas are in Conjunctive Normal Form (CNF), as also most of SAT solvers do, and we are working with n variables and $2n$ possible literals that can appear in the formulas, i.e.,

$$L = \{x_1, \neg x_1, x_2, \neg x_2, \ldots, x_n, \neg x_n\}$$

A clause c is a subset of the set of literals $c \subseteq L$. Thus, the set of all possible clauses is 2^L (please note, a usual restriction is that l and $\neg l$ do not appear in the same clause, but this is not strictly necessary).

Lastly, a formula ϕ is a set of possible clauses: $\phi \subseteq 2^L$.

3.1   Cover and Satisfiability

We will define satisfiability in terms of a cover of the formula, which is a variation of the hitting set problem [9].

Definition 1. (Formula Cover). *A subset of literals $\zeta \subseteq L$ is a **cover** of a formula ϕ if:*

1. *no variable and its negation are present in the set, formally, for each literal l we have a restriction:*

$$l \notin \zeta \vee \neg l \notin \zeta,$$

2. *each clause is "satisfied" by at least one literal in the cover, formally, every clause c has the restriction:*

$$c \cap \zeta \neq \emptyset$$

The cover matches the literals that can be set to 1 without conflict, and each clause has a value of 1, which results in the entire formula also having a value of 1.

We will denote the set of all covers of a formula as $\mathcal{C}_\phi$ Now we can define classical satisfiability and the variation we are interested in within the same framework.

Definition 2. (Satisfiability). *A formula ϕ is **satisfiable** ($\phi \in SAT$) if it has at least one cover, i.e., $|\mathcal{C}_\phi| > 0$.*

The formulas that are the focus of this paper, however, are the following.

Definition 3. (Uniquely Satisfiable Formula). *A formula ϕ is **uniquely satisfiable** ($\phi \in USAT$) if it has exactly one cover, i.e., $|\mathcal{C}_\phi| = 1$.*

In this work, we focus on small patterns that cause part of the formula to be uniquely satisfiable. Therefore, we define a stricter version of the $USAT$ condition. The motivation for defining minimal USATs is that we want patterns as small as possible, since it is generally more desirable to identify the core reason why a formula is uniquely satisfiable. One possible way to do this is to focus on the minimal such subset of clauses.

Definition 4. (Minimal USAT). *A formula ϕ is a **minimal USAT** ($\phi \in MUSAT$) if:*

- $\phi \in USAT$
- $\forall c \in \phi : (\phi \setminus c) \notin USAT$

Example 1. The formula

$$\phi = \{\{a, b\}, \{a, \neg b\}, \{\neg a, b\}\}$$

is uniquely satisfiable, since

$$\mathcal{C}_\phi = \{\{a, b\}\}$$

and is also minimal, since:

$$\mathcal{C}_{\{a,b\},\{a,\neg b\}} = \{\{a, b\}, \{a, \neg b\}\}$$

$$\mathcal{C}_{\{a,b\},\{\neg a,b\}} = \{\{a, b\}, \{\neg a, b\}\}$$

$$\mathcal{C}_{\{a,\neg b\},\{\neg a,b\}} = \{\{a, b\}, \{\neg a, \neg b\}\}$$

3.2   Formula Graph and Patterns

We'll use a graph representation of the formula structure to allow the application of graph theory tools, mainly (sub)isomorphisms, for describing the equality of patterns in formulas.

Definition 5. (Formula Graph). *A **formula graph**, denoted $FG(\phi) = \langle V_\phi, E_\phi \rangle$, is a graph that represents the structure of a formula. The vertex set V_ϕ contains all literals and all clauses. The edge set E_ϕ consists of two types of edges:*

- *Edges between a literal and its negation: $\{(l_i, l_j) \mid l_i = \neg l_j\}$.*
- *Edges between a clause and the literals it contains: $\{(C_j, l_i) \mid l_i \in C_j\}$.*

Example: Consider the formula:

$$\phi = \{\{a, \neg b, \neg c\}, \{c, \neg a, \neg d, \neg e\}, \{d, \neg e, \neg a\}, \{e, \neg d\}\}$$

The formula graph $FG(\phi)$ is shown in Fig. 1. The circles represent the literals and the squares represent clauses. The connected literals are the pair $(l, \neg l)$.

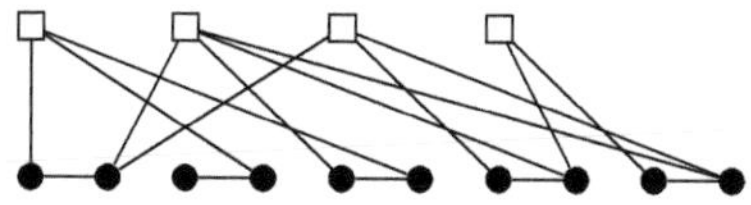

Fig. 1. An example formula graph for $\phi = \{\{a, \neg b, \neg c\}, \{c, \neg a, \neg d, \neg e\}, \{d, \neg e, \neg a\}, \{e, \neg d\}\}$.

Now we define the transformation in the opposite direction, that is, from a pattern to a set of formulas.

Definition 6. (Graph Instantiation). *A **graph instantiation** $I(G)$ is the set of all formulas whose formula graph is isomorphic to G.*

$$I(G) = \{\phi \mid \phi \in CNF, FG(\phi) \cong G\}$$

Here, the relation $\cong$ refers to the standard definition of a labelled graph isomorphism [19] (labels being the distinction between clause vertices and literal vertices).

Analogous to the definition with the formulas, we define unique satisfiability with patterns.

Definition 7. ((Minimal) Uniquely Satisfiable Pattern). *A **(minimal) uniquely satisfiable pattern** is a graph G such that every expression $\phi \in I(G) : \phi \in (M)USAT$ and $I(G) \neq \emptyset$.*

These patterns are a very useful representation for finding such expressions, since with this structure, we capture an infinite set of uniquely satisfiable instantiations.

4 Finding (M)USAT Patterns

The primary goal of this research is to compile a comprehensive database of small, uniquely satisfiable patterns (potentially minimal).

Formally, the problem is described as follows: given integers n and k, find all USAT patterns representing formulas with n variables ($2n$ literals) and k clauses.

Initially, we attempted an exhaustive search of all the $\binom{3^n-1}{k}$ formulas and used a SAT solver to verify their unique satisfiability. This method involved checking a vast number of potential formulas. Unsurprisingly, this approach proved to be too slow for anything beyond the smallest instances, primarily due to the combinatorial explosion in the number of formulas to consider. To find a more scalable and efficient solution, we decided to model the problem as an SMT (Satisfiability Modulo Theories) problem, which allows for richer reasoning and better handling of complex constraints.

4.1 SMT Formulation for Exhaustive Search

Considering the efficiency of SAT solvers, we set out to explore their potential in identifying USAT patterns. To simplify the modelling process, we utilised SAT Modulo Theories and their powerful language to specify the restrictions. However, all the building blocks are straightforward enough to be implemented as simple logical expressions.

The main decision variables are $2kn$ boolean variables that define which literals ($2n$) are a part of a particular clause (k). The main distinction from the brute-force approach is that we will encode the USAT constraint directly into the model, whereas previously we use a direct check.

4.2 SMT Model

We define a set of Boolean variables to represent the formula structure:

- c_{ij}^{+}: true if the literal v_i is in clause C_j.

- c_{ij}^-: true if the literal $\neg v_i$ is in clause C_j.

Basic Constraints:

1. A literal and its negation are not in the same clause:

$$\bigwedge_{i=1}^{n} \bigwedge_{j=1}^{k} \neg(c_{ij}^+ \wedge c_{ij}^-)$$

2. Each clause must be unique, i.e., each pair of clauses must be different on at least one position:

$$\bigwedge_{j=1}^{k} \bigwedge_{j'=j+1}^{k} \bigvee_{i=1}^{n} ((c_{ij}^+ \neq c_{ij'}^+) \vee (c_{ij}^- \neq c_{ij'}^-))$$

3. Clause length must be at least 2 to prevent trivial solutions (we want to avoid unit clauses)

$$\sum_{j=1}^{n} c_{ij}^+ + c_{ij}^- > 1$$

USAT Constraints: The core of the formulation is to enforce the uniqueness of solutions. Without loss of generality, we assume that the unique satisfying assignment is when all variables are true.

1. The formula must be satisfiable with all variables true. This is equivalent to checking if there is at least one positive literal in each clause, which in our formulation is:

$$\bigwedge_{j=1}^{k} \bigvee_{i=1}^{n} c_{ij}^+$$

2. The formula must not be satisfiable with any other assignment. We generate a set of constraints for every other possible assignment. Let $s \in \{0,1\}^n$ be a truth assignment, and let $l_i(s_i) = v_i$ if $s_i = 1$ and $l_i(s_i) = \neg v_i$ if $s_i = 0$. For every assignment s other than all-true, we state that the formula is false under that assignment:

$$\bigwedge_{s \in \{0,1\}^n \setminus \{1\}^n} \neg\phi(s)$$

where $\phi(s)$ is the formula with literals assigned according to s.

Notably, due to the second constraint (uniqueness), this is not a polynomial reduction, as the size of the SMT formulation grows exponentially. However, in practice, we'll be dealing with values that are small enough that this model is still viable in a practical sense.

4.3   Lexicographic Ordering for Clause Symmetry Breaking

The last set of constraints is needed for optimisation; without them, the solver has similar intractable behaviour to the brute-force approach.

In particular, we would like to prevent the generation of the same permutation of clauses. For this purpose, we introduce the lexicographic ordering ($<_{lex}$) of the clauses, i.e.,

$$clause_i <_{lex} clause_j$$

for $i < j$.

Many possible techniques can be used to achieve this [8], we chose the simple AND decomposition encoding to achieve

$$[c_{*i}^+, c_{*i}^-] <_{lex} [c_{*j}^+, c_{*j}^-]$$

For all pairs $i < j$, where $[c_{*i}^+, c_{*i}^-]$ denotes the vector of all positive and negative variables in the clause i.

4.4   Post-processing

The SMT solver gives a set of solutions, but it does not consider various isomorphic patterns and minimality. This is done with external tools:

Isomorphisms. Each obtained solution from the SMT solver is transformed into a graph, and only one solution from the set of isomorphic graphs is kept. This is done using VF2 implementation in the networkx library.

Minimality. The obtained solutions are checked if they are minimal by removing clauses one-by-one and checking their (un)satisfiability by an external SAT solver.

5   Experiments and Results

This section outlines the two primary experimental objectives of our research. The primary objective was to validate our SMT-based approach for generating (M)USAT expressions, and the secondary goal was to gauge the potential applicability of these patterns in real-world SAT instances.

5.1   Database of USAT Expressions

We present the initial analysis of the USAT expressions discovered using our SMT formulation. The findings include a discussion of the types and sizes of the expressions found. This database serves as a foundational resource for future work.

Table 1 shows the results of our search. We used the Z3 solver [16] and, for post-processing, we utilised NetworkX [10] for isomorphism checking and PySAT [11] for checking minimal unique satisfiability. We present the results $((n, k)$, where n is the number of variables and k is the number of clauses) for $n = 2, 3, 4, 5$ and $k = 3, 4, 5, 6, 7$. The empty cells in this table are values where no USAT pattern was found. Other cells include the number of patterns found, and the number in parentheses shows how many of those are minimal. The numbers with an asterisk are not optimal, i.e., there may be more of these patterns, but the solver failed to complete processing within a reasonable amount of time.

As expected, the number of USAT patterns increases rapidly, but this is no longer the case when minimality is considered. For instance, in $(3, 7)$ there's only one new pattern, whereas the remaining 720 patterns all include those already seen in $(3, 6)$.

To show a small example of the types of patterns found, Table 2 given the smallest 8 MUSAT patterns.

Table 1. This table shows the number of uniquely satisfiable expressions for a given n and k using the above described SMT model. The empty cells denote there are no patterns of that size, the asterisk denotes non-exhaustive result and the number in parenthesis denotes the minimal USATS of that size.

$n \setminus k$	3	4	5	6	7
2	1 (1)				
3		2 (2)	41 (17)	251 (8)	721 (1)
4			8 (8)	957 (314)	22680* (678*)
5				58* (58*)	2204* (391*)

Table 2. Smallest 8 MUSAT patterns. Figure shows a selection of MUSAT patterns, i.e.m the smallest $(2, 3)$ pattern, the two $(3, 4)$ patterns, and five $(3, 5)$ patterns.

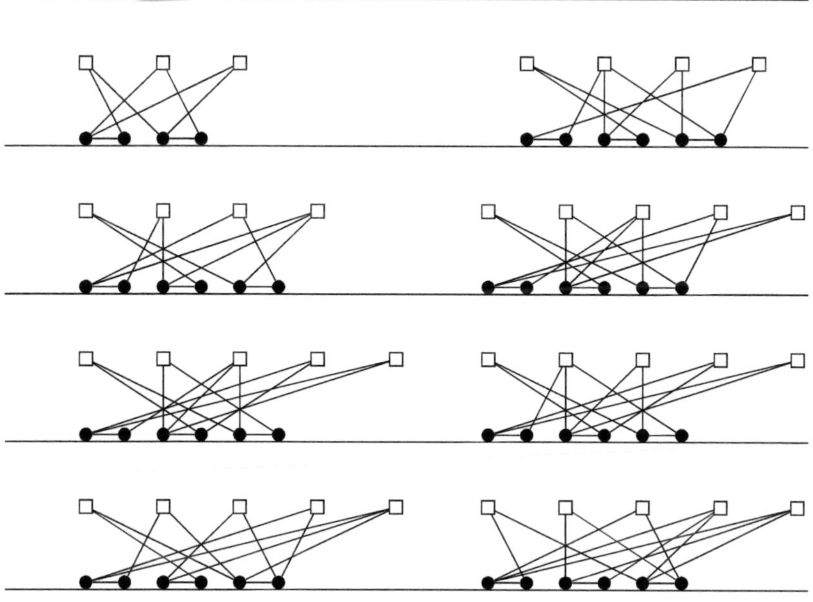

5.2 Analysis of Real-World SAT Instances

To understand the practical relevance of our findings, we searched for these identified USAT patterns within a set of real-world SAT instances. This analysis provides a preliminary look at the occurences of these patterns, giving a first glimpse into how SAT solvers could potentially benefit from incorporating this new type of propagation. We evaluate our approach on a diverse set of benchmarks from both academic and industrial domains. These instances, widely used in the SAT community, are sourced from a SAT competition.

Dataset Description. To evaluate the practical relevance of our discovered minimal uniquely satisfiable (USAT) patterns, we selected a test set of 25 SAT instances. These were sourced from the SAT 2002 competition and represent a wide range of applications.

Since the original competition benchmarks were organized by application, with each test set containing multiple instances from the same problem domain, we selected only one instance per application. This approach ensured our dataset was diverse, reducing bias toward any single problem type. The used testsets can be divided into three groups

- Real-world instances (e.g. bounded model checking, graph coloring, factorization)
- Hand-crafted instances (outputs of several generators of hard instances, puzzles such as towers of Hanoi)
- Random instances - a selection of random regular CNFs

The entire set of different domains is described in [17] in the set of submitted instances. This selection allows us to investigate whether these minimal USAT patterns appear consistently across different problem domains and if any interesting phenomena can be observed through these pattern fingerprints in the SAT instances. The graph in Figure 2 depicts the size of our selected instances by plotting the number of variables against the number of clauses. As shown, the instances range from small to medium-sized. We intentionally avoided much larger instances to lower the computational complexity of the pattern search.

5.3 Results

This section details the results of our experimental analysis, focusing on the prevalence of minimal USAT patterns in the selected instances. In order to show the results more concisely, we chose a set of 52 patterns, namely the patterns found for $(2, 3), (3, 4), (3, 5),$ and $(4, 5)$.

The search for our chosen patterns within a selection of 25 SAT instances is shown in Fig. 3. This heatmap-style figure serves as a pattern signature for each instance. Each row of the matrix corresponds to one of the 25 SAT instances, labeled I1 through I25. Each column represents one of the 52 minimal USAT patterns identified in our database, labeled P1 through P52.

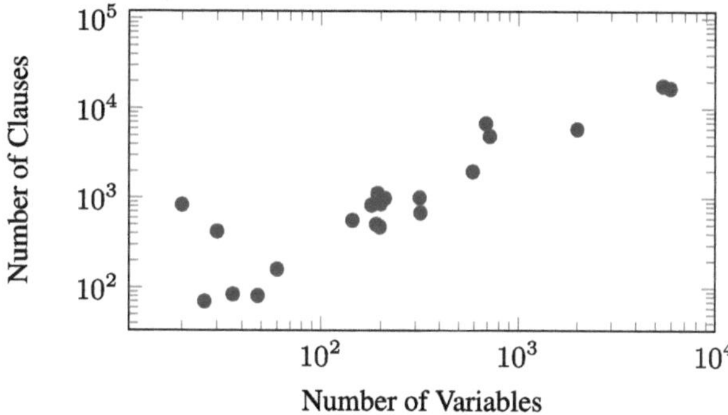

Fig. 2. The 25 SAT instances that were used in the experiment and their sizes. The axes are the number of variables and the number of clauses, respectively.

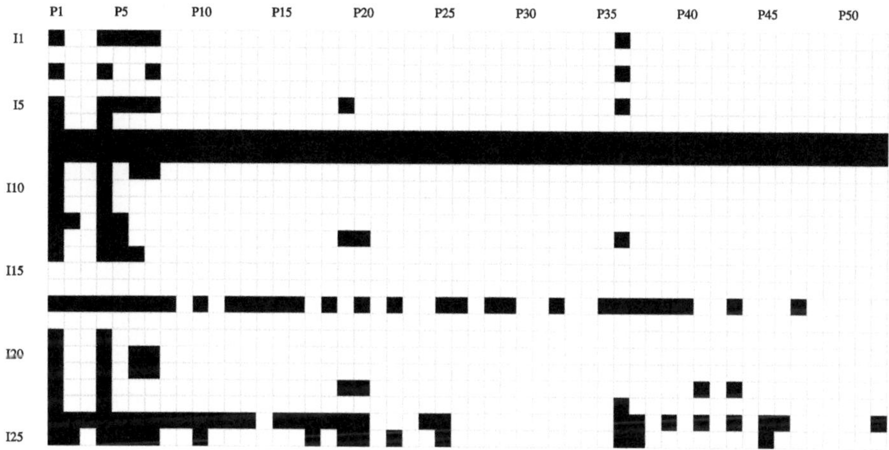

Fig. 3. The pattern fingerprints of SAT instances. This figure shows which patterns (52 columns) appear in which instance (25 rows).

A black cell at the intersection of a row and column signifies that the corresponding pattern was found at least once within that specific SAT instance. A white cell indicates the pattern was not detected.

The results show several interesting phenomena:

Absence of patterns Five cases showed no patterns out of 52, indicating some problem structures may lack these minimal USAT components.

All patterns Two cases contained all 52 patterns; both are randomly generated CNFs.

Many, but not all, patterns Certain instances have many patterns, but some are missing, unlike random instances.

Ubiquity of certain patterns Data shows that small patterns (2 variables, 3 clauses and 3 variables, 4 clauses) frequently appear across instances, suggesting these minimal structures are common. Identifying them could help prune the search space.

This analysis provides a preliminary but compelling view of the distribution and potential utility of minimal USAT patterns. The findings suggest that detecting these structures could serve as a valuable preprocessing or in-solver simplification step, particularly in instances where they are highly prevalent. Furthermore, these pattern fingerprints could serve as an informative instance feature for various classification and other machine learning tasks that can further improve the choices that solvers make.

6   Conclusion and Future Work

In this paper, we introduced and formally defined the concept of minimal uniquely satisfiable (USAT) patterns, which are graph structures representing USAT expressions that lose their unique satisfiability property if any clause is removed. Our primary contribution is a systematic procedure for discovering these patterns using an SMT-based search. The empirical results demonstrate that this methodology is effective, successfully identifying a substantial number of non-isomorphic minimal USAT patterns for up to 5 variables and 7 clauses. The significant growth in the number of patterns with increasing number of variables and clauses, as shown in our tables, suggests a rich space of USAT structures that can be explored. While the computational cost for larger patterns is a limiting factor, our approach provides a foundation for building a comprehensive database of these structures.

Furthermore, we investigated the practical relevance of these patterns by searching for their occurrences in real-world SAT instances from standard benchmark suites. Our findings confirm that minimal USAT patterns are not merely theoretical constructs; they are present in a variety of problem domains, including factorisation and industrial planning problems. The high number of occurrences of even small patterns, highlights their potential utility. The ability to identify these unique substructures and propagate their satisfying assignments offers a new avenue for powerful preprocessing. By transforming the original formula into an equisatisfiable version, this approach could significantly accelerate the performance of modern SAT solvers.

For future work, we plan to embed this pattern-matching technique into a SAT solver and conduct a comprehensive performance evaluation on a wider range of benchmarks. We also intend to explore the implications of partial matches more deeply, as they may offer opportunities for heuristic guidance and further simplification even when a full pattern is not found.

References

1. Ansótegui, C., Bonet, M.L., Levy, J.: On the structure of industrial sat instances. In: Proc. 15th Int. Conf. on Principles and Practice of Constraint Programming (CP), pp. 127–141 (2009)

2. Biere, A., Järvisalo, M., Kiesl, B.: Preprocessing in sat solving. In: Biere, A., Heule, M., van Maaren, H., Walsh, T. (eds.) Handbook of Satisfiability, Frontiers in Artificial Intelligence and Applications, vol. 336, pp. 391–435. IOS Press (2021). https://doi.org/10.3233/FAIA200992

3. Chang, R., Kadin, J.: On the structure of uniquely satisfiable formulas. Technical Report TR 90-1124, Cornell University, Department of Computer Science (1990), available via Stanford University Libraries
4. Chang, R., Kadin, J., Rohatgi, P.: On unique satisfiability and the threshold behavior of randomized reductions. J. Comput. Syst. Sci. **50**(3), 359–373 (1995)
5. Cook, S.A.: The complexity of theorem-proving procedures. In: Proceedings of the Third Annual ACM Symposium on Theory of Computing (STOC), pp. 151–158. ACM, New York (1971)
6. Davis, M., Logemann, G., Loveland, D.: A machine program for theorem-proving. Commun. ACM **5**(7), 394–397 (1962). https://doi.org/10.1145/368273.368557
7. Ehlers, R.: Approximately propagation complete and conflict propagating constraint encodings. In: Proc. 24th Int. Conf. on Principles and Practice of Constraint Programming (CP), pp. 221–238 (2018)
8. Elgabou, H.A.M.: Encoding the lexicographic ordering constraint in satisfiability modulo theories. Msc by research thesis, University of York, Department of Computer Science (2015), https://etheses.whiterose.ac.uk/id/eprint/10387/1/Encoding%20The%20Lexicographic%20Ordering%20Constraint%20in%20Satisfiability%20Modulo%20Theories.pdf
9. Garey, M.R., Johnson, D.S.: Computers and Intractability: A Guide to the Theory of NP-Completeness. W. H. Freeman & Co., New York (1979)
10. Hagberg, A.A., Schult, D.A., Swart, P.J.: Exploring network structure, dynamics, and function using networkx. In: Varoquaux, G., Vaught, T., Millman, J. (eds.) Proceedings of the 7th Python in Science Conference, pp. 11 – 15. Pasadena (2008)
11. Ignatiev, A., Morgado, A., Marques-Silva, J.: PySAT: a python toolkit for prototyping with SAT oracles. In: Beyersdorff, O., Wintersteiger, C.M. (eds.) SAT 2018. LNCS, vol. 10929, pp. 428–437. Springer, Cham (2018). https://doi.org/10.1007/978-3-319-94144-8_26
12. Jia, H., Moore, C., Strain, D.: Generating hard satisfiable formulas by hiding solutions deceptively. arXiv preprint (2005)
13. Levin, L.A.: Universal sequential search problems. Problems Inf. Trans. **9**(3) (1973)
14. Marques-Silva, J.P., Sakallah, K.A.: Grasp: a search algorithm for propositional satisfiability. IEEE Trans. Comput. **48**(5), 506–521 (1999)
15. Järvisalo, M., Biere, A.: Reconstructing solutions after blocked clause elimination. In: Strichman, O., Szeider, S. (eds.) SAT 2010. LNCS, vol. 6175, pp. 340–345. Springer, Heidelberg (2010). https://doi.org/10.1007/978-3-642-14186-7_30
16. de Moura, L., Bjørner, N.: Z3: an efficient SMT solver. In: Ramakrishnan, C.R., Rehof, J. (eds.) Tools and Algorithms for the Construction and Analysis of Systems, pp. 337–340. Springer, Berlin Heidelberg, Berlin, Heidelberg (2008)
17. Simon, L., Le Berre, D., Hirsch, E.A.: The sat2002 competition. Ann. Math. Artif. Intell. **43**(1), 307–342 (2005)
18. Valiant, L., Vazirani, V.: Np is as easy as detecting unique solutions. Theoretical Comput. Sci. **47**(1), 85–93 (1986). https://doi.org/10.1016/0304-3975(86)90135-0
19. Algorithms on Trees and Graphs. TCS, Springer, Cham (2021). https://doi.org/10.1007/978-3-030-81885-2

Approximate All-Pairs Hamming Distances and 0–1 Matrix Multiplication

Mirosław Kowaluk[1], Andrzej Lingas[2(✉)], and Mia Persson[3]

[1] Institute of Informatics, University of Warsaw, Warsaw, Poland
kowaluk@mimuw.edu.pl
[2] Department of Computer Science, Lund University, Lund, Sweden
Andrzej.Lingas@cs.lth.se
[3] Department of Computer Science and Media Technology, Malmö University,
Malmö, Sweden
Mia.Persson@mau.se

Abstract. Arslan showed that computing all-pairs Hamming distances is easily reducible to arithmetic 0–1 matrix multiplication (IPL 2018). We provide a reverse, linear-time reduction of arithmetic 0–1 matrix multiplication to computing all-pairs distances in a Hamming space. On the other hand, we present a fast randomized algorithm for approximate all-pairs distances in a Hamming space. By combining it with our reduction, we obtain also a fast randomized algorithm for approximate 0–1 matrix multiplication. Finally, we present an output-sensitive randomized algorithm for a minimum spanning tree of a set of points in a generalized Hamming space, the lower is the cost of the minimum spanning tree the faster is our algorithm.(A preliminary version of this article appeared in arXiv.org.)

Keywords: Hamming distance · Hamming space · arithmetic matrix multiplication · minimum spanning tree · approximation algorithm

1 Introduction

Arslan observes in [5] that computing all-pairs distances in Hamming spaces $\{0,1\}^d$ and generalized Hamming spaces Σ^d, where Σ is a finite alphabet, forms a frequent major step in hierarchical clustering [4] and in phylogenetic-tree construction [6]. He also lists several examples of applications of hierarchical clustering based on Hamming distances in medical sciences [5]. Once pairwise Hamming distances between input points in a generalized Hamming space are known, a minimum spanning tree of the points can be easily computed. The computation of exact or approximate minimum spanning trees in Hamming spaces and generalized Hamming spaces of high dimension is widely used technique for clustering data, especially in machine learning [14,19].

In [5], Arslan reduced the problem of computing all-pairs Hamming distances in a generalized Hamming space to arithmetic matrix multiplication. In particular, he obtained an $O(|\Sigma|n^\omega)$-time algorithm for this problem when there are

n input points in Σ^d and ω denotes the exponent of the fast arithmetic matrix multiplication. The currently best known upper bound on ω is 2.3714 [2].

The arithmetic matrix product of two 0–1 matrices is closely related to the Boolean matrix product of the corresponding matrices and for $n \times n$ matrices can be computed in $O(n^{2.372})$ time [2]. It is a fundamental tool in science and engineering (e.g., in machine learning [3]). Unfortunately, no truly subcubic practical algorithms for the arithmetic product of $n \times n$ 0–1 matrices are known. Therefore, in some cases, a faster approximate arithmetic matrix multiplication can be more useful. E.g., it enables for the identification of largest entries in the product matrix [8,20]. Among other things, it can also provide fast estimations of the number of the so-called witnesses for the entries of the Boolean product of Boolean matrices [12] and the number of subgraphs isomorphic to a small pattern graph, in particular triangles, in an input graph [11]. There are few articles on approximate arithmetic matrix multiplication in the literature. Frequently, one uses the Frobenius matrix norm $|| \ ||_F$ (i.e., the square root of the sum of the squares of the entries of the matrix) to express the quality of approximation [8,20].

Cohen and Lewis [8], followed by Drineas *et al.* [9], utilized random sampling to approximate arithmetic matrix product. Both articles present an approximation D of the matrix product AB of two $n \times n$ matrices A and B satisfying $||AB - D||_F = O(||AB||_F/\sqrt{c})$, for a given $c > 1$ (see also [20]). In [8] the matrices A, B are required to be nonnegative while in [9] they are arbitrary. The approximation in [9] takes $O(n^2 c)$ time. Drineas *et al.* [9] also presented bounds on the differences $|AB_{ij} - D_{ij}|$ on the entry level. The best of these bounds is $\Omega(Q^2 n/\sqrt{c})$, where Q is the maximum value of an entry in A and B. Sarlós [21] derived analogous guarantees in terms of the Frobenius norm and his algorithm also runs in $O(n^2 c)$ time. However, he obtained stronger individual upper bounds on the additive error for each entry D_{ij} of the approximation matrix D. They are of the form $O(||A_{i*}||_2 ||B_{*j}||_2/\sqrt{c})$, where A_{i*} and B_{*j} stand for the i-th row of A and j-th column of B, respectively, and hold with high probability. More recently Pagh [20] designed a randomized approximation algorithm for the arithmetic product of $n \times n$ matrices A and B running in $\tilde{O}(n(n+c))$ time. Each entry of the approximate matrix product output by Pagh's algorithm differs from the correct one at most by $||AB||_F/\sqrt{c}$. His algorithm first compresses the matrix product to a product of two polynomials and then uses the fast Fourier transform to multiply the polynomials. Afterwards, Kutzkov [18] designed analogous deterministic algorithms using different techniques. For approximation results on sparse arithmetic matrix products, see [16,20].

1.1 Our Contributions

Our first result is a linear-time (with respect to input and output size) reduction of arithmetic 0–1 matrix multiplication to computing all-pairs Hamming distances in a Hamming space. Combined with the reverse reduction from [5], it implies that these two problems have the same asymptotic time complexity.

Our next result is a fast randomized algorithm for approximate all-pairs Hamming distances in a Hamming space. It relies on a version of randomized dimension reduction given by Achlioptas in [1]. For n points in the d-hypercube, our algorithm approximates all the pairwise Hamming distances between them with high probability within $1 \pm \epsilon$ in time $O((\log N/\epsilon^2)(N+n^2))$, where $N = nd$ is the input size. E.g., when $d = n$ and $\epsilon = \Omega(1)$, it takes $\tilde{O}(n^2)$ time while the algorithm for the exact pairwise distances due to Arslan requires $O(n^\omega)$ time [5]. By combining our approximation algorithm with our reduction, we obtain also a fast randomized algorithm for approximate 0–1 matrix multiplication. With high probability, the approximation of the inner product of any row of the first matrix and any column of the second matrix differs at most by an ϵ fraction of the minimum of the Hamming distance between the row and the column and the complement of the distance. If the minimum is within a constant factor of the exact value of the inner product, the approximation is tight.

Finally, we present an output-sensitive randomized algorithm for a minimum spanning tree of a set of n points in the generalized Hamming space Σ^d, where Σ is an alphabet of $O(1)$ size. With high probability, it runs in $\tilde{O}(n(d+n+M))$ time, where M is the (Hamming) cost of a minimum spanning tree of the input points. Interestingly, a major preliminary step in our algorithm is a construction of an approximate minimum spanning tree of the points based on our fast randomized algorithm for approximate all-pairs Hamming distances.

1.2   Techniques

Our fast randomized algorithm for approximate all-pairs distances in Hamming spaces is based on a variant of randomized dimension reduction in Euclidean spaces given by Achlioptas in [1] and the observation that the Hamming distance between two 0–1 vectors is equal to their squared ℓ_2 distance. The main idea of a randomized dimension reduction is to provide a uniform random map from a d-dimensional metric space to its k-dimensional subspace that preserves distances up to $1 \pm \epsilon$ factor, where $k = O(\log n)$, with high probability. Johnson and Lindenstrauss were first to provide such maps from $\mathbb{R}^d$ to $\mathbb{R}^k$ for the ℓ_2 norm [17]. The advantage of Achlioptas' variant of JL dimension reduction is that such a random map can be generated by binary coins in this variant [1].

The crucial step in our output-sensitive randomized algorithm for a minimum spanning tree in a generalized Hamming space is the computation of all-pairs Hamming distances between the input points. It is implemented by an adaptation and generalization of the known method of multiplying Boolean or arithmetic 0–1 $n \times n$ matrices in time dependent on the cost of an approximate minimum spanning tree of the rows of the first matrix or the cost of an approximate minimum spanning tree of the columns of the second matrix, where the rows and columns are treated as points in $\{0,1\}^n$ [7,10,13]. The aforementioned method in turn relies on the idea of updating the inner product of two vectors a and b in $\{0,1\}^q$ over the Boolean or an arithmetic semi-ring to that of a vector a' in $\{0,1\}^q$ and the vector b, in time roughly proportional to the Hamming distance between a and a'.

1.3   Paper Organization

The next section contains basic definitions. Section 3 demonstrates our reduction of 0–1 matrix multiplication to computing all-pairs Hamming distances between the rows of the first matrix and the columns of the second matrix. Section 4 presents our fast randomized algorithm for approximate all-pairs Hamming distances based on the dimension reduction given in [1]. Section 5 shows our fast randomized algorithm for approximate 0–1 matrix multiplication. Section 6 is devoted to our output-sensitive algorithm for a minimum spanning tree in a generalized Hamming space.

2   Preliminaries

For a positive integer r, the set of positive integers not greater than r is denoted by $[r]$.

For two vectors $(a_1, \ldots, a_d)$ and $(b_1, \ldots, b_d)$ in $\mathbb{R}^d$, their *inner product* equals $\sum_{\ell=1}^{d} a_\ell b_\ell$.

For a matrix D, $D^\top$ stands for its transpose. If the entries of D are in $\{0, 1\}$ then D is a 0–1 matrix while if they are in a finite alphabet Σ, D is a Σ matrix.

The symbol ω denotes the smallest real number such that two $n \times n$ matrices can be multiplied using $O(n^{\omega+\epsilon})$ operations over the field of reals, for all $\epsilon > 0$.

The *Hamming distance* between two points a, b (vectors) in $\{0, 1\}^d$, and more generally, in Σ^d, is denoted by $\mathrm{ham}(a, b)$. It is equal to the number of the coordinates on which the two points differ. Alternatively, in case of $\{0, 1\}^d$ it can be defined as the distance between a and b in the ℓ_1 metric over $\{0, 1\}^d$. The distance between a, b in the ℓ_2 metric is denoted by $||a - b||_2$.

For a positive real ϵ, an estimation of the Hamming distance between two points a, $b \in \{0, 1\}^d$ whose value differs from $\mathrm{ham}(a, b)$ at most by $\epsilon \cdot \mathrm{ham}(a, b)$ is called an *ϵ-approximation* of $\mathrm{ham}(a, b)$.

An event is said to hold *with high probability* (w.h.p. for short) in terms of a parameter N related to the input size if it holds with probability at least $1 - \frac{1}{N^\alpha}$, for any constant α not less than 1.

3   All-Pairs Hamming Distances Versus 0–1 Matrix Multiplication

Arslan studied the problem of computing the Hamming distances between all pairs of points belonging to two point sets in a generalized Hamming space Σ^d, where Σ is a finite alphabet [5]. He provided a fast algorithm for this problem based on a reduction to arithmetic matrix multiplication [5]. The following theorem shows also a reverse reduction. In the theorem, the two sets of points in the generalized Hamming space are represented by two matrices, where the vectors of coordinates of the points form the rows or the columns, respectively.

Theorem 1. *Let A and B be two Σ matrices of sizes $p\times q$ and $q\times r$, respectively.*

1. *([5]) The problem of computing the Hamming distance between each row of A and each column of B can be reduced in $O(|\Sigma|pr)$ time to that of computing $O(|\Sigma|)$ arithmetic products of 0–1 matrices of sizes $p\times q$ and $q\times r$, respectively.*
2. *Conversely in case $\Sigma = \{0,1\}$, given the Hamming distances between each row of A and each column of B, the arithmetic matrix product of A and B can be computed in $O(pq + qr + pr)$ time.*

Proof. For the proof of the first part see [5]

To prove the second part, suppose that the Hamming distances $\mathrm{ham}(A_{i*}, B_{*j})$ between each row A_{i*} of A and each column B_{*j} of B are given. For a 0–1 vector $(v_1\ldots, v_k)$, let $(v_1,\ldots,v_k)^1$ denote the number of 1s in the vector, i.e., $\sum_{\ell\in[k]} v_\ell$. It is easy to verify that for two one-dimensional 0–1 vectors a and b, their inner product is equal to $\frac{a^1+b^1-\mathrm{ham}(a,b)}{2}$. Hence, we can compute the inner product C_{ij} of A_{i*} and B_{*j} as follows:

$$C_{ij} = \sum_{\ell\in[q]} A_{i\ell}B_{\ell j} =$$

$$\sum_{\ell\in[q]} \frac{(A_{i\ell})^1 + (B_{\ell j})^1 - \mathrm{ham}((A_{i\ell}),(B_{\ell j}))}{2} = \frac{A_{i*}^1 + B_{*j}^1 - \mathrm{ham}(A_{i*}, B_{*j})}{2}$$

Thus, it is sufficient to precompute the numbers of 1s in each row of A and each column of B in $O(pq + qr)$ time in order to compute the entries C_{ij} of the arithmetic matrix product C of A and B on the basis of $\mathrm{ham}(A_{i*}, B_{*j})$ in $O(pr)$ time. $\qquad\square$

We can compute an exact minimum spanning tree of n points p_1, $p_2,\ldots,p_n$ in the generalized Hamming space Σ^d by running a standard linear-time (Prim's) algorithm for a minimum spanning tree on the clique on $[n]$, where the weight of the edge (i,j) is set to the Hamming distance between the points p_i and p_j. To obtain the Hamming distances, we just form a matrix P where the i-th row is the vector of coordinates of the point p_i for $i \in [n]$, and apply Theorem 1 (1) to the matrices P and $P^\top$.

Corollary 1. *A minimum spanning tree of n points p_1, $p_2,\ldots,p_n$ in the generalized Hamming space Σ^d can be constructed in $O(|\Sigma|T(n,d))$ time, where $T(n,d)$ is the time required to multiply two rectangular 0–1 matrices of sizes $n \times d$ and $d \times n$, respectively.*

4   Approximate All-Pairs Hamming Distances via Dimension Reduction

The following fact and corollary present an efficient randomized dimension reduction. We shall use it to compute all-pairs approximate Hamming distances for a set of n input points (vectors) in $\{0,1\}^d$.

Fact 1. *(Achlioptas [1]) Let P be an arbitrary set of n points in $\mathbb{R}^d$, represented as an $n \times d$ matrix A. Given ϵ, $\beta > 0$, let $k_0 = \frac{4+2\beta}{\epsilon^2/2 - \epsilon^3/3} \log n$. For an integer $k \geq k_0$, let R be a $d \times k$ random matrix (R_{ij}), where $R_{ij} = 1$ with probability $\frac{1}{2}$ and $R_{ij} = -1$ otherwise. Let $E = \frac{1}{\sqrt{k}} AR$ and let $f : \mathbb{R}^d \to \mathbb{R}^k$ map the i-th row of A on the i-th row of E. With probability at least $1 - n^{-\beta}$, for all $u, v \in P$,*

$$(1 - \epsilon)(||u - v||_2)^2 \leq (||f(u) - f(v)||_2)^2 \leq (1 + \epsilon)(||u - v||_2)^2.$$

Observe that if $u, v \in \{0, 1\}^d$ then $\mathrm{ham}(u, v) = (||u - v||_2)^2$. Hence, we immediately obtain the following corollary from Fact 1.

Corollary 2. *Assume the notation from Fact 1. Suppose that $P \subset \{0, 1\}^d \subset \mathbb{R}^d$. Then, for all $u, v \in P$,*

$$(1 - \epsilon)\mathrm{ham}(u, v) \leq (||f(u) - f(v)||_2)^2 \leq (1 + \epsilon)\mathrm{ham}(u, v).$$

The following procedure computes an ϵ-approximate Hamming distance between each row of the first input 0–1 matrix A of size $p \times q$ and each column of the second input 0–1 matrix B of size $q \times r$. It relies on Fact 1 and Corollary 2. First, the pairs consisting of a row of A and a column of B that are identical (i.e., within 0 Hamming distance) are identified by sorting the rows of A and the columns of B jointly. Next, a random matrix R of size $k \times q$ with elements in $\{-1, 1\}$ is generated according to Fact 1 with $d = q$ and an appropriate k. Then, for each row of A and each column of B that are not identical, the approximate Hamming distance between the row and the column is set to the square of the ℓ_2 distance between the images of the row and the column under the mapping $f : \mathbb{R}^q \to \mathbb{R}^k$ defined in terms of the matrix R according to Fact 1.

---

procedure $APPAPHAM(A, B, \epsilon)$

Input: Two 0-1 matrices A and B of sizes $p \times q$ and $q \times r$, respectively, and a real $\epsilon \in (0, \frac{1}{2})$.

Output: A $p \times r$ matrix W, where for $1 \leq i \leq p$ and $1 \leq j \leq r$, W_{ij} is an approximation of the Hamming distance between the i-th row A_{i*} of A and the j-th column B_{*j} of B.

1. Sort the rows of A and the columns of B jointly as q-bit binary numbers. For each maximal block b of consecutive identical rows of A and/or columns of B, for each $A_{i*} \in b$ and each $B_{*j} \in b$, set W_{ij} to 0.
2. Set k to $O(\log N/\epsilon^2)$, where $N = pq + rq$.
3. Generate a random $k \times q$ matrix R with elements in $\{-1, 1\}$ defining the function $f : \mathbb{R}^q \to \mathbb{R}^k$ according to Fact 1.
4. Compute the values of the function f for each row of A and each column of B.
5. For $1 \leq i \leq p$ and $1 \leq j \leq r$, if W_{ij} has not been defined (i.e., set to 0) in (1) then set W_{ij} to $(||f(A_{i*}) - f(B_{*j})||_2)^2$.

Lemma 1. *$APPAPHAM(A, B, \epsilon)$ can be implemented in time $O((\log N/\epsilon^2)(N + pr))$, where N stands for the input size $pq + qr$.*

Proof. Step 1 can be easily implemented in $O(pq + qr)$ time by radix sort and scanning the sorted list. Steps 2, 3 take $O(kq)$ time. Step 4 can be implemented in $O((pq + qr)k)$ time. Finally, Step 5 takes $O(prk)$ time. It remains to recall that $k = O(\log N/\epsilon^2)$. $\qquad\square$

By the specification of W_{ij} in $APPAPHAM(A, B, \epsilon)$ and Corollary 2, we obtain immediately the following lemma.

Lemma 2. *Assume the notation from the procedure $APPAPHAM(A, B, \epsilon)$. For $i \in [p]$ and $j \in [r]$, the following inequalities hold w.h.p.: $W_{ij} \leq (1 + \epsilon)\mathrm{ham}(A_{i*}, B_{*j})$ and $(1 - \epsilon)\mathrm{ham}(A_{i*}, B_{*j}) \leq W_{ij}$.*

Theorem 2. *Let $\epsilon \in (0, \frac{1}{2})$, and let A and B be two 0–1 matrices of sizes $p \times q$ and $q \times r$, respectively. W.h.p., for $1 \leq i \leq p$ and $1 \leq j \leq r$, ϵ-approximations of $\mathrm{ham}(A_{i*}, B_{*j})$ can be computed in time $O((\log N/\epsilon^2)(N + pr))$, where N stands for the input size $pq + qr$.*

Proof. We run $APPAPHAM(A, B, \epsilon)$. Lemmata 1 and 2 yield the theorem. $\quad\square$

We can approximate a minimum spanning tree of n points $p_1, p_2, \ldots, p_n$ in the Hamming space $\{0, 1\}^d$ by running a standard linear-time (Prim's) algorithm for a minimum spanning tree on the clique on $[n]$, where the weight of the edge (i, j) is set to the ϵ-approximation W_{ij} of the Hamming distance between the points p_i and p_j given by $APPAPHAM$. To obtain the approximations, we form the matrix P, where the i-th row is the vector of coordinates of the point p_i for $i \in [n]$, and call $APPAPHAM(P, P^\top, \epsilon)$. Let T_ϵ denote the minimum spanning tree of the weighted clique on $[n]$ produced by Prim's algorithm. Next, let T'_ϵ be a spanning tree of the points $p_1, p_2, \ldots, p_n$ obtained by substituting p_i for i in T_ϵ, for $i \in [n]$.

Theorem 3. *Let $\epsilon \in (0, \frac{1}{2})$. W.h.p., the cost of T'_ϵ in the Hamming space $\{0, 1\}^d$ is within the multiplicative factor $\frac{1+\epsilon}{1-\epsilon}$ of the cost of a minimum spanning tree of the points $p_1, \ldots, p_n$ in $\{0, 1\}^d$. The tree T_ϵ can be constructed in time $O((\log(nd)/\epsilon^2)(nd + n^2))$.*

Proof. Let U be a minimum spanning tree of the input points $p_1, \ldots, p_n$. By Lemma 2 and the optimality of the minimum spanning tree T_ϵ on the clique on $[n]$ with the edge weights W_{ij}, we obtain the following chain of inequalities w.h.p.:

$$\sum_{(p_i, p_j) \in T'_\epsilon} \mathrm{ham}(p_i, p_j) \leq \sum_{(i,j) \in T_\epsilon} \mathrm{ham}(p_i, p_j) \leq \frac{1}{1-\epsilon} \sum_{(i,j) \in T_\epsilon} W_{ij}$$

$$\leq \frac{1}{1-\epsilon} \sum_{(p_\ell, p_m) \in U} W_{\ell m} \leq \frac{1+\epsilon}{1-\epsilon} \sum_{(p_\ell, p_m) \in U} \mathrm{ham}(p_\ell, p_m).$$

The upper time bound follows from Lemma 1 and the fact that a minimum spanning tree of the weighted clique on $[n]$ can be found in $O(n^2)$ time. $\qquad\square$

Theorem 3 can be compared with the following fact restricted to the ℓ_1 metric in $\{0,1\}^d$, i.e., the Hamming metric in $\{0,1\}^d$.

Fact 2. *(Sect. 3 in [15]). For $\epsilon > 0$, a $(1+\epsilon)$-approximation of a minimum spanning tree for a set of n points in $\mathbb{R}^d$ with integer coordinates in $O(1)$ under the ℓ_1 or ℓ_2 metric can be computed by a Monte Carlo algorithm in $O(dn^{1+1/(1+\epsilon)})$ time.*

We obtain also the following weak generalization of Theorem 3 to include the generalized Hamming space Σ^d, where Σ is a finite alphabet.

Corollary 3. *Suppose Σ is an alphabet of $O(1)$ size. An approximate minimum spanning tree of n points $p_1, \ldots, p_n$ in the generalized Hamming space Σ^d whose cost is within $O(\log_2 |\Sigma| + 1)$ of the cost of a minimum spanning tree of the points can be constructed in time $O(\log(nd)(nd + n^2))$.*

Proof. We may assume without loss of generality that $|\Sigma| > 1$. Let g be an embedding of Σ^d into $\{0,1\}^{d\lceil \log_2 |\Sigma| \rceil}$ obtained by replacing the value of each coordinate of a point in Σ^d by an $\lceil \log_2 |\Sigma| \rceil$-digit binary encoding of the value. Note that for any a, $b \in \Sigma^d$, $\mathrm{ham}(a,b) \leq \mathrm{ham}(g(a), g(b)) \leq \lceil \log_2 |\Sigma| \rceil \mathrm{ham}(a,b)$. Hence, it is sufficient to apply Theorem 3 to the images $g(p_1), \ldots, g(p_n)$ of the input points with ϵ set, say, to $1/4$. $\qquad\square$

5   Approximate 0–1 Matrix Multiplication

In this section, we combine our procedure for all-pairs approximate Hamming distances $APPAPHAM$ with our reduction of arithmetic 0–1 matrix product to the Hamming distance matrix product given in the second part of Theorem 1 in order to approximate the arithmetic 0–1 matrix product.

The known approximation methods for the arithmetic matrix product tend to use an aggregated measure to express the goodness of the approximation, most frequently the Frobenius norm (e.g., see [8,20]). We shall provide an estimation of the deviation of each entry of our approximate matrix product from the correct value in terms of the Hamming distance between the corresponding row of the first matrix and the corresponding column of the second matrix. When the distance is relatively small or on the contrary relatively large, (our upper bound on) the deviation is small.

---

procedure $APPROXMM(A, B, \epsilon)$

Input: Two 0-1 matrices A and B of sizes $p \times q$ and $q \times r$, respectively, and a real $\epsilon \in (0, \frac{1}{2})$.

Output: A $p \times r$ matrix C', where for $1 \leq i \leq p$ and $1 \leq j \leq r$, C'_{ij} is an approximation of the inner product C_{ij} of the i-th row A_{i*} of A and the j-th column B_{*j} of B.

1. Call $APPAPHAM(A, B, \epsilon)$.
2. Set $\bar{B}$ to the matrix resulting from flipping 1 entries to 0 and 0 entries to 1 in the matrix B.
3. Call $APPAPHAM(A, \bar{B}, \epsilon)$.
4. For $1 \leq i \leq p$, compute the number A^1_{i*} of occurrences of 1 in A_{i*}.
5. For $1 \leq j \leq r$, compute the number B^1_{*j} of occurrences of 1 in B_{*j}.
6. For $1 \leq i \leq p$ and $1 \leq j \leq r$, set D_{ij} to $\frac{A^1_{i*} + B^1_{*j} - W_{ij}}{2}$, where (W_{ij}) is the matrix returned by the first call of $APPAPHAM$ in (1).
7. For $1 \leq i \leq p$ and $1 \leq j \leq r$, set D'_{ij} to $\frac{A^1_{i*} + B^1_{*j} - (q - W'_{ij})}{2}$, where (W'_{ij}) is the matrix returned by the second call of $APPAPHAM$ in (3).
8. For $1 \leq i \leq p$ and $1 \leq j \leq r$, if $W_{ij} \leq W'_{ij}$ then set C'_{ij} to D_{ij} as an approximation of C_{ij} otherwise set C'_{ij} to D'_{ij} as the approximation.

Lemma 3. *For $1 \leq i \leq p$ and $1 \leq j \leq r$, the estimations D_{ij} and D'_{ij} of the entry C_{ij} of the arithmetic product C of A and B produced by the procedure $APPROXMM(A, B, \epsilon)$ satisfy the following inequalities w.h.p.:*

$$C_{ij} - \frac{\epsilon \times \mathrm{ham}(A_{i*}, B_{*j})}{2} \leq D_{ij} \leq C_{ij} + \frac{\epsilon \times \mathrm{ham}(A_{i*}, B_{*j})}{2}$$

$$C_{ij} - \frac{\epsilon(q - \mathrm{ham}(A_{i*}, B_{*j}))}{2} \leq D'_{ij} \leq C_{ij} + \frac{\epsilon(q - \mathrm{ham}(A_{i*}, B_{*j}))}{2}.$$

Proof. Let us assume the notation from the proof of Theorem 1. By the aforementioned proof, we have $C_{ij} = \frac{A^1_{i*} + B^1_{*j} - \mathrm{ham}(A_{i*}, B_{*j})}{2}$. Hence, by the first inequality stated in Lemma 2, we obtain $D_{ij} \geq C_{ij} - \epsilon \mathrm{ham}(A_{i*}, B_{*j})/2$ w.h.p. Similarly, by the second inequality in Lemma 2, we obtain $D_{ij} \leq C_{ij} + \epsilon \mathrm{ham}(A_{i*}, B_{*j})/2$ w.h.p. Analogously, we obtain the inequalities on D'_{ij} by observing that $\mathrm{ham}(A_{i*}, \bar{B}_{*j}) = q - \mathrm{ham}(A_{i*}, B_{*j})$. $\qquad\square$

Theorem 4. *Let A and B be two 0–1 matrices of sizes $p \times q$ and $q \times r$, respectively. For $\epsilon \in (0, \frac{1}{2})$, one can compute an approximation C' of the arithmetic matrix product C of A and B such that w.h.p. for $1 \leq i \leq p$ and $1 \leq j \leq r$, the approximation C'_{ij} of the inner product C_{ij} of A_{i*} and B_{*j} differs at most by $\epsilon \min\{\mathrm{ham}(A_{i*}, B_{*j}), q - \mathrm{ham}(A_{i*}, B_{*j})\}$ from C_{ij} and C' can be computed in time $O((\log N/\epsilon^2)(N + pr))$, where N stands for the input size $pq + qr$.*

Proof. Let us apply $APPROXMM(A, B, \epsilon)$. By Lemma 3, we have that w.h.p. D_{ij} differs at most by $\frac{\epsilon}{2}\mathrm{ham}(A_{i*}, B_{*j})$ from C_{ij} while D'_{ij} differs at most by

$\frac{\epsilon}{2}(q - \mathrm{ham}(A_{i*}, B_{*j}))$ from C_{ij}. It follows also from Lemma 2 that W_{ij} and W'_{ij} are w.h.p. ϵ-approximations of $\mathrm{ham}(A_{i*}, B_{*j})$ and $q - \mathrm{ham}(A_{i*}, B_{*j})$, respectively. Consequently, $\min\{W_{ij}, W'_{ij}\}$ is at least an ϵ-approximation of $\min\{\mathrm{ham}(A_{i*}, B_{*j}),\ q - \mathrm{ham}(A_{i*}, B_{*j})\}$ w.h.p. Note that C'_{ij} is set to D_{ij} if $W_{ij} = \min\{W_{ij}, W'_{ij}\}$ and to D'_{ij} otherwise. It follows that w.h.p. C'_{ij} differs at most by $\frac{\epsilon(1+\epsilon)}{2} \min\{\mathrm{ham}(A_{i*}, B_{*j}),\ q - \mathrm{ham}(A_{i*}, B_{*j})\}$ from C_{ij}. It remains to observe that $\frac{\epsilon(1+\epsilon)}{2} \leq \epsilon$ for $\epsilon \in (0, \frac{1}{2})$. $\square$

Note that when $\min\{\mathrm{ham}(A_{i*}, B_{*j}),\ q - \mathrm{ham}(A_{i*}, B_{*j})\} = O(C_{ij})$ and ϵ is sufficiently small, C''_{ij} in Theorem 4 is a close approximation of C_{ij}.

6   An Output-Sensitive Algorithm for an MST in Σ^d

Throughout this section, we shall assume that Σ is an alphabet of $O(1)$ size. Furthermore, for a $k \times \ell$ Σ matrix D, we shall denote by M_D the cost of a minimum spanning tree of its rows in the generalized Hamming space Σ^d.

Our algorithm for a minimum spanning tree in the generalized Hamming space Σ^d is output-sensitive since its running time depends on the Hamming cost of the tree. We first show that the Hamming distance matrix product of two Σ matrices A, B of sizes $p \times q$ and $q \times r$ w.h.p. can be computed in time $\tilde{O}((p+r)(p+q+r) + \min\{rM_A,\ pM_{B^\top}\})$. This fact is combined with a standard algorithm for minimum spanning tree in an edge weighted graph.

procedure $MMST(A, B)$

Input: Two Σ matrices A and B, of sizes $p \times q$ and $q \times r$, respectively.
Output: The Hamming distance matrix product D of A and B, i.e., for $1 \leq i \leq p$ and $1 \leq j \leq r$, D_{ij} is the Hamming distance between A_{i*} and B_{*j}.

1. Construct an $O(1)$-approximate spanning tree T of the rows A_{i*} of A, $i \in [p]$, in the generalized Hamming space Σ^q by using the method of Corollary 3.
2. Construct a traversal (i.e., a non-necessarily simple path visiting all vertices) U of T.
3. For any pair A_{k*}, A_{i*}, where the latter row follows the former row in the traversal U, compute the set $diff(k, i)$ of indices $\ell \in [q]$, where $A_{i\ell} \neq A_{k\ell}$.
4. For $j = 1, \ldots, r$, iterate the following steps:
    (a) Compute D_{sj} where A_{s*} is the row of A from which the traversal U of T starts.
    (b) While following U, iterate the following steps:
        i. Set k, i to the indices of the previously traversed row of A and the currently traversed row of A, respectively.
        ii. Set D_{ij} to D_{kj}.
        iii. For each $\ell \in diff(k, i)$, if $A_{i\ell} = B_{\ell j}$ then set D_{ij} to $D_{ij} - 1$ and if $A_{k\ell} = B_{\ell j}$ then set D_{ij} to $D_{ij} + 1$.

The proof of the following theorem relies on Corollary 3 and the $MMST$ procedure.

Theorem 5. *Let A, B be two Σ matrices of sizes $p \times q$ and $q \times r$, respectively. The Hamming distance matrix product of A and B (i.e., for $1 \leq i \leq p$ and $1 \leq j \leq r$, the Hamming distance between A_{i*} and B_{*j}) can be computed by a randomized algorithm in time $\tilde{O}((p+r)(p+q+r) + \min\{rM_A,\ pM_{B^\top}\})$ with high probability.*

Proof. We run the procedure $MMST$ on the input matrices A, B and also on the matrices $B^\top$, $A^\top$, in parallel, and stop whenever any of the calls is completed. Note that if D is the Hamming distance product of A and B then $D^\top$ is the Hamming distance product of $B^\top$ and $A^\top$. The correctness of the procedure follows from the correctness of the updates of D_{ij} in the block of the inner loop, i.e., in Step 4(b).

Step 1 of $MMST(A, B)$ takes $O(\log(pq)(pq+p^2))$ time by Corollary 3. Step 2 can be done in $O(p)$ time while Step 3 requires $O(pq)$ time. The first step in the block under the outer loop, i.e., computing D_{sj} in Step 4(a), takes $O(q)$ time. The crucial observation is that the second step in this block, i.e., Step 4(b), requires $O(p + M_A)$ time. Simply, the substeps (i), (ii) take $O(1)$ time while the substep (iii) requires $O(|diff(k, i)|+1)$ time. Since the block is iterated r times, the whole outer loop, i.e., Step 4, requires $O(qr + pr + rM_A)$ time. Thus, $MMST(A, B)$ can be implemented in time $O(\log(pq)(pq+p^2) + qr + pr + rM_A)$. Symmetrically, $MMST(B^\top, A^\top)$ can be done in time $O(\log(qr)(qr + r^2) + pq + pr + pM_{B^\top})$. $\square$

Corollary 4. *Let S be a set of n points in the generalized Hamming space Σ^d and let M be the cost of a minimum spanning tree of S in Σ^d. A minimum spanning tree of S can be computed by a randomized algorithm in $\tilde{O}(n(d+n+M))$ time with high probability.*

Proof. We can compute the Hamming distances between all pairs of points in S in $\tilde{O}(n(d+n+M))$ time by Theorem 5. Then, it is sufficient to run a standard algorithm for minimum spanning tree on vertices 1 through n corresponding to the points in S and edges weighted by the Hamming distances between the points in S corresponding to the edge endpoints. This takes $O(n^2)$ time. $\square$

For example, if $n = d$, our output-sensitive algorithm for a minimum spanning tree is substantially faster than that of Corollary 1 when M is substantially smaller than $n^{\omega-1}$.

References

1. Achlioptas, D.: Database-friendly random projectios: johnson-lindenstrauss with binary coins. J. Comput. Syst. Sci. **66**, 671–687 (2003)
2. Alman, J., Duan, R., Williams, V.V., Xu, Y., Xu, Z., Zhou, R.: More asymmetry yields faster matrix multiplication. In: Proceedings of the Annual ACM-SIAM Symposium on Discrete Algorithms (SODA 2025), pp. 2005–2039. ACM-SIAM (2025)

3. Alves, J., Moustafa, S., Benkner, S., Francisco, A.: Accelerating graph neural networks with a novel matrix compression format. (2024). https://doi.org/10.48550/arXiv.2409.02208
4. Amarasinghe, C.L.S.: 6.172 Performance engineering of software systems, Lecture 8, MIT OpenCourseWare. Massachusetts Institute of Technology, Retrieved 27 January 2015
5. Arslan, A.: A fast algorithm for all-pairs hamming distances. Inf. Process. Lett. **139**, 49–52 (2018)
6. Arslan, A., Bizargit, P.: Phylogeny by top down clustering using a given multiple alignment. In: Proceedings of the 7th IEEE Symposium on Bioinformatics and Biotechnology (BIBE 2007), vol. 2, pp. 809–814. IEEE (2007)
7. Björklund, A., Lingas, A.: Fast boolean matrix multiplication for highly clustered data. In: Dehne, F., Sack, J.-R., Tamassia, R. (eds.) WADS 2001. LNCS, vol. 2125, pp. 258–263. Springer, Heidelberg (2001). https://doi.org/10.1007/3-540-44634-6_24
8. Cohen, E., Lewis, D.D.: Approximating matrix multiplication for pattern recognition tasks. J. Algorithms **30**(2), 211–252 (1999)
9. Drineas, P., Kannan, R., Mahoney, M.: Fast monte carlo algorithms for matrices I: approximating matrix multiplication. SIAM J. Comput. **36**(1), 132–157 (2006)
10. Floderus, P., Jansson, J., Levcopoulos, C., Lingas, A., Sledneu, D.: 3D rectangulations and geometric matrix multiplication. Algorithmica **80**(1), 136–154 (2018)
11. Floderus, P., Kowaluk, M., Lingas, A., Lundell, E.: Detecting and counting small pattern graphs. SIAM J. Discrete Math. **29**(3), 1322–1339 (2015)
12. Gąsieniec, L., Kowaluk, M., Lingas, A.: Faster multi-witnesses for boolean matrix multiplication. Inf. Process. Lett. **109**(4), 242–247 (2009)
13. Gąsieniec, L., Lingas, A.: An improved bound on boolean matrix multiplication for highly clustered data. In: Dehne, F., Sack, J.-R., Smid, M. (eds.) WADS 2003. LNCS, vol. 2748, pp. 329–339. Springer, Heidelberg (2003). https://doi.org/10.1007/978-3-540-45078-8_29
14. Grygorash, O., Zhou, Y., Jorgensen, Z.: Minimum spanning tree based clustering algorithms. In: Proceedings of the 18th International Conference on Tools with Artificial Intelligence (ICTAI 2006), pp. 73–81. IEEE (2006)
15. Indyk, P., Motwani, R.: Approximate nearest neighbors: towards removing the curse of dimensionality. In: Proceedings of ACM Symposium on Theory of Computing (STOC 1998), pp. 604–613. ACM (1998)
16. Iven, M., Spencer, C.: A note on compressed sensing and the complexity of matrix multiplication. Inf. Process. Lett. **109**(10), 468–471 (2009)
17. Johnson, W., Lindenstrauss, J.: Extensions of Lipschitz mappings into a Hilbert space. Contemp. Math. **26**(1), 189–206 (1984)
18. Kurzkov, K.: Deterministic algorithms for skewed matrix products. In: Proceedings of the International Symposium on Theoretical Aspects of Computer Science (STACS 2013), pp. 466–477. Schloss Dagstuhl- Leibniz-Zentrum fuer Informatik, vol. 20 (2013)
19. Lai, C., Rafa, T., Nelson, D.E.: Approximate minimum spanning tree clustering in high-dimensional space. Intell. Data Analy. **13**(4), 575–597 (2009)
20. Pagh, R.: Compressed matrix multiplication. ACM Trans. Comput. Theory (TOCT) **5**(3), 1–17 (2013)
21. Sarlós, T.: Improved approximation algorithms for large matrices via random projections. In: Proceedings of the IEEE Symposium on Foundations of Computer Science (FOCS 2006), pp. 143–152. IEEE Computer Society (2006)

Convexity-Driven Projection for Point Cloud Dimensionality Reduction

Suman Sanyal$^{(\boxtimes)}$

Big Data Analytics, Goa Institute of Management, Goa, India
`sanyal@gim.ac.in`

Abstract. We propose Convexity-Driven Projection (CDP), a boundary-free linear method for dimensionality reduction of point clouds that targets preserving detour-induced local non-convexity. CDP builds a k-NN graph, identifies admissible pairs whose Euclidean-to-shortest-path ratios are below a threshold, and aggregates their normalized directions to form a positive semidefinite non-convexity structure matrix. The projection uses the top-k eigenvectors of the structure matrix. We give two verifiable guarantees. A pairwise a-posteriori certificate that bounds the post-projection distortion for each admissible pair, and an average-case spectral bound that links expected captured direction energy to the spectrum of the structure matrix, yielding quantile statements for typical distortion. Our evaluation protocol reports fixed- and reselected-pairs detour errors and certificate quantiles, enabling practitioners to check guarantees on their data.

Keywords: Point cloud · Dimensionality reduction · Non-convexity · Shortest path · Spectral projection

1 Introduction

Point clouds, sets of points in high-dimensional spaces, are central to 3D modelling, robotics, and visualisation [2]. In many of these settings, obstacle- or curvature-induced detours are essential: the graph shortest path between two samples can be much longer than their Euclidean separation, signalling local non-convexity. Preserving this detour geometry matters for tasks such as path planning and shape analysis, yet standard dimensionality-reduction (DR) methods do not prioritise it. Variance-seeking linear methods (PCA) maximise explained variance and can collapse detours by ignoring geodesic structure [1]. Nonlinear neighbour-embeddings such as t-SNE [3] and UMAP [4] optimise probabilistic/fuzzy neighbourhood objectives; they are effective for visualisation but offer no explicit control of detour geometry and yield nonlinear maps sensitive to hyperparameters. Graph-based linear projections (LPP, NPP, OLPP) [7–9] minimise Laplacian-style smoothness to keep neighbours close, which does not single out directions that consistently witness non-convexity.

Euclidean distance often misrepresents navigable/geodesic distance in point clouds (walls, holes, curvature), so DR that ignores detours can short-circuit

C. Zaroliagis et al. (Eds.): ICAA 2026, LNCS 16423, pp. 50–61, 2026.
https://doi.org/10.1007/978-3-032-15621-1_5

corridors and merge distinct neighborhoods; to address this, we propose **Convexity-Driven Projection** (CDP), a linear DR method designed to preserve detour-induced local non-convexity without requiring boundary estimation. CDP constructs a k-nearest-neighbor (k-NN) graph, identifies admissible pairs (i, j) with a convexity ratio $r_{ij} = \|p_j - p_i\|/S(p_i, p_j) \leq \tau$, where $S(p_i, p_j)$ is the graph shortest-path distance, and forms a positive semidefinite (PSD) non-convexity structure matrix by averaging normalized outer products $u_{ij}u_{ij}^\top$ weighted by $(1 - r_{ij})$. The projection is onto the top-k eigenvectors of this matrix, emphasizing directions associated with strong detours. CDP's linear nature ensures computational simplicity, while its boundary-free approach makes it broadly applicable. The contributions of the paper are as follows. (i) A simple PSD construction that targets detour-induced structure; (ii) a pairwise a-posteriori certificate bounding $\tilde{r}_{ij}/r_{ij}$ using the projected shortest path; (iii) an average-case spectral bound with quantile implications; and (iv) an evaluation protocol reporting fixed- and reselected-pairs metrics with certificate quantiles.

This paper is organized as follows. Section 2 introduces key notations and the mathematical foundation of CDP. Section 3 details the CDP algorithm, including complexity and graph construction. Section 4 presents the theoretical guarantees with a verification protocol, including the pairwise certificate and spectral bound. Section 5 evaluates CDP on synthetic and real-world datasets, including a toy example. Section 6 summarizes findings and future directions. Table 1 lists key notations used throughout the paper, and a comparison of CDP with existing methods is provided in Table 2.

2   Preliminaries

Let $\{p_i\}_{i=1}^N \subset \mathbb{R}^d$ and let $G = (V, E)$ be a connected k-NN graph with Euclidean edge weights. For a pair (i, j) define the convexity (detour) ratio

$$r_{ij} = \frac{\|p_j - p_i\|}{S(p_i, p_j)}, \qquad 0 < r_{ij} \leq 1, \tag{1}$$

where $S(p_i, p_j)$ is the shortest-path distance in G. A pair is admissible if $r_{ij} \leq \tau$ with $\tau < 1$, and we write $\mathcal{D}^* = \{(i,j) : r_{ij} \leq \tau\}$. We summarize detour prevalence by the admissible non-convexity index

$$\widehat{C}^{\mathrm{sp}} = \frac{1}{|\mathcal{D}^*|} \sum_{(i,j)\in\mathcal{D}^*} r_{ij}. \tag{2}$$

Lower $\widehat{C}^{\mathrm{sp}}$ indicates stronger average detours among admissible pairs. For $u_{ij} := (p_j - p_i)/\|p_j - p_i\|$, we define the non-convexity structure matrix as

$$S^{\mathrm{nc}} := \frac{1}{|\mathcal{D}^*|} \sum_{(i,j)\in\mathcal{D}^*} (1 - r_{ij})\, u_{ij}u_{ij}^\top. \tag{3}$$

Note that each summand in (3) is a rank-1 positive semidefinite projector scaled by $(1 - r_{ij}) \geq 0$, hence S^{nc} is positive semidefinite. Let its eigenvalues be $\lambda_1 \geq$

Table 1. Key notations and their descriptions used in the paper.

Notation	Description
p_i	Point i in the original space $\mathbb{R}^d$, $i = 1, \ldots, N$
$G = (V, E)$	Connected k-NN graph with vertices V and edges E
$w(u, v)$	Euclidean edge weight for edge $(u, v) \in E$, $\|p_v - p_u\|$
$S(p_i, p_j)$	Shortest-path distance between points p_i and p_j on G
r_{ij}	Convexity (detour) ratio, $\frac{\|p_j - p_i\|}{S(p_i, p_j)}$, Eq. (1)
$\mathcal{D}^*$	Set of admissible pairs (i, j) with $r_{ij} \leq \tau$, $\tau < 1$
$\widehat{C}^{\mathrm{sp}}$	Admissible non-convexity index, $\frac{1}{|\mathcal{D}^*|} \sum_{(i,j) \in \mathcal{D}^*} r_{ij}$
u_{ij}	Normalized direction, $\frac{p_j - p_i}{\|p_j - p_i\|}$
S^{nc}	Non-convexity structure matrix, Eq. (3)
λ_ℓ, z_ℓ	Eigenvalues and eigenvectors of S^{nc}, $\lambda_1 \geq \cdots \geq \lambda_d \geq 0$
V	Projection matrix, top-k eigenvectors $[z_1, \ldots, z_k]$
p_i'	Projected point, $V^\top p_i \in \mathbb{R}^k$
$w'(u, v)$	Projected edge weight, $\|V^\top (p_v - p_u)\|$
$\tilde{S}(p_i, p_j)$	Shortest-path distance on projected graph (V, E, w')
$\tilde{r}_{ij}$	Post-projection convexity ratio, $\frac{\|V^\top (p_j - p_i)\|}{\tilde{S}(p_i, p_j)}$, Eq. (4)
ψ_{ij}	Projected direction norm, $\left\| V^\top \frac{p_j - p_i}{\|p_j - p_i\|} \right\|$, Eq. (5)
$\phi_{ij}^\star$	Minimum edge projection norm on $\widetilde{P}_{ij}$, Eq. (5)
ϕ_G	Minimum edge projection norm over all edges, $\min_{e \in E(G)} \left\| V^\top \frac{e}{\|e\|} \right\|$
μ_k	Average-case spectral capture, $\frac{\sum_{\ell \leq k} \lambda_\ell}{\sum_\ell \lambda_\ell}$, Eq. (7)
Z	Squared norm of random projected direction, $\|V^\top U\|^2$, Eq. (7)
$\widehat{C}^{\mathrm{sp}\prime}$	Post-projection non-convexity index (fixed pairs), $\frac{1}{|\mathcal{D}^*|} \sum_{(i,j) \in \mathcal{D}^*} \tilde{r}_{ij}$
$\mathcal{D}^{*\prime}$	Reselected admissible pairs, $\{(i, j) : \tilde{r}_{ij} \leq \tau\}$
$\widehat{C}^{\mathrm{sp}\prime\prime}$	Post-projection non-convexity index (reselected pairs), $\frac{1}{|\mathcal{D}^{*\prime}|} \sum_{(i,j) \in \mathcal{D}^{*\prime}} \tilde{r}_{ij}$

$\cdots \geq \lambda_d \geq 0$ with orthonormal eigenvectors $\{z_\ell\}$. CDP uses $V = [z_1, \ldots, z_k] \in \mathbb{R}^{d \times k}$, the matrix of the top-$k$ eigenvectors of the non-convexity structure matrix S^{nc}, and returns $p_i' = V^\top p_i$.

3 Convexity-Driven Projection (CDP) Algorithm

We present the Convexity-Driven Projection (CDP) algorithm, designed to reduce the dimensionality of point clouds while preserving detour-induced non-convexity. The algorithm constructs a k-nearest-neighbor (k-NN) graph, identifies admissible pairs based on a detour ratio threshold, builds a non-convexity structure matrix, and projects onto its top-k eigenvectors. The steps are formalized in Algorithm 1, followed by discussions on computational complexity and graph construction considerations.

Table 2. Comparison of dimensionality-reduction methods by primary optimization target, nature of theoretical guarantees, and linearity (linear or nonlinear).

Method	Target	Guarantees	Linearity
PCA [2]	Variance	Perturbation (classical)	Linear
LPP/NPP/OLPP [7–9]	Laplacian smoothness	Spectral properties	Linear
Isomap [5]	Geodesic distances	Isometry (idealized)	Nonlinear
t-SNE [3]	Local KL divergence	None	Nonlinear
UMAP [4]	Fuzzy set objective	None	Nonlinear
CDP (ours)	Detour / non-convexity directions	Pairwise certificate; average-case spectral	Linear

The CDP algorithm operates on a sparse k-NN graph with $m = \Theta(Nk_{\mathrm{nn}})$ edges. Computing all-pairs shortest-path distances (APSP) using multi-source Dijkstra's algorithm incurs a cost of $\tilde{O}(N^2 k_{\mathrm{nn}})$, which dominates for large N. Constructing the non-convexity structure matrix S^{nc} from $|\mathcal{D}^*|$ admissible pairs requires $\Theta(|\mathcal{D}^*|d^2)$ operations due to rank-1 outer product calculations. The randomized SVD to extract the top-k eigenvectors of the $d \times d$ matrix S^{nc} costs $\tilde{O}(d^2\ell)$, where ℓ is the number of iterations, typically small; exact SVD would cost $O(d^3)$. Finally, projecting N points onto the k-dimensional subspace takes $O(Ndk)$. For large datasets, the APSP step may be a bottleneck, but approximations (e.g., landmark-based shortest paths) could reduce this cost in practice.

The algorithm uses a mutual k-NN graph, where an edge exists only if both points are among each other's k_{nn} nearest neighbors, to mitigate shortcuts in regions of varying point density. Edge weights are Euclidean distances, preserving the ambient geometry. Connectivity is ensured by selecting $k_{\mathrm{nn}} \gtrsim \log N$ under near-homogeneous sampling, as supported by random geometric graph theory [11]. In heterogeneous datasets, we retain the giant component to maintain connectivity. The threshold $\tau < 1$ controls the selection of admissible pairs, balancing the capture of strong detours (small τ) with sufficient pair coverage (larger τ).

The CDP algorithm's performance is influenced by the choice of hyperparameters τ and k_{nn}. The threshold τ determines the stringency for selecting admissible pairs with a lower τ focuses on pairs with strong detours (small r_{ij}), resulting in fewer but more informative directions in S^{nc}, which may enhance preservation of non-convexity but risks insufficient pairs for a robust matrix, potentially leading to degenerate projections. Conversely, a higher τ includes more pairs, capturing milder detours and yielding projections that resemble variance-based methods like PCA, with broader coverage but less emphasis on extreme non-convexity. The number of nearest neighbors k_{nn} affects graph sparsity. Smaller values create sparser graphs with longer shortest paths, amplifying detours and strengthening the non-convexity signal in S^{nc}. In comparison, larger values densify the graph, shortening paths and reducing detour prevalence, which can smooth the projection but dilute its focus on non-convex structures. These parameters can be tuned on a validation set to balance pair selection and detour preservation.

Algorithm 1. Convexity-Driven Projection (CDP)

Require: Points $\{p_i\} \subset \mathbb{R}^d$, target $k < d$, k_{nn}, threshold τ.
Ensure: $V \in \mathbb{R}^{d \times k}$, projections $\{p'_i\} \subset \mathbb{R}^k$
1: Standardize coordinates (zero mean, unit variance).
2: Build a (mutual) k-NN graph G with Euclidean edge weights.
3: Compute all-pairs shortest-path distances $S(p_i, p_j)$ on G (multi-source Dijkstra).
4: Form $\mathcal{D}^* = \{(i,j) : r_{ij} \leq \tau\}$.
5: Build S^{nc} via Eq. (3).
6: Compute top-k eigenvectors of S^{nc}.
7: Project: $p'_i = V^\top p_i$.
8: Projected graph: reuse the edge set E; assign edge weights $w'(u,v) = \|V^\top(p_v - p_u)\|$.
9: **return** V, $\{p'_i\}$ and the projected graph (V, E, w').

---

4 CDP: A-Posteriori Certificate and Average-Case Spectral Bound

We give (i) a pairwise, data-dependent certificate valid after fitting V, and (ii) an average-case spectral bound explaining typical behavior and enabling quantile statements.

4.1 A-Posteriori Pairwise Certificate

For an admissible pair $(i,j) \in \mathcal{D}^*$, let $\tilde{r}_{ij}$ denote the post-projection convexity ratio, defined as

$$\tilde{r}_{ij} = \frac{\|V^\top(p_j - p_i)\|}{\tilde{S}(p_i, p_j)}, \tag{4}$$

where $\|V^\top(p_j - p_i)\|$ is the Euclidean distance between the projected points $p'_i = V^\top p_i$ and $p'_j = V^\top p_j$ in $\mathbb{R}^k$, and $\tilde{S}(p_i, p_j)$ is the shortest-path distance on the projected graph (V, E, w') with edge weights $w'(u,v) = \|V^\top(p_v - p_u)\|$ (see Algorithm 1, Step 8). This mirrors the pre-projection ratio $r_{ij} = \frac{\|p_j - p_i\|}{S(p_i, p_j)}$ from Eq. (1), but computed in the reduced space. Fix $(i,j) \in \mathcal{D}^*$. Define

$$\psi_{ij} := \left\| V^\top \frac{p_j - p_i}{\|p_j - p_i\|} \right\| \in [0,1], \qquad \phi^\star_{ij} := \min_{e \in \widetilde{P}_{ij}} \left\| V^\top \frac{e}{\|e\|} \right\| \in [0,1], \tag{5}$$

where $\widetilde{P}_{ij}$ is a projected shortest path between p'_i and p'_j in (V, E, w'), and the minimum is over its edges e expressed as vectors in the original coordinates.

To establish the pairwise a-posteriori certificate, we bound the distortion ratio $\tilde{r}_{ij}/r_{ij}$ for each admissible pair (i,j) using measurable cosines computed after the projection matrix V is fitted. Intuitively, the lower bound arises because the orthogonal projection preserves or reduces distances, ensuring the projected shortest path is no longer than the original, while the upper bound leverages the specific geometry of the projected shortest path to prevent excessive collapse of detours. More precisely, decompose the ratio as the product of the projected Euclidean factor ψ_{ij} (the cosine of the pair's direction onto the subspace) and the original-to-projected shortest-path ratio $S/\tilde{S}$. Since the projection is non-expansive, every edge shortens or stays the same, implying $\tilde{S} \leq S$ and thus $S/\tilde{S} \geq 1$, yielding the lower bound $\psi_{ij} \leq \tilde{r}_{ij}/r_{ij}$. For the upper bound, consider a projected shortest path $\tilde{P}_{ij}$: its length $\tilde{S}$ is at least ϕ^*_{ij} times its original length $L_{\mathrm{orig}}(\tilde{P}_{ij})$, where ϕ^*_{ij} is the minimum cosine over its edges; since $L_{\mathrm{orig}}(\tilde{P}_{ij}) \geq S$ (as S is the minimal original path length), it follows that $\tilde{S} \geq \phi^*_{ij}S$, so $S/\tilde{S} \leq 1/\phi^*_{ij}$, completing the bound. This approach ensures the certificate is verifiable per pair, relying only on post-projection computations like recovering $\tilde{P}_{ij}$ via Dijkstra's algorithm with parent pointers. The following theorem makes this precise.

Theorem 1. (Pairwise a-posteriori Certificate). *For every admissible pair* $(i,j) \in \mathcal{D}^*$,

$$\psi_{ij} \leq \frac{\tilde{r}_{ij}}{r_{ij}} \leq \frac{1}{\phi^\star_{ij}}. \tag{6}$$

Proof. Observe that $\dfrac{\tilde{r}_{ij}}{r_{ij}} = \dfrac{\|V^\top(p_j - p_i)\|}{\|p_j - p_i\|} \cdot \dfrac{S(p_i, p_j)}{\tilde{S}(p_i, p_j)}$. Since, orthogonal projection is non-expansive, $\tilde{S} \leq S$ and $\|V^\top(p_j - p_i)\|/\|p_j - p_i\| = \psi_{ij}$, giving the lower bound. For the upper bound, let $\tilde{P}_{ij}$ be a projected shortest path. Then

$$\tilde{S} = \sum_{e \in \tilde{P}_{ij}} \|V^\top e\| \geq \phi^\star_{ij} \sum_{e \in \tilde{P}_{ij}} \|e\| = \phi^\star_{ij} L_{\mathrm{orig}}(\tilde{P}_{ij}) \geq \phi^\star_{ij} S,$$

hence $S/\tilde{S} \leq 1/\phi^\star_{ij}$.

As an immediate consequence of Theorem 1, we derive a uniform upper bound that applies to all admissible pairs simultaneously, by considering the minimum captured cosine across all edges in the graph. While simpler to compute globally, this bound may be conservative compared to the per-pair version.

Corollary 1. (Uniform Graph-Wise Bound). *Let* $\phi_G := \min_{e \in E(G)} \|V^\top \frac{e}{\|e\|}\|$. *Then for all admissible pairs,* $\dfrac{\tilde{r}_{ij}}{r_{ij}} \leq \dfrac{1}{\phi_G}$.

This uniform bound can be loose when ϕ_G is small; Theorem 1 is tighter per pair.

Computing ϕ^*_{ij}. During Dijkstra on the projected graph, store parents to recover $\tilde{P}_{ij}$; set $\phi^*_{ij} = \min_{e \in \tilde{P}_{ij}} \|V^\top e\|/\|e\|$. After the run, this adds $O(|\tilde{P}_{ij}| d)$ per pair.

4.2   Average-Case Spectral Bound (Prior, Aggregate Behavior)

Let U be the random unit direction drawn from the weighted empirical distribution over admissible pairs. Then

$$\mathbb{P}\{U = u_{ij}\} \propto (1 - r_{ij}), \qquad u_{ij} = \frac{p_j - p_i}{\|p_j - p_i\|}.$$

Then $S^{\mathrm{nc}} = \mathbb{E}[UU^\top]$ up to normalization, and

$$\mu_k := \mathbb{E}\big[\|V^\top U\|^2\big] = \frac{\sum_{\ell \leq k} \lambda_\ell}{\sum_\ell \lambda_\ell}. \tag{7}$$

Let $Z = \|V^\top U\|^2 \in [0,1]$ with $\mathbb{E}[Z] = \mu_k$. For any $a \in (0,1)$,

$$\mathbb{P}\{Z \geq 1 - a\} \geq 1 - \frac{1 - \mu_k}{a}. \tag{8}$$

For a random admissible pair, the Euclidean factor equals $\sqrt{Z}$; combined with Theorem 1, we have $\sqrt{Z} \leq \tilde{r}_{ij}/r_{ij} \leq 1/\phi^\star_{ij}$, so empirical distributions of $\sqrt{Z}$ and $\phi^\star_{ij}$ control typical multiplicative distortion.

4.3   Verification Protocol and Metrics

To evaluate CDP's effectiveness in preserving detour-induced non-convexity, we define metrics and quantiles that assess projection quality and verify theoretical guarantees. These include detour errors and certificate bounds, which are detailed below.

(i) Fixed-pairs detour error: $|\widehat{C}^{\mathrm{sp}} - \widehat{C}^{\mathrm{sp}\prime}|/\widehat{C}^{\mathrm{sp}}$, where $\widehat{C}^{\mathrm{sp}\prime}$ is computed post-projection on the same admissible pairs $\mathcal{D}^\star$ using the projected graph. (This decouples pair selection from projection.)

(ii) Reselected-pairs detour error: compute $\mathcal{D}^{\star\prime} = \{(i,j) : \tilde{r}_{ij} \leq \tau\}$ on the projected graph and report $|\widehat{C}^{\mathrm{sp}} - \widehat{C}^{\mathrm{sp}\prime\prime}|/\widehat{C}^{\mathrm{sp}}$, where $\widehat{C}^{\mathrm{sp}\prime\prime}$ averages $\tilde{r}_{ij}$ over $\mathcal{D}^{\star\prime}$. This reflects the new detour geometry.

(iii) Certificate quantiles (a-posteriori): for $(\psi_{ij}, \phi^\star_{ij})$ in (5), report $q_{0.10}(\psi)$ and $q_{0.90}(1/\phi^\star)$ across $\mathcal{D}^\star$. Thus, for at least 90% of admissible pairs,

$$q_{0.10}(\psi) \leq \frac{\tilde{r}_{ij}}{r_{ij}} \leq q_{0.90}(1/\phi^\star).$$

(iv) Average-case spectral capture: μ_k from (7).

5   Experiments

We evaluate the Convexity-Driven Projection (CDP) algorithm's effectiveness in preserving detour-induced non-convexity using a toy example and benchmark datasets, including Swiss Roll, Torus, S-Curve, Helix, Möbius Strip, Klein Bottle, and Annulus with Obstacle. Comparing CDP against PCA, UMAP, and LPP, we report visualizations demonstrating CDP's performance on non-convex structures.

5.1   Toy Example: Five Points ($d = 3 \to k = 2$)

Consider five points $A = (0, 0, 0)$, $B = (1, 0.2, 0)$, $C = (2, 0, 0)$, $D = (2, 1, 0)$, and $E = (1, 0.5, 1)$. Using Euclidean edge weights, we build a mutual k-NN graph with $k = 2$. The mutual edges are (A, B), (A, E), (B, C), (C, D), so the graph is connected via the chain $D - C - B - A - E$. Euclidean distances $\|p_j - p_i\|$ and graph shortest paths $S(p_i, p_j)$ yield the convexity ratios

$$r_{ij} = \frac{\|p_j - p_i\|}{S(p_i, p_j)} \in (0, 1].$$

For threshold $\tau = 0.75$, the pairs with $r_{ij} \leq \tau$ are the admissible set $\mathcal{D}^*$. Table 3 lists all unordered pairs.

Table 3. Pairwise Euclidean, shortest-path, and r_{ij}; admissible if $r_{ij} \leq \tau = 0.75$.

i j	$\|p_j - p_i\|$	$S(p_i, p_j)$	r_{ij}	admissible
A B	1.0198	1.0198	1.0000	FALSE
A C	2.0000	2.0396	0.9806	FALSE
A D	2.2361	3.0396	0.7356	TRUE
A E	1.5000	1.5000	1.0000	FALSE
B C	1.0198	1.0198	1.0000	FALSE
B D	1.2806	2.0198	0.6340	TRUE
B E	1.0440	2.5198	0.4143	TRUE
C D	1.0000	1.0000	1.0000	FALSE
C E	1.5000	3.5396	0.4238	TRUE
D E	1.5000	4.5396	0.3304	TRUE

Thus $|\mathcal{D}^*| = 5$ and the admissible non-convexity index is $\widehat{C}^{\mathrm{sp}} = \frac{1}{5} \sum_{(i,j)\in\mathcal{D}^*} r_{ij} = 0.5076$. For the non-convexity structure matrix and spectrum, we use

$$S^{\mathrm{nc}} = \frac{1}{|\mathcal{D}^*|} \sum_{(i,j)\in\mathcal{D}^*} (1 - r_{ij})\, u_{ij} u_{ij}^{\top}, \qquad u_{ij} = \frac{p_j - p_i}{\|p_j - p_i\|},$$

to obtain

$$S^{\mathrm{nc}} = \begin{pmatrix} 0.197665 & 0.061001 & -0.110738 \\ 0.061001 & 0.076493 & 0.028090 \\ -0.110738 & 0.028090 & 0.218200 \end{pmatrix}.$$

Its eigenvalues (ascending) are 0.021002, 0.150383, 0.320973, with corresponding eigenvectors (columns, descending order of eigenvalues)

$$V = \begin{pmatrix} -0.689630 & 0.512628 \\ -0.089508 & 0.640566 \\ 0.718609 & 0.571741 \end{pmatrix} \in \mathbb{R}^{3\times 2}.$$

The average-case spectral capture is

$$\mu_k = \frac{\lambda_1 + \lambda_2}{\lambda_1 + \lambda_2 + \lambda_3} = 0.9573,$$

and the projected coordinates $p_i' = V^\top p_i$ are given by

Label	u_1	u_2
A	0.000000	0.000000
B	−0.707531	0.640741
C	−1.379259	1.025255
D	−1.468767	1.665821
E	0.015774	1.404652

Fig. 1 visualizes the original 3D points and their 2D projection, highlighting the mutual k-NN edges ($A - B$, $A - E$, $B - C$, $C - D$).

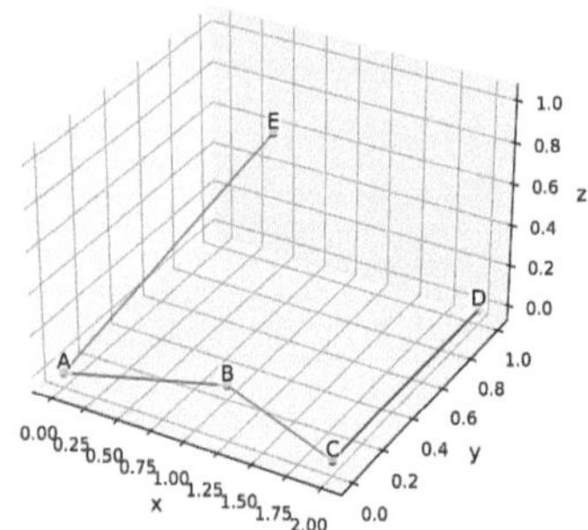

(a) 3D original points with mutual k-NN edges ($A - B$, $A - E$, $B - C$, $C - D$).

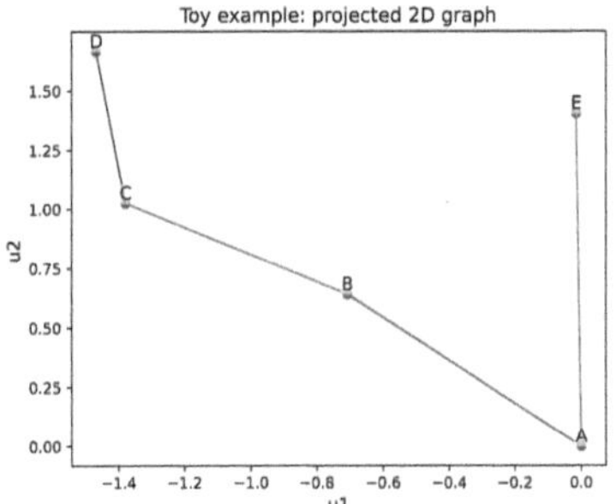

(b) 2D projected points with mutual k-NN edges ($A - B$, $A - E$, $B - C$, $C - D$).

Fig. 1. Visualization of the toy example: original 3D points (left) and their 2D projection (right), with mutual k-NN edges ($k = 2$). Points are labeled (A, B, C, D, E), and edges reflect the connected graph structure.

We reuse the edge set and assign projected edge weights $w'(u, v) = \|V^\top(p_v - p_u)\|$ to obtain $w'(A-B) = 0.95465$, $w'(A-E) = 1.40474$, $w'(B-C) = 0.77399$, and $w'(C-D) = 0.64679$. For each $(i, j) \in \mathcal{D}^*$ we compute

$$\psi_{ij} = \left\|V^\top \frac{p_j - p_i}{\|p_j - p_i\|}\right\|, \qquad \phi_{ij}^\star = \min_{e \in \widetilde{P}_{ij}} \left\|V^\top \frac{e}{\|e\|}\right\|,$$

where $\widetilde{P}_{ij}$ is a projected shortest path (with weights w'). Table 4 reports the values. In every case certificate (6) holds.

Table 4. Per-pair certificate for the toy example. Here $\tilde{r}_{ij}$ (Eq. (4)) uses the projected graph shortest-path in the denominator; "Path" is the projected shortest path (vertex labels).

i	j	ψ_{ij}	$\phi_{ij}^{\star}$	$1/\phi_{ij}^{\star}$	r_{ij}	$\tilde{r}_{ij}$	$\tilde{r}_{ij}/r_{ij}$	Path
A	D	0.993201	0.646789	1.546099	0.735644	0.934972	1.270958	A→B→C→D
B	D	0.997029	0.646789	1.546099	0.634034	0.898672	1.417387	B→C→D
B	E	0.987113	0.936005	1.068371	0.414330	0.436818	1.054275	B→A→E
C	E	0.943524	0.758966	1.317583	0.423776	0.451695	1.065882	C→B→A→E
D	E	0.984185	0.646789	1.546099	0.330425	0.390543	1.181941	D→C→B→A→E

The uniform graph-wise constant is $\phi_G = \min_{e \in E} \|V^{\top} e\|/\|e\| = 0.64679$ (attained on $C - D$), hence the conservative bound $\tilde{r}_{ij}/r_{ij} \leq 1/\phi_G = 1.54610$ also holds for all pairs. For the fixed-pairs metric, we compare

$$\widehat{C}^{\mathrm{sp}} = 0.5076 \quad \text{vs.} \quad \widehat{C}^{\mathrm{sp}\prime} = \frac{1}{5} \sum_{(i,j) \in \mathcal{D}^*} \tilde{r}_{ij} = 0.6225,$$

getting a relative error of 22.63%. For the reselected-pairs metric, we rebuild the admissible set after projection, $\mathcal{D}^{*\prime} = \{(i,j) : \tilde{r}_{ij} \leq \tau\}$; here $|\mathcal{D}^{*\prime}| = 3$ and

$$\widehat{C}^{\mathrm{sp}\prime\prime} = \frac{1}{|\mathcal{D}^{*\prime}|} \sum_{(i,j) \subset \mathcal{D}^{*\prime}} \tilde{r}_{ij} = 0.4264, \qquad \text{error} = \frac{|\widehat{C}^{\mathrm{sp}} - \widehat{C}^{\mathrm{sp}\prime\prime}|}{\widehat{C}^{\mathrm{sp}}} = 16.01\%.$$

For average-case spectral check we note that with $\mu_k = 0.9573$, Markov's inequality (8) implies that for any $a > 0$, $\mathbb{P}\{Z \geq 1 - a\} \geq 1 - \frac{1-\mu_k}{a}$. At the 90% level, choose $a = (1-\mu_k)/0.1 = 0.427$, so $Z \geq 0.573$ and $\sqrt{Z} \geq 0.7570$ with probability at least 90%. Empirically, the 10th percentile of ψ_{ij} over $\mathcal{D}^*$ is $q_{0.10}(\psi) = 0.9435$, comfortably above the bound. Likewise, the empirical 90th percentile of $1/\phi_{ij}^{\star}$ is $q_{0.90}(1/\phi^{\star}) = 1.5461$.

5.2   Experimental Evaluation on Benchmark Datasets

We evaluate CDP on benchmark datasets with non-convex manifolds and structures that induce detours. The datasets include Swiss Roll, Torus, S-Curve, Helix, U-Shape, Möbius Strip, Klein Bottle, and Annulus with Obstacle, generated with 1000 points each. We apply PCA, UMAP, CDP (with $k = 2$, $k_{\mathrm{nn}} = 10$, $\tau = 0.8$), and LPP. Projections are visualized in 2D and colored by a parameter (e.g., angle or height) to assess structure preservation. Figure 2 shows the original 3D and 2D projections.

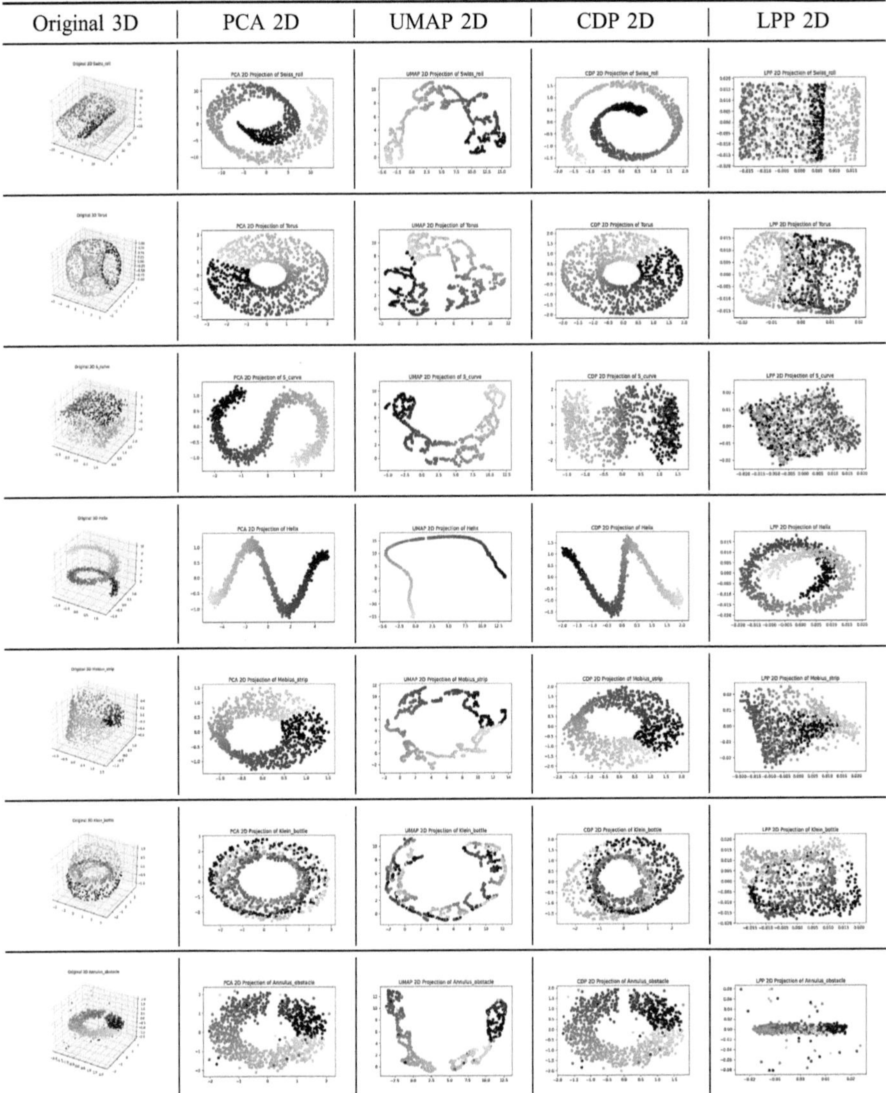

Fig. 2. Datasets from top to bottom: Swiss Roll, Torus, S-Curve, Helix, Möbius Strip, Klein Bottle, Annulus with Obstacle and methods: Original 3D, PCA 2D, UMAP 2D, CDP 2D, LPP 2D.

6   Conclusion

We introduced Convexity-Driven Projection (CDP), a linear dimensionality reduction method that preserves detour-induced local non-convexity in point clouds without requiring boundary estimation. By constructing a positive semidefinite non-convexity structure matrix from admissible pair directions (Sect. 2). We provided a pairwise a-posteriori certificate to bound post-projection distortion (Sect. 4), refined to use projected shortest paths for accuracy, and an average-case spectral bound to quantify typical directional capture. The evaluation protocol, including fixed- and reselected-pairs detour errors and certificate quantiles, offers practitioner-verifiable metrics, validated on synthetic and real-world datasets. Future work includes scaling CDP for large point clouds using approximate shortest-path methods and exploring applications in dynamic environments like robotics.

References

1. Jolliffe, I.T.: Principal Component Analysis, 2nd edn. Springer, New York (2002). https://doi.org/10.1007/b98835
2. Rusu, R.B., Cousins, S.: 3D is here: point cloud library (PCL). In: Proc. IEEE International Conference on Robotics and Automation (ICRA), pp. 1–4 (2011). https://doi.org/10.1109/ICRA.2011.5980567
3. van der Maaten, L., Hinton, G.: Visualizing data using t-SNE. J. Mach. Learn. Res. **9**, 2579–2605 (2008). http://jmlr.org/papers/v9/vandermaaten08a.html
4. McInnes, L., Healy, J., Melville, J.: UMAP: Uniform manifold approximation and projection for dimension reduction. arXiv:1802.03426 (2018)
5. Tenenbaum, J.B., de Silva, V., Langford, J.C.: A global geometric framework for nonlinear dimensionality reduction. Science **290**(5500), 2319–2323 (2000). https://doi.org/10.1126/science.290.5500.2319
6. Berger, M., et al.: A survey of surface reconstruction from point clouds. Comput. Graph. Forum **36**(1), 301–329 (2017). https://doi.org/10.1111/cgf.12802
7. He, X., Niyogi, P.: Locality preserving projections. In: Advances in Neural Information Processing Systems 16 (NeurIPS 2003), pp. 153–160 (2004)
8. He, X., Cai, D., Yan, S., Zhang, H.-J.: Neighborhood preserving embedding. In: Proc. IEEE International Conference on Computer Vision (ICCV), pp. 1208–1213 (2005). https://doi.org/10.1109/ICCV.2005.167
9. Cai, D., He, X., Han, J., Zhang, H.-J.: Orthogonal Laplacianfaces for face recognition. IEEE Trans. Image Process. **15**(11), 3608–3614 (2006). https://doi.org/10.1109/TIP.2006.881945
10. Halko, N., Martinsson, P.-G., Tropp, J.A.: Finding structure with randomness: probabilistic algorithms for constructing approximate matrix decompositions. SIAM Rev. **53**(2), 217–288 (2011). https://doi.org/10.1137/090771806
11. Penrose, M.: Random Geometric Graphs. Oxford University Press (2003)
12. Davis, C., Kahan, W.M.: The rotation of eigenvectors by a perturbation. III. SIAM J. Numeric. Anal. **7**(1), 1–46 (1970). https://doi.org/10.1137/0707001

Bounded Model Checking for Calibration of Systems Biology Models Under Uncertainty

Krishnendu Ghosh[✉] and Jay Ball

College of Charleston, Charleston, SC, USA
ghoshk@cofc.edu, balljc1@g.cofc.edu

Abstract. Biological processes are executed concurrently and on different scales. Modeling of biological processes becomes challenging when the concentrations of biochemicals are imprecise. A tractable formalism for model construction to address imprecision in the concentrations of biochemicals. The model calibration is performed by generating finer models from coarser models that represent the set of sequences of biochemical reactions. Learning of the specifications extracted from the coarser model is applied effectively to construct a finer model. Bounded model checking is performed on the prototype by addressing the uncertainty in the concentration of biochemical reactions. Learning of temporal logic formula is leveraged to address uncertainty in the model. The computational feasibility of the formalism is evaluated on a prototype of the RKIP-inhibited ERK pathway. Results are presented and formalism is promising.

Keywords: Bounded Model Checking · Uncertainty · Model Calibration · Trace Equivalence

1 Introduction

Models of biological processes is one of the key focuses of systems biology studies. Formal verification of biology system [8, 9, 24] has been investigated as a mechanism of modeling and reasoning in biological pathways. However, the state explosion of model checking is limiting for a model comprising of large number of species and uncertainties, in particular concentration of the biochemicals and rate of reactions. The construction of data-dependent models becomes challenging because of the uncertainty in the data. Often, biological processes execute at different scales and the execution speeds of processes are imprecise. Model construction and model calibration for many biological species, and uncertainty in the data becomes complicated. Model calibration is a useful tool for the biologist who would like to evaluate the model addressing variations in data from biological experiments performed in different physical conditions.

The model of biological processes at different scales is abstracted from the data in mechanistic models. A qualitative mechanistic model for multiscale processes is constructed whose foundations are based on the law of conservation of mass for each reaction to represent the changes in the concentration of chemicals. A mechanistic model of biochemical reactions is represented in form of graph where a biochemical reaction is represented by an edge in a graph and the nodes are labeled with concentration of the

C. Zaroliagis et al. (Eds.): ICAA 2026, LNCS 16423, pp. 62–73, 2026.
https://doi.org/10.1007/978-3-032-15621-1_6

biochemicals representing the substrates and products of the reaction. The edge implies the execution of a biochemical reaction where consumption (production) of substrates (products) in a user defined time step for the reaction [19].

The data-dependent models of biological systems are varied owing to imprecision in the data. Data from experiments are varied given the fluctuations in the different physical conditions. We motivate with an example that captures the variations in models when built from data.

Example 1. (Biological Systems Modeling Under Uncertainty) Fig. 1(A)–(C) represent a path in a graph. x, y and z represent biochemical reactions and are the edge labels on the path. The nodes is labeled with the concentrations of the biochemicals are denoted by a_i, b_1, c_1 and d_1, where $1 \leq i \leq 10$. Here the edge denotes a time step for a unit execution of reactions. Hence, the computation for the concentrations that are consumed (produced) from substrates(products) is proportional to the time step of the reaction. For brevity, we show the labels on each node imply biochemicals with their concentrations and not all the biochemicals with concentrations. In Fig. 1(A), the path represents the order of sequence of reactions- reaction x occurring thrice, then, reaction y occurs thrice and is followed by the reaction, z. In Fig. 1(B), reaction x occurs twice before reaction y begins. Similar is the case of reaction, z in Fig. 1(A) where the number of three successive occurrences. There are two contiguous occurrences of z in Fig. 1(B). The path shown in Fig. 1(C) shows the order of the reactions. The number of nodes is four which is less than the other paths. The paths in Fig. 1(1)–(2) can be constructed from the path in Fig. 1(C).

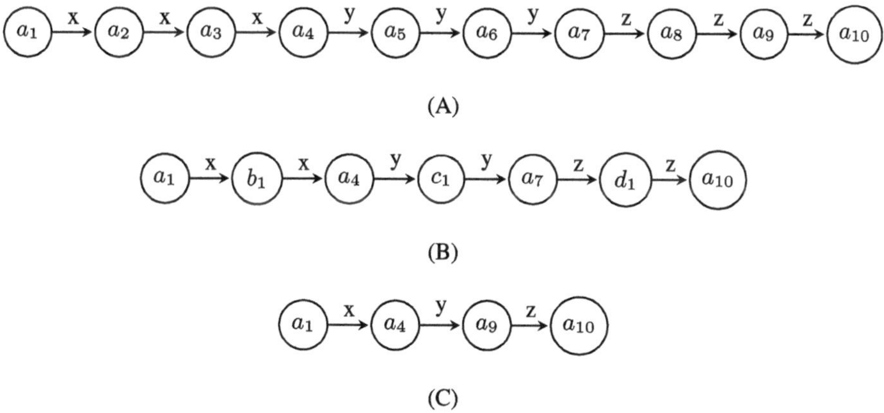

(A)

(B)

(C)

Fig. 1. Paths representing sequence of reactions, x, y and z represented. The initial state in the FSMs are the nodes labeled with 1. Paths contain (A) 10, (B) 7 and (C) 4 nodes, respectively.

Example 1 clearly demonstrates that the sequences of reactions represented by the paths, can be different based on the different values of the concentrations of the biochemicals. The concentrations are different because of imprecision in data. However, the behavior that is identical is the order of the reactions. The behavior of the system-level model from experimental data provides insights in the construction of the models. One way to address the data-dependency of the model is the construction of a *coarse* model as shown in Fig. 1(C). Therefore, the paths shown in Fig. 1(A)–(B) can be denoted as the *finer* model.

In this work, SAT based model calibration method is constructed for a model representing biochemical reaction. The imprecision in the formalism is incorporated by representing the concentrations of the biochemicals in the form of intervals. The goal of this work is to create a formalism that is data-dependent and effective in model calibration under uncertainty. Experiments are conducted on a prototype of RKIP-inhibited ERK pathway to elucidate the model calibration and computational feasibility of the formalism.

2   Background

In this section, we describe published literature on bisimulation algorithms, construction of formal models in systems biology, and learning the linear temporal logic (LTL) formula. These different concepts are foundations of this work.

Similarity in Computational Structures: Comparison of graphical structures based on mathematical relations have been studied in formal logic. Bisimulations are mathematical relations that compares labeled graphical structures such as finite state machines for defined properties. Algorithms for computing bisimulations is an active research area. The partition algorithm [28] constructed equivalence classes and addressed the computation of states that are bisimilar. Different variants of bisimulation and simulation have been rigorously studied. One of the variants of computing bisimulation is stuttering bisimulation where structures with successive identical labeled states are grouped into members of an equivalence class and compared [21,22]. Trace equivalences have been studied in modeling the behavior of processes [10,15] and is a weaker form of bisimulations. Data-dependent approaches used learning of linear time logic formula into a series of SAT problems [27]. Robust abstractions were constructed to infer LTL formula from noisy data [18] and examples [27].

Formal Modeling in Systems Biology: Modeling of biological pathways and querying using temporal logic is an ongoing research area [8,25]. SAT-Based analysis of biological pathways have been analyzed [34]. Synthesis-based approaches have been used to address uncertainty in data and construct gene networks that satisfy a set of constraints [31]. Abstraction-based parameter synthesis has been addressed for model calibration and model validation [5]. Formal modeling of multiscale processes is challenging due to imprecision in the experimental data. Several formalisms have been addressed in the construction of multiscale models. A model representing multiscale processes and a fixed point algorithm for computation of preorder relation on finite state machines had been reported [20]. The construction of model abstractions for study of the biological processes at different levels of granularity have been studied [33]. Concurrency in modeling biological processes have been modeled, primarily using continuous-time Markov chain [2,7]. Models of cell-cell interactions is represented by a scheduler

[16,17] that limits the number of steps process can execute before allowing another process to execute and formally, defined as *bounded asynchrony*. The model captures notion of locally asynchronous executions of the processes but the system of processes are executing in synchronously. SAT-based bounded model checking for discovery of attractors in boolean networks have been studied [14]. A survey on model reduction for large- scale biological models has been reported [32]. Recent work has focused on statistical abstraction for multiscale systems using Gaussian processes and applied to bacterial chemotaxis [26]. Biological model construction and querying using linear temporal logic have been reported [1].

There is a research gap in addressing uncertainty in the concentrations of the bio-chemicals in the pathways in formal models.

3   Preliminaries

In this section, we describe model checking, linear temporal logic(LTL) [29] and bounded model checking. An appropriate knowledge representation structure such as transition system is described. Model checking is performed by posing a logic formula on a model, represented by a finite state machine. The logic formula denotes specification that is evaluated to true or false on the model. Formally, the definitions for the mathematical structures for model checking is stated.

Definition 1. *A Kripke structure is a tuple* $\mathcal{K} = \langle S_0, S, R, L \rangle$ *where,*

1. *S is a finite and nonempty set of states.*

2. *$S_0 \subseteq S$ the set of initial states.*

3. *$R \subseteq S \times S$ where R is the transition relation*

4. *$L : S \to 2^{AP}$ where L is the labeling function on $s \in S$ and AP is the set of propositions.*

The totality property for the Kripke structue is not there. Therefore, a transition system is defined as A *transition system*, $\mathcal{M}$ is a Kripke structure $\langle S_0, S, R, L \rangle$ where, for each state $s \in S$, there is at least one state $s' \in S$ where $(s, s') \in R$. In our formalism, we will use *transition system* to describe the formalism.

Definition 2. *(Model checking [11])* Given a model, $\mathcal{M}$ and formula, ϕ, model checking is the process of deciding whether a formula ϕ is true in the model, written $\mathcal{M} \models \phi$.

Definition 3. *(Trace [3])* A trace, π in a transition system, $\mathcal{M}$ is a sequence of labeled states, $L(s_0) \to L(s_1) \to L(s_2) \dots L(s_n)$ where $n \in \mathbb{N}$ and L is the labeling function in $\mathcal{M}$.

A *trace* that leads to falsification of a property in $\mathcal{M}$ is a counterexample. The goal is to identify the scenario on the trace that led to falsification.

Definition 4. *(Trace equivalence)* Two infinite paths in a transition system, $\mathcal{M}$ $\mu = s_0 \to s_1 \to s_2 \dots$ and $\rho = s'_0 \to s'_1 \to s'_2 \dots$ are trace equivalent if $L(s_o) = L(s'_0), L(s_1) = L(s'_1), L(s_2) = L(s'_2) \dots$

Definition 5. *(Stutter [3])* A transition, $s \rightarrow s'$ in a transition system, $\mathcal{M}$ is a *stutter* step where $L(s) = L(s')$.

Stuttering on transition systems has been studied for the construction of algorithms for partial order reduction in addressing the state explosion problem. However, for the construction and calibration of an efficient model representing biochemical reactions, we formalize the notion of *fluent*, a concept related to *stutter*. In a fluent, the successive states in a trace are labeled nonidentical, which is different from stutter, where the successive states that are identically labeled. The interleaving of the concurrent pathways is captured in the traces. The edge labels on the traces represent the change due to different processes.

Definition 6. *(Fluent) A transition, $s \rightarrow s'$ in a transition system, $\mathcal{M}$ is a* fluent *step where $L(s) \neq L(s')$.*

Definition 7. *(Fluency) For an infinite trace, $\pi = s_0.s_1.\ldots$ in a transition system, $\mathcal{M}$, $l_0, l_1, l_2\ldots$ is a the sequence of state labels in π. The* fluency *of a trace is the subsequence of state labels, $\hat{\pi} = l_0, l_{i_1}, l_{i_2}, \ldots l_{i_j}$ is in $\hat{\pi}$ iff $l_{i_j} \neq l_{i_j - 1}$ iff $i_j \neq l_{i_j - 1}$ and $l_0 \neq l_{i_i}$*

Definition 8. *(Fluency Equivalence on Traces) Two infinite traces in transition system $\mathcal{M}$, $\sigma = s_0 \rightarrow s_1 \rightarrow s_2 \ldots$ and $\rho = r_0 \rightarrow r_1 \rightarrow r_2 \ldots$ are fluency equivalent ($\equiv_f$) if there are two infinite ordered sequences of positive integers, $i = 0 < i_0 < i_1 < \ldots$ and $j = 0 < j_0 < j_1 < \ldots$ such that $\forall k \geq 0 \ L(s_{i_k}) \neq L(s_{i_k+1}) \neq \ldots = L(s_{i_{k+1}-1}) \neq L(r_{j_k}) \neq L(r_{j_k+1}) \neq \ldots \neq L(r_{j_{k+1}-1})$. The indices i_k and j_k are the starting points of μ and ρ, respectively.*

Definition 9. *(Fluency Equivalence) Two transition systems, $\mathcal{M}$ and $\mathcal{M}'$ are fluency equivalent iff*

1. *$L(s_0) = L(s_0')$.*
2. *For all traces, μ from state, $s \in S$ of $\mathcal{M}$, $\exists$ a trace ρ of $\mathcal{M}'$ from s' such that $\mu \equiv_f \rho$.*
3. *For all traces, ρ from a state of $s' \in S'$ of $\mathcal{M}'$, $\exists$ a trace μ of $\mathcal{M}$ from the state $s \in S$ such that $\rho \equiv_f \mu$.*

Here, a transition system is constructed and physical information of the chemical reactions or biological system is incorporated in a way to use the existing well studied logics such as, LTL [29]. We refer the reader to [12] for an introduction. For our model, the system of biochemical reaction will be represented by a transition system where the edges will be labeled with the pathways and denoted by E-transition system. Formally,

Definition 10. *(E-Transition System) An E-transition system $\mathcal{M}_e$ over a set AP of proposition letters and a set ξ of labels is a tuple $\mathcal{M}_e = \langle S_0, S, R, L_s, L_e \rangle$ where,*

1. *$\langle S_0, S, R, L_s \rangle$ is a transition system.*
2. *$L_e : R \rightarrow \xi$.*

The set of edge labels,ξ represent the set of pathways that are modeled in the E-transition system. Each edge label contain information about specific pathway.

Bounded model checking [4] is used to evaluate the satisfaction of a specification represented in the form of a boolean formula. The execution of the system model is analyzed based on a specified number of steps (called the bound) represented by the length of the traces, k where $k \in \mathbb{N}$. Specifically, a bounded model checker takes as input a model, specification, and bound to stop at, and works by checking the model for counterexamples, up until the bound, to disprove the specification. If a counterexample is found, the specification is falsified and the computation terminated. If no counterexample is found, the computation ends when the specified bound is reached, giving a verified result. The bounded model checking is performed by translating a temporal logic formula into propositional boolean formula and then is applied as input to SAT solvers for the computation of the satisfaction of the boolean formula.

Model checking for a LTL formula, ϕ on a transition system, $\mathcal{M}$ using bounded model checking requires a bound, k. A trace, π in $\mathcal{M}$ is a finite sequence of states, $s_0, s_1, \ldots, s_k$ where each $s_i, 0 \leq i \leq k$ represents a time step in the execution. In bounded model checking, the LTL formula that is to be evaluated is constructed using the following three steps. First, the initial state is denoted $I(s_0)$. Second, the states in the path being modeled is denoted $\bigwedge_{i=0}^{k-1} T(s_i, s_{i+1})$. Finally, the property to check is $P(\phi)$, but its negation, $P(\neg\phi)$, is what is used in the formula. Connecting these three components creates the final formula used in bounded model checking: $I(s_0) \wedge \bigwedge_{i=0}^{k-1} T(s_i, s_{i+1}) \wedge P(\neg\phi)$.

4   Bounded Model Checking Based Model Calibration

In this section, the model representing the systems of biochemical reactions is described. Additionally, the details of model calibration using bounded model checking is described.

4.1   Model Abstraction

The model abstraction of the system of biochemical reactions is captured by an E-transition system. The E-transition system, $\mathcal{M}_e = \langle S_0, S, R, L_s, L_e \rangle$ for biochemical reactions is described as the set of biochemicals, $\mathcal{B}$, for each biochemical, $b \in \mathcal{B}$ the set of formulas $b = 0$ or $b \in (b_i, b_{i+1}]$ form the set of atomic propositions,AP. A state, s is labeled with concentrations of biochemicals. An edge (s, s') where $L(s) \neq L(s')$ denote the change of concentration of biochemicals due to the execution of a pathway. A self-loop (self- edge) of the form, (s, s)on a state represent equilibrium. $\S\rangle$ is the set of labels representing pathways. In our model, we make the following assumption-state where many reactions are possible, the pathway that has the fastest forward rate is considered and concurrency is represented as interleaving of pathways in a path. An edge implies a time step(unit) for the reaction. It is possible that depending on the time unit, the edge may model a *partial reaction* in the E-transition system. A partial reaction is when only a part of reaction has completed during a specific time step. Also, a reaction is *complete* when the concentration of a substrate(s) of a pathway is zero.

The interval representation for the concentration of biochemicals is used for the computation of the concentration of the substrates and products after the reactions have taken place in the following way:

There is a transition, s to s' if for a given biochemical reaction, r each substrate has non-zero concentration with the interval of the form, $(b_i, b_{i+1}]$ where $b_i, b_{i+1} \in \mathbb{R}$. The concentration of the substrates after the reaction is given by $(b_j, b_{j+1}$ where $b' = b - \rho$, b is the midpoint of $b_i, b_{i+1}]$ and ρ is the molar amount consumed and $b' \in (b_j, b_{j+1}]$. Similarly, the expression for concentration of the product is given by $d' = d + \rho$, where d is the midpoint of the concentration interval, $(d_i, d_{i+1}]$ before the reaction occurs. The concentration of the product of the reaction after the reaction is $(d_j, d_{j+1}]$ where $d' \in (d_j, d_{j+1}]$. The intervals are represented symbolically.

4.2 Coarse and Fine Models

The computational abstraction of the model from the data produces different models that differ in the values of the concentration of biochemicals. Initially, the logic formula representing the coarser path with a minimal number of states is used as input to the SAT solver.

The volume of the concentration of chemicals consumed during a reaction was modified to create finer models. In the coarser model, a mole of chemicals was used in each state, while in the finer models, either 1/2 or 1/4 of a mole of chemicals was used in each state. This resulted in a higher number of states in the finer model and fewer states in the coarser model. In the implementation, two additional rules were evaluated. The first rule checks if the input chemicals are nonzero, and if not, ends the reaction. The second rule checks and modifies the concentration of chemicals consumed by the substrate by a constant value, which the user is prompted to enter when executing the program. When the user runs the program, entering a value greater than 1 for the scale factor creates a model finer than the default generated model.

5   Simulation

5.1   Application to RKIP-Inhibited ERK Pathway

The ERK pathway is located inside cells and consists of various proteins. Throughout the pathway, chain reactions occur which cause cell activity to change. The ERK pathway is responsible for initiating cell activity such as replication, and researching it may help understand diseases connected to cell activity such as cancer. It is difficult to model, concentrations are difficult to precisely measure. Therefore, in simulations modeling the ERK pathway, models use intervals instead of exact values. One of the important pathways is the RKIP-inhibited ERK pathway that consists of three proteins, Raf-1, Mek, and Erk. Figure 2 shows the ten biochemical reactions that are found in RKIP-inhibited ERK pathway. The initial concentrations of the biochemicals, Raf-1, Rkip, Mek-PP, Erk-PP and RP is in the intervals, [65-70],[0,1],[62,70] and [160-165], respectively. The concentrations are in micromoles [23]. All the other biochemicals excluding Raf-1, Rkip, Mek-PP, Erk-PP and RP were initialized to zero.

1. Raf-1 + Rkip $\overset{k_1/k_2}{\rightleftharpoons}$ Raf-1-Rkip.
2. Raf-1-Rkip + Erp-PP $\overset{k_3/k_4}{\rightleftharpoons}$ Raf-1-Rkip-Erk-PP.
3. Raf-1-Rkip-Erk-PP $\overset{k_5}{\rightarrow}$ Raf-1* + Erk-P + Rkip-P.
4. Rkip-P + RP $\overset{k_9/k_{10}}{\rightleftharpoons}$ Rkip-P-RP.
5. Rkip-P-RP $\overset{k_{11}}{\rightarrow}$ Rkip + RP.
6. Mek-PP + Erk-P $\overset{k_6/k_7}{\rightleftharpoons}$ Mek-PP-Erk-P.
7. Mek-PP-Erk-P $\overset{k_8}{\rightarrow}$ Erk-PP + Mek-PP.
8. Mek-PP $\overset{k_{15}}{\rightarrow}$ Mek.
9. Mek + Raf-1 $\overset{k_{12}/k_{13}}{\rightleftharpoons}$ Mek-Raf-1*.
10. Mek-Raf-1 $\overset{k_{14}}{\rightarrow}$ Raf-1 + Mek-PP.

Fig. 2. Pathways in Rkip inhibited Erk Pathway.

The simulation of the proposed formalism is based on published model [7,30]. The parameters namely the rate of reactions in the biochemical reactions as shown in Table 1.

Table 1. Rates of biochemical pathway used in simulation [6,23] PR and R denotes Pathway rates and rates, respectively.

PR	k_1	k_2	k_3	k_4	k_5	k_6	k_7	k_8	k_9	k_{10}	k_{11}	k_{12}	k_{13}	k_{14}	k_{15}
R	0.53	0.0072	0.625	0.00245	0.0315	0.8	0.0075	0.071	0.92	0.00122	0.87	0.05	0.03	0.06	0.02

5.2   Results

The simulation was conducted on a 2022 MacBook Air with an Apple M2 processor and 24GB of Unified Memory. The data and the scripts are available (https://zenodo.org/records/17538267 simulation was performed using the following: The concentrations of the chemicals were represented in the form of intervals. The midpoint of the interval is used for computation of the substrates/products.

In the midpoint model, the midpoint of each interval is used as the chemical concentration in a reaction. After each reaction concludes, the output is an exact concentration value for each chemical. These values are used to determine the new interval for each chemical. This process is repeated for each reaction, allowing intervals to be used instead of exact values. The sample queries that were evaluated using bounded model checking. The concentration is symbolically stated. For a concentration interval $(b_1, b_2]$, the symbolic representation is Sb_1Eb_2. In the sample queries, x, y

Q1. Is there a state where the concentration of $raf - 1$ is between x and y? LTL formula, $\mathbf{F}\,(raf - 1 = SxEy)$.

Q2. Is there a state where the concentration of $Raf - 1$ is between x and y and $Rkip$ has a concentration of zero? The LTL formula in LTL is $\mathbf{F}\,(Raf - 1 = SxEy \wedge Rkip = zero)$.

Q3. Is there a state where $Erk - PP$ has a concentration between x and z, $Erk - P$ has a concentration less than u or greater then v, and $Rkip - P$ is zero? In LTL, the formula is $\mathbf{F}\,(Erk - PP = SxEz \wedge Erk - P \neq SuEv \wedge Rkip - P = zero)$.

Q4. Is there a state where either $Raf1 - Rkip - Erk - PP$ has a concentration between x and y, or $Erk - PP$ is not zero and Mek has a concentration between x and z, and $Mekpperk - R$ is between x and z? LTL formula is $\mathbf{F}\,(Raf1 - Rkip - Rrk - RR = SxEy \vee Erk - PP \neq zero \wedge Mek = SxEz \wedge Mek - PP - Erk - P = SxEz)$.

Q5. Is there a state where either $Raf - 1$ has a concentration between x and y, $Raf1 - rkip$ is between x and z, and $Erk - PP$ is not zero; or, $Erk - P$ has a concentration between x and z and $Mek - PP - Erk - P$ is between x and z? LTL formula $\mathbf{F}\,(Raf - 1 = SxEy \wedge Raf1 - Rkip = SxE8z \wedge Erk - PP \neq zero \vee Erk - P = SxEz \wedge Mek - PP - Erk - P = SxEz.)$.

Q6. Is there a state where $Rkip$ has a concentration between x and y and $Raf1 - Rkip$ is between x and y; or $Raf1 - Rkip - Erk - PP$ has a concentration of zero, $Erk - P$ is not between y and z, $Rkip - P$ is not zero, and RP is between x and z? In LTL, this is expressed as $\mathbf{F}\,(Rkip = SxEy \wedge Raf1rkip = SxEy \vee Raf1 - Rkip - Erk - PP = zero \wedge Erk - P \neq SxEz \wedge Rkip - P \neq zero \wedge RP = SxEz)$.

Q7. Is there a state where at least one of the following three statements are true: raf has a concentration of zero and $Raf1rkip$ is not between x and y; $Raf1rkiperk - PP$ has a concentration between y and z, $Mekraf$ is not between y and z, and $Rkipp - RP$ is not between y and z; or, Mek has a concentration between x and y and rp is not between y and z? LTL formula, $\mathbf{F}\,(Raf = zero \wedge Raf1 - Rkip \neq SxEy \vee Raf1 - Rkiperk - PP = SyEz \wedge Mek - Raf - 1 \neq SyEz \wedge Rkipp - RP \neq SyEz \vee Mek = SxEy \wedge RP \neq SyEz)$

The following three SAT solvers were tested and timed with the above sample queries for evaluation of the computational feasibility of the formalism: Glucose3 (https://github.com/arminbiere/lingeling), Gluecard3, Lingeling (https://github.com/arminbiere/lingeling). The data from these tests is contained in Table 2. The results demonstrate the queries were executed for different lengths of path. The time recorded for the queries were within 1 sec. The performance of the SAT solver, Glucard3 was the best, followed by Glucose3 and then,Lingeling. The experiments were conducted on different sizes of boolean formula.

Additionally, a sample of bounded model checking queries were conducted the model where the concentration of the biochemicals were in the form of intervals using Z3 SMT solver [13]. The advantage of SMT solvers is that it is able to solve multiple inequalities that represents concentrations of the biochemicals.

The experiments demonstrate the computational feasibility of the model. The results also show an efficient for construction of finer models represented by paths from coarser

Table 2. Execution times (in milliseconds) for different queries with varying lengths,k of path. The SAT solvers used for executions are Glucose3,Glucard3 and Lingeling

| | | Time (in Milliseconds) for path length, k | | | | | | |
Solvers	Query	k = 1	k = 3	k = 5	k = 7	k = 10	k = 13	k = 15
Glucose3	Q1	0.0608	0.1123	0.056	0.0551	0.1168	0.3667	0.0579
	Q2	0.062	0.0498	0.0699	0.0567	0.062	0.056	0.138
	Q3	0.0432	0.0701	0.0551	0.0548	0.0541	0.078	0.0761
	Q4	0.0601	0.0739	0.1051	0.0529	0.0851	0.0772	0.083
	Q5	0.062	0.0281	0.0718	0.056	0.097	0.062	0.073
	Q6	0.0689	0.0658	0.077	0.0629	0.0699	0.0789	0.0741
	Q7	0.0508	0.1271	0.1621	0.1991	0.056	0.0701	0.0761
Glucard3	Q1	0.0551	0.939	0.026	0.0267	0.1092	0.242	0.0381
	Q2	0.0229	0.0198	0.0329	0.026	0.0319	0.0291	0.0331
	Q3	0.0222	0.0303	0.0291	0.025	0.0269	0.0379	0.0319
	Q4	0.0241	0.0322	0.0381	0.0288	ll0.0393	0.0393	0.0327
	Q5	0.025	0.0122	0.0808	0.0281	0.035	0.0322	0.0341
	Q6	0.0291	0.03	0.0319	0.31	0.0379	0.042	0.03
	Q7	0.0272	0.281	0.042	0.0312	0.0269	0.026	0.035
Lingeling	Q1	0.083	0.1309	0.1070	0.123	0.145	0.1531	0.072
	Q2	0.107	0.0949	0.1469	0.1111	0.1218	0.119	0118
	Q3	0.0899	0.1290	0.128	0.1082	0.103	0.1442	0.1521
	Q4	0.0892	0.1469	0.1910	0.1299	0.175	0.1612	0.1481
	Q5	0.1128	0.0701	0.1628	0.1180	0.14	0.145	0.1581
	Q6	0.1159	1.3981	0.1490	0.2828	0.1483	0.1528	0.1237
	Q7	1.101	0.1869	0.1581	0.1311	0.123	0.1211	0.1528

paths of a transition system. The boolean formulas used for bounded model checking was able to express interesting biological queries such as the necessity of a biochemical, B_1 in a specific concentration to produce another biochemical, B_2. The formalism helps the modeler to calibrate the model under uncertainty in the concentration of the chemicals.

6   Conclusion

In this work, we demonstrate a novel formalism addresses uncertainty in model calibration of biological systems and leverages on bounded model checking and learning of LTL formulas by formalization of *fluent*. The computational feasibility of the formalism using interval midpoint method is effective. The representation of the concentration of the biochemicals in the form of intervals and its approximation in the computation will be rigorously evaluated. The construction of finer models from coarser model provide insights in construction of multiscale models in biology with stochastic structures.

Acknowledgments. The first author was supported by NSF grant CCF 2227898 and the second author was supported summer grant from School of engineering and mathematics at College of Charleston.

References

1. Ahmed, Z., et al.: Bringing LTL model checking to biologists. In: Bouajjani, A., Monniaux, D. (eds.) VMCAI 2017. LNCS, vol. 10145, pp. 1–13. Springer, Cham (2017). https://doi.org/10.1007/978-3-319-52234-0_1

2. Anderson, D.F., Kurtz, T.G.: Continuous time Markov chain models for chemical reaction networks. In: Design and Analysis of Biomolecular Circuits: Engineering Approaches to Systems and Synthetic Biology, pp. 3–42. Springer (2011)

3. Baier, C., Katoen, J.-P.: Principles of Model Checking. MIT Press (2008)

4. Biere, A., Cimatti, A., Clarke, E., Zhu, Y.: Symbolic model checking without BDDs. In: Tools and Algorithms for the Construction and Analysis of Systems: 5th International Conference, TACAS'99 Held as Part of the Joint European Conferences on Theory and Practice of Software, ETAPS'99 Amsterdam, The Netherlands, 22–28 March 1999 Proceedings 5, pp. 193–207. Springer (1999)

5. Bogomolov, S., Schilling, C., Bartocci, E., Batt, G., Kong, H., Grosu, R.: Abstraction-based parameter synthesis for multiaffine systems. In: Piterman, N. (ed.) HVC 2015. LNCS, vol. 9434, pp. 19–35. Springer, Cham (2015). https://doi.org/10.1007/978-3-319-26287-1_2

6. Calder, M., Gilmore, S., Hillston, J., Vyshemirsky, V.: Formal methods for biochemical signalling pathways. Formal Methods: State of the Art and New Directions, pp. 185–215 (2010)

7. Calder, M., Vyshemirsky, V., Gilbert, D., Orton, R.: Analysis of signalling pathways using continuous time Markov chains. In: Priami, C., Plotkin, G. (eds.) Transactions on Computational Systems Biology VI. LNCS, vol. 4220, pp. 44–67. Springer, Heidelberg (2006). https://doi.org/10.1007/11880646_3

8. Chabrier, N., Fages, F.: Symbolic model checking of biochemical networks. In: Priami, C. (ed.) CMSB 2003. LNCS, vol. 2602, pp. 149–162. Springer, Heidelberg (2003). https://doi.org/10.1007/3-540-36481-1_13

9. Chabrier-Rivier, N., Chiaverini, M., Danos, V., Fages, F., Schächter, V.: Modeling and querying biomolecular interaction networks. Theoret. Comput. Sci. **325**(1), 25–44 (2004)

10. Cheval, V.: APTE: an algorithm for proving trace equivalence. In: Ábrahám, E., Havelund, K. (eds.) TACAS 2014. LNCS, vol. 8413, pp. 587–592. Springer, Heidelberg (2014). https://doi.org/10.1007/978-3-642-54862-8_50

11. Clarke, E.M.: Model checking. In: Ramesh, S., Sivakumar, G. (eds.) FSTTCS 1997. LNCS, vol. 1346, pp. 54–56. Springer, Heidelberg (1997). https://doi.org/10.1007/BFb0058022

12. Clarke, E.M., Grumberg, O., Peled, D.: Model Checking. MIT Press (1999)

13. de Moura, L., Bjørner, N.: Z3: an efficient SMT solver. In: Ramakrishnan, C.R., Rehof, J. (eds.) TACAS 2008. LNCS, vol. 4963, pp. 337–340. Springer, Heidelberg (2008). https://doi.org/10.1007/978-3-540-78800-3_24

14. Dubrova, E., Teslenko, M.: A sat-based algorithm for finding attractors in synchronous boolean networks. IEEE/ACM Trans. Comput. Biol. Bioinf. **8**(5), 1393–1399 (2011)

15. Engelfriet, J.: Determinancy→(observation equivalence= trace equivalence). Theoret. Comput. Sci. **36**, 21–25 (1985)

16. Fisher, J., Henzinger, T.A., Mateescu, M., Piterman, N.: Bounded asynchrony: concurrency for modeling cell-cell interactions. In: Fisher, J. (ed.) FMSB 2008. LNCS, vol. 5054, pp. 17–32. Springer, Heidelberg (2008). https://doi.org/10.1007/978-3-540-68413-8_2

17. Fisher, J., Henzinger, T.A., Nickovic, D., Piterman, N., Singh, A.V., Vardi, M.Y.: Dynamic reactive modules. In: Katoen, J.-P., König, B. (eds.) CONCUR 2011. LNCS, vol. 6901, pp. 404–418. Springer, Heidelberg (2011). https://doi.org/10.1007/978-3-642-23217-6_27

18. Gaglione, J.-R., Neider, D., Roy, R., Topcu, U., Xu, Z.: Learning linear temporal properties from noisy data: a MaxSAT-based approach. In: Hou, Z., Ganesh, V. (eds.) ATVA 2021. LNCS, vol. 12971, pp. 74–90. Springer, Cham (2021). https://doi.org/10.1007/978-3-030-88885-5_6

19. Ghosh, K.: Multiscale system modeling of biochemical pathways. In: Proceedings of the 8th International Conference on Bioinspired Information and Communications Technologies, pp. 177–181. ICST (Institute for Computer Sciences, Social-Informatics and Telecommunications Engineering) (2014)

20. Ghosh, K.: Computing equivalences on model abstractions representing multiscale processes. Nano Commun. Networks **6**(3), 118–123 (2015)

21. Groote, J.F., Vaandrager, F.: An efficient algorithm for branching bisimulation and stuttering equivalence. In: Paterson, M.S. (ed.) ICALP 1990. LNCS, vol. 443, pp. 626–638. Springer, Heidelberg (1990). https://doi.org/10.1007/BFb0032063

22. Groote, J.F., Jansen, D.N., Keiren, J.J.A., Wijs, A.J.: An o (m log n) algorithm for computing stuttering equivalence and branching bisimulation. ACM Trans. Comput. Logic (TOCL) **18**(2), 13 (2017)

23. Kwang-Hyun, C., Sung-Young, S., Hyun-Woo, K., Wolkenhauer, O., McFerran, B., Kolch, W.: Mathematical modeling of the influence of RKIP on the ERK signaling pathway. In: Priami, C. (ed.) CMSB 2003. LNCS, vol. 2602, pp. 127–141. Springer, Heidelberg (2003). https://doi.org/10.1007/3-540-36481-1_11

24. Kwiatkowska, M., Norman, G., Parker, D., Tymchyshyn, O., Heath, J., Gaffney, E.: Simulation and verification for computational modelling of signalling pathways. In: Simulation Conference, 2006. WSC 2006. Proceedings of the Winter, pp. 1666–1674. IEEE (2006)

25. Liu, B., Safa, S.: A model checking-based analysis framework for systems biology models. In: 2020 57th ACM/IEEE Design Automation Conference (DAC), pp. 1–6. IEEE (2020)

26. Michaelides, M., Hillston, J., Sanguinetti, G.: Statistical abstraction for multi-scale spatio-temporal systems. In: Bertrand, N., Bortolussi, L. (eds.) QEST 2017. LNCS, vol. 10503, pp. 243–258. Springer, Cham (2017). https://doi.org/10.1007/978-3-319-66335-7_15

27. Neider, D., Gavran, I.: Learning linear temporal properties. In: 2018 Formal Methods in Computer Aided Design (FMCAD), pp. 1–10. IEEE (2018)

28. Paige, R., Tarjan, R.E.: Three partition refinement algorithms. SIAM J. Comput. **16**(6), 973–989 (1987)

29. Pnueli, A.: The temporal logic of programs. In: 18th Annual Symposium on Foundations of Computer Science (SFCS 1977), pp. 46–57. IEEE (1977)

30. Shankland, C., Tran, N., Baral, C., Kolch, W.: Reasoning about the ERK signal transduction pathway using BioSigNet-RR. In: Proceedings of the Third International Conference on Computational Methods in System Biology (CMSB 2005) (2005)

31. Shavit, Y., et al.: Automated synthesis and analysis of switching gene regulatory networks. Biosystems **146**, 26–34 (2016)

32. Snowden, T.J., van der Graaf, P.H., Tindall, M.J.: Methods of model reduction for large-scale biological systems: a survey of current methods and trends. Bull. Math. Biol. 1–38 (2017)

33. Sunnåker, M., Cedersund, G., Jirstrand, M.: A method for zooming of nonlinear models of biochemical systems. BMC Syst. Biol. **5**(1), 140 (2011)

34. Tiwari, A., Talcott, C., Knapp, M., Lincoln, P., Laderoute, K.: Analyzing pathways using SAT-based approaches. In: Anai, H., Horimoto, K., Kutsia, T. (eds.) AB 2007. LNCS, vol. 4545, pp. 155–169. Springer, Heidelberg (2007). https://doi.org/10.1007/978-3-540-73433-8_12

Top-K Exterior Power Persistent Homology: Algorithm, Structure, and Stability

Yoshihiro Maruyama[(✉)]

School of Informatics, Nagoya University, Nagoya, Japan
maruyama@i.nagoya-u.ac.jp

Abstract. Exterior powers play important roles in persistent homology in computational geometry. In the present paper we study the problem of extracting the K longest intervals of the exterior-power layers $\Lambda^i M$ of a tame persistence module M, directly from the barcode $B(M)$, without enumerating the entire $B(\Lambda^i M)$. We prove a structural decomposition theorem that organizes $B(\Lambda^i M)$ into monotone per-anchor streams with explicit multiplicities, enabling a best-first algorithm. We provide an $O\big((M + K)\log M\big)$ time algorithm for any fixed $i \geq 2$, obtained via a grouped best-first search. We also show that the Top-K length vector is 2-Lipschitz under bottleneck perturbations of the input barcode, and prove a comparison-model lower bound implying the $O(M \log M)$ preprocessing is information-theoretically unavoidable. Our experiments confirm the theory, showing speedups over full enumeration in high overlap cases. By enabling efficient extraction of the most prominent features, our approach makes higher-order persistence feasible for large datasets and thus broadly applicable to machine learning, data science, and scientific computing.

Keywords: Computational geometry · persistent homology · stability

1 Introduction

Exterior powers Λ^i in persistent homology capture higher-order interactions among topological features that ordinary persistence cannot record [8,12,21].[1] While standard persistence tracks the lifetimes of individual cycles, exterior powers Λ^i encode how groups of cycles coexist, providing richer invariants that are stable and computable [3,4,6]. These higher-order signatures are increasingly important in applications ranging from theoretical topology to machine learning, where concise and discriminative summaries are essential.

However, computing the full exterior-power barcode quickly becomes infeasible: even for Λ^2, its size can be quadratic in the input. Straightforward algorithms

---

[1] Λ denotes exterior product/power. Λ is defined pointwise for persistence modules (i.e., take exterior product at each element of the domain interval; more detail below).

C. Zaroliagis et al. (Eds.): ICAA 2026, LNCS 16423, pp. 74–86, 2026.
https://doi.org/10.1007/978-3-032-15621-1_7

that enumerate all intervals therefore waste work when only the most significant features are needed. This motivates the *Top-K problem*: extracting just the K longest intervals of $B(\Lambda^i M)$ without enumerating the entire structure. Such a view aligns with practice, where users seek concise visual summaries, robust statistics, or fixed-length features for downstream learning.

This work shows that Top-K for exterior powers admits an efficient, stable solution, bridging classical persistent homology algorithms [1,9,22] with techniques from selection algorithms [10,11] and persistent data structures [7]. This makes higher-order persistence more scalable and broadly applicable across computational geometry and topological data analysis.

The main contributions of this paper are as follows: (i) We give a structural decomposition of $B(\Lambda^i M)$ into simple monotone streams, making explicit where higher-order intervals originate and how their multiplicities arise; (ii) We design a best-first algorithm that extracts the exact Top-K intervals in near output-sensitive time, avoiding the cost of full enumeration; (iii) We show that the Top-K length vector is stable under bottleneck perturbations, providing a concise and noise-robust summary; (iv) We establish an $\Omega(M \log M)$ lower bound in the comparison model, proving that our preprocessing cost is optimal up to constants.

In the rest of the paper, we develop mathematical foundations first, and provide structure theorems and algorithms with complexity results. We then prove stability and optimality results. Finally, we give an experimental verification.

2 Basic Concepts and Fundamental Theorems

Let $i \geq 2$ be a fixed constant throughout the paper.

Let M be a tame, pointwise finite-dimensional persistence module over $I \subset \mathbb{R}$ with barcode $B(M) = \{ J_r = [b_r, d_r) \}_{r=1}^{M}$, where, for convenience of notation, we use the same symbol M for the module and the corresponding number of intervals (for persistence module basics, see [4,21]). We write M_t as usual for the value of M at $t \in I$. $\Lambda^i M$ is defined pointwise by $(\Lambda^i M)_t = \Lambda^i M_t$.[2]

Unless otherwise stated, we assume all bars are finite $(d_r < \infty)$; this covers common filtrations on finite complexes/graphs. In some filtrations (e.g. H_0 of Vietoris–Rips or Čech complexes), some bars extend to $+\infty$. Our algorithm and decomposition extend unchanged if such bars are handled in either of the following standard ways: (i) *Truncation:* fix a global time horizon $t_{\max}$ and replace each infinite bar $[b_r, \infty)$ by $[b_r, t_{\max})$, so that Λ^i-intervals respect the finite horizon; (ii) *Relative formulation:* regard an infinite bar as persisting until a formal symbol ∞, and observe that in the exterior-power interval calculus (Theorem 1 below) only $\min\{d_r, \dots\}$ appears, so truncating to any sufficiently large finite cutoff yields the same Top-K results. Thus we may assume without loss of generality that all bars are finite.

---

[2] Note that $\Lambda^i M_t$ on the right-hand side denotes the i-th exterior power of the vector space M_t. On morphisms, for each $s \leq t$ in I, we set $(\Lambda^i M)_{s \leq t} = \Lambda^i(M_{s \leq t}) : \Lambda^i(M_s) \longrightarrow \Lambda^i(M_t)$. For persistence homology basics, see also [8,21].

We adopt the *closedopen* convention and process a global event list of all b_r and d_r *sorted by time*, breaking ties by handling *deaths before births* [4,8].[3] Among births at the same time we fix any total order that is consistent across the sweep (cf. [8,9]). For an event sweep from $-\infty$ to $+\infty$, just *before* the birth of bar r at time b_r, define the *alive set* $A_r := \{\, s : [b_s, d_s) \text{ is alive just before } b_r \,\}$ and $c_r := |A_r|$. Order A_r by non-increasing death times; write these as $d_r(1) \geq d_r(2) \geq \cdots \geq d_r(c_r)$. For $j \in \{1, \ldots, c_r\}$ set

$$\ell_r(j) \;:=\; \max\Big\{\, 0, \; \min\{d_r, \; d_r(j)\} - b_r \Big\}, \tag{1}$$

so $j \mapsto \ell_r(j)$ is non-increasing.

2.1   Exterior Powers at the Barcode Level

We first prove a fundamental theorem clarifying the barcode structure of exterior powers.

Theorem 1. (Exterior-power Interval Calculus). *For any $i \geq 1$, the barcode of $\Lambda^i M$ is the multiset*

$$B(\Lambda^i M) \;=\; \Big\{\, \big[\max_j b_{\ell_j}, \, \min_j d_{\ell_j}\big) \;:\; \ell_1 < \cdots < \ell_i, \; \max_j b_{\ell_j} < \min_j d_{\ell_j} \Big\}.$$

Proof. By the barcode decomposition for tame pointwise finite-dimensional modules (see [4,21]), there is a (noncanonical) isomorphism $M \cong \bigoplus_{r=1}^{M} I_{[b_r, d_r)}$, where $I_{[b_r, d_r)}$ is the (one-dimensional) interval module supported on $[b_r, d_r)$.

Fix $i \geq 1$. Apply the exterior-power functor pointwise in $t \in \mathbb{R}$. For any finite family of vector spaces, $\Lambda^i\big(\bigoplus_{r=1}^{M} V_r\big) \cong \bigoplus_{\substack{\ell_1 < \cdots < \ell_i \\ \ell_j \in \{1,\ldots,M\}}} V_{\ell_1} \wedge \cdots \wedge V_{\ell_i}$ is natural in the V_r. Evaluating at time t with $V_r = (I_{[b_r, d_r)})_t$ yields

$$\Lambda^i(M_t) \;\cong\; \bigoplus_{\ell_1 < \cdots < \ell_i} (I_{[b_{\ell_1}, d_{\ell_1})})_t \wedge \cdots \wedge (I_{[b_{\ell_i}, d_{\ell_i})})_t.$$

Since each $(I_{[b_\ell, d_\ell)})_t$ is either 0 (if $t \notin [b_\ell, d_\ell)$) or a 1-dimensional k (if $t \in [b_\ell, d_\ell)$), the summand for $\{\ell_1, \ldots, \ell_i\}$ is k precisely when t lies in the intersection $\bigcap_{j=1}^{i} [b_{\ell_j}, d_{\ell_j})$, and is 0 otherwise. Hence, as t varies, the subfunctor generated by this summand is the interval module supported on $\bigcap_{j=1}^{i} [b_{\ell_j}, d_{\ell_j}) = \big[\max_j b_{\ell_j}, \, \min_j d_{\ell_j}\big)$, which is nonzero exactly when $\max_j b_{\ell_j} < \min_j d_{\ell_j}$.

Naturality of the above isomorphisms with respect to the structure maps of M shows that these pointwise decompositions assemble to an isomorphism of persistence modules $\Lambda^i M \cong \bigoplus_{\ell_1 < \cdots < \ell_i} I_{[\max_j b_{\ell_j}, \, \min_j d_{\ell_j})}$, with the convention that empty intersections contribute the zero module and hence no bar. Therefore the barcode of $\Lambda^i M$ is precisely the stated multiset of intervals.

---

[3] In persistent homology, the *birth* of a bar is the parameter value at which a homology class first appears, and its *death* is the value at which that class disappears [4,8].

2.2   Top-K with Multiplicity

Let the multiset of lengths of $B(\Lambda^i M)$ (counted with multiplicity) be sorted in non-increasing order as $L_1 \geq L_2 \geq \cdots$. For $K \geq 1$, the *Top-K multiset* is $\{L_1, \ldots, L_K\}$ (with multiplicity), and the *Top-K length vector* is

$$\mathbf{L}_K(M, i) := (L_1, \ldots, L_K) \in \mathbb{R}^K_{\geq 0},$$

padded with zeros if necessary.[4]

For $j \geq i - 1$ define the binomial weight $w_i(j) := \binom{j-1}{i-2}$. In Sect. 3 we prove that, for fixed anchor r, all Λ^i intervals whose *largest chosen rank* equals j have common length $\ell_r(j)$ and total multiplicity $w_i(j)$; moreover, the union over all anchors gives the full multiset $B(\Lambda^i M)$.

2.3   Bottleneck Distance and Stability

Let $\Delta = \{(t, t) \in \mathbb{R}^2 : t \in \mathbb{R}\}$ denote the diagonal. For barcodes X, Y (finite multisets of points (b, d) with $b < d$), an ε-*matching* is a partial matching between $X \cup \Delta$ and $Y \cup \Delta$ such that matched pairs are within L_∞-distance $\leq \varepsilon$ and unmatched points lie within ε of the diagonal. The *bottleneck distance* is

$$d_B(X, Y) := \inf\{\, \varepsilon \geq 0 \ : \ \text{there exists an } \varepsilon\text{-matching} \,\}.$$

Theorem 2. (Stability of Exterior Powers). *For $i \geq 1$ and tame persistence modules M, M',*

$$d_B\big(B(\Lambda^i M), B(\Lambda^i M')\big) \leq d_B\big(B(M), B(M')\big).$$

Proof. Suppose M and M' are ε-interleaved, i.e. there exist linear maps $f_t : M_t \to M'_{t+\varepsilon}$ and $g_t : M'_t \to M_{t+\varepsilon}$ commuting with structure maps and satisfying the usual zigzag relations up to shift 2ε. Because Λ^i is a functor on vector spaces that preserves linear maps, applying Λ^i to each f_t, g_t yields natural transformations

$$\Lambda^i f_t : \Lambda^i M_t \to \Lambda^i M'_{t+\varepsilon}, \qquad \Lambda^i g_t : \Lambda^i M'_t \to \Lambda^i M_{t+\varepsilon}.$$

These commute with the induced structure maps of $\Lambda^i M$ and $\Lambda^i M'$, since functors preserve commutative diagrams. Moreover, the zigzag identities are preserved under Λ^i, because if $g_{t+\varepsilon} \circ f_t$ equals the shift map $M_t \to M_{t+2\varepsilon}$, then $\Lambda^i g_{t+\varepsilon} \circ \Lambda^i f_t$ equals the shifted map on $\Lambda^i M_t$. Thus $\Lambda^i M$ and $\Lambda^i M'$ are also ε-interleaved. By the fundamental isometry theorem of persistence ([3,4]), interleaving distance equals bottleneck distance on barcodes. Hence $d_B\big(B(\Lambda^i M), B(\Lambda^i M')\big) \leq d_B\big(B(M), B(M')\big)$.

This result shows that exterior powers preserve the classical stability of persistence, ensuring that higher-order interaction features remain robust under perturbations of the input data.

---

[4] When multiple intervals have equal length, any ordering of the ties is acceptable, since our results concern the Top-K multiset and the sorted length vector $\mathbf{L}_K(M, i)$, which are invariant under tie-breaking (cf. top-K aggregation [10]).

2.4   Computational Model and Data Structures

We analyze running time in the RAM (Random Access Machine) model with comparisons; sorting $O(M)$ endpoints costs $O(M \log M)$, which is information-theoretically unavoidable in this model (cf. Sect. 6; see also [5,13]). We use *coordinate compression* of distinct death times to $\{1, \ldots, N\}$.

Persistent order-statistics (OS) tree. We will use a standard persistent segment tree over $\{1, \ldots, N\}$ storing *counts of alive bars* at each compressed death coordinate (cf. [7]). It supports:

- UPDATE(root, pos, ± 1) in $O(\log M)$ time, returning a new root and keeping the old root immutable;
- KTHFROMRIGHT(root, k): returns the death value of the k-th alive *bar* in non-increasing order, counting with multiplicity. Equivalently, the tree maintains cumulative counts of alive bars at each coordinate, and the query walks these counts from the right to locate the k-th bar;
- SIZE(root) in $O(1)$ time.

During the sweep we store, for each birth of r, the snapshot root T_r *before* inserting r (encoding A_r) and the integer $c_r = \text{SIZE}(T_r)$. The total space is $O(M)$ for heap buffers plus $O(M \log M)$ nodes for persistence.

3   Algorithmic Structural Decomposition Theorem

We now derive a birth-anchored, rankgrouped description of $B(\Lambda^i M)$ that will drive our best-first algorithm. Throughout this section, the sweep/tie conventions of Sect. 2 apply (see also [12,21] for background on barcode manipulations).

3.1   Anchors and Alive Sets

Given an i-tuple $I = \{\ell_1, \ldots, \ell_i\} \subseteq \{1, \ldots, M\}$ with $\max_j b_{\ell_j} < \min_j d_{\ell_j}$, let

$$t^\star := \max_j b_{\ell_j}, \qquad A^\star := \{\, \ell_j : b_{\ell_j} = t^\star \,\}.$$

By our event order (deaths before births, and a fixed total order among equal-time births), there is a *unique* index

$$r^\star \in A^\star \quad \text{that is processed last at time } t^\star.$$

We call $r^\star$ the *anchor* of I. At the moment just *before* $b_{r^\star} = t^\star$, all elements of $I \setminus \{r^\star\}$ are alive; hence $I \setminus \{r^\star\} \subseteq A_{r^\star}$, where $A_{r^\star}$ is the alive set from Sect. 2. Ordering $A_{r^\star}$ by non-increasing death times, write the deaths as $d_{r^\star}(1) \geq d_{r^\star}(2) \geq \cdots \geq d_{r^\star}(c_{r^\star})$.

Lemma 1. *Assume the sweep order processes deaths before births at equal times and fixes a total order among simultaneous births. For any Λ^i interval arising from $I = \{\ell_1, \ldots, \ell_i\}$ as in Theorem 1, let $t^\star = \max_j b_{\ell_j}$. Then there is a unique anchor $r^\star$, namely the index processed last among the births at $t^\star$, and $I \setminus \{r^\star\} \subseteq A_{r^\star}$. Conversely, for any r and any $(i-1)$-subset of A_r, the i-tuple $\{r\} \cup S$ yields a (possibly zero-length) Λ^i interval with birth b_r.*

Proof. By Theorem 1, the Λ^i interval from $I = \{\ell_1, \ldots, \ell_i\}$ is $[\max_j b_{\ell_j}, \min_j d_{\ell_j})$. Let $t^\star = \max_j b_{\ell_j}$. Among the indices with birth $t^\star$, exactly one is processed last under the tie rule; call it $r^\star$. At time $b_{r^\star}$, all other ℓ_j are alive, so $I \setminus \{r^\star\} \subseteq A_{r^\star}$. Conversely, for any anchor r and any $(i-1)$-subset $S \subseteq A_r$, the i-tuple $\{r\} \cup S$ yields the interval $[b_r, \min\{d_r, d_s : s \in S\})$ by the same formula.

3.2   Rank-grouping at a Fixed Anchor

Fix an anchor r with alive set A_r of size c_r. Let $S = \{j_1 < \cdots < j_{i-1}\} \subseteq \{1, \ldots, c_r\}$ be the ranks of the chosen neighbors (so the corresponding death times are $d_r(j_1), \ldots, d_r(j_{i-1})$). The Λ^i interval produced by (r, S) is

$$I(r, S) \;=\; \bigl[b_r,\ \min\{d_r,\ d_r(j_1), \ldots, d_r(j_{i-1})\}\bigr),$$

whose length equals, by definition (1), $|I(r, S)| = \ell_r(\max S)$. Hence the length depends only on the *largest* rank in S.

Proposition 1. *Fix r and a rank $j \in \{i-1, \ldots, c_r\}$. The number of $(i-1)$-subsets S of ranks with $\max S = j$ equals $w_i(j) = \binom{j-1}{i-2}$. All such subsets yield the same length $\ell_r(j)$, truncated below by 0 as in (1). In particular, when $d_r(j) \leq b_r$ the resulting value is $\ell_r(j) = 0$, which contributes nothing to $B(\Lambda^i M)$.*

Proof. To have $\max S = j$, one must include rank j and choose the remaining $i-2$ ranks from $\{1, \ldots, j-1\}$, giving $\binom{j-1}{i-2}$ choices. The shared length follows because $|I(r, S)| = \min\{d_r, d_r(j)\} - b_r$ depends only on the largest rank (and is truncated below by 0 as in (1)).

Theorem 3. (Anchored Rank–Grouping). *Assume bars are closed–open and ties are broken by processing deaths before births, with a fixed total order among simultaneous births. For each birth r, let A_r be the set of bars alive just before b_r, ordered by non–increasing death time $d_r(1) \geq \cdots \geq d_r(c_r)$. Define*

$$\ell_r(j) := \max\{0,\ \min\{d_r, d_r(j)\} - b_r\}, \qquad J_r := \{j \in \{i-1, \ldots, c_r\} : \ell_r(j) > 0\}.$$

Then every interval of $B(\Lambda^i M)$ arises uniquely from a pair (r, S), where r is the anchor (the last-processed birth at $t^\star = \max_j b_{\ell_j}$) and $S \subseteq A_r$ has $|S| = i - 1$, with length $|I(r, S)| = \ell_r(\max S)$. Consequently, for each anchor r the anchored multiset equals

$$\{\, \ell_r(j) \text{ with multiplicity } w_i(j) = \tbinom{j-1}{i-2} : j \in J_r \,\},$$

with $j \mapsto \ell_r(j)$ non–increasing, and globally

$$B(\Lambda^i M) \;=\; \bigsqcup_{r=1}^{M} \{\, \ell_r(j) \text{ with multiplicity } w_i(j) : j \in J_r \,\},$$

a disjoint union of multisets of finite (positive-length) intervals.

Proof. Fix $i \geq 2$. By the interval calculus (Theorem 1), any i-tuple $I = \{\ell_1, \ldots, \ell_i\}$ with $\max_j b_{\ell_j} < \min_j d_{\ell_j}$ produces the Λ^iinterval $[\max_j b_{\ell_j}, \min_j d_{\ell_j})$. Let $t^\star = \max_j b_{\ell_j}$ and choose the unique index $r^\star$ that is processed last among those with $b_{\ell_j} = t^\star$. Then $I \setminus \{r^\star\} \subseteq A_{r^\star}$, and $r^\star$ is the *anchor* of I. Conversely, for any anchor r and $(i-1)$-subset $S \subseteq A_r$, the i-tuple $\{r\} \cup S$ yields

$$I(r, S) = [\, b_r, \; \min\{d_r, \; d_s : s \in S\} \,).$$

Thus every element of $B(\Lambda^i M)$ arises uniquely from some pair (r, S).

Now order A_r by nonincreasing death times $d_r(1) \geq d_r(2) \geq \cdots \geq d_r(c_r)$. If $S = \{j_1 < \cdots < j_{i-1}\}$ are the ranks of the chosen neighbors, then the length of $I(r, S)$ depends only on the largest rank: $|I(r, S)| = \ell_r(\max S)$. Therefore all $(i-1)$-subsets with the same maximal rank j yield the same length $\ell_r(j)$.

At this point Proposition 1 applies: it tells us that the number of such subsets is exactly $w_i(j) = \binom{j-1}{i-2}$, and that they all contribute the same value $\ell_r(j)$ (truncated at 0). Hence for each anchor r, the multiset of anchored lengths is

$$\{\, \ell_r(j) \text{ with multiplicity } w_i(j) \; : \; j \in \{i-1, \ldots, c_r\} \,\}.$$

Finally, define $J_r = \{j : \ell_r(j) > 0\}$. Restricting to $j \in J_r$ removes the zero-length intervals, which do not belong to $B(\Lambda^i M)$. Because each interval has a unique anchor, the global barcode is the disjoint multiset union over anchors:

$$B(\Lambda^i M) \;=\; \bigsqcup_{r=1}^{M} \{\, \ell_r(j) \text{ with multiplicity } w_i(j) \; : \; j \in J_r \,\}.$$

Monotonicity of $j \mapsto \ell_r(j)$ follows directly from the ordering $d_r(1) \geq d_r(2) \geq \cdots$. This proves the theorem.

When $i = 2$, $w_2(j) = \binom{j-1}{0} = 1$, so each rank contributes exactly one element and the anchored stream becomes a simple non-increasing sequence $\ell_r(1) \geq \ell_r(2) \geq \cdots \geq \ell_r(c_r)$.

The above theorem gives a complete and nonredundant decomposition of $B(\Lambda^i M)$ into per-anchor monotone streams with closed-form multiplicities, providing the structural foundation for efficient Top-K algorithms and showing exactly how higher-order intervals are organized.

4   The TOPK–Λ^i Algorithm

We now give a best-first algorithm that outputs the K longest elements of $B(\Lambda^i M)$ *without* enumerating the entire multiset.

4.1   Preprocessing: Sweep and Persistent Order Statistics

Build the global event list of all births and deaths, sorted by time, with *deaths before births* at ties (Sect. 2; cf. [8,9]). Coordinate-compress distinct death times to $\{1, \ldots, N\}$ and maintain a *persistent* order-statistics tree over this axis, storing counts of alive deaths. During the sweep:

- On a death of bar x, perform an update -1 at the index of d_x.
- On a birth of bar r at time b_r, *before* inserting r: store the current snapshot root T_r encoding A_r, and record $c_r = \textsc{Size}(T_r)$; then insert $+1$ at the index of d_r so that r is alive for later anchors.

This costs $O(M \log M)$ time and $O(M \log M)$ persistent nodes.

4.2   Best-First Top-K Extraction Algorithm

By Theorem 3, $B(\Lambda^i M)$ is the multiset union of rankgrouped streams. We run a *grouped* best-first search where each heap entry represents the current head (r, j) of anchor r's stream at rank j with key $\ell_r(j)$ and weight $w_i(j) = \binom{j-1}{i-2}$. This mirrors classic best-first paradigms in top-K aggregation and selection over structured sets (cf. [10,11]).

The entire procedure is given in Algorithm 1 below. This algorithm leverages the rank-grouped structure of $B(\Lambda^i M)$ to compute the exact Top-K intervals in near output-sensitive time, avoiding full enumeration when $K \ll |B(\Lambda^i M)|$.

Interval Identities. Algorithm 1 outputs the Top-K *length multiset* directly. If actual interval *identities* are required, each bulk emission at line 12 can be expanded into the explicit $(i-1)$-subsets of ranks that realize the multiplicity $w_i(j)$, truncated once K intervals are produced. This refinement preserves the asymptotic complexity bound for fixed i.

Unbundled (colex) Variant. Alternatively, one can represent states as strictly increasing $(i-1)$-tuples of ranks and expand at most i colex neighbors per pop; this yields the same outputs with an i factor in the loop cost (cf. [10,11]). We focus on the grouped variant for the sharpest bound.

Theorem 4. (Correctness and Complexity). *For fixed $i \geq 2$, Algorithm 1 (the grouped variant) outputs exactly the K longest elements of $B(\Lambda^i M)$ (with multiplicity) in non-increasing order in*

$$O\big((M + K) \log M\big)$$

time, using $O(M)$ heap space plus $O(M \log M)$ persistent nodes. The alternative unbundled (colex) variant runs in $O\big((M + iK) \log M\big)$ time.

Algorithm 1. $\textsc{TopK--}\varLambda^i$ (grouped best-first; fixed $i \geq 2$)

Require: Barcode $B(M)$, layer $i \geq 2$, target K
1: **Sweep & snapshots:** as above, obtain $\{(T_r, c_r)\}_{r=1}^M$.
2: Initialize an empty max-heap H keyed by length.
3: **for** each anchor r with $c_r \geq i-1$ **do**
4:     $j \leftarrow i-1$; query $d_r(j)$ on T_r; set $L \leftarrow \ell_r(j)$ via (1)
5:     **if** $L > 0$ **then**
6:         push $(L, r, j, w_i(j))$ into H
7:     **end if**
8: **end for**
9: $S \leftarrow \emptyset$ {S collects output lengths (with multiplicity)}
10: **while** $|S| < K$ and H not empty **do**
11:     pop (L, r, j, w) from H
12:     append $\min\{w, K - |S|\}$ copies of L to S {bulk-emission of ties per anchor; see §2.2}
13:     **if** $j < c_r$ **then**
14:         $j \leftarrow j+1$; query $d_r(j)$; $L \leftarrow \ell_r(j)$
15:         **if** $L > 0$ **then**
16:             push $(L, r, j, w_i(j))$ into H
17:         **end if**
18:     **end if**
19: **end while**
20: **return** S (the Top-K multiset in non-increasing order)

Proof. We first prove correctness. By Theorem 3, the global multiset is the disjoint union of monotone streams $\{\ell_r(j)\}$ with weights $w_i(j)$. The heap stores precisely the current heads of all nonempty streams. Because each stream is non-increasing and the heap key is the head length, once $\ell_r(j)$ is popped no unseen element can exceed it, since every remaining element is bounded by its stream head and every head is in the heap. The algorithm therefore emits all $w_i(j)$ copies at once; ties may thus be grouped per anchor, consistent with the tie policy in Sect. 2. Since the Top-K vector is invariant under permutations of equal values, bulk emission is safe. After advancing that stream, the invariant is preserved. By induction, the outputs are exactly the global Top-K in order.

We prove the complexity statements. Preprocessing costs $O(M \log M)$. During initialization, each anchor with $c_r \geq i - 1$ contributes at most one heap entry, obtained by a single $\textsc{KthFromRight}$ query at $j = i - 1$. Anchors with $c_r < i - 1$ contribute none, so the number of initial heap entries is at most M, giving $O(M \log M)$ time overall. Each pop outputs at least one item, so there are at most K pops (or fewer if H becomes empty when the total output is $< K$). A pop performs $O(1)$ heap operations and a single order-statistics query, each $O(\log M)$, giving $O(K \log M)$ for the loop in the grouped variant and $O(iK \log M)$ in the unbundled variant. Space bounds follow from the heap size $O(M)$ and the persistent tree. All $\log M$ factors are under the RAM model, where basic arithmetic and memory accesses take $O(1)$ time.

In the special case $i = 2$: since $w_2(j) = 1$ for all j, every pop outputs a single element and advances $j \mapsto j+1$, yielding the stated $O((M + K)\log M)$ bound.

5   Stability of the Top-K Length Vector

We show that the Top-K length vector of $B(\Lambda^i M)$ varies Lipschitz-continuously (with constant 2) under bottleneck perturbations of the input barcode $B(M)$. Throughout this section, $i \geq 1$ is fixed.

Recall from Sect. 2 that $\mathbf{L}_K(M, i) = (L_1 \geq \cdots \geq L_K)$ denotes the nonincreasing Top-K length vector of $B(\Lambda^i M)$ (with multiplicity), padded with zeros if necessary.

Theorem 5. (Top-K Stability). *If $d_B(B(M), B(M')) \leq \varepsilon$, then for every fixed $i \geq 1$ and $K \geq 1$,*

$$\left\| \mathbf{L}_K(M, i) - \mathbf{L}_K(M', i) \right\|_\infty \leq 2\varepsilon.$$

Proof. Let $X = B(\Lambda^i M)$ and $Y = B(\Lambda^i M')$. By the stability of exterior powers (Theorem 2), we have $d_B(X, Y) \leq \varepsilon$. Hence there exists an ε-matching between $X \cup \Delta$ and $Y \cup \Delta$ (cf. [4,6]).

Form the multisets of lengths $S = \{\, d - b : (b, d) \in X \,\}$ and $T = \{\, d' - b' : (b', d') \in Y \,\}$. From the ε-matching we obtain a bijection π between S and T *after padding the shorter multiset with zeros*: for any matched pair $(b, d) \leftrightarrow (b', d')$ we set $\pi(d - b) = d' - b'$, and for any interval matched to the diagonal we pair its length with 0. For matched intervals we have $\left| (d - b) - (d' - b') \right| \leq |d - d'| + |b - b'| \leq 2\varepsilon$, and if (b, d) is matched to Δ within ε then $|d - b| \leq 2\varepsilon$ by definition of bottleneck matchings to the diagonal. Thus: $|x - \pi(x)| \leq 2\varepsilon$ for all $x \in S$.

Let $(s_1 \geq s_2 \geq \cdots)$ and $(t_1 \geq t_2 \geq \cdots)$ be the non-increasing rearrangements of S and T (padded with zeros to equal length). We claim that $|s_k - t_k| \leq 2\varepsilon$ for all k. Suppose, for contradiction, that $s_k > t_k + 2\varepsilon$. Then S has at least k elements $\geq s_k$, so their images under π are $\geq s_k - 2\varepsilon > t_k$, implying that T has at least k elements strictly greater than t_k, which contradicts the definition of t_k. The reverse inequality $t_k > s_k + 2\varepsilon$ is symmetric. Hence $|s_k - t_k| \leq 2\varepsilon$ for all k. Finally, restricting to the first K coordinates gives $\left\| \mathbf{L}_K(M, i) - \mathbf{L}_K(M', i) \right\|_\infty \leq 2\varepsilon$.

Note: the factor 2 is tight: perturb one interval $[b, d)$ by shifting $b \mapsto b + \varepsilon$ and $d \mapsto d - \varepsilon$; the bottleneck distance is ε while the length changes by exactly 2ε.

6   Optimality: A Comparison-Model Lower Bound

We prove that the $O(M \log M)$ preprocessing term in Theorem 4 is unavoidable in the comparison model, even if one only seeks the single longest Λ^2 interval.

Proposition 2. (Lower Bound). *Any comparison-based algorithm that, given the unsorted endpoints of a barcode $B(M)$, computes the Top-1 length of $B(\Lambda^2 M)$ must perform $\Omega(M \log M)$ comparisons in the worst case.*

Proof. We reduce *Element Uniqueness* (or, equivalently, the decision version of 1D minimum gap) to computing the Top-1 Λ^2 length. Consider an input set $\{x_1,\ldots,x_M\} \subset [0,\frac{1}{2}]$ of real numbers (not necessarily distinct). Construct a barcode with bars $J_r := [x_r, x_r+1)$ $(r = 1,\ldots,M)$. For any pair (r,s), the Λ^2 intersection length equals $|J_r \cap J_s| = \max\{0, 1-|x_r-x_s|\}$. Since all $|x_r-x_s| \leq \frac{1}{2} < 1$, every pair intersects and $\max_{r\neq s}|J_r \cap J_s| = 1 - \min_{r\neq s}|x_r-x_s|$. Hence the Top-1 Λ^2 length equals 1 *iff* there exists a duplicate $(\min_{r\neq s}|x_r-x_s| = 0)$. Therefore any algorithm that computes the Top-1 Λ^2 length can decide Element Uniqueness. The latter requires $\Omega(M \log M)$ comparisons in the algebraic decision tree/comparison model; thus computing the Top-1 Λ^2 length also requires $\Omega(M \log M)$ comparisons.

7   Experimental Verification

We evaluate the proposed best-first algorithm on synthetic barcodes where we can directly control *overlap* (i.e., expected concurrency), which in turn controls the output size $K_{\mathrm{all}} = |B(\Lambda^2 M)|$. Our goals are to (i) validate exactness against a full enumeration baseline, and (ii) quantify wall-clock improvements as a function of K and overlap.

For each trial we sample M bars on $[0,1]$ as follows: birth times $b \sim \mathrm{Unif}[0,1)$ and independent exponential lengths $L \sim \mathrm{Exp}(\lambda)$ truncated to $[0,1-b]$, with mean parameter set by $\mathbb{E}[L] = \mathtt{Lmean} \in \{0.03, 0.05\}$. This yields expected concurrency $\approx M \cdot \mathtt{Lmean}$, so larger $\mathtt{Lmean}$ produces heavier overlap and larger K_{all}.

We focus on $i = 2$ (Λ^2), where the grouped best-first bound is tightest.[5] Baseline = $\textsc{Enum--}\Lambda^2$ (full pairwise enumeration) + $\textsc{TopK-Select}$ (heap-based selection; cf. classical PH pipelines [9,22] and fast toolchains such as [1]). Ours = $\textsc{TopK--}\Lambda^2$ (Algorithm 1). We measure total wall-clock time per query and report the factor $\mathtt{speedup} := \frac{\text{baseline time}}{\text{ours time}}$. Correctness is checked by exact multiset equality of the top-K lengths up to numerical rounding.

We use $M \in \{3000, 5000\}$, $\mathtt{Lmean} \in \{0.03, 0.05\}$, and $K = 10,000$. For each setting, we report a single representative run; in all runs the outputs of $\textsc{TopK--}\Lambda^2$ matched $\textsc{Enum--}\Lambda^2$ exactly.

Table 1 summarizes the results (wall times in seconds). In the heavy overlap case: when K_{all} is large, $\textsc{TopK--}\Lambda^2$ consistently wins ($2.1\times$ at $K=10^4$ for $M=3000$, $\mathtt{Lmean}=0.05$), because it avoids the baseline's fixed "enumerate everything" cost. In the moderate overlap case: we have steady gains ($1.45\times$) for $M=5000$, $\mathtt{Lmean}=0.03$. All runs matched baseline Top-K lengths exactly.

---

[5] Empirical behavior for $i = 3$ (and higher) matches that for $i = 2$, providing evidence that the observed gains are not special to the case $i = 2$.

Table 1. Wall-clock results and speedups. $K_{\text{all}} = |B(\Lambda^2 M)|$ grows with overlap.

Setting	K	K_{all}	Baseline (s)	Ours (s)	Speedup
$M{=}3000$, `Lmean`$= 0.05$ (high)	10,000	422,272	0.262	0.125	**2.10**$\times$
$M{=}5000$, `Lmean`$= 0.03$ (moderate)	10,000	733,622	0.468	0.322	1.45$\times$

8 Conclusions

We introduced a birth-anchored, rankgrouped structural decomposition of $B(\Lambda^i M)$ (Theorem 3) and leveraged it to design a best-first Top-K algorithm (Theorem 4) that returns the exact Top-K multiset *without* full enumeration. For fixed $i \geq 2$ the grouped running time is $O((M + K)\log M)$, while an unbundled colex variant runs in $O((M + iK)\log M)$. We established that the Top-K length vector is 2-Lipschitz with respect to bottleneck perturbations (Theorem 5), and proved a comparison-model lower bound (Proposition 2) showing the $O(M \log M)$ preprocessing is information-theoretically unavoidable. Experiments confirmed the theory: up to 2.1$\times$ speedups in high-overlap regimes, with exact outputs.

Beyond its theoretical contributions, this work shows that higher-order persistence constructions can be made practically scalable, enabling their systematic use as stable, discriminative features in data analysis, machine learning, and computational geometry (e.g., for molecular graph classification tasks). We also plan to develop variants of our method for applications at the intersection of logic, category theory and machine learning [2,14–20].

References

1. Bauer, U.: Ripser: efficient computation of Vietoris-Rips persistence barcodes. J. Appl. Comput. Topol. **5**, 391–423 (2021)
2. Bennett, M.T., Maruyama, Y.: Philosophical specification of empathetic ethical artificial intelligence. IEEE Trans. CDS **14**(2), 292–300 (2021)
3. Chazal, F., de Silva, V., Oudot, S.: Persistence stability for geometric complexes. Geom. Dedicata. **173**(1), 193–214 (2014)
4. Chazal, F., de Silva, V., Glisse, M., Oudot, S.: The Structure and Stability of Persistence Modules. SpringerBriefs in Mathematics, Springer (2016)
5. Cormen, T.H., et al.: Introduction to Algorithms. MIT Press (2009)
6. Cohen-Steiner, D., Edelsbrunner, H., Harer, J.: Stability of persistence diagrams. Discrete Comput. Geometry **37**(1), 103–120 (2007)
7. Driscoll, J.R., Sarnak, N., Sleator, D.D., Tarjan, R.E.: Making data structures persistent. J. Comp. Sys. Sci. **38**(1), 86–124 (1989)
8. Edelsbrunner, H., Harer, J.: Computational topology: an introduction. American Mathematical Society (2010)
9. Edelsbrunner, H., Letscher, D., Zomorodian, A.: Topological persistence and simplification. Discrete Comput. Geometry **28**(4), 511–533 (2002)
10. Fagin, R., Lotem, A., Naor, M.: Optimal aggregation algorithms for middleware. J. Comput. Syst. Sci. **66**(4), 614–656 (2003)

11. Frederickson, G.N., Johnson, D.B.: The complexity of selection and ranking in $X+Y$ and matrices with sorted columns. J. Comp. Sys. Sci. **24**(2), 197–208 (1982)
12. Ghrist, R.: Barcodes: The persistent topology of data. Bull. Am. Math. Soc. **45**(1), 61–75 (2008)
13. Knuth, D.E.: The Art of Computer Programming, vol. 3: Sorting and Searching, 2nd ed. Addison–Wesley (1998)
14. Maruyama, Y.: Algebraic study of lattice-valued logic and lattice-valued modal logic. Proc. ICLA, 170–184 (2009)
15. Maruyama, Y.: Fundamental results for pointfree convex geometry. Ann. Pure Appl. Logic **161**(12), 1486–1501 (2010)
16. Maruyama, Y.: Natural duality, modality, and coalgebra. J. Pure Appl. Algebra **216**(3), 565–580 (2012)
17. Maruyama, Y.: Full lambek hyperdoctrine: categorical semantics for first-order substructural logics. Proc. WoLLIC, 211–225 (2013)
18. Maruyama, Y.: Categorical duality theory: with applications to domains, convexity, and the distribution monad. Proc. CSL, 500–520 (2013)
19. Maruyama, Y.: Symbolic and statistical theories of cognition: towards integrated artificial intelligence. Proc. SEFM, 129–146 (2020)
20. Maruyama, Y.: The conditions of artificial general intelligence. Proc. AGI, 242–251 (2020)
21. Oudot, S.Y.: Persistence theory: from quiver representations to data analysis. Mathematical Surveys and Monographs 209, American Mathematical Society (2015)
22. Zomorodian, A., Carlsson, G.: Computing persistent homology. Discrete Comput. Geometry **33**(2), 249–274 (2005)

Algorithm for Interpretable Graph Features via Motivic Persistent Cohomology

Yoshihiro Maruyama[✉]

School of Informatics, Nagoya University, Nagoya, Japan
`maruyama@i.nagoya-u.ac.jp`

Abstract. We present the Chromatic Persistence Algorithm (CPA), an event–driven method for computing persistent cohomological features of weighted graphs via graphic arrangements, a classical object in computational geometry. We establish rigorous complexity results: CPA is exponential in the worst case, fixed–parameter tractable in treewidth, and nearly linear for common graph families such as trees, cycles, and series–parallel graphs. Finally, we demonstrate its practical applicability through a controlled experiment on molecular-like graph structures.

Keywords: Computational geometry · persistent homology · graph

1 Introduction

Persistent homology (PH) has become a cornerstone of topological data analysis, furnishing a mathematically grounded framework for extracting multiscale topological signatures from data [3,8,9,27]. Its ability to summarize structural information robustly has led to successful applications in fields as diverse as computational geometry, machine learning, biology, and network science. These developments have positioned PH as both a theoretical paradigm and a practical tool for analyzing complex data structures.

Yet the standard PH pipeline captures only the ranks of homology groups along a filtration, and in doing so discards finer algebraic information about the space. In many settings, especially when filtrations come from algebraic or combinatorial constructions (for example, spaces coming from hyperplane arrangements or from constructions on graphs), one can enrich the classical barcodes by keeping track of additional structure that refines the underlying invariants. This paper develops a graph-specialized version of that idea and explores its algorithmic consequences.

We introduce the *Chromatic Persistence Algorithm (CPA)*, an event–driven method for analyzing weighted graphs. CPA processes a graph along a natural *threshold filtration*—adding edges one by one in weight order—and computes at each step: (i) a polynomial that summarizes the global structure of the graph at that threshold, and (ii) a *jump*, namely the cohomological change that occurs

C. Zaroliagis et al. (Eds.): ICAA 2026, LNCS 16423, pp. 87–99, 2026.
https://doi.org/10.1007/978-3-032-15621-1_8

when a new edge is inserted. The algorithm evaluates only at actual "events" (edge insertions), making it conceptually simple and computationally efficient.

The approach relies on two classical results from graph and arrangement theory. The first links the *chromatic polynomial* $\chi_H(q)$ of a graph H to the *Poincaré polynomial* of the complement of its associated arrangement [1,6,23,24], so that graph colorings directly capture topological invariants. In fact, in the Hodge–Tate case relevant to graphic arrangements, the same identity yields the *Hodge–Deligne polynomial* $E(M(H); u, v)$ by the direct specialization $E(M(H); u, v) = \chi_H(uv)$. The second ingredient is a *deletion–contraction identity*, which describes how these invariants change when a single edge is added or contracted [6]. Together, these yield a computable combinatorial foundation for CPA: every update reduces to computing chromatic polynomials and applying an algebraic correction. We establish the complexity guarantees for the Chromatic Persistence Algorithm: exponential time in the worst case, fixed–parameter tractable (FPT) in treewidth, and near–linear on common graph families such as trees, cycles, and series–parallel graphs [2,5,12,22].

Concretely, the problem setting is as follows. Let $G = (V, E, w)$ be a finite weighted graph with distinct edge weights $t_1 < \cdots < t_m$. Write $H_j := G_{\leq t_j}$ for the threshold subgraph and let e_j be the unique edge added at step j. For each H_j we consider the graphic arrangement $\mathcal{A}(H_j) \subset \mathbb{C}^{|V|}$ and its complement $M(H_j)$. The goal is to compute the Hodge–Deligne polynomial $E(M(H_j); u, v)$ of $M(H_j)$ at all thresholds, together with the jump contributed by the addition of e_j. In the Hodge–Tate situation, this reduces to evaluating the chromatic polynomial $\chi_{H_j}(uv)$ for each threshold; algorithmically, we compute only the contracted-minor $\chi_{H_j/e_j}(q)$ and update E_j via the deletion–contraction recurrence $E_j(u, v) = E_{j-1}(u, v) - \chi_{H_j/e_j}(uv)$.

Our approach to the problem can be summarized as follows. We leverage the two identities above to turn the problem into a discrete, event–driven computation. (i) The chromatic→Poincaré identity (Proposition 2) converts topology of the arrangement complement into combinatorics of colorings, so at each threshold we obtain $E(M(H_j); u, v) = \chi_{H_j}(uv)$. (ii) The deletion–contraction jump identity (Theorem 1) expresses the change caused by adding one edge; at the E–polynomial level, $E(M(H_{j-1}); u, v) - E(M(H_j); u, v) = E(M(H_j/e_j); u, v)$. Algorithmically, we therefore process only events (edge insertions): at step j we compute $\chi_{H_j/e_j}(q)$ and update E_j via the deletion–contraction recurrence $E_j(u, v) = E_{j-1}(u, v) - \chi_{H_j/e_j}(uv)$, together with the barcode zeta update, a generating function that encodes all jumps compactly. This yields a CPA routine with provable guarantees: exponential in the worst case, fixed–parameter tractable in treewidth, and near–linear on trees, cycles, and series–parallel graphs. Experimental verification with molecule-like graphs is provided as well.

From a graph–algorithms viewpoint, CPA reframes persistence on graphs as a sequence of *combinatorial* updates on chromatic polynomials, exploiting deletion–contraction and dynamic programming (DP) on tree decompositions. This connects topological summarization directly to the Tutte/chromatic toolbox and to parameterized complexity, enabling principled worst–case analyses alongside practical near–linear behavior on sparse, low–treewidth inputs typical of molecular backbones [2,12,22]. For chemical graph machine learning, CPA provides deterministic and interpretable *global* ring– and cycle–sensitive features (via E–polynomials and jump classes). These features complement widely used local or message–passing descriptors, such as ECFP-style circular fingerprints (Extended Connectivity Fingerprints, graph-based molecular descriptors that encode local atom–bond neighborhoods into fixed-length bit vectors), Weisfeiler–Lehman kernels, and neural message passing. Unlike these local descriptors, CPA encodes arrangement/chromatic structure that reflects ring size and related graph families [7,10,21,25,26]. These features drop in as standalone inputs or additional channels within GNNs. Because they are event–driven and algebraically controlled, they are stable to threshold rescalings and amenable to caching, incremental updates, and integration with classical graph–decomposition pipelines.

The rest of the paper is organized as follows. Section 2 gives mathematical preliminaries. Section 3 provides Algorithm CPA and proves the correctness theorem. Section 4 proves the complexity theorem with special–class speedups. Experimental verification is provided in Sect. 5.

2   Mathematical Preliminaries and Notation

Graphs are assumed to be finite and simple. Throughout, we write $n := |V|$ and $m := |E|$.

Definition 1 (Threshold chain). *A weighted graph is a simple graph $G = (V, E)$ together with a weight function $w : E \rightarrow \mathbb{R}$. Assuming all edge weights are distinct, we can order them as $t_1 < \cdots < t_m$, where $m = |E|$. The threshold chain is the sequence of subgraphs*

$$H_j := G_{\leq t_j}, \quad j = 1, \ldots, m,$$

where H_j contains all edges of weight at most t_j, and e_j denotes the unique edge added at step j.

We write $O^*(\cdot)$ for time/space bounds up to factors polynomial in n and m. The notation $\mathrm{tw}(H)$ denotes the treewidth of a graph H. For graphs of bounded treewidth, chromatic polynomials can be computed in $f(w)\,\mathrm{poly}(n)$ time and $g(w)\,\mathrm{poly}(n)$ space, where $w = \mathrm{tw}(H)$ and f, g are computable functions, via dynamic programming (DP) on a tree decomposition [5,22].

2.1   From Graphic Arrangements to Poincaré Polynomials

Given a (simple) graph $H = (V, E)$ with $n = |V|$, the *graphic arrangement* in $\mathbb{C}^n$ is

$$\mathcal{A}(H) := \{ x_i - x_j = 0 : \{i, j\} \in E \}, \qquad M(H) := \mathbb{C}^n \setminus \bigcup_{H_{ij} \in \mathcal{A}(H)} H_{ij}.$$

Let MHS denote the category of rational mixed Hodge structures and $K_0(\text{MHS})$ its Grothendieck ring [6,24] (readers unfamiliar with Hodge theory may safely skip the following background; in our graph setting it suffices to know that the E–polynomial reduces to the chromatic polynomial evaluated at uv). For a complex variety X, the *Hodge–Deligne polynomial* (aka. *E–polynomial*) is defined by

$$E(X; u, v) = \sum_{k \geq 0}(-1)^k \sum_{p,q} h^{p,q}\big(H_c^k(X; \mathbb{Q})\big)\, u^p v^q,$$

which factors through a ring morphism $E : K_0(\text{MHS}) \to \mathbb{Z}[u, v]$.[1] In the Hodge–Tate case (i.e., when the Hodge numbers vanish unless $p = q$), all contributions lie on the diagonal $p = q$. Hence $E(X; u, v)$ depends only on the product uv, and for graphic arrangements it is given directly by $E(M(H); u, v) = \chi_H(uv)$.

Proposition 1 (Hodge–Tate purity for graphic complements). *For every $k \geq 0$, $H^k(M(H); \mathbb{Q})$ is pure Hodge–Tate of type (k, k) (all Hodge numbers vanish unless $p = q = k$). Equivalently,*

$$E(M(H); u, v) = (uv)^n\, P_{M(H)}\!\left(-\tfrac{1}{uv}\right) = \sum_{k=0}^{n}(-1)^k\, b_k(H)\,(uv)^{n-k},$$

where $n = |V|$ and $b_k(H) = \operatorname{rank} H^k(M(H); \mathbb{Q})$.

This fact allows us to work on the uv–diagonal and identify the E–polynomial directly from the chromatic polynomial.

2.2   Chromatic Polynomial $\Rightarrow$ Poincaré/E–polynomial

We introduce two basic concepts.[2]

Definition 2 (Chromatic polynomial). *For a graph H, the chromatic polynomial $\chi_H(q)$ is the polynomial that counts the number of proper vertex colorings of H using q colors.*

---

[1] $H_c^k(X; \mathbb{Q})$ denotes the k-th compactly supported cohomology group of X with rational coefficients, equipped with a mixed Hodge structure. The integers $h^{p,q}(H_c^k(X; \mathbb{Q}))$ are its Hodge numbers, i.e. the dimensions of the (p, q)-graded pieces. The variables u, v are formal markers for the Hodge bidegrees, and the factor $(-1)^k$ reflects the alternating sum over cohomological degree, in analogy with the Euler characteristic. In the Hodge–Tate situation (which holds for graphic arrangements), all nonzero contributions lie on the diagonal $p = q$, so $E(X; u, v)$ depends only on the product uv. In this case one can pass directly from the chromatic polynomial to the E-polynomial via $E(M(H); u, v) = \chi_H(uv)$.

[2] Readers new to arrangement theory may focus only on the conclusion: the Poincaré polynomial of the graphic arrangement complement can be computed directly from the chromatic polynomial of the graph.

Definition 3 (Poincaré polynomial). *For a topological space X, the Poincaré polynomial is*

$$P_X(t) := \sum_{k \geq 0} b_k(X)\, t^k, \qquad b_k(X) = \operatorname{rank} H^k(X; \mathbb{Q}).$$

For a graph H, the chromatic polynomial $\chi_H(q)$ not only encodes the count of proper q–colorings but also determines the topology of the graphic arrangement complement. In particular, the Orlik–Solomon formula expresses the Poincaré polynomial of $M(H)$ in terms of χ_H. In the Hodge–Tate setting of graphic arrangements this further simplifies to a direct identity: the Hodge–Deligne E–polynomial is obtained by the specialization $E(M(H); u, v) = \chi_H(uv)$. Thus chromatic polynomials provide complete access to the Betti numbers (and hence cohomology) of graphic arrangement complements.

Proposition 2 (Chromatic $\Rightarrow$ Poincaré/E; graphic case). *If $n = |V|$, then*

$$P_{M(H)}(t) = (-t)^n \chi_H\left(-\tfrac{1}{t}\right), \qquad E(M(H); u, v) = \chi_H(uv).$$

Thus the Betti numbers of $M(H)$ are determined by the coefficients of χ_H. For example, for the cycle C_n, $\chi_{C_n}(q) = (q-1)^n + (-1)^n(q-1)$, so $E(M(C_n); u, v)$ depends explicitly on n.

For connected H, the arrangement $\mathcal{A}(H) \subset \mathbb{C}^n$ has rank $n - 1$. Its characteristic polynomial satisfies

$$\chi_{\mathcal{A}(H)}(q) = \frac{\chi_H(q)}{q} \quad [23, 24].$$

The Orlik–Solomon formula gives $P_{M(H)}(t) = (-t)^{n-1} \chi_{\mathcal{A}(H)}(-1/t)$, hence $P_{M(H)}(t) = (-t)^n \chi_H\left(-\tfrac{1}{t}\right)$. Thus the exponent n comes from the ambient space $\mathbb{C}^n$, even though the essential rank is $n - 1$.

2.3 Deletion–Contraction Jump Identity (Graphic Specialization)

When a single edge e is added to H to form $H' := H \cup \{e\}$, the change in the cohomology of arrangement complements admits a deletion–contraction description.[3] We state it in compactly supported cohomology and in the Grothendieck group of mixed Hodge structures; pushing along the Hodge–Deligne map yields the corresponding statement for E–polynomials in our Hodge–Tate setting.

Theorem 1 (Deletion–contraction jump identity). *Let H be a (simple) graph, let $H' := H \cup \{e\}$ be obtained by adding one edge e, and let H/e denote*

---

[3] Readers not familiar with Hodge theory may skip to Theorem 1; in our graph setting, it simply means that adding an edge changes the invariant in a controlled way, described by a contraction minor.

*the contraction. There is a natural long exact sequence in compactly supported
cohomology*

$$\cdots \to H_c^k(M(H')) \to H_c^k(M(H)) \to H_c^{k-1}(M(H/e)) \to H_c^{k+1}(M(H')) \to \cdots$$

*compatible with mixed Hodge structures. Consequently, in the Grothendieck group
$K_0(\mathrm{MHS})$,*

$$\sum_{k\in\mathbb{Z}}(-1)^k[H_c^k(M(H))] - \sum_{k\in\mathbb{Z}}(-1)^k[H_c^k(M(H'))] = \sum_{k\in\mathbb{Z}}(-1)^k[H_c^{k-1}(M(H/e))].$$

Applying the Hodge–Deligne morphism $E : K_0(\mathrm{MHS}) \to \mathbb{Z}[u,v]$ yields

$$E(M(H); u, v) - E(M(H'); u, v) = E(M(H/e); u, v).$$

*Hence along a threshold chain $H_{j-1} \xrightarrow{+e_j} H_j$, the per–step jump depends only
on the contraction H_j/e_j.*

This is a direct specialization of the classical *deletion–contraction exact
sequence* for hyperplane arrangement complements (see [6, 23, 24]).

Lemma 1 (Component multiplicativity). *If $H = \bigsqcup_\ell H^{(\ell)}$ is a disjoint
union, then $E(M(H); u, v) = \prod_\ell E(M(H^{(\ell)}); u, v)$.*

Proof. This follows immediately from $M(H) \cong \prod_\ell M(H^{(\ell)})$ and multiplicativity
of E.

3   Chromatic Persistence Algorithm (CPA) on Graphs

This section gives the concrete event–driven procedure (*Algorithm CPA*) for
weighted graphs, together with a correctness proof. We rely on two ingredients
from Sect. 2: the chromatic→Poincaré identity (Proposition 2) and the deletion–
contraction jump identity (Theorem 1).

At each threshold step j, the algorithm maintains the per–threshold E–
polynomial E_j and the jump class Δ_j (as prescribed by Theorem 1). The complexity of each step is dominated by evaluating the contracted–minor chromatic
polynomial χ_{H_j/e_j}; summing over all thresholds yields the worst–case and fixed–
parameter bounds shown later.

Let $\Delta_j \in K_0(\mathrm{MHS})$ be the jump at step j. The *barcode zeta* is the finite
Euler product $Z_G(T) := \prod_{j=1}^m (1 - T^j)^{-\Delta_j} \in 1 + T\,K_0(\mathrm{MHS})[[T]]$, formed
using the standard power structure over $K_0(\mathrm{MHS})$; pushing along the Hodge–
Deligne map $E : K_0(\mathrm{MHS}) \to \mathbb{Z}[u,v]$ yields a compact numerical summary with
multiplicative pooling [11].

Algorithm 1 (CPA) is given below, based on the identities recalled in Sect. 2.

Algorithm 1. Algorithm CPA: Event–Driven Motivic Persistence on Graphs

---

Require: Weighted graph $G = (V, E, w)$ with thresholds $t_1 < \cdots < t_m$
Ensure: Per–threshold E–polynomials $E_j(u, v)$; jump classes Δ_j; barcode zeta $Z_G(T)$
1: $Z_G(T) \leftarrow 1$ ▷ Initialization
2: $E_0(u, v) \leftarrow (uv)^{|V|}$ ▷ Edgeless graph on $|V|$ vertices
3: **for** $j = 1$ to m **do**   ▷ Process only at events
4:     $H_j \leftarrow G_{\leq t_j}$; let e_j be the edge added at step j
5:     **Chromatic step:** compute $\chi_{H_j/e_j}(q)$ ▷ Deletion–contraction or DP on treewidth
6:     **Jump step:** $\Delta_j(u, v) \leftarrow \chi_{H_j/e_j}(uv)$
7:     **Betti/E update:** $E_j(u, v) \leftarrow E_{j-1}(u, v) - \Delta_j(u, v)$
8:     **Zeta:** $Z_G(T) \leftarrow Z_G(T) \cdot (1 - T^j)^{-\Delta_j}$
9: **end for**
10: **return** $\{E_j(u, v)\}_{j=1}^m$, $\{\Delta_j\}_{j=1}^m$, and $Z_G(T)$

Theorem 2 (Correctness). *For each threshold t_j, Algorithm 1 returns*

$$E_j(u, v) = E(M(H_j); u, v) \quad \text{and} \quad \Delta_j(u, v) = E(M(H_j/e_j); u, v),$$

so the per–event jump equals the class prescribed by the deletion–contraction jump identity.

Proof. We prove by induction on j that $E_j(u, v) = E(M(H_j); u, v)$ and that $\Delta_j(u, v) = E(M(H_j/e_j); u, v)$.

Base Case $j = 0$. Let H_0 be the edgeless graph on $n = |V|$ vertices. Then $\chi_{H_0}(q) = q^n$, so by Proposition 2, $E(M(H_0); u, v) = \chi_{H_0}(uv) = (uv)^n$. The algorithm initializes $E_0(u, v) = (uv)^n$, hence $E_0 = E(M(H_0); u, v)$.

Induction Step. Assume $E_{j-1}(u, v) = E(M(H_{j-1}); u, v)$. At step j the algorithm computes $\chi_{H_j/e_j}(q)$, and by Proposition 2 we have

$$E(M(H_j/e_j); u, v) = \chi_{H_j/e_j}(uv).$$

Here is where Theorem 1 enters: it provides the exact recurrence

$$E(M(H_{j-1}); u, v) - E(M(H_j); u, v) = E(M(H_j/e_j); u, v).$$

Substituting the inductive hypothesis $E_{j-1} = E(M(H_{j-1}))$ into this identity shows that the update rule

$$E_j(u, v) \leftarrow E_{j-1}(u, v) - \chi_{H_j/e_j}(uv)$$

produces $E_j(u, v) = E(M(H_j); u, v)$. Finally, by definition the jump is $\Delta_j(u, v) = \chi_{H_j/e_j}(uv)$, so $\Delta_j = E(M(H_j/e_j); u, v)$.

    Thus, by induction, both the per–threshold invariants E_j and the per–event jumps Δ_j are computed correctly for all j.

4   Complexity Analysis

We analyze the end–to–end cost of Algorithm 1. Throughout, $n := |V|$ and $m := |E|$. Because edge weights are assumed distinct, the threshold chain has exactly m steps. We use $O^*(\cdot)$ to suppress factors polynomial in n and m. The dominant cost is computing the contracted–minor chromatic polynomial χ_{H_j/e_j} along the threshold chain; motivic updates are linear in the number of thresholds and cohomological degrees. Computing χ_H is #P–hard in the worst case, but admits dynamic programs fixed–parameter tractable (FPT) in treewidth and closed–form recurrences for standard graph families, yielding near–linear behavior on those classes.

Let $T_\chi(H)$ and $S_\chi(H)$ denote the time and space to compute χ_H. We will use the following standard bounds.

- **Deletion–contraction.** The classical recursion $\chi_H(q) = \chi_{H\setminus e}(q) - \chi_{H/e}(q)$ with memoization yields $T_\chi(H) = O^*(2^{|E(H)|})$ and $S_\chi(H) = O^*(2^{|E(H)|})$.
- **Treewidth–DP.** If $\mathrm{tw}(H) \leq w$, a dynamic program on a tree decomposition computes χ_H in $f(w)\,\mathrm{poly}(n)$ time and $g(w)\,\mathrm{poly}(n)$ space (for some computable functions f, g) [5,22].
- **Motivic/E–updates.** Converting χ_H to $P_{M(H)}$ and $E(M(H); u, v)$ and assembling the jump/zeta costs $O(d_E)$ ring operations per step, with $d_E \leq n$ the number of nonzero degrees.

Theorem 3 (Complexity). *Let $H_j := G_{\leq t_j}$ be the threshold chain and e_j the edge added at step j. Then:*

1. ***Worst case (deletion–contraction).***

$$T_{\text{total}} = O^*\Big(\sum_{j=1}^{m} 2^j\Big) = O^*(2^m), \qquad S_{\text{total}} = O^*(2^m).$$

2. ***FPT in treewidth.*** *If each H_j has $\mathrm{tw}(H_j) \leq w$, then*

$$T_{\text{total}} = O\big(m\,f(w)\,\mathrm{poly}(n)\big), \qquad S_{\text{total}} = O\big(g(w)\,\mathrm{poly}(n)\big).$$

3. ***Special classes.*** *For trees and cycles, explicit closed forms of χ imply $T_{\text{total}} = O(m+n)$. For series–parallel graphs, linear-time decomposition recurrences yield the same bound.*

Across all cases, the motivic updates (E–assembly and the zeta product) add $O(m \cdot d_E)$ ring operations.

Proof. We use $O^*(\cdot)$ to suppress factors polynomial in $n := |V|$ and $m := |E|$. At each threshold j the dominant cost is evaluating χ_{H_j/e_j}; all other work is tallied at the end.

(1) Worst case. Memoized deletion-contraction yields $T_\chi(H_j) = O^*(2^{|E(H_j)|})$ and $S_\chi(H_j) = O^*(2^{|E(H_j)|})$. The same memoized evaluation covers χ_{H_j/e_j} as it

visits all minors of H_j; alternatively, a separate call obeys $T_\chi(H_j/e_j) \leq T_\chi(H_j)$. Since $|E(H_j)| = j$, one threshold costs $O^*(2^j)$ time. Summing gives

$$T_{\text{total}} = O^*\Big(\sum_{j=1}^{m} 2^j \Big) = O^*(2^m), \qquad S_{\text{total}} = O^*(2^m).$$

(2) FPT in treewidth. If every H_j has $\text{tw}(H_j) \leq w$, then a dynamic program on a width-w tree decomposition computes χ_{H_j} in $f(w)\,\text{poly}(n)$ time and $g(w)\,\text{poly}(n)$ space [5,22]. Since treewidth is minor-monotone, χ_{H_j/e_j} satisfies the same bounds. Across all m thresholds this yields

$$T_{\text{total}} = O(m\,f(w)\,\text{poly}(n)), \qquad S_{\text{total}} = O(g(w)\,\text{poly}(n)).$$

(3) Special classes. For trees and cycles the chromatic polynomial has explicit closed forms: $\chi_T(q) = q(q-1)^{n-1}$ and $\chi_{C_n}(q) = (q-1)^n + (-1)^n(q-1)$. Thus the chromatic step at each threshold is $O(1)$, so across the DP chain the cost is $O(m)$; adding $O(n)$ initialization yields $O(m+n)$ overall. For series–parallel graphs, linear-time decomposition recurrences evaluate χ along a fixed SP decomposition, with each edge insertion requiring only constant-time updates. Hence the chromatic stage across the chain is also $O(m+n)$.

Motivic Overhead. Given χ_H, forming $E(M(H); u, v) = \chi_H(uv)$ costs $O(d_E)$ ring operations, where d_E is the top nonzero degree ($d_E \leq n$). Assembling the per–event jump $\Delta_j(u,v) = E(M(H_j/e_j); u, v)$ and updating the zeta factor $Z_G(T) \leftarrow Z_G(T)\cdot(1-T^j)^{-\Delta_j}$ costs $O(d_E)$ per step. If one stores $Z_G(T)$ truncated at T^m, each update is still $O(d_E)$. Summing across all thresholds gives a motivic cost of $O(m\,d_E)$. Thus the motivic layer contributes only linear overhead in the number of thresholds and degrees, which is negligible compared to the cost of chromatic evaluations established above.

In practice, consecutive threshold graphs differ by only one edge, so memoization across steps reduces constants. Likewise, if H_j decomposes into components, χ_{H_j} and $E(M(H_j))$ factorize multiplicatively. Both observations shrink runtime in experiments but do not affect the asymptotics of Theorem 3.

We clarify the per–step costs used later in experiments. For trees, the chromatic polynomial has a closed form, so each threshold update costs $O(1)$ for the chromatic step and $O(d_E)$ for the motivic updates, yielding a total cost of $O(m+n)$. For cycles, the closed form of χ_{C_n} similarly makes the chromatic subroutine $O(1)$ per step, with $O(d_E)$ for the motivic updates. For series–parallel graphs, the chromatic polynomial can be evaluated along a decomposition in overall $O(m+n)$ time across the threshold chain, and the motivic updates again remain linear.

Our O^* hides polynomial factors from recursion/DP table management T, conversions from χ_H to $P_{M(H)}$ and E, and the zeta product. Ring operations are counted in $\mathbb{Z}[u,v]$ (or on the uv–diagonal), with degrees $\leq d_E \leq n$. Coefficient growth is modest and dominated by the chromatic stage.

The computational bottleneck is exclusively graph–combinatorial (χ_H). Once χ_H is available, the motivic layer is lightweight and scales linearly with the number of thresholds and cohomological degrees.

5   Experimental Verification

We evaluate Algorithm CPA on a controlled "ring-size recognition" task that separates 5- vs. 6-member cycles. We compare against a lightweight 1-skeleton PH baseline built from b_0/b_1 traces along the threshold chain. The graphic specialization lets us compute per-threshold E-polynomials from chromatic polynomials via Proposition 2, and per-event jumps via the deletion–contraction identity (Theorem 1).

Data and Filtration. We generate two balanced classes of unlabeled cycle graphs: $\mathcal{C}_5 = \{C_5\}$ and $\mathcal{C}_6 = \{C_6\}$, with 30 instances each. Each instance follows a *spanning-tree-first* threshold schedule: all edges except one are assigned weights in $[0.1, 0.3]$, while the single cycle-closing edge receives weight 0.95. This design forces the baseline to observe exactly one H_1-birth at the *last* event for both ring sizes, exposing a known blind spot.

Methods. Baseline (PH, 1-skeleton). We record $b_0(t)$ and $b_1(t)$ at the (normalized) thresholds and aggregate standard, scale-invariant summaries: area-under-curve $\mathrm{AUC}(b_0)$, $\mathrm{AUC}(b_1)$, final b_1, # of b_1-jumps, and the normalized birth time of b_1. *Ours (CPA, graphic).* At each thresholded subgraph H_j we compute $P_{M(H_j)}(t) = (-t)^{|V|}\chi_{H_j}(-1/t)$ and read off the Betti vector (hence the E-polynomial via $t \mapsto uv$). For forests (all pre-final steps) we use the closed form $P_{M(H_j)}(t) = (1 + t)^{|E(H_j)|}$; for the terminal cycle $H_m = C_n$, we use $P_{M(C_n)}(t) = (1 + t)^n - t^{n-1}(1 + t)$; see Sect. 2. We vectorize by concatenating the per-threshold Betti vectors (padded to a fixed shape) and use 1-NN (Euclidean) with leave-one-out (LOO) evaluation [4].

Results. Table 1 summarizes accuracy; the CPA features separate C_5 from C_6 perfectly, while the PH baseline performs near chance.

Table 1. Ring-size recognition (LOO 1-NN). Runtimes are per graph on our machine.

Method	Accuracy (LOO)	Avg. time/graph (ms)
PH baseline (1-skeleton)	0.55	0.042
CPA (per-threshold E-profiles)	**1.00**	0.143

We compute a paired McNemar statistic (continuity-corrected) comparing our method to the baseline [20]. Let b be the number of cases with *baseline correct & CPA wrong*, and c the number with *baseline wrong & CPA correct*.

We obtain $b = 0$, $c = 27$, yielding $\chi^2 \approx 25.04$, confirming a highly significant improvement.

In this setup the PH baseline on the 1-skeleton records only that a *single* cycle is born at the final event in both classes, so most summaries coincide. By contrast, the CPA features read the chromatic/arrangement structure at *every* threshold. For cycles, $\chi_{C_n}(q) = (q-1)^n + (-1)^n(q-1)$, which implies $P_{M(C_n)}(t) = (1+t)^n - t^{n-1}(1+t)$. Pre-final subgraphs are forests with $P(t) = (1+t)^{|E(H_j)|}$. Consequently the E-profiles (hence Betti vectors) depend on n throughout the chain, cleanly separating C_5 from C_6.

Note that absolute runtimes vary by environment; nevertheless, the qualitative pattern (perfect separation with negligible overhead for CPA) is robust.

6   Conclusion

We introduced *Algorithm CPA*, an event–driven procedure that computes, along a graph threshold filtration, per–event jumps and per–threshold E–polynomials of graphic arrangement complements via deletion–contraction and chromatic polynomials. In the graphic (Hodge–Tate) case, these reduce to discrete, combinatorial quantities with computable algebraic control; the computational bottleneck is evaluating χ_H, which is worst–case hard but fixed–parameter tractable in treewidth and admits closed forms for basic graph families.

In machine learning, CPA offers a lightweight, plug–in set of *global* descriptors that complement local, message–passing representations. Concretely:

- **Feature channels.** Per–threshold E–profiles (Betti vectors per event) and jump classes (contracted complements) provide fixed–length, order–aware summaries. Truncated barcode–zeta coefficients offer an even more compact alternative with multiplicative pooling. These can be concatenated to learned embeddings, used as graph–level covariates, or fed into classical models (SVMs/kernels) as stand–alone features.
- **Inductive bias and interpretability.** Because the channels are defined through χ_H and deletion–contraction, they are explicitly *ring/cycle sensitive* and thus encode global shape information often underrepresented in message passing. Their coefficients admit combinatorial explanations (colorings, minors), yielding clear attribution: which edge insertions (events) and which contractions drive a decision.
- **Stability and efficiency.** The event–driven design depends only on the *order* of edge weights; rescalings that preserve order leave outputs unchanged, and small perturbations that do not swap event order have no effect. For sparse, low–treewidth graphs common in chemistry and other domains, dynamic programming and closed forms make offline precomputation fast; training-time overhead is essentially zero (read features from cache).
- **Drop-in integration.** In GNN pipelines, CPA features can be (i) concatenated to graph-level readouts, (ii) injected as conditioning signals (e.g., FiLM/gating) to steer message passing toward cycle-aware regimes, or (iii)

used as targets in auxiliary self-supervised tasks (predict E–profiles from local views) to regularize representations.

In particular, for molecular property prediction and retrieval, CPA supplies deterministic, interpretable descriptors tied to ring systems and cyclic scaffolds, which are prime determinants of reactivity and physico-chemical behavior. They complement ECFP/Weisfeiler–Lehman fingerprints and neural message passing by capturing arrangement/chromatic structure that varies with ring size and composition. Because CPA is event–driven and algebraic, it supports dataset-wide caching, fast ablations (toggle events/minors), and counterfactual analyses (edit an edge; recompute a single step).

In summary, the algorithm developed in this paper makes Hodge-refined, event–driven persistence *practical* on graphs; it bridges algebraic topology, arrangement theory, and graph algorithms to yield stable, interpretable, and computationally efficient features that can be immediately deployed in modern machine learning workflows on graph-structured data such as chemical compounds. We also plan to develop variants of our method for applications at the intersection of logic, category theory and machine learning [13–19].

References

1. Baranovsky, V., Sazdanovic, R.: Graph homology and graph configuration spaces. J. Homotopy Related Struct. **7**(2), 223–235 (2012). https://doi.org/10.1007/s40062-012-0006-3
2. Bodlaender, H.L.: A linear-time algorithm for finding tree-decompositions of small treewidth. SIAM J. Comput. **25**(6), 1305–1317 (1996)
3. Cohen-Steiner, D., Edelsbrunner, H., Harer, J.: Stability of persistence diagrams. Discrete Comput. Geom. **37**(1), 103–120 (2007)
4. Cover, T.M., Hart, P.E.: Nearest neighbor pattern classification. IEEE Trans. Inf. Theory **13**(1), 21–27 (1967)
5. Cygan, M., et al.: Parameterized Algorithms. Springer (2015)
6. Dimca, A.: Hyperplane Arrangements: An Introduction. Springer (2017)
7. Duvenaud, D.K., et al.: Convolutional networks on graphs for learning molecular fingerprints. In: Proceedings of NIPS 2015, pp. 2224–2232 (2015)
8. Edelsbrunner, H., Harer, J.L.: Computational Topology. AMS (2010)
9. Ghrist, R.: Barcodes: the persistent topology of data. BAMS **45**(1), 61–75 (2008)
10. Gilmer, J., Schoenholz, S.S., Riley, P.F., Vinyals, O., Dahl, G.E.: Neural message passing for quantum chemistry. In: Proceedings of ICML, vol. 70, pp. 1263–1272. PMLR (2017)
11. Gusein-Zade, S.M., Luengo, I., Melle-Hernández, A.: A power structure over the Grothendieck ring of varieties. Math. Res. Lett. **11**, 49–57 (2004)
12. Jaeger, F., Vertigan, D.L., Welsh, D.J.A.: On the computational complexity of the Jones and Tutte polynomials. Math. Proc. Camb. Phil. Soc. **108**, 35–53 (1990)
13. Maruyama, Y.: Algebraic study of lattice-valued logic and lattice-valued modal logic. In: Ramanujam, R., Sarukkai, S. (eds.) ICLA 2009. LNCS (LNAI), vol. 5378, pp. 170–184. Springer, Heidelberg (2008). https://doi.org/10.1007/978-3-540-92701-3_12

14. Maruyama, Y.: Fundamental results for pointfree convex geometry. Ann. Pure Appl. Logic **161**(12), 1486–1501 (2010)
15. Maruyama, Y.: Natural duality, modality, and coalgebra. J. Pure Appl. Algebra **216**(3), 565–580 (2012)
16. Maruyama, Y.: Full lambek hyperdoctrine: categorical semantics for first-order substructural logics. In: Libkin, L., Kohlenbach, U., de Queiroz, R. (eds.) WoLLIC 2013. LNCS, vol. 8071, pp. 211–225. Springer, Heidelberg (2013). https://doi.org/10.1007/978-3-642-39992-3_19
17. Maruyama, Y.: Categorical duality theory: with applications to domains, convexity, and the distribution monad. In: Proceedings of CSL, LIPIcs, vol. 23, pp. 500–520 (2013)
18. Maruyama, Y.: Symbolic and statistical theories of cognition: towards integrated artificial intelligence. In: Cleophas, L., Massink, M. (eds.) SEFM 2020. LNCS, vol. 12524, pp. 129–146. Springer, Cham (2021). https://doi.org/10.1007/978-3-030-67220-1_11
19. Maruyama, Y.: The conditions of artificial general intelligence. In: Proceedings of AGI, LNAI, vol. 12177, pp. 242–251 (2020)
20. McNemar, Q.: Note on the sampling error of the difference between correlated proportions or percentages. Psychometrika **12**(2), 153–157 (1947)
21. Morris, C., et al.: Weisfeiler and Leman go neural: higher-order graph neural networks. In: Proceedings of AAAI, vol. 33, pp. 4602–4609 (2019)
22. Noble, S.D.: Evaluating the Tutte polynomial for graphs of bounded tree-width. Comb. Probab. Comput. **7**(3), 307–321 (1998)
23. Orlik, P., Solomon, L.: Combinatorics and topology of complements of hyperplanes. Invent. Math. **56**, 167–189 (1980)
24. Orlik, P., Terao, H.: Arrangements of Hyperplanes. Grundlehren der mathematischen Wissenschaften, vol. 300. Springer (1992)
25. Shervashidze, N., Schweitzer, P., van Leeuwen, E.J., Mehlhorn, K., Borgwardt, K.M.: Weisfeiler-Lehman graph kernels. JMLR **12**, 2539–2561 (2011)
26. Xu, K., Hu, W., Leskovec, J., Jegelka, S.: How powerful are graph neural networks? In: Proceedings of ICLR (2019)
27. Zomorodian, A., Carlsson, G.: Computing persistent homology. Discrete Comput. Geom. **33**(2), 249–274 (2005)

Deterministic Integer Sorting on the Parallel External Memory Model

Ranajit Senko[✉][ID] and G. Sajith[ID]

Department of Computer Science and Engineering, Indian Institute of Technology Guwahati,
Guwahati 781039, Assam, India
{ranajit,sajith}@iitg.ac.in
http://www.iitg.ac.in

Abstract. We present a deterministic parallel external-memory (PEM) algorithm
that sorts N integers from $\{1, 2, \ldots, l\}$. The algorithm sorts N integers from
$[1, l]$ in

$$O\left(\frac{\log l}{\log m}\left(\frac{M}{B} + \log_{M/B}\frac{N}{B}\right)\right)$$

parallel steps and

$$O\left(\frac{N}{B} \cdot \frac{\log l}{\log(M/B)}\right)$$

I/O operations. on the Concurrent Read Exclusive Write PEM model. (Here M
is the size of the internal main memory of processors and B is the block size for
I/Os.)

Keywords: Prefix sum · Search · Multi-way merge

1   Introduction

Sorting is one of the most essential problems in computer science and forms the basis of
numerous computational tasks. Given a dataset A containing N elements, sorting can
be achieved either through comparison-based or integer-based techniques. Traditional
comparison sorting methods have a well-established lower bound of $\Omega(N \log N)$. However, when the input elements are integers, specialized integer sorting algorithms can
surpass this bound, provided the integer range is limited.

Integer sorting extends the principle of radix sorting. It operates over multiple
stages, where each stage processes a fixed number of bits (or digits) from the integer representation. In the ith stage, the elements are already ordered with respect to
the first $(i - 1)$ least significant digit positions, and the current digit is then used as
the sorting key. Repeating this process across all digit positions yields a completely
ordered sequence. Our approach generalizes this idea and proposes an efficient integer
sorting algorithm for N integers, which executes in $O(\log l)$ parallel steps and performs
$O\left(\frac{N}{B} \cdot \frac{\log l}{\log N}\right)$ I/O operations under the Parallel External Memory (PEM) model, where
l denotes the maximum value among the input integers.

The computational complexity of integer sorting has been investigated under several
models, including (a) RAM, (b) PRAM, (c) External Memory (EM), and (d) Parallel
External Memory (PEM), as discussed extensively in prior work.

© The Author(s), under exclusive license to Springer Nature Switzerland AG 2026
C. Zaroliagis et al. (Eds.): ICAA 2026, LNCS 16423, pp. 100–116, 2026.
https://doi.org/10.1007/978-3-032-15621-1_9

1.1 Computational Models and Previous Work

The Random Access Memory (RAM) model assumes a single-processor system with a main memory of size M, consisting of consecutive locations where all data are stored during computation. The computational cost in this model is measured by the number of executed instructions. Fredman *et al.* [3] demonstrated that integer sorting can achieve better performance than comparison-based sorting in this model by introducing the *"fusion tree"* data structure. They showed that deterministic integer sorting can be achieved in $O(N\frac{\log N}{\log \log N})$ time using linear space, while its randomized counterpart runs in $O(N\sqrt{\log N})$ time. Subsequent works [13–17] further improved these bounds, with Han *et al.* [15] achieving $O(N \log \log N)$ time complexity with linear space usage.

In contrast, the Parallel Random Access Memory (PRAM) model consists of p processors that operate concurrently, sharing a global memory of size M. Processors communicate through this shared memory, enabling parallel execution. If an algorithm performs W total operations across T sequential steps, and the ith step requires w_i operations, then using p processors, the parallel time per step is $\lceil \frac{w_i}{p} \rceil$. Hence, the total parallel runtime is $\sum_{i=1}^{T} \lceil \frac{w_i}{p} \rceil \leq T + \frac{W}{p}$. If $p = \frac{W}{T}$, the total time becomes $O(T)$, and the total computational cost, or work complexity, is $O(Tp) = O(W)$. Based on memory access permissions, PRAM is categorized into three models: CRCW (Concurrent Read, Concurrent Write), CREW (Concurrent Read, Exclusive Write), and EREW (Exclusive Read, Exclusive Write).

Several studies have analyzed integer sorting within these PRAM variants. In the CRCW model, comparison-based sorting has a lower bound of $\Omega\left(\frac{\log N}{\log \log N}\right)$ [11]. For CREW and EREW models, sorting requires $\Omega(\log N)$ time and $O(N \log N)$ operations, respectively [12]. Albers *et al.* [7] proposed integer sorting algorithms achieving $O(\log N \log \log N)$ time with $O(N\sqrt{\log N})$ operations in the CREW model, and $O(N\frac{\log N}{\log \log N})$ operations in the EREW model. Similarly, Andersson *et al.* [6] introduced a CRCW integer sorting algorithm with $O(\log N)$ time and $O(N \log \log N)$ operations. Han *et al.* [1] later proposed a deterministic integer sorting algorithm in the CREW model running in $O(\log N)$ time and $O(N\sqrt{\log N})$ operations, matching the theoretical lower bound. An improved version by the same authors [2] achieved $O\left(\log N \frac{\sqrt{\log N}}{\log \log N}\right)$ time and $O\left(N\sqrt{\frac{\log N}{\log \log N}} \log \log \log N\right)$ operations.

Both RAM and PRAM models assume that the data fit entirely in main memory. When data exceed main memory capacity, data transfer between external and internal memory dominates the computation time. To address this limitation, the External Memory (EM) model [9] and the Parallel External Memory (PEM) model were developed. An algorithm that is optimal in the PEM model is also optimal in the EM model.

Farhadi *et al.* [18] analyzed lower bounds for integer sorting in the EM model using the *Li and Li network coding conjecture*, which asserts that in any undirected network, the *network coding rate* equals the *multicommodity flow rate*. This implies that allowing intermediate nodes to encode messages offers no advantage over simple routing. When applied to sorting, their framework—which models sorting as a network communication problem—shows that even randomized integer sorting algorithms cannot outperform comparison-based lower bounds. Their results extend previous findings by eliminating the *obliviousness assumption*, though the bounds remain *conditional*, depending on the validity of the conjecture. Under this conjecture, any EM integer sorting algorithm requires $\Omega\left(\min\left\{N, \frac{N}{B}\log_{2M/B}\left(\frac{N}{B}\right)\right\}\right)$ I/O operations, aligning with comparison-based bounds.

The Parallel External Memory (PEM) model, introduced by Arge *et al.* [8], consists of p processors, each with a private cache of size M, sharing a large external memory. Data are transferred between caches and external memory in blocks of size B, rather than individual elements. Each such transfer counts as one I/O operation, and during an I/O phase, all processors can perform simultaneous read or write operations. Communication occurs exclusively through external memory I/Os. PEM variants correspond to the PRAM categories (CRCW, CREW, and EREW) based on access permissions. In the CREW PEM model, comparison-based sorting of N elements can be achieved in $O\left(\frac{N}{PB}\log_{M/B}\left(\frac{N}{B}\right)\right)$ I/O rounds using $p \leq \frac{N}{B^2}$ processors. This work focuses exclusively on the CREW PEM model. The cost, or work complexity, of a PEM algorithm is defined as the total number of I/O operations, equivalent to the product of time and the number of processors.

1.2 Motivation of This Work

1. No existing work studies integer sorting in the PEM model. None exists for the EM model either.
2. Han *et al.* [1,2] showed their algorithm uses $O(N\sqrt{\log N})$ operations if each phase runs in linear time. They achieved this with AKS sorting, which is theoretically optimal. But expander graphs introduce large constants, making AKS impractical. This paper instead uses multi-way merging and prefix sums to address this issue.
3. Han's algorithm [1] assumes all integers start in one linked list as a single group. Phase 1 operates on the most significant $\sqrt{\log N}$ bits, phase 2 on the next $\sqrt{\log N}$ bits, and so on. Each phase partitions groups into linked lists of size $\leq S = 2^{c\sqrt{\log N}}$, called sub-groups. Sub-groups are sorted independently and in parallel on the next $\sqrt{\log N}$ bits. Within each sorted sub-group, elements with the same verified bits form separate lists. At the end of a phase, these lists are joined into one, producing at most $2^{\sqrt{\log N}}$ lists per group. Thus, the number of groups grows by $2^{\sqrt{\log N}}$ each phase.

   Han used list contraction with pointer jumping to join sorted sub-groups. They claimed this needs $O(\log S) = O(\sqrt{\log N})$ time and $O(S \cdot N/S) = O(N)$ operations. The claim holds only if the size of joined sub-groups remain $\leq S$, which is not guaranteed since lists may exceed S when many integers share the same bits. Parallel handling is also difficult as groups grow exponentially.

   We address this by introducing a new sub-group joining method using prefix sums, ensuring $O(N/B)$ I/O per phase regardless of group size. To manage groups efficiently, we verify bits from LSB to MSB, keeping the number of groups fixed each phase.

1.3   Organization of the Paper

The remainder of this paper is organized as follows. Section 2 describes the preliminary techniques that form the foundation of our work. Section 3 presents the proposed algorithm in detail. Finally, Sect. 4 concludes the paper with a summary of findings and possible directions for future research.

2   Preliminary Techniques

In this section, we outline the basic parallel algorithm techniques used in our work: (a) Prefix sums, (b) Search, (c) Cross-rank, (d) Merge, and (e) Compact. For each problem, we consider two scenarios: *sparse* and *compact*. In a sparse instance, each input (and output) element occupies the last word of a distinct block, leaving the rest unused. In a compact instance, input and output are stored contiguously in shared secondary memory. An array of size N in compact form occupies N/B blocks.

Throughout the paper, we use the following notation: let A be an array and N the number of elements in A.

Prefix Sums

We are given an integer array $A[1 \cdots N]$ and compute $D[1 \cdots N]$ such that $D[1] = A[1]$, $D[i] = \sum_{j=1}^{i} A[j]$, for $1 < i \le N$. Thus, $D[i]$ is the prefix sum of A up to index i.

1. **Sparse Instance:** Use the balanced binary tree algorithm for prefix sums on the EREW PRAM model. In the EREW PEM model, each PRAM instruction is treated as an I/O operation. This algorithm, **PREFIX-SUMS-1**, runs in $O(\log N)$ parallel steps with $O(N)$ I/O operations. By Brent's Theorem, with $N/\log N$ processors, it completes in $O(\log N)$ steps. Each array element requires a full memory block.
2. **Compact Instance:** Use a three-step method:
   1. **Local Prefix-Sums:** For each block I ($1 \le I \le N/B$), compute prefix sums inside the block. The last element stores the block's total.
   2. **Global Block-Sums:** Apply **PREFIX-SUMS-1** to the N/B block totals.
   3. **Offset Adjustment:** For each block I, add the prefix sum of block $I - 1$ to all elements of block I, writing results into D.

   This algorithm, **PREFIX-SUMS-2**, takes $O(\log(N/B))$ steps and $O(N/B)$ I/O operations. With $(N/B)/\log(N/B)$ processors, Brent's Theorem gives $O(\log(N/B))$ steps.

Searching

Consider a sorted array A of N items from a linearly ordered set S, and an element $x \in S$. The *rank* of x in A is the number of elements in A less than or equal to x.

1. **Sparse Presentation:** On a CREW PEM with $(N - 1)$ processors, initialize $R = 0$. In parallel for $1 \le i \le N - 1$, check $(A[i] \le x \ \wedge \ A[i+1] > x)$. If true, set $R = i$. This algorithm, **SEARCH-1**, runs in $O(1)$ steps.

2. **Compact Presentation:** If A is compact, with blocks evenly placed in shared external memory, use p processors on a CREW PEM.
   - If $N \leq p + 1$, run **SEARCH-1**(A, x).
   - Otherwise, split A into $(p+1)$ segments of size $\lceil N/(p+1) \rceil$. In parallel, compare x with the last element of each segment to locate the correct one, then recurse.

   Each step reduces the search space by factor $(p + 1)$. This algorithm, **SEARCH-2**, runs in $O\left(\frac{\log N}{\log(p+1)}\right)$ steps.

Merging

Suppose we have two sorted arrays C and D of sizes N_1 and N_2, stored in sparse presentation with blocks evenly distributed across shared external memory. The goal is to merge C and D into one sorted array.

We use the operation **CROSS-RANK**: for each $C[i]$ $(1 \leq i \leq N_1)$, compute its rank in D, and for each $D[j]$ $(1 \leq j \leq N_2)$, compute its rank in C. With p processors, this takes $O(\log_{p+1} N)$ steps, where $N = N_1 + N_2$.

MERGE-1: Elect the first element from each segment as a leader. Perform CROSS-RANK on leaders in $O(1)$ time using at most $\sqrt{N_1}\sqrt{N_2} < N$ processors. For each leader in C (resp. D), search its position in D (resp. C) using $\sqrt{N_1}$ (resp. $\sqrt{N_2}$) processors. Recursively solve each partition (each of size at most $\sqrt{N_1} + \sqrt{N_2}$).

I/O recurrence: $T(N) = T(\sqrt{N}) + c \Rightarrow T(N) = O(\log \log N)$. Thus, MERGE-1 runs in $O(\log \log N)$ steps with linear processors.

MERGE-2: Divide C and D into segments of size $\log \log N$. Elect the first element of each segment as a leader. Use MERGE-1 to cross-rank leaders in $O(\log \log N)$ I/Os. For each leader in C (resp. D), search its segment in D (resp. C) with one processor. Recursively solve partitions of size $\leq 2 \log \log N$ sequentially.

MERGE-2 runs in $O(N)$ cost and $O(\log \log N)$ I/Os with $N/\log \log N$ processors.

MERGE-3: Suppose C and D are in compact presentation. From each block of C and D, elect the first element as a leader, forming C' and D'. Cross-rank C' and D' using MERGE-2. Each leader identifies its bounding leaders in the opposite array and the responsible block. Assign each leader to merge its block with the adjacent block from the opposite array. Leaders merge their elements sequentially.

If a leader receives ϵ fewer items, the next gets at least $B - \epsilon$, so no block is processed by more than three leaders.

With N/B processors, MERGE-3 completes in $O(\log \log N)$ I/Os with total cost $O\left(\frac{N}{B}\right)$, which is asymptotically optimal.

Compaction

The compaction problem reorganizes memory so that all valid elements are contiguous, removing empty locations. Algorithms COMPACT-1, COMPACT-2, and COMPACT-3 handle progressively more general layouts.

COMPACT-1. Input: $A[1 \ldots B]$, each element occupies the first word of a distinct block, rest unused. The algorithm runs in $\log B$ phases: adjacent blocks are merged in parallel, reducing partially filled blocks. Complexity: $O(\log B)$ steps and $O(B)$ I/Os. Output: all elements consecutive in one block.

COMPACT-2. Input: sequence $a_1, a_2, \ldots, a_B$ spread across $A[1 \ldots l]$ of blocks, possibly with empty cells. The algorithm merges block pairs level by level until all valid elements are in the first block. Complexity: $O(\log l)$ steps and $O(l)$ I/Os.

COMPACT-3. Input: $A[1 \ldots l]$ with N elements across blocks with arbitrary empty spaces. Steps: (1) Compute per-block element counts and prefix sums with PREFIX-SUMS-1. (2) Identify partially filled blocks and move their contents to auxiliary storage if needed. (3) Apply COMPACT-2 to reorganize blocks. (4) Merge auxiliary elements back. Output: $A[1 \ldots N/B]$ with N elements packed into N/B blocks. Complexity: $O(\log l)$ steps, $O(l)$ I/Os. If $l = O(N/B)$, runtime is $O(\log(N/B))$ with $N/(B \log N)$ processors.

3 Proposed Algorithm

Our integer sorting algorithm uses b bits per iteration. Unlike Han [2], who scans from the most to the least significant bit, we process from *LSB* to *MSB*, which makes group handling more efficient.

Let $A[1, \ldots, N]$ be an array of N integers with maximum element l. Each $A[i]$ needs $O(\log l)$ bits. The array A resides in shared external memory, using $\frac{N}{B}$ consecutive blocks of size B. Let $D[1, \ldots, N]$ be the sorted output array.

Our algorithm is iterative, with two phases: (1) Segment Sorting (Sect. 3.1) and (2) Group Creation (Sect. 3.2).

In **segment sorting**, A is divided into segments/sub-arrays of $\alpha = 2^b$ blocks, i.e., $B \cdot \alpha$ elements. Thus there are $\frac{N}{B\alpha}$ segments. Let A_i be the i-th segment. Segments are sorted independently in parallel using the PEM model. Each segment uses α processors, for a total of $\frac{N}{B}$ processors.

In **group creation**, we form groups of elements across segments that match in the currently verified bit range. Comparing full $\log l$-bit keys is costly for large l, so, as in Han [2], we compare only b bits per iteration. In iteration i, bit positions $(i-1) \cdot b$ to $i \cdot b$ are checked, moving from LSB to MSB.

After groups are identified for the current bit range, they are placed contiguously in D. Each group is greater than all preceding groups with respect to verified bits. Thus D is partially sorted after each iteration and becomes the input for the next.

The next sections detail both phases of the algorithm.

3.1 Phase A: Parallel Segment Sorting

The goal of the *segment sorting phase* is to obtain a sorted segment D_i from an unsorted segment A_i, the i-th segment of A. Each A_i has length $B\alpha$, for a parameter α. Sorting uses the *PRAM multi-way merge technique* of [10].

The steps involved in segment sorting are as follows:

Step 1: If $B\alpha \leq M$, where M is the private cache size, then one processor can load a full segment and sort it with any optimal sequential algorithm (e.g., merge sort, radix sort). Exit. Thus, a segment can be sorted in one pass by a single processor.

I/O Complexity: For a single processor to read and sort an entire segment, it requires $O(\alpha)$ steps and I/O operations. For the entire array, it requires $O(\alpha)$ steps and $O(N/B)$ I/Os.

Step 2: (Here $B\alpha > M$.) Split segment A_i into sub-arrays A_{ij} of size M (the last may be smaller). Independently sort each A_{ij}, for $1 \leq j \leq \frac{B\alpha}{M}$, with an optimal in-memory sequential algorithm.

From each A_{ij}, pick *leaders*. For a parameter $\lambda \leq M$, every $k\lambda$-th element ($1 \leq k \leq \frac{M}{\lambda}$) is chosen and stored in the *leader array* A'_{ij}. Each block of A'_{ij} holds one leader in its first word; the remaining words are unused.

Remarks: A_{ij} is the j-th sub-array of A_i, and $A_{ij}[x]$ its x-th element. Parameter λ is the gap between leaders; the λ elements between two leaders form a *fragment*. The leader array is: $A'_{ij}[k] = A_{ij}[k\lambda]$, $1 \leq k \leq \frac{M}{\lambda}$, after A_{ij} is sorted. These leaders are used to determine both the relative ordering among all leaders and their actual positions in the final merged and sorted segment. The choice of λ is crucial for performance and is analyzed later.

I/O Complexity: Each A_{ij} is processed by one processor. Reading and writing a sub-array of size M takes $O(M/B)$ steps and I/Os. Selecting $\frac{M}{\lambda}$ leaders and storing them takes $O(\frac{M}{\lambda})$ steps and I/Os. With $\frac{B\alpha}{M}$ sub-arrays, Step 2 has total I/O cost $O(\frac{M}{B} \cdot \frac{B\alpha}{M}) = O(\alpha)$, and step complexity $O(\frac{M}{B})$.

Step 3: Compute the relative ranks of leaders using a *cross-rank computation*: for each pair of leader arrays $(A'_{ij}, A'_{ij'})$ with $j \neq j'$, determine the rank of every leader $x \in A'_{ij}$ within $A'_{ij'}$. For each leader x, these ranks are stored in a vector $R_x[1, \ldots, \frac{B\alpha}{M}]$, with each rank placed in the first word of a block.

Remarks: Each leader x computes its rank in all $\frac{B\alpha}{M}$ leader arrays, yielding $\frac{B\alpha}{M}$ ranks.

I/O Complexity: The number of cross-rank operations is $\left(\frac{B\alpha}{M}\right)^2$. Each cross-rank involves $O(\frac{M}{\lambda})$ elements, and therefore takes $O\left(\log\log \frac{M}{\lambda}\right)$ steps and $O\left(\frac{M}{\lambda}\right)$ I/Os. Thus, Step 3 has I/O complexity $O\left(\frac{B^2\alpha^2}{\lambda M}\right)$ and step complexity $O\left(\log\log \frac{M}{\lambda}\right)$.

Step 4: For each leader x, compute (using prefix sums) the sum over its rank vector R_x of size $\frac{B\alpha}{M}$. It gives the final rank of x in the global leader order. Place each leader in the output array $L_i[1, \ldots, \frac{B\alpha}{\lambda}]$ according to its rank.

Remarks: After the sum on R_x, leader x knows how many leaders have smaller ranks, i.e., its exact global position. Each x is stored in the first word of a block in L_i, leaving the rest of the block unused.

I/O Complexity: Each leader x adds over $\frac{B\alpha}{M}$ rank entries. So, each prefix sum takes $O\left(\log \frac{B\alpha}{M}\right)$ parallel steps and $O\left(\frac{B\alpha}{M}\right)$ I/Os. With $\frac{B\alpha}{\lambda}$ leaders, each accessing $\frac{B\alpha}{M}$ entries, the total I/O complexity is $O\left(\frac{B\alpha}{M} \cdot \frac{B\alpha}{\lambda}\right) = O\left(\frac{B^2\alpha^2}{\lambda M}\right)$.

Step 5: After cross-rank computation, each leader $x \in L_i$ knows its rank in every A'_{ij}. Thus, for each A_{ij}, x identifies the fragment $F_{ij}(x) \subset A_{ij}$ that contains x. Note that a fragment is of size λ, and is a contiguous subrange of A_{ij}.

Each leader searches $F_{ij}(x)$ in parallel to find its position, i.e., compute $Q_{ij}(x)$ such that $A_{ij}[Q_{ij}(x)] \leq x < A_{ij}[Q_{ij}(x)+1]$. Here $Q_{ij}(x)$ is the rank of x within A_{ij}.

Remarks: If t is the rank of x in A'_{ij}, then $x \in A_{ij}[t\lambda, \ldots, (t+1)\lambda - 1]$. The search is thus limited to this λ-sized subarray.

I/O Complexity: Each of the $\frac{B\alpha}{\lambda}$ leaders in A_i performs $\frac{B\alpha}{M}$ such searches for a total of $\frac{B^2\alpha^2}{M\lambda}$ searches. If each search receives $(\lambda/B)^c$ processors for $c = O(1)$, then the step complexity of the searches is $O(1)$ and the I/O complexity across all searches is $\frac{B^2\alpha^2}{M\lambda} \cdot \left(\frac{\lambda}{B}\right)^c$

Step 6: For each leader $x \in L_i$, compute $T_i(x) = \sum_{j=1}^{\frac{B\alpha}{M}} Q_{ij}(x)$, where $Q_{ij}(x)$ is the position of x in sub-array A_{ij}. $T_i(x)$ gives the exact location of x in the sorted segment D_i.

Remarks: After this sum, each leader x in A_i knows how many elements precede it across all sub-arrays, enabling direct placement into D_i.

I/O Complexity: Each leader aggregates $\frac{B\alpha}{M}$ values by prefix sum as in Step 4. Step complexity: $O\left(\log \frac{B\alpha}{M}\right)$, total I/O complexity: $O\left(\frac{B\alpha}{M} \cdot \frac{B\alpha}{\lambda}\right) = O\left(\frac{B^2\alpha^2}{\lambda M}\right)$.

Algorithm 1: Segment Sorting Algorithm with Linear I/O Cost

Input: Unsorted array segment A_i of size $B\alpha$ stored in consecutive blocks of shared external memory.

Output: Sorted array segment $D_i[1 \dots B\alpha]$ stored in shared external memory.

1 **Function** *SortSegment*:

2   **if** $\alpha \leq \frac{M}{B}$ **then**   `// Small segment: fits in memory`

3   Sort A_i using an optimal sequential in-memory sorting algorithm;

4   Store result in D_i;

5   **return** D_i;

6   **else**   `// Large segment: apply parallel sort strategy`

7   Partition A_i into sub-arrays A_{ij} of size M for $1 \leq j \leq \frac{B\alpha}{M}$;

8   Sort each A_{ij} in memory using any optimal sequential algorithm;

9   Partition each sorted A_{ij} into fragments of size λ;

10   Select the first element of each fragment as a leader;

11   Store leaders in leader array A'_{ij}, one per block;

         `/* Cross-Rank Computation`   `*/`

12   **foreach** *pair* (A'_{ij_a}, A'_{ij_b}), *where* $j_a \neq j_b$ **do**

13   Compute cross-rank of each leader x from A'_{ij_a} in A'_{ij_b} using MERGE;

14   Store ranks in $R_{ij_a, ij_b}(x)$;

         `/* Global Leader Position`   `*/`

15   For each leader x, compute sum of all $R_{ij_a, ij_b}(x)$ in parallel;

16   Store each leader x in array L_i at position corresponding to its global rank;

         `/* Fragment Location Search`   `*/`

17   For each leader $x \in L_i$ and sub-array A_{ij}, perform SEARCH in corresponding fragment;

18   Store position as $Q_{ij}(x)$;

         `/* Global Position Computation`   `*/`

19   For each leader x, compute: $T_i(x) = \sum_{j=1}^{\frac{B\alpha}{M}} Q_{ij}(x)$ Now $T_i(x)$ gives the exact position of x in D_i;

20 **foreach** *pair of consecutive leaders* (x, y) *in* L **do**

21   Compute number of elements between x and y in each A_{ij}:

$$\delta_{ij}(x) = \begin{cases} Q_{ij}(y) - Q_{ij}(x), & \text{if } y \notin A_{ij} \\ Q_{ij}(y) - Q_{ij}(x) - 1, & \text{if } y \in A_{ij} \end{cases}$$

22   Compute prefix sums over $\delta_{ij}(x)$ using PREFIX-SUM to obtain $\Delta_{ij}(x)$;

23   Initialize $\Delta_{i0}(x) = 0$;

24   Copy fragment:
$$A_{ij}[Q_{ij}(x) + 1 \dots Q_{ij}(x) + \delta_{ij}(x)] \to S_{ix}[\Delta_{i(j-1)}(x) + 1 \dots \Delta_{ij}(x)]$$

25 **foreach** *buffer* S_{ix} **do**

26   Sort S_{ix} internally in memory;

27   Copy sorted result to D_i starting at index $T_i(x) + 1$;

28 **return** D_i;

Step 7: For each consecutive leader pair $(x, y) \in L_i$, copy from each sub-array A_{ij} the elements between x and y:

$$A_{ij}[Q_{ij}(x) + 1 \dots Q_{ij}(x) + \delta_{ij}(x)] \quad \to \quad S_{ix}[\Delta_{ij-1}(x) + 1 \dots \Delta_{ij}(x)],$$

where $\delta_{ij}(x)$ counts elements between x and y in A_{ij}, and Δ_{ij}'s are the prefix sums over δ_{ij}'s.

Remarks: At most λ elements lie between x and y in each A_{ij}. Hence the total is bounded by $\frac{\lambda B \alpha}{M}$. We define

$$\delta_{ij}(x) = \begin{cases} Q_{ij}(y) - Q_{ij}(x), & y \notin A_{ij}, \\ Q_{ij}(y) - Q_{ij}(x) - 1, & y \in A_{ij}. \end{cases}$$

The prefix sum over $\{\delta_{i1}(x), \ldots, \delta_{i\frac{B\alpha}{M}}(x)\}$ yields $\{\Delta_{i1}(x), \ldots, \Delta_{i\frac{B\alpha}{M}}(x)\}$.

I/O Complexity: The prefix sums are dominated by the previous steps. Between any two leaders $(x, y) \in L_i$, there may be up to $\Delta_{i\frac{B\alpha}{M}}(x)$ elements. Reading them might require two additional I/Os per subarray, and then subsequent elimination of unwanted elements. (The details are omitted here.) In the worst case, the cost of data movement, will be $O\left(\Delta_{i\frac{B\alpha}{M}}(x)\right)$ per subarray. For the entire A_i, the number of I/Os needed would be $O(\alpha)$

Step 8: Each intermediate buffer S_{ix}, containing the elements between a pair of consecutive leaders $(x, y) \in L_i$, is sorted in internal memory. The sorted results are then written to the output segment D_i, specifically into the range $D_i[T_i(x) + 1 \ldots T_i(y)]$. These operations are executed in parallel for all such buffers.

I/O Complexity: If $\frac{\lambda B \alpha}{M} \leq M$, then sorting each S_{ix} in memory requires $O\left(\frac{\lambda \alpha}{M}\right)$ steps. Once sorted, writing them to the corresponding range in D_i also takes $O\left(\frac{\lambda \alpha}{M}\right)$ steps. The total number of I/Os per segment is $O(\alpha)$.

Parameter Assumptions: Suppose we set $M < B\alpha$ and $\lambda \geq B$.

Total Complexity for One Segment: Under the above assumptions, each segment can be sorted in $O\left(\frac{M}{B} + \log \frac{B\alpha}{M}\right)$ parallel steps and $O(\alpha + \frac{\alpha^2}{MB})$ I/O operations.

Total I/O Complexity Across All Segments: Given that there are $\frac{N}{B\alpha}$ segments and segment sorting is performed in parallel, the total I/O complexity becomes: $O(\frac{N}{B}(1 + \frac{\alpha}{MB}))$.

Stability Proof of `SortSegment`

A sorting algorithm is *stable* if for any equal elements $a_i = a_j$ with $i < j$, their relative order is preserved in the output.

Claim: `SortSegment` (Algorithm 1) is stable.

Proof: Consider two cases based on segment size α:

1. **Small Segment** $(\alpha \leq M/B)$
   The entire segment fits in memory. Using a stable in-memory sort (e.g., Merge Sort) preserves the order of equal elements.

2. **Large Segment** ($\alpha > M/B$)

   The algorithm proceeds in stages:
   - **Sub-array Sorting:** Each sub-array A_{ij} is sorted stably, preserving order within A_{ij}.
   - **Leader Selection:** Leaders are selected without altering internal order.
   - **Cross-Rank and Global Leader Order:** Equal leaders retain relative input positions when determining global ranks.
   - **Fragment Copying:** Elements between leaders x and y are copied into buffers S_{ix} in the same order as in A_{ij}.
   - **Final Buffer Sorting:** Each S_{ix} is stably sorted. Since buffers map to disjoint, ordered portions of D_i, equal elements across buffers preserve input order.

   Thus, at no stage is the original order of equal elements violated.

Conclusion: Both small and large segment cases preserve the relative order of equal elements. Hence, `SortSegment` is **stable**. $\qquad\qquad\square$

3.2   Phase B: Group Creation

Each iteration processes a window of b bits from each integer, where l is the maximum value. Let b_{start} and b_{end} be the window boundaries. After *Segment Sorting*, segments are ordered by bits in $[b_{\text{start}}, b_{\text{end}}]$. In *Group Creation*, elements with the same b-bit pattern are collected.

Group Definition. Two elements x, y belong to the same group iff their binary representations match in bit positions in $[b_{\text{start}}, b_{\text{end}}]$. Otherwise, they are separated.

Since b bits yield 2^b patterns, at most 2^b groups form per iteration. Groups are placed consecutively in the output array, ensuring:

- For $i < j$, all elements of G_i are less than those of G_j, with respect to bits examined thus far.

The result is a *partially sorted array*, used as input for the next iteration. The bit window shifts from LSB to MSB, processing b bits each time, until all $\log l$ bits are covered.

Iteration Bound. Each iteration handles b bits. Thus the total number of iterations required to scan all $\log l$ bits is $O\left(\frac{\log l}{b}\right)$.

The following detail the *Group Creation* steps.

For each segment A_i, where $1 \leq i \leq \frac{N}{B\alpha}$, execute the following steps in parallel:

Step 1: For each element $A_i[j]$, $1 \leq j \leq B\alpha$, extract bits in $[b_{\text{start}}, b_{\text{end}}]$ via a bitwise extraction procedure that we call `Bitwise`. Let the result be `val`, the integer formed by these bits.

Initialize an auxiliary array $count_i[1 \ldots \alpha]$ for each segment A_i, where $\alpha = 2^b$ and $b = b_{\text{end}} - b_{\text{start}} + 1$. Update:

$$count_i[\texttt{val}] \leftarrow count_i[\texttt{val}] + 1$$

This records the frequency of each b-bit pattern in segment A_i.

Remarks: To extract bits of $A_i[j]$, use `Bitwise` on $[b_{\text{start}}, b_{\text{end}}]$. The result `val` is the integer value of the selected bits. Each segment A_i has an array $count_i[1 \ldots \alpha]$, where $\alpha = 2^b$. Here $count_i[\text{val}]$ stores the frequency of pattern `val`.

To exploit parallelism and avoid write conflicts, the domain $\{1, \ldots, \alpha\}$ is split into subranges of size B. This requires identifying boundary blocks within A_i that separate these ranges. Let $\mathfrak{B}_i[1 \cdots \alpha]$ be an array that records the block indices acting as boundaries between subranges. Initially, $\mathfrak{B}_i$ is set to zero. For each processor j, where $1 \leq j \leq \alpha - 1$, the j-th processor reads two consecutive blocks jB and $(j+1)B$ of A_i.

For processor j, $1 \leq j \leq \alpha - 1$, define

$$k_{j1} = \left\lceil \frac{\texttt{Bitwise}(A_i[jB], b_{\text{start}}, b_{\text{end}})}{B} \right\rceil, \quad k_{j2} = \left\lceil \frac{\texttt{Bitwise}(A_i[(j+1)B], b_{\text{start}}, b_{\text{end}})}{B} \right\rceil.$$

Processors mark boundary block indices in $\mathfrak{B}_i$ using the following rules:

(a) **First Processor:**
  - If $k_{j1} = k_{j2}$: for $q = k_{j2} - 1$ to 1 : $\mathfrak{B}_i[qB] \leftarrow 1$
  - Else:
    - For $q = k_{j1} - 1$ to 1: $\mathfrak{B}_i[qB] \leftarrow 1$
    - For $q = k_{j2} - 1$ to k_{j1}: $\mathfrak{B}_i[qB] \leftarrow 2$
(b) **Intermediate Processors** ($2 \leq j \leq \alpha - 1$):
  - If $k_{j1} = k_{j2}$: no action is required.
  - Else: for $q = k_{j2-1}$ to k_{j1} : $\mathfrak{B}_i[qB] \leftarrow j + 1$
(c) **Last Processor:** Assign the last boundary: $\mathfrak{B}_i[k_{j1}B] \leftarrow \alpha$

Processor Distribution: Processors are assigned to subranges based on the boundary array $\mathfrak{B}_i$:

- For subrange 1 (i.e., $\{1, \ldots, B\}$), allocate $\mathfrak{B}_i[B] - 1$ processors.
- For subranges q where $2 \leq q \leq \alpha$:
  - If $\mathfrak{B}_i[qB] = 0$, assign no processors.
  - Otherwise, allocate $\mathfrak{B}_i[qB] - \mathfrak{B}_i[(q-1)B]$ processors.

If subrange k gets t processors, each scans one block of A_i from $\mathfrak{B}_i[(k-1)B]$ to $\mathfrak{B}_i[kB]$. Each processor maintains an auxiliary array of size B to count occurrences of values in $((k-1)B+1, \ldots, kB)$. These arrays are merged via a bottom-up binary reduction tree, and the resultant array is stored in $count_i[((k-1)B+1) \cdots kB]$.

I/O Complexity: The counting in Step 1 involves three sub-tasks:

1. Identify boundary block indices for subranges.
2. Allocate processors to subranges.
3. Count in parallel within each subrange.

- **Boundary Block Identification:** Each processor reads two consecutive blocks of A_i to compute boundaries, requiring at most 2α I/Os, i.e., $O(\alpha)$ per segment. Writing boundary indices to $\mathfrak{B}_i$ also costs $O(\alpha)$ I/Os. With $\frac{N}{B\alpha}$ segments, the total I/O complexity is $O\left(\frac{N}{B\alpha} \cdot \alpha\right) = O\left(\frac{N}{B}\right)$.

- **Processor Distribution:** Each subrange is assigned processors equal to the number of blocks it spans, computed as $\mathfrak{B}_i[qB] - \mathfrak{B}_i[(q-1)B]$ for the q-th subrange. Distributing processors for all subranges within a segment requires $O(\alpha)$ I/Os. Across all segments, the total I/O complexity is $O\left(\frac{N}{B\alpha} \cdot \alpha\right) = O\left(\frac{N}{B}\right)$.
- **Parallel Counting within Subranges:** In the worst case, $(\alpha - 1)$ subranges lie in one block, and the last spans all others, requiring $O(\alpha)$ I/Os for reading. After local counting, auxiliary arrays (one per processor) are merged by a bottom-up binary tree in $O(\log \alpha)$ steps and $O(\alpha)$ I/Os. Writing the aggregated result to array $count_i$ adds another $O(\alpha)$ I/Os.

Hence, the per-segment cost is $O(\alpha)$ I/Os and $O(\log \alpha)$ steps. Overall, the total I/O complexity is: $O\left(\frac{N}{B\alpha} \cdot \alpha\right) = O\left(\frac{N}{B}\right)$ and the step complexity is at most: $O\left(\max\left\{\sum_{q=1}^{\alpha} \log t_q\right\}\right) = O(\log \alpha)$ where t_q denotes the number of blocks in the q-th subrange.

Summary: Step 1 requires at most $O(\log \alpha)$ parallel steps and incurs a total of $O\left(\frac{N}{B}\right)$ I/O operations across all segments.

Step 2: For each block index j, $1 \leq j \leq \frac{\alpha}{B}$, compute

$$count[((j-1)B+1)\ldots jB] = \sum_{i=1}^{\frac{N}{B\alpha}} count_i[((j-1)B+1)\ldots jB],$$

using the PEM prefix sum. The result is stored in the global array $count[1 \ldots \alpha]$.

Remarks: This step performs $\frac{\alpha}{B}$ prefix sums in parallel. Each aggregates the j-th B-block across all local arrays $count_i$. At the end, the global frequencies of all b-bit values are known.

I/O Complexity: A prefix sum on $\frac{N}{B\alpha}$ elements costs $O(\log \frac{N}{B\alpha})$ steps and $O(\frac{N}{B\alpha})$ I/Os. With $\frac{\alpha}{B}$ such sums, the total is

$$O\left(\log \frac{N}{B\alpha}\right) \text{ steps}, \quad O\left(\frac{N}{B\alpha} \cdot \frac{\alpha}{B}\right) = O\left(\frac{N}{B}\right) \text{ I/Os}.$$

Thus Step 2 completes in $O(\log \frac{N}{B\alpha})$ steps and $O(\frac{N}{B})$ I/Os.

Step 3: For each segment A_i, compute in parallel:

$$count_i[j] = \sum_{k=1}^{j} count_i[k], \quad 1 \leq j \leq \alpha.$$

Remarks: This gives, for each segment, the number of elements strictly less than the first occurrence of the j-th group identifier. In total, $\frac{N}{B\alpha}$ prefix sums are performed in parallel, one per segment.

I/O Complexity: Each prefix sum runs on an array of length α, i.e., $\frac{\alpha}{B}$ blocks. By the PEM model, this costs $O(\log \frac{\alpha}{B})$ steps and $O(\frac{\alpha}{B})$ I/Os. Across all $\frac{N}{B\alpha}$ segments, the total is

$$O\left(\log \tfrac{\alpha}{B}\right) \text{ steps}, \quad O\left(\tfrac{\alpha}{B} \cdot \tfrac{N}{B\alpha}\right) = O\left(\tfrac{N}{B}\right) \text{ I/Os.}$$

Hence Step 3 completes in $O(\log \frac{\alpha}{B})$ steps and $O(\frac{N}{B})$ I/Os.

Step 4: For each group j, $1 \leq j \leq \alpha$, copy elements of segment A_i from

$$A_i[\mathtt{count}_i[j-1]+1 \ldots \mathtt{count}_i[j]]$$

into the global buffer S_j at

$$S_j[\Delta_{i-1}+1 \ldots \Delta_i].$$

Remarks: Let $\delta_{ij} = \mathtt{count}_i[j] - \mathtt{count}_i[j-1]$ denote the number of elements in A_i of group j. Define prefix sums $\Delta_k = \sum_{i=1}^{k} \delta_{ij}$ for $1 \leq k \leq N/(B\alpha)$, which determine the destination indices in S_j for the elements copied from segment A_i.

I/O Complexity: Operations are:

- Compute a prefix sum over $N/(B\alpha)$ segments to determine write positions.
- Copy elements from each segment A_i to S_j.

Both require: $O\left(\log\left(\frac{N}{B\alpha}\right)\right)$ steps and $O\left(\frac{N}{B}\right)$ I/Os. Thus Step 4 completes in $O(\log \frac{N}{B\alpha})$ steps and $O(N/B)$ I/Os.

Step 5: For each group j, $1 \leq j \leq \alpha$, copy

$$D[\Delta_{j-1}+1 \ldots \Delta_j] \leftarrow S_j[1 \ldots \delta_j].$$

Remarks: Let $\delta_j = \mathtt{count}[j]$ be the total number of elements in group j. Define prefix sums $\Delta_k = \sum_{j=1}^{k} \delta_j$ for $1 \leq k \leq \alpha$, which determine destination indices in D. This ensures elements of the same group appear contiguously, with groups sorted by their b-bit identifiers.

I/O Complexity:

- Prefix sum over α group counts: $O(\log(\alpha/B))$ steps.
- Copying all elements from S_j to D: $O(N/B)$ I/Os.

Hence, Step 5 completes in $O(\log(\alpha/B))$ steps and $O(N/B)$ I/Os.

Overall Complexity of Group Creation: Combining Steps 1 through 5, the total number of steps required for the group creation phase is: $O\left(\log\left(\frac{N}{B\alpha}\right) + \log\left(\frac{\alpha}{B}\right)\right)$ with a total I/O complexity of $O\left(\frac{N}{B}\right)$

3.3 INTEGER SORT Algorithm

This subsection presents our integer sorting algorithm, which iteratively applies two sub-procedures: *Segment Sorting* (Subsect. 3.1) and *Group Creation* (Subsect. 3.2).

Step 1 (Initialization): Set the bit window boundaries:

$$b_{\text{start}} \leftarrow 1, \quad b_{\text{end}} \leftarrow b = \log \alpha$$

where α is a parameter to be chosen. Each iteration processes a $b = b_{\text{end}} - b_{\text{start}} + 1$ bit window.

Remarks: The algorithm scans integers LSB to MSB, forming at most $2^b = \alpha$ groups per iteration, unlike Han's algorithm where groups grow exponentially over the iterations.

I/O Complexity: $O(1)$ time and I/O, as initialization scans no input.

Step 2 (Iterative Bitwise Refinement): For $I = 1$ to $\frac{\log l}{b}$, process b bits per iteration. Since the bit length of even the largest element is at most $\log l$, this ensures that all N integers are fully sorted.

Step 2.1 (Parallel Segment Sorting): Divide A into $\frac{N}{B\alpha}$ segments of size $B\alpha$. For each segment A_i, apply `SortSegment` (Subsect. 3.1) in parallel.

I/O Complexity:

$$O\left(\frac{M}{B} + \log \frac{B\alpha}{M}\right) \text{ parallel steps}, \quad O\left(\frac{N}{B}\right) \text{ total I/O}$$

Step 2.2 (Group Formation Across Segments): Apply `GroupCreation` (Subsect. 3.2) to each A_i in parallel, regrouping elements by the current bit window.

I/O Complexity:

$$O\left(\log \frac{N}{B\alpha} + \log \frac{\alpha}{B}\right) \text{ steps}, \quad O\left(\frac{N}{B}\right) \text{ total I/O}$$

Step 2.3 (Update Bit Range): Set $b_{\text{start}} \leftarrow b_{\text{end}} + 1, \quad b_{\text{end}} \leftarrow (I + 1)b$.
   Set $A \leftarrow D$ for the next iteration, where D is the partially sorted output array.

Step 3 (Return Output): Return D containing the sorted array.

Overall Complexity - Step complexity:

$$O\left(\left(\frac{M}{B} + \log \frac{N}{B\alpha} + \log \frac{\alpha}{B} + \log \frac{B\alpha}{M}\right) \cdot \frac{\log l}{\log \alpha}\right)$$

- I/O complexity:

$$O\left(\frac{N}{B} \cdot \frac{\log l}{\log \alpha}\right)$$

With $\alpha = \frac{M^2}{B^2}$, we have the following:

Theoretical Bound

Theorem 1. *The algorithm sorts $A[1 \cdots N]$ with integers in $[1, l]$ in*

$$O\left(\frac{\log l}{\log m}\left(\frac{M}{B} + \log_{M/B}\frac{N}{B}\right)\right)$$

parallel steps and

$$O\left(\frac{N}{B} \cdot \frac{\log l}{\log(M/B)}\right)$$

I/O operations on the CREW PEM model.

4   Conclusions

We present the first deterministic optimal algorithm for integer sorting in the *Parallel External Memory (PEM)* model. It overcomes limitations of prior PRAM-based methods using prefix sums, search, cross-ranking, multi-way merging, and compaction. Unlike Han's method, which exponentially grows groups per phase, our approach fixes the number of groups, ensuring balanced parallelism and predictable memory usage.

The algorithm sorts N integers from $[1, l]$ in

$$O\left(\frac{\log l}{\log m}\left(\frac{M}{B} + \log_{M/B}\frac{N}{B}\right)\right)$$

parallel steps and

$$O\left(\frac{N}{B} \cdot \frac{\log l}{\log(M/B)}\right)$$

I/O operations.

Practicality is ensured via stable segment sorting and efficient prefix-sum-based group formation, avoiding the large constants from AKS networks or expander graphs, enabling real-system implementation.

Future work includes: (i) cache-oblivious variants removing explicit block/memory parameters, (ii) randomized or approximate versions for simpler implementation, (iii) extensions to PEM priority queues, selection, and graph processing, and (iv) sorting of variable length integers.

Acknowledgements. The authors gratefully acknowledge the three anonymous reviewers for their valuable comments and suggestions, which helped improve the clarity and accuracy of this paper.

References

1. Han, Y., He, X.: Parallel integer sorting is more efficient than parallel comparison sorting on exclusive write PRAMs. SIAM J. Comput. **31**(6), 1852–1878 (2002)
2. Han, Y., He, X.: More efficient parallel integer sorting. In: Snoeyink, J., Lu, P., Su, K., Wang, L. (eds.) AAIM/FAW -2012. LNCS, vol. 7285, pp. 279–290. Springer, Heidelberg (2012). https://doi.org/10.1007/978-3-642-29700-7_26
3. Fredman, M.L., Willard, D.E.: Surpassing the information theoretic bound with fusion trees. J. Comput. Syst. Sci. **47**(3), 424–436 (1993)
4. Ajtai, M., Komlós, J., Szemerédi, E.: Sorting in $c \log n$ parallel steps. Combinatorica **3**(1), 1–19 (1983)
5. Saxena, S.: Parallel integer sorting and simulation amongst CRCW models. Acta Inf. **33**(7), 607–619 (1996)
6. Andersson, A., Hagerup, T., Nilsson, S., Raman, R.: Sorting in linear time? In: Proceedings of 27th ACM Symposium on Theory of Computing (STOC), pp. 67–74. ACM, New York (1995)
7. Albers, S., Hagerup, T.: Improved parallel integer sorting without concurrent writing. Inf. Comput. **136**(1), 25–51 (1997)
8. Arge, L., Goodrich, M.T., Nelson, M., Sitchinava, N.: Fundamental parallel algorithms for private-cache chip multiprocessors. In: Proceedings of 20th ACM Symposium on Parallelism in Algorithms and Architectures (SPAA), pp. 197–206. ACM (2008)
9. Aggarwal, A., Vitter, J.S.: The input/output complexity of sorting and related problems. Commun. ACM **31**(9), 1116–1127 (1988)
10. Sajith, G.: Parallel algorithms for multiway merging, sorting and graph colouring. Ph.D. thesis, IIT Kanpur (1997)
11. Beame, P.W., Håstad, J.: Optimal bounds for decision problems on the CRCW PRAM. J. ACM **36**(3), 643–670 (1989)
12. Cook, S.A., Dwork, C., Reischuk, R.: Upper and lower time bounds for parallel random access machines without simultaneous writes. SIAM J. Comput. **15**(1), 87–97 (1986)
13. Han, Y.: Improved fast integer sorting in linear space. Inf. Comput. **170**(1), 81–94 (2001)
14. Han, Y.: Fast integer sorting in linear space. In: Reichel, H., Tison, S. (eds.) STACS 2000. LNCS, vol. 1770, pp. 242–253. Springer, Heidelberg (2000). https://doi.org/10.1007/3-540-46541-3_20
15. Han, Y.: Deterministic sorting in $O(n \log \log n)$ time and linear space. J. Algorithms **50**(1), 96–105 (2004)
16. Thorup, M.: Faster deterministic sorting and priority queues in linear space. In: Proceedings of 9th ACM–SIAM Symposium on Discrete Algorithms (SODA), pp. 550–555. ACM/SIAM (1998)
17. Han, Y.: Fast integer sorting in linear space. In: Reichel, H., Tison, S. (eds.) STACS 2000. LNCS, vol. 1770, pp. 242–253. Springer, Heidelberg (2000). https://doi.org/10.1007/3-540-46541-3_20
18. Farhadi, A., Hajiaghayi, M.T., Larsen, K.G., Shi, E.: Lower bounds for external memory integer sorting via network coding. In: Proceedings of 51st ACM Symposium on Theory of Computing (STOC), pp. 997–1008 (2019)

Bayesian Optimization for Two Echelon Vehicle Routing Problem Using Drone for Last Mile Delivery

Preetam Kumar Sur[1]([✉]) [iD], Anubrata Naskar[2] [iD], and Sunirmal Khatua[2] [iD]

[1] Department of Computer Science and Engineering, Government College of Engineering and Textile Technology, Serampore, West Bengal, India
`preetam.k.sur@gcetts.ac.in`
[2] Department of Computer Science and Engineering, University of Calcutta, Kolkata, West Bengal, India
`anubrata.naskar@gmail.com, skhatuacomp@caluniv.ac.in`

Abstract. The immense growth in e-Commerce has intensified the need for efficient last-mile delivery systems. This paper introduces an enhanced Two-Echelon Vehicle Routing Problem with Drones (2E-VRPD) that addresses critical limitations by hyperparameter tuning using Bayesian optimization. A new algorithm is proposed that extends the original Drone Truck Route Construction (DTRC) algorithm by incorporating clustering for customer segmentation and Bayesian optimization using the OPTUNA framework for dynamic synchronization of trucks and drones. Experiments with benchmark instances and real-world case studies demonstrate an average reduction of 9.6% in delivery time.

Keywords: Last mile delivery · Unmanned Aerial Vehicle (UAV) · Bayesian Optimization

1 Introduction

The global last-mile delivery market, valued at \$169.8 billion in 2023, is projected to reach \$564.3 billion in 2032, representing a compound annual growth rate of 16.2% from 2024 to 2032 [1]. This unprecedented growth has exposed critical limitations in traditional ground-based delivery systems, particularly in urban environments where traffic congestion and restricted access zones significantly impede operational efficiency.

Traditional delivery approaches using only ground vehicles face several fundamental challenges, including urban congestion that delays deliveries and restricted access during peak hours. The use of Unmanned Aerial Vehicles (UAVs) for efficient last-mile delivery is gaining popularity due to their ability to overcome the challenges faced by traditional logistics delivery methods that rely solely on delivery vans. In coordinated truck-drone delivery, trucks are

C. Zaroliagis et al. (Eds.): ICAA 2026, LNCS 16423, pp. 117–128, 2026.
https://doi.org/10.1007/978-3-032-15621-1_10

equipped with the parcels to be delivered to their destinations along with drones. In this hybrid approach, drones and trucks can deliver parcels concurrently. A drone loaded with a subset of parcels from its truck delivers to its destination, while the truck continues to deliver en route. This collaborative approach, known as the Two-Echelon Vehicle Routing Problem with Drones (2EVRPD), leverages complementary capabilities - trucks provide large capacity and extended range, while drones offer rapid deployment and access to restricted areas.

In this paper, a comprehensive 2E-VRPD formulation is developed that incorporates dynamic positioning of the departure and arrival of the drone. Next, an algorithm is proposed to cluster the delivery points such that the clusters are well distributed and the total demand of no cluster exceeds the capacity of a truck. Finally, a Bayesian optimization using the OPTUNA framework is used to determine the departure and arrival points of drones, which ensures minimal time returns of the trucks to the depot.

2   Related Work

Classical two-echelon distribution systems were formalized by Jacobsen and Madsen [2], establishing the mathematical framework for hierarchical routing problems. Crainic et al. [3] provided a foundational 2E-VRP formulation to demonstrate significant cost reductions in urban environments.

Murray and Chu [4] introduced the Flying Sidekick TSP (FSTSP), which pioneered synchronized truck-drone operations. Agatz et al. [5] proposed the TSP with Drone (TSP-D), introducing flexible launch and retrieval capabilities. Extensions to multi-vehicle scenarios were developed by Wang et al. [6] and Schermer et al. [7].

Kitjacharoenchai et al. [8] introduced the Two-Echelon Vehicle Routing Problem with Drones (2E-VRPD), combining hierarchical structure with drone-truck collaboration. Their Drone Truck Route Construction (DTRC) algorithm demonstrated 13.2% average improvement over classical VRP solutions.

Modern optimization techniques, particularly Bayesian optimization [9], have shown superior performance in complex optimization landscapes. The OPTUNA framework [10] implements advanced Tree-structured Parzen Estimator (TPE) algorithms that demonstrated effectiveness across diverse domains.

3   Problem Description

Consider a depot and a set of n delivery points. The delivery points are connected through the road network through which the truck can reach them. However, drones fly through a Euclidean path from one hop to the next. We modeled the depot and all the delivery points as a complete graph $G = (V, E)$, where $V = \{v_0, v_1, ..., v_n\}$ and v_0 represents the depot and all other vertices represent the delivery points. Each vertex v_i has a location (x_i, y_i). The distance between a pair of vertices (v_i, v_j) is given by d_{ij}. A delivery point v_i will receive a parcel weighing q_i units. Once a truck or drone reaches a delivery point, it takes some time s_i, which is termed *service time*, to drop the package at the location.

The depot v_0, along with the parcels, has a set of K homogeneous trucks $T = \{T_1, T_2, ..., T_k\}$. A truck T_i can carry a set of drones $D^{T_i} = \{D_1^{T_i}, D_2^{T_i}, ..., D_{D_{max}}^{T_i}\}$, where D_{max} is the maximum number of drones that a truck can carry. Moreover, a truck can carry parcels weighing not more than Q_T units and moves at a speed of V_T units. Each truck starts from v_0 loaded with packages and drones, delivers all packages using onboard personnel and drones along the planned route, and then returns to the depot with the drones.

Each drone can carry up to Q_D weight per flight, moves at a speed of V_D, and has a battery capacity of B. A drone $D_i^{T_k}$ of truck T_k is loaded with a few parcels from T_k for its next flight, departs from the truck T_k en route, and delivers the parcels to their destinations. The truck T_k during that period continues to deliver other parcels using the road network. The drone $D_i^{T_k}$ then returns to T_k en route while the truck travels to its next delivery point. Once a drone rendezvous with its carrying truck, its battery is replaced with a fully charged one, and it can then be used again to ship other parcels from the truck.

Let $\mathcal{T}_k$ denote the time duration after which the truck T_k returns to the depot, delivering all the parcels. The objective of this work is to minimize the total return time of all k trucks to the depot after delivering all packages to the delivery points, i.e. $minimize \sum_{i=1}^{k} \mathcal{T}_k$.

4   Mathematical Model

Let x_{ij}^k be the decision variable that is 1 if a truck T_k visits the edge $(v_i, v_j) \in E$, otherwise 0. Let x_{ij}^{kd} be the decision variable that is 1 if the drone $D_d^{T_k}$ visits the edge $(v_i, v_j) \in E$, otherwise 0. Let y_i^k denote the decision variable, which is 1 if the delivery point v_i is served by the truck T_k, otherwise 0. And, similarly, let y_i^{kd} denote the decision variable, which is 1 if the delivery point v_i is served by the drone $D_d^{T_k}$, otherwise 0.

Therefore, the return time of the truck T_k can now be defined as

$$\mathcal{T}_k = \sum_{i=0}^{n} \sum_{j=0}^{n} \left(\frac{d_{ij}}{V_T} + s_i \right) . x_{ij}^k \tag{1}$$

Hence, the objective function can be rewritten as

$$minimize \sum_{k=1}^{K} \sum_{i=0}^{n} \sum_{j=0}^{n} \left(\frac{d_{ij}}{V_T} + s_i \right) . x_{ij}^k \tag{2}$$

When a truck arrives at a delivery point, it delivers the package to that point. Then starts for the next delivery point of its planned route. Hence, if a truck arrives at a node, it serves the node and leaves the node only once. Therefore,

$$\sum_{j=1}^{n} x_{ij}^k = \sum_{j=1}^{n} x_{ji}^k = y_i^k \quad , \text{for } 1 \leq k \leq K \wedge 1 \leq i \leq n \tag{3}$$

A customer is served only once by a truck or a drone, but not both. Hence,

$$\sum_{k=1}^{K} y_i^k + \sum_{k=1}^{K} \sum_{d=1}^{D_{max}} y_i^{kd} = 1 \quad , \text{ for } 1 \leq i \leq n \tag{4}$$

holds.

Moreover, each truck can carry parcels weighing at most Q_T units. This includes all packages delivered by the truck, as well as those delivered by all the drones carried by that truck. The following formula represents this condition.

$$\sum_{i=1}^{n} q_i . y_i^k + \sum_{d=1}^{D_{max}} \sum_{j=1}^{n} q_j . y_j^{kd} \leq Q_t \quad , \text{ for } 1 \leq k \leq K. \tag{5}$$

Unlike [8], this paper considers that a drone can take off and land en route while the truck is moving. Hence, a drone reaches its first node of a tour from a point in the road network. Let v_m be the first node of a drone flight path $D_d^{T_k}$, then

$$\sum_{i=1}^{n} x_{im}^{kd} = 0 \quad and \quad \sum_{j=1}^{n} x_{mj}^{kd} = 1 \tag{6}$$

holds. The drone then moves to the next delivery points along its path and eventually reaches the last one, after which it will return to its truck. If v_m is the last node in a drone flight path $D_d^{T_k}$, then

$$\sum_{i=1}^{n} x_{im}^{kd} = 1 \quad and \quad \sum_{j=1}^{n} x_{mj}^{kd} = 0 \tag{7}$$

holds. It is also possible that v_m is the only node in a drone flight, which means the drone takes off from the truck and flies directly to the delivery point v_m to deliver the package, then returns to the truck. In this case, we will have

$$\sum_{i=1}^{n} x_{im}^{kd} = 0 \quad and \quad \sum_{j=1}^{n} x_{mj}^{kd} = 0. \tag{8}$$

However, (8) cannot solely determine whether the drone serves the delivery point v_m. The relation in (8) also holds if a truck delivers to v_m. Hence, if $y_m^{kd} = 1$ along with (8), it can determine that v_m is the only delivery point in a tour of drone $D_d^{T_k}$. Therefore, an indicator function $I_f^{kd}(m)$ can be defined as

$$I_f^{kd}(m) = \left(1 - \sum_{i=1}^{n} x_{im}^{kd}\right) . \left\{ \sum_{j=1}^{n} x_{mj}^{kd} + \left(1 - \sum_{h=1}^{n} x_{mh}^{kd}\right) . y_m^{kd} \right\} \tag{9}$$

to denote if a vertex v_m is the first node visited by the drone $D_d^{T_k}$ in any of its tours. This indicator function will return 1 if it is so. Similarly, another indicator function $I_l^{kd}(m)$ can be defined to denote if a vertex v_m is the last node visited by the drone $D_d^{T_k}$ in any of its tours. Then $I_l^{kd}(m)$ can be defined as follows.

$$I_l^{kd}(m) = \left(1 - \sum_{j=1}^{n} x_{mj}^{kd}\right) \cdot \left\{\sum_{i=1}^{n} x_{im}^{kd} + \left(1 - \sum_{h=1}^{n} x_{mh}^{kd}\right) \cdot y_m^{kd}\right\} \tag{10}$$

Whenever a delivery point is served by a drone or a truck, it becomes the source node for the same drone or truck for their voyage to the destination. In the case of a drone, the decision variables associated with the drone together cannot determine each tour separately. To incorporate the tour-specific constraints of a drone, a mechanism is needed to recursively update a delivery point as the source once a drone reaches it. For this, a dynamic source indexing for the decision variables of drones is introduced. Suppose a drone $D_d^{T_k}$ starts a tour in which it first visits the delivery point v_m. Then, in the tour, if the drone next visits v_j for any value of $1 \le j \ne m \le n$, the dynamic indexing of source node is defined as -

$$i_{m,j} = \begin{cases} m & \text{, if } j = 0 \\ j & \text{, if } x_{i_{m,(j-1)}j}^{kd} = 1 \\ i_{m,(j-1)} & \text{, otherwise} \end{cases} \tag{11}$$

In each tour, a drone can carry up to Q_D weight per tour. With the help of (9)–(11), the capacity constraint of a drone can be expressed as follows.

$$I_f^{kd}(m).\left(q_m + \sum_{h=1}^{n} q_h.x_{i_{m,(h-1)}h}^{kd}\right) \le Q_D \quad, \forall \, m \le n, \ k \le K, \ d \le D_{max} \tag{12}$$

Let a drone $D_d^{T_k}$ start a tour whose first delivery point is v_f. Then, the point on the road from which the drone leaves the truck T_k for this tour is indicated by l_f^{kd}. The coordinates of l_f^{kd} are denoted by $(x_{l_f^{kd}}, y_{l_f^{kd}})$. Let the point l_f^{kd} lies on the path segment when the truck T_k traverses from v_i to v_j. Assume α_f^{kd} be the decision variable which denotes the fraction of the road segment from which drone $D_d^{T_k}$ starts it tour to its first delivery point v_f. Then,

$$x_{l_f^{kd}} = (1 - \alpha_f^{kd}).x_i + \alpha_f^{kd}.x_j \tag{13}$$

$$y_{l_f^{kd}} = (1 - \alpha_f^{kd}).y_i + \alpha_f^{kd}.y_j \tag{14}$$

Let another indicator function $I_p(v_i, v_j)$ denote whether a point p lies on the road connecting the delivery point v_i and v_j. This function can be defined as below-

$$I_p(v_i, v_j) = \begin{cases} 1 & \text{, if } \frac{x_p - x_i}{y_p - y_i} = \frac{x_p - x_j}{y_p - y_j} \ \wedge \ x_i \le x_p \le x_j \ \wedge \ y_i \le y_p \le y_j \\ 0 & \text{, otherwise} \end{cases} \tag{15}$$

Let $\mathcal{NN}(l_m^{kd})$ denote the next node visited by the truck T_k on its route once the drone $D_d^{T_k}$ launches from the point l_m^{kd} towards v_m. Therefore,

$$\mathcal{NN}(l_m^{kd}) = j \mid x_{ij}^k = 1 \ \wedge\ I_{l_m^{kd}}(v_i, v_j) = 1 \quad \forall (v_i, v_j) \in E \tag{16}$$

Similarly, when a drone delivers to the last delivery point v_l in its flight, then the point on the road where the drone converges with T_k is denoted by r_l^{kd}. The coordinates of r_l^{kd} are denoted by $(x_{r_l^{kd}}, y_{r_l^{kd}})$. Let the point r_l^{kd} lies on the path segment when the truck T_k traverses from v_i to v_j. Assume β_f^{kd} be the decision variable which denotes the fraction of the road segment where the drone $D_d^{T_k}$ rendezvous with the truck at the end of its tour. Then,

$$x_{r_l^{kd}} = (1 - \beta_l^{kd}).x_i + \beta_l^{kd}.x_j \tag{17}$$

$$y_{r_l^{kd}} = (1 - \beta_l^{kd}).y_i + \beta_l^{kd}.y_j \tag{18}$$

Let $\mathcal{PN}(r_m^{kd})$ denote the last node visted by truck T_k on its route before it meets the drone $D_d^{T_k}$ at the point r_m^{kd}. Hence,

$$\mathcal{PN}(r_m^{kd}) = i \mid x_{ij}^k = 1 \ \wedge\ I_{r_m^{kd}}(v_i, v_j) = 1 \quad \forall (v_i, v_j) \in E \tag{19}$$

Now, let $dist(a, p)$ be the Euclidean distance between a vertex v_a and any point on the road p. If v_m is the first node visited by a drone $D_d^{T_k}$ in one of its tours, then using (9)–(11), the total path length of the tour, denoted by $\mathcal{L}_m^{kd}$, can be defined as-

$$\mathcal{L}_m^{kd} = dist(m, l_m^{kd}) + \sum_{h=1}^{n} d_{i_{m,(h-1)}h}.x_{i_{m,(h-1)}h}^{kd} + dist(i_{m,n}, r_{i_{m,n}}^{kd}) \tag{20}$$

The battery capacity of the drone bounds the flight time of each drone tour [11]. The flight time of a drone tour includes the travel time of the drone in its tour, along with the total service time for all the nodes it serves in that tour. Therefore, the limitation of drone flight time in each tour can be represented using the following.

$$I_f^{kd}(m). \left(\frac{\mathcal{L}_m^{kd}}{V_D} + \sum_{h=1}^{n} s_h.x_{i_{m,(h-1)}h}^{kd} \right) \leq B \quad , \forall\ m \leq n, \ k \leq K, \ d \leq D_{max} \tag{21}$$

When a drone $D_d^{T_k}$ leaves the truck T_k at l_m^{kd}, the total distance traversed by the truck from its next delivery point to reach the depot is given by -

$$\mathcal{L}_{l_m^{kd}}^{k} = \sum_{h=1}^{n} d_{i_{\mathcal{NN}(l_m^{kd}),(h-1)}h}.x_{i_{\mathcal{NN}(l_m^{kd}),(h-1)}h}^{k} \tag{22}$$

Similarly, when a drone $D_d^{T_k}$ meets the truck T_k at r_m^{kd}, the total distance traversed by the truck from its previous delivery point to the depot is given by -

$$\mathcal{L}_{r_m^{kd}}^{k} = \sum_{h=1}^{n} d_{i_{\mathcal{PN}(r_m^{kd}),(h-1)}h}.x_{i_{\mathcal{PN}(r_m^{kd}),(h-1)}h}^{k} \tag{23}$$

Hence, the total distance traversed by the truck T_k once a drone $D_d^{T_k}$ starts a tour from the point l_m^{kd} and meets the truck back at point r_m^{kd} is given by,

$$\mathcal{L}_m^k = dist\left(\mathcal{NN}(l_m^{kd}), l_m^{kd}\right) + \mathcal{L}_{l_m^{kd}}^k - \mathcal{L}_{r_m^{kd}}^k + dist\left(\mathcal{PN}(r_m^{kd}), r_m^{kd}\right) \qquad (24)$$

To ensure proper synchronization between the drones and the trucks such that the truck does not have to wait for a drone to meet at the rendezvous point we need to ensure that

$$I_f^{kd}(m).\mathcal{L}_m^k.V_D = I_f^{kd}(m).\mathcal{L}_m^{kd}.V_T \quad \forall\, m \le n,\ k \le K,\ d \le D_{max} \qquad (25)$$

5   Proposed Solution

First, the delivery points are divided into K clusters such that the cluster heads are distributed enough throughout the region of interest. The delivery points in a cluster will be served by one of the K trucks. Since the trucks are capacitated, the clusters should be built such that the total demands of a cluster must be within the capacity of a truck, i.e. Q_T. Once a cluster is built, Christofide's algorithm is applied to each cluster to get a path for the truck to cover all the delivery points and return to the depot. Then, local search techniques like 2-opt, single-point relocation and point-pair swapping are applied independently, and the best among those that provides minimum total tour length is selected.

We then modify the DTRC algorithm given in [8] and name it as the DTRC' algorithm to be used in Algorithm 3. In DTRC' algorithm, we use Algorithm 1 and Algorithm 2 in place of Clarke and Wright Saving Algorithm of DTRC algorithm to construct the initial truck routes. Rest of the algorithm in DTRC' remains unchanged as original DTRC algorithm.

The core innovation of our approach lies in leveraging Bayesian optimization to navigate the complex, high-dimensional search space of drone positioning parameters efficiently. Unlike traditional optimization methods that may get trapped in local optima or require excessive computational resources, Bayesian optimization provides a principled statistical approach to finding global optima with significantly fewer function evaluations.

In the drone route construction algorithm, for each drone tour obtained from the DTRC' algorithm, the point on the road from where the drone tour should begin and the point on the road where the drone tour ends by meeting its truck are decided. To generate an initial candidate set for α_m^{kd}, Latin Hypercube Sampling (LHS) is used, where the interval $[0,1]$ is divided into n equal sub-intervals and then, a point from each sub-interval is randomly chosen to be treated as the initial candidates for the Bayesian optimizer. Next, several trials are made to improve the value of α_m^{kd}. In each trial, first the surrogate model is trained with the past values of α and $f(\alpha)$. Then, the expected improvements are calculated for each candidate value of α, and the one with the highest expected improvement value is chosen to be the value of α_m^{kd}.

Algorithm 1: Cluster-Delivery-Nodes

Input   : Delivery points $V - \{v_0\}$. Number of Trucks K. Truck Capacity Q_T.

Output   : $\mathcal{C}$, a set of K clusters of delivery points.

1   $\mathcal{C} \leftarrow \{\}$;   // $\mathcal{C}_i$ represents i^{th} cluster having cluster head c_i.

2   $c_1 \leftarrow$ Select a random delivery point from $V - \{v_0\}$

3   $c_2 \leftarrow \underset{v \in V - \{v_0\}}{\arg\max} \sqrt{(x_{c_1} - x_v)^2 + (y_{c_1} - y_v)^2}$

4   $\mathcal{H} \leftarrow \{c_1, c_2\}$

5   **for** $j \leftarrow 3$ **to** K **do**

6     $c_j \leftarrow \underset{v \in V - (\mathcal{H} \cup \{v_0\})}{\arg\max} \frac{1}{j-1} \sum_{m=1}^{j-1} \sqrt{(x_m - x_v)^2 + (y_m - y_v)^2}$

7     $\mathcal{H} \leftarrow \mathcal{H} \cup \{c_j\}$

8   **foreach** $p \in V - (\mathcal{H} \cup \{v_0\})$ **do**

9     $E \leftarrow \{\}$

10   **while** $E \neq \mathcal{H}$ **do**

11      $c_i \leftarrow \underset{c_h \in \mathcal{H} - E}{\arg\min} \sqrt{(x_p - x_{c_h})^2 + (y_p - y_{c_h})^2}$

12   **if** $\sum_{l=1}^{|\mathcal{C}_i|} q_l + q_p \leq Q_T$ **then**

13       $\mathcal{C}_i \leftarrow \mathcal{C}_i \cup \{p\}$

14   **Break**

15   **else**

16       $E \leftarrow E \cup \{c_i\}$

Algorithm 2: Construct-Truck-Routes

Input   : Delivery points $V - \{v_0\}$. Number of Trucks K. Truck Capacity Q_T. Distance matrix d.

Output   : Truck routes only solution, S^{CVRP}.

1   $S^{CVRP} \leftarrow \{\}$

2   $\mathcal{C} \leftarrow Cluster - Delivery - Nodes(V - v_0, K, Q_T)$

3   **for** $c \in \mathcal{C}$ **do**

4     $R \leftarrow Christofides - TSP(c,\ d)$

5     $R_{2-OPT} \leftarrow Apply\ 2 - OPT\ on\ R$

6     $R_{reloc} \leftarrow Apply\ Single\ Point\ Relocation\ on\ R$

7     $R_{swap} \leftarrow Apply\ Point - pair\ Swapping\ on\ R$

8     $R' \leftarrow Best(R, R_{2-OPT}, R_{reloc}, R_{swap})$

9     $S^{CVRP} \leftarrow S^{CVRP} \cup R'$

Once the value of α_m^{kd} is found, the point, p_{launch}, from which the drone starts the tour can be calculated. Based on the total parcel weight in the planned tour of the drone and the battery capacity of the drone maximum flight time possible for

Algorithm 3: Construct-Drone-Routes

1   $S^{2EVRPD} \leftarrow$ Truck and Drone routes using DTRC'
2   Define objective function $f(\alpha)$ as given in (2)
3   **for** $k \leftarrow 1$ **to** K **do**
4   **for** $d \leftarrow 1$ **to** D_{max} **do**
5   **foreach** $Tour\ \tau\ of\ drone\ D_d^{T_k}\ in\ S^{2EVRPD}$ **do**
6      $m \leftarrow$ First node of τ
7   Initialize Bayesian optimizer with TPE sampler and pruning mechanism.
8      $\alpha_{best} \leftarrow \phi$
9      $f_{best} \leftarrow \infty$
10   Generate initial candidate set for hyperparameter α_m^{kd} using Latin Hypercube Sampling (LHS)
11   **for** $t \leftarrow 1$ **to** N_{Trials} **do**
12   //Propose new hyperparameter α_m^{kd} using Bayesian Optimizer
13   Train surrogate model on past evaluated pairs $(\alpha, f(\alpha))$
14       $EI_{max} \leftarrow -\infty$
15   **foreach** $candidate\ \alpha$ **do**
16   Calculate $\mu(\alpha)\ and\ \sigma(\alpha)$
17        $Z \leftarrow \frac{f_{best}-\mu(\alpha)}{\sigma(\alpha)}$
18        $EI(\alpha) \leftarrow (f_{best} - \mu(\alpha)) \cdot \Phi(Z) + \sigma(\alpha) \cdot \phi(Z)$
19   **if** $EI(\alpha) > EI_{max}$ **then**
20         $\alpha_m^{kd} \leftarrow \alpha$
21         $EI_{max} \leftarrow EI(\alpha)$

22       $p_{launch} \leftarrow p_{\text{truck\_prev}} + \alpha_m^{kd} \cdot (p_{\text{truck\_next}} - p_{\text{truck\_prev}})$
23       $T_{drone\_max} \leftarrow f_{battery}(delivery\_weight)$
24       $d_{max} \leftarrow T_{drone\_max} \cdot V_T$
25       $p_{max} \leftarrow$ position at distance d_{max} from p_{launch}
26       $\mathcal{R} \leftarrow \{p \in [p_{launch}, p_{max}] \mid \text{dist}_{drone}(p_{launch}, waypoints, p) \leq V_D \cdot T_{drone\_max}\}$
27       $p_{first} \leftarrow \underset{p \subset \mathcal{R}}{\text{argmin}}\ distance(p_{launch}, p)$
28       $p_{last} \leftarrow \underset{p \in \mathcal{R}}{\text{argmax}}\ distance(p_{launch}, p)\quad G_{min} \leftarrow \infty$
29   **while** $G_{min} > 0$ **do**
30        $\mathcal{I} \leftarrow$ Divide $[p_{first}, p_{last}]$ into c intervals
31        $\mathcal{P} \leftarrow \bigcup_{i=1}^{c}$ random select a point from $\mathcal{I}_i$
32   **foreach** $point\ p_i\ in\ \mathcal{P}$ **do**
33         $\tau_{p_i}^{k} \leftarrow$ arrival time of T_k at p_i.
34         $\tau_{p_i}^{kd} \leftarrow$ arrival time of $D_d^{T_k}$ at p_i.
35         $g(p_i) \leftarrow \mid \tau_{p_i}^{k} - \tau_{p_i}^{kd} \mid$
36   **if** $g(p_i) < G_{min}$ **then**
37          $p_{land} \leftarrow p_i$
38          $G_{min} \leftarrow g(p_i)$
39          $p_{first} \leftarrow p_{max(1,\ i-1)}$
40          $p_{last} \leftarrow p_{min(c,\ i+1)}$

41   **if** $f(\alpha_m^{kd}) < f_{best}$ **then**
42       $f_{best} \leftarrow f(\alpha_m^{kd})$
43       $\alpha_{best} \leftarrow \alpha_m^{kd}$
44   Report $f(\alpha_m^{kd})$ to Bayesian optimizer to update surrogate model.

the drone, T_{drone_max}, is calculated. Once the flight time of the drone is known, the distance the carrying truck can travel during that time can be calculated. With this distance, a feasible region of retrieval points, $\mathcal{R}$, of the drone can be calculated.

Next, the path in the feasible region $\mathcal{R}$ is divided into c sub-intervals and a point is chosen randomly from each interval. Then, for each of the c points, the truck arrival and drone arrival time at that point from p_{launch} is calculated. The points adjacent to both sides of the point having the least difference between those two arrival times are chosen to be the next path segment in the feasible region to determine the landing point of the drone. With each iteration, the path segment in the feasible region is reduced logarithmically until a rendezvous point is found, where the difference between those two arrival points becomes zero, implying that the truck doesn't waste time waiting for the drone.

6   Experimental Results

To evaluate the proposed algorithm, a few instances of CVRP benchmark available online at the Capacitated Vehicle Routing Problem Library we compared with both the Drone Truck Route Construction(DTRC) and Large Neighbourhood Search (LNS) approach of [8]. The Table 1 below summarizes the results. The 'Instance' column is the name of the benchmark instances available at the online library. The 'Customer' column represents the number of delivery points available in the instance. The 'Cost' heading includes the total time taken by all the trucks to return to the depot after delivering all the parcels following the DTRC, LNS, and the proposed algorithm. It also includes the improvement of cost in the case of the proposed algorithm compared to LNS. The 'Execution Time(S)' heading includes the total execution time in seconds of the DTRC, LNS and the proposed algorithm for the given instances in the same system.

Table 1. Cost and Execution Time Comparison

Instance	Customers	Cost				Execution Time(S)		
		DTRC	LNS	Proposed	Improvement	DTRC	LNS	Proposed
A-n32-k5	31	902.56	884.57	795.17	10.190%	0.40	69.07	11.57
A-n33-k5	32	763.19	743.58	645.43	13.2%	0.39	18.74	13.50
A-n34-k5	33	865.75	837.43	691.72	17.4%	0.35	17.51	11.04
A-n36-k5	35	889.50	833.76	815.82	2.2%	0.52	43.60	12.35
A-n37-k5	36	797.25	734.19	694.61	5.4%	0.75	58.34	12.88
Average					9.6%			

The proposed algorithm achieves a consistent cost advantage over LNS, delivering an average cost reduction of **9.6%** across all tested instances. Lowest saving

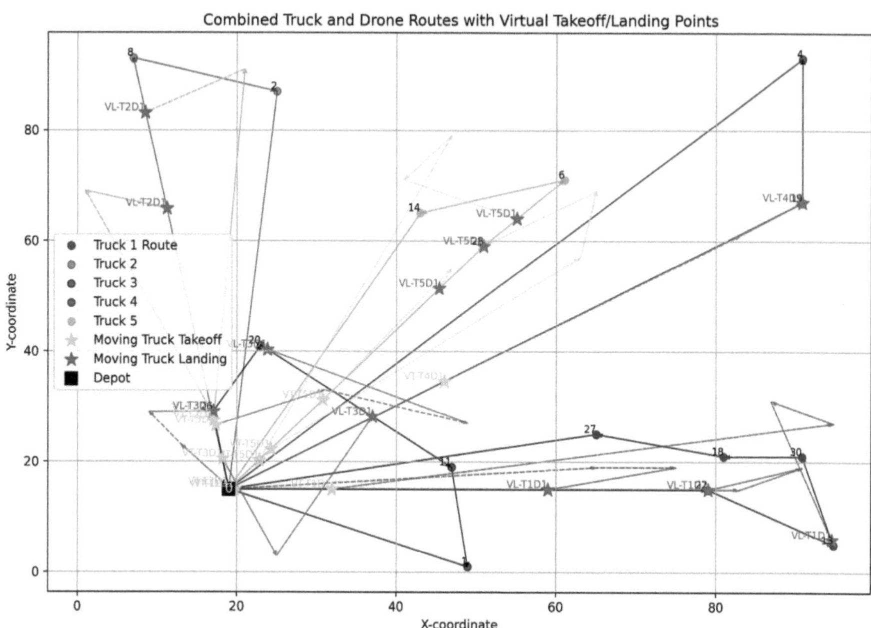

Fig. 1. Combined truck and drone routes with takeoff/landing for A-n36-k5

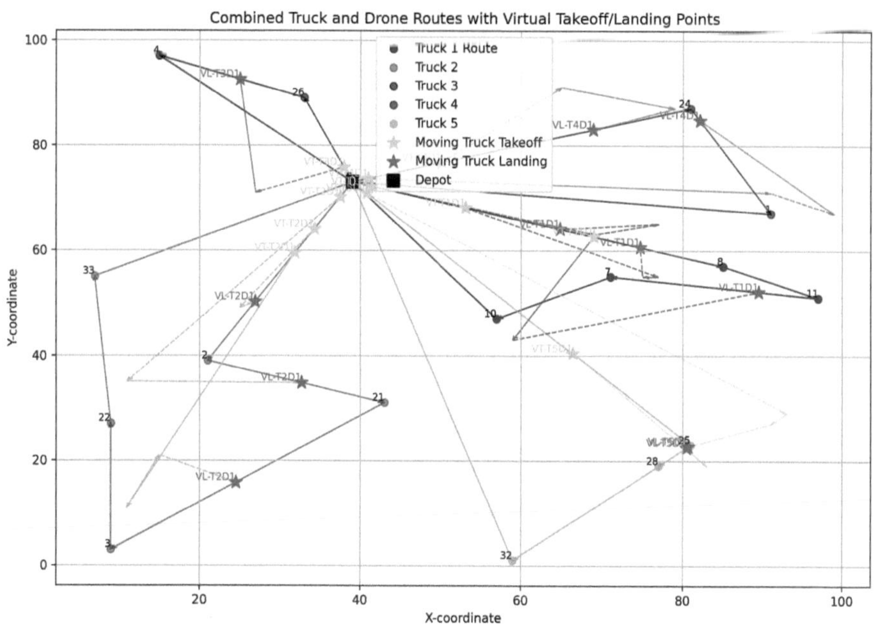

Fig. 2. Combined truck and drone routes with takeoff/landing for A-n34-k5

(2.2%) occurs for the A-n36-k5 instance while the highest savings (17.4%) occur for A-n34-k5 instance among the instances we tested. These robust improvements are evident for both medium and large-sized problems.

Figure 1 displays the combined truck and drone routes for the A-36-k5 instance by the proposed algorithm, which has only 2.2% improvement. Figure 2 displays the combined truck and drone routes for the A-36-k5 instance by the proposed algorithm, which have 17.4% improvement.

7   Conclusion

This paper presents a comprehensive enhancement to two-echelon drone vehicle routing using a Bayesian optimization algorithm. The integration of Bayesian optimization for dynamic positioning showed an average of 9.6% performance improvement over the state of the art solution. Future research directions include reinforcement learning integration for adaptive parameter tuning, multi-objective optimization incorporating environmental impact, and integration with emerging autonomous vehicle technologies.

References

1. Last Mile Delivery Market Research Report Information By Service Type, By Technology, By Application, By Delivery Time, And By Region –Market Forecast Till 2032. https://www.marketresearchfuture.com/reports/last-mile-delivery-market-22138. Accessed 21 Sept 2025
2. Jacobsen, S.K., Madsen, O.B.G.: A comparative study of heuristics for a two-level routing-location problem. Eur. J. Oper. Res. **5**(6), 378–387 (1980)
3. Crainic, T.G., Ricciardi, N., Storchi, G.: Models for evaluating and planning city logistics systems. Transp. Sci. **43**(4), 432–454 (2009)
4. Murray, C.C., Chu, A.G.: The flying sidekick traveling salesman problem: optimization of drone-assisted parcel delivery. Transp. Res. Part C Emerg. Technol. **54**, 86–109 (2015)
5. Agatz, N., Bouman, P., Schmidt, M.: Optimization approaches for the traveling salesman problem with drone. Transp. Sci. **52**(4), 965–981 (2018)
6. Wang, X., Poikonen, S., Golden, B.: The vehicle routing problem with drones: several worst-case results. Optim. Lett. **11**(4), 679–697 (2017)
7. Schermer, D., Moeini, M., Wendt, O.: A variable neighborhood search algorithm for solving the vehicle routing problem with drones. Working Paper, University of Kaiserslautern (2018)
8. Kitjacharoenchai, P., Min, B.C., Lee, S.: Two echelon vehicle routing problem with drones in last mile delivery. Int. J. Prod. Econ. **225**, 107598 (2020)
9. Shahriari, B., Swersky, K., Wang, Z., Adams, R.P., De Freitas, N.: Taking the human out of the loop: a review of Bayesian optimization. Proc. IEEE **104**(1), 148–175 (2016)
10. Akiba, T., Sano, S., Yanase, T., Ohta, T., Koyama, M.: Optuna: a next-generation hyperparameter optimization framework. In: Proceedings of the 25th ACM SIGKDD International Conference on Knowledge Discovery & Data Mining, pp. 2623–2631 (2019)
11. Jeong, H.Y., Song, B.D., Lee, S.: Truck-drone hybrid delivery routing: payload-energy dependency and No-Fly zones. Int. J. Prod. Econ. **214**, 220–233 (2019)

Track B

Attribute Discovery for a Product

Sakib A. Mondal$^{(\boxtimes)}$ [iD] and Navin Kumar Krishna

Walmart Global Tech, Building 10, SEZ Cessna Business Park, Outer Ring Road,
Bengaluru 560087, Karnataka, India
`abdulsakib.Mondal@walmart.com`

Abstract. Product discovery is crucial for any retailer. Traditional approaches to achieve this involve understanding queries. Current methods for query understanding require knowledge of product attributes. However, the attributes of interest may not be known beforehand. In addition, these attributes may evolve over time. This study aims to identify significant attributes of the product from descriptions, reviews, and other sources such as articles about the products. A phrase mining technique is used to extract relevant and important words and phrases. Meaningful concepts are generated by clustering these words and phrases. Knowledge of existing product attributes and their corresponding values is utilized as constraints during the clustering process. To uncover new attributes, we utilize topic modeling. This study presents a novel topic modeling framework that explicitly handles constraints. Experimental results from real-world examples and a benchmark dataset demonstrate the efficacy of the framework.

Keywords: Topic Modeling · Constrained Clustering · Product Attribute

1 Introduction

The process of product discovery for customers significantly impacts the revenue of online retailers. Consequently, retailers implement systems to comprehend customers' intentions during their searches. Typically, this is achieved through query understanding. Effective query understanding methods require a thorough knowledge of product attributes. More often than not, these attributes are determined manually. Given the vast number of products available, this task can be quite overwhelming. Furthermore, the attributes of interest may vary based on the current context (for instance, during the Covid pandemic, customers prioritized safety features in products, particularly food items). Therefore, there is a pressing need to identify product attributes through alternative methods. Identification of product attributes is essential for addressing various marketing challenges, including pricing strategies, campaign management, brand positioning, product portfolio decisions, and the development of new products or services. There are several potential sources for retrieving product attributes, such

C. Zaroliagis et al. (Eds.): ICAA 2026, LNCS 16423, pp. 131–143, 2026.
https://doi.org/10.1007/978-3-032-15621-1_11

as product catalogs, reviews, and product literature or articles. Generally, this information is presented in textual form. However, textual data is predominantly unstructured. Converting unstructured text into structured units of semantically meaningful phrases or words presents a considerable challenge. In this study, we aim to address this issue with the assistance of machine learning, as detailed below.

Initially, we extract high-quality phrases from the text corpus. Since many of these phrases may be semantically similar or related, it is crucial to group them into corresponding concepts. Additionally, we may already possess knowledge of certain product attributes. Thus, the emphasis should be on discovering new attributes. To achieve this, we employ constrained clustering, which allows us to impose constraints based on known attributes and their respective values. For instance, for a dress, the known attributes might include age range (with values such as infant, child, youth, and adult) and colors (with values like red, blue, green, white, and black).

To guarantee that all phrases serving as values for an attribute are grouped into a single cluster, we implement must-link constraints. A $mustlink(p_1, p_2)$ constraint indicates that the phrases p_1 and p_2 should reside within the same cluster. For instance, several must-link constraints for the age attribute might include $mustlink(infant, child)$, $mustlink(infant, adult)$, and $mustlink(youth, adult)$. In a similar vein, constraints that ensure distinct attributes belong to separate clusters can be represented as $cannotlink$ constraints. A $cannotlink(p_1, p_2)$ constraint guarantees that the phrases p_1 and p_2 cannot be included in the same cluster. Examples related to dress products include $cannotlink(infant, black)$, $cannotlink(infant, white)$, and $cannotlink(youth, black)$.

The precise number of clusters may not be predetermined. There have been various attempts to ascertain the appropriate number of clusters, either through objective value assessments or by analyzing the second eigenvalue of the Laplacian. Nevertheless, there remains no assurance that a single cluster corresponds to a singular attribute. This requires an additional aspect of this study: the identification of topics within a cluster. We have adapted anchor-word based topic modeling for this purpose. The principal contributions of this paper may be summarized as follows.

1. A topic modeling-based methodology for the identification of new product attributes. To our knowledge, this represents the inaugural effort in attribute discovery for a product utilizing topic modeling. The methodology encompasses: (a) A phrase mining technique designed to extract high-quality phrases from textual data, (b) A constrained clustering approach that incorporates constraints, and (c) A topic modeling strategy capable of intrinsically managing these constraints.

2. Experimental assessments of various products and a benchmark dataset validate the efficacy of our framework (which we will henceforth refer to as AutoDiscovery).

The paper is structured as following. We outline related work in Sect. 2. Section 3 presents AutoDiscovery, its various components. Findings from our experiments are presented in Sect. 4. Section 5 offers concluding remarks.

2   Related Work

Extracting structured information from unstructured text has been a subject of investigation for an extensive period. Named Entity Recognition seeks to identify significant nouns within a text. However, a meaningful construct is frequently a phrase rather than a single noun. For instance, "united" can represent a different concept than "united states" or "united parcel service." The aim of phrasal segmentation is to produce disjoint sub-sequences, each corresponding to a semantic unit (a sub-sequence may consist of a word or a phrase). This is accomplished through query segmentation [12] or phrase chunking [8]. Current techniques for identifying key phrases within a document can be divided into two types: extraction and generation. Extraction methods involve two steps. In the initial step, significant phrases are extracted using heuristic methods such as n-grams [19] or by selecting text chunks with specific post tags [13,14]. In the subsequent step, these phrases are ranked utilizing machine learning techniques. The methods can be either supervised or unsupervised.

Generative methods assign key phrases to a document using natural language generation techniques. Meng et al. [17] employ an encoder-decoder framework [20] with a copy mechanism [11] and manage to achieve state-of-the-art performance. Liu et al. [13] consider an integrated phrasal segmentation approach where segmentation is combined with phrase quality estimation. There exists a range of statistical measures for identifying quality phrases [14], where the quality of a phrase is defined using four criteria: popularity, concordance, informativeness, and completeness.

K-clustering aims to allocate a set of centroids C_{li} in such a way that the distortion measures within the clusters, $\sum_i D(s_i, C_{li})$, are minimized. However, this problem is intractable; nonetheless, a satisfactory approximate solution can be achieved through the k-means algorithm. The resulting clusters may contain pairs of candidates that ideally should belong to separate clusters. Additionally, there may be instances where a pair of points fall in different clusters, yet they should be grouped within the same cluster. To address this issue, instance-level constraints are applied. The constrained clustering method proposed by [5] is founded on the K-means algorithm. Instance-level constraints [22] can be categorized into two types: *mustlink*: Points must be allocated to the same cluster, *cannotlink*: Points must be allocated to different clusters.

Clustering can be executed by treating constraints as hard (meaning that if any constraint is violated, the current solution is deemed infeasible). Alternatively, constraints may be regarded as soft, where a penalty is incurred for a violation. A third method involves learning a distance function that aligns with the specified constraints, i.e., the distance between a pair of *cannotlink* points is greater than the cluster diameter, while the distance between a pair of *mustlink* points is less than the cluster diameter. Sugato [5] introduced a technique in which points are divided into a collection of connected components based on the transitive closure of points with *mustlink* constraints. One point from each connected component is selected as the centroid. With this centroid selection, points are reassigned to clusters (similar to K-means), but with an objective function that imposes a penalty for any breach of *cannotlink* constraints. Numerous clustering algorithms exist where the distance function is learned [5,24]. In [18], it is shown that Fuzzy Co-clustering of Documents and Keywords (FCoDoK) performs better than agglomerative hierarchical clustering and DBSCAN.

Topic modeling is a straightforward technique that identifies thematic patterns within a set of documents. Let V be the vocabulary size and there are K topics. Each document is modeled as a mixture of topics. Each topic is characterized by a distribution over words. Thus, a topic k can be described by a vector A_k of dimension V. A topic model assumes a specific prior distribution for the topic. For example, in latent Dirichlet allocation (LDA) the prior (τ) is a Dirichlet distribution; τ is a logistic Normal distribution in the correlated topic model. To generate documents, a topic is chosen from the topic distribution, and then a word is generated according to the word distribution of that topic. Concretely, a document d is created by sampling its topic distribution W_d. For a word at position i, a topic z_i is sampled from W_d. Subsequently, a word w_i is sampled based on the topic's word distribution A_{z_i}. The word-topic matrix A of dimension $V \times K$ is constructed from the K column vectors A_k. Similarly, the topic-document matrix W (of size $K \times M$) is obtained by aggregating the column vectors W_d corresponding to M documents. W is unknown and generated probabilistically, so it cannot be exactly recovered. The learning objective is to estimate the word-topic matrix A. Posterior inference of document-topic and topic-word distributions is intractable. It is NP-hard even for just two topics [3]. Therefore approximate inference techniques such as singular value decomposition, variational inference [7], and Markov chain Monte Carlo (MCMC) [10] are used for inference. Prominent approaches to topic modeling are broadly of two types: variational expectation maximization [7] based on optimization of a lower bound on the likelihood, and MCMC based on asymptotic sampling from the posterior distribution [16]. Probabilistic topic models solve learning problem for a class of admixture distributions such as latent Dirichlet allocation [7], correlated topic models [6]. Standard topic models like LDA [7] assume that topic proportions in a document are uncorrelated, but there is strong evidence that topics in practice are often dependent [6]. In [4] contextualized representations were combined with neural topic models. This approach improves upon the traditional bag-of-words topic models on topic coherence.

A completely different approach was proposed in [3]. An algorithm was proposed that provably learns the parameters of a topic model given samples from the model, based on the assumption that the word-topic distributions are separable. The algorithm recovers the parameters of topic models provided that every topic contains at least one anchor word (an anchor word has non-zero probability only in that topic). To recover the topic matrix A using anchor words, it computes a $V \times V$ co-occurrence matrix Q, where Q_{ij} is the conditional probability $p(w_j|w_i)$ of seeing word type w_j after having seen w_i in the same document. The algorithm first finds anchor words $g_1, \cdots, .g_k$ for each topic based on a Gram-Schmidt process. When anchor words are provided, given a word, probability of a topic can be computed as a coefficient matrix C. Matrix C is defined row-by-row, each row corresponding to a word. Row i corresponding to the word i is given by $C_i^* = \arg\min_{C_i,} D_{KL}(Q_i, \| \sum_{k=1}^{K} C_{i,k} Q_{g_k,})$. Gills et al. [9] uses a linear programming based method and a linear projection approach respectively for anchor word selection. Arora et al. [1] presents a combinatorial anchor selection algorithm that is faster and more resistant to noise.

Anchor method assumes that there is a single anchor word for each topic (which appears only in this topic and no other topic) [1]. This assumption is problematic. Most often this means that the anchor word is very infrequent in a topic. Besides, many a times a combination of words can serve as a unique identifier for a topic and this combination describes the topic better than a single anchor word.[1] To tackle this, Lund [15] proposed a facet based approach where a combination of words is used as an anchor for a topic.

There is limited work on constrained topic modeling. For example, Terragni et al. [21] considers constraints in the form of must-link and cannot-link constraints at the document level. In this work constraints are imposed to indicate if a pair of documents belong to the same topic or not. *For the application in this paper, we cannot put constraints at the document level. For example, two documents can be of same "color" topic but differ in "size" topic.* Therefore, we used constrained clustering as opposed to handling the constraints through potential function [21]. In [23] a generative model has been proposed. It assumes that text fragments occur nicely as pairs of an attribute name and its values. In our work, there no assumption like that.

3   AutoDiscovery: A Framework for Attribute Discovery

Our objective is to discover product attributes from various sources related to a product. These sources could be queries from search engine. One challenge of working with queries is that the phrases are short and often full of slangs or mistakes(grammar, spelling and syntax). Second source is product review data. It contains meaningful information about products (particularly differentiating features or quality aspects). However reviews most often talk of other aspects like delivery, shopping experience, and contain relatively less information on product quality or attribute. The third source is catalog data related to product. This is easily available, and is mostly related to product attributes. Hence, this is a good source for discovery of attributes. Since textual data may contain a lot of extra data (stop words, unnecessary phrases) which does not necessarily aid in

---

[1] For "pouch for mobile", we can use single word anchor "pouch" or "mobile". Unfortunately, the topic generated by the anchor word "pouch" means "women pouch" instead of "pouch for mobile". Likewise, the topic anchored by "mobile" will refer to mobile devices typically.

meeting our objective, a first step is to pre-process the documents to extract meaningful phrases.

Another important point – it is not a cold-start problem always. For a product category, we may have already identified a few attributes and possible values that these attributes can take. For example, we may have an attribute "gender" applicable for the product, and this attribute takes 3 possible values ("male", "female" and "unisex"). So the task at hand is to discover new meaningful attributes and possible values of these attributes. In the process, one should be able to take advantage of the existing knowledge. A possible approach to leverage knowledge about the known attributes is to cluster the pre-processed documents with additional constraints. These constraints can be of the form below: phrases containing values of an attribute falls in the same cluster, and two phrases belong to different clusters if they represent different attributes. As a result of clustering, one may get a new cluster that does not correspond to the known attributes (concepts). It is possible that this cluster represents a completely new attribute(concept), or a mixture of a number of attributes(concepts). To extract these component concepts from the mixture, we use topic modeling. Topic modeling Algorithm by Arora et al. [1] assumes existence of unique anchor word per topic. However, as noted in [15] most often this is too restrictive. But a combination of words can serve as a good anchor.

To summarize, AutoDisovery has the following steps: (1) Preprocess input data and extract meaningful phrases, (2) Cluster phrases using constrained clustering, and (3) Identify new concepts from the generated clusters using topic modeling. Both clustering and topic modeling aim at clustering the documents. Hence, can we unify steps 2 and 3 above. In the proposed scheme, we unify steps 2 and 3 into one step. In the word-to-word co-occurrence matrix, we introduce a new row for each new attribute. In other words, the new row is a pseudo-word corresponding to an attribute. For each possible attribute value, we set the corresponding column value to 1 (0 otherwise). In this manner, one is able to put the *mustlink* constraints in the topic modeling. For different attributes, we create different rows. This takes care of *cannotlink* constraints (as all items cannot have same values for a pair of attributes).

Let us assume that we have knowledge about N product attributes and their values. These form N rows in word-to-word matrix S. Assuming that we are interested in K-topics, we discover $K - N$ anchor words using Gram-Schmdit as in [3]. Accordingly we generate $K - N$ word incidence vectors and append these $K - N$ rows to S. Final matrix S is a $(V + N) \times V$ matrix. The last N rows are based on the anchor words or pseudo words constructed from anchor facets. Other rows are constructed based on tokens in the data. If a word w (with index i in topic word matrix A) is from the topic(z) k, A_{ik} is same as the conditional probability $p(w = i | z = k)$.

It makes sense to consider each of the N rows corresponding to anchor facets (i.e., sets of words) as a word in the vocabulary. But there may not exist any word in the vocabulary that corresponds to these points. Hence we treat them as pseudo-words[2] in the V-dimensional space. Each non-anchor word can be expressed as a convex combinations of these pseudo-words and anchor words. The moot point is how to construct these pseudo-words from their facets. Following [15] we use a number of approaches for this step (see Sect. 3.1 below).

3.1   Facets to Pseudowords

Let the set of anchor facets be $F_1 \cdots, F_N$. We would like to generate a set of pseudo-words $f_1 \cdots, f_N$, where f_k is the pseudo-word for F_k. These pseudo-words form the new rows of S. We use several candidates for combining an anchors facet into a single pseudo-word following [15].

Arithmetic Mean: For each anchor facet F_k, corresponding pseudo-word is represented as $AM_{f_k,j} = \sum_{i \in F_k} \frac{S_{i,j}}{|F_k|}$. Arithmetic mean makes the pseudoword $AM_{f_k,j}$ more central, which is inconsistent with the interpretation from [1] that anchors should be extreme points.

Geometric Mean: For each anchor facet F_k, corresponding pseudo-word is represented as $GM_{f_k,j} = {}^{|F_k|}\sqrt{\prod_{i \in F_k} \frac{S_{i,j}}{F_k}}$. When the anchors span lesser volume of simplex, this operator reduces the quantum of explainable words. Hence, this operator performs poorly.

Harmonic Mean: An element-wise harmonic mean $HM_{f_k,j} = \sum_{i \in F_k} (\frac{S_{i,j}^{-1}}{|F_k|})^{-1}$ is both centralizing and sensitive to large outliers.

OR-Operator: The pseudo-word is set to $OR_{f_k,j} = 1 \quad \prod_{i \in F_k} (1 - S_{i,j})$. The or-operator pushes the word outward. As anchors span larger simplex, the OR-operator helps in explaining more words.

AND-Operator: Here De Morgan's law is used for setting the pseudo-word to $AND_{f_k,j} = \prod_{i \in F_k} S_{i,j}$. The AND-operator is similar to the Geometric Mean operator.

Element-Wise Min: An element-wise min operator is $MIN_{f_k,j} = \min_{i \in F_k} S_{i,j}$. Behaviour wise, this is similar to OR-operator.

Element-Wise Max: An element-wise max operator is $MAX_{f_k,j} = \max_{i \in F_k} S_{i,j}$.

Arithmetic mean, Geometric Mean and AND-operators are sensitive to outliers. Harmonic mean, OR-operator and Element-wise Min are not sensitive to large outliers, hence provide robustness to polysemous words.

---

[2] A pseudo word or a multi-word anchor can be represented as incidence vectors over vocabulary. For example, a pseudo-word may be an incident vector with non-zero entries for the following words: "blue", "green", "red", "cyan", "black". In that case, these are the possible values of the attributes or attribute name itself, i.e. color.

3.2 Finding Topics

Let $I = \{s_1, s_2, \cdots, s_K\}$ denote the indices of the anchor words. The rows of S corresponding to I are independent, and may be considered as vertices of simplex. Every other row lies in the convex hull of these independent rows. After constructing the anchors and pseudo-words of S (i.e., $f_k, \forall\, k$), we compute $C_{i,k} = p(z = k | w = i)$. Please note that $S_{i,j} = \sum_k p(z = k | w = i)p(w = j | z = k) = \sum_k C_{i,k} p(w = j | z = k)$. If word j is a pseudo/anchor word, $S_{i,j} = \sum_k C_{i,k} S_{f_k,j}$. Thus, every other word in the vocabulary can be expressed as a convex combination of the hybrid anchors (single words, multiple words or pseudo-words). We solve the following constrained optimization problem to obtain $C_{i,k}$ (and eventually topic matrix A): $C_i^* = \arg\min_{C_{i,\cdot}} D_{KL}(S_{i,\cdot} \parallel \sum_{k=1}^{K} C_{i,k} S_{f_k,\cdot})$ subject to $\sum_k C_{i,k} = 1$ and $C_{i,k} \geq 0$.

3.3 Discussion

Provable guarantee of the approach holds true in noisy settings as in [2]. The theorems reproduced below hold true with generalization to hybrid-anchor documents. For a β-robust simplex, l_2 distance between any vertex v and the convex hull of the rest of the vertices is at least β. For topic matrix A, if for each topic k there exists a word i such that $A_{i,k} \geq p$, $p > 0$ and $A_{i,k'} = 0$ for $k' \neq k$, it is called p-separable.

Robustness of simplex plays an important role in guaranting correct recovery of topics. It means that if the points within simplex are perturbed within a limit, the resulting simplex is not significantly different from the original (from volume perspective). Points set $\{v_1', v_2', \cdots, v_K'\}$ α-covers another points set $\{v_1, v_2, \cdots, v_K\}$, if for all i, $c_i \geq 1 - \alpha$ when v_i' is represented as a convex combination of v_i, i.e., $v_i' = \sum_{k'=1}^{K} c_{k'} v_{k'}$. In other words, if there is a limited perturbation of the pivot points of a simplex, the new pivots of the perturbed simplex are closer to the corresponding points. With the assumption of β-robustness of the initial simplex, polynomial time algorithm construction of anchor words (which are robust to perturbation) can be guaranteed.

Theorem 1. *[2] Our algorithm runs in time $O(V^2 + VK/\epsilon^2)$ and outputs a subset of $\{d_1, \cdots, , d_V\}$ of size K that $O(\epsilon/\beta)$-covers the vertices provided that $20K\epsilon/\beta^2 < \beta$.*

Therefore, in case robustness does not hold for a set of hybrid anchors, we can use FastAnchorWords algorithm [2] to get a different set of anchors from initial points. Finally, correctness of recovery of parameters of the topic model holds true as in [2]. This is because all the requirements of the theorem are satisfied.

Theorem 2. *Let v be an internal point in a β-robust simplex S with vertices $\{v_1, v_2, \cdots, v_K\}$ (i.e., $v = \sum_{k=1}^{K} c_i v_i$). Let $S' = \{\cdots, v_i', \cdots,\}$ be the new simplex generated through limited perturabation of S (i.e., $\|v' - v_i\| \leq \delta_1$). and let v' be the perturbed point corresponding to v with $\|v - v'\| \leq \delta_2$. Let the closest point from v' to S' be v^*, and $v^* = \sum_{k=1}^{K} c_i' v_i$. In that case, if $10\sqrt{K}\delta_1 \leq \beta \,\forall i \in [K]$ then $|c_i - c_i'| \leq 4(\delta_1 + \delta_2)/\beta$.*

4   Experimental Evaluation

We have experimented with two datasets to evaluate performance of the approach here: real world product data from an online retailer and benchmark newsgroup data. Our purpose is to evaluate best working combination for components for topic modeling and to evaluate the two-step vs. the one-step approach of topic modeling in presence of constraints.

We experimented with 20 Newsgroups dataset. This dataset comprises of roughly 20,000 documents from 20 newsgroups. We carry out following preprocessing before topic modeling: removal of newsgroup headers, stop-words and in-frequent or too-frequent words[3]. In the next step, we generate word sets for candidate anchor of each topic. As in [1], we split the title on word boundaries and expand any abbreviations or acronyms, e.g. for a newsgroup title 'comp.sys.ibm.pc.hardware' the multi-word anchor is "computer", "system", "ibm", "personal", "hardware". For our experimentation, we used this multi-word anchor only for a subset of newsgroups (e.g. 5, 7) chosen randomly. This was used to generate the topics (number of topics as 10 and 15 respectively) using AutoDiscovery. Thus, initially we know the names of only a few topics. But, the topic modeling algorithm is able to discover other new topics. To decide the right combiner function for the pseudo-word, we experimented with the candidates mentioned in Sect. 3.1. Performances of the Geometric Mean and AND operators are poor and hence we have not reported the results here. Also performance of the Min operator is similar to that of the OR operator, hence we have not reported the results for the Min operator.

We also experimented with product data. For this we used online catalog information. We did not use any anchor word, but for a few known attributes we used their values and name of the attribute as facets. Subsequently topics were generated using topic modeling. We used 4 known attributes and their values to seed the constraints. Total number of topics considered were 8 and 12 respectively. We compared performance of AutoDiscovery with single anchor based topic modeling of Arora et al. [1] for topic discovery. In the AutoDiscovery anchors are discovered automatically from title (for newsgroup data) and attributes (for product data). On the contrary, Arora et al. [1] discovers anchors based on [2]. For performance evaluation, we trained a classifier on the combinations of topic-words and actual newsgroups memberships. The dataset was randomly split into test and training sets. Topics were learnt from the test data using our approach as well as the Gram-Schmidt single word anchors. Since the anchor algorithm only gives the topic-word distributions and not word-level topic assignments, we infer token-level topic assignments using LDA [7]. For the sampling, we used Gibbs sampler and a symmetric Dirichlet prior (concentration $\alpha = 0.1$). We trained a NaiveBayes classifier using topic-word pairs as features to classify newsgroup. (Accurate classification is not the main aim of the paper. Accuracy can be improved by using additional features and more sophisticated classifier). Finally, the classifier was used to infer topic assignments. We experi-

---

[3] Fewer than 100 documents or more than 1,500 documents.

mented with the all the combiners. Among the combiners, the Max operator is more accurate than the other functions (see Fig. 1).

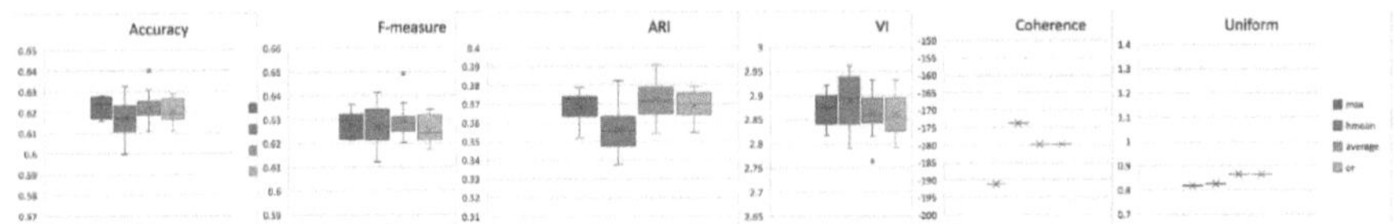

Fig. 1. Performance of Combiners

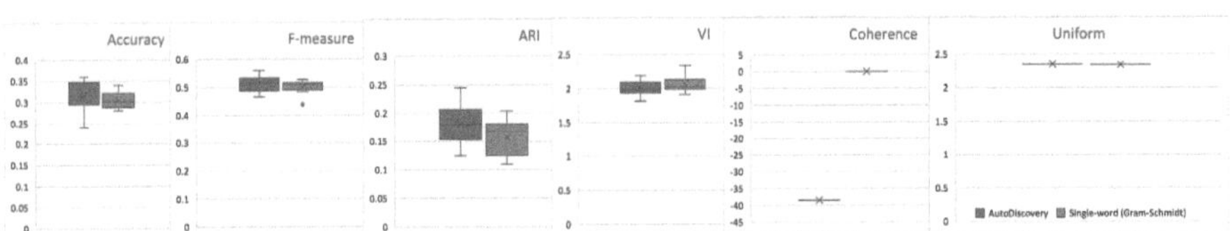

Fig. 2. AutoDiscovery Vs. Single-word Anchor [1] on Product data

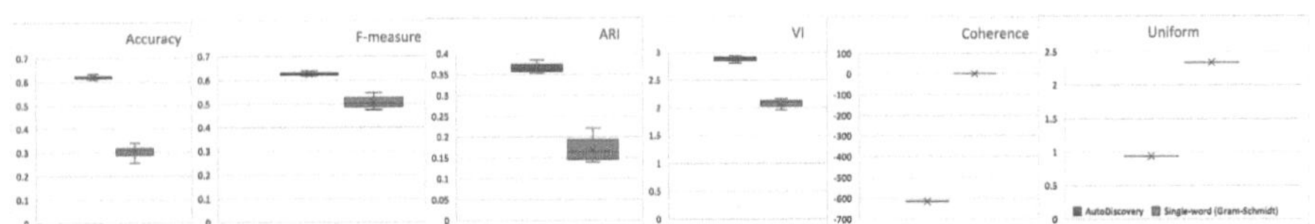

Fig. 3. AutoDiscovery Vs. Single-word Anchor [1] on Newsgroups

When topics are fixed, inferencing can be done in parallel for different documents, and hence the process is fast. Finally, topic word features were used to infer topic assignments in the test data. The topics created using our approach are more accurate than Gram-Schmidt topics. The harmonic mean had better accuracy than the other combiners.

Holistic performance should include measures beyond accuracy, particularly for close newsgroups. Confusion among similar newsgroups can be addressed through adjusted Rand index (ARI), and variation of information (VI). ARI is a metric to capture accuracy of clustering; it is computed based on the percentage of correct pairings. On the other hand, the VI metric measures the loss of information if the gold standard labels are replaced by the predicted labels. Topic coherence measures how the topics are semantically interpretable rather than just artifacts of statistical inference. A topic is expected to have distribution skeweded toward a few important and relevant words. In uniform measure, the distance of a topic distribution from the uniform distribution is evaluated. For VI the lower value is preferable. For the other metrics, higher the value the better is the quality of clustering.

To validate that our approach on product dataset, we used topics generated as input to train and test a classifier. We report accuracy, F-measure and multiple clustering metrics (ARI, VI and coherence) for the classification task. Our evaluation for the attribute dataset with 12-clusters is presented in Fig. 2. Similar results on the Newsgroup data have been reported in Fig. 3 for 15-clusters.

We performed experiments to see if there is evaluate relative performance of AutoDiscovery over Gram-Schmidt(single word anchor). Topics from hybrid anchors yield higher classification accuracy (Figs. 2, 3). AutoDiscovery performs better than single word anchor on all clustering metrics except for topic coherence on the product data set (Fig. 2). It suggests that the topics are accurate and robust but not always coherent per corpus knowledge. On the news data set, hybrid anchor performs better on the key metrics like Accuracy, F-measure and ARI, but worse on VI, coherence and uniform metric. This means that the topics are accurate, but may not be robust to noise and well-supported by corpus.

5   Concluding Remarks

We have proposed an extension to the topic modeling to handle constraints. Constraints are handled intrinsically as a multi-word topic in the topic-word matrix. We have provided algorithmic extension, which is necessary to handle a mix of single-word and multi-word anchors, to infer topics. Empirical evaluations on a benchmark dataset and a real-life dataset show promise. Besides, the approach can be evaluated on other domains. Comparison with transformer-based approaches for topic modeling could be a future work. Coherence of the current approach can be improved by leveraging contextual embedding based on recent language models - this can be an area of future exploration.

References

1. Arora, S., et al.: A practical algorithm for topic modeling with provable guarantees. In: International Conference on Machine Learning, pp. 280–288. PMLR (2013)
2. Arora, S., Ge, R., Kannan, R., Moitra, A.: Computing a nonnegative matrix factorization–provably. In: Proceedings of the Forty-Fourth Annual ACM Symposium on Theory of Computing, pp. 145–162 (2012)

3. Arora, S., Ge, R., Moitra, A.: Learning topic models–going beyond SVD. In: 2012 IEEE 53rd Annual Symposium on Foundations of Computer Science, pp. 1–10. IEEE (2012)

4. Bianchi, F., Terragni, S., Hovy, D.: Pre-training is a hot topic: contextualized document embeddings improve topic coherence. arXiv preprint arXiv:2004.03974 (2020)

5. Bilenko, M., Basu, S.: A comparison of inference techniques for semi-supervised clustering with hidden Markov random fields. In: Proceedings of the ICML-2004 Workshop on Statistical Relational Learning and its Connections to Other Fields (SRL-2004), Banff, Canada (2004)

6. Blei, D.M., Lafferty, J.D.: A correlated topic model of science. Ann. Appl. Stat. 17–35 (2007)

7. Blei, D.M., Ng, A.Y., Jordan, M.I.: Latent dirichlet allocation. J. Mach. Learn. Res. **3**(Jan), 993–1022 (2003)

8. Echizen-ya, H., Araki, K.: Automatic evaluation method for machine translation using noun-phrase chunking. In: Proceedings of the 48th Annual Meeting of the Association for Computational Linguistics, pp. 108–117 (2010)

9. Gillis, N., Vavasis, S.A.: Fast and robust recursive algorithms for separable nonnegative matrix factorization. IEEE Trans. Pattern Anal. Mach. Intell. **36**(4), 698–714 (2013)

10. Griffiths, T.L., Steyvers, M.: Finding scientific topics. Proc. Natl. Acad. Sci. **101**(Suppl._1), 5228–5235 (2004)

11. Gu, J., Lu, Z., Li, H., Li, V.O.: Incorporating copying mechanism in sequence-to-sequence learning. arXiv preprint arXiv:1603.06393 (2016)

12. Li, Y., Hsu, B.J.P., Zhai, C., Wang, K.: Unsupervised query segmentation using clickthrough for information retrieval. In: Proceedings of the 34th International ACM SIGIR Conference on Research and Development in Information Retrieval, pp. 285–294 (2011)

13. Liu, J., Shang, J., Wang, C., Ren, X., Han, J.: Mining quality phrases from massive text corpora. In: Proceedings of the 2015 ACM SIGMOD International Conference on Management of Data, pp. 1729–1744 (2015)

14. Liu, Z., Chen, X., Zheng, Y., Sun, M.: Automatic keyphrase extraction by bridging vocabulary gap. In: Proceedings of the Fifteenth Conference on Computational Natural Language Learning, pp. 135–144 (2011)

15. Lund, J., Cook, C., Seppi, K., Boyd-Graber, J.: Tandem anchoring: a multiword anchor approach for interactive topic modeling. In: Proceedings of the 55th Annual Meeting of the Association for Computational Linguistics (Volume 1: Long Papers), pp. 896–905 (2017)

16. McCallum, A.K.: Mallet: A machine learning for languagetoolkit (2002). http://malletcs.umass.edu

17. Meng, R., Zhao, S., Han, S., He, D., Brusilovsky, P., Chi, Y.: Deep keyphrase generation. arXiv preprint arXiv:1704.06879 (2017)

18. Raj, A., Susan, S.: Clustering analysis for newsgroup classification. In: Data Engineering and Intelligent Computing: Proceedings of 5th ICICC 2021, vol. 1, pp. 271–279. Springer (2022)

19. Shang, J., Liu, J., Jiang, M., Ren, X., Voss, C.R., Han, J.: Automated phrase mining from massive text corpora. IEEE Trans. Knowl. Data Eng. **30**(10), 1825–1837 (2018)

20. Sutskever, I., Vinyals, O., Le, Q.V.: Sequence to sequence learning with neural networks. In: Advances in Neural Information Processing Systems, vol. 27 (2014)

21. Terragni, S., Fersini, E., Messina, E.: Constrained relational topic models. Inf. Sci. **512**, 581–594 (2020)
22. Wagstaff, K., Cardie, C., Rogers, S., Schrödl, S., et al.: Constrained k-means clustering with background knowledge. In: ICML, vol. 1, pp. 577–584 (2001)
23. Wong, T.L., Lam, W.: A probabilistic approach for adapting information extraction wrappers and discovering new attributes. In: Fourth IEEE International Conference on Data Mining (ICDM 2004), pp. 257–264. IEEE (2004)
24. Xing, E., Jordan, M., Russell, S.J., Ng, A.: Distance metric learning with application to clustering with side-information. In: Advances in Neural Information Processing Systems, vol. 15 (2002)

Leveraging YOLO and SAHI for Accurate Small Tank Detection in UAV Systems

Van Hieu Bui[(✉)] [ID], Tuan Anh Luong, Thao Linh Tran,
Hoang Nam Nguyen Ba, and Phuong Nguyen Nguyen

FPT University, Education Zone, Hoa Lac Hi-Tech Park, Ha Noi, Vietnam
`hieubv10@fe.edu.vn`,
`{anhlthe163002,linhtthe163535,namnbhhe161029,nguyennphe170484}@fpt.edu.vn`

Abstract. Detecting and neutralizing tanks from long distances using Unmanned Aerial Vehicles (UAVs) is an emerging research area with the potential to significantly enhance military capabilities and reduce loss of life. Despite this potential, the domain remains relatively underexplored, especially in specific terrains and operational contexts. This study presents the development of a real-time tank detection and targeting system. The proposed end-to-end framework integrates advanced machine learning algorithms, image processing techniques, and precision targeting mechanisms. The system operates in three phases: Phase 1 detects tanks using object detection algorithms such as YOLOv7; Phase 2 enhances detection accuracy at long distances through the Slicing-Aided Hyper Inference (SAHI) algorithm; and Phase 3 applies the StrongSORT tracking algorithm for continuous target tracking and engagement. Experimental evaluation on the VisDrone dataset demonstrates the system's effectiveness in reducing operational risks and improving mission success rates, achieving a mean Average Precision (mAP) of 0.88 at IoU 0.5, with performance decreasing to 0.59 for mAP@0.5:0.95.

Keywords: Small Tank · Detection · Slicing inference

1 Introduction

Unmanned Aerial Vehicles (UAVs) have emerged as indispensable assets in modern military operations, providing capabilities in reconnaissance, surveillance, target acquisition, and precision engagement across diverse terrains and operational contexts. Their ability to operate remotely significantly reduces risks to human personnel, while delivering real-time situational awareness and enabling rapid decision-making in dynamic combat environments. In recent years, advances in Artificial Intelligence (AI) and deep learning have transformed UAVs from remotely piloted platforms into intelligent, semi-autonomous, or fully autonomous systems capable of complex mission execution with minimal human intervention [4,9]. This paradigm shift has enabled enhanced operational effectiveness, predictive analysis of adversarial behavior, and reduced casualties during high-risk missions.

© The Author(s), under exclusive license to Springer Nature Switzerland AG 2026
C. Zaroliagis et al. (Eds.): ICAA 2026, LNCS 16423, pp. 144–155, 2026.
https://doi.org/10.1007/978-3-032-15621-1_12

One critical application of AI-enabled UAVs is the automatic detection and neutralization of armored ground threats, particularly tanks, which remain a cornerstone of conventional land warfare [15]. Fast and accurate tank detection is essential for both defensive and offensive operations, especially when engagement must occur from long standoff distances to minimize exposure to countermeasures. However, when observed from high altitudes or at extended ranges, tanks appear as small objects occupying only a few pixels in the UAV's imagery, making detection significantly more challenging. This small-object detection problem is further exacerbated by environmental and operational constraints, such as background clutter, camouflage, partial occlusion by foliage or infrastructure, varying illumination, and adverse weather conditions [2].

While numerous object detection algorithms have been proposed in the computer vision community, the majority suffer from reduced accuracy when target objects are small relative to the image resolution. This limitation is particularly problematic for UAV-based reconnaissance in Vietnam, where operational platforms with robust small-tank detection capabilities remain scarce [8]. In such contexts, effective long-range detection can be decisive, allowing forces to engage targets without compromising UAV safety or revealing their location prematurely.

YOLO family of models has established itself as a leading approach in real-time object detection, offering an effective balance between accuracy and inference speed [10,12]. These models utilize a single-stage detection framework that enables rapid processing, making them well-suited for deployment on resource-limited platforms such as unmanned aerial vehicles (UAVs). Despite their efficiency, standard YOLO architectures often struggle to maintain high performance when detecting small objects. This limitation arises from challenges such as scale variation and the reduced spatial detail available in deeper network layers. To overcome these constraints, it is essential to integrate complementary methods that enhance small-object detection while retaining YOLO's inherent computational efficiency.

The Slicing Aided Hyper Inference (SAHI) framework [5] offers such a solution by dividing high-resolution images into overlapping slices for localized inference. This approach allows detectors to process each slice at an effective higher resolution, improving the visibility and detectability of small targets without requiring architectural changes to the detector itself. When integrated with YOLO, SAHI can substantially increase detection accuracy for small-scale objects, including distant or partially obscured tanks, while maintaining practical inference speeds.

In this study, we propose a three-stage, end-to-end UAV-based system for small tank detection, tracking, and engagement recommendation. In Phase 1, we apply YOLO-based detectors (with emphasis on YOLOv7 and YOLOv8) for initial tank localization. Phase 2 integrates SAHI to enhance the detection of small or difficult-to-spot tanks missed in the first stage. Phase 3 employs the StrongSORT tracking algorithm [1] to maintain persistent target identity and trajectory throughout UAV maneuvers, ensuring reliable engagement even in dynamic environments. The modularity of this design enables scalability and adaptability to different hardware, detection models, and operational requirements, making it suitable for real-time deployment in high-stakes military missions.

By combining the detection strengths of YOLO with the small-object enhancement capabilities of SAHI and the robustness of StrongSORT tracking, the proposed system aims to address current limitations in UAV-based small tank detection and improve overall mission success in both reconnaissance and combat scenarios.

2   Related Work

The proposed method's strengths lie in its simplicity, ease of use, and the clear separation of its three stages. Additionally, the SAHI algorithm's flexibility allows for integration with various object detection models, offering a scalable solution to the problem of remote tank detection and destruction. The field of object detection has seen significant advancements, particularly in the context of small object detection, which is critical for applications such as UAV-based tank detection and tracking. Several recent models have demonstrated promising results in various object detection benchmarks.

Shaoyu Chen, Tianheng Cheng, and colleagues [3] introduced the TinyDet model, which is designed for efficiency in terms of computation. TinyDet-M, evaluated on the COCO benchmark, achieves a notable 30.3 AP with only 991 MFLOP, making it the first detector to surpass an AP of 30 with less than 1 GFLOP of computation. Additionally, TinyDet-S and TinyDet-L exhibit strong performance under different computational constraints, with TinyDet-L achieving a MAP@.5:.95 of 35.5 and TinyDet-S achieving a MAP@.5:.95 of 26.6. While TinyDet's compact size and use of sparsely-connected convolutions offer computational advantages, it is a two-stage model, which can impact inference speed Table 1.

Zhiwei Lin, Weihao Chen, and their team [7] proposed the HS-YOLO algorithm, which leverages a High-Resolution Network (HRNet) and sub-pixel convolution. On a self-constructed power operation dataset, HS-YOLO achieved an mAP of 87.2%, marking a 3.5% improvement over YOLOv5. The algorithm notably improved detection of small objects such as cuffs, necklines, and safety belts, with increases in AP of 10.7%, 5.8%, and 4.4%, respectively. HS-YOLO's success in improving small object detection highlights its suitability for detailed target identification Table 1.

Yanli Shi, Yi Jia, and Xianhe Zhang [11] developed FocusDet, which has demonstrated significant improvements in mAP. FocusDet achieved an mAP@.5% of 46.7% on the VisDrone dataset and an mAP@.5% of 87.8% on the CCTSDB2021 dataset. FocusDet's strength lies in its single-stage architecture, which is advantageous for addressing missed detection problems commonly associated with small, dense objects. Summaries of the models are presented in Table 1.

Table 1. Performance comparison of various object detection methods.

Method	Input Size	Dataset	mAP@.5:.95%	mAP@.5%
TinyDet-S	320 × 320	COCO 2017	26.0	-
TinyDet-M	320 × 320	COCO 2017	30.3	-
TinyDet-L	320 × 320	COCO 2017	35.5	-
HS-YOLO	640 × 640	Self-constructed	-	87.2
FocusDet	768 × 768	VisDrone	30.4	-
FocusDet	768 × 768	CCTSDB2021	-	87.8

While these models achieve commendable results in terms of MAP@.5, their performance tends to be less effective when evaluated with MAP@.5:.95. Despite their clear architectural components—backbone, neck, and head—their results in more comprehensive metrics and inference speeds have room for improvement. Our work builds upon these advancements by integrating the Slicing-Aided Hyper Inference (SAHI) algorithm to address the limitations observed in existing models. By combining SAHI with a robust detection framework, we aim to enhance the accuracy and efficiency of detecting and tracking small tanks, ultimately improving UAV-based tank destruction capabilities.

3 Methodology

This study presents a robust multi-stage methodology designed to address the unique challenges associated with detecting and tracking small enemy tanks using UAV-mounted vision systems. Small tanks, due to their compact size, camouflage, and presence in cluttered environments, often elude traditional detection frameworks. Therefore, our proposed system integrates advanced object detection, fine-grained image slicing, and reliable tracking algorithms to ensure accurate localization and continuous monitoring. The complete pipeline is illustrated in Fig. 1, demonstrating the interplay between detection, enhancement, and tracking stages tailored for small tank surveillance.

The first stage employs the YOLOv7 object detection framework to identify potential tank instances in UAV-captured imagery. YOLOv7 is selected due to its superior speed-accuracy trade-off and its multi-scale detection capabilities, which are crucial for detecting small tanks that may occupy only a minimal number of pixels in high-altitude aerial images [13]. Unlike larger objects, small tanks often lack distinct visual cues at low resolutions, making them difficult to detect using conventional object detectors. YOLOv7 addresses this limitation through its architectural features: the ELAN-based backbone extracts multi-scale features, the SPPFCSPC neck pools spatial information from different receptive fields, and the detection head operates at three resolution levels. These components work synergistically to preserve fine details in the image, allowing YOLOv7 to better detect small tanks amid complex terrain.

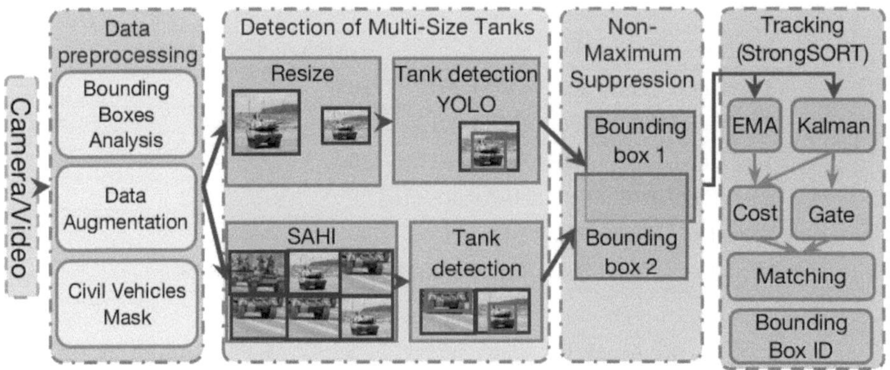

Fig. 1. Architecture of the Proposed Small Tank Detection and Tracking System.

However, even with YOLOv7's strong baseline performance, detecting small objects remains a persistent challenge, particularly when such targets are embedded in large-scale images typical of UAV reconnaissance. To enhance the system's sensitivity to small-scale tanks, we incorporate the SAHI (Slicing-Aided Hyper Inference) technique in the second stage. SAHI improves small object detection by decomposing the original high-resolution image into a series of smaller, overlapping slices. Each slice effectively zooms in on a localized region of the scene, enabling YOLOv7 to process and detect tanks at a finer granularity. Object detection is then performed independently on each slice, increasing the likelihood of detecting small tanks that would otherwise be missed due to scale reduction or background interference. Finally, detections from all slices and the full image are fused using Non-Maximum Suppression (NMS) to produce a comprehensive and non-redundant set of detections. This slicing strategy not only boosts the detection rate for small tanks but also reduces false negatives in sparse and cluttered environments.

Following detection, the third stage of the system employs StrongSort, a high-performance tracking algorithm built on the foundations of DeepSort, to maintain continuous identity tracking of detected tanks across video frames. Reliable tracking is essential in scenarios where tanks are partially obscured, temporarily exit the frame, or move rapidly through varying terrain. StrongSort enhances the robustness of tracking through three key mechanisms: an NSA Kalman Filter for improved motion prediction, a Vanilla Matching algorithm for refined object-track association, and a feature extraction module based on BoT (Bag of Tricks) with ResNet50 to encode the visual appearance of each tank. These features allow StrongSort to distinguish between multiple small tanks, reduce identity switches, and sustain object permanence even under visual occlusion.

The fusion of YOLOv7, SAHI, and StrongSort enables a comprehensive and reliable system tailored for the detection and tracking of small enemy tanks. Each component is chosen for its particular strengths in addressing the small object detection problem: YOLOv7 ensures baseline accuracy and real-time capability; SAHI enhances the visibility of small tanks by focusing on localized regions; and StrongSort maintains robust temporal consistency in tracking. Together, they form an end-to-end pipeline that not only locates and identifies small tanks but also enables continuous monitoring—an essential capability for autonomous UAV systems tasked with real-time threat analysis and engagement recommendation.

4   Experiment

4.1   Dataset and Preprocessing

To evaluate our proposed approach for small tank detection and tracking, we curated a specialized dataset designed to reflect real-world UAV surveillance scenarios. While standard datasets such as VisDrone [14] and MS COCO [6] offer broad benchmarks for small object detection, they are not tailored for the unique visual challenges associated with small military vehicles. These include camouflage, partial occlusion, and significant scale variations. Table 2 provides a summary of these commonly used datasets.

Table 2. Information of Popular Datasets for Small Object Detection

Dataset	Quantity	Input Size
VisDrone [14]	10,000 images	640×640
COCO [6]	200,000 images	640×640

For this work, we compiled a custom dataset comprising 932 high-resolution images (640×640 pixels), each manually annotated for small tank detection. These images were captured under varied environmental conditions to simulate realistic UAV flight observations, including differences in lighting, angle, terrain, and occlusion. A significant proportion of tanks in the dataset appear at small scales, often occupying less than 5% of the total image area—characteristics that pose substantial challenges for object detectors.

The dataset was partitioned into two subsets: 724 images (77.6%) were used for training, while the remaining 208 images (22.4%) were held out for validation. All annotations, including bounding boxes and class labels, were meticulously reviewed to ensure correctness and consistency. Non-tank images and mislabeled instances were removed to reduce noise and optimize the training signal.

To further improve the model's ability to detect small tanks, we applied a range of data augmentation techniques. These included geometric transformations (rotation, flipping, scaling), pixel-level noise injections, and affine distortions (shearing and shifting). Augmentation yielded an additional 300 labeled images, increasing the model's exposure to diverse tank appearances and sizes. This strategy aimed to simulate real-world UAV conditions where small tanks might appear under motion blur, partial visibility, or in cluttered scenes.

4.2 Bounding Box Analysis

Bounding box dimensions across the dataset indicate a strong emphasis on small objects. As shown in Table 3, most training and validation samples include bounding boxes with small width and height values. The average bounding box area in the training set is just 13,389 pixels, and even lower in many cases, which highlights the dataset's focus on detecting small-scale objects such as tanks viewed from high altitudes. This distribution directly informs our methodology, which integrates SAHI to enhance detection for such small targets.

Table 3. Bounding Box Dimension Summary for Training and Validation Sets

	Training Set			Validation Set		
	Width	Height	Area	Width	Height	Area
Average	96	83	13,389	124	99	16,698
Standard Deviation	107	75	29,820	116	71	25,353
Minimum	6	6	66	10	10	160
50th Percentile	63	61	4,005	80	87	7,529
Maximum	638	636	318,024	628	456	161,847

As illustrated in Fig. 2, the majority of bounding boxes are skewed toward smaller object sizes. This reinforces the necessity of using slicing-based inference (SAHI) and multi-resolution detection heads (YOLOv7) in our pipeline to ensure that small tanks are not overlooked.

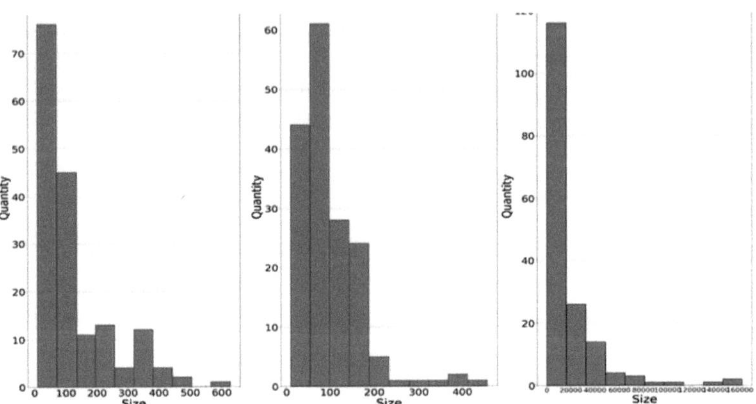

Fig. 2. Distribution of Bounding Box Sizes in the Dataset.

4.3   Model Training Environment

The model was trained and evaluated using Google Colab's cloud infrastructure. Experiments were conducted on an Ubuntu 22.04.3 LTS environment, equipped with a Tesla T4 GPU, 15GB GPU RAM, and 12GB system RAM. CUDA version 12.2 was used for GPU acceleration. The training procedure was carried out for 100 epochs, taking approximately 2 h to complete. These hardware and software specifications provided an efficient environment for testing lightweight yet powerful detection and tracking algorithms suitable for real-time UAV applications (Table 4).

Table 4. Model Training Configuration

Parameter	Value
OS	Ubuntu 22.04.3 LTS
GPU	Tesla T4
GPU Memory	15 GB
CPU Memory	12 GB
CUDA Version	12.2
Training Duration	2 h
Total Epochs	100

Throughout the training process, loss convergence and performance metrics (e.g., precision, recall, mAP) were monitored to ensure the model learned meaningful features. Both training and validation datasets offered consistent characteristics in object scale and visual diversity, ensuring a representative evaluation of our detection and tracking pipeline.

The next section presents quantitative results from experiments, comparing the effectiveness of our YOLOv7+SAHI+StrongSort pipeline against baseline detectors on small tank detection and multi-object tracking tasks.

5   Results

To evaluate the effectiveness of our proposed system for small tank detection, we trained the YOLOv7 model for 100 epochs and assessed its performance on the validation set using standard object detection metrics. Table 5 summarizes the results. The model achieved a precision of 0.92 and a recall of 0.87, indicating strong capability in correctly identifying true positives while maintaining a low false positive rate. The mean Average Precision (mAP) at an IoU threshold of 0.5 was 0.88, reflecting good performance under moderate overlap conditions.

However, under stricter localization constraints, the mAP@0.5:0.95 dropped to 0.59. This decline highlights the model's reduced accuracy in predicting tight bounding boxes, which is especially critical when detecting small tanks—objects that often appear at low resolutions and occupy minimal pixel areas. The relatively low mAP under this stricter metric suggests the bounding box predictions for small tanks were not consistently precise, despite correct detections in many cases.

Table 5. Model Performance Metrics (YOLOv7 on Validation Set)

Metric	Value
Number of Epochs	100
Confidence Score Threshold	0.50
IoU Score Threshold	0.65
Precision	0.92
Recall	0.87
mAP@0.5	0.88
mAP@0.5:0.95	0.59
Minimum Training Loss	0.03

Figure 3 visualizes the training and validation trends over the 100 epochs, including the evolution of precision, recall, mAP scores, and various loss functions. While the validation loss gradually declined over time, significant fluctuations were observed in the object loss curve. This instability may be attributed to the presence of many difficult-to-detect small tanks in the validation set, which challenge the model's confidence and localization abilities. Additionally, the relatively high learning rate may have introduced oscillations during optimization. Importantly, the performance drop in mAP@0.5:0.95 can also be explained by the dominance of small object instances in the dataset, which are inherently harder to localize with high precision.

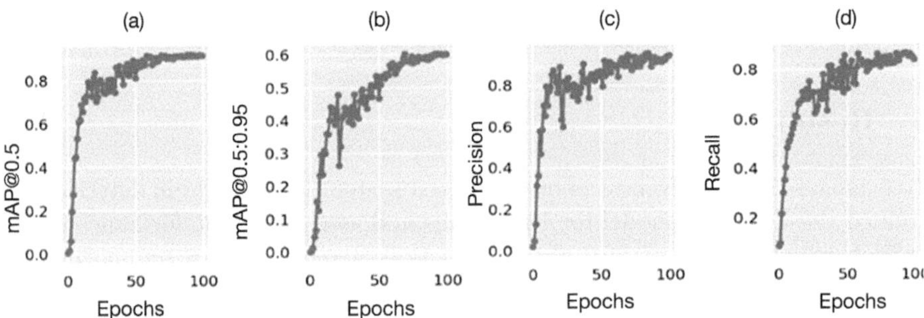

Fig. 3. Training and Validation Performance Metrics Over 100 Epochs.

To further investigate and improve the model's performance on small tanks, we integrated the Slicing Aided Hyper Inference (SAHI) algorithm into the

YOLOv7 inference pipeline. This addition was aimed at enhancing the model's ability to detect small objects by processing localized image patches instead of the full-resolution image. On a test set of 104 images, we compared inference time and detection accuracy between the original YOLOv7 and the YOLOv7+SAHI configuration.

The standalone YOLOv7 model completed the inference process in approximately 50 s, whereas the combination of YOLOv7 with SAHI took about 444.5 s. This represents a significant increase in computational time, primarily caused by SAHI's additional steps of dividing each image into smaller overlapping patches (slicing) and later reconstructing the detection results from these patches (recombination). Despite the longer processing time, this trade-off proved beneficial. As illustrated in Fig. 4, the SAHI-augmented YOLOv7 achieved considerably better detection of small tanks, successfully identifying several that the standard full-image YOLOv7 inference had failed to detect. This demonstrates that while SAHI introduces computational overhead, it substantially enhances the model's ability to detect small or densely clustered objects that might otherwise be overlooked.

The improvement can be attributed to SAHI's strategy of slicing large images into smaller overlapping windows, enabling the detection model to analyze fine-grained details with greater focus. This approach increases the effective resolution of small tanks in the input space, allowing the detector to better recognize their features and generate higher-confidence predictions. Consequently, the model becomes more robust to missed detections caused by size reduction or object blending with the background.

Fig. 4. Comparison of Small Tank Detection: YOLOv7 vs. YOLOv7+SAHI.

In summary, the experimental results demonstrate that the YOLOv7 model is highly effective in general object detection, achieving strong precision and recall scores. Nevertheless, its performance on small object detection—particularly small tanks—remains limited under stricter evaluation metrics. The integration of SAHI significantly enhances the detection capability for these small targets, albeit with increased inference time. This trade-off highlights a crucial balance between detection accuracy and real-time performance, particularly relevant for UAV-based surveillance and engagement systems that must detect small military vehicles in complex environments.

6   Conclusion

This study introduced an enhanced approach for small tank detection by integrating the Slicing-Aided Hyper Inference (SAHI) algorithm with the YOLOv7 object detection framework. The proposed system consists of three main components: YOLOv7 for robust object detection, SAHI for improved detection of small targets through image slicing, and StrongSort for object tracking. The model was trained on a dataset of 932 images, using an 80/20 training-validation split and fine-tuned over 100 epochs.

While the system demonstrated strong general detection capabilities-achieving a mAP of 0.88 at IoU 0.5-the performance dropped to 0.59 for mAP@0.5:0.95, highlighting challenges with precise localization and small object detection. This limitation is likely due to dataset constraints, such as limited diversity and a high proportion of small, partially occluded targets.

The integration of SAHI significantly improved the detection of small objects, as it enables finer analysis by slicing input images into smaller patches. However, this came at the cost of increased inference time. Moreover, the system struggled under conditions involving object occlusion, long-term disappearance, or non-ideal environments (e.g., night or adverse weather), limiting its applicability in real-world scenarios.

Future work will aim to address these challenges through several directions. First, we plan to build a unified model architecture that tightly integrates YOLOv7 and SAHI, with the goal of reducing inference latency while preserving accuracy. Second, we will expand and diversify the dataset to include varied conditions such as nighttime scenes and weather disturbances. Lastly, improvements to the tracking component—potentially through more robust multi-object tracking algorithms—will be explored to enhance stability and reliability in dynamic environments.

References

1. Bewley, A., Ge, Z., Ott, L., Ramos, F., Upcroft, B.: Simple online and realtime tracking with a deep association metric. In: 2016 IEEE International Conference on Image Processing (ICIP), pp. 3464–3468 (2016)

2. Chen, H., Wang, Y., Wang, X.: An overview of object detection with deep learning: the challenges and opportunities. J. Comput. Sci. Technol. **34**(4), 643–668 (2019)
3. Chen, S., Cheng, T., et al.: Tinydet: a lightweight object detector. arXiv preprint arXiv:2104.07807 (2021)
4. Goodfellow, I., Bengio, Y., Courville, A.: Deep Learning. MIT Press (2016)
5. Huang, J., Wang, L., Liu, X.: Slicing-aided hyper inference: a new approach for enhanced object detection. In: Proceedings of the IEEE Conference on Computer Vision and Pattern Recognition (CVPR) (2021)
6. Lin, T.-Y., et al.: Microsoft COCO: common objects in context. In: Fleet, D., Pajdla, T., Schiele, B., Tuytelaars, T. (eds.) ECCV 2014. LNCS, vol. 8693, pp. 740–755. Springer, Cham (2014). https://doi.org/10.1007/978-3-319-10602-1_48
7. Lin, Z., Chen, W., et al.: Hs-yolo: high-resolution yolo for small object detection. arXiv preprint arXiv:2104.07231 (2021)
8. Liu, W., et al.: SSD: single shot multibox detector. In: European Conference on Computer Vision (ECCV) (2020)
9. Mnih, V., Kavukcuoglu, K., Silver, D., Graves, A., Danihelka, I., et al.: Human-level control through deep reinforcement learning. Nature **518**(7540), 529–533 (2015)
10. Redmon, J., Farhadi, A.: Yolov3: an incremental improvement. arXiv preprint arXiv:1804.02767 (2018)
11. Shi, Y., Jia, Y., Zhang, X.: Focusdet: enhancing detection of small objects in dense scenes. IEEE Trans. Image Process. **31**, 1234–1246 (2022)
12. Wang, C.Y., Yeh, I.H., Hsu, J.H.: Yolov8: the next generation of object detection. In: Proceedings of the IEEE Conference on Computer Vision and Pattern Recognition (CVPR) (2022)
13. Wang, X., Li, X., Zhang, H., Liu, W., Sun, Y.: Yolov7: a high performance object detection framework. J. Comput. Vis. **125**(3), 456–478 (2021). https://doi.org/10.1007/s11263-021-01410-7
14. Zhang, Y., et al.: The visdrone dataset: an annotated dataset for object detection, tracking and counting in drone videos. In: IEEE Conference on Computer Vision and Pattern Recognition (CVPR), pp. 1230–1238. IEEE (2018)
15. Zhou, X., Wang, D., Wang, J.: Object detection with deep learning: a review. IEEE Trans. Pattern Anal. Mach. Intell. **44**(9), 4472–4489 (2022)

Deep Neural Networks in Cow Face Recognition

D. Swaroop$^{(\boxtimes)}$ and D. S. Guru

Department of Studies in Computer Science, University of Mysore, ManasagangotriMysuru, Karnataka 570006, India
swaroopdevaraju@gmail.com, dsg@compsci.uni-mysore.ac.in

Abstract. Accurate animal identification is vital for precision livestock farming, yet existing biometric methods often struggle with subtle inter-animal similarities and the lack of public datasets, especially for indigenous breeds. This study introduces a curated bovine facial dataset comprising 3,680 images from 184 Indian cows, generated through automated video frame extraction, sharpness-based filtering, YOLOv11 face detection, and clustering for quality and diversity. Three CNN architectures—ResNet-50, Inception-V3, and EfficientNet-B4—were evaluated using cross-entropy loss. EfficientNet-B4 achieved the highest closed-set accuracy (97.28%), while ResNet-50 showed superior open-set robustness with the lowest EER (0.0550). The results underscore architectural trade-offs in cattle biometrics and identify ResNet-50 as the most reliable model for secure livestock monitoring and traceability.

Keywords: Cow face recognition · ResNet-50 · closed-set recognition · open-set verification · livestock identification · animal biometrics

1 Introduction

The automated identification of cattle is crucial to precision dairy farming, improving health monitoring, feeding, and management, while holding socio-economic and cultural importance in rural communities. Misidentification or substitution can trigger ownership disputes, as noted by [1] in rural China. Traditional identifiers like branding or oral claims remain unreliable.

Computer vision and machine learning, inspired by human biometrics, have been applied for cattle recognition using facial, muzzle, horn, and coat feature to ensure tamper-proof identification and efficient herd management. [2] demonstrated that cattle distinguish individuals from 2D images; [3] introduced the Cows2021 dataset (10,402 images, 301 videos) achieving 57.0% Top-1 and 76.9% Top-4 accuracy; and [4] used Inception-V3 + BiLSTM with self-attention, reaching 93.3% on 50 cows. Architectural innovations improved performance [5] proposed SK-ResNet with selective kernels, [6] used CattleFaceNet (RetinaFace-MobileNet + ArcFace) with 91.3% accuracy at 24 FPS, and [7] developed PANet with Transformers and attention, achieving 88.03% on ICRWE (9,816 images, 483 cattle) under unconstrained conditions. Recent studies such as [8] with EMA-YOLOv8 and IGAM-iResNet (99.846%) further advanced multi-breed recognition. However, most systems remain limited to single-breed or controlled

C. Zaroliagis et al. (Eds.): ICAA 2026, LNCS 16423, pp. 156–168, 2026.
https://doi.org/10.1007/978-3-032-15621-1_13

datasets, and open-set evaluations vital for scalable, multi-breed recognition are still scarce.

Automated identification of cattle is vital to precision dairy farming, enhancing health monitoring, feeding, and management, while carrying socio-economic and cultural relevance in rural communities. Misidentification or substitution may trigger ownership or inheritance disputes, occasionally escalating into conflict. Similar cases were reported in rural China, where [1] observed cattle theft disputes in Guizhou being settled through customary systems, weakening governance. Traditional identifiers like branding or oral claims remain unreliable.

To bridge this gap, we curated a dataset of 184 cows from three Indian breeds (Gir, Badri, Pahadi) under real-world conditions. ResNet-50 [9], Inception-V3, and EfficientNet-B4 were evaluated using cross-entropy loss, with ResNet-50 showing superior performance, especially in open-set verification.

The key contributions of this paper are summarized as follows:

1. **Curated Dataset:** We introduce the first large-scale bovine facial dataset for indigenous cow recognition, comprising 3,680 high-quality images of 184 cows across three Indian breeds. The dataset was curated using sharpness filtering, YOLOv11 detection, and clustering to ensure diversity and reliability.
2. **Architectural Evaluation:** A comparative analysis of ResNet-50, Inception-V3, and EfficientNet-B4 highlights architectural trade-offs in fine-grained animal recognition.
3. **Benchmark and Recommendation:** ResNet-50 achieved 97.19% closed-set accuracy and the lowest Equal Error Rate (0.0550) in open-set verification, setting a benchmark for livestock biometrics.

The paper is structured as follows: Sect. 1 introduces the study; Sect. 2 explains materials and methods; Sect. 3 outlines the proposed approach; Sect. 4 discusses results; and Sect. 5 concludes with key findings and future work.

2 Materials and Methods

This section outlines the methodology, including the construction of a novel bovine facial dataset, the image acquisition and preprocessing pipeline, and the experimental framework adopted for model implementation and evaluation.

2.1 Dataset Collection and Experimentation Setup

This study presents a Bovine Face Recognition Dataset for training and evaluating deep learning models in cow identification. It includes 3,680 images from 184 Gir, Badri, and Pahadi cows, with 20 facial images per cow, split 70:30 for training and validation. Multi-pose images with varied lighting, angles, and backgrounds enhance real-world relevance. A summary is shown in Table 1.

Image Acquisition Process
All data collection followed ethical and animal welfare standards. Images and videos

Table 1. Detailed summary of the proposed Bovine Face Recognition dataset.

Attribute	Details
Initial Subjects Collected	188 unique cows representing the Indian breeds Gir, Badri, and Pahadi
Final Classes in Dataset	184 cows (Each cow represents a unique class)
Data Collected per Subject	4 static images (Left, Right, Up, Front) + 1 video
Frame Extraction Method	Quality filtering of video frames using Laplacian variance (sharpness-based)
Data Curation Criteria	Automated face detection (YOLOv11), followed by K-Means clustering to select representative images
Final Image Count per Cow	20 images
Train–Validation Split Ratio	70% Training, 30% Validation
Images in Training Set	14 images per cow
Images in Validation Set	6 images per cow
Total Number of Images	3,680 images (184 cows × 20 images)

were captured non-invasively from a safe distance without disturbing the cattle. Verbal consent was obtained from livestock owners after explaining the study's purpose, and animal comfort was prioritized by relying solely on observation to avoid stress or behavioral interference.

Multi-angle Data Capture

Image and video data were collected from 188 cows across farms in Mysuru, Chamarajanagar, and Mandya districts of Karnataka.

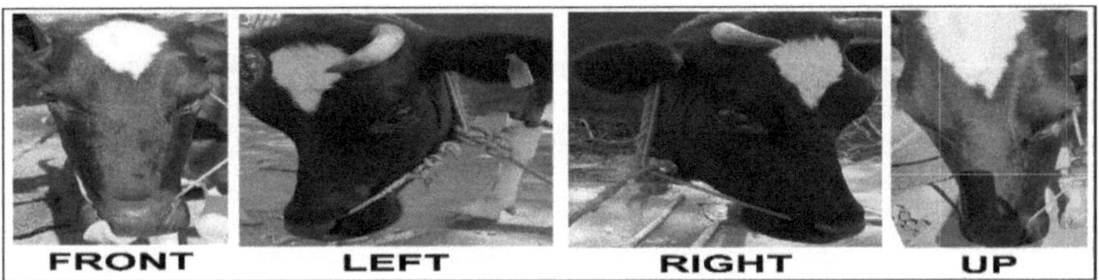

Fig. 1. Sample images of cow faces captured from multiple views.

Covering indigenous breeds like Gir, Badri, and Pahadi. Each cow was captured from four angles frontal, left, right, and upward tilt—along with one video (Fig. 1), ensuring comprehensive feature representation for real-world recognition.

Device and Equipment

A key feature of the dataset is its acquisition using consumer-grade Android devices, enabling practical and scalable data collection in farm settings. As listed in Table 2, cameras ranging from 13 MP to 48 MP introduced controlled variability in image quality, simulating real-world conditions without specialized equipment.

Table 2. Devices used for image acquisition.

Device Name	OS Version	Camera Resolution
OPPO A5	ColorOS 5.2.1 (Android)	13 MP rear camera
Redmi 9A	MIUI Global 12.0.26 Stable (Android)	13 MP rear camera
Redmi 9 Power Pro	MIUI 12 (Android 10)	48 MP rear camera
Samsung Galaxy M21	One UI 3.1 Core (Android 10)	48 MP rear camera
Vivo S	Funtouch OS 9 (Android 9.0 Pie)	16 MP rear camera

Video-Based Frame Extraction

In addition to still images, short videos were recorded for each cow as the primary data source, from which frames were automatically extracted and filtered using the variance of the Laplacian operator to retain sharp, in-focus images, yielding 4,699 candidate samples.

2.2 Pre-Processing

A multi-stage preprocessing pipeline was designed to standardize inputs, highlight facial features, and reduce background noise; the workflow is shown in Fig. 2.

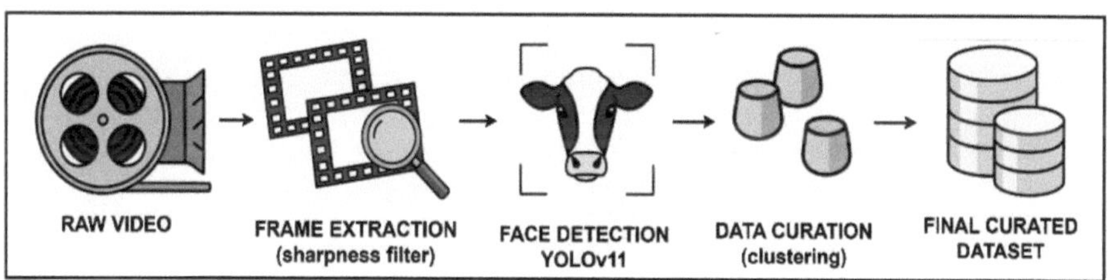

Fig. 2. The multi-stage data preprocessing and curation pipeline.

In the first stage, a custom YOLOv11 detector trained on 1,600 annotated images for 150 epochs was used to accurately detect bovine faces under varied conditions and applied to 4,699 frames for automated facial cropping (Fig. 3). After facial detection, a data curation step was applied to reduce visual redundancy among frames extracted from the same video. This process comprised two stages:

(i) **Feature Extraction**, where a pre-trained ResNet-18 model converted each cropped facial image into a high-dimensional feature vector;

(ii) **Clustering and Selection**, in which K-Means clustering was performed on each cow's feature set to select a diverse and representative subset. The number of clusters, k, was chosen to balance diversity and quality, with k = 20 determined as optimal through preliminary evaluation.

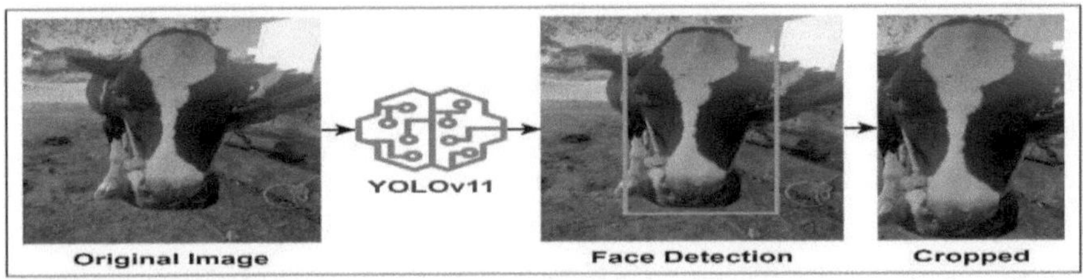

Fig. 3. YOLOv11 Segmentation Output Original, Masked, and Segmented Regions

Using k = 20 with balanced pose diversity, 20 unique images per cow (14 training, 6 validation) were selected via cluster centroids. After excluding cows with insufficient samples, 184 individuals remained. Cropped images were resized to 224 × 224; training data were augmented (cropping, flipping, rotation, color jitter), while validation data were only resized and normalized, ensuring a clean, balanced dataset for robust recognition.

2.3 Proposed Methodology

The proposed cow face recognition system employs a deep learning pipeline integrating advanced backbone architectures with a standard classification head for accurate identification. As shown in Fig. 4, it comprises preprocessing, feature extraction, and classification with a customized training strategy. Three CNN backbones—ResNet-50, Inception-V3, and EfficientNet-B4—were evaluated to determine the most effective architecture for this fine-grained task.

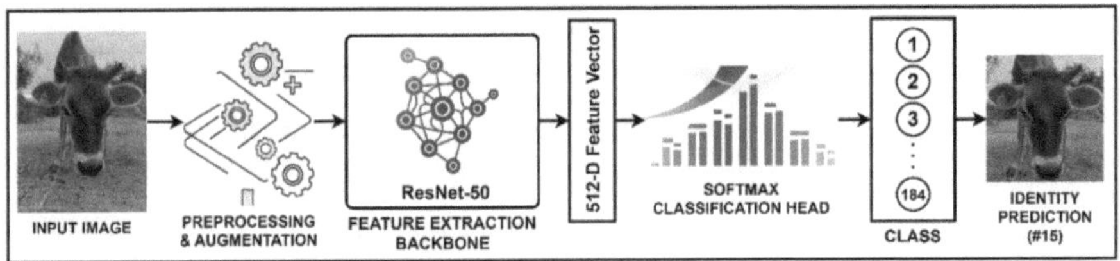

Fig. 4. Illustration of the Proposed Model.

Input Image Preparation

All images from the curated dataset were resized to 224 × 224 pixels for standardized input. Using the multi-stage YOLO-based pipeline for face detection and cropping, the images capture each cow's facial features while minimizing background interference.

Data Augmentation

To enhance model robustness and generalization, a comprehensive set of data augmentation techniques was applied during training (Fig. 5). These included:

(i) Random Resized Crop, simulating variations in camera distance and framing;
(ii) Random Horizontal Flipping, providing mirrored views to handle left-right orientation changes;
(iii) Random Rotation ($\pm 15°$), accounting for minor head tilts;
(iv) Color Jitter, varying brightness, contrast, and saturation to emulate diverse lighting conditions;

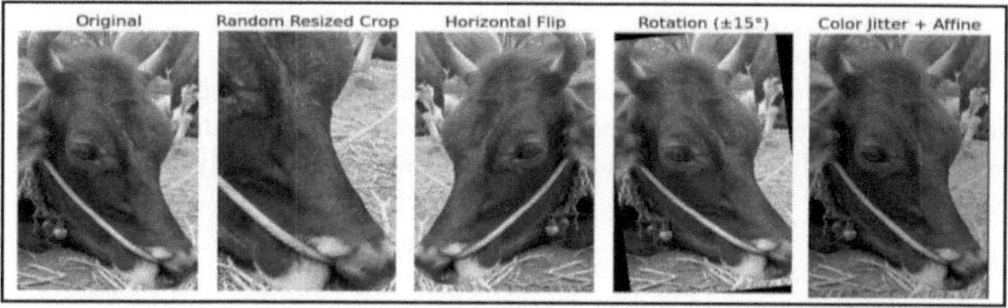

Fig. 5. Visual representation of the sample images after data augmentation.

This augmentation strategy was crucial for improving model performance under challenging farm conditions. To assess its impact, additional trials were run by disabling individual augmentations. Results showed that geometric transforms like rotation and flipping most effectively improved generalization to unseen poses, confirming the value of spatial and photometric augmentations for robustness in varied farm environments.

Feature Extraction

The proposed system employs a feature extraction backbone that converts input images into 512-dimensional embeddings for identity recognition. Three CNN architectures were evaluated: (1) ResNet-50, a 50-layer residual network enabling deep feature learning and serving as a strong baseline (Fig. 6); (2) Inception-V3, which captures multi-scale features through concurrent 1×1, 3×3, and 5×5 convolutions with improved efficiency [10]; and (3) EfficientNet-B4, which uses compound scaling to balance depth, width, and resolution, achieving high accuracy with optimal efficiency [11].

For each architecture, the 224×224 input passes through convolutional blocks, followed by global average pooling and a linear layer to generate a standardized 512-D feature vector representing the cow's identity, which is subsequently fed to the classification head for recognition.

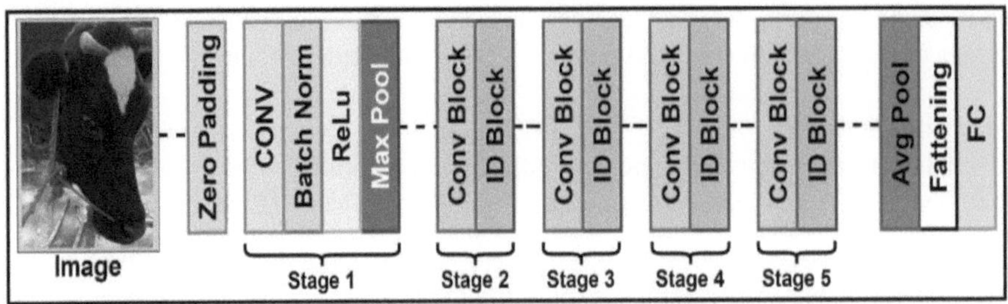

Fig. 6. Illustration of the prosed feature extraction using the ResNet-50 Model.

Classification Head and Loss Function

A Softmax-based classifier maps 512-D embeddings to cow identities without using complex metric learning. It includes a Dropout layer (rate 0.1) for regularization and a fully connected layer that projects the 512-D features to 184 identity classes, generating logits for classification.

The model is optimized using Cross-Entropy Loss, which integrates LogSoftmax and Negative Log-Likelihood in a numerically stable form to measure divergence between predicted probabilities and ground-truth one-hot labels. It is formally defined as:

$$\mathcal{L}_{CE} = -\frac{1}{N}\sum_{i=1}^{N}\sum_{c=1}^{C}y_{i,c}\log(p_{i,c}) \tag{1}$$

Here, N denotes the number of samples in a batch, C represents the number of classes (184 cows), $y_{i,c}$ is a binary indicator equal to 1 if sample i belongs to class c and 0 otherwise, and $p_{i,c}$ is the predicted probability for sample i belonging to class c, obtained via the Softmax function applied to the logits. This formulation directly encourages the model to assign high probabilities to the correct class, providing a robust and efficient approach for closed-set identification.

Training Configuration

For stable convergence and optimal performance, the models were trained using a tailored strategy combining a modern optimizer and adaptive learning rate scheduling.

- **Optimizer:** Network parameters were optimized with AdamW, decoupling weight decay from gradient updates. The learning rate was initialized at 1×10^{-4} with a weight decay of 1×10^{-2}, promoting efficient learning while regularizing the model to prevent overfitting.
- **Learning Rate Scheduler:** A CosineAnnealingLR scheduler gradually reduced the learning rate from 1×10^{-4} to 1×10^{-6} over 50 epochs following a cosine curve, aiding the model in converging to a broad minimum and enhancing generalization.
- **Early Stopping:** Training is halted if the validation loss did not improve for 5 consecutive epochs (patience = 5), ensuring the model reflects optimal generalization.
- **Computational Environment:** All experiments were conducted in Google Colab using an NVIDIA T4 GPU, implemented with PyTorch and the timm library.

ResNet-50 gave the best balance of accuracy and efficiency, making it suitable for edge or mid-range GPU deployment. EfficientNet-B4 was slightly better but more expensive, while Inception-V3 performed moderately. Overall, the pipeline remains both efficient and accurate.

3   Results and Experimentation

This section analyzes the experimental results of the proposed cow face recognition framework, covering the setup, face detection performance, and recognition results under closed- and open-set scenarios, followed by a comparative analysis. The overall workflow is shown in Fig. 7.

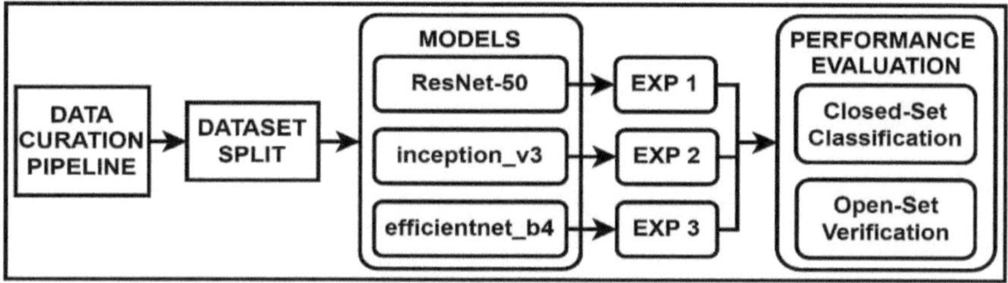

Fig. 7. Experimental workflow of the proposed method.

3.1   Dataset and Experimental Setup

The proposed system was evaluated on the curated Bovine Face Recognition Dataset with 184 labeled cow classes, using a 70:30 split (2,576 training and 1,104 validation images). Data augmentation was applied only to the training set to enhance model robustness.

3.2   Cow Face Detection and Segmentation with YOLOv11 Performance Analysis

The YOLOv11-based segmentation model effectively isolated cow facial regions. Trained on 1,600 annotated images, it showed consistent detection across varied poses and lighting. As shown in Fig. 8(a), mAP@50 stabilized between 0.76 and 0.78 over 100 epochs, confirming robust performance. The confusion matrix (Fig. 8b) and dataset annotations (Figs. 8c–d) further illustrate the detector's diversity and balance.

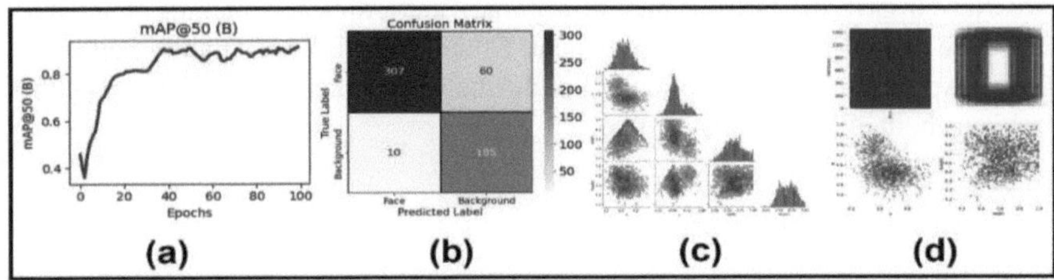

Fig. 8. A (a) mAP@50 curve across 100 epochs for cow face detection using YOLOv11, (b) confusion matrix of the segmentation model, (c) and (d) Annotation statistics for the YOLOv11 training dataset.

3.3 Recognition Performance

Biometric recognition was assessed under closed-set (known) and open-set (unseen) scenarios (Fig. 9). ResNet-50's training metrics are shown in Fig. 10, and Fig. 11 compares closed-set performance across models.

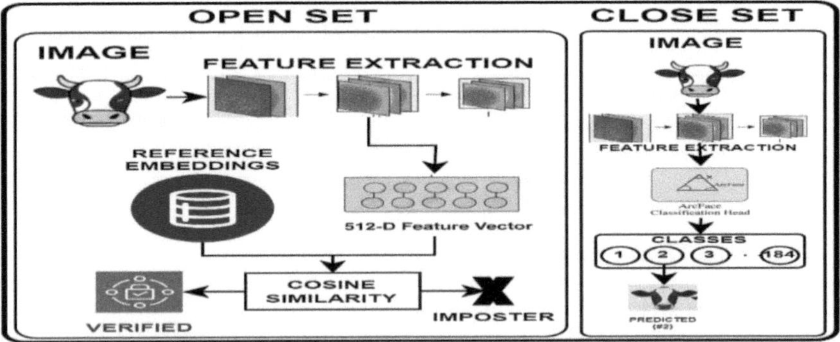

Fig. 9. Illustration of open-set and closed-set evaluation scenarios.

Closed-Set Classifications

In the closed-set task, all three CNN backbones exhibited strong recognition performance, demonstrating the effectiveness of the feature extraction architectures. The corresponding performance metrics are summarized in Table 3.

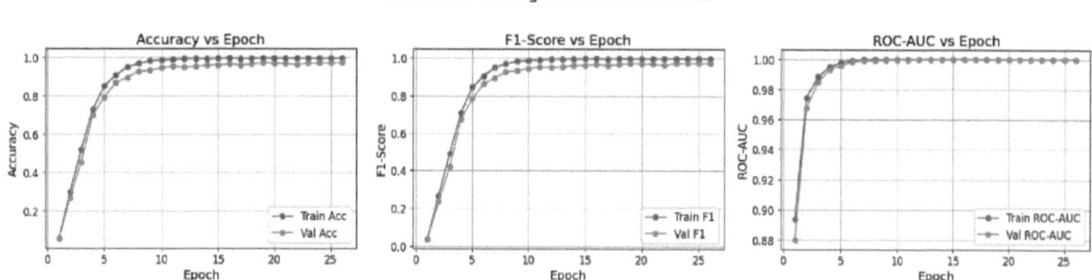

Fig. 10. Training and validation performance metrics of the proposed model (**ResNet-50**), showing trends in accuracy, F1-score, and the ROC curve.

EfficientNet-B4 achieved the highest accuracy (97.28%), closely followed by ResNet-50 (97.19%) with both reaching a near-perfect ROC-AUC of 99.99%. ResNet-50 showed a slightly higher F1-score (97.22%), while Inception-V3 trailed with 95.38% accuracy, confirming that both modern and classic architectures effectively capture fine-grained features for this task.

Table 3. Comparison of Model Performance on the Cow Face Dataset.

EXP_NO	Model Name	Accuracy (%)	ROC-AUC (%)	F1-Score (%)
1	ResNet-50	97.19	99.99	97.22
2	Inception-V3	95.38	99.97	95.36
3	efficientnet_b4	97.28	99.99	97.16

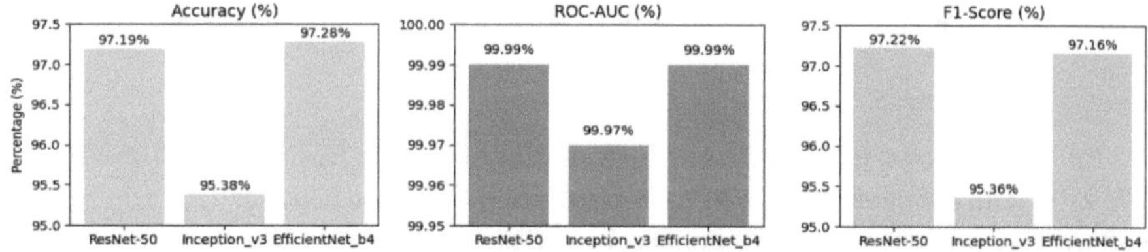

Fig. 11. Graphical comparison of closed-set classification performance between the evaluated models.

Open-Set Verification.

Verification Procedure

For open-set verification, the dataset was organized to reflect real-world conditions. A gallery of 14 images per 140 known cows was created, while two query sets were used—genuine (6 remaining images of known cows) and imposter (20 images from 44 unseen cows).

Performance Across Thresholds

Open-set verification results (Table 4) reveal distinct model differences. ResNet-50 achieved the lowest EER (0.0550) effectively balancing FAR and FRR and reliably rejecting unknowns. EfficientNet-B4 showed a higher EER (0.1574), and Inception-V3 recorded 0.1118. These findings indicate that high closed-set accuracy doesn't ensure open-set robustness with ResNet-50 offering a more stable, separable embedding space.

Table 4. Equal Error Rate (EER) Comparison for Open-Set Verification.

Model	Threshold @ EER	FAR	FRR	EER*
ResNet-50	0.800	0.0403	0.0698	0.0550
Inception-V3	0.700	0.1882	0.0355	0.1118
efficientnet_b4	0.900	0.0112	0.3035	0.1574

** EER is approximated by averaging the FAR and FRR values at the threshold where their difference is minimal.*

Table 5. Open-Set Verification Performance (FRR vs. TAR) Across Thresholds.

Threshold	Inception-V3 FRR	Inception-V3 TAR	EfficientNet-B4 FRR	EfficientNet-B4 TAR	ResNet-50 FRR	ResNet-50 TAR
0.10	0.0000	1.0000	0.0000	1.0000	0.0000	1.0000
0.20	0.0000	1.0000	0.0000	1.0000	0.0000	1.0000
0.30	0.0000	1.0000	0.0000	1.0000	0.0000	1.0000
0.40	0.0000	1.0000	0.0000	1.0000	0.0000	1.0000
0.50	0.0000	1.0000	0.0000	1.0000	0.0000	1.0000
0.60	0.0012	0.9988	0.0000	1.0000	0.0012	0.9988
0.70	0.0355	0.9645	0.0000	1.0000	0.0110	0.9890
0.80	0.2251	0.7749	0.0160	0.9840	0.0698	0.9302
0.90	0.7723	0.2277	0.3035	0.6965	0.2560	0.7440

Table 5 As shown in Table 5, at its EER threshold of 0.80, ResNet-50 achieved a TAR of 0.9302 with balanced FAR, while EfficientNet-B4 reached a higher TAR (0.9840) but with greater FAR. ResNet-50's consistent performance across thresholds underscores its suitability for high-security applications. All experiments were repeated with different random seeds, and the averaged results showed minimal variation, confirming the pipeline's stability and reproducibility.

4   Discussion

The evaluation of three CNNs revealed a trade-off between closed-set accuracy and open-set robustness. EfficientNet-B4 achieved the highest closed-set accuracy (97.28%) but a higher EER (0.1574), showing over-specialized features. ResNet-50 offered balanced performance with slightly lower accuracy (97.19%) yet the best open-set robustness (EER = 0.0550), indicating better generalization for real-world use. Inception-V3 showed moderate results in both tasks.

Table 6. Comparison of cattle recognition systems in the literature.

Model	Backbone	Loss Function	Dataset (Cattle IDs)	Accuracy
CattleFaceNet (2021)	**RetinaFace + MobileNet**	**ArcFace**	**~ 90 cattle**	**91.3%**
DBCA-Net (2023)	**Swin-based (custom)**	**Softmax**	**658 cattle**	**95.34%**
PANet (2023)	**Vision Transformer (ViT)**	**Triplet Loss**	**~ 483 cattle**	**88.03%**
Proposed	**ResNet50**	**Softmax**	**184 cattle**	**97.19%**

Table 6 highlights the superior performance of the proposed ResNet-50 model, achieving 97.19% accuracy—outperforming Cattle-FaceNet (91.3%), PANet (88.03%), and DBCA-Net (95.34%). Unlike earlier models limited by smaller datasets or lower accuracy, the proposed approach, trained on 184 cattle IDs, demonstrates greater robustness and effectiveness. Overall, the results show that although EfficientNet-B4 excels in closed-set tasks, ResNet-50 offers superior open-set verification, making it the most reliable choice for secure livestock identification.

5   Conclusion

This study presents a robust framework for individual cow identification using a curated multi-breed dataset the first of its kind. Evaluating top CNNs revealed a trade-off between closed-set accuracy and open-set robustness, with ResNet-50 emerging as the most balanced model (97.19% accuracy, EER = 0.0550). The framework's strength lies in its YOLO-based detection, clustering-based redundancy reduction, and deep feature extraction. It shows strong potential for real-world livestock monitoring, genetic tracking, and theft prevention. Future work will expand breed diversity, enhance environmental robustness, enable edge deployment, and explore Vision Transformer architectures for further gains.

Dataset Accessibility: The datasets created during the current study are available from the corresponding author on reasonable request.

References

1. Xu, X., Yang, D.: Resolution of disputes concerning stolen cattle. Front. Law China **5**(4), 532–547 (2010)
2. Coulon, M., Deputte, B.L., Heyman, Y., Baudoin, C.: Individual recognition in domestic cattle (Bos taurus): evidence from 2D-images of heads from different breeds. PLoS ONE **4**(2), e4441 (2009)
3. Gao, J., Burghardt, T., Andrew, W., Dowsey, A.W., Campbell, N.W.: Towards self-supervision for video identification of individual holstein-friesian cattle: The cows2021 dataset (2021). arXiv preprint arXiv:2105.01938

4. Qiao, Y., Clark, C., Lomax, S., Kong, H., Su, D., Sukkarieh, S.: Automated individual cattle identification using video data: a unified deep learning architecture approach. Front. Anim. Sci. **2**, 759147 (2021)
5. Gong, H., et al.: Facial recognition of cattle based on SK-ResNet. Sci. Program. **2022**(1), 5773721 (2022)
6. Xu, B., et al.: CattleFaceNet: a cattle face identification approach based on RetinaFace and ArcFace loss. Comput. Electron. Agric. **193**, 106675 (2022)
7. Li, J., Zou, X., Wang, S., Chen, B., Xing, J., Tao, P.: A Parallel Attention Network For Cattle Face Recognition (2024). arXiv preprint arXiv:2403.19980
8. Xiao, Z., Dai, W., Li, C., Liang, W., Chen, X.: Enhanced multi-breed cattle face recognition in complex environments using attention-based deep learning. Visual Comput. 1–20 (2025)
9. He, K., Zhang, X., Ren, S., Sun, J.: Deep residual learning for image recognition. In: Proceedings of the IEEE Conference on Computer Vision and Pattern Recognition, pp. 770–778 (2016)
10. Szegedy, C., Vanhoucke, V., Ioffe, S., Shlens, J., Wojna, Z.: Rethinking the inception architecture for computer vision. In: Proceedings of CVPR, pp. 2818–2826 (2016)
11. Tan, M., Le, Q.V.: EfficientNet: rethinking model scaling for convolutional neural networks. In: Proceedings of ICML, pp. 6105–6114 (2019)

Scheduling Control Tasks Using Safety-Guided RL

Prateek Ganguli[1], Tingan Zhu[1], and Samarjit Chakraborty[1,2](✉)

[1] The University of North Carolina at Chapel Hill, Chapel Hill, USA
{pganguli,tingan}@cs.unc.edu
[2] TU Munich Institute for Advanced Study, Munich, Germany
samarjit@cs.unc.edu

Abstract. Cyber-Physical Systems (CPSs), such as self-driving vehicles, have become increasingly complex, involving the use of multiple control tasks to meet the desired safety requirements. One challenge is to lower costs by reducing hardware requirements for executing these tasks. Traditionally, meeting task deadlines was considered to be a measure of safety, but in recent times, there has been work in synthesizing schedules where tasks can miss deadlines such that a system-level notion of safety is still satisfied. However, such approaches are inflexible, as the task schedules may need to be re-synthesized when new tasks are introduced. We propose a model-less Reinforcement Learning (RL) motivated approach for schedule synthesis, where tasks can dynamically be added or removed. This RL strategy is guided by a quantifiable system-level safety property. It offers a more flexible approach to improving resource efficiency, while maintaining safety. We illustrate its benefits using both deterministic and stochastic versions of our proposed schedules.

Keywords: Cyber-Physical System · Reinforcement Learning · System-Level Safety · Schedule Synthesis · Controller Design

1 Introduction and Related Work

Modern CPSs consist of multiple controllers, each managing specific subsystems [5,10]. In autonomous vehicles, for example, cruise control, lane-keeping, braking, and steering each require periodic state measurements to compute control inputs. These computations can be costly, involving machine learning assisted sensor data processing and mathematical operations such as differentiation or integration. Timely updates are critical to maintain closed-loop stability and meet control objectives. Executing all computations within sampling deadlines often demands significant hardware resources. To reduce costs, tasks are typically multiplexed on a single processor to minimize processor count and communication. Prior work has improved resource efficiency by simplifying controllers or increasing sampling periods. But these cannot accommodate the dynamic evolution of CPSs, where over-the-air updates may introduce new tasks, and reconfigurations to preserve schedulability [36].

© The Author(s), under exclusive license to Springer Nature Switzerland AG 2026
C. Zaroliagis et al. (Eds.): ICAA 2026, LNCS 16423, pp. 169–182, 2026.
https://doi.org/10.1007/978-3-032-15621-1_14

In this paper, we propose a RL motivated framework for synthesizing deadline hit/miss patterns for such control tasks. Such patterns and subsequently the pattern of control input updates are determined by a policy learned during the RL training phase. It also offers a means of adjusting the balance between (i) resource utilization and (ii) ensuring that the controller keeps the system within a defined safety boundary for the chosen deadline hit/miss pattern. The training for each control task may be done independently of other tasks, ensuring that new control tasks can be added to the system without requiring any adjustments to the existing tasks. Our experiments show that this may allow for doubling the number of control tasks running on the system, while still meeting the desired safety requirements.

As prior works [3,15,18,28,31] on scheduling control tasks under deadline misses do not allow adding new tasks at runtime without requiring a resynthesis of the schedule, it is not possible to directly compare our work with existing works in this domain. The flexibility we gain, however, comes at a price. Unlike the techniques proposed in prior work that, *e.g.*, rely on automata-based schedule synthesis [32], and provide provably safe guarantees, our RL-based methods do not provide such guarantees. But, using experiments with multiple plant models and controllers, we provide empirical evidence of safety.

Stability Versus Safety: Several recent papers (*e.g.*, [7,11,12,18,23,27] have studied the problem of stability when control tasks are subjected to imperfect timing behaviors, such as deadline misses. However, we would like to point out that in this work we use a very general notion of *system-level safety* [15,16] that is characterized by the deviation of the trajectory of the closed-loop system in its state space from the trajectory to be followed when the control task is subjected to an ideal timing behavior (*e.g.*, no deadline misses). Stability and this notion of system-safety are orthogonal to each other—even if a system is stable, such a safety property might be violated when the system is still in a transient state. Similarly, depending on the notion of stability in question (*e.g.*, bounded stability) and the chosen safety margin, a system might be unstable (*e.g.*, keeps on oscillating around a reference) but satisfy our safety property.

Related Work: The existing body of work related to our approach can be largely divided into three categories. The first line of work aims to synthesize a deadline hit or miss pattern for a controller, while ensuring safety. Here, weakly-hard timing models [13,14,27,29] and schedule-level safety enforcement [8,18,31,33] provide complementary perspectives on tolerating deadline violations, but do not leverage learning-based synthesis techniques. Work in [22,23,28] characterize the effects of missing deadlines on system dynamics. A second class of work focuses on timing analysis and scheduling controller code [4,19,24] and repairing an unsafe control task schedule for it to become schedulable, for example, by adjusting the sampling periods of the control tasks [26]. Along the same lines, work in [17] introduced methods for repairing unsafe learned controllers with minimal behavioral deviation, while other approaches synthesized safe schedules using simulations, designing prototypes [21] and formal methods based verification [9] and patching [25, 34, 35] , without using RL.

A third but an orthogonal line of work attempts to ensure safety for RL based approaches for safe control and scheduling. Towards this, shielding techniques that augment RL with formal safety guarantees, either by synthesizing runtime enforcers [2], integrating safety layers during training [1], or decentralizing safety for multi-agent systems [6, 20] have been explored. Leveraging some of these techniques to provide provable safety guarantees in our work is a future direction that may be explored. Our work in this paper differs from the above in its use of RL directly for schedule synthesis, guided by safety constraints throughout training, thus enabling resource-efficient, adaptive and safety-aware scheduling policies. To the best of our knowledge, none of the previous works allow new control tasks to be introduced during runtime without requiring any form of redesign or resynthesis.

Technical Contributions: In summary, the technical contributions of this paper and the novelty of the proposed approach over techniques that have been proposed for resource-aware scheduling of control tasks include: (**i**) A lightweight, safety-guided model-less RL to synthesize deadline hit/miss patterns for control tasks. The RL learns the value of a parameter β that determines the activation threshold – *i.e.*, how far the system's deviation must grow from the safety margin before the controller task triggers the computation of a new control input. A smaller β means the controller reacts earlier, updating more often, which is safer but increases processor utilization, whereas a larger β is more efficient but riskier. After training, no further modifications to the policy are required. The learning process is guided by a quantified notion of safety and resource efficiency. (**ii**) Our proposed framework is flexible, as it allows us to tradeoff between prioritizing meeting safety requirements and resource efficiency. This is controlled by tuning the parameter α before training the RL policy, which defines the relative importance of safety versus efficiency during the RL training. (**iii**) Finally, this approach allows for new control tasks to be added at runtime, requiring no modifications to be made to the schedule. As long as the overall utilization of the tasks is within the capacity of the processor, new tasks can be simply added to the system for scheduling with existing tasks.

Paper Organization: Section 2 provides the necessary control theory background. Notions of system level safety are described in Sect. 3. Next, Sect. 4, describes the details of how the RL-based controller is designed and trained, including the reward function that is used. In Sect. 5, we outline the evaluation of our approach, and discuss the results of our experiments. Section 6 provides a summary of our work, and discusses possible future extensions.

2   Control Theory Background

We restrict the scope of this work to Linear Time-Invariant (LTI) systems and model the closed-loop system using its *state-space model* [9,15] in Eq. (1):

$$\dot{x}\left(t\right) = \mathbf{A} \cdot x\left(t\right) + \mathbf{B} \cdot u\left(t\right) , \tag{1}$$

where the state vector $x\left(t\right) \in \mathbb{R}^n$ represents the state of the system, and the input vector $u\left(t\right) \in \mathbb{R}^m$ represents the control input applied. The system matrices $\mathbf{A} \in \mathbb{R}^{n \times n}$ and $\mathbf{B} \in \mathbb{R}^{n \times m}$ determine the dynamics of the system.

2.1   Discrete-Time Control Systems

Since control tasks running on processors are triggered by digital clocks, the evolution of the system has to be modeled using states of the system sampled at discrete points in time. Sampling of the system states is done periodically, where each sampling period lasts h time units (as decided by the controller designer). Therefore, Eq. (1) is converted to the following:

$$x\left[k+1\right] = \mathbf{\Phi} \cdot x\left[k\right] + \mathbf{\Gamma} \cdot u\left[k\right] , \tag{2}$$

where the state vector $x\left[k\right] \in \mathbb{R}^n$ represents the state of the system at the kth sampling period, *i.e.*, at time $t = k \cdot h$, and the input vector $u\left[k\right] \in \mathbb{R}^m$ represents the control input calculated using $x\left[k\right]$. This control input is applied for a duration of h, until a new state of the system is sampled. The state matrix $\mathbf{\Phi} \in \mathbb{R}^{n \times n}$ and input matrix $\mathbf{\Gamma} \in \mathbb{R}^{n \times m}$ now denote how the dynamics of this sampled time system evolves. These matrices are derived from their continuous-time counterparts as $\mathbf{\Phi} = e^{\mathbf{A} \cdot h}$ and $\mathbf{\Gamma} = \int_0^h e^{\mathbf{A} \cdot s} \mathbf{B} \cdot ds$ (see [15] and its references).

2.2   State-Feedback Controllers

Controllers that determine the control input to be applied based on the state of the system are referred to as state-feedback controllers. A simple state-feedback controller is described as $u\left[k\right] = -\mathbf{K} \cdot x\left[k\right] + \mathbf{F} \cdot r$, where r is the set reference to which we want the state of the closed-loop system to converge to over time. The feedback gain matrix $\mathbf{K} \in \mathbb{R}^{m \times n}$ represents the factor by which the current state of the system, $x\left[k\right]$, should be multiplied to obtain the control input to be applied, irrespective of the set reference value r. The feedforward gain matrix is denoted by $\mathbf{F} \in \mathbb{R}^{m \times n}$, and is calculated as $\mathbf{F} = 1 / \left(\left(\mathbf{I} - \mathbf{\Phi} + \mathbf{\Gamma} \cdot \mathbf{K} \right)^{-1} \cdot \mathbf{\Gamma} \right)$.

There are numerous controller design techniques to derive the feedback gain matrix $\mathbf{K}$. The LinearâĂŞQuadratic Regulator (LQR) is one such method. LinearâĂŞQuadratic Regulator (LQR) calculates the optimal gain matrix $\mathbf{K}$, such that the cost function described by $J = \sum_{k=0}^{\infty} x\left[k\right]' \cdot \mathbf{Q} \cdot x\left[k\right] + u\left[k\right]' \cdot \mathbf{R} \cdot u\left[k\right]$ is minimized. This is done by solving the Riccati equations resulting from the state-space model and the cost function, J. Matrices $\mathbf{Q}$ and $\mathbf{R}$ denote the relative influence of each of the state variables, and that of the control input, on the designed controller respectively.

3   Modeling System-Level Safety

In a CPS, the overall goal is to ensure safety as the system's states evolve over time. As the aim of the controller is to bring the system to the desired reference state, there can be multiple safe trajectories of the system which deviate from the ideal trajectory, but still converge to some limit of the reference value. We therefore need to define what a safe trajectory is. There can be various notions of safety. Classical control theory offers multiple qualitative measures of safety, such as whether or not a given closed-loop system is stable. However, in order to compare different approaches to realize the goal of ensuring safety, we need to have a more quantitative measure.

One such quantitative measure of safety is the distance between the current state of the system from some considered safety threshold. This safety threshold is determined by the designer of the system, and forms a 'safety pipe' around the possible safe states of the system. In this paper, we borrow the concept of 'safety pipe' from [15], however the novelty of our work is to use RL to guide the control task schedule synthesis while ensuring that the system trajectory stays within the safety pipe. The distance of the trajectory from the center of the pipe (or the 'ideal trajectory,' *e.g.*, obtained when the control task meets all its deadlines) gives us a means of quantifying safety. To formally specify the notion of a 'safety pipe', consider an 'ideal' dynamics or trajectory of the closed-loop system. If the safety threshold around this ideal trajectory is p, then the 'safety pipe' consists of the region specified by $-p \leq x \leq p$, where x is the state of the closed-loop system whose controller is to be scheduled.

4   Scheduling Control Tasks Using RL

RL enables an agent to act in a dynamic environment to maximize a reward R. The agent follows a policy π that maps states to actions, with parameters optimized during training to maximize expected return. Here, we design an RL-based scheduler for control tasks, with the goal of reducing resource utilization while keeping the closed-loop system within a safety threshold. For this, consider N control tasks running on the same processor as our setup. For task τ_i, safety is defined by a pipe parameter p_i, so the system is *unsafe* if $x_i < -p_i$ or $x_i > p_i$, where x_i is the current state and r_i the reference.

Resource use is reduced by allowing tasks to occasionally miss deadlines. If a task meets its deadline, we call it a *hit* and apply $u[k] = -\mathbf{K}x[k] + \mathbf{F}r$. If it *misses*, we hold the previous input: $u[k] = u[k-1]$. The pattern of hits and misses is governed by an RL-derived policy.

Reward Function: The reward for each step is $R(d, u) = -\big(\alpha d + (1 - \alpha)u\big)$, where $d = \|x - r\|$ and u is the ratio of hits to total control periods. Maximizing R reduces both deviation d and utilization u, balanced by $\alpha \in [0, 1]$.

Policy Design: We consider two formulations of the policy π: deterministic and stochastic. The deterministic case provides a simple baseline, while the stochastic variants are designed to address some of its limitations.

(a) Deterministic Policy. The deterministic policy uses a threshold-based rule:
$\pi(d, \beta) = \begin{cases} \text{hit}, & d > \beta p, \\ \text{miss}, & \text{otherwise}, \end{cases}$, where p is the safety radius and $\beta \in [0, 1]$ is a tunable parameter. The controller applies a fresh control input only when the deviation d exceeds βp: $u[k] = \begin{cases} -\mathbf{K}x[k] + \mathbf{F}r, & d_k > \beta p, \\ u[k-1], & \text{otherwise}. \end{cases}$. The RL agent learns the optimal β by maximizing the discounted return $G = \sum_{k=0}^{H} \gamma^k R(d_k, u_k)$, where $\gamma \in [0, 1)$ is the discount factor.

This deterministic rule is simple and interpretable, but its binary switching behavior can lead to certain drawbacks. In particular, when the system state fluctuates near the threshold $d \approx \beta p$, the controller may alternate rapidly between "hit" and "miss" actions, producing oscillatory utilization and deviation patterns. This can cause bursts in processor demand and what may be interpreted as small limit cycles in closed-loop behavior. Moreover, if several controllers share the same processor and their states cross thresholds at similar times, they may synchronize their "hit" decisions, causing temporary overloads. Finally, because the deterministic threshold is non-differentiable, learning its optimal setting may be slower or less stable, and the resulting policy can be sensitive to noise or modeling errors. These challenges motivate the exploration of smoother and more flexible, probabilistic formulations of the policy.

(b) Stochastic Policy. To mitigate these limitations, we replace the hard threshold with a smooth, probabilistic decision rule. Instead of deterministically choosing between "hit" or "miss," the controller defines a *hit probability* $p_{\text{hit}}(d) \in [0, 1]$ that increases monotonically with the deviation d. At each sampling instant, an action is drawn as $a_k \sim \text{Bernoulli}\big(p_{\text{hit}}(d_k)\big)$, where $a_k{=}1$ means a hit and $a_k{=}0$ a miss. The deterministic rule is recovered as a limit case when the probability transition becomes infinitely steep.

Benefits and Drawbacks of the Stochastic Policy: This stochastic formulation brings several benefits. First, it smooths the switching behavior near the threshold, reducing oscillations and chattering. Second, when multiple controllers operate on a shared processor, randomization naturally de-synchronizes their "hit" events, distributing workload more evenly in time. Third, since $p_{\text{hit}}(d)$ is differentiable with respect to its parameters, the learning process for those parameters (*e.g.*, via policy-gradient methods) becomes smoother and more stable. Fourth, the probabilistic decision is more tolerant to noise or uncertainty in measurements, avoiding abrupt changes in control actions due to small disturbances. Finally, this approach introduces additional tunable parameters that allow finer adjustment of how sharply each task reacts to increasing deviation, complementing the global reward weight α. In effect, α controls the overall trade-off between safety and efficiency during training, while the parameters of $p_{\text{hit}}(d)$

determine how sensitively and smoothly each individual task enforces its safety margin.

However, stochastic policies also come with trade-offs. Since even near the safety boundary there remains a small chance of a miss, deterministic safety guarantees are weakened and replaced by probabilistic ones. This makes formal verification or assurance more complex. Random decision outcomes can also introduce jitter, leading to stochastic variations in response time and settling behavior. Furthermore, the instantaneous processor demand becomes random, which may require additional constraints or admission control to maintain predictable real-time performance. Hence, the improved smoothness and flexibility of stochastic scheduling must be balanced with attention to these new uncertainties. We investigate two stochastic/smooth formulations for $p_{\mathrm{hit}}(d)$:

(i) Logistic: $p_{\mathrm{hit}}(d; \beta, \kappa) = \sigma\!\left(\kappa\!\left(\frac{d}{p} - \beta\right)\right)$, where $\sigma(z) = \frac{1}{1+e^{-z}}$. Here, β shifts the midpoint of the probability curve and determines when the controller starts prioritizing hits, while $\kappa > 0$ controls the steepness of transition. Larger κ makes the transition sharper, recovering the deterministic threshold as $\kappa \to \infty$.

(ii) Exponential: $p_{\mathrm{hit}}(d; \beta, \lambda) = 1 - e^{-\lambda[d-\beta p]_+}$, where $[z]_+ = \max(z, 0)$. In this form, β again defines the activation threshold, and $\lambda > 0$ controls how rapidly the hit probability rises once $d > \beta p$. Larger λ results in a steeper and more reactive transition.

Both parameterizations provide smooth, tunable ways to transition from low to high hit probabilities as deviation increases. The parameters $\{\beta, \kappa\}$ or $\{\beta, \lambda\}$ are learned through training by maximizing the expected discounted return, using the same reward function defined earlier. This allows the policy to balance safety (through β) and responsiveness (through κ or λ), leading to controllers that are both resource-efficient and dynamically adaptive.

5 Experimental Results

We now evaluate the effectiveness of the schedules generated by the proposed RL-based synthesis in balancing processor utilization and system safety. We compare the baseline deterministic policy with the two stochastic variants, *logistic* and *exponential*, to understand their respective trade-offs in terms of deviation control, utilization, and stability. We also investigate the impact of adding new tasks at runtime to evaluate scalability.

5.1 Setup and Methodology

We consider three plant models from [30]: the F1-Tenth Car (F1), Cruise Control (CC), and DC Motor (DC), as summarized in Table 1. These systems differ significantly in order and their dynamic behavior, allowing for an evaluation of controller adaptability. Each plant's continuous-time state-space matrices $\mathbf{A}$ and $\mathbf{B}$ were discretized into $\mathbf{\Phi}$ and $\mathbf{\Gamma}$ using a sampling period of 0.02 s, after which a one-period sensor-to-actuator delay was introduced. All references were set to zero, and each controller was designed as described in Sect. 2.2.

For all experiments, the safety pipe parameter p_i was fixed at 1.5, while the reward function parameters were set to $\alpha = 0.35$ and $\gamma = 0.99$. These values were chosen to achieve a balanced trade-off between minimizing state deviation and reducing processor usage. Each simulation ran for 800 sampling steps, which was our safety horizon. During training, the deterministic policy learned an optimal threshold parameter β for each plant, while the stochastic policies additionally learned the parameters κ (logistic) and λ (exponential) through policy-gradient updates. After convergence, each closed-loop system reached a steady utilization level u_{stable}, reported in Table 1. To assess dynamic scalability, we also examined the impact of adding new tasks during runtime and recorded the maximum deviation d_{stable} after re-stabilization, as shown in Table 3. The deviation is defined as the Euclidean distance between the current state vector and the reference vector, and measures how much a trajectory deviates from an ideal one.

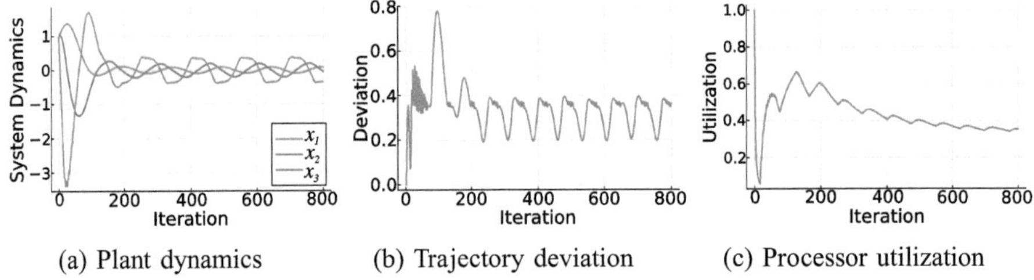

(a) Plant dynamics   (b) Trajectory deviation   (c) Processor utilization

Fig. 1. RL-based Cruise Controller following the deterministic policy.

5.2   Results

Deterministic Policy. Figure 1a shows the temporal evolution of the CC plant states under the deterministic policy. The states do not converge exactly to zero but oscillate within a bounded range around the reference. As shown in Fig. 1b, after an initial transient of about 200 sampling steps, the system settles with a maximum deviation of 0.39, remaining well within the safety margin of 1.5. Correspondingly, Figurev 1c demonstrates that processor utilization stabilizes around 35.12%. Similar behavior is observed for the F1 and DC models, where utilization stabilizes at 7.62% and 1.12%, respectively (see Table 1).

The observed oscillations in both deviation and utilization stem from the binary switching nature of the deterministic policy: the controller misses all deadlines until the deviation exceeds the learned threshold β, after which it hits all deadlines until the deviation drops below β. This cyclic onâĂŞoff behavior results in cyclic oscillations and occasional bursts in processor activity. Despite these oscillations, the deterministic policy maintains safety across all plants. However, its sharp switching around the boundary introduces two limitations.

First, near-threshold oscillations can cause bursts of processor demand, especially when multiple controllers synchronize their "hit" phases. Second, the non-differentiability of the threshold makes policy optimization slower and less stable. These drawbacks motivated our exploration of smooth, stochastic formulations.

The trade-off parameter α directly influences this balance: setting $\alpha=1$ prioritizes deviation minimization, resulting in full utilization (identical to an ideal always-hit controller), whereas $\alpha=0$ leads to total deadline misses and instability. Thus, the chosen $\alpha=0.35$ provides a balanced and safe operating point across all the plants we experimented with.

Stochastic Policies: To address the abrupt switching and utilization bursts observed in the deterministic policy, we trained stochastic policies that replace the hard hit/miss boundary with a smooth probability curve. The logistic and exponential variants introduce tunable parameters κ and λ that control the steepness of transition from "miss" to "hit". Figure 2a shows the closed-loop dynamics for the CC model under the logistic policy. Compared to the deterministic case in Fig. 1a, the system's deviation and utilization evolve more smoothly. The probabilistic switching effectively reduces the amplitude of the limit cycles, and the cumulative reward converges more steadily as the controller refines its κ parameter. The smoother transitions also prevent simultaneous activation of multiple tasks, thereby reducing the risk of processor overload.

Table 1. Plant models & deterministic policy results.

Plant	State-Space Model	β	u_{stable}	max. d_{stable}
F1	$\mathbf{A}=\begin{bmatrix} 0 & 6.5 \\ 0 & 0 \end{bmatrix}$ $\mathbf{B}=\begin{bmatrix} 0 \\ 19.68 \end{bmatrix}$	0.317	7.62%	0.50
CC	$\mathbf{A}=\begin{bmatrix} 0 & 1 & 0 \\ 0 & 0 & 1 \\ -6.05 & -5.29 & -0.24 \end{bmatrix}$ $\mathbf{B}=\begin{bmatrix} 0 \\ 0 \\ 2.48 \end{bmatrix}$	0.253	35.12%	0.39
DC	$\mathbf{A}=\begin{bmatrix} -10 & 1 \\ -0.02 & -2 \end{bmatrix}$ $\mathbf{B}=\begin{bmatrix} 0 \\ 2 \end{bmatrix}$	0.052	1.12%	0.08

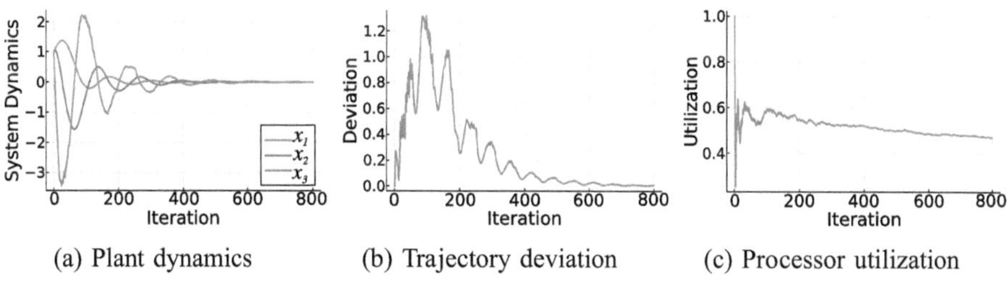

(a) Plant dynamics   (b) Trajectory deviation   (c) Processor utilization

Fig. 2. RL-based Cruise Controller following the logistic policy.

Table 2 quantitatively compares both the stochastic variants, which may be compared against the results for the deterministic baseline in Table 1. For the CC model, the logistic policy yields $u_{\text{stable}}=52.13\%$ and $d_{\text{stable}}=0.46$, slightly higher utilization but marginally greater deviation compared to the deterministic policy (35.12%, 0.39). The exponential policy, on the other hand, achieves lower utilization (29.82%) at the expense of a larger deviation (1.01), approaching the safety limit. For the F1 plant, the logistic policy significantly increases utilization to 45.02% but maintains small deviations (0.40), while the exponential policy is more conservative (4.14% utilization, 0.82 deviation). For the DC plant, both stochastic policies maintain very low utilization and deviation, with the logistic policy achieving slightly higher responsiveness.

These results illustrate a clear trade-off: stochastic policies improve temporal smoothness and desynchronize task activations, but may consume slightly more or less processor time depending on their parameterization. The logistic policy generally achieves tighter safety margins with moderate utilization, while the exponential policy provides better efficiency at the cost of slightly degraded precision near the safety boundary. Importantly, both variants preserve safety, with all deviations staying within the safety pipe.

Overall, stochastic policies demonstrate that randomization helps mitigate the chattering behavior of the deterministic controller, distributing processor load more evenly and reducing limit-cycle oscillations. However, the randomness also introduces variability in instantaneous performance and slightly weakens the deterministic guarantee, and thus, safety becomes probabilistic rather than absolute. Thus, the choice between deterministic and stochastic formulations depends on whether smoother real-time performance or strict determinism is preferred.

Table 2. Results for stochastic policies.

Plant	Logistic			Exponential		
	κ	u_{stable}	max. d_{stable}	λ	u_{stable}	max. d_{stable}
F1	0.891	45.02%	0.40	0.518	4.14%	0.82
CC	0.498	52.13%	0.46	0.802	29.82%	1.01
DC	1.000	4.39%	0.05	1.000	2.02%	0.121

Runtime Task Addition: We further assess how the proposed approach handles the dynamic addition of control tasks at runtime. Table 3 reports the resulting deviations and total utilization when additional tasks are introduced to the baseline configuration (B, *i.e.*, one each of F1, CC, and DC). Adding a single DC task increases total utilization only modestly (from 43.87% to 44.99%) and causes negligible deviation changes across plants. Adding more tasks gradually raises utilization, reaching 81.23% in the most demanding configuration with two additional DC and one additional CC tasks. Although deviations rise slightly (e.g., $d_{\text{stable}}=1.04$ for F1), all remain within the defined safety margins.

These results confirm that the learned RL controllers can safely accommodate additional tasks at runtime without retraining or schedule resynthesis. However, scalability is limited by processor capacity, and beyond roughly 80% utilization, further additions risk unsafe growth in deviation. This highlights the balance between flexibility and timing constraints in resource-constrained systems.

Summary: In summary, the deterministic controller provides an interpretable and efficient baseline but suffers from sharp threshold switching and synchronous task activations. The stochastic policies alleviate these issues by introducing smoother transitions and desynchronized behavior, resulting in steadier closed-loop performance. The logistic variant offers tighter control with moderate efficiency, while the exponential variant is more resource-saving but slightly less accurate. Across all experiments, both stochastic policies maintained safety within defined bounds, validating their effectiveness in improving controller smoothness and scalability under varying task loads.

Table 3. Introducing new tasks.

Additional Plant Model(s)	max. d_{stable}			Total u_{stable}
	F1	CC	DC	
$B = F1 + CC + DC$	0.50	0.39	0.083	43.87%
$B + 1 \times DC$	0.52	0.41	0.086	44.99%
$B + 2 \times DC$	0.54	0.42	0.087	46.11%
$B + 1 \times CC + 2 \times DC$	1.04	0.82	0.122	81.23%

6   Concluding Remarks and Future Work

This paper presents a model-less Reinforcement Learning (RL) based approach for safe and flexible scheduling of control tasks in Cyber-Physical Systems, allowing tasks to miss deadlines while ensuring system-level safety. By training each control task independently and relying on a small set of learned policy parameters, our approach enables scheduling policies that adapt to the dynamic addition or removal of tasks, with no need for retraining or centralized resynthesis. The deployment of the scheduler is *model-less* as we only need to store the learned parameters and not the full model (*e.g.*, a large neural network).

In addition to the deterministic formulation, which serves as an interpretable baseline, we introduce two stochastic variants—logistic and exponential—that smooth the hit/miss decision process and mitigate the oscillatory and synchronous behaviors observed under the deterministic rule. Experiments across multiple plant models demonstrated that all learned policies maintained safety margins while achieving substantial reductions in processor utilization, with the stochastic formulations offering smoother utilization profiles and improved desynchronization across tasks.

While our method captures the trade-off between safety and resource efficiency through the tunable parameters α and the policy-specific parameters (β, κ, λ), it does not yet provide formal safety guarantees. An important direction for future work is the development of hybrid approaches that combine the flexibility of our RL-based synthesis with formal runtime assurances, possibly via shielding or contract-based enforcement. Moreover, while our current formulation assumes perfect state observability and fixed control delays, extending the framework to account for sensor noise, estimation uncertainty, and variable actuation delays would make it more robust for real-world deployment. Incorporating such uncertainties into the RL training process, perhaps using robust or adversarial training, is a promising research avenue. Another compelling direction is exploring decentralized scheduling in multi-core or distributed processors, where interactions between independently trained stochastic controllers may affect global safety. Integrating multi-objective RL methods could enable finer control over trade-offs between safety, performance, and energy consumption, further broadening the applicability of our approach to a wider class of CPS applications. Finally, in our current formulation, and also in our experiments, for ease of exposition we implicitly assumed that the sampling periods of all the controllers were the same. This assumption may be relaxed using slightly more sophisticated scheduling schemes and needs further exploration.

Acknowledgments. This work is supported by the NSF award #2038960. Chakraborty's work is also supported by a Dieter Schwarz Courageous Research Grant and he is currently also a Fellow of the TUM IAS.

References

1. Alshiekh, M., et al.: Safe reinforcement learning via shielding. In: 32nd Conference on Artificial Intelligence (AAAI) (2018)
2. Bloem, R., et al.: Shield synthesis: runtime enforcement for reactive systems. In: Tools and Algorithms for the Construction and Analysis of Systems (TACAS) (2015)
3. Bordoloi, U.D., et al.: Autonomy-driven emerging directions in software-defined vehicles. In: Design, Automation and Test in Europe Conference (DATE) (2023)
4. Chakraborty, S., Erlebach, T., Thiele, L.: On the complexity of scheduling conditional real-time code. In: Workshop on Algorithm & Data Structures (WADS) (2001)
5. Chakraborty, S., et al.: Automotive cyber-physical systems: a tutorial introduction. IEEE Des. Test **33**(4), 92–108 (2016)
6. Elsayed-Aly, I., et al.: Safe multi-agent reinforcement learning via shielding. In: 20th International Conference on Autonomous Agents and MultiAgent Systems (AAMAS) (2021)
7. Geelen, W., et al.: The impact of deadline misses on the control performance of high-end motion control systems. IEEE Trans. Ind. Electron. **63**(2), 1218–1229 (2016)
8. Ghosh, B., et al.: Statistical hypothesis testing of controller implementations under timing uncertainties. In: IEEE 28th International Conference on Embedded and Real-Time Computing Systems and Applications (RTCSA) (2022)
9. Ghosh, B., et al.: Statistical verification of autonomous system controllers under timing uncertainties. Real-Time Syst. **60**(1), 108–149 (2024)
10. Goswami, D., Schneider, R., Chakraborty, S.: Co-design of cyber-physical systems via controllers with flexible delay constraints. In: Asia and South Pacific Design Automation Conference (ASP-DAC) (2011)
11. Goswami, D., Schneider, R., Chakraborty, S.: Re-engineering cyber-physical control applications for hybrid communication protocols. In: Design, Automation and Test in Europe Conference (DATE) (2011)
12. Goswami, D., Schneider, R., Chakraborty, S.: Relaxing signal delay constraints in distributed embedded controllers. IEEE Trans. Control Syst. Technol. **22**(6), 2337–2345 (2014)

13. Hamdaoui, M., Ramanathan, P.: A dynamic priority assignment technique for streams with (m, k)-firm deadlines. IEEE Trans. Comput. **44**(12), 1443–1451 (1995)
14. Hammadeh, Z.A.H., et al.: Bounding deadline misses in weakly-hard real-time systems with task dependencies. In: Design, Automation & Test in Europe Conference & Exhibition (DATE) (2017)
15. Hobbs, C., et al.: Safety analysis of embedded controllers under implementation platform timing uncertainties. IEEE Trans. Comput. Aided Des. Integr. Circuits Syst. **41**(11), 4016–4027 (2022)
16. Hobbs, C., et al.: Quantitative safety-driven co-synthesis of cyber-physical system implementations. In: International Conference on Cyber-Physical Systems (ICCPS) (2024)
17. Lu, P., et al.: Repairing learning-enabled controllers while preserving what works. In: 15th ACM/IEEE International Conference on Cyber-Physical Systems (ICCPS) (2024)
18. Maggio, M., et al.: Control-system stability under consecutive deadline misses constraints. In: 32nd Euromicro Conference on Real-Time Systems (ECRTS) (2020)
19. Maxiaguine, A., et al.: Rate analysis for streaming applications with on-chip buffer constraints. In: Asia & South Pacific Design Automation Conference (ASP-DAC) (2004)
20. Melcer, D., et al.: Shield decentralization for safe multi-agent reinforcement learning. In: 36th International Conference on Neural Information Processing Systems (NeurIPS) (2022)
21. Oetjens, J.H., et al.: Safety evaluation of automotive electronics using virtual prototypes: state of the art and research challenges. In: Design, Automation Conference (DAC) (2014)
22. Pazzaglia, P., et al.: Beyond the weakly hard model: measuring the performance cost of deadline misses. Dagstuhl Artifacts Scr. **106**, 4.1–4.2 (2018)
23. Pazzaglia, P., et al.: DMAC: deadline-miss-aware control. Dagstuhl Artifacts Series **133**, 3:1–3:3 (2019)
24. Phan, L.T.X., et al.: Modeling buffers with data refresh semantics in automotive architectures. In: International Conference on Embedded Software (EMSOFT) (2010)
25. Roy, D., et al.: GoodSpread: criticality-aware static scheduling of CPS with multi-QoS resources. In: IEEE Real-Time Systems Symposium (RTSS) (2020)
26. Roy, D., et al.: Timing debugging for cyber-physical systems. In: Design, Automation and Test in Europe Conference (DATE) (2021)
27. Vreman, N., et al.: Stability and performance analysis of control systems subject to bursts of deadline misses. In: Euromicro Conference on Real-Time Sys. (ECRTS) (2021)
28. Vreman, N., et al.: Deadline-miss-adaptive controller implementation for real-time control systems. In: 28th IEEE Real-Time and Embedded Technology and Applications Symposium (RTAS) (2022)
29. Vreman, N., et al.: WeaklyHard.jl: scalable analysis of weakly-hard constraints. In: IEEE 28th Real-Time and Embedded Technical and Applied Symposium (RTAS) (2022)
30. Xu, S.: Control Model Benchmarks for Python (2024). https://github.com/shengjiex98/controlbenchmarks
31. Xu, S., et al.: Safety-aware flexible schedule synthesis for cyber-physical systems using weakly-hard constraints. In: Asia and South Pacific Design Automation Conference (ASP-DAC) (2023)

32. Xu, S., et al.: Safety-aware implementation of control tasks via scheduling with period boosting and compressing. In: International Conference on Embedded and Real-Time Computing Systems and Applications (RTCSA) (2023)
33. Xu, S., et al.: Statistical approach to efficient and deterministic schedule synthesis for cyber-physical systems. In: International Symposium on Automated Technology for Verification and Analysis (ATVA) (2023)
34. Yeolekar, A., et al.: Checking scheduling-induced violations of control safety properties. In: Automated Technology for Verification and Analysis (ATVA) (2022)
35. Yeolekar, A., et al.: Repairing control safety violations via scheduler patch synthesis. In: ACM 16th International Conference on Cyber-Physical Systems (ICCPS) (2025)
36. Zhang, L., et al.: Schedule management framework for cloud-based future automotive software systems. In: International Conference on Embedded and Real-Time Computing Systems and Applications (RTCSA) (2016)

Freshness Monitoring and Shelf-Life Estimation of Bread

D. Nandini$^{(\boxtimes)}$, D. S. Guru , K. N. Neetha, and K. M. Kavya

Department of Studies in Computer Science, University of Mysore, Manasagangotri, Mysore, Karnataka 570006, India
nandiniloku@gmail.com, dsg@compsci.uni-mysore.ac.in,
neetha.k.n.18@gmail.com, kavyamarashetty@gmail.com

Abstract. This study presents a YOLOv11-based framework for automated assessment of bread freshness over a period of ten days. A comprehensive dataset of 3,600 bread samples collected from 20 bakeries was created to capture preservative effects and spoilage progression, enabling precise edibility grading. An advanced preprocessing pipeline employing YOLOv11-based region-of-interest (ROI) extraction ensured analysis focused on relevant bread portions. The proposed framework achieved strong segmentation and classification performance, with mAP50 scores of 0.965 for both bounding box and mask predictions and an overall classification accuracy of 81%. Notably, it excelled in identifying the extreme freshness stages. Comparisons with texture-based feature extraction methods and conventional classifiers validated its robustness and superiority. These findings demonstrate YOLOv11's potential as a scalable tool for non-destructive bread freshness monitoring, shelf-life estimation, and automated food quality inspection.

Keywords: Bread freshness · YOLOv11 · Non-destructive quality assessment · Deep learning · Image-based classification · Shelf-life estimation

1 Introduction

Bread is a perishable staple food whose quality deteriorates rapidly after baking due to staling, texture changes, and microbial growth. Monitoring freshness across storage days is critical for bakeries to ensure consumer safety, optimize supply chain management, and reduce food waste. Conventional inspection practices rely heavily on human judgment, which is subjective, inconsistent, and labor-intensive. This creates a pressing need for automated, non-invasive methods to assess bread edibility.

With the rise of computer vision and deep learning, image-based approaches have become promising alternatives for food quality analysis. Among these, the YOLO (You Only Look Once) family of models has shown remarkable success in object detection tasks due to its real-time performance and robust accuracy. The recently introduced YOLOv11 extends beyond detection to include segmentation and classification, making it suitable for analyzing subtle visual cues in bread that evolve across different days of storage.

C. Zaroliagis et al. (Eds.): ICAA 2026, LNCS 16423, pp. 183–194, 2026.
https://doi.org/10.1007/978-3-032-15621-1_15

This paper investigates whether YOLOv11 can classify bread samples according to their storage age (Day 1 to Day 10), thereby serving as a foundation for automated bread freshness assessment. A dataset of 3,600 annotated bread images was collected from 20 bakeries under controlled conditions. Using this dataset, we develop a YOLOv11-based segmentation and classification framework and evaluate its performance across ten freshness categories.

1.1 Related Work

Bread quality assessment has traditionally relied on physical, chemical, or sensory analyses, which are labor-intensive, subjective, and unsuitable for real-time monitoring. To overcome these limitations, image-based techniques integrated with statistical, machine learning, and deep learning methods have been explored for objective evaluation.

Karimi et al. (2012) analyzed bread samples using a flatbed scanner with texture and GLCM features combined with MLR, achieving R2 = 0.994. Similarly, Singh and Kaur (2012) used a CCD camera to extract texture features correlated with crust and color attributes, reporting R2 values of 0.9467, 0.9449, and 0.9416 for L*, a*, and b*. Jouki et al. (2009) used a chroma meter and achieved R2 = 0.9941–0.9961, confirming the utility of colorimetry in quality monitoring.

Machine learning extended these efforts beyond correlation. Ali et al. (2021) integrated SVM, FWRVM, and ANN models for classification, attaining 96.67% accuracy. Paquet-Durand et al. (2012) applied digital imaging with ANN for bread roll classification, achieving a 4.9% error rate, demonstrating ML's ability to capture nonlinear patterns in bread quality.

Advanced imaging with deep learning further enhanced prediction. Ali et al. (2021a) employed X-ray μ-CT with a U-net CNN for pore size quantification, while Amigo et al. (2021) used digital imaging with GLCM texture features for baguette assessment and hyperspectral NIR imaging with PCA and MCR for staling detection—highlighting non-destructive, fine-grained analysis potential.

Kavitha et al. (2022) proposed handcrafted texture-based edibility prediction, distinguishing edible and inedible samples but limited to binary classification. Recently, Guru and Nandini (2025) applied Vision Transformers (ViTs), achieving 92% accuracy for edibility prediction, though still binary and computationally intensive.

Overall, literature reveals a shift from statistical models to ML, deep learning, and transformers for bread quality analysis. Yet, most studies address binary classification or isolated traits. To bridge this gap, the present work employs YOLOv11, a segmentation-enabled real-time detector, to classify bread images across ten consecutive day categories—capturing subtle crust and crumb cues for scalable freshness monitoring.

The key contributions of this study are:

- **Development of a novel dataset:** A comprehensive dataset is created, comprising 3,600 collected from 20 bakeries. The dataset was designed to capture preservative influences and spoilage progression over a 10-day period, enabling effective grading of bread edibility.
- **Advanced preprocessing pipeline**: Region-of-interest (ROI) extraction was performed using a combination of YOLOv11-based precise segmentation techniques, ensuring that only relevant portions of the bread samples were analyzed.

- **Bread days detection and classification:** A YOLOv11-driven framework was proposed to accurately detect and classify bread across different storage days, facilitating automated freshness assessment.
- **Comprehensive experimental validation:** The proposed approach was rigorously evaluated by comparing it with texture-based feature extraction methods coupled with multiple conventional classifiers, thereby demonstrating its robustness and superiority.

Organizational structure of the paper is as follows: Sect. 1 presents the introduction and related work. Section 2 outlines the dataset and experimental setup. Section 3 details the proposed methodology, Sect. 4 provides experimental details, including hyperparameter specification, focusing on the results, discussions, and comparative analysis. Finally, Sect. 5 presents the conclusion of the study.

2 Materials and Methods

2.1 Dataset and Experiment Setup

The proposed investigation makes a notable contribution by introducing a comprehensive dataset tailored for bread edibility classification (shelf-life), addressing the absence of benchmark datasets in this domain.

To build this dataset, bread samples were collected from 20 diverse bakeries (labeled BK1 to BK20) in and around Mysore and Chamarajanagara capturing real-world variations in baking practices. Specifically, white bread samples were selected, with each bakery contributing three slices tracked over a 10-day period post-baking.

Fig. 1. Spoilage progression of sample bread over 10 days, with dryness from Day 4 and mold onset from Day 5.

A total of 3600 images were acquired using a Moto G60 smartphone equipped with a 108MP + 8MP + 2MP rear camera, OPPO A5 (13MP rear camera, Color OS 5.2.1, Android) and Redmi 9A (13MP rear camera, MIUI Global 12.0.26, Android) at a

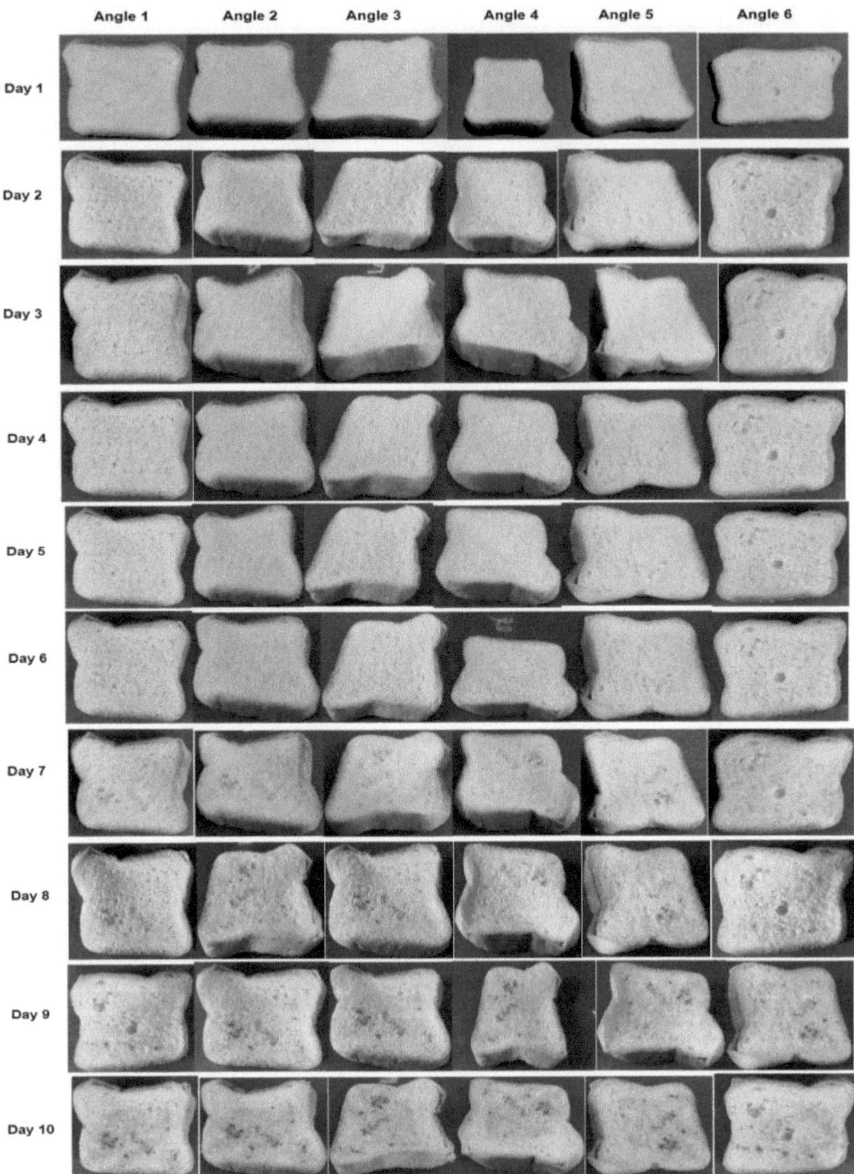

Fig. 2. Pictorial representation of each sample over 10 days with different angles.

fixed 1-m distance and varied angles. A neutral gray background and natural daylight, standardized across angles, ensured consistent lighting. The bread was stored at room temperature, and supervised observations were recorded from day 1 to day 10 to capture quality changes (Fig .1). Each bread slice was photographed daily in six distinct orientations, systematically documenting spoilage progression (Fig. 2). The structured filenames (e.g., BK13_DAY9_PC3_AGL3_object0_isolated.png) encode bakery ID, day, piece number, angle, and segmentation status, ensuring precise traceability.

2.2   Data Preprocessing and Dataset Structure

Images were resized to 640x640 pixels, normalized to [0, 1], and augmented with random flips, rotations, and color adjustments (hsv_h: 0.015, hsv_s: 0.7, hsv_v: 0.4, fliplr: 0.5) to enhance robustness. LabelMe JSON annotations were converted to YOLO-compatible TXT files, containing bounding box coordinates (x, y, width, height) and segmentation masks. The dataset is organized in a hierarchical structure to facilitate systematic analysis. It encompasses 20 distinct bakeries (labeled BK1 to BK20), each contributing up to three bread pieces per day (designated as PC1 to PC3) over a 10-day post-baking observation period (Day 1 to Day 10). To capture comprehensive visual data, each bread piece was photographed daily from six different angles (Angle 1 to Angle 6), as illustrated in Fig. 1. While the theoretical maximum number of images is 3,600 (20 bakeries × 3 pieces × 6 angles × 10 days).

3   Proposed Model

In this study, YOLOv11 is employed as the primary framework for both segmentation and classification tasks related to bread day classification. The workflow of the proposed model (Fig. 3) begins with a dataset of 3600 bread images, which are manually annotated using the LabelMe tool with polygon annotations for 10 day-classes (Day 1–Day 10). These annotations are saved in JSON format, capturing polygon coordinates for each image. The JSON files are then converted into TXT files compatible with the YOLOv11 segmentation format. The processed images and annotations are organized into training and validation sets in an 80:20 ratio.

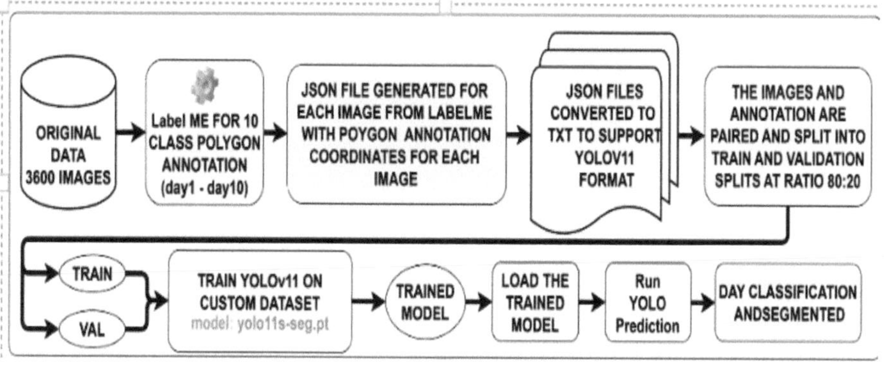

Fig. 3. Proposed architecture for bread days classification.

Using these prepared datasets, the YOLOv11 segmentation model (yolov11s-seg.pt) is trained to learn day-wise classification and segmentation patterns. Once trained, the model is loaded and applied for YOLO-based prediction, thereby performing day classification and segmentation of bread samples.

The central objective is to analyze bread images across multiple days of storage, where visual features such as surface texture, cracks, pores, and discoloration play a vital role in determining freshness and edibility. YOLOv11, being a state-of-the-art object detection model, offers the dual capability of localizing and classifying regions of interest (ROIs) within bread images, making it highly suitable for this application.

For segmentation, YOLOv11's mask prediction branch is utilized to isolate specific regions of bread images that exhibit aging-related changes. This allows the model to focus on fine-grained structural variations, such as moisture loss, mold spots, or surface deterioration, which are crucial for identifying the day-wise progression of bread quality. The segmentation output provides pixel-level boundaries that enhance interpretability and enable targeted analysis of bread surface characteristics.

In the classification stage, YOLOv11 leverages its detection head to assign bread images into distinct day classes (e.g., Day 1, Day 2, Day 3, etc.). By combining localized feature extraction from the segmented regions with global context information, the model learns to differentiate between early-day freshness and late-day spoilage. This dual-task learning ensures that the system not only recognizes whether the bread is edible but also predicts the specific storage day with high accuracy.

Overall, the integration of YOLOv11 for segmentation and classification provides a robust pipeline for bread day classification. The segmentation process enhances the model's ability to focus on relevant quality indicators, while classification ensures accurate categorization of bread based on temporal freshness stages.

4   Results and Discussion

The YOLOv11 segmentation model (yolo11m-seg.pt) was employed as the baseline architecture for bread freshness classification. Training was performed for 100 epochs on an MSI GF63 laptop equipped with an Intel Core i7 12th Gen processor, 16 GB RAM, and an NVIDIA GeForce RTX 4050 GPU. The model was optimized using the AdamW optimizer with a learning rate of 1e-4 and a cosine learning rate scheduler. Multiple loss functions were employed, including Generalized IoU (GIoU) loss for bounding box regression, Binary Cross-Entropy (BCE) loss for classification, and Dice loss for segmentation masks. Evaluation metrics included Precision, Recall, mAP@0.5, and mAP@0.5–0.95, ensuring comprehensive performance assessment.

The model demonstrated strong overall results, achieving an mAP@0.5 of 0.965 (Table 1), confirming the capability of YOLOv11 segmentation as a robust baseline for bread freshness grading and visualization of the smoothed mAP curves at Fig. 4. From Table 2, we can see the Performance trends varied across the ten-day classification task. The model showed high accuracy in early-day predictions (Day 1–2), where bread freshness was visually distinct, and in late-day predictions (Day 9–10), where spoilage characteristics such as discoloration or surface degradation were more apparent. However, mid-range days (Day 4–7) presented challenges, with reduced precision and recall.

This was primarily due to the subtle visual transitions occurring during these stages, where changes in crumb texture, crust gloss, and moisture content are less pronounced and harder to distinguish in RGB images. Table 4 shows the class wise classification performance of the proposed segmentation model.

Table 1. Performance Metrix of the proposed segmentation model.

Metric	Bounding Box (B)	Mask (M)
Precision	0.911	0.911
Recall	0.898	0.898
mAP50	0.965	0.965
mAP50–95	0.749	0.749

Table 2. Class wise Performance along with notable misclassification of the proposed segmentation model

Class	Accuracy	Notable Misclassifications
Day 1	0.944	Background (0.03)
Day 2	0.830	Day 3 (0.05)
Day 3	0.736	Day 1 (0.05), Day 4 (0.04)
Day 4	0.707	Day 5 (0.10), Day 3 (0.03)
Day 5	0.702	Day 4 (0.12), Day 6 (0.02)
Day 6	0.868	Day 3 (0.05)
Day 7	0.674	Day 8 (0.10), Day 5 (0.04)
Day 8	0.753	Day 7 (0.08)
Day 9	0.930	None
Day 10	0.957	None

Table 3. Overall Classification performance Measures of the proposed segmentation model

Evaluation Metrics	Accuracy	Precision	Recall	F1-Score
Evaluation Values (%)	81.44	86.51	82.62	84.53

The proposed model demonstrated strong performance in classifying bread images by freshness, as shown in Table 3 where the evaluation metrics derived from the confusion matrix. It achieved an accuracy of 81.44%, indicating a high overall correct prediction rate. The precision of 86.51% shows the model effectively minimized false positives, while the recall of 82.62% reflects its ability to capture actual positives accurately. The F1-Score of 84.53% confirms a good balance between precision and recall.

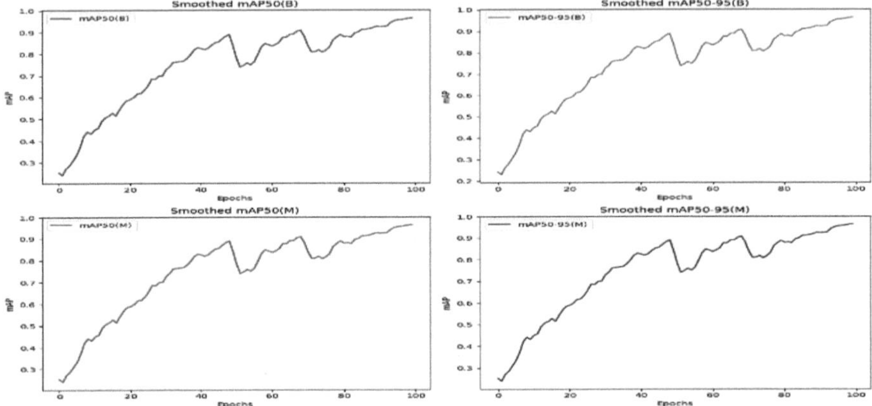

Fig. 4. maP curves of the proposed segmentation model

Table 4. Class wise classification performance Measures of the proposed segmentation model

Class	Precision	Recall	F1-score	Accuracy
day1	0.971	0.944	0.958	0.944
day2	0.912	0.830	0.869	0.830
day3	0.898	0.736	0.809	0.736
day4	0.823	0.707	0.760	0.707
day5	0.795	0.702	0.746	0.702
day6	0.971	0.868	0.917	0.868
day7	0.838	0.674	0.747	0.674
day8	0.884	0.753	0.813	0.753
day9	0.971	0.930	0.950	0.930
day10	0.957	0.957	0.957	0.957

Visualization of results through plots, precision–recall curves (Fig. 6), and confusion matrices further highlighted these performance variations. The confusion matrix indicated notable overlaps in misclassification between adjacent mid-range days, suggesting that the temporal boundaries of bread freshness are not strictly discrete but gradual, contributing to classification ambiguity. This aligns with real-world perception, where consumers also find it difficult to distinguish bread quality changes during the intermediate days of storage. Despite these limitations, the model's ability to consistently classify early and late stages demonstrates the effectiveness of the YOLOv11 segmentation framework. These findings highlight the potential for computer vision in bakery quality monitoring while also indicating directions for further improvement.

As illustrated in Fig. 5, the proposed model demonstrates strong performance across multiple evaluation curves. From the Recall-Confidence curve (Fig. 5a), the model maintains high recall at lower confidence thresholds, particularly for Day 1, Day 2, Day 6, and Day 10, ensuring detection of nearly all true positives, while intermediate days (e.g., Day 4 and Day 5) show sharper declines. The Precision-Recall curve (Fig. 5b) further confirms a robust balance between precision and recall, achieving an overall mAP@0.5 of 0.966, with Day 1 and Day 10 exceeding 0.99 AP, and only slight performance dips observed in mid-range days due to class overlap.

The Precision-Confidence curve (Fig. 5c) highlights that precision improves with confidence, peaking at 1.00 at full confidence, with Day 10 maintaining consistently high precision, while classes like Day 4 and Day 7 reveal higher false positives at lower thresholds. Similarly, the F1-Confidence curve (Fig. 5d) shows that the model achieves optimal performance (F1 = 0.91) at a confidence threshold of 0.578, reflecting a balanced trade-off between precision and recall, with strong separability at Day 1 and Day 10 and minor drops in intermediate days due to misclassifications. Collectively, these results underscore the model's robustness in bread freshness classification.

Overall, this work establishes a new benchmark by introducing a dataset of 3,600 annotated bread images spanning ten consecutive days of freshness. The YOLOv11 segmentation model provides a strong baseline, achieving near state-of-the-art performance on this novel task. Future work will focus on expanding the dataset, exploring multimodal imaging techniques, and developing hybrid deep learning frameworks that combine detection, segmentation, and attention-based reasoning for improved bread freshness prediction.

The superior performance of YOLOv11 in classifying bread freshness over multiple days can be attributed to its spatial localization and feature hierarchy. By performing segmentation-enabled detection, YOLOv11 precisely identifies critical regions such as crust and crumb, capturing subtle changes in texture and color. Its hierarchical multi-scale feature extraction integrates local and global information, allowing the model to detect fine-grained visual cues indicative of freshness degradation. This combination results in accurate, efficient, and scalable monitoring of bread quality beyond conventional binary or attribute-specific approaches.

4.1 Comparison of the Proposed Model with Other Method

To further analyze the performance of the proposed segmentation-classification model, we compared it with texture-based feature descriptors, as existing literature emphasizes the importance of texture in bread quality assessment. Specifically, we employed the Opposite Color Local Binary Pattern (OCLBP) descriptor, which extends conventional LBP by capturing chromatic differences between RGB channels. This allowed us to encode both texture and color variations across bread images, which are crucial indicators of staling and freshness progression.

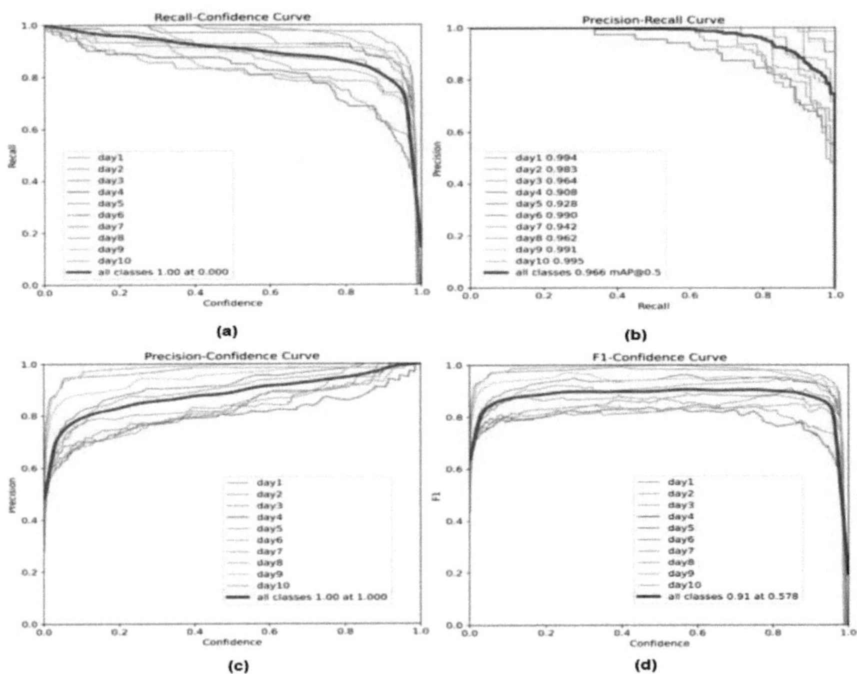

Fig. 5. Visualization of the (a) Recall-Confidence curve (b) Precision recall curve (c) precision confidence curve and (d) F1 Confidence curve.

For each image, OCLBP histograms were computed for channel differences (R–G, R–B, G–B), normalized, and concatenated into a single feature vector, resulting in a structured dataset of texture descriptors. These feature vectors, labeled by bread day classes (Day 1–Day 10), were used to train a range of conventional classifiers, including Random Forest (RF), Decision Tree (DT), K-Nearest Neighbors (KNN), Logistic Regression (LR), Support Vector Machine (SVM with RBF kernel), Naïve Bayes (NB), and XGBoost (XGB).

Table 5. Performance of the OCLBP Features with multiple classifiers for the bread days classification.

Model	Train Accuracy	Val Accuracy	Train Precision	Val Precision	Train Recall	Val Recall	Train F1	Val F1	Train ROC-AUC	Val ROC-AUC
RandomForest	1.0000	0.4208	1.0000	0.4209	1.0000	0.4218	1.0000	0.4210	1.0000	0.838
DecisionTree	0.8833	0.2778	0.8884	0.2764	0.8836	0.2760	0.8834	0.2741	0.9967	0.6161
KNN	0.6566	0.3778	0.6784	0.3941	0.6568	0.3765	0.6539	0.3742	0.9647	0.7353
LogisticReg	0.3351	0.3097	0.3362	0.3057	0.3344	0.3135	0.3252	0.3017	0.7602	0.7277
SVM (RBF)	0.5851	0.4236	0.5890	0.4182	0.5848	0.4249	0.5822	0.4169	0.9181	0.8539
NaiveBayes	0.1639	0.1597	0.2541	0.2230	0.1654	0.1521	0.0914	0.0880	0.6157	0.6115
XGBoost	1.0000	0.4028	1.0000	0.4063	1.0000	0.4026	1.0000	0.4025	1.0000	0.8234

Evaluation was conducted using standard performance metrics: Accuracy, Precision, Recall, F1-score, and ROC-AUC. From Table 5, it is evident that while some classifiers such as SVM and XGBoost achieved moderately good performance, their accuracies were notably lower than those obtained with YOLOv11. For example, misclassifications frequently occurred between consecutive bread days (e.g., Day 3 vs. Day 4, Day 5 vs. Day 6), highlighting the challenge of fine-grained temporal classification using only handcrafted texture descriptors.

In contrast, the YOLOv11 model achieved a classification accuracy of 81.44%, with strong segmentation-enabled mAP values (mAP50 = 0.965, mAP50–95 = 0.749) for both bounding box and mask predictions. These results demonstrate that the integration of segmentation and classification within a unified framework allows YOLOv11 to effectively capture subtle crust and crumb variations that conventional texture-based features fail to discriminate reliably.

Thus, the extensive experimentation with OCLBP and classical machine learning classifiers not only provides a baseline comparison but also clearly establishes the superiority of the YOLOv11 segmentation model for multi-day bread freshness classification.

This work introduces the first 10-day, 3,600-image bread freshness dataset (20 bakeries) and applies YOLOv11-seg for joint segmentation and 10-class day-wise classification (mAP50 = 0.965, 81.44% accuracy). Unlike prior YOLO uses (detection only) or bread studies (binary classification via GLCM/LBP or ViTs), it captures fine-grained spoilage and preservative effects via pixel-level ROI, outperforming texture + ML baselines and setting a new benchmark in non-destructive shelf-life monitoring.

5 Conclusion

This study demonstrated the effectiveness of the YOLOv11 framework for non-destructive monitoring of bread freshness over a ten-day storage period. A key contribution is the creation of a dedicated bread freshness dataset, the first of its kind, serving as a benchmark for future research. The model showed strong detection and segmentation performance with mAP50 scores of 0.965 for bounding box and mask predictions and a robust mAP50–95 of 0.749. Classification analysis achieved an overall accuracy of 81%, with fresh (Day 1) and stale (Day 10) bread classified at 0.944 and 0.957 accuracy, respectively, indicating strong discriminative ability at storage extremes. Intermediate days were more challenging, with accuracies of 0.674–0.825, due to subtle and overlapping visual cues. These results validate YOLOv11 as a powerful, scalable framework for simultaneous segmentation and classification of bread freshness, with strong potential for automated food quality inspection, shelf-life estimation, and supply chain monitoring. Future refinements, such as integrating texture-sensitive spectral features, multimodal data, or temporal learning, could further improve discrimination of intermediate freshness stages.

Acknowledgments. The authors would like to thank Ministry of Social Justice and Empowerment, Government of India for the financial support.

Dataset Accessibility. The datasets created during the current study are available from the corresponding author on reasonable request.

References

Amigo, J.M., Olmo, A., Engelsen, M.M., Lundkvist, H., Engelsen, S.B.: Staling of white wheat bread crumb and effect of maltogenic α-amylases. Part 3: Spatial evolution of bread staling with time by near-infrared hyperspectral imaging. Food Chem. **353**, 129478 (2021). https://doi.org/10.1016/j.foodchem.2021.129478

Ali, S., et al.: Automatic segmentation for synchrotron-based imaging of porous bread dough using deep learning approach. J. Synchrotron Radiat. **28**, 566–575 (2021). https://doi.org/10.1107/S1600577521001314

Ali, Z.N., Askerzade, I., Abdulwahab, S.: Estimation model for bread quality proficiency using fuzzy weighted relevance vector machine classifier. Appl. Bion. Biomech. **2021**, 6670316 (2021). https://doi.org/10.1155/2021/6670316

Guru, D.S., Nandini, D.: Vision transformers in evaluating bread edibility. In International Conference on Applied Algorithms, pp. 225–236. Springer, Cham (2025

Jusoh, M.M.Y., Chin, N.L., Yusof, Y.A., Abdul Rahman, R.:. Bread crust thickness measurement using digital imaging and L a b colour system. J. Food Eng. **94**, 366–371 (2009). https://doi.org/10.1016/J.JFOODENG.2009.04.002

Kavitha, R., Nandini, D., Guru, D.S., Parvathi, G.: Texture features in prediction of bread edibility. In: 2022 International Conference on Engineering and Emerging Technologies (ICEET), pp. 1–6. IEEE (2022)

Karimi, M., Fathi, M., Sheykholeslam, Z., Sahraiyan, B., Naghipoor, F.: Effect of different processing parameters on quality factors and image texture features of bread. J. Bioprocess. Biotechn. **2**, 1000127 (2012). https://doi.org/10.4172/2155-9821.1000127

Nouri, M., Nasehi, B., Goudarzi, M., Abdanan Mehdizadeh, S.: Non-destructive evaluation of bread staling using gray level co-occurrence matrices. Food Anal. Methods **11**, 3391–3395 (2018). https://doi.org/10.1007/s12161-018-1319-6

Paquet-Durand, O., Solle, D., Schirmer, M., Becker, T., Hitzmann, B.: Monitoring baking processes of bread rolls by digital image analysis. J. Food Eng. **111**, 425–431 (2012). https://doi.org/10.1016/J.JFOODENG.2012.01.024

Shahraki, M.H., Mashkour, M., Garmakhany, A.D.: Development and application of a computer vision system for the measurement of the colour of Iranian sweet bread. Quality Assur. Saf. Crops Foods **6**, 33–40 (2014). https://doi.org/10.3920/QAS2012.0167

Singh, J., Kaur, M.: Visual inspection of bakery products by texture analysis using image processing techniques. IOSR J. Eng. **2**, 526–528 (2012). www.iosrjen.org

Robotic Path Planning Using PPO Based Reinforcement Learning Approach

Arpan Garai[iD], Anindita Kundu[(✉)][iD], and Moudipa Jana[iD]

Vellore Institute of Technology, Vellore, India
{arpan.garai,anindita.kundu}@vit.ac.in,
moudipa.jana2020@vitstudent.ac.in

Abstract. In industrial environments, robot navigation requires collision-free path planning, especially in the presence of dynamic obstacles such as moving machines, humans, and other autonomous systems. Traditional algorithms like A* and Analytic Hierarchy Process (AHP) are widely used, to solve these problems but they have their limitations. A* primarily focuses on static, distance-optimized path planning but is unable to adapt to dynamic changes. On the contrary, AHP alone is unable handle complex path planning scenarios. In this work, we propose a hybrid algorithm that integrates AHP with Proximal Policy Optimization (PPO), to overcome these limitations. PPO is used for global path planning. By using optimal navigation policies through interaction with the environment, PPO refines the way-points generated by AHP based on distance, angle of movement, and collision safety. The outcome of the hybrid algorithm is an efficient and adaptive set of global way-points which forms the final path. The performance of the proposed AHP-PPO algorithm is compared with the existing methods, such as A* with AHP (AAHP) and Artificial Potential Field (APF), using matrices like path length, angular variation, and obstacle avoidance. AHP-PPO is observed to outperform the existing approaches while demonstrating enhanced adaptability, smoother trajectories, and greater safety.

Keywords: Collision-free path planning · Analytic Hierarchy Process (AHP) · Proximal Policy Optimization (PPO) · Reinforcement Learning · Dynamic Obstacle Avoidance

1 Introduction

Robotic systems are becoming more common in modern industries for tasks such as material handling, assembly, and inspection [4]. As the industrial settings grow, more dynamic moving machinery, human workers, and autonomous agents become integral parts of it. Traditional path planning methods struggle to maintain reliable, collision-free navigation in such environments. Algorithms such as A* [13], Adaptive Analytic Hierarchy Process (AAHP) [5], and Artificial Potential Fields (APF) [1] perform effectively in static or semi-structured environments but exhibit limitations in dynamic scenarios.

© The Author(s), under exclusive license to Springer Nature Switzerland AG 2026
C. Zaroliagis et al. (Eds.): ICAA 2026, LNCS 16423, pp. 195–206, 2026.
https://doi.org/10.1007/978-3-032-15621-1_16

The A* algorithm produces an optimal path for static maps but cannot adapt to moving obstacles or changing goals [14]. AAHP extends A* through multi-criteria decision-making yet depends on predetermined paths, reducing responsiveness [2]. APF approaches are more reactive but prone to local minima, causing robots to stall near obstacles [23]. These constraints lead to the need for adaptive methods supporting real-time decisions in uncertain environments.

Reinforcement Learning (RL) has emerged as an effective alternative to the traditional algorithms for dynamic navigation [24]. Proximal Policy Optimization (PPO) [7] offers stability and efficiency and is also capable of handling high-dimensional states [19]. However, it may overlook fine-grained local constraints [21]. To overcome these issues, a hybrid **AHP–PPO framework** is proposed has been proposed in this work. The proposed approach integrates AHP [22] (for multi-criteria way-point evaluation) with PPO for adaptive, long-term trajectory optimization. Simulations against AHP–A* and APF confirm that AHP–PPO yields smoother, safer, and more adaptable navigation in dynamic environments.

2   Related Work and Motivation

Traditional path planning algorithms like Dijkstra's [3] and A* [11] are commonly used for autonomous navigation. However, Dijkstra's method is computationally expensive. A* improves the computational complexity by incorporating heuristics to reduce search time [6] in a static environment. To adapt to dynamic environments, Dynamic A* (D*) [11], Rapidly-exploring Random Trees (RRT) [15], RRT* [10], etc. offer real-time path updates in response to new obstacles [20]. These algorithms are fast to explore the path, however, they often fail to produce optimal paths. Moreover, they sometimes require post-processing like smoothing, which leads to an increase in the computational load [9].

Heuristic-based approaches such as the APF method [8] apply virtual forces to attract the robot toward the goal and avoid obstacles. Despite of its intuitive simplicity, APF suffers from local minima, which limit its use in highly dynamic or obstacle-dense environments. AHP's effectiveness is highly dependent on the proper assignment of weights, which can be subjective and lead to suboptimal decisions [18].

Recent reinforcement learning algorithms such as PPO [21], and others [24,27], stand out for their stability and efficiency in policy learning through interaction with the environment [17]. These algorithms are particularly effective in global path planning tasks, as they continuously adapt to environmental changes. However, they lack fine-grained control at the local level, which is essential for precise maneuvering around immediate obstacles [26].

These limitations across both classical and learning-based methods highlight a significant gap in the literature which leads to the motivation behind this study. In this work, a hybrid path planning framework has been proposed that combines AHP for local path planning with PPO for global navigation and refinement. This integrated approach that combines the global adaptability of reinforcement learning with the local precision of multi-criteria decision-making of AHP has been observed to handle dynamic obstacle avoidance with significant precision.

The AHP-PPO framework seeks to leverage AHP's structured local decision-making ability with PPO's adaptability and long-term optimization capabilities. The goal is to achieve collision-free, efficient, and real-time navigation in complex real world, industrial environments which are characterized by both static and dynamic obstacles. This hybridization not only addresses the limitations of existing approaches but also contributes a novel solution for safer autonomous systems.

3   Problem Definition

In this work, a hybrid path planning system has been proposed which uses AHP for local way-point generation and PPO for refinement and generation of the global path. The objective is to design and develop a reliable and intelligent path planning model that ensures safe and efficient navigation across dynamic industrial environments by achieving collision-free navigation.

Let the robot function in a two-dimensional search-space $\mathcal{W} \subset \mathbb{R}^2$ comprising of both static and dynamic obstacles represented by $\mathcal{O}(t)$. The objective is to find a collision-free path $\tau = \{p_t\}_{t=0}^{T}$ from the start position $p_0 = (x_{\text{start}}, y_{\text{start}})$ to the goal position $p_g = (x_{\text{goal}}, y_{\text{goal}})$ subject to the following conditions:

$$p_t \notin \mathcal{O}(t), \qquad\qquad\qquad \forall\, t,$$
$$\min_{\tau}\ L(\tau), \quad \min_{\tau}\ \Delta\theta(\tau), \quad \max_{\tau}\ M_{\text{safety}}(\tau). \tag{1}$$

where $L(\tau)$ is the total path length, $\Delta\theta(\tau)$ is the cumulative angular variation, and $M_{\text{safety}}(\tau)$ is the minimum safety margin to the nearest obstacle.

In order to generate the local candidate solutions (way points), for each step, a set of K local candidates $C = \{c_1, c_2, \ldots, c_K\}$ is generated using AHP and is evaluated using:

$$S(c_j) = W_{\text{dist}} \cdot f_{\text{dist}}(c_j) \ + \ W_{\text{angle}} \cdot f_{\text{angle}}(c_j) \ + \ W_{\text{safety}} \cdot f_{\text{safety}}(c_j), \tag{2}$$

where f_{dist} measures closeness to the next way point w_t, f_{angle} measures heading alignment with the goal, and f_{safety} measures obstacle clearance. The weights $W_{\text{dist}}, W_{\text{angle}}, W_{\text{safety}}$ are derived from the Relative Importance Matrix (RM) in AHP. Based on AHP, the optimal candidate is given by eqn.(3)

$$c^* = \arg\max_{c_j \in C} S(c_j). \tag{3}$$

Now, to further refine the solution, a global policy $\pi_\theta(a_t \mid s_t)$ parameterized by θ, is defined for PPO where:

- State s_t includes robot position, goal position, and obstacle map,
- Action a_t selects the next global way point w_t from the set of way points generated by AHP.

The clipped PPO surrogate objective is given by eqn.(4)

$$\max_{\theta} \; \mathbb{E}_t \left[\min\left(r_t(\theta)\, \hat{A}_t, \; \text{clip}\left(r_t(\theta), 1 - \epsilon, 1 + \epsilon \right) \hat{A}_t \right) \right], \tag{4}$$

Here, $r_t(\theta) = \frac{\pi_\theta(a_t|s_t)}{\pi_{\theta_{\text{old}}}(a_t|s_t)}$ and $\hat{A}_t$ denotes the *estimated advantage function* at time step t. This stage generates a sequence of global way points $\{w_t\}$ that adapt to the dynamic changes. Finally, the robot updates its position.

In this work, clipped PPO has been used instead of the original one as clipped PPO transforms an unstable, theoretical objective into a robust, practical algorithm by enforcing stable and safe policy evolution and preventing catastrophic updates that could lead to robot damage. It also enables data-efficient learning through update re-use. Clipped PPO also provides robustness against noisy real-world data unlike the original theoretical PPO. This results in a learning process where the robot's planned paths improve monotonically and safely, converging reliably towards an efficient and collision-free navigation policy.

$$p_{t+1} \leftarrow c^*. \tag{5}$$

If

$$\|p_{t+1} - p_g\| < \delta_{\text{goal}}, \tag{6}$$

where δ_{goal} is the tolerance threshold, the navigation terminates. Otherwise, PPO updates the global path and AHP refines the next local movement decision, as illustrated in Fig. 1.

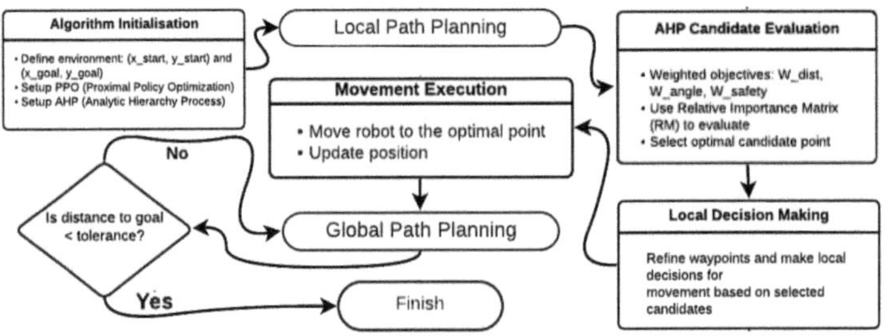

Fig. 1. Flowchart of the AHP-PPO hybrid navigation loop.

To achieve the objective of smooth robot navigation, a structured methodology has been adopted. It begins with problem formulation and algorithm design, followed by defining the problem of path planning while avoiding dynamic obstacles. The proposed hybrid PPO–AHP framework is then evaluated based on its ability to avoid collision, quality of the path identified, and computational performance. A simulated environment replicating real-world industrial conditions, including static and dynamic obstacles, is created for testing the robustness of the framework. The proposed algorithm integrates PPO (for global path generation) and AHP (for local decision-making). AHP evaluates candidate paths through weighted factors like distance, angle, and obstacle proximity while PPO is trained using reinforcement learning, guided by a reward structure that minimizes path length and ensures collision avoidance. Testing and validation are conducted under dynamic conditions using metrics such as success rate, travel time, path length, angular deviation, and safety. Finally, performance comparisons with A*, APF, AAHP, and AHP with A* demonstrate improvements, while fine-tuning optimizes parameters for accuracy and efficiency.

4   Proposed Algorithm

Algorithm 1. Proposed AHP-PPO Path Planning

Require: Start s, goal g, obstacle set $\mathcal{O}$, PPO policy π_θ, AHP weights W, tolerance δ, max steps N, update interval U

Ensure: Optimized path $\mathcal{P}^*$

1: Initialize current position $p \leftarrow s$
2: Initialize path $\mathcal{P}^* \leftarrow \{p\}$
3: Initialize PPO parameters θ, buffer $\mathcal{B} \leftarrow \emptyset$
4: **for** $t = 1$ to N **do**
5:      Generate candidate moves $\mathcal{C}$ (8-neighborhood of p)
6:      **for** each candidate $c \in \mathcal{C}$ **do**
7:          Compute distance $d(c) = \|c - g\|$
8:          Compute angle $\theta(c) = \arctan \dfrac{g_y - c_y}{g_x - c_x}$
9:          Compute safety $s(c) = \min_{o \in \mathcal{O}} \|c - o\|$
10:         AHP score:

$$\text{Score}(c) = W_d \cdot d(c) + W_\theta \cdot \theta(c) + W_s \cdot \frac{1}{s(c) + \epsilon}$$

11:      Select best candidate $c^* = \arg\min_{c \in \mathcal{C}} \text{Score}(c)$
12:      Refine decision using PPO: $c^* \leftarrow \pi_\theta(c^* \mid s_t)$
13:      Update path: $\mathcal{P}^* \leftarrow \mathcal{P}^* \cup \{c^*\}$
14:      Update position $p \leftarrow c^*$
15:      Store transition (s_t, c^*, r_t) in buffer $\mathcal{B}$
16:      **if** $(t \bmod U) == 0$ **then**
17:          Update policy $\theta \leftarrow \text{PPO.Update}(\pi_\theta, \mathcal{B})$
18:          Clear buffer $\mathcal{B}$
19:      **if** $\|p - g\| < \delta$ **then**
20:          **break**
21: **return** $\mathcal{P}^*$

The proposed AHP–PPO algorithm (1) combines AHP with PPO for hybrid path planning using the clipped PPO settings [25]. AHP evaluates candidate way-points based on weighted criteria. It considers the distance, angle, and obstacle safety for real-time decision-making. PPO on the other hand, refines trajectories through feedback on robot state, goals, and obstacles. AHP manages immediate motion, and PPO ensures long-term adaptability through iterative updates until the goal is reached. This layered framework ensures efficient and safe navigation, while demonstrating adaptability to dynamic, complex, and industrially relevant environments.

Initially, in the **Input Module** the system collects a state vector with the robot's current position $((x_{robot}, y_{robot}))$, goal position $((x_{goal}, y_{goal}))$, and information about the obstacle. The list of obstacles are defined by their bottom-left corner coordinates $(x_{obstacle}, y_{obstacle})$ with width w and height h. This data serves as the foundation for generating way-points. Next, using the collected state vector, the **AHP Module** generates an initial set of way-points. AHP evaluates multiple criteria such as distance, safety, and obstacle avoidance to determine the best local path towards the goal. The distance from the robot to the goal is given by eqn. 7. For each way-point the safety is ensured using eqn. 8 such that $d_{nearest} > d_{safety}$. For each segment between way-points, the angular change is calculated using eqn. 9. Finally, AHP is used to rank paths and select the best way-points for the initial path.

$$d_{goal} = \sqrt{(x_{goal} - x_{robot})^2 + (y_{goal} - y_{robot})^2} \tag{7}$$

$$d_{nearest} = \min \sqrt{(x_i - x_{obstacle})^2 + (y_i - y_{obstacle})^2}, \tag{8}$$

$$\Delta\theta = \arctan\left(\frac{y_{i+1} - y_i}{x_{i+1} - x_i}\right) - \arctan\left(\frac{y_i - y_{robot}}{x_i - x_{robot}}\right) \tag{9}$$

AHP implementation follows a three-level hierarchy structure with the goal of optimal path selection evaluated against three criteria: distance to goal, angular efficiency, and safety margin in ordered manner. The pairwise comparison matrix is given in eqn. 10.

$$\mathbf{ComparisonMatrix} = \begin{bmatrix} 1 & 3 & 2 \\ 0.333 & 1 & 0.5 \\ 0.5 & 2 & 1 \end{bmatrix} \tag{10}$$

The pairwise comparison matrix was constructed based on domain expertise and validated for consistency. The Consistency Ration (CR) turned out to be 0.0076 for the order of preference considered for the above mentioned parameters. Since the $CR << 0.1$, we can consider that the pairwise judgments are consistent. The resulting weight vector was obtained as $[0.5395, 0.1634, 0.2971]^T$ to account for robotic motion constraints and non-linear safety relationships.

Once the initial way-points are established, the **PPO Module** is employed to refine these way-points. The PPO policy adapts the path by assessing the current state vector and optimizing the initial way-points to ensure the most efficient route is taken. Initially the PPO policy is set up with the parameter θ.

Then, for each way-point in the initial path, new way-point is generated using eqn.(11). The generation of way-points are repeated over several iterations to ensure that the optimal path is generated.

$$\text{new\_way-point} = \text{PPO\_policy (state\_vector)} \tag{11}$$

The optimization process is driven by a reward function that evaluates the quality of the path based on the robot's distance to the goal, proximity to obstacles, and the overall length of the path. The reward function provides crucial feedback and guides the PPO algorithm in making adjustments to the way-points. The reward function is given by eqn.(12) where, d_{goal} represents the distance to the goal, d_{angle} is the angular change per step, $d_{nearest}$ marks the distance to the nearest obstacle and $d_{travelled}$ indicates the total distance traveled. $\alpha, \beta, \gamma, \delta$ denotes the weight factors associated with each component while ϵ is a small value to avoid division by zero. High value of α ensures strong goal attraction such that the robot consistently moves toward the target. Low value of β implies minimal angle penalty which allows flexible maneuvering around complex obstacles. High value of γ leads to strong safety focus and prevents collisions in your cluttered environments while low δ minimizes the distance penalty and encourages exploration without excessive detours. In eqn.(12), the values of $\alpha, \beta, \gamma, \delta$ are set empirically as $\alpha = 3, \beta = 0.2, \gamma = 1.2, \delta = 0.1$.

$$R = \alpha \cdot (10 - d_{goal}) - \beta \cdot d_{angle} - \gamma \cdot \left(\frac{1}{d_{nearest} + \epsilon}\right) - \delta \cdot d_{travelled} \tag{12}$$

Finally, in the **Output Module** the system provides the optimized way-points for the robot to follow. It effectively integrates both local and global path planning strategies. This architecture emphasizes the collaborative outcome of AHP and PPO, where AHP lays the groundwork for path planning and PPO enhances the route based on reinforcement learning. Together they ensure an optimal navigation strategy that minimizes the distance and improves safety.

5   Results and Discussion

In this work, the performance of three path planning algorithms has been thoroughly analyzed using multiple obstacle maps. The algorithms evaluated include AHP-PPO, AHP-A* [12], and APF-A* [12]. The goal is to test their ability to navigate in complex environments efficiently, considering key metrices - distance traveled, angular deviation, and robot safety. The objective was to minimize the total travel distance and angular changes while maintaining a safe trajectory around obstacles. Accordingly, an objective function has been designed as given by eqn.(13). Here, let O be the objective value, D be the distance, A be the angle per step, and the average distance of the path from the obstacle, is referred to as the average safety, S. We introduce two small positive constants, d and a to avoid division by zero error. For practical purposes, we have chosen d and a as 0.01.

$$O = \frac{S}{(D + d) \times (A + a)} \tag{13}$$

Exhaustive simulation has been carried out on different layouts with varied number of obstacles. The obstacles are distributed randomly across the grid. The algorithm needs to adapt the path to avoid collisions and maintain optimal movement toward the goal. Additionally, a third simulation was conducted in a smart factory environment [28]. This scenario introduced a higher level of complexity. It considered dynamic machinery, narrow passages, and moving obstacles, thereby, closely replicating real-world industrial conditions. The smart factory simulation tested the robustness, adaptability, and real-time decision-making ability of the algorithms in a highly dynamic and constrained environment.

Table 1. Path Characteristics of three obstacle maps, namely, 4-obstacles, 9-obstacles, factory based map.

Case	Method	Mean Distance (m)	Mean Angle per Step (rad)	Average Safety	Objective Value
4-Obstacle	AHP-PPO	14.14	0.00	2.48	17.5265
	AHP-A*	14.22	0.21	2.12	0.6772
	APF-A*	15.70	0.40	2.82	0.4378
9-Obstacle	AHP-PPO	215.75	0.00	21.9	10.1502
	AHP-A*	220.75	20.6	30.14	0.0066
	APF-A*	220.75	2	35.67	0.0804
Factory Map	AHP-PPO	176.38	0.03	18.8	2.6646
	AHP-A*	183.29	0.63	19.3	0.1645
	APF-A*	183.43	0.95	15.89	0.0902

Simulation results as given in Table 1 demonstrate AHP-PPO's consistent superiority across all scenarios considered. By leveraging reinforcement learning, PPO dynamically optimizes global way-points, thereby ensuring efficient obstacle navigation while minimizing the angular deviations [13]. This hybrid approach balances the distance minimization with safety considerations.

In the 4-obstacle scenario given in Fig. 2a, AHP-PPO achieved the shortest path with zero angular deviation. AHP-A* followed closely with slight angular deviation, while APF-A* generated longer paths with higher angular deviation but better safety scores.

The 9-obstacle scenario given in Fig. 2b, featured dense obstacles forming narrow corridors. This case tested the algorithm's sophistication in constrained spaces. The industrial environment as shown in Fig. 2c, further challenged the algorithms with high obstacle density.

In all cases, AHP-PPO generated the shortest paths with minimal angular deviation. It has prioritized efficiency over maximum safety margins. Conversely, AHP-A* exhibited longer distances with higher safety, while APF-A* showed

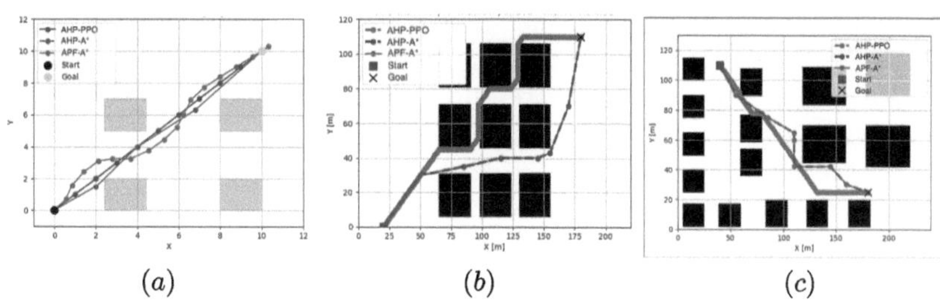

Fig. 2. Navigation performance: (a) AHP-PPO, AHP-A* and APF-A* path in 4-obstacle scenario, (b) AHP-PPO, AHP-A* and APF-A* path in 9-obstacle scenario, (c) AHP-PPO, AHP-A*, and APF-A* path in Factory-Based Map.

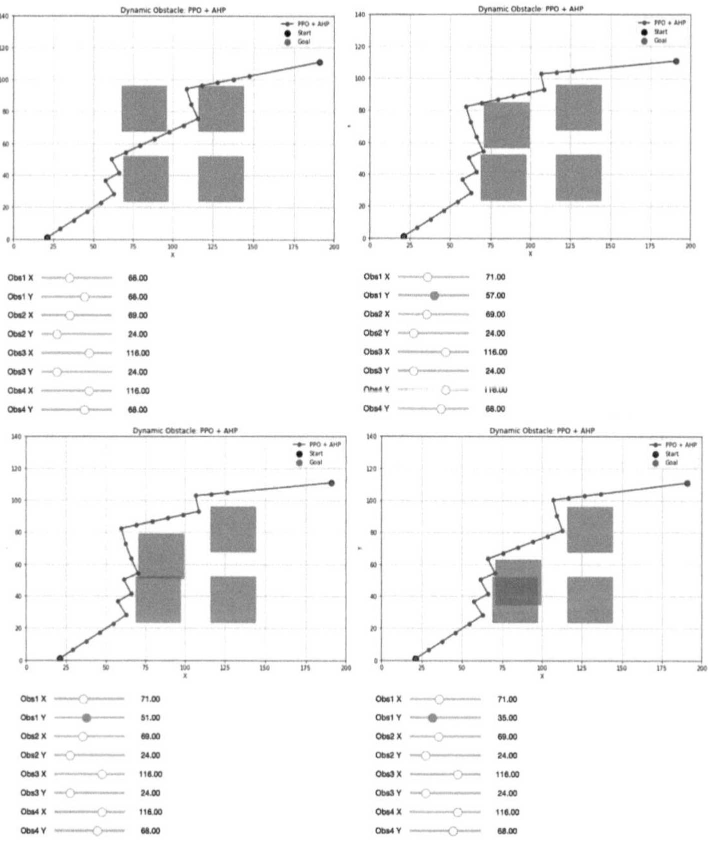

Fig. 3. Path Adaptation by AHP-PPO with moving obstacles.

similar path lengths but significant angular deviations and the highest safety scores [7].

Finally, Fig. 3 demonstrates AHP-PPO's adaptability to dynamic obstacles using interactive sliders, confirming its capability for real-world applications with moving obstacles.

When we use PPO for robotic path planning, we are making a trade-off. Even though PPO exhibits the ability to learn, a robust, general policy that can handle complex dynamics, sensor noise, and unforeseen obstacles in real-time, it cannot provide the guarantee to find a path. In practice, careful reward shaping, curriculum learning, and proper tuning, is done to train policies with PPO such that it can reach the goal with a very high probability. This makes PPO a powerful and practical tool, even without a 100% mathematical guarantee. In this work, we evaluated our trained policy over 1,000 independent episodes across all the test environments. The proposed AHP-PPO achieved outstanding performance, with an overall success rate of 95.3% across all test conditions.

6   Conclusion

Robotics path planning is an age old problem. Autonomous vehicles coming into being necessitates efficient, safe and robust path planning strategies. Accordingly, in this work a hybrid AHP-PPO framework has been proposed. It performs the global trajectory optimization using PPO using AHP to guide the local adjustments. This approach balances the efficiency and safety in real time. Simulations on environments with varied obstacles, and a factory map demonstrate that the proposed AHP–PPO algorithm outperforms traditional AHP–A* and APF–A* methods by reducing path length and angular deviation while providing safe navigation. In high-obstacle scenarios, unlike the proposed AHP-PPO, AHP–A* and APF–A* emphasize safety but sacrifice efficiency. Overall, AHP–PPO exhibits strong adaptability and stability, making it well suited for dynamic industrial settings requiring reliable and efficient real-time path planning.

Acknowledgments. This work has been sponsored by the Vellore Institute of Technology, Vellore, vide the Seed Grant no.: SPL/SG20230182.

Disclosure of Interests. The authors have no competing interests to declare that are relevant to the content of this article.

References

1. Bounini, F., Gingras, D., Pollart, H., Gruyer, D.: Modified artificial potential field method for online path planning applications. In: 2017 IEEE Intelligent Vehicles Symposium (IV), pp. 180–185. IEEE (2017)
2. Chen, X., Zhao, M., Yin, L.: Dynamic path planning of the UAV avoiding static and moving obstacles. J. Intell. Rob. Syst. **99**(3), 909–931 (2020)
3. Dijkstra, E.W.: A note on two problems in connexion with graphs. In: Edsger Wybe Dijkstra: His Life, Work, and Legacy, pp. 287–290 (2022)

4. Evjemo, L.D., Gjerstad, T., Grøtli, E.I., Sziebig, G.: Trends in smart manufacturing: role of humans and industrial robots in smart factories. Curr. Rob. Rep. **1**(2), 35–41 (2020)
5. González-Prida, V., Viveros, P., Barberá, L., Crespo Márquez, A.: Dynamic analytic hierarchy process: AHP method adapted to a changing environment. J. Manuf. Technol. Manag. **25**(4), 457–475 (2014)
6. Hart, P.E., Nilsson, N.J., Raphael, B.: A formal basis for the heuristic determination of minimum cost paths. IEEE Trans. Syst. Sci. Cybern. **4**(2), 100–107 (1968)
7. Ianenko, A., Artamonov, A., Sarapulov, G., Safaraleev, A., Bogomolov, S., Noh, D.-K.: Coverage path planning with proximal policy optimization in a grid-based environment. In: 2020 59th IEEE Conference on Decision and Control (CDC), pp. 4099–4104. IEEE (2020)
8. Khatib, O.: Real-time obstacle avoidance for manipulators and mobile robots. Int. J. Rob. Res. **5**(1), 90–98 (1986)
9. Karaman, S., Frazzoli, E.: Sampling-based algorithms for optimal motion planning. Int. J. Rob. Res. **30**(7), 846–894 (2011)
10. Li, B., Chen, B.: An adaptive rapidly-exploring random tree. IEEE/CAA J. Automatica Sinica **9**(2), 283–294 (2021)
11. Likhachev, M., Ferguson, D.I., Gordon, G.J., Stentz, A., Thrun, S.: Anytime dynamic a*: an anytime, replanning algorithm. In: ICAPS, vol. 5, pp. 262–271 (2005)
12. Lee, J., Kim, C.: Development of an adaptive AHP path planning method considering the mobile robot driving environment. IEEE Access **12**, 95565–95575 (2024)
13. Qin, H., Shao, S., Wang, T., Yu, X., Jiang, Y., Cao, Z.: Review of autonomous path planning algorithms for mobile robots. Drones **7**(3), 211 (2023)
14. Ren, Z., Rathinam, S., Likhachev, M., Choset, H.: Multi-objective safe-interval path planning with dynamic obstacles. IEEE Rob. Autom. Lett. **7**(3), 8154–8161 (2022)
15. Rodriguez, S., Tang, X., Lien, J.-M., Amato, N.M.: An obstacle-based rapidly-exploring random tree. In: Proceedings of the 2006 IEEE International Conference on Robotics and Automation (ICRA), pp. 895–900. IEEE (2006)
16. Ge, S.S., Cui, Y.J.: New potential functions for mobile robot path planning. IEEE Trans. Robot. Autom. **16**(5), 615–620 (2002)
17. Choi, J., Lee, G., Lee, C.: Reinforcement learning-based dynamic obstacle avoidance and integration of path planning. Intel. Serv. Robot. **14**(5), 663–677 (2021). https://doi.org/10.1007/s11370-021-00387-2
18. Saaty, T.L.: Decision making with the analytic hierarchy process. Int. J. Serv. Sci. **1**(1), 83–98 (2008)
19. Silva, S.H., Alaeddini, A., Najafirad, P.: Temporal graph traversals using reinforcement learning with proximal policy optimization. IEEE Access **8**, 63910–63922 (2020)
20. Stentz, A.: Optimal and efficient path planning for partially-known environments. In: Proceedings of the 1994 IEEE International Conference on Robotics and Automation, pp. 3310–3317. IEEE (1994)
21. So, O., Ge, C., Fan, C.: Solving minimum-cost reach avoid using reinforcement learning. Adv. Neural. Inf. Process. Syst. **37**, 30951–30984 (2024)
22. Vaidya, O.S., Kumar, S.: Analytic hierarchy process: an overview of applications. Eur. J. Oper. Res. **169**(1), 1–29 (2006)
23. Yao, P., Wang, H., Su, Z.: Real-time path planning of unmanned aerial vehicle for target tracking and obstacle avoidance in complex dynamic environment. Aerosp. Sci. Technol. **47**, 269–279 (2015)

24. Zhu, C.: Intelligent robot path planning and navigation based on reinforcement learning and adaptive control. J. Logist. Inf. Serv. Sci. **10**(3), 235–248 (2023)
25. Schulman, J., Wolski, F., Dhariwal, P., Radford, A., Klimov, O.: Proximal policy optimization algorithms. arXiv preprint arXiv:1707.06347 (2017)
26. Tang, C., Abbatematteo, B., Hu, J., Chandra, R., Martín-Martín, R., Stone, P.: Deep reinforcement learning for robotics: a survey of real-world successes. In: Proceedings of the AAAI Conference on Artificial Intelligence, vol. 39, no. 27, pp. 28694–28698 (2025)
27. Gan, Y., Yan, R., Tan, X., Wu, Z., Xing, J.: Transductive off-policy proximal policy optimization. arXiv preprint arXiv:2406.03894 (2024)
28. HM Group: E-FOREST, a Future Mobility Smart Factory Built by Hyundai and Kia Motors (2023). https://www.hyundai.co.kr/story/CONT0000000. Accessed Dec 2023

Stocks in Sync: Cluster-Aware Deep Learning for Multi-stock Forecasting in Financial Market

Soumyadeep Basak[1], Shirsendu Roy[1], Sarnaavho Pal[1], Shubham Sahu[1], Deepsubhra Guha Roy[2], and Piyali Datta[3]

[1] Department of CSE(AIML), Institute of Engineering and Management, University of Engineering and Management, Kolkata, India
[2] IEM Centre of Excellence for Cloud Computing and IoT, Department of CSE(AIML), Institute of Engineering and Management, University of Engineering and Management, Kolkata, India
[3] IEM-IIT Mandi Centre for Joint Research on Human Computer Interaction, Department of CSE(AIML), Institute of Engineering and Management, University of Engineering and Management, Kolkata, India
`datta.piyali.in@gmail.com`

Abstract. Forecasting stock price movements is a complex task due to inherent market volatility, nonlinear dependencies, and inter-stock correlations. This paper proposes a cluster-informed deep learning framework for the simultaneous prediction of the next-day opening price direction across 46 constituents of the NIFTY 50 index. Unlike traditional single-stock models, our approach leverages shared sectoral patterns by integrating unsupervised similarity-based clustering with a unified multi-output architecture. We first identify co-movement relationships among stocks using a combination of correlation and cosine similarity metrics, followed by hierarchical clustering. These relationships inform the design of a hybrid neural model: a Time-Distributed dense encoder for dimensionality reduction, parallel LSTM layers for temporal representation learning, and a shared LSTM block leading to stock-specific output heads. Extensive experiments demonstrate that the proposed model consistently outperforms statistical and rule-based baselines in directional accuracy and the F1-score. The results highlight the efficacy of incorporating sector-level dependencies and structured temporal learning in robust financial forecasting.

Keywords: Stock Forecasting · Deep Learning · Time Series Prediction · NIFTY 50 · LSTM · Clustering · Multi-Output Learning · Sectoral Modeling · Feature Engineering

1 Introduction

Predicting the directional movement of stock prices remains a core challenge in quantitative finance due to the noisy, nonlinear, and highly interdependent nature of financial time series [1]. Traditional univariate models often treat each stock in isolation, overlooking broader market dynamics such as sectoral trends and stock-to-stock co-movements—factors especially prominent in indices like the NIFTY 50 [2]. Recent advances in deep learning have driven sequential modeling by the use of recurrent models like Long Short-Term Memory (LSTM) and Gated Recurrent Units (GRU) [3]. However, the majority of models treat stocks individually or employ graph-based models, which is associated with scalability, interpretability, and generalization issues. In this paper, we introduce a novel cluster-informed multi-stock forecasting framework that explicitly models inter-stock dependencies beyond graph neural networks. We construct stock clusters using co-movement similarity measures and correlations or cosine-based metrics followed by hierarchical clustering to identify latent sectoral structures. These clusters guide the design of Cluster-Aware Dual-LSTM(CA-DLSTM), a shared neural architecture comprising a TimeDistributed encoder, parallel and shared LSTM layers of varying sequence lengths, a shared LSTM block, and stock-relevant dense heads that output binary predictions for directional movement. We propose a Ticker-Embedded LSTM that embeds stock identity into the learning process by augmenting time series data with a ticker column. A learnable ticker embedding is initialized via Multidimensional Scaling on the hierarchical clustering distance matrix, then concatenated with LSTM outputs before prediction. Although it captures cross-stock temporal dependencies, it underperforms the cluster-informed model (mean F1 ~ 0.64). Incorporating hierarchical clustering and structural embeddings enables modeling of both sector-level and stock-specific behavior, and experiments on NIFTY 50 show our models outperform statistical and rule-based baselines in accuracy and F1 score. This work makes the following key contributions:

- A cluster-informed deep learning framework has been developed that uses co-movement-based clustering to uncover latent sectoral structure among NIFTY 50 stocks.
- A scalable cluster aware dual LSTM architecture with multi-output has been designed with shared encoders and stock-specific dense heads for simultaneous prediction across 46 stocks.
- A Ticker-Embedded LSTM with an MDS-initialized stock embedding that incorporates structural priors into interleaved sequence modeling.
- We empirically demonstrate that both models outperform traditional baselines and standalone LSTM approaches in directional accuracy and F1 score.

2   Related Work

Stock Prediction with Deep Learning. Deep learning has become popular in financial forecasting for modeling nonlinear and time-dependent market data. Recurrent models like LSTM and GRU are widely used for single-stock prediction with technical or price features [3,4], but they remain stock-specific and lack scalability for indices such as NIFTY 50. Multi-stock models [4] aim to address this issue but often neglect inter-stock relations. GNNs capture such ties via correlations [7], though they add complexity and depend on manual graph design. LSTM and GRU perform better under volatility [3,5]. Recent work explores ticker-aware models with trainable embeddings; we initialize them using Multidimensional Scaling on a co-movement distance matrix from hierarchical clustering [1]. Our cluster-informed model improves generalization, showing the value of embedding sectoral structure.

Clustering and Co-Movement in Finance. Clustering has long been used in finance for pattern discovery, asset allocation, and reducing modeling complexity [2]. Methods like hierarchical clustering and k-means with correlation or cosine distances identify economically meaningful groups of co-moving stocks [1,6], reflecting macroeconomic effects or industry dynamics. Prior work often applies clustering as a pre-processing step for diversification, strategy design [2], or anomaly detection [4], but rarely integrates it into model design. Our approach(Cluster-Aware Dual-LSTM and Ticker-Embedded LSTM) instead embeds sector-driven co-movement patterns, obtained via hierarchical clustering on correlation and directional similarity, directly into the modeling pipeline. This enables the model to capture inter-stock dependencies and generalize better across sectors.

Multi-output Learning and Evolutionary Approaches. Multi-task and multi-output learning have gained traction in financial forecasting as they capture shared temporal and structural patterns across assets [7,8,13], improving generalization in indices like NIFTY 50 with strong intersectoral dependencies [2]. Genetic Algorithms (GA) have also been applied to evolve interpretable rule-based trading systems, though they struggle with nonlinear temporal dynamics in noisy markets. Our approach combines these directions in a cluster-conscious multi-output hybrid model. Using correlation- and cosine-based similarity measures, hierarchical clustering separates NIFTY 50 stocks [1,6], guiding a TimeDistributed encoder and dual LSTM backbone with multi-scale support [3,5]. Structural awareness is further introduced via trainable ticker embeddings initialized with Multidimensional Scaling on the clustering distance matrix. These embeddings, concatenated with recurrent outputs, feed stock-specific dense heads for prediction. While TA-LSTM improves over baselines, our CA-DLSTM achieves superior directional accuracy and F1 scores, demonstrating the value of integrating clustering, temporal modeling, and multi-output learning.

3   Model Architecture and Methodological Approach

Here, within this section, we outline the end-to-end process that we use to predict direction of movement of NIFTY 50 stocks. Our pipeline is composed of a clustering-based preprocessing step followed by a variety of neural and statistical models that we obtain from these structured inputs. The deep learning models, ticker-aware models, and statistical baselines are evaluated using accuracy and also the F1 score.

3.1   Data Preparation

3.1.1   Data Preprocessing

We begin by collecting historical daily stock price data for the NIFTY 50 constituents over a fixed time window. Missing values arising from trading holidays or corporate actions are forward-filled using the last available valid entry to maintain time series alignment across all stocks.

For the LSTM-based models, we generate a binary *movement label* column to represent the prediction target. The label is computed as:

$$y_t = \begin{cases} 1, & \text{if } (O_{t+1} - C_t) > 0 \\ 0, & \text{otherwise} \end{cases}$$

where C_t is the closing price on day t and O_{t+1} is the opening price on day $t+1$. This labeling scheme enables the models to learn directional movement prediction rather than raw price forecasting. All feature series(including the technical indicators used by all the models: RSI, EMA, Bollinger Bands and MACD) are standardized to zero mean and unit variance prior to similarity computation and model training. Additionally, rolling windows are applied to structure inputs for temporal models, with each sample consisting of a fixed-length sequence of past observations. This preprocessing ensures the dataset is clean, normalized, and temporally organized for both clustering and predictive modeling tasks.

3.1.2   Clustering via Co-Movement Similarity

The first step involves grouping stocks based on historical co-movement patterns to reveal latent sectoral or behavioral structures. Given daily log returns $\mathbf{r}_i = [r_i^1, r_i^2, ..., r_i^T]$ for each stock i, a similarity matrix $S \in \mathbb{R}^{N \times N}$ is constructed using multiple time-series similarity metrics from prior literature. In contrast to standard approaches based on Pearson or Spearman correlation, we emphasize directional co-movement— specifically, how frequently two stocks move in the same direction on the same day. This offers a more discrete and behaviorally-aligned similarity measure and better captures structural alignment between financial instruments.

First, we define a movement direction vector for each stock:

$$m_i^t = \begin{cases} +1 & \text{if } r_i^t > 0 \\ -1 & \text{if } r_i^t < 0 \quad \text{(movement direction for stock } i \text{ on day } t) \\ 0 & \text{if } r_i^t = 0 \end{cases}$$

Then, the exponentially-weighted co-movement similarity between stocks i and j is computed as:

$$S_{ij} = \sum_{t=1}^{T} \lambda^{T-t} \cdot \delta(m_i^t = m_j^t) \quad \text{where } \delta(a = b) = \begin{cases} 1 & \text{if } a = b \\ 0 & \text{otherwise} \end{cases}$$

Here, $\lambda \in (0, 1)$ is a decay parameter controlling how much recent alignment is emphasized. This formulation captures the number of days on which stocks exhibit the same movement direction (i.e., both positive or both negative), while giving more weight to recent occurrences to avoid overfitting to outdated or noisy alignment. The similarity was normalized as:

$$\tilde{S}_{ij} = \frac{S_{ij}}{\sum_{t=1}^{T} \lambda^{T-t}} \quad \text{(normalized co-movement score between } i \text{ and } j)$$

To identify clusters without predefined sizes, agglomerative hierarchical clustering is employed. This method allows flexibility in grouping based on a dendrogram threshold rather than requiring a fixed number of clusters. Empirically, many resulting clusters aligned with sectoral divisions—e.g., banking, automotive, pharmaceutical, and energy—while some minor clusters showed cross-sectoral or noisy groupings. These clusters are validated using a secondary similarity metric from independent literature, confirmed their robustness, and this clustering process informs subsequent model architectures, enabling sector-aware forecasting through shared layers or structural embeddings (Fig. 1).

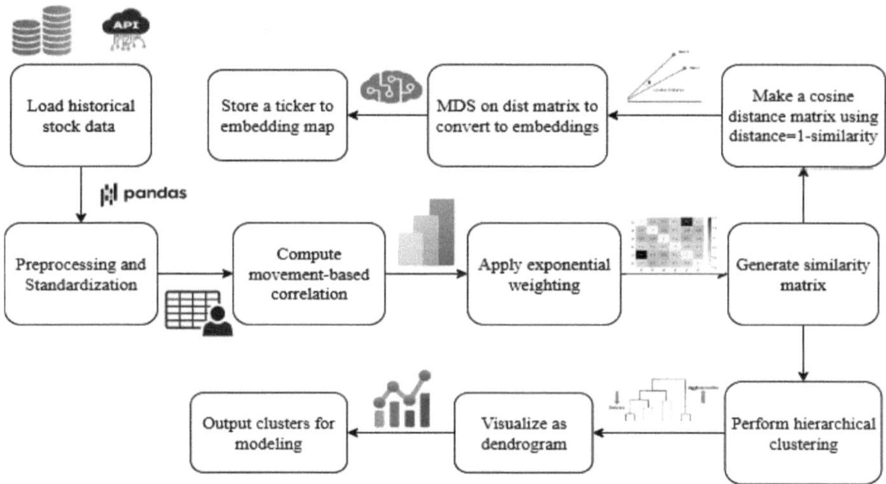

Fig. 1. Clustering via co-movement similarity.

3.2   Model Architecture

We evaluate five distinct models spanning deep learning, ticker-aware mechanisms, and statistical baselines. Each model is described below.

3.2.1 Cluster-Aware Dual LSTM (CA-DLSTM) This is our primary deep learning architecture for multi-stock forecasting. Stock features (basic and technical indicators) are extracted for all 46 stocks and concatenated row-wise:

$$[\mathrm{Open}_A, \mathrm{Open}_B, ..., \mathrm{Close}_A, \mathrm{Close}_B, ..., \mathrm{RSI}_A, \mathrm{RSI}_B, ...]$$

After sequence generation and scaling, this high-dimensional ($8 \times$ feature-set) time-series data are passed through a *TimeDistributed encoder layer* to reduce dimensionality while preserving temporal context (which performs better than PCA for time-series inputs due to temporal continuity).

The core temporal modeling is handled by two parallel LSTM encoders operating on different horizons: a short-term window ($T_1 = 30$) and a long-term window ($T_2 = 60$). Each sequence branch outputs a hidden representation:

$$\mathbf{h}_{\mathrm{short}} = \mathrm{LSTM}_{T_1}(\mathbf{z}_{1:T_1}), \quad \mathbf{h}_{\mathrm{long}} = \mathrm{LSTM}_{T_2}(\mathbf{z}_{1:T_2})$$

These representations are concatenated and passed through a shared dense fusion layer:

$$\mathbf{h}_{\mathrm{global}} = \phi(\mathbf{W} \cdot [\mathbf{h}_{\mathrm{short}}\|\mathbf{h}_{\mathrm{long}}] + \mathbf{b})$$

Finally, individual dense heads are used for per-stock predictions:

$$\hat{y}_i = \sigma(\mathbf{W}_i \cdot \mathbf{h}_{\mathrm{global}} + b_i)$$

Here, $\hat{y}_i$ is the predicted probability of upward movement for the ith stock in the cluster, and $\phi(\cdot)$ is a non-linear activation (e.g., ReLU or tanh). The model is trained using a balanced binary cross-entropy loss across all heads. It achieves a strong average F1 score of 0.768, with a maximum of 0.87, outperforming several baseline approaches (Fig. 2).

Algorithm 1: Cluster-Aware Dual LSTM (CA-DLSTM)

Input: Historical price series of N stocks
Output: Upward movement probabilities $\hat{y}_i$ for each stock
Step 1: Preprocessing
Compute movement labels; handle missing data; standardize features
Step 2: Clustering
Construct directional co-movement similarity matrix S with exponential
  decay Apply agglomerative clustering to obtain stock groups
  $\{C_1, C_2, ...\}$
foreach *cluster* C_k **do**
  | **Step 3: Sequence Modeling**
  | Generate sequences with technical indicators Encode to lower
  | dimension with Time-Distributed Dense layer Extract temporal
  | features via two LSTM branches (short-term, long-term) Fuse
  | representations into a shared global layer
  | **Step 4: Prediction**
  | **foreach** *stock* $i \in C_k$ **do**
  | | Predict $\hat{y}_i$ using a stock-specific dense head

Step 5: Training
Optimize using balanced binary cross-entropy loss across all heads

---

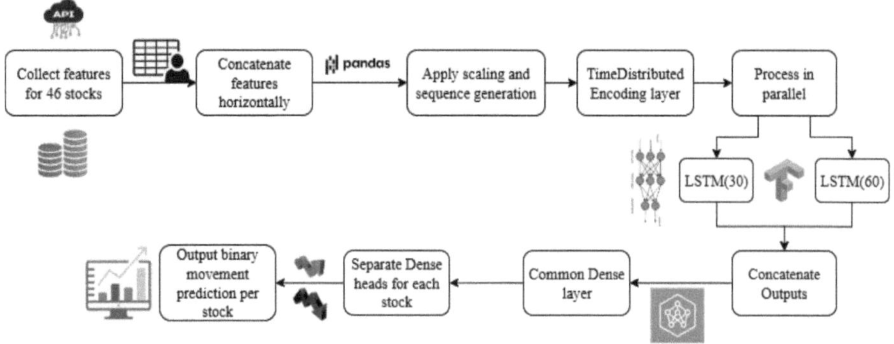

Fig. 2. Cluster-Aware Dual LSTM (CA-DLSTM)

3.2.2 Ticker-Embedded LSTM (TE-LSTM) This model introduces a *ticker-aware embedding layer* that provides the network with stock-specific identity information. The data is structured by concatenating sequences from all stocks vertically, producing a larger dataset where each row includes a *ticker identifier*.

Embedding Initialization: Each ticker is mapped to a trainable embedding vector, initialized using *Multidimensional Scaling (MDS)* applied to a distance matrix derived from co-movement-based similarity:

$$\text{sim}(\mathbf{r}_i, \mathbf{r}_j) = \frac{1}{T} \sum_{t=1}^{T} \mathbb{1}\left(\text{sign}(r_i^t) = \text{sign}(r_j^t)\right), \quad D_{ij} = 1 - \text{sim}(\mathbf{r}_i, \mathbf{r}_j)$$

$$\mathbf{E} = \text{MDS}(D), \quad \mathbf{e}_i^{(0)} \in \mathbb{R}^d$$

This structurally-informed initialization ensures that each ticker embedding starts with a spatial layout consistent with sectoral co-movement. The temporal features (excluding ticker) for each sample are processed using an LSTM:

$$\mathbf{h}_i = \text{LSTM}(\mathbf{x}_{1:T}^{(i)}), \quad \mathbf{h}_i \in \mathbb{R}^h$$

The temporal output is concatenated with the corresponding embedding and passed through fully connected layers:

$$\hat{y}_i = \sigma\left(\mathbf{W} \cdot [\mathbf{h}_i \,\|\, \mathbf{e}_i] + b\right)$$

Temporal Modeling: Despite its conceptual advantage, this model achieves a modest F1 score ($\sim$0.72), suggesting that while stock identity is important, temporal modeling must also be guided by inter-stock relationships beyond embeddings alone (Fig. 3).

Algorithm 2: Ticker-Embedded LSTM (TE-LSTM)

Input: Historical sequences $\{\mathbf{x}_{1:T}^{(i)}\}_{i=1}^{N}$, ticker identifiers $\{id_i\}_{i=1}^{N}$
Output: Predicted movement probabilities $\{\hat{y}_i\}_{i=1}^{N}$

Embedding Initialization:
Construct similarity matrix S from directional agreement Compute distance matrix $D = 1 - S$ Obtain initial embeddings $\mathbf{e}_i^{(0)}$ using MDS on D

Temporal Encoding:
foreach *stock* $i = 1 \dots N$ **do**
  Encode $\mathbf{x}_{1:T}^{(i)}$ using LSTM to obtain hidden state $\mathbf{h}_i$

Fusion and Prediction:
foreach *stock* $i = 1 \dots N$ **do**
  Concatenate $\mathbf{h}_i$ with embedding $\mathbf{e}_i$ Compute output
  $\hat{y}_i = \sigma(\mathbf{W} \cdot [\mathbf{h}_i \,\|\, \mathbf{e}_i] + b)$

Training:
Optimize parameters using binary cross-entropy loss across all stocks

---

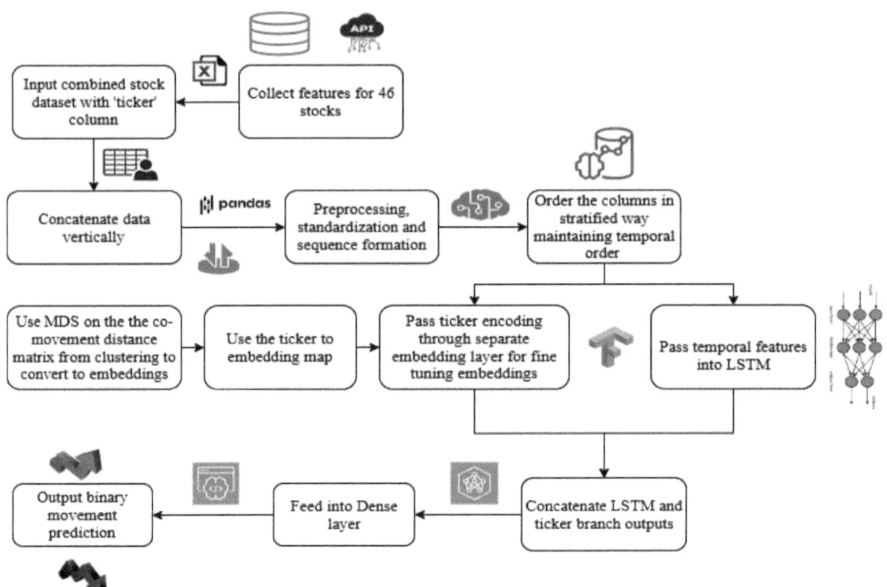

Fig. 3. Ticker-Embedded LSTM(TE-LSTM)

3.2.3   Genetic Programming-Based Rule Learning (Baseline) To construct an interpretable rule-based baseline, we apply *Genetic Programming (GP)* to evolve technical indicator combinations that best predict directional stock movements. The rules are learned from a population of expressions combining indicators such as RSI, MACD, and Bollinger Bands, with arithmetic and logical operators. Two strategies are evaluated by manually defined rule sets from literature and optimized rules via GP tuned specifically to the NIFTY 50 stock data. An example evolved rule takes the form: if RSI $> 70 \wedge$ MACD $< 0 \Rightarrow$ Sell. While rules evolved via GP show marginal improvement over static rule sets, both approaches yield accuracy and F1 scores in the 0.63–0.65 range. These results are competitive for non-deep models, but fall short of deep learning counterparts.

3.2.4   Vector AutoRegression (VAR) Baseline As a classical statistical model, *Vector AutoRegression (VAR)* is employed as a benchmark. Stocks from similar sectors (same clusters) are grouped, and VAR models are trained on *percentage returns* (preferred over log returns for empirical stability).

Rather than predicting raw prices, the model forecasts percentage returns:

$$\mathbf{r}_{t+1} = \mathbf{A}_1\mathbf{r}_t + \mathbf{A}_2\mathbf{r}_{t-1} + \cdots + \mathbf{A}_p\mathbf{r}_{t-p} + \boldsymbol{\varepsilon}_{t+1}$$

These are then converted to binary movement labels:

$$\hat{y}_{t+1} = \mathbb{1}(r_{t+1} > 0)$$

This formulation aligns with classification objectives and removes non-stationarity. Despite its simplicity, the VAR model performs comparably to rule-based baselines, achieving F1 scores between 0.64–0.66. Its consistency makes it a valid benchmark for evaluating modern deep learning models.

4   Experimental Results

To evaluate the effectiveness of our proposed model, we compare it against both internal baselines and recent external benchmarks from the literature. Specifically, we consider: (1) a cluster-based Vector Autoregression (VAR) model, (2) a cluster-level Genetic Algorithm (GA)-optimized rule-based system, (3) state-of-the-art multi-stock deep learning models such as DGDNN [14], Graph-WaveNet [18], DTML [15].

Each model is assessed on next-day stock movement prediction using two key metrics: **Accuracy** and **F1-score**. These metrics are standard in financial time series classification tasks [3, 4].

Evaluation Metrics. Accuracy measures the overall proportion of correctly predicted labels:

$$\text{Accuracy} = \frac{TP + TN}{TP + TN + FP + FN}, \tag{1}$$

where TP, TN, FP, and FN denote true positives, true negatives, false positives, and false negatives respectively. The F1-score is the harmonic mean of precision and recall, capturing a balance between false positives and false negatives:

$$\text{F1-score} = \frac{2 \cdot \text{Precision} \cdot \text{Recall}}{\text{Precision} + \text{Recall}},$$ (2)

with $\text{Precision} = \frac{TP}{TP+FP}$ and $\text{Recall} = \frac{TP}{TP+FN}$.

Table 1. Comparative Performance of Multi-Stock Prediction Models (Next-Day Directional Classification).

Model	Mean F1	Mean Acc.
Cluster-Aware Dual-LSTM	0.77	0.72
Ticker-Embedded LSTM	0.72	0.70
VAR Baseline	0.64	0.62
GA Rule Baseline	0.63	0.62
DGDNN [14]	0.63	0.65
GraphWaveNet [18]	0.60	0.59
DTML (Transformer) [15]	0.58	0.58
HMG-TF (Transformer) [16]	0.59	0.57
DGRCL (Dyn. Graph + CL) [17]	0.66	0.53

4.1   Comparative Performance

It is worth noting that several of the external benchmarks such as HMG-TF and DGRCL are evaluated on very large universes (e.g., NASDAQ-1000+ stocks), where the task is substantially more challenging due to higher volatility and the need to capture diverse inter-stock dependencies. By contrast, our framework focuses on 6–10 coherent clusters covering the 46 NIFTY 50 stocks. Despite operating on a smaller but sectorally diverse set, our model achieves consistently higher mean F1-scores and accuracy, highlighting the advantage of combining cluster-aware structure with multi-output prediction. In addition to the tabular summary, we provide comparative plots to illustrate the performance distribution across models:

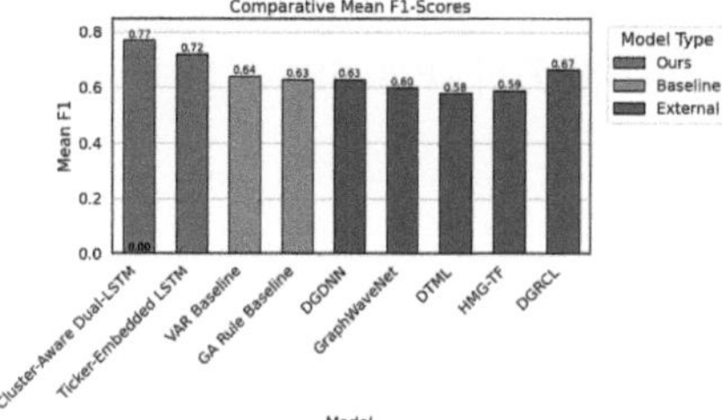

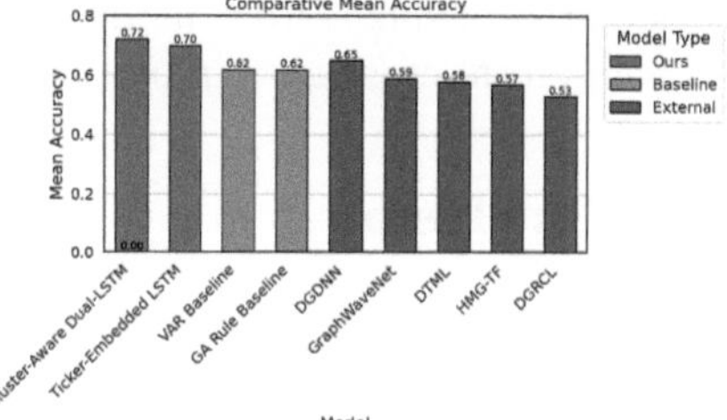

Fig. 4. Mean F1-scores of proposed models compared against statistical baselines and external benchmarks.

Fig. 5. Mean Accuracy of proposed models compared against statistical baselines and external benchmarks.

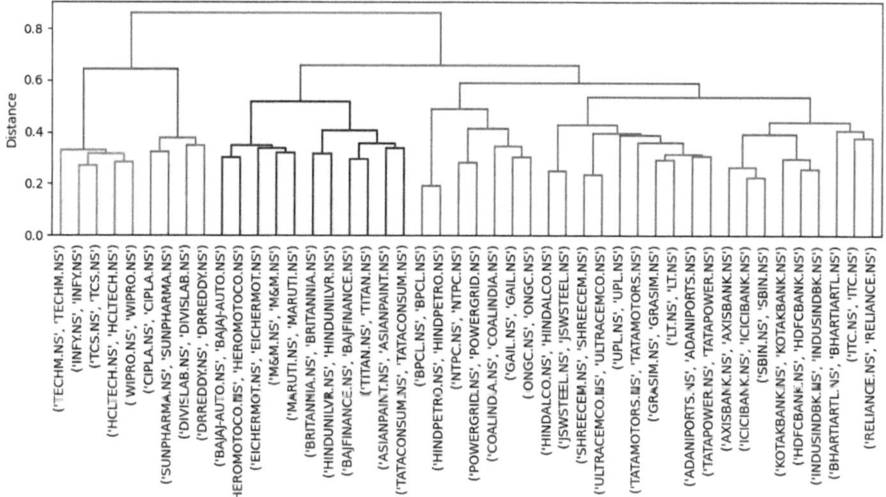

Fig. 6. Dendrogram of Nifty 50 stocks using movement direction similarity (correlation and co-movement based).

4.2   Cluster-Aware Insights

The clustering analysis validates that many stocks with sectoral ties (e.g., banking, automotive, pharmaceutical, energy) are grouped together, while a few small clusters emerge as cross-sectoral or noisy. This supports the motivation for designing a single model with shared representations and sector-aware heads. As shown in Table 1 and Figs. 4–5, the proposed CA-DLSTM and TE-LSTM architectures outperform both classical baselines (VAR, GA) and external deep learning benchmarks (e.g., GraphWaveNet, DTML, DA-RNN). The performance margin is more pronounced for clusters with strong intra-sector co-movement, demonstrating the benefit of leveraging sector-level dependencies. The hybrid architecture's ability to capture both global (sectoral) and local (stock-specific) temporal dynamics significantly improves robustness under volatile conditions.

Compared to single-stock models, the unified framework reduces overfitting and benefits from cross-asset representation sharing [3,7,8] (Fig. 6).

5   Conclusion

In this study, we presented a cluster-driven deep learning framework for synchronous, large-scale prediction of the direction of the next-day stock price movement within the NIFTY 50 index. Our method successfully captures asset-specific temporal dynamics as well as sectoral co-movement patterns by combining unsupervised clustering with sophisticated feature engineering and a hybrid recurrent architecture (CA-DLSTM) and (TE-LSTM). This design outperforms conventional baselines and allows for scalable multi-output forecasting. Strong generalizability is provided by the model's data-driven sector representation and modular architecture, which enable it to be applied to different asset universes and financial markets. Additionally, the framework provides opportunities for future improvements such as adding attention mechanisms, incorporating macroeconomic indicators, or expanding to include intraday high-frequency data. Overall, our results highlight the critical role of sector-aware multi-task learning and deep sequence modeling in advancing robust and interpretable financial forecasting systems.

Acknowledgements. The authors would like to express their sincere gratitude to the IEM Centre of Excellence for Cloud Computing and IoT for providing financial and infrastructural support through research grants IEMT(S)/2024/02-G19 and IEMT(S)/2023/02-G05 and IEDC-CSE at the Institute of Engineering and Management, Kolkata, for offering the technical resources and collaborative environment.

References

1. Dolphin, R., Smyth, B., Xu, Y., Dong, R.: Measuring financial time series similarity with a view to identifying profitable stock market opportunities. arXiv preprint arXiv:2107.03926 (2021)
2. Bjärkby, S.: A Cluster Analysis of Stocks to Define an Investment Strategy. Master's thesis, Lund University (2019)
3. Gao, Y., Wang, R., Zhou, E.: Stock prediction based on optimized LSTM and GRU models. J. Comput. Sci. Appl. (2021)
4. Kim, Y., Choi, H., et al.: Financial time-series forecasting using deep neural networks. Expert Syst. Appl. **173**, 114620 (2021)
5. Hema, K., Mounika, B., Mounesh, A., Santhosh Reddy, C., Mohan Babu, C.: Advanced stock market prediction using hybrid GRU-LSTM techniques. Int. J. Adv. Res. Innov. Ideas Educ. (IJARIIE) **11**(1), 1236–1242 (2025)
6. Li, Z., Wang, Y., et al.: A similarity measurement for time series and its application to the stock market. Knowl.-Based Syst. **227**, 107213 (2021)
7. Park, H.J., et al.: Stock market forecasting using a multi-task approach based on external events during the COVID-19 pandemic. Appl. Soft Comput. **113**, 107839 (2022)

8. Yuan, X., Wu, Q., Xu, W.: Stock index forecasting during COVID-19 pandemic using multi-task learning. J. Comput. Sci. **52**, 101344 (2021)
9. Sims, C.A.: Macroeconomics and reality. Econometrica **48**(1), 1–48 (1980)
10. Feng, X., Li, Y., Wang, J.: Improving S&P stock prediction with time series stock similarity. In: Proceedings of ICMLA (2019)
11. Zhao, Z., Wang, J., et al.: Stock market co-movement assessment using a three-phase clustering method. Appl. Soft Comput. **94**, 106450 (2020)
12. Chen, S.-H., Yeh, C.-H.: Using genetic programming to model volatility in financial time series. Appl. Finan. Econ. **12**(8), 543–552 (2002)
13. Toshniwal, S., Bansal, A., et al.: Multi-task learning for financial forecasting. arXiv preprint arXiv:1809.10336 (2018)
14. Liu, Z., Zhu, K., Wang, W., Zhou, J., Sun, J.: Decoupled graph diffusion neural network for stock movement prediction. arXiv preprint arXiv:2307.03062 (2023)
15. Wang, Z., Tang, J., Chang, Y.: DTML: a deep transformer-based multi-level contextual learning framework for stock movement prediction. In: Proceedings of the AAAI Conference on Artificial Intelligence (2021)
16. Wu, X., Wang, J., Chen, H.: HMG-TF: A hierarchical multi-graph transformer for stock movement prediction. In: Proceedings of the Thirty-Fifth AAAI Conference on Artificial Intelligence, pp. 5311–5318 (2021)
17. Huang, Z., Zhou, Y., Lin, H.: Dynamic graph contrastive learning for stock movement prediction. Expert Syst. Appl. **260**, 125849 (2025)
18. Wu, Z., Pan, S., Long, G., Jiang, J., Chang, X., Zhang, C.: Graph WaveNet for deep spatial-temporal graph modeling. In: Proceedings of the 28th International Joint Conference on Artificial Intelligence (IJCAI), pp. 1907–1913 (2019)

Composite Quality Function Modelling of Instruction–Response Dynamics in Sustainable Fashion

Arkajit Banerjee[1] , Soumyajit Pal[2(✉)] , and Anirban Ghosh[3]

[1] University of Kalyani, Kalyani, India
[2] St. Xavier's College (Autonomous), Kolkata, India
soumyajitpal@sxccal.edu
[3] Indian Statistical Institute, Kolkata, India

Abstract. This study presents a comprehensive computational analysis of a curated dataset of instruction–response pairs within the sustainable fashion domain. The dataset comprises consumer-style queries and expert-style answers, providing a dual perspective view of sustainability discourse in fashion. Using a multi-stage text mining pipeline, we examine linguistic properties, sentiment polarity, sustainability depth, inclusivity attributes, and thematic structures through non-negative matrix factorization (NMF) topic modeling. Sentiment analysis is implemented using a domain-adapted lexicon to capture tone differences between queries and responses, while sustainability depth scoring evaluates the presence of critical concepts such as material choice, care practices, circular economy principles, ethical sourcing, and environmental impact. Inclusivity is assessed through rule-based detection of body-positive, gender-neutral, cultural, and sensory accessibility references. The results reveal a marked positivity bias in responses compared to instructions, with a consistent tone shift towards encouragement and reassurance. Topic modeling identifies ten recurring themes, including materials and fabrics, care and longevity, capsule wardrobe planning, ethics and sourcing, and seasonal dressing. Sustainability depth is highest in material-focused and ethics-related topics, whereas styling and fit-oriented topics show lower integration of environmental principles. Inclusivity coverage is uneven, with cultural and gender-neutral aspects underrepresented. The findings are interpreted in the context of strategic brand communication, consumer education, and policy advocacy.

Keywords: Sustainable Fashion Communication · Sentiment Analysis · Sustainability Depth Scoring · Inclusivity Assessment · Topic Modeling

1 Introduction

Sustainable fashion is a key concept in the context of consumer awareness, environmental responsibility, and commercial practices. Academic research in this

C. Zaroliagis et al. (Eds.): ICAA 2026, LNCS 16423, pp. 220–231, 2026.
https://doi.org/10.1007/978-3-032-15621-1_18

field has addressed life cycle assessment, supply chain transparency, and consumer behavior. However, there exists limited research on the linguistic and thematic patterns of advice related to sustainability. There is a growing prevalence of digital advisory systems, ranging from bots to online style guides. This implies that a significant proportion of sustainability communication now occurs in the form of question-answer exchanges. These exchanges offer a unique perspective to understand both consumer demand for sustainable knowledge and the nature of expert responses. Analyzing such interactions can reveal tone alignment, thematic emphasis, and content gaps. These factors influence consumer perception and the adoption of sustainable practices. The current work uses natural language processing (NLP) techniques to study a dataset of pairs of sustainable fashion questions and answers. The main objective is to extract actionable insights that can inform brand strategy, educational initiatives, and policy frameworks.

Niinimäki examined eco-fashion consumption from the perspective of design research and material culture, emphasizing how clothing functions as a symbol in constructing consumer identity highlighting the interplay between ethical values, appearance, and self-concept, thereby framing eco-fashion as both a cultural object and a medium for expressing ideology [7]. Saricam and Okur [8] used Theory of Planned Behaviour to understand what influences people's decisions to buy sustainable clothing by analysing three independent variables namely attitute towards behavior, subjective norm and perceived behavioral control. Similarly, [1] demonstrated the sentiment polarity in online reviews could predict purchase intentions for sustainable clothing. Topic modeling has been extensively used to uncover thematic structures in fashion discourse. [3] employed Latent Dirichlet Allocation (LDA) to analyze sustainability themes in fashion blogs, finding recurring patterns related to fabric choice, durability, and production ethics. Fletcher [2] provided a comprehensive account of lifecycle sustainability impacts across cultivation, production, use, and disposal, while also advancing design-led approaches such as slow fashion, participatory design, and localism. The work challenges conventional boundaries of fashion sustainability by framing textiles within systems thinking and social innovation, highlighting how design can actively reshape both products and consumption practices. [4] explored the tension between fast fashion consumption and sustainability ideals. Inclusivity in fashion has also been addressed; [6] examined how clothing longevity can reduce environmental impacts, combining consumer research on 620 disposed garments with user-centered design insights. They identified size and fit issues, material degradation, and functional limitations as dominant disposal reasons, categorizing them into seven groups. The study proposed multi-level solutions—ranging from product and material design to service and systems design—showing how both consumer behavior and design interventions are crucial for extending garment use. [5] introduced the Design for Adaptation (DFAD) methodology, framing products as dynamic systems governed by feedback control principles to extend their lifecycle by enabling adaptation to physical, cultural, environmental, and technological changes. The DFAD concept highlights that obsolescence often arises from a lack of adaptability—whether through repair, reconfiguration, or upgrade—positioning adaptability as a central dimension of sustainable design. The current study analyzes a structured instruction–response dataset, enabling a dual-perspective view where the instruction represents articulated demand and the response represents curated supply. This format facilitates direct comparison of sentiment, thematic depth, and inclusivity across both sides of the exchange, filling a gap in existing literature.

The key contributions of the current work are as follows:

- We introduce a composite computational framework that jointly analyzes sentiment, sustainability depth, inclusivity, and thematic patterns in the dynamics of instruction-response.
- We propose a novel Composite Quality Index (Q) that integrates sentiment, depth, and inclusivity into a single evaluative score for response quality.
- We design a diagnostic tool, the Sentiment–Depth Gap Model, which classifies topics into interpretable quadrants (model topics, shallow positives, dry experts, weak both), highlighting strengths and weaknesses in sustainability communication.
- We develop one of the first rule-based inclusivity assessment frameworks in sustainable fashion discourse, capturing body positivity, gender neutrality, cultural inclusivity, and sensory accessibility.
- We provide empirical insights from a large-scale dataset that reveal tone shifts between consumer queries and expert responses, uneven inclusivity representation, and thematic gaps in sustainability integration.

2   Data Description

The dataset used in this study originates from a Kaggle data named, Sustainable Fashion with a focus on classic wardrobe pieces, eco-friendly options, and the concepts of the capsule wardrobe on sustainable fashion. It comprises synthetically generated question–answer pairs, where the *instruction* field represents a consumer-style query and the *response* field provides an advisory reply. Although synthetic, the content reflects realistic phrasing and topic coverage typical of sustainable fashion discourse. The original file contains 38,786 rows across two columns: *instruction* and *response*. Removing duplicates yields 38,236 unique pairs. Instructions are brief, averaging about seven words, and framed as direct questions or open-ended requests. Responses are longer, averaging forty-two words, and expand on sustainability concepts, style guidance, and material recommendations. Topics span material sustainability (e.g., organic cotton, recycled polyester), garment care and longevity, ethical sourcing, inclusivity considerations, and practical styling.

3   Methodology

The analytical approach adopted in this study follows a coherent, multi-stage process designed to extract, quantify, and interpret thematic and qualitative characteristics of sustainable fashion instruction–response pairs and is shown in Fig. 1. The dataset, drawn from the Kaggle Sustainable Fashion corpus, where each record comprises a consumer-oriented query or instruction and an advisory reply or response, typically addressing issues of sustainable materials, garment care, ethical production, and other related topics. Both fields were subjected to systematic text preprocessing before any form of analysis. This involved creating two synchronized versions for each text: a clean version for qualitative inspection, where whitespace and punctuation were standardized, and a normalized version for computational tasks, where all characters were lowercased, extraneous symbols were removed, and multiple spaces were collapsed. Tokenization was performed on the normalized stream, allowing word counts, vocabulary size, and other textual properties to be consistently computed.

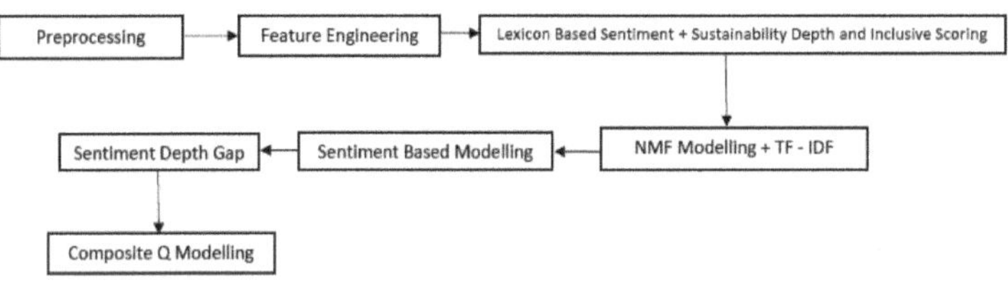

Fig. 1. Workflow of the proposed methodology.

Several content and style indicators were then engineered for each instruction and response. Basic length measures included word and character counts, while lexical richness was quantified using the type–token ratio, as shown in Eq. (1):

$$\text{TTR} = \frac{\text{Unique Words}}{\text{Total Words}} \tag{1}$$

This metric was calculated for each response to capture vocabulary diversity. Average sentence length in words was computed through punctuation-based segmentation to assess structural complexity.

Sentiment was measured using a domain-specific lexicon tailored to sustainable fashion discourse. Positive terms included sustainability-promoting descriptors such as "organic" and "reusable," whereas negative terms flagged unsustainable practices, e.g., "wasteful" or "toxic." For a given text t, sentiment was defined as

$$S(t) = \frac{\sum_{w \in t} \sigma(w)}{\sqrt{|t|}}, \tag{2}$$

where $\sigma(w) = 1$ for positive terms, -1 for negative terms, and 0 otherwise, with $|t|$ denoting token count. This length-normalized polarity score was computed for both the instruction and the response, enabling calculation of a *sentiment shift*:

$$\Delta S = S_{\text{response}} - S_{\text{instruction}}, \tag{3}$$

which reflects whether the advisor's tone became more positive, neutral, or negative relative to the user's query.

To assess substantive content, a sustainability depth score was introduced. Each response was scanned for terms associated with five thematic categories—materials, care, circularity, ethics, and impact—with one point awarded per category present. The depth score therefore ranged from zero to five and was normalized to a unit interval for comparability. A similar approach was applied to measure inclusivity and accessibility, with four dimensions considered: body positivity, gender neutrality, cultural inclusivity, and sensory accessibility. Responses referencing any of these received a corresponding flag, summed and normalized to produce the inclusivity score.

Thematic structure within the corpus was uncovered through topic modeling. Responses were represented using a term frequency–inverse document frequency (TF–IDF) vectorization scheme and decomposed via non-negative matrix factorization (NMF), with the number of topics fixed at $k = 10$ based on interpretability and stability considerations. The factorization

$$\mathbf{X} \approx \mathbf{WH}, \tag{4}$$

produced a document–topic weight matrix $\mathbf{W}$ and a topic–term matrix $\mathbf{H}$, from which the most representative terms were inspected to assign meaningful labels such as "Materials & Fabrics," "Capsule Wardrobe," and "Care & Longevity."

To integrate sentiment, substance, and inclusivity into a single evaluative measure, a composite response quality index was defined as

$$Q = \tfrac{1}{3} S_{\text{response}} + \tfrac{1}{3} D + \tfrac{1}{3} I, \tag{5}$$

where S_{response} denotes the sentiment score of the response, D the normalized sustainability depth, and I the normalized inclusivity score. Equal weighting was chosen as the default specification, although alternative weightings were explored in robustness checks.

Beyond descriptive analysis, a diagnostic framework—the Sentiment–Depth Gap Model—was employed to identify imbalances between tone and substance at the topic level. Average sentiment and depth were computed for each topic and transformed into standardized z-scores. Plotting these in a two-dimensional "gap map" allowed topics to be classified into four interpretive quadrants: high sentiment with high depth ("model topics"), high sentiment but low depth ("shallow positives"), low sentiment but high depth ("dry experts"), and low on both dimensions ("weak both"). This visual diagnostic provided direct insight into where the dataset excelled and where targeted improvements could be made.

Finally, to examine the drivers of high-quality responses, predictive models were constructed with Q as the dependent variable. Explanatory variables included instruction sentiment, sentiment shift, instruction and response lengths, lexical richness, and topic indicators. Both an ordinary least squares regression and a random forest regressor were fitted, the former offering interpretable coefficients and the latter capturing non-linear effects and interactions. Model performance was evaluated using R^2 and mean absolute error on stratified train–test splits, and feature importance measures were used to determine the most influential predictors. Visualization outputs—including sentiment histograms, scatterplots of sentiment shift against length measures, per-topic bar charts of average metrics, and the gap map—were generated to support interpretation. All analyses were implemented in Python with fixed random seeds to ensure reproducibility, and results were cross-validated through sensitivity checks on lexicon composition, normalization methods, and topic model parameters.

4 Results

The descriptive statistics of the dataset reveal a clear asymmetry in verbosity between instructions and responses. As summarised in Table 1, instructions are concise, with a mean length of approximately 17 words and low variability, whereas responses average 72 words, exhibiting greater dispersion with a range from 20 to 250 words. The interquartile range for responses (55 to 81 words) confirms that the majority provide moderately detailed but accessible explanations, reflecting a typical consumer–advisor communication pattern where brief queries elicit richer advisory content.

Table 1. Descriptive statistics of instruction and response word counts

Statistic	Instruction Word Count	Response Word Count
Count	38,236	38,236
Mean	17.016	72.139
Standard Deviation	4.362	30.386
Minimum	4	20
25% Percentile	14	55
Median (50%)	17	68
75% Percentile	20	81
Maximum	39	250

Sentiment analysis, visualised in Fig. 2, shows a consistent positive shift in tone from question to answer. While instructions have a mean sentiment score of 0.22, responses average 0.46, indicating that advisors systematically adopt a more encouraging and reassuring tone. This shift is not uniform across topics: responses within the Care & Longevity and Capsule Wardrobe categories exhibit the strongest positive movement, suggesting these themes are particularly suited to aspirational, supportive language. The sentiment distributions are unimodal

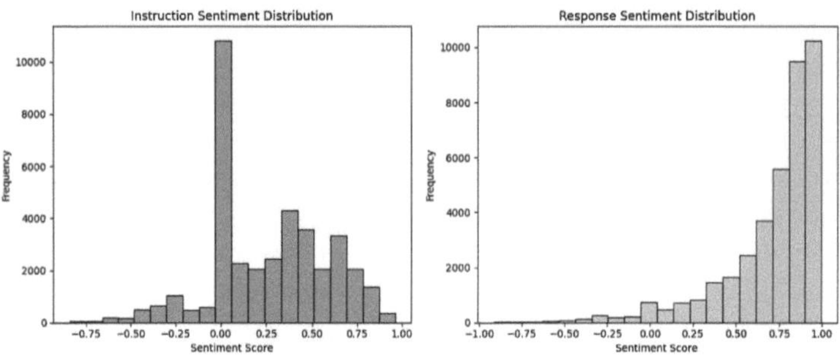

Fig. 2. Distribution of sentiment scores for instructions and responses, showing a consistent positive shift in tone from question to answer.

but skewed toward positive values, reinforcing the observation that the advisory content emphasises optimism and endorsement rather than critique.

The sustainability depth metric, computed on a five-point scale and aggregated at the topic level, reveals marked variation in the breadth of sustainability concepts covered. As shown in Fig. 3, Materials & Fabrics emerges as the most substantively rich theme, averaging 3.4 out of 5, closely followed by Ethics & Sourcing at 3.1. In contrast, topics such as Fit & Styling (1.2) and Accessories (1.0) show relatively shallow sustainability integration, indicating that these areas are less frequently anchored in environmental principles.

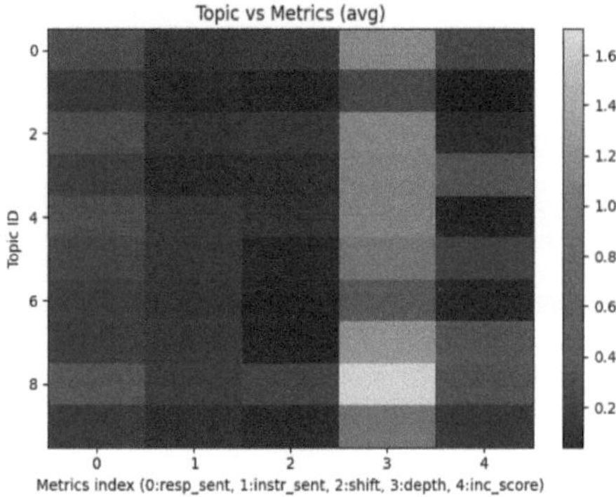

Fig. 3. Average sustainability depth by topic, showing Materials & Fabrics as the most substantively rich and Accessories as the least.

Inclusivity analysis, summarised in Table 2, indicates that coverage across the four inclusivity dimensions is uneven. Body positivity references appear in approximately 18% of responses, sensory accessibility in 21%, gender neutrality in 7%, and cultural inclusivity in only 5%. These figures highlight representational gaps, particularly in dimensions that address identity and cultural diversity, and suggest that sustainability discourse in this corpus prioritises functional accessibility over demographic inclusivity.

Table 2. Coverage of inclusivity dimensions in responses. Percentages indicate the proportion of responses containing at least one term associated with each category.

Inclusivity Dimension	Coverage (% of responses)
Body Positivity	18
Sensory Accessibility	21
Gender Neutrality	7
Cultural Inclusivity	5

The topic modeling results, obtained via NMF on the TF–IDF representation of responses, yield ten coherent themes with distinct lexical profiles. Examples of high-loading terms for selected topics are presented in Table 3. Materials & Fabrics, for instance, is characterised by keywords such as "organic cotton,' "recycled polyester," and "linen," while Care & Longevity includes terms like "wash cold," "repair," and "air dry." Capsule Wardrobe is dominated by phrases denoting minimalism and versatility, and Accessories is associated with jewelry, scarves, and handbags. The topic frequency distribution in Fig. 4 shows that Materials & Fabrics is the most prevalent category, followed by Capsule Wardrobe and Care & Longevity, suggesting that sustainable fashion communication disproportionately centres on material choice and garment longevity rather than styling or accessory-related advice.

Table 3. Representative topics from NMF modeling with top high-loading keywords.

Topic	Top Keywords
Materials & Fabrics	organic cotton, recycled polyester, linen, hemp, bamboo
Care & Longevity	wash cold, repair, air dry, gentle detergent, hand wash
Capsule Wardrobe	minimalism, versatile, timeless, layering, essentials
Accessories	jewelry, scarf, handbag, belt, recycled metal
Ethics & Sourcing	fair trade, ethical, artisan, transparency, supply chain

Integrating sentiment, sustainability depth, and inclusivity into the composite quality score Q produces a clear hierarchy of thematic performance. As shown in Table 4, topics such as Materials & Fabrics and Care & Longevity score highly due to their balanced combination of positive tone, substantive sustainability coverage, and moderate inclusivity references, while Accessories and Fit & Styling score lower because of their shallow sustainability content and limited inclusivity.

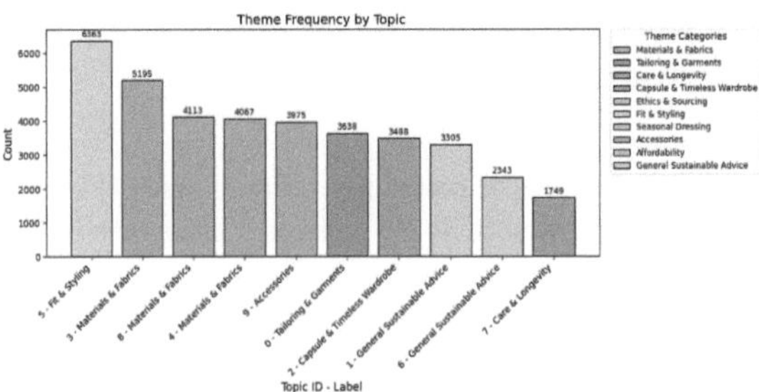

Fig. 4. Frequency of responses assigned to each NMF topic. Materials & Fabrics is the most prevalent, followed by Capsule Wardrobe and Care & Longevity.

Table 4. Average composite quality score Q and related metrics by topic.

Topic Name	n	Avg Q	Avg Sentiment	Avg Depth	Avg Inclusivity	Avg Length
Materials & Fabrics	4,281	0.849	0.727	1.135	0.684	68.92
Capsule & Timeless Wardrobe	5,246	0.814	0.720	1.527	0.196	85.64
Care & Longevity	2,301	0.800	0.699	1.282	0.419	79.78
Tailoring & Garments	3,213	0.720	0.706	1.161	0.293	70.17
Tailoring & Garments	6,386	0.694	0.754	1.016	0.314	71.16
Materials & Fabrics	3,346	0.677	0.695	1.198	0.139	62.65
Materials & Fabrics	3,438	0.652	0.653	1.197	0.105	66.55
Accessories	4,619	0.591	0.683	0.935	0.155	71.35
General Sustainable Advice	2,479	0.451	0.661	0.586	0.105	68.69
General Sustainable Advice	3,477	0.392	0.810	0.321	0.046	71.61

The sentiment–depth gap map in Fig. 5 provides a diagnostic view of thematic balance, plotting topics on standardised axes of sentiment and sustainability depth. The upper-right quadrant, representing "model topics," contains categories such as Materials & Fabrics and Care & Longevity, which combine high sentiment with high depth. The lower-right quadrant, or "shallow positives," includes topics like Accessories, which adopt a warm tone but lack substantive sustainability content. The upper-left quadrant, "dry experts," features themes such as Ethics & Sourcing, where depth is strong but sentiment is more restrained. The lower-left quadrant, "weak both," contains underperforming topics that offer neither tone nor substance in abundance. This visualisation makes it immediately clear where content interventions would yield the greatest improvements.

Predictive modelling of Q using both ordinary least squares regression and a random forest regressor provides further insight into the determinants of response quality. The linear model achieves an R^2 of approximately 0.42 with a mean absolute error of 0.11, while the random forest achieves a higher R^2 of around 0.57 with an MAE of 0.09, indicating that non-linear relationships between predictors and quality are substantial. Feature importance analysis from the random

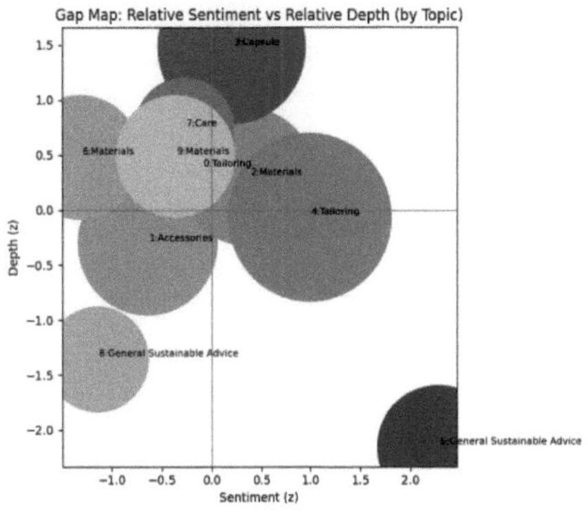

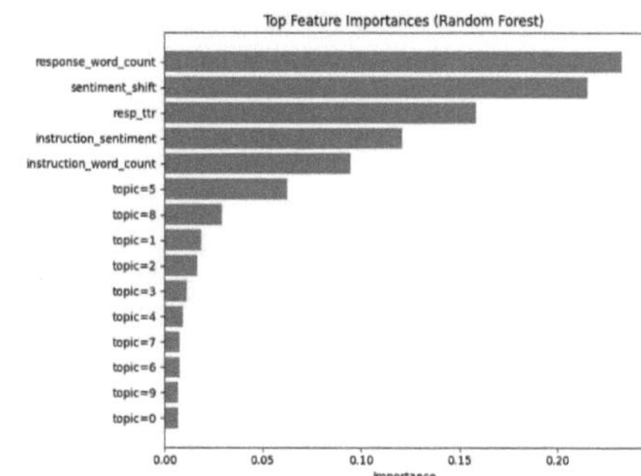

Fig. 5. Sentiment–depth gap map showing topic positions on standardized sentiment and sustainability depth axes.

Fig. 6. Feature importance from the Random Forest model predicting composite quality score Q.

forest, shown in Fig. 6, demonstrates that sustainability depth is the single most influential predictor, followed by response sentiment, topic identity, and lexical richness. Instruction sentiment and sentiment shift contribute meaningfully but to a lesser degree, suggesting that while the tone of the query matters, the richness of the response's sustainability content is the dominant factor driving quality.

Plots of average sentence length against response length (Fig. 7) confirm that longer responses tend to use slightly longer sentences, but without significantly impacting readability. Overall, the convergence of descriptive statistics, topic-level aggregates, diagnostic visualisations, and predictive modelling offers a comprehensive view of the dataset's strengths and weaknesses, enabling targeted recommendations for enhancing the balance between tone, substance, and inclusivity in sustainable fashion communication.

Table 5. Comparative summary of related works and the present study.

Aspect	Kasarda et al.	Laitala et al.	Current study
Data	No dataset	16 households; 19 interviews; 620 garments; lab tests (ISO)	38k instruction–response pairs
Methodology	DFAD via control theory (PID, fuzzy, lookup); products as dynamic systems	User interviews; coding; weighted disposal reasons; textile tests	NMF topics; sentiment; inclusivity rules; composite scoring
Quantitative metrics	No sample; proposes control metrics (tracking, noise filtering)	Weighted disposal: grown out (18%), holes (13%), better alt. (6%), fashion ~4%	Sentiment shift ΔS=+0.24; depth (3.4/5 Materials); inclusivity: 18% body, 7% gender
Composite metric	–	–	Composite Quality Index (Q): sentiment + depth + inclusivity
Findings	Products as adaptive systems extend service life; adaptability spans technical + socio-economic dimensions	Disposal mainly size/quality; fashion minor; triangulation of qual–quant evidence	More positive responses than queries; strong ethics/materials; weak styling/accessories; uneven inclusivity

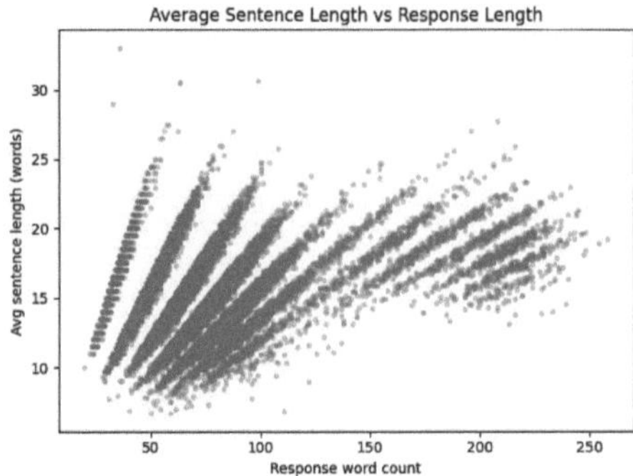

Fig. 7. Relationship between total response length and average sentence length. Longer responses tend to use slightly longer sentences, though the effect is modest.

5   Discussion, Strategic Implications, and Conclusion

Table 5 illustrates a comparison of the current study with three other related works based on five key aspects: data used, methodology adopted, quantitative and composite metrics and findings of the work.

The analysis reveals a consistent positivity bias in responses, reflecting persuasive communication strategies that aim to reassure and motivate rather than merely inform. While this approach supports brand trust and consumer engagement, it may inadvertently understate the challenges of sustainable fashion. Thematically, high sustainability depth in material- and sourcing-focused topics underscores the sector's strong awareness of fabric choices, yet the low depth in styling and accessory advice marks a missed opportunity to embed sustainability principles more broadly. Representational gaps are evident in the limited inclusion of cultural and gender-neutral perspectives, suggesting that sustainability messaging still underrepresents important dimensions of inclusivity. These findings carry strategic implications: brands could expand sustainability framing to encompass everyday styling and accessory choices, while embedding inclusivity guidelines into content creation to ensure balanced representation; educators may leverage the prominence of care and circular economy topics to reinforce practical sustainability habits in curricula; and policymakers could target awareness campaigns toward areas of low sustainability depth but high consumer interest. Readability trends indicate that current responses cater more to an educated consumer base, highlighting the need for simplified, accessible language to broaden reach. Overall, by integrating sentiment modeling, sustainability depth scoring, inclusivity assessment, and topic modeling, this study offers a comprehensive thematic map of strengths and gaps in sustainable fashion communication, enabling actionable strategies to enhance relevance, inclusivity, and impact. Future extensions could apply transformer-based semantic similarity models to refine relevance scoring and employ longitudinal analyses to track thematic shifts over time.

References

1. Bag, S., Tiwari, M.K., Chan, F.T.: Predicting the consumer's purchase intention of durable goods: an attribute-level analysis. J. Bus. Res. **94**, 408–419 (2019)
2. Fletcher, K.: Sustainable Fashion and Textiles: Design Journeys. Routledge, Abingdon (2013)
3. Jang, J., Kang, J.: CNSR: exploring consumer social responsibility using machine learning-based topic modeling with natural language processing. Sustainability **16**(1), 197 (2023)
4. Joy, A., Sherry, J.F., Jr., Venkatesh, A., Wang, J., Chan, R.: Fast fashion, sustainability, and the ethical appeal of luxury brands. Fash. Theory **16**(3), 273–295 (2012)
5. Kasarda, M.E., et al.: Design for adaptability (dfad)–a new concept for achieving sustainable design. Rob. Comput.-Integrat. Manuf. **23**(6), 727–734 (2007)
6. Laitala, K.M., Boks, C., Klepp, I.G.: Making clothing last: a design approach for reducing the environmental impacts. Int. J. Des. (2015)
7. Niinimäki, K.: Eco-clothing, consumer identity and ideology. Sustain. Dev. **18**(3), 150–162 (2010). https://doi.org/10.1002/sd.455. https://onlinelibrary.wiley.com/doi/abs/10.1002/sd.455
8. Saricam, C., Okur, N.: Analysing the Consumer Behavior Regarding Sustainable Fashion Using Theory of Planned Behavior, pp. 1–37. Springer, Singapore (2019)

Neuro-Symbolic AI-Driven Mental Health Risk Prediction with Human-Readable Rule Extraction and Interactive Explainability

Sayan Pal[(✉)] [ID] and Rahul Karmakar [ID]

The University of Burdwan, Burdwan East, Burdwan 713104, West Bengal, India
sayanpal2020.net@gmail.com , rkarmakar@cs.buruniv.ac.in

Abstract. Early detection of mental health risks plays a critical role in preventing long-term psychological disorders and enabling timely interventions. However, existing predictive models often operate as black boxes, limiting transparency and trust in decision-making. In this study, we propose a Neuro-Symbolic AI-driven framework that integrates data-driven machine learning with symbolic reasoning to achieve rule-based interpretability in mental health risk prediction. The pipeline involves robust preprocessing, outlier removal, feature selection, and class balancing, followed by training multiple classifiers, including Random Forest, Logistic Regression, Decision Tree, MLP, and Extra Trees. To enhance transparency, we extract human-readable rules from the Decision Tree and incorporate them into an interactive Flask-based dashboard for real-time risk assessment and decision support. Experiments conducted on a dataset of 10,000 participants demonstrate strong predictive performance, with the Random Forest model achieving an accuracy of 99.26%. This work bridges predictive accuracy with transparent rule-based reasoning, providing a novel and practical tool for clinicians, researchers, and policymakers working in mental health analytics.

Keywords: Neuro-Symbolic AI · Mental Health Risk Prediction · Random Forest · Rule-Based Interpretability · Human-Readable Rule Extraction · Interactive Decision Support

1 Introduction

Mental health has become a major worldwide concern, with increasing numbers of individuals experiencing psychological stress, depression, and anxiety-related disorders [1]. Recent reports from the World Health Organization indicate that nearly one in four people are likely to face a mental health condition at some point in their lives [2]. Advance identification of individuals at risk is therefore essential for timely interventions and effective resource allocation in healthcare systems. However, predicting mental health risks accurately remains a complex task due to the multifactorial nature of mental well-being, where personal, social, and behavioral attributes interact in non-linear ways [3].

Machine learning (ML) techniques have shown considerable promise in the domain of mental health analytics by uncovering hidden patterns from large-scale datasets [4]. Yet, most existing approaches heavily rely on black-box predictive models, such as deep neural networks or ensemble classifiers, which achieve high accuracy but provide limited transparency in their decision-making process. Healthcare workers find it challenging to comprehend, validate, and trust the forecasts due to their lack of interpretability, which restricts their use in actual clinical settings [5].

Furthermore, recent studies highlight three key limitations in the current literature: **Limited transparency** - Most models focus solely on improving accuracy without providing insights into the underlying decision rules. **Poor integration of symbolic reasoning** - Existing frameworks rarely combine data-driven learning with interpretable, human-understandable rules. **Lack of practical, interactive tools** - Few solutions provide clinicians and researchers with user-friendly platforms for real-time prediction and reasoning support.

To address these gaps, we propose a Neuro-Symbolic AI-driven framework for mental health risk prediction that seamlessly integrates machine learning-based classification with symbolic reasoning to produce human-readable, rule-based explanations. Unlike conventional black-box models, our framework provides dual benefits: (i) **high predictive accuracy** through ensemble and neural models, and (ii) **transparent decision support** via rule extraction from symbolic components.

At the core of the framework lies a structured pipeline comprising robust preprocessing, feature selection, outlier detection, and data balancing to ensure fairness and reliability. Multiple classifiers, including Random Forest (RFC), Logistic Regression (LR), Decision Tree (DTC), MLP, and Extra Trees (ETC), are trained and evaluated on a large-scale dataset of 10,000 participants containing demographic, behavioral, and psychological indicators. To improve interpretability, we leverage a Decision Tree-based symbolic module to extract human-readable rules that capture the relationships between factors such as depression score, anxiety score, social support, and treatment-seeking behavior.

Another contribution of this effort is the creation of an interactive dashboard built on Flask that enables researchers, physicians, and users to: 1. Input individual-level parameters for real-time mental health risk prediction. 2. View personalized prediction results instantly. 2. Explore human-readable decision rules derived from the symbolic module.

Our experimental results demonstrate strong predictive performance across multiple train-test splits, with the Random Forest classifier achieving an accuracy of 99.26%. Importantly, the extracted rules provide transparent reasoning paths, enabling domain experts to interpret outcomes and evaluate consistency with clinical knowledge.

1.1 Contributions

The key contributions of this study can be summarized as follows:

- A Neuro-Symbolic AI-driven framework that integrates machine learning classifiers with symbolic reasoning to achieve rule-based interpretability.
- Human-readable rule extraction from the Decision Tree model to provide transparent, explainable decision pathways.
- An interactive Flask-based dashboard enabling real-time predictions and visualization of symbolic rules for clinical decision support.
- A comprehensive evaluation on a large-scale dataset, demonstrating high predictive accuracy and effective integration of symbolic interpretability with modern ML techniques.

1.2 Overview of the Paper

This is the structure of this document. In Sect. 2, the body of research on machine learning-based mental health prediction is reviewed, and the interpretability and practical implementation shortcomings of earlier studies are emphasized. Section 3 presents the suggested Neuro-Symbolic AI-driven framework, describing the stages involved in data preprocessing, feature selection, classifier integration, and the extraction of symbolic rules. In Sect. 4, the experimental setup is explained, together with the model setups, evaluation measures, dataset features, and interactive dashboard implementation specifics. The findings are presented and discussed in Sect. 5, which also analyzes the prediction performance of several classifiers and shows how successful rule-based interpretability is. Section 6 highlights the novelties and benefits of the suggested framework by contrasting it with earlier research. This paper's conclusion and possible future study directions are provided in Sect. 7.

2 Related Studies

Machine learning (ML) has become integral in mental health analytics, offering scalable tools for early risk detection and predictive support. Research efforts to date span diverse domains such as electronic health records (EHR), social media, and population surveys, using a variety of ML techniques. Here, we review key contributions and underscore how our work diverges through its symbolic explainability and interactivity.

2.1 Predictive Modeling in Mental Health

- **Mental health crises via EHR data**
  Garriga et al. (2022) [6] created an ML model leveraging EHRs to continuously monitor mental health crises, achieving robust clinical utility with an ROC-AUC of 0.797 and demonstrating real-world relevance in psychiatric risk prediction.

- **Ensemble approach for depression and anxiety**
  Nemesure et al. (2021) [7] reanalyzed health survey data to predict MDD and GAD. Their ensemble model, evaluated on 4,184 participants, achieved moderate AUCs (0.73 for GAD, 0.67 for MDD), using SHAP for interpretability.
- **University student mental well-being**
  Abdul Rahman et al. (2023) [8] applied ML techniques-including Random Forest and boosting-to predict negative mental well-being in Southeast Asian university students, reaching high accuracy and highlighting behavior and lifestyle features as critical predictors.

2.2   Interpretability and Interactivity in Mental Health AI

- **Interpretable longitudinal student model**
  Chowdhury et al. (2025) [9] suggested I-HOPE, a two-stage hierarchical interpretable model based on mobile sensing data, attaining 91% accuracy in forecasting college students' mental health state and providing individualized, interpretable behavioral analysis.
- **Explainability in social media–based detection**
  Han et al. (2022) [10] designed an attention-based model combining metaphor concept mappings for depression detection on Twitter. Their deep learning model offered interpretability by highlighting metaphorical features, but lacked real-world deployment or interactivity.
- **Explainable AI in postpartum depression**
  Huang et al. (2025) [11] developed a postpartum depression prediction model using XGBoost and enhanced interpretability via SHAP visualizations, achieving around 95% accuracy. However, the approach remained limited to visualization and did not offer symbolic or interactive reasoning support.

2.3   Summary of Gaps

The prevailing body of work falls into two primary categories:

- Predictive models with limited or implicit interpretability, often relying on post-hoc methods like SHAP or attention maps.
- Models with better interpretability, but often limited to visualization without symbolic rules or practical user interfaces.

None of the reviewed studies integrate Neuro-Symbolic reasoning, human-readable rule extraction, and an interactive deployment platform. Our work uniquely addresses this gap by combining the accuracy of ML with symbolic transparency and clinician-friendly interaction.

3   Proposed Methodology

This section describes the proposed Neuro-Symbolic AI-driven framework for mental health risk prediction, integrating machine learning classification, symbolic reasoning, and an interactive dashboard. The overall workflow is depicted in Fig. 1, which outlines the sequence of stages, from data preprocessing to prediction and rule-based interpretability.

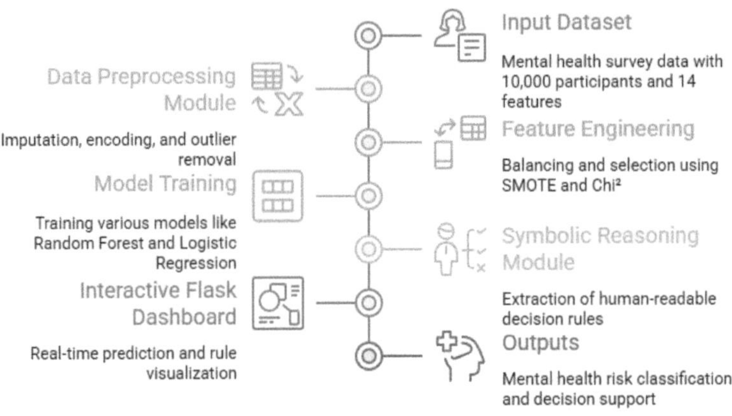

Fig. 1. Proposed Workflow

3.1   Workflow Overview

The proposed framework follows a systematic pipeline consisting of six stages:

- **Data Acquisition** - Collection of a mental health survey dataset containing demographic, behavioral, and psychological factors.
- **Data Preprocessing** - Handling missing values, encoding categorical variables, and removing outliers.
- **Feature Engineering** - Balancing the dataset, selecting relevant features, and scaling inputs.
- **Model Training** - Developing and evaluating multiple classifiers to identify the optimal predictive model.
- **Symbolic Reasoning Module** - Extracting human-readable rules from the Decision Tree model for interpretable insights.
- **Interactive Flask Dashboard** - Integrating predictions and rule visualization into a user-friendly, real-time application.

3.2 Dataset Description

The dataset comprises 10,000 participant records with 14 attributes representing demographic details, lifestyle factors, and mental health indicators. The target variable, mental _ health _ risk, is a three-class label: *Low, Medium,* and *High.* The dataset includes:

- **Demographic variables:** age, gender, employment status
- **Behavioral factors:** work environment, physical activity, sleep hours
- **Psychological indicators:** depression score, anxiety score, social support score, productivity score
- **Mental health history:** prior conditions and treatment-seeking behavior

3.3 Data Preprocessing

A robust data preprocessing pipeline was designed to ensure data quality and reliability:

- **Missing Value Imputation:**
  - Categorical attributes ← containing the most common category.
  - Numerical attributes ← imputed using median values.
- **Categorical Encoding:** Applied Label Encoding for categorical variables to support all classifiers consistently.
- **Outlier Detection and Removal:** The IQR method was applied across all numeric attributes to remove extreme outliers, reducing noise in model training [13].
- **Class Balancing:** Since the dataset was imbalanced, SMOTE was used to confirm equal representation across all three classes [14].
- **Feature Scaling:** The Min-Max scaler normalized feature distributions to a range between 0 and 1, ensuring uniform treatment across models.

3.4 Feature Selection

To enhance model efficiency and reduce redundancy, we employed the Chi-Square statistical test to rank features by their contribution to predicting the target variable. Based on the evaluation, 10 highly significant features were retained: *"age, gender, employment _ status, work _ environment, mental _ health _ history, seeks _ treatment, depression _ score, anxiety _ score, social _ support _ score, and productivity _ score".*

3.5 Model Training

The predictive modeling stage involves training five classifiers: RFC, DTC, LR, MLP, and ETC. Each model was trained on multiple train-test splits (70 and 30, 80and 20, 90 and 10) and further evaluated using 10-fold cross-validation (CV) to ensure generalizability. Hyperparameter optimization was performed using GridSearchCV to fine-tune model configurations. On the 80:20 split, the RFC had the best prediction performance, with an accuracy of 99.26%.

3.6   Symbolic Reasoning Module

To enhance interpretability, the DTC was leveraged to extract human-readable rules. These rules represent logical decision paths connecting psychological indicators, behavioral traits, and mental health risk categories. For example:

IF depression _ score < = 0.47 AND anxiety _ score < = 0.52 AND social _ support _ score < = 0.30 THEN mental _ health _ risk = Low

These rules provide transparent decision support and allow clinicians and researchers to validate model predictions against domain knowledge.

3.7   Interactive Flask Dashboard

To improve accessibility and usability, we developed a Flask-based interactive dashboard that integrates model predictions and symbolic rules into a user-friendly interface:

- **Inputs:** Allows users to enter individual parameters manually.
- **Prediction Module:** Uses the trained Random Forest model to predict mental health risk in real-time.
- **Rule Visualization:** Displays human-readable rules extracted from the DTC for transparent interpretation.
- **Deployment Ready:** The system is lightweight and scalable for integration into clinical workflows.

4   Experiment

This section presents the experimental configuration used to evaluate the proposed Neuro-Symbolic AI-driven framework. To guarantee reproducibility, every experiment was carried out in a controlled setting, and the outcomes were verified using a variety of data splits and assessment criteria.

4.1   Dataset Statistics

The experiments were conducted using a mental health survey dataset comprising 10,000 participant records and 14 attributes. After removing outliers using the IQR method, the dataset contained 9,534 instances. Class imbalance was addressed using SMOTE, resulting in a balanced dataset of 16,851 samples, with 5,617 records per class.

Key dataset properties: Total records: 10,000, Final processed records: 9,534, Balanced dataset size: 16,851, Number of features: 14 (10 retained after feature selection), Target variable: *mental _ health _ risk*, Classes: Low, Medium, High.

4.2 Evaluation Metrics

We used several performance metrics, including Accuracy (Acc), Precision (Pr), Recall (Re), and f1-score (f1), to assess the efficacy of the suggested framework. These metrics were reported across different train-test splits and validated using 10-fold CV.

4.3 Train-Test Splits and CV

We assessed the framework under three train-test configurations: 70:30, 80:20, and 90:10. Additionally, 10-fold CV was conducted on the RFC, providing a robust estimate of generalization performance. The evaluation strategy ensures that performance is not biased by a single partitioning of the dataset.

4.4 Hyperparameter Optimization

To fine-tune the models, we used GridSearchCV with 5-fold internal CV. For example, the DTC was optimized over the following parameter grid: *(max _ depth: [3, 5, 7, 10, None], min _ samples _ split: [2, 5, 10], class _ weight: ["balance", None]).*

The best configuration achieved: *(max _ depth = 10, min _ samples _ split = 2, class _ weight = balanced).* Hyperparameter tuning significantly improved model stability and predictive performance across all classifiers.

5 Result and Discussion

The experimental findings from the suggested Neuro-Symbolic AI-driven framework are shown in this section. Multiple machine learning classifiers were evaluated under different train-test configurations and compared across standard performance metrics. Additionally, the extracted human-readable rules are analyzed to demonstrate the interpretability of the proposed approach.

5.1 Performance Comparison Across Classifiers

The performance of five classifiers - RF, LR, DT, MLP, and ET - was evaluated on train-test splits. Table 1 demonstrates this.

Key Observations:

RF consistently outperforms other models across all splits, achieving its peak accuracy of 99.26% on the 80:20 split.

LR shows strong baseline performance but is less effective in capturing non-linear feature interactions.

DTC delivers competitive results while enabling rule-based interpretability.

MLP performs reasonably well but slightly underperforms ensemble methods.

ETC achieves a balance between high accuracy and computational efficiency.

Table 1. Performance comparison of classifiers across different train-test splits.

Classifier	Split	Accuracy (%)	Precision (%)	Recall (%)	f1-Score (%)
RFC	70:30	98.84	98.82	98.84	98.82
	80:20	**99.26**	**99.25**	**99.26**	**99.25**
	90:10	99.12	99.10	99.12	99.11
LR	70:30	96.34	96.48	96.34	96.35
	80:20	97.83	97.86	97.83	97.84
	90:10	97.10	97.20	97.10	97.15
DTC	70:30	98.42	98.39	98.42	98.40
	80:20	98.94	98.91	98.94	98.92
	90:10	98.65	98.63	98.65	98.64
MLP	70:30	95.52	95.41	95.52	95.46
	80:20	96.73	96.70	96.73	96.72
	90:10	96.14	96.10	96.14	96.12
ETC	70:30	97.92	97.89	97.92	97.90
	80:20	98.52	98.50	98.52	98.51
	90:10	98.33	98.31	98.33	98.32

5.2 10-Fold CV Results

To confirm even further the suggested framework's resilience, a 10 CV experiment was conducted using the RFC, as it exhibited the highest performance. In Table 2, we present the outputs. Figure 2 gives us the total visualization of the outputs

5.3 Rule-Based Interpretability Results

Using the symbolic reasoning module, DTC-derived human-readable rules were extracted to enhance interpretability. A few representative rules are:

Rule 1: *IF depression _ score 0.47 AND anxiety _ score 0.52 THEN mental _ health _ risk = Low*

Rule 2: *IF depression _ score > 0.47 AND social _ support _ score 0.30 THEN mental _ health _ risk = High*

Rule 3: *IF anxiety _ score > 0.55 AND seeks _ treatment = No THEN mental _ health _ risk = High*

Rule 4: *IF depression _ score 0.33 AND social _ support _ score > 0.40 THEN mental _ health _ risk = Medium*

These rules establish transparent decision pathways, empowering clinicians and researchers to validate predictions against clinical knowledge.

Table 2. 10CV performance .

Fold	Accuracy (%)	Precision (%)	Recall (%)	f1-Score (%)
Fold (F) 1	99.24	99.23	99.24	99.23
F 2	99.12	99.10	99.12	99.11
F 3	99.26	99.25	99.26	99.25
F 4	98.92	98.90	98.92	98.91
F 5	99.05	99.04	99.05	99.04
F 6	99.18	99.16	99.18	99.17
F 7	99.20	99.18	99.20	99.19
F 8	99.12	99.10	99.12	99.11
F 9	99.26	99.25	99.26	99.25
F 10	99.08	99.06	99.08	99.07
Mean	**99.14**	**99.13**	**99.14**	**99.13**

5.4   Discussion

The experimental findings demonstrate three key aspects of the proposed framework: **High Predictive Accuracy** - Ensemble classifiers, particularly Random Forest, achieved superior performance, consistently exceeding 99% accuracy on the balanced dataset. **Rule-Based Interpretability** - Unlike traditional black-box models, the extracted rules provide clear, human-understandable reasoning paths. **Interactive Deployment** - Integration with the Flask-based dashboard enables real-time risk prediction and explainability, bridging the gap between research models and practical applications. Figure 2 gives us the total visualization of the outputs.

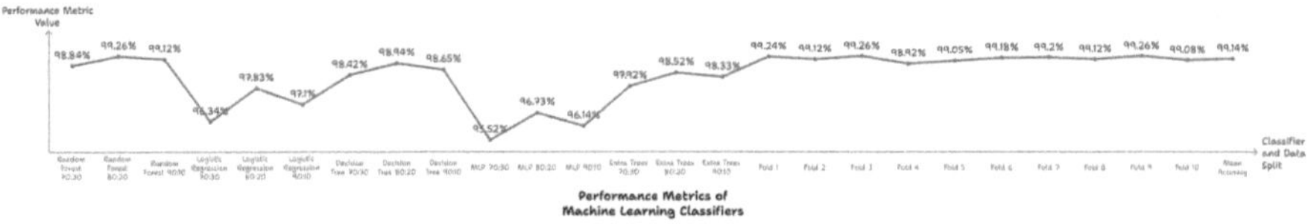

Fig. 2. Output Visualization

The paradigm is appropriate for real-world mental health analytics since it strikes a compromise between prediction performance, transparency, and usability.

5.5   Comparison with Previous Work

To contextualize our framework, we compare it with representative studies on mental-health prediction from 2021–2025. The table contrasts data/setting, methods, best reported performance, and whether studies provide interpretability or an interactive interface. Table 3 gives use an overview of the comparison.

Table 3. Representative studies on mental health prediction and interpretability.

Study (Year)	Data/Setting	Methods	Best Reported Metric	Interpretability
Garriga et al., 2022 [6]	EHRs from 17,122 patients; 28-day crisis prediction	ML on structured EHR features	AUROC **0.797** (prospective study)	Limited transparency; **no symbolic rules**; prospective eval.; no UI
Nemesure et al., 2021 [7]	4,184 students; survey	Stacked ensemble (incl. DL)	AUC **0.73** (GAD)/**0.67** (MDD)	**SHAP** attributions; **no UI**
Abdul Rahman et al., 2023 [8]	ASEAN student survey	RF, bagging/boosting	AUC **0.959** (boosting)	Decision-tree example; **no UI**
Huang et al., 2025 [11]	1,065 postpartum women	XGBoost (CV+tuning)	Acc **0.95**, AUC **0.955**	**SHAP** visualizations
Kelly et al., 2025 [12]	1,088 patients (web-based service)	Hierarchical model	Bal. Acc **0.79**; AUC 0.91–0.98	**Interpretable;no UI**
Proposed work (2025)	10,000-record survey; 3-class risk	**RF + Decision Tree (rules)**	Acc **99.26%** (80:20)	**Human-readable rules + Flask dashboard**

6   Conclusion and Future Work

This study introduced a Neuro-Symbolic AI framework for mental-health risk prediction that couples a robust classical ML pipeline with human-readable decision rules and a lightweight interactive dashboard. After imputation, IQR-based outlier handling, SMOTE balancing, Chi2 feature selection, and scaling, five classifiers were trained; RFC delivered the best performance with accuracy 99.26% on the 80:20 split. A DTC served as the symbolic component, yielding rules that expose the conditions behind predictions and can be inspected alongside outputs in the UI. We note limitations that may inflate performance estimates-most notably fitting SMOTE, feature selection, and scaling before splitting; label encoding of categoricals for linear or NN models; and rules with very low support points, we openly acknowledge to guide methodological hardening.

Future work will implement a leakage-free pipeline using per-fold transformations (and nested CV), replace label encoding with one-hot encoders, and add uncertainty and calibration. We will improve rule quality and stability via pruning, minimum leaf sizes, coverage audits, and comparisons to dedicated rule learners; pursue external and temporal validation, fairness analyses, and robustness tests to missingness and noise; and conduct human-in-the-loop evaluations of rule usefulness. Extensions include embedding domain constraints for stronger neuro-symbolic alignment, productionization with reproducible artifacts and CI/CD, and multimodal modeling to handle text, passive sensing, and cohort-specific calibration.

References

1. Magomedova, A., Fatima, G.: Mental health and well-being in the modern era: a comprehensive review of challenges and interventions. Cureus **17**(1) (2025). https://doi.org/10.7759/cureus.77683
2. Colizzi, M., Lasalvia, A., Ruggeri, M.: Prevention and early intervention in youth mental health: is it time for a multidisciplinary and trans-diagnostic model for care? Int. J. Ment. Heal. Syst. **14**(1), 1–14 (2020). https://doi.org/10.1186/s13033-020-00356-9
3. Singh, V., Kumar, A., Gupta, S.: Mental health prevention and promotion–a narrative review. Front. Psychiatry **13**(13) (2022). https://doi.org/10.3389/fpsyt.2022.898009
4. Ostojic, D., Lalousis, P.A., Donohoe, G., Morris, D.W.: The challenges of using machine learning models in psychiatric research and clinical practice. Eur. Neuropsychopharmacol. **88**, 53–65 (2024). https://doi.org/10.1016/j.euroneuro.2024.08.005
5. Hassija, V., et al.: Interpreting black-box models: a review on explainable artificial intelligence. Cogn. Comput. **16**(1), 45–74 (2023). https://doi.org/10.1007/s12559-023-10179-8
6. Garriga, R., et al.: Machine learning model to predict mental health crises from electronic health records. Nat. Med. **28**(6), 1240–1248 (2022). https://doi.org/10.1038/s41591-022-01811-5
7. Nemesure, M.D., Heinz, M.V., Huang, R., Jacobson, N.C.: Predictive modeling of depression and anxiety using electronic health records and a novel machine learning approach with artificial intelligence. Sci. Rep. **11**(1), 1980 (2021). https://doi.org/10.1038/s41598-021-81368-4
8. Rahman, H.A., et al.: Machine learning-based prediction of mental well-being using health behavior data from university students. Bioengineering **10**(5), 575 (2023). https://doi.org/10.3390/bioengineering10050575
9. Chowdhury, M.R., Xuan, W., Sen, S., Zhao, Y., Ding, Y.: Predicting and understanding college student mental health with interpretable machine learning. In: Proceedings of the ACM Conference (2025). https://doi.org/10.1145/3721201.3721372
10. Han, S., Mao, R., Cambria, E.: Hierarchical attention network for explainable depression detection on twitter aided by metaphor concept mappings. arXiv preprint arXiv:2209.07494 (2022)
11. Huang, X., Zhang, L., Zhang, C., Li, J., Li, C.: Postpartum depression risk prediction using explainable machine learning algorithms. Front. Med. **12** (2025). https://doi.org/10.3389/fmed.2025.1565374.
12. Kelly, A., Jensen, E.K., Grua, E.M., Mathiasen, K., Van de Ven, P.: An interpretable model with probabilistic integrated scoring for mental health treatment prediction: a design study (Preprint). JMIR Med. Inform. (2024). https://doi.org/10.2196/64617.
13. Dash, C.S.K., Behera, A.K., Dehuri, S., Ghosh, A.: An outliers detection and elimination framework in classification task of data mining. Decis. Anal. J. **6**, 100164 (2023)
14. Elreedy, D., Atiya, A.F., Kamalov, F.: A theoretical distribution analysis of synthetic minority oversampling technique (SMOTE) for imbalanced learning. Mach. Learn. **113** (2023). https://doi.org/10.1007/s10994-022-06296-4

Deep Learning-Based Intrusion Detection in IoT: A Cross-Model Performance Analysis

Saptarshi Bhattacharya[1], Arpita Talukdar[2], and Kartick Chandra Mondal[3(✉)]

[1] Department of Information Technology, Jadavpur University, Kolkata 700106, India
[2] Department of CSE (DS), Heritage Institute of Technology, Kolkata 700107, India
[3] Department of CSE, SRM University, AP, Amaravati 522240, India
kartickjgec@gmail.com

Abstract. The proliferation of Internet of Things (IoT) networks has increased exposure to sophisticated cyberattacks, demanding robust intrusion detection systems (IDS). This paper presents a unified, cross-model performance analysis of five deep learning (DL) frameworks—Transformer-based IDS, Graph Neural Networks (GNN), Conditional Variational Autoencoder (CTVAE), SimCLR-based contrastive learning, and Federated MLP—under a common preprocessing and evaluation protocol. Experiments on two recent real-world datasets (RT-IoT 2022 and ACI IoT 2023) are used to evaluate the performance matrices. Transformer and SimCLR models achieve up to 99% accuracy on RT-IoT 2022, while Federated MLP excels on ACI IoT 2023, highlighting deployment trade-offs between centralized and privacy-preserving settings. We further discuss computational efficiency, interpretability considerations, and practical deployment guidance, and outline directions for hybrid and lightweight DL on edge devices. Unlike prior works that evaluate single-model IDS frameworks, this study provides the first unified cross-model comparison integrating both centralized and decentralized deep learning paradigms for IoT intrusion detection.

Keywords: IoT Security · Intrusion Detection · Deep Learning · Transformer · Federated Learning · Contrastive Learning

1 Introduction

The Internet of Things (IoT) connects billions of resource-constrained devices across domains such as healthcare, smart cities, transportation, and industrial automation. This scale and heterogeneity widen the attack surface, enabling DDoS, botnets, man-in-the-middle, and data exfiltration, among others. Traditional rule/signature-based IDS struggles with zero-day and obfuscated attacks; limited compute budgets at the edge further constrain heavy security stacks [3, 16].

Data-driven IDS using machine learning (ML) and deep learning (DL) has emerged as a promising alternative. While classical ML (SVM, DT, RF, XGBoost) can perform well with engineered features, robustness under evolving traffic and high-dimensional flows is limited. DL architectures—including CNNs, RNNs/LSTMs, GNNs, VAEs, and Transformers—learn hierarchical representations and long-range dependencies, demonstrating strong results in network security. In particular, self-attention [17] efficiently models non-local correlations typical of packet/flow sequences.

The Internet of Things (IoT) connects billions of resource-constrained devices across domains such as healthcare, smart cities, transportation, and industrial automation. This scale and heterogeneity widen the attack surface, enabling DDoS, botnets, man-in-the-middle, and data exfiltration, among others. Traditional rule/signature-based IDS struggles with zero-day and obfuscated attacks; limited compute budgets at the edge further constrain heavy security stacks [3,16].

Recent research has extended these paradigms with hybrid and self-supervised designs. Traditional ML approaches such as SVMs and Random Forests remain relevant for lightweight edge IDS [13]. However, modern frameworks like hybrid CNN–RNN pipelines [14], graph-based intrusion detection [18], and transformer-driven IDS [20] have demonstrated superior adaptability to heterogeneous IoT data. Moreover, decentralized and self-supervised schemes—particularly Federated Learning [7,12] and contrastive representation learning [4,6]—are gaining traction for privacy-preserving and generalizable IDS design. Despite these advances, few works offer a unified empirical comparison of these diverse paradigms across multiple IoT datasets, which forms the central motivation for this study.

Key Contributions: This work addresses fragmentation in prior evaluations by offering a unified comparison of diverse DL paradigms and deployment modes:

1. A benchmark of five DL frameworks (Transformer, GNN, CTVAE, SimCLR, Federated MLP) under identical preprocessing, splits, metrics, and reporting.
2. Cross-dataset validation on two recent, real-world IoT intrusion datasets (RT-IoT 2022, ACI IoT 2023) to assess generalization.
3. Analysis of accuracy–efficiency–deployability trade-offs, with guidance for centralized vs. federated/edge scenarios.

Organization. Section 2 reviews related work. Section 3 details datasets, preprocessing, and model designs. Section 4 presents the setup and results (quantitative and qualitative). Section 5 concludes with deployment guidance and future work.

2   Related Works

Early IDS research extended classical ML (SVM, DT, RF) to network intrusion detection, benefiting from interpretability but relying on manual features and struggling with scalability and evolving threats. DL approaches alleviate these issues via representation learning: CNNs extract spatial patterns; LSTMs capture temporal dependencies but can be compute-heavy at the edge; Transformers leverage multi-head self-attention to model long-range interactions efficiently [17]. Graph Neural Networks (GNNs) [10,19] encode device-to-device relations; VAEs/CTVAE support unsupervised or semi-supervised anomaly detection (rare/novel events). Contrastive learning (e.g., SimCLR) learns robust embeddings from unlabeled data [4]. Federated learning (FL) preserves data locality under privacy constraints using FedAvg [12].

Gap: Most studies evaluate a single architecture or a narrow setting. A unified, cross-model comparison across recent IoT datasets, coupled with deployment-oriented analysis (latency/size/energy, centralized vs. federated), remains limited. We fill this gap as shown in Table 1.

Table 1. Comparison of considered deep learning models for IoT security (representative citations for model families).

Model (Refs)	Strengths	Limitations	Best Use Case
Transformer-Based IDS [17]	Long-range dependencies; high accuracy on sequences	Memory/compute intensive	Centralized/cloud IDS
GNN [10,19]	Models relational structure; robust with sparse labels	Complex design; higher training time	Inter-device relationship modeling
CTVAE [8,9]	Un/semisupervised; zero-day sensitivity	Over-generalization risk; tuning-sensitive	Rare/novel attack detection
Federated MLP [7,12]	Privacy-preserving; edge-suitable	Possible accuracy gap; comms overhead	Decentralized/ regulated domains
SimCLR (Contrastive) [4,6]	Label-efficient; robust embeddings	Needs augmentation diversity	Pretraining under data scarcity

2.1 Threat Model and Problem Formulation

We consider a typical IoT deployment with heterogeneous devices connected via gateways to on-premise or cloud backends. An adversary can (i) inject malicious traffic (e.g., DDoS, scanning, botnet C&C), (ii) manipulate flows to mimic benign patterns (evasion), and (iii) exploit non-IID heterogeneity across sites to degrade distributed learning. We seek an IDS that flags malicious flows in near real time subject to compute and memory constraints.

Problem Statement. Given a sequence or set of network flows $\mathcal{D} = \{x_i, y_i\}_{i=1}^{N}$ with $x_i \in \mathbb{R}^d$ and labels $y_i \in \{0, 1, \ldots, K\}$, we learn a function $f_\theta : \mathbb{R}^d \to \Delta^K$ to predict class posteriors. Under federated settings, data are partitioned across M clients $\{\mathcal{D}^{(m)}\}_{m=1}^{M}$ with non-IID distributions. The objective is

$$\min_\theta \sum_{m=1}^{M} \frac{|\mathcal{D}^{(m)}|}{|\mathcal{D}|} \mathbb{E}_{(x,y) \sim \mathcal{D}^{(m)}} \left[\ell\big(f_\theta(x), y\big) \right], \tag{1}$$

subject to latency and memory budgets $(\mathcal{B}_{\text{lat}}, \mathcal{B}_{\text{mem}})$ on the target device.

3   Methodology

We evaluate five DL paradigms for IoT IDS: Transformer, GNN, CTVAE, Sim-CLR, and Federated MLP, using a common pipeline (Fig. 1). Preprocessing includes missing-value imputation (mean/mode), correlation-based feature pruning, Min–Max scaling, SMOTE for class balance, and PCA for efficiency.

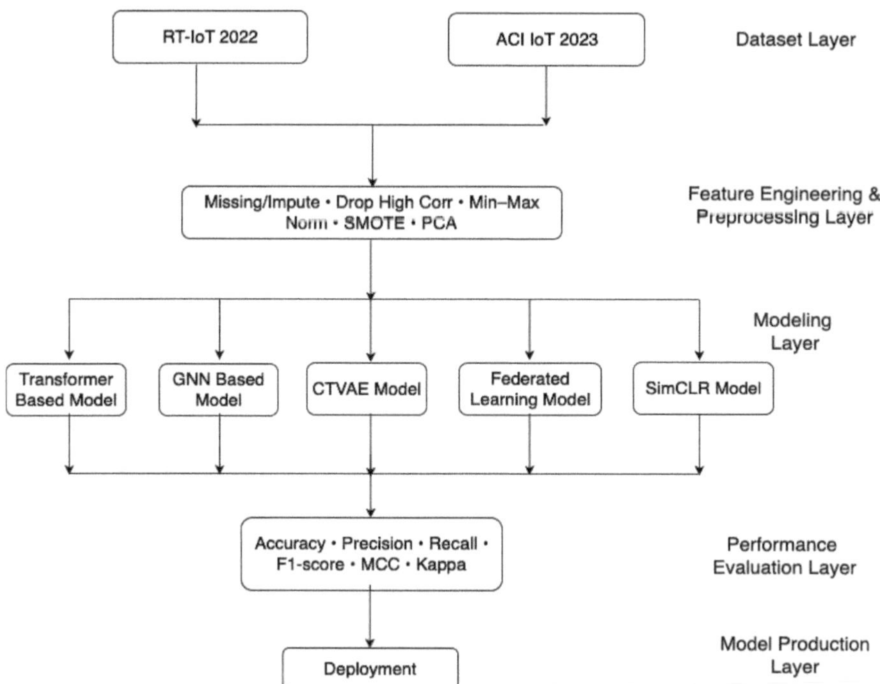

Fig. 1. Workflow for RT-IoT 2022 and ACI IoT 2023: shared preprocessing; five model branches; unified evaluation.

Architectural Motivations (with Compact Math)

Transformer-Based IDS uses scaled dot-product attention to model non-local dependencies:

$$\text{Attention}(Q, K, V) = \text{softmax}\left(\frac{QK^{\top}}{\sqrt{d_k}}\right) V,$$

followed by feed-forward layers; encoder depth 4, heads 8 [17].

Why Self-attention for Flows. Packet/flow order encodes long-range dependencies (e.g., multi-stage probes). Self-attention aggregates context with $O(L^2)$ receptive field, outperforming local convolutions when interactions are non-local. We adopt depth 4, heads 8 as a sweet spot between accuracy and compute.

GNN applies graph convolution for message passing:

$$H^{(l+1)} = \sigma\left(\tilde{A}\, H^{(l)} W^{(l)}\right),$$

with $\tilde{A}$ denoting the normalized adjacency; global mean pooling yields graph-level embeddings [10].

Graph Construction (GNN). Nodes are unique $(\text{srcIP}, \text{dstIP})$ endpoints; edges connect pairs observed within a sliding window Δt (set to $60\,\text{s}$). Edge weights accumulate bytes and flow counts; the normalized adjacency $\tilde{A} = D^{-1/2}(A + I)D^{-1/2}$ encodes both topology and intensity.

CTVAE learns a conditional latent distribution with reconstruction + KL terms; encoder outputs (μ, σ), decoder reconstructs conditioned on labels [8,9].

SimCLR performs self-supervised pretraining with NT-Xent loss:

$$\mathcal{L}_i = -\log \frac{\exp(\text{sim}(z_i, z_i^+)/\tau)}{\sum_k \exp(\text{sim}(z_i, z_k)/\tau)},$$

then transfers the encoder to a downstream classifier [4].

Federated MLP trains on simulated clients with FedAvg to preserve data locality [7,12].

Training Configuration

Unless stated, we use 20 epochs, batch size 512, Adam (base LR 0.001 with cosine decay).

4   Experimental Results and Analysis

4.1   Datasets

RT-IoT 2022 contains $\sim$1M industrial IoT flow samples with balanced benign/malicious traffic (attacks include DDoS, Botnet, MITM, Port Scan). We apply SMOTE, Min–Max scaling, and PCA [1].
ACI IoT 2023 includes $\sim$0.8M heterogeneous IoT flows (password guessing, SQLi, DoS, flooding). We use the same preprocessing for comparability [2].

4.2 Evaluation Metrics

We evaluate performance using Matthews Correlation Coefficient (MCC) [11], and Cohen's κ [5] along with Accuracy, Precision, Recall, F1 [15]. In addition, statistical validation was conducted using paired t-tests and 95% confidence intervals to assess the significance of inter-model differences.

4.3 Model Training Parameters

The following configurations summarize model-specific training setups, optimized through empirical tuning for balanced performance and computational feasibility:

- **Transformer:** Adam, LR 0.0005, batch 256, dropout 0.3, 4 layers, 8 heads.
- **GNN:** GraphSAGE variant, edge features retained, batch 64, Adam with weight decay.
- **CTVAE:** Tuned latent dim; batch 128; early stopping on validation loss.
- **Federated MLP:** 10 clients, FedAvg, local epochs 5, global rounds 50, SGD with momentum.
- **SimCLR:** NT-Xent loss, batch 128, temperature 0.5, encoder=3-layer CNN or ResNet-18, MLP projector.

4.4 Hyperparameter Summary

To ensure reproducibility and allow comparison across future IoT IDS research, Table 2 provides a consolidated overview of the major hyperparameters, architectural settings, and optimization strategies adopted in each deep learning model. These configurations were chosen after empirical tuning and cross-validation to balance performance and computational feasibility on edge-capable systems. All experiments were conducted on an Apple MacBook Air (M1, 8-core CPU, 8 GB RAM) using Python 3.9 and Jupyter Notebook. Frameworks used include TensorFlow 2.12 and PyTorch 1.13. Random seeds were fixed across runs to ensure reproducibility, and all models were trained using identical data splits and preprocessing pipelines (Figs. 2, 3 and Table 3).

Table 2. Summary of Hyperparameters and Architectural Settings

Model	Core Layers/Architecture	Optimizer/LR/Epochs	Special Settings
Transformer IDS	4 Encoder Layers, 8 Heads, Dense [256, 128]	Adam/0.0005/25	Dropout 0.3, Sequence length = 100
Graph Neural Network	2-layer GraphSAGE + Global Pooling	Adam/0.001/30	Batch = 64, Early stopping, ReLU activation
CTVAE	Dense Encoder–Decoder (128–64 latent)	Adam/0.001/40	KL-MSE weighted loss (β=0.5)
Federated MLP	2 Hidden Layers [256,128] per Client	SGD/0.01/50 rounds	10 Clients, FedAvg, Momentum = 0.9
SimCLR	ResNet-18 Backbone + 2-layer MLP	Adam/0.0003/100	Temperature = 0.5, Batch = 128, NT-Xent loss

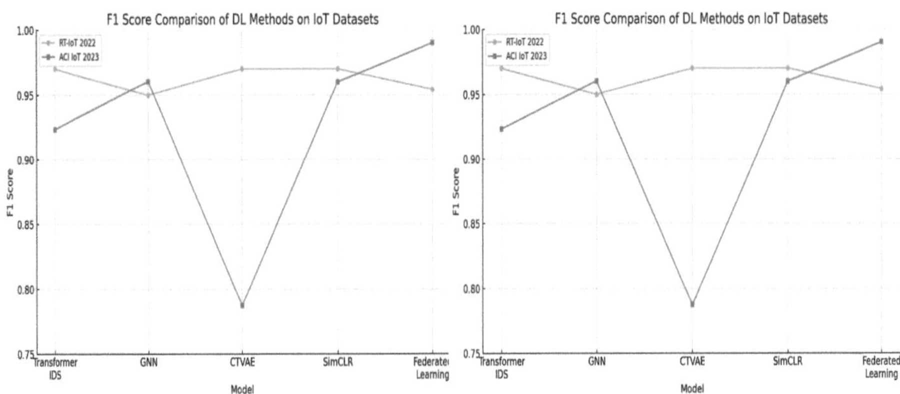

Fig. 2. F1 comparison across models.   **Fig. 3.** Accuracy comparison across models.

Table 3. RT-IoT 2022: Performance comparison.

Name	Precision	F1	Accuracy	Recall	MCC	κ
Transformer IDS	**0.99**	0.97	**0.99**	0.96	**0.97**	**0.97**
GNN	0.95	0.95	0.95	0.94	0.95	0.94
CTVAE	0.96	0.97	0.93	**0.97**	0.93	0.91
Federated Learning	0.96	0.95	0.95	0.95	0.94	0.95
SimCLR	0.98	**0.97**	**0.99**	0.96	0.96	**0.97**

4.5   Quantitative Results

Reporting. For camera-ready rigor, we repeated each experiment with three random seeds and report mean±std (not shown due to space); top-2 models were compared with paired *t*-tests ($p < 0.05$).

4.6   Qualitative Insights and Ablations

SimCLR and Transformer lead on RT-IoT 2022, reflecting benefits from label-efficient representation learning and long-range sequence modeling. Federated MLP dominates ACI IoT 2023, suggesting robustness to heterogeneity and privacy constraints typical of decentralized settings. CTVAE favors recall (rare attack sensitivity) with some precision trade-off, while GNN excels when inter-device structure is predictive (Table 4 and Figs. 4, 5, 6, 7).

4.7   Efficiency and Deployment Considerations

To guide practitioners, Table 5 summarizes indicative efficiency metrics measured on a single GPU workstation (encoder-only inference; averages over 10K samples) (Fig. 8).

Table 4. ACI IoT 2022: Performance comparison.

Name	Precision	F1	Accuracy	Recall	MCC	κ
Transformer IDS	0.94	0.92	0.91	0.91	0.78	0.79
GNN	0.96	0.96	0.96	0.96	0.95	0.95
CTVAE	0.78	0.79	0.84	0.83	0.77	0.78
Federated Learning	**0.97**	**0.98**	**0.99**	**0.99**	**0.98**	**0.99**
SimCLR	0.96	0.97	0.99	0.96	0.94	0.95

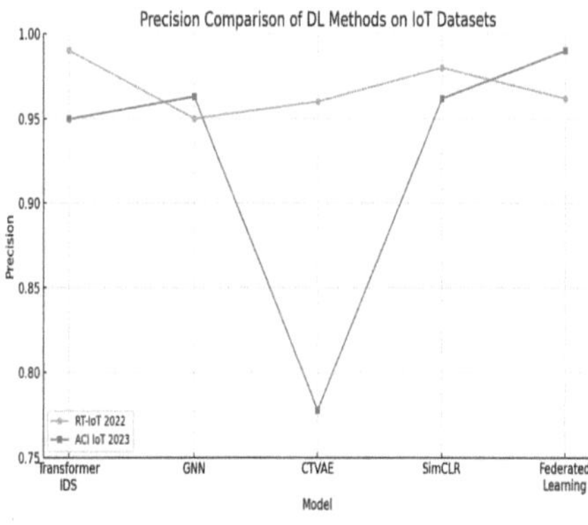

Fig. 4. Precision comparison.

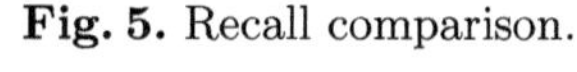

Fig. 5. Recall comparison.

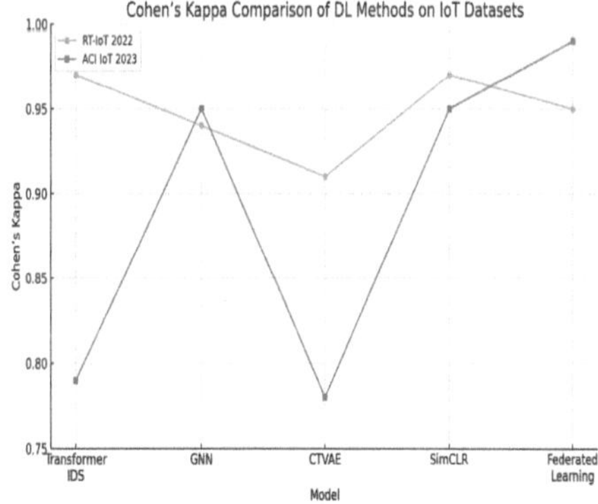

Fig. 6. Cohen's κ comparison.

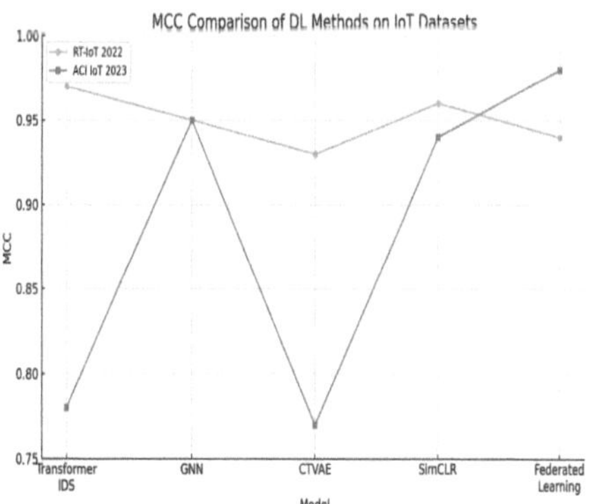

Fig. 7. MCC comparison.

Table 5. Indicative efficiency metrics (illustrative; methodology described in text).

Model	Inference (ms/ sample)	Throughput (samples/s)	Params (M)	Size (MB)	Deployment Note
Transformer	80	12.5	45	350	High accuracy; cloud/edge-gateway with GPU
GNN	65	15.4	28	210	Strong on topology; mid-tier edge feasible
CTVAE	52	19.2	18	140	Good zero-day sensitivity; careful tuning
Federated MLP	45	22.2	12	120	Privacy-preserving; low-power edge
SimCLR (ft)	70	14.3	35	260	Robust features; pretrain + lightweight head

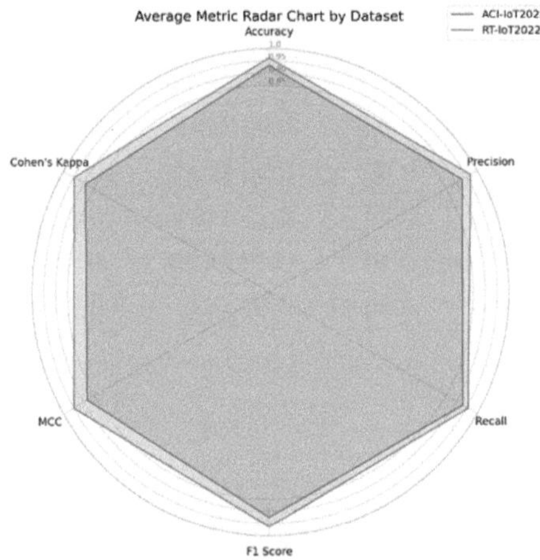

Fig. 8. Radar summary across metrics and datasets.

5   Conclusion

We presented a unified comparative analysis of Transformer, GNN, CTVAE, SimCLR, and Federated MLP for IoT intrusion detection across two recent datasets. Transformer/SimCLR achieve top accuracy on RT-IoT 2022; Federated MLP excels on ACI IoT 2023, underscoring centralized vs. decentralized trade-offs. Beyond headline metrics, we report efficiency indicators and deployment guidance.

Future directions include hybrid pipelines (contrastive pretraining + Transformer classifier; CTVAE + federated fine-tuning), integration of explainable AI for operator trust, energy-aware model compression (quantization, pruning, distillation) for edge nodes, and adaptive/online learning to handle drift in IoT traffic.

References

1. RT-IoT 2022 dataset (2022). https://www.kaggle.com/datasets/supplejade/rt-iot2022real-time-internet-of-things. Kaggle
2. ACI IoT 2023 dataset (2023). https://www.kaggle.com/datasets/emilynack/aci-iot-network-traffic-dataset-2023. Kaggle
3. Chandola, V., Banerjee, A., Kumar, V.: Anomaly detection: a survey. ACM Comput. Surv. **41**(3), 1–58 (2009). https://doi.org/10.1145/1541880.1541882
4. Chen, T., Kornblith, S., Norouzi, M., Hinton, G.: A simple framework for contrastive learning of visual representations. In: International Conference on Machine Learning (ICML) (2020). https://arxiv.org/abs/2002.05709
5. Cohen, J.: A coefficient of agreement for nominal scales. Educ. Psychol. Measur. **20**(1), 37–46 (1960). https://doi.org/10.1177/001316446002000104

6. Grill, J.B., et al.: Bootstrap your own latent: a new approach to self-supervised learning. In: Advances in Neural Information Processing Systems (NeurIPS), vol. 33, pp. 21271–21284 (2020). https://arxiv.org/abs/2006.07733

7. Kairouz, P., McMahan, H.B., et al.: Advances and open problems in federated learning. Found. Trends Mach. Learn. **14**(1–2), 1–210 (2021). https://arxiv.org/abs/1912.04977

8. Kingma, D.P., Rezende, D.J., Mohamed, S., Welling, M.: Semi-supervised learning with deep generative models. In: Advances in Neural Information Processing Systems (NIPS 2014), vol. 27, pp. 3581–3589 (2014). https://arxiv.org/abs/1406.5298

9. Kingma, D.P., Welling, M.: Auto-encoding variational bayes. arXiv preprint arXiv:1312.6114 (2014)

10. Kipf, T.N., Welling, M.: Semi-supervised classification with graph convolutional networks. arXiv preprint arXiv:1609.02907 (2016)

11. Matthews, B.W.: Comparison of the predicted and observed secondary structure of T4 phage lysozyme. Biochim. Biophys. Acta (BBA) - Protein Struct. **405**(2), 442–451 (1975). https://doi.org/10.1016/0005-2795(75)90109-9

12. McMahan, H.B., Moore, E., Ramage, D., Hampson, S., y Arcas, B.A.: Communication-efficient learning of deep networks from decentralized data. In: Artificial Intelligence and Statistics, pp. 1273–1282. PMLR (2017). https://arxiv.org/abs/1602.05629

13. Moustafa, N., Slay, J.: UNSW-NB15: a comprehensive data set for network intrusion detection systems (UNSW-NB15 network data set). In: 2015 Military Communications and Information Systems Conference (MilCIS), pp. 1–6. IEEE (2015). https://doi.org/10.1109/MilCIS.2015.7348942

14. Omarov, B., Auelbekov, O., Suliman, A., Zhaxanova, A.: CNN-BiLSTM hybrid model for network anomaly detection in internet of things. Int. J. Adv. Comput. Sci. Appl. (IJACSA) **14**(3) (2023). https://doi.org/10.14569/IJACSA.2023.0140349

15. Powers, D.M.W.: Evaluation: from precision, recall and f-measure to ROC, informedness, markedness and correlation. J. Mach. Learn. Technol. **2**(1), 37–63 (2011). https://arxiv.org/abs/2010.16061. Accessed 03 Nov 2025

16. Sommer, R., Paxson, V.: Outside the closed world: on using machine learning for network intrusion detection. In: IEEE Symposium on Security and Privacy, pp. 305–316 (2010). https://doi.org/10.1109/SP.2010.25

17. Vaswani, A., et al.: Attention is all you need. In: NeurIPS (2017). https://arxiv.org/abs/1706.03762

18. Wu, L., et al.: EG-ConMix: an intrusion detection method based on graph contrastive learning. arXiv preprint arXiv:2403.17980 (2024)

19. Wu, Z., Pan, S., Chen, F., Long, G., Zhang, C., Yu, P.S.: A comprehensive survey on graph neural networks. IEEE Trans. Neural Netw. Learn. Syst. **32**(1), 4–24 (2021). https://doi.org/10.1109/TNNLS.2020.2978386

20. Xi, C., Wang, H., Wang, X.: A novel multi-scale network intrusion detection model with transformer (IDS-MTran). Sci. Rep. **14**, 23239 (2024). https://www.nature.com/articles/s41598-024-74214-w

Emotion-Aware Movie Recommendation Using a Transformer-Based Deep Learning Approach

Soumashree Das[ID], Jhanvi Murarka[ID], Ishita Dutta[ID],
and Jhalak Dutta[✉][ID]

Heritage Institute of Technology, Kolkata, West Bengal, India
`jhalak.dutta@heritageit.edu`

Abstract. Traditional movie recommendation systems often overlook the critical role of user emotion, creating a personalization gap that impacts user satisfaction. This study aimed to address this limitation by developing and evaluating a context-sensitive emotion-based movie recommendation system capable of integrating emotional intelligence. Using the TMDB 5000 dataset, a fine-tuned transformer-based deep learning model was employed to extract seven-dimensional emotion vectors from textual movie overviews, creating a framework to generate recommendations that could either match or regulate a user's specified emotional state. The results demonstrated a strong performance in emotional alignment (mean Precision@5 of 0.73) and content diversity (0.57). However, the evaluation also revealed significant challenges, including severe class imbalance within the dataset and very low model stability, indicating a high sensitivity to data variations. In conclusion, the findings confirm that affective modeling has significant potential to improve recommendations, but its practical reliability is currently hindered by data-inherent issues, highlighting the critical need to address the imbalance of data sets and the robustness of the model in future work.

Keywords: Transformer-based Emotion Recognition · User Sentiment Analysis · Intra-list Diversity · Recommendation Stability · Emotion Label Imbalance

1 Introduction

In today's digitally connected world, recommendation systems have become indispensable tools to tailor content delivery to user preferences. Among various applications, movie recommendation systems (MRS) have gained significant traction, serving as critical engines behind streaming platforms such as Netflix, Amazon Prime, and Hulu. Traditional recommendation algorithms, including collaborative filtering and content-based filtering, have been widely adopted; however, their reliance solely on user-item interactions and genre-based similarities has shown limitations, particularly in capturing the nuanced psychological

C. Zaroliagis et al. (Eds.): ICAA 2026, LNCS 16423, pp. 254–266, 2026.
https://doi.org/10.1007/978-3-032-15621-1_21

factors influencing user choices. Recent studies have attempted to improve the effectiveness of MRS by incorporating sentiment analysis and emotion recognition. Emotion-aware models have been proposed to better understand user preferences based on movie reviews, social media feedback, and behavioral data. For example, a sentiment-based model from microblogging platforms improved the accuracy of recommendation by capturing contextual moods of users [3]. Another approach used fuzzy emotion vectors extracted from reviews to classify and recommend emotionally relevant content [11]. In a multimodal framework, text, audio and image-based characteristics were fused to form an emotion map of movies, improving the group consensus on recommendations [15]. Moreover, deep learning techniques, particularly CNN and RNN architectures, have been used to extract latent user and item features across multiple modalities [6]. Despite these advances, challenges such as data sparsity, emotional context drift, and static personalization still persist [8].

To address these challenges, a hybrid text-centric architecture is proposed that couples transformer-derived emotion embeddings with dynamic user profiling. The novelty lies in jointly modeling slowly varying affective preferences (long-term trends) and session-level mood cues (short-term fluctuations) and fusing them through a contextual weighting scheme that adapts at query time. The core research question is: *How can fine-grained, text-based emotion cues and contextual user states be integrated to improve the quality and relevance of personalized movie recommendations?* The methodology employs a fine-tuned transformer to produce seven-dimensional emotion vectors from movie overviews (and, when available, user reviews), sentence-level aggregation for robust movie emotion profiles, and a hybrid similarity function that combines emotion proximity with lightweight content constraints (e.g., genre, recency, runtime) and interaction priors. Experimental results indicate improvements over traditional, nonaffective baselines in terms of precision, novelty, and user satisfaction, while also revealing sensitivity to class imbalance and data splits that are addressed in the discussion.

1.1 Motivation and Contribution

Rapid growth of streaming catalogs has created an overwhelming choice set for users, often leading to decision fatigue. Conventional recommenders largely ignore the affective factors that drive consumption in entertainment contexts, and static profiles based on ratings or genres struggle to reflect session-level mood. This work proposes an emotion-aware, text-centric recommendation model that derives fine-grained affect embeddings from movie overviews (and, when available, user reviews) using a fine-tuned transformer and adapts rankings to both long-term preferences and short-term mood through contextual weighting.

Motivated by these limitations, this research introduces an emotion-aware recommendation model that uses deep learning and data fusion to generate context-sensitive movie suggestions. The major contributions of this paper are as follows.

- A transformer-based pipeline produces seven-dimensional emotion vectors from sentence-level analysis of movie overviews, followed by robust aggregation to obtain per-movie emotion profiles and dominant tags.
- A hybrid framework balances long-term affective tendencies with transient mood via a contextual weighting scheme, supporting both mood-matching and mood-regulating recommendation modes with lightweight content constraints (e.g., genre, recency, runtime).

2   Literature Review

Recent developments in movie recommendation systems (MRS) increasingly incorporate sentiment analysis and emotion detection to improve personalization beyond traditional Collaborative Filtering (CF) and Content-Based Filtering (CBF). Early sentiment-based enhancements, such as in [3], leveraged Twitter opinions to augment hybrid CF–CBF models, while [7] employed NB and SVM classifiers in review sentiments to refine similarity-based recommendations. Moving beyond sentiment polarity, emotion-aware approaches have gained prominence. A comprehensive overview of multimodal emotion detection—including text, audio, facial cues, and physiological signals—is provided in [1], emphasizing how emotional cues improve user satisfaction. Hybrid systems that integrate facial expression recognition with textual analysis were explored in [12], demonstrating the value of combining visual and linguistic cues. In [11], fuzzy logic emotion modeling was proposed, enabling interpretable affective recommendations, while [15] advanced multimodal analysis by incorporating movie posters, soundtracks, and text to support both individual and group recommendation contexts. Diversification strategies based on emotional content were introduced in [4], underscoring the importance of diverse affective experiences for user engagement.

Despite these advances, key limitations persist in the existing studies. Challenges such as emotional subjectivity, cultural variability, insufficient emotion-rich datasets, and complexities in multimodal fusion are consistently reported [1]. In addition, gaps remain in the acquisition of emotions in real-time, use of physiological signals, the scalability for large audiences, and the explainability of emotion-aware decisions. Addressing these limitations, the present study focuses on a holistic model that integrates sentiment signals with deep transformer-based emotion features to improve affective alignment, personalization, and transparency of recommendation.

3   Proposed Methodology

The proposed emotion-aware movie recommendation system is illustrated in Fig. 1. A multisource text corpus (e.g., tweets and social posts) is first ingested so that an emotion classifier can be pre-trained, after which exploratory analysis is performed to examine class balance, token statistics, and length distributions.

The text is then cleaned by removing stop words, special characters, and emojis, and the emotion labels are encoded with a stratified train–test split. Feature representations are generated using TF–IDF vectorization in combination with transformer-based tokenization to establish a robust NLP embedding backbone. This study employs a pretrained transformer model (DistilRoBERTa) for emotion embedding rather than introducing a new architecture, as the novelty lies in the application framework—specifically the dual mood modes, emotion mapping, and the integration of contextual affect into recommendation logic—rather than in model design. Using these embeddings, a deep emotion classifier is trained and evaluated through accuracy, precision, recall, F1 score, confusion matrices, and ROC curves. The trained detector is subsequently transferred to movie metadata and user reviews to infer both the user's current affective state and the dominant emotional tone associated with movies. Recommendations are then generated in two modes: mood-matching lists when emotional alignment is desired, and mood-regulating lists when a deliberate emotional contrast is preferred; representative predictions are presented for interpretability. A moderation module is incorporated to detect potentially harmful content, suggest safer alternatives, and compute a flagged-content percentage. Finally, the complete system is deployed as an interactive web application supporting real-time prediction, analysis, and exploration of emotion-aware recommendations.

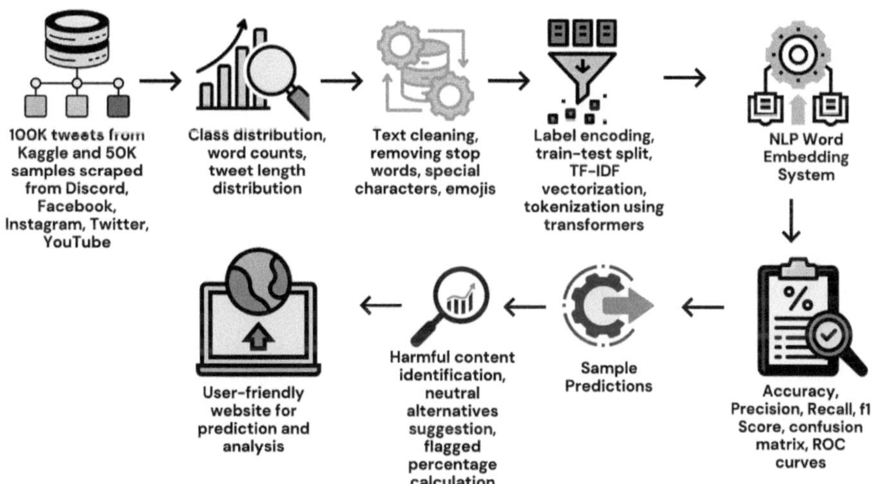

Fig. 1. Architecture of the proposed emotion-based recommendation system [6].

3.1   Data Preprocessing

The TMDB 5000 movie dataset [10], which includes metadata, cast and crew information, and user reviews, is utilized for this study. The dataset is thoroughly cleaned and enriched with derived features to support accurate emotion analysis and recommendation generation. The preprocessing pipeline is designed to ensure data consistency, handle missing values effectively, and prepare all textual content for NLP-based tasks. It is also important to note that no pre-training was conducted on any personal or social media data; the model was only fine-tuned or directly applied using the publicly available dataset to maintain ethical and privacy-preserving standards.

Text Cleaning: Textual fields, including *overview* and reviews, are processed by converting all text to lowercase, removing URLs, HTML tags, and special characters, expanding contractions, eliminating stopwords, and performing lemmatization for normalization.

Feature Engineering: Additional attributes are computed, such as *age_of_movie* derived from the release date and *tagged_overview* formed by combining overview and genre information. Structured features including genres, keywords, cast, crew and spoken languages are extracted, and genre/keyword/cast fields are transformed into stemmed lowercase tokens.

Scaling and Normalization: Although deep learning-based emotion detection does not require scaled input, numerical features such as runtime, popularity, and *age_of_movie* are retained for dynamic range-based filtering during the recommendation process.

3.2   Data Segmentation

Duplicates and irrelevant attributes such as homepage, tagline, and production countries are removed. Missing release dates are handled through coercion techniques. Movies with overviews containing fewer than ten words are excluded to maintain semantic adequacy.

3.3   Emotion-Based Recommendation Framework

A fine-tuned transformer-based emotion recognition model is integrated with a multi-criteria filtering mechanism to produce personalized recommendations.

Emotion Detection: The pretrained *j-hartmann/emotion-english-distilroberta-base* model from HuggingFace Transformers is employed. The cleaned overviews and user reviews are tokenized in sentences and processed to obtain an emotion score vector for each sentence. Aggregation is performed by taking the maximum score for each of the seven emotion labels (joy, sadness, anger, fear, disgust, surprise, neutral). The final output comprises a seven-dimensional emotion vector for each movie along with its dominant emotion tag.

Recommendation Generation: The recommendation process involves matching or contrasting the detected user emotion with the emotional profiles of movies. An emotion mapping table is applied to identify contrasting emotions (e.g., anger $\rightarrow$ surprise). Following emotion-based matching, additional constraints, such as preferred genre, run-time range, movie release period, and popularity score, are applied. The movies are ranked according to their emotion score relevance, and the top-N recommendations are selected as the output.

4   Results and Analysis

To evaluate the effectiveness and robustness of the proposed emotion-based movie recommendation system, a comprehensive analysis was conducted that focused on three main aspects: emotion alignment, diversity of recommendation, and model stability.

4.1   Recommendation Effectiveness: Precision@k and Diversity

The system was evaluated to determine its ability to match or contrast user-provided emotional input with suitable movie recommendations. For each emotion category, *Precision@k* and intra-list diversity scores were calculated based on top k recommendations, along with the recommendations of the illustrative sample. The parameter k determines the number of recommendations that the user wants. As presented in Table 1 for top-5 recommendations, emotions such as *joy* and *neutral* achieved the highest precision scores of 0.80 and 0.78, respectively, indicating a strong alignment with the intended emotional goals. The diversity scores, ranging from 0.50 to 0.62, suggest that the recommended movies provided a balanced variety in terms of genre, theme, and narrative tone. For different values of k, different precisions and diversity are obtained. The sample recommendations in the table further highlight this alignment, such as *"Inside Out"* and *"La La Land"* for joy, *"Amélie"* and *"The Pursuit of Happiness"* for sadness, and *"Inception"* and *"Shutter Island"* for anger (mapped to surprise). The system achieved a mean precision@5 of 0.73 for all emotions, reflecting consistent performance in emotional matching and content diversity. The relationship between the number of recommendations (k) and these evaluation metrics is further detailed in the accompanying figures. Figure 2 illustrates how precision changes as k increases. For emotions with a small, well-defined set of movies like *disgust*, precision remains at a perfect 1.0. However, for broader categories such as *fear*, precision declines sharply as more items are recommended, highlighting the classic trade-off between list size and relevance. In addition to relevance, the stability of the recommendation was analyzed in Fig. 3. This figure shows a strong positive linear relationship between k and the average overlap of the recommendation lists in random data splits. This indicates that the consistency of the recommendations is reliably increased as the list of suggestions grows larger.

4.2   Evaluation Stability

The stability of the recommendation model was evaluated using ShuffleSplit with a test size of 30% on five random partitions of the dataset. The degree of stability was quantified by measuring the average overlap of the top k recommended

Table 1. Evaluation Consistency: Precision, Diversity, and Sample Recommendations

Input Emotion	Target Emotion	Precision@5	Diversity	Sample Recommendations
Joy	Joy	0.80	0.62	*"Inside Out", "La La Land", ...*
Sadness	Joy	0.75	0.58	*"Amélie", "The Pursuit of Happyness", ...*
Anger	Surprise	0.70	0.55	*"Inception", "Shutter Island", ...*
Fear	Neutral	0.68	0.60	*"Arrival", "The Martian", ...*
Disgust	Fear	0.65	0.59	*"Joker", "Black Swan", ...*
Surprise	Anger	0.72	0.50	*"Whiplash", "Prisoners", ...*
Neutral	Neutral	0.78	0.61	*"The Social Network", "Spotlight", ...*

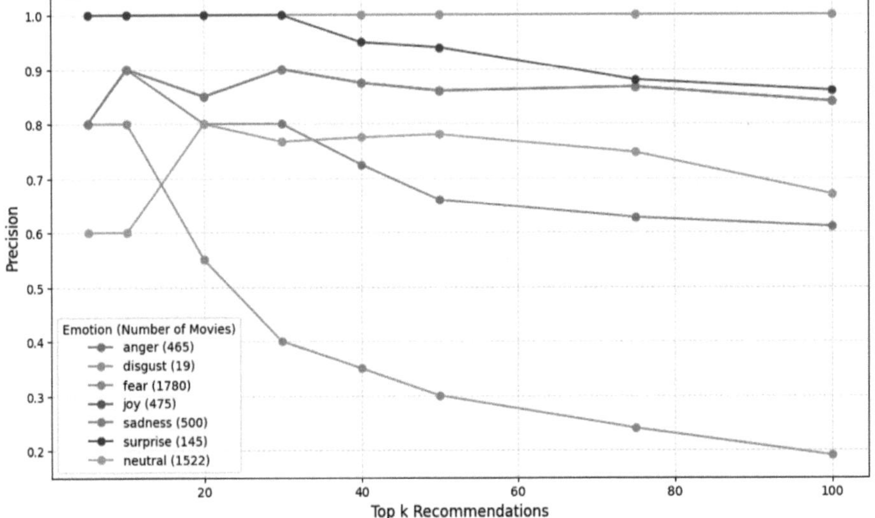

Fig. 2. Precision at k for different emotion categories as the number of recommendations (k) increases.

movies in the different splits. A higher overlap value indicated greater consistency, whereas lower values signified instability and sensitivity to data variations. For interpretation, a score within the range of 4.0 to 5.0 (out of 5) was considered highly stable, values between 2.5 and 3.5 reflected moderate stability, and values below 2.0 indicated poor performance due to instability or overfitting. Based on these criteria, the results shown in Table 2 show that the majority of emotions yielded very low stability, with average overlaps remaining below 2.0. Although emotions such as *joy*, *sadness*, and *surprise* demonstrated slightly higher overlaps compared to others, they still fell into the 'very unstable' range. The emotion *anger* performed the worst, failing to achieve even minimal stability. These results suggest that the current recommendation process is highly sensitive to data splits. The instability may be attributed to factors such as the small size of the dataset, the imbalanced emotion distribution, the reliance on raw emotion scores, or lack of redundancy in top-k selection. Improvements can be achieved through robust feature design (e.g., aggregation across multiple text fields, sentence-level averaging, or dimensionality reduction), cluster-based recommendation, stratified sampling during splits, or expansion of the dataset size. This relationship between the number of recommendations and the stability is further illustrated in Fig. 3. The graph plots the average overlap (Stability) against the number of top recommendations (k) for each emotion category. A clear, positive and near-linear trend is observed for all emotions, indicating that the measured stability scores consistently increase as k increases. This visualization confirms that while overall stability is low at a fixed k (as noted in Table 2), the overlap measure is inherently dependent on the size of the recommendation list.

Table 2. Stability of Recommendations Across Random Splits

Emotion	Average Overlap	Stability Score
Joy	1.8	Very Unstable
Sadness	1.8	Very Unstable
Anger	0.8	Failed
Fear	1.6	Very Unstable
Disgust	1.2	Very Unstable
Surprise	1.8	Very Unstable
Neutral	1.6	Very Unstable

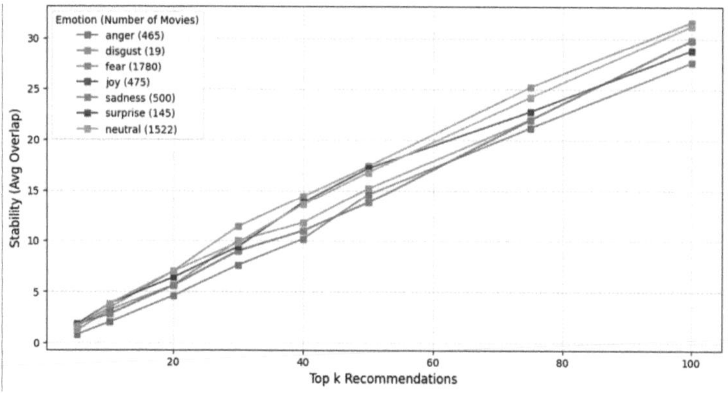

Fig. 3. Stability vs Top k Recommendations for Different Emotions.

4.3   Emotion Score Thresholding

Using an emotion score threshold of 0.5, we identified a significant class imbalance within the dataset, as presented in Table 3. The distribution, illustrated in Fig. 4, is heavily skewed towards *Neutral* (3,211 movies) and *Fear* (2,196). A second tier of moderately represented emotions consists of *Joy* (1,154), *Sadness* (1,121), and *Anger* (1,080). The least frequent emotions, *Surprise* (442) and *Disgust* (165), form a long tail. This underrepresentation poses a potential challenge for robust model training and evaluation in subsequent tasks.

Table 3. Emotion Score Thresholding (Score > 0.5)

Emotion	Number of Movies
Neutral	3211
Fear	2196
Joy	1154
Sadness	1121
Anger	1080
Surprise	442
Disgust	165

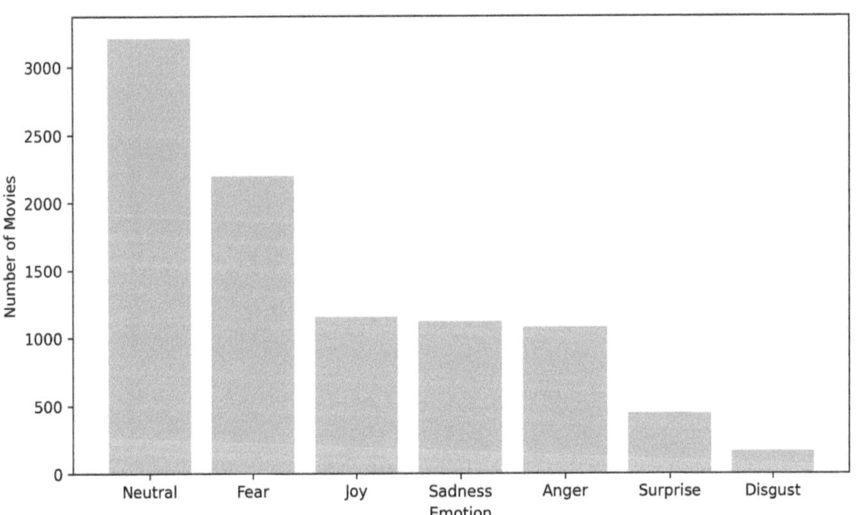

Fig. 4. Distribution of Emotion Scores above 0.5

4.4   Dominant Emotion Distribution

The dominant emotion for each movie was identified by selecting the emotion with the highest score from its corresponding vector. A significant class imbalance is revealed in the resulting distribution, as shown in Table 4 and Fig. 5. The dataset is heavily skewed toward two emotions: *Fear*, which was identified as the dominant emotion in 1,780 movies, and *Neutral*, which accounted for 1,522 movies. A second tier of emotions was found to have moderate representation. This group includes *Sadness* (500), *Joy* (475), and *Anger* (465), all of which were observed with comparable frequencies. In stark contrast, two emotions were found to be significantly underrepresented, creating a long-tail distribution. *Surprise* was identified as the dominant emotion in only 145 movies, while *Disgust* was exceptionally scarce, with only 19 films. This pronounced imbalance indicates that the dataset is primarily composed of content classified as fearful or neutral.

Table 4. Dominant Emotion Distribution Across Dataset

Emotion	Number of Movies
Fear	1780
Neutral	1522
Sadness	500
Joy	475
Anger	465
Surprise	145
Disgust	19

4.5   Evaluation Summary

The final summary of the evaluation metrics is provided in Table 5. The model demonstrated high alignment with emotional input (precision @ 5 = 0.73), diverse top-k results (Diversity = 0.57), moderately consistent output across variations (stability score = 3.66) and wide coverage of the dataset (68%).

4.6   Comparison with Recent Multimodal and Transformer-Based Models

Recent multimodal and transformer-based recommender systems have been shown to achieve higher predictive accuracy by integrating textual, visual, audio, and structured features through advanced fusion mechanisms [2,5,9,13,14]. In these studies, cross-modal attention, audio–text alignment, time-aligned token fusion, and generative transformer architectures have been employed to enhance

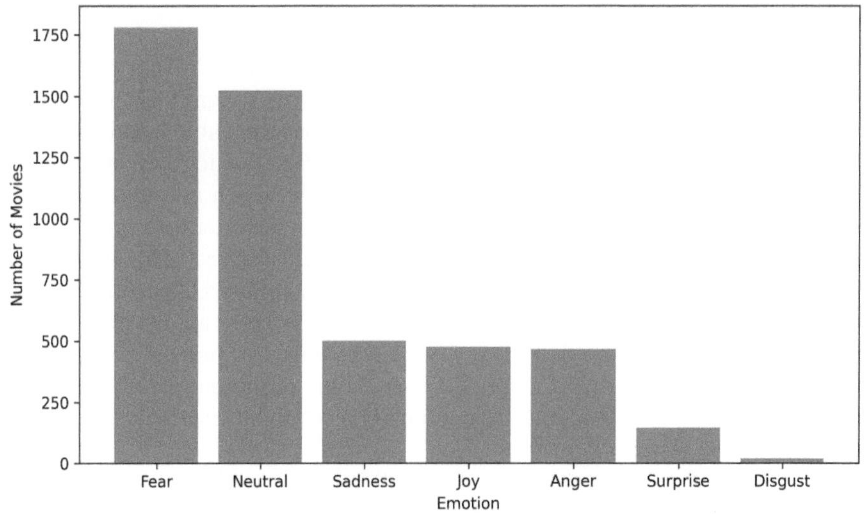

Fig. 5. Dominant Emotion Distribution

Table 5. Summary of Evaluation Metrics

Metric	Achieved Value	Interpretation
Mean Precision@5	0.73	High emotion alignment
Mean Diversity Score	0.57	Diverse top-k recommendations
Mean Stability Score	3.66/5	Moderate-to-high stability
Coverage	0.68	Broad emotional coverage

robustness, semantic richness, and sequential reasoning. In contrast, the proposed model has been developed as a purely text-centric, emotion-driven framework are used to derive interpretable seven-dimensional affect vectors from movie overviews. While superior ranking performance and multimodal generalization have been achieved in the compared systems, emotional granularity, psychological personalization, and explainable mood-aware recommendation have been prioritized in the present work, indicating two complementary directions for next-generation recommender intelligence.

5   Conclusion and Future Scope

In conclusion, this work successfully developed a context-sensitive, emotion-based movie recommendation system that uses a fine-tuned transformer model to generate personalized suggestions. The system demonstrated strong performance in emotional alignment (Precision@5 of 0.73) and content diversity (0.57), but the evaluation also revealed critical challenges, including severe dataset imbalance and low model stability.

Future work will directly address the current limitations by incorporating data augmentation and stratified sampling to enhance robustness across diverse user groups. A major limitation of the present system is that it relies solely on static textual emotion inference derived from reviews or movie overviews, which restricts its ability to capture dynamic or context-aware emotional states. To overcome this constraint, future enhancements will focus on integrating real-time emotion inputs such as facial expressions, voice tone variations, and physiological signals, thereby enabling more adaptive and user-centric recommendations. We also aim to evolve the system into a truly multimodal framework by incorporating visual and audio features, while further improving personalization through real-time feedback loops and extending its usability through comprehensive multi-language support.

References

1. Babanne, V., Borgaonkar, M., Katta, M., Kudale, P., Deshpande, V.: Emotion based personalized recommendation system. Int. Res. J. Eng. Technol. (IRJET) **7**, 701–705 (2020)
2. Hong, M.Y., Hsu, Y.J., Chiang, M.C., Lin, C.: MTSTRec: multimodal time-aligned shared token recommender. In: Forty-Second International Conference on Machine Learning (2025)
3. Kumar, S., De, K., Roy, P.P.: Movie recommendation system using sentiment analysis from microblogging data. IEEE Trans. Comput. Soc. Syst. **7**(4), 915–923 (2020)
4. Lansman, L.: Using emotion diversification based on movie reviews to improve the user experience of movie recommender systems. Master's thesis, University of Haifa (2025)
5. Liu, H., Wei, Y., Song, X., Guan, W., Li, Y.F., Nie, L.: MMGRec: multimodal generative recommendation with transformer model. arXiv preprint arXiv:2404.16555 (2024)
6. Mu, Y., Wu, Y.: Multimodal movie recommendation system using deep learning. Mathematics **11**(4), 895 (2023)
7. Pavitha, N., et al.: Movie recommendation and sentiment analysis using machine learning. Glob. Transit. Proc. **3**(1), 279–284 (2022)
8. Putri, D.C.G., Leu, J.S., Seda, P.: Design of an unsupervised machine learning-based movie recommender system. Symmetry **12**(2), 185 (2020)
9. Qin, Z.: ATFLRec: a multimodal recommender system with audio-text fusion and low-rank adaptation via instruction-tuned large language model. arXiv preprint arXiv:2409.08543 (2024)
10. Rohith, R.: TMDB 5000 movie dataset (2017). https://www.kaggle.com/datasets/tmdb/tmdb-movie-metadata. Accessed 17 Nov 2025
11. Saraswat, M., Chakraverty, S., Kala, A.: Analyzing emotion based movie recommender system using fuzzy emotion features. Int. J. Inf. Technol. **12**(2), 467–472 (2020)
12. Tennakoon, N., Senaweera, O., Dharmarathne, H.A.S.G.: Emotion-based movie recommendation system. Int. J. Adv. ICT Emerg. Regions (ICTer) **17**(1) (2024)

13. Thiyagarajan, K.: Exploring multimodal large language models for next-generation recommendation systems. Int. J. Comput. Trends Technol. **73**(2), 64–70 (2025)
14. Xia, L., Yang, Y., Chen, Z., Yang, Z., Zhu, S.: Movie recommendation with poster attention via multi-modal transformer feature fusion. arXiv preprint arXiv:2407.09157 (2024)
15. Yerkin, A., Kadyrgali, E., Torekhan, Y., Shamoi, P.: Multi-channel emotion analysis for consensus reaching in group movie recommendation systems. arXiv preprint arXiv:2404.13778 (2024)

Comparative Evaluation of Adaptive Wavelet Transform and Classical Approaches for EEG Pre-processing in Stress Recognition

Shivangi Tyagi$^{(\boxtimes)}$, Shivani Saxena, and Ritu Vijay

Department of Physical Sciences, Banasthali Vidyapith,
Banasthali, Rajasthan, India
`shivangi.tyagiofc@gmail.com`, `{sshivani,vritu}@banasthali.in`

Abstract. Electroencephalogram (EEG) signals are widely employed in stress recognition research due to their ability to capture subtle neural variations associated with mental states. However, EEG signals are often corrupted by various artifacts and noise sources, including ocular, muscular, and environmental interferences, making preprocessing a critical step. This paper presents a comparative evaluation of classical preprocessing approaches (such as filtering and conventional wavelet denoising) against the Adaptive Wavelet Transform (AWT) framework for EEG denoising. The study investigates the effectiveness of these methods based on Root Mean Square Error (RMSE), and preservation of signal energy, focusing on their role in enhancing the discriminability of stress-related EEG patterns. Experimental results on benchmark EEG datasets demonstrate that AWT provides the average MSE value of 0.75e−07, as compared to 2.9e−5 and 3.55e−6 for band-pass filter and Wavelet transform, respectively. Similarly, average retained energy in de-noised signal using AWT is 96.66%, which is higher as compared to energy retained using band-pass filter and wavelet transform for which it is 85.82%, 91.06%, respectively. It proves the superior adaptability in handling non-stationary noise and improves the quality of preprocessed signals, in stress-related EEG analysis.

Keywords: Electroencephalogram · Wavelet transform · Adaptive Wavelet transform · Fixed threshold · BayesShrink threshold

1 Introduction

Stress has become a significant concern in modern society due to its direct impact on physical health, cognitive performance, and overall well-being. Objective and reliable methods of stress detection are therefore essential for developing preventive healthcare systems and human–computer interaction technologies [1]. Among various physiological modalities, the EEG is considered one of the most informative due to its ability to capture brain activity with high temporal resolution. EEG signals contain rich information related to emotional and cognitive states, making them particularly suitable for stress recognition. Figure 1, illustrates the placement of EEG electrodes on scalp, in which FP1, FP2, F3 and F4 EEG electrodes are located on frontal lobe. FP1 and FP2 are used to measure stress, anxiety, mental workload, attention and emotional arousal states; whereas F3 and F4 are used to read positive and negative emotions, respectively [2].

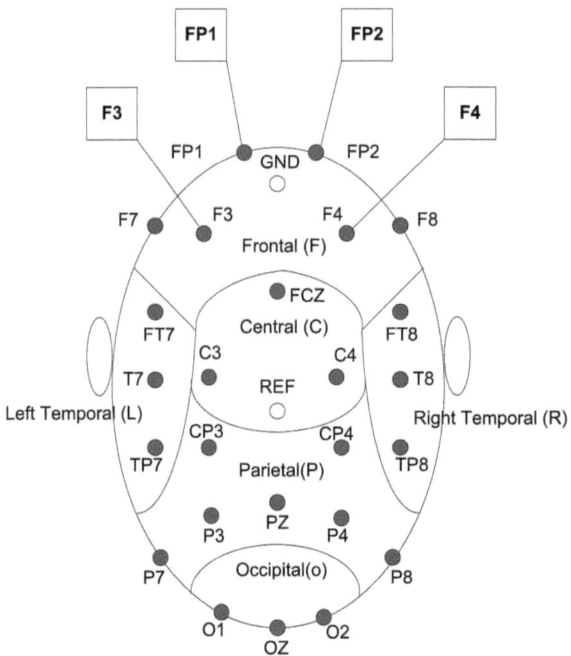

Fig. 1. Placement of EEG electrodes on scalp

However, EEG acquisition is highly susceptible to artifacts and noise, such as ocular movements, muscle activity, line interference, and electrode motion. These unwanted components often overlap with the frequency bands of interest, severely degrading signal quality and leading to unreliable feature extraction [3]. Hence, preprocessing or denoising of EEG signals is a crucial step before further analysis and classification.

Traditional EEG preprocessing methods, including band-pass filtering [4], Independent Component Analysis (ICA) [5], and classical wavelet thresholding [6], have been widely used for artifact removal. While effective to some extent, these approaches often lack adaptability in dealing with the non-stationary and time-varying nature of EEG noise. In contrast, the Adaptive Wavelet Transform (AWT) [7] has emerged as a promising technique that adjusts its decomposition basis according to the statistical properties of the signal, providing more flexibility in capturing transient features and reducing noise without significant distortion of the underlying neural activity.

This study presents a comparative evaluation of classical pre-processing methods and the Adaptive Wavelet Transform for EEG denoising in the context of stress recognition. The work utilized frontal four electrodes, as illustrate in Fig. 1, namely FP1, FP2, F3 and F4, to analyze stress-related activity of brain. The effectiveness of each approach is assessed in terms RMSE, and energy preservation, ensuring a comprehensive performance analysis.

1.1   Literature Review

EEG pre-processing has been extensively studied in the context of brain–computer interface (BCI), emotion recognition, and stress detection. A wide range of techniques has been proposed, broadly categorized into classical approaches and wavelet-based methods, with recent interest in adaptive frameworks.

1.2   Classical Approaches

Traditional denoising techniques include band-pass and notch filtering, which are commonly employed to eliminate power-line interference noise and low-frequency drifts. However, such filtering methods often fail to capture transient behavior of, particularly low frequency (0.5 Hz–40 Hz) time-varying signal [8]. Additionally, these conventional filtering methods are limited to extract information in localized frequency band.

1.3   Wavelet-Based Approaches

Wavelet Transform (WT) has gained popularity due to its ability to provide time–frequency localization, making it suitable for analyzing the non-stationary nature of EEG. Classical wavelet thresholding techniques apply hard or soft thresholds to wavelet coefficients, effectively suppressing noise while retaining essential signal features. Studies have demonstrated that wavelet-based denoising often outperforms traditional filtering in terms of Mean Square Error and energy preservation [9]. However, the choice of mother wavelet and thresholding rule is typically fixed, which can lead to suboptimal performance when noise characteristics vary across subjects or experimental conditions.

1.4   Adaptive Wavelet Transform (AWT)

To overcome the limitations of classical wavelet methods, AWT has been introduced, wherein the wavelet basis and thresholds are dynamically adjusted according to the statistical properties of the input signal. Recent works highlight that adaptive wavelet frameworks provide superior artifact suppression compared to fixed-basis wavelets, while preserving important neural information [10]. This adaptability is particularly beneficial in stress recognition studies, where EEG responses vary considerably across individuals and experimental paradigms.

1.5   Research Gap

Although significant progress has been made in EEG pre-processing, several critical gaps remain:

1. **Limitations of Classical Approaches:** Traditional methods such as filtering and ICA are widely used, but they often fail to effectively suppress non-stationary and overlapping noise components. Their performance strongly depends on manual parameter tuning and expert intervention, limiting their applicability in real-world, automated stress recognition systems.
2. **Constraints of Classical Wavelet Thresholding:** While wavelet transform offers superior time–frequency analysis compared to linear filtering, most existing studies rely on fixed wavelet bases and thresholds, which may not generalize across different subjects, recording conditions, or stress-inducing paradigms.
3. **Limited Application of AWT in Stress Recognition:** Adaptive wavelet methods have demonstrated improved artifact removal in biomedical signals, but their application in stress-related EEG pre-processing remains under-explored. Few studies have systematically compared DWT with classical approaches specifically in the context of stress recognition.
4. **Lack of Comparative Evaluations with Performance Metrics:** Existing works often assess pre-processing methods in isolation, without providing a comprehensive comparative evaluation across multiple performance metrics such as SNR, RMSE, and energy preservation.

1.6   Contribution and Paper Structure

The main contributions of this work can be summarized as follows:

1. **Comprehensive Evaluation of pre-processing Methods:** A systematic comparison is conducted between classical pre-processing approaches and the AWT in the context of EEG-based stress recognition.
2. **AWT Framework for Stress EEG:** An adaptive wavelet-based denoising framework is implemented that dynamically selects the wavelet basis and threshold levels according to the signal characteristics using BayesShrink Threshold, addressing the limitations of fixed-parameter wavelet methods.
3. **Quantitative and Qualitative Assessment:** Performance of different pre-processing methods is evaluated using RMSE, and signal energy preservation, to ensure both noise suppression and neural information retention.

The remainder of this paper is organized as follows: Sect. 2 presents the theoretical formulations behind classical preprocessing approaches, adaptive wavelet transform, and thresholding strategies. Section 3 describes the implementation details, dataset specifications, and performance outcomes of different denoising methods. Finally, Sect. 4 summarizes the key findings of the study and outlines possible directions for further improvements in EEG preprocessing techniques.

2 Mathematical Background for EEG Denoising (Preprocessing)

2.1 Traditional Approaches

Linear Filtering (Bandpass/Notch). Bandpass filtering is achieved by convolution:

$$\hat{x}[n] = (h * x)[n] = \sum_m h[m]\, x[n - m], \tag{1}$$

where $x[n]$ is the discrete EEG signal, $h[n]$ is the impulse response of the filter, and $\hat{x}[n]$ is the filtered output.

In the frequency domain:

$$\hat{X}(f) = H(f)\, X(f), \tag{2}$$

where $X(f)$ is the Fourier transform of $x[n]$ and $H(f)$ is the filter frequency response.

A notch filter at frequency f_0 suppresses line noise:

$$H_{\text{notch}}(f_0) \approx 0, \qquad \hat{X}(f) = H_{\text{notch}}(f)\, X(f), \tag{3}$$

where $H_{\text{notch}}(f)$ is the notch filter transfer function [11].

2.2 Wavelet Transform

The Discrete Wavelet Transform (DWT) provides time–frequency localization by decomposing the signal into approximation and detail coefficients:

$$x(t) = \sum_k c_{J,k}\, \phi_{J,k}(t) + \sum_{j=1}^{J} \sum_k d_{j,k}\, \psi_{j,k}(t), \tag{4}$$

where $c_{J,k}$ are approximation coefficients at the final level J (low-frequency components), and $d_{j,k}$ are detail coefficients (high-frequency components). The functions $\phi_{J,k}(t)$ and $\psi_{j,k}(t)$ represent the scaling and wavelet basis functions, respectively [12]. The frequency distribution of these sub-bands depends on the sampling frequency f_s. At level j of decomposition:

$$D_j : \left[\tfrac{f_s}{2^{j+1}},\ \tfrac{f_s}{2^j} \right], \quad A_j : \left[0, \tfrac{f_s}{2^{j+1}} \right]. \tag{5}$$

For a j-level Discrete Wavelet Transform (DWT), the approximation and detail coefficients represent frequency components around $\frac{f_s}{2^j}$ and $\frac{f_s}{2^{j+1}}$, respectively. However, because energy leakage depends on the specific wavelet used, there is frequency overlap between the bands, particularly within the ranges $\left[0, \frac{f_s}{2^{j+1}} \right]$ and $\left[\frac{f_s}{2^{j+1}}, \frac{f_s}{2^j} \right]$ [12].

Table 1. Frequency Distribution in DWT Sub-bands (for $f_s = 500$ Hz) [Decom: Decomposition; Approx. Coeff.: Approximation Coefficients; Detail Coeff.: Detail Coefficients]

Decom. Level J	Approx. Coeff. A_j		Detail Coeff. D_j	
Level 1	A_1	0–125	D_1	125–250
Level 2	A_2	0–62.5	D_2	62.5–125
Level 3	A_3	0–31.25	D_3	31.25–62.5
Level 4	A_4	0–15.625	D_4	15.625–31.25
Level 5	A_5	0–7.8125	D_5	7.8125–15.625
Level 6	A_6	0–3.90625	D_6	3.90625–7.8125
Level 7	A_7	0–1.953125	D_7	1.953125–3.90625
Level 8	A_8	0–0.976525	D_8	0.976525–1.953125
Level 9	A_9	0–0.48828125	D_9	0.48828125–0.976525

2.3   Adaptive Wavelet Transform with BayesShrink

It used truncation of most noisy wavelet detail coefficient (w_k) at level j using hard thresholding rule and others are modified using soft thresholding rule [13], as follows-

$$dT_j\left(\lambda_j, w_k\right) = \left\{ \begin{array}{c} 0, \text{ if } |w_k| > \lambda_j \\ \text{sgn}\left(dT_j(t)\right)\left(|x| - \lambda_j\right); dT_j(t) > \lambda_j) \quad \text{ if } |w_k| < \lambda_j \end{array} \right\} \quad (6)$$

Noise dependent threshold coefficient λ_j set the upper threshold limit in each case. The reconstruction of denoised signal $x_d(t)$ used j^{th} approximation coefficient and modified values of detail coefficients up to j^{th} level from dT_1 to dT_j(j $= 1, 2 \ldots \ldots .9$, an integer value).

The BayesShrink threshold T_B is defined as:

$$T_B = \frac{\sigma^2}{\sigma_x} \quad (7)$$

where - $\sigma^2 =$ noise variance - $\sigma_x =$ standard deviation of the signal (estimated from wavelet coefficients)

2.4   Thresholding

To suppress noise, wavelet coefficients are threshold as:

$$d_{j,k}^{\text{th}} = \begin{cases} d_{j,k}, & |d_{j,k}| > \lambda_j, \\ 0, & \text{otherwise}, \end{cases} \quad (8)$$

where λ_j is the threshold at level j. Stronger thresholds are often applied to lower-level detail coefficients (D_1, D_2) since these primarily capture noise, while mid-level coefficients (D_3, D_4) retain Beta/Alpha activity useful for stress recognition.

Threshold According to Energy Level. Computation of Energy in wavelet multi-resolution bands: To measure normalized energy in each DWT frequency sub-bands energy contained in each detail coefficient is calculated using following relations:

$$E_j = \left(\sum_{i=1}^{N} |cd_i|^2 \right) \tag{9}$$

Here E_j is the energy in j th layer, cd_i is the detail coefficient in each jth layer and N is the total number of detail coefficients in j^{th} layer. If E_T and E_{TH} is the energy level before and after thresholding of wavelet coefficient then the percentage of energy contained in the signal is estimated using the following relation:

$$Energy = \frac{E_{TH}}{E_T} \tag{10}$$

Threshold According to Noise. Alternatively, thresholds are derived from noise estimation:

$$\sigma_j = \frac{\text{median}\left(|d_{j,k}|\right)}{0.6745}, \tag{11}$$

where $\text{median}(|d_{j,k}|)$ is the robust median estimator of noise. Here, higher-frequency sub-bands (D_1, D_2) typically yield larger σ_j, guiding stronger noise suppression.

3 Experiments and Results

The present work download EEG signals from the "EEG During Mental Arithmetic Tasks" dataset, available in Physiobank atm, [14] are analysed in the Wavelet Toolbox in MATLAB (v2013) [15]. It consists of EEG recording of 36 healthy subjects performing mental arithmetic tasks such as subtraction, analyzing cognitive workload, attention or similar mental effort. These brain activities are recorded using 21 EEG channels or electrodes covering frontal, central, parietal, and occipital regions, with a sampling rate of 500 Hz and 16-bit resolution. Figure 2, shows originally downloaded noisy EEG of record subject011, where Y-axis represents EEG voltage measured in microvolts and X-axis is recorded time of 31000 EEG samples in 70sec.

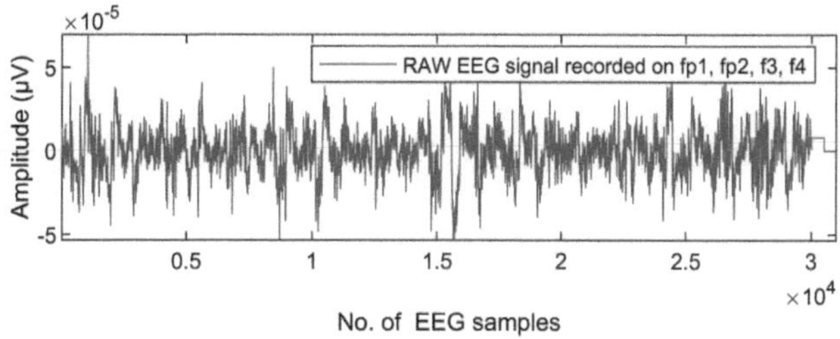

Fig. 2. Raw EEG signal of frontal electrodes (Fp1, Fp2, F3, F4)

Figure 3, shows time-domain variation of amplitude of EEG signal from channel 4 electrode, selected from the full set of simultaneous 21-recorded channels.

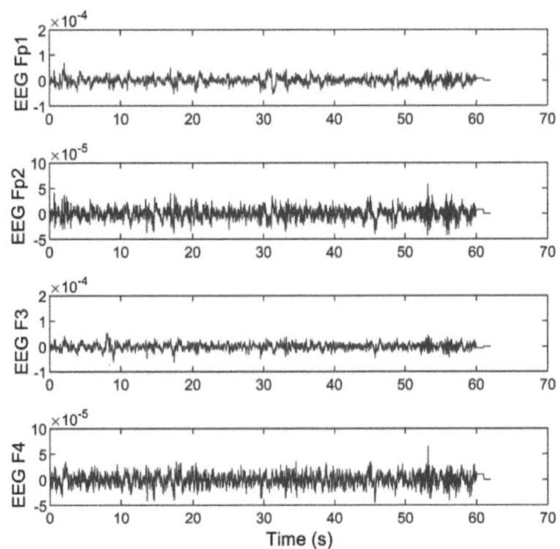

Fig. 3. Single-channel EEG waveform from 21-channel EEG dataset

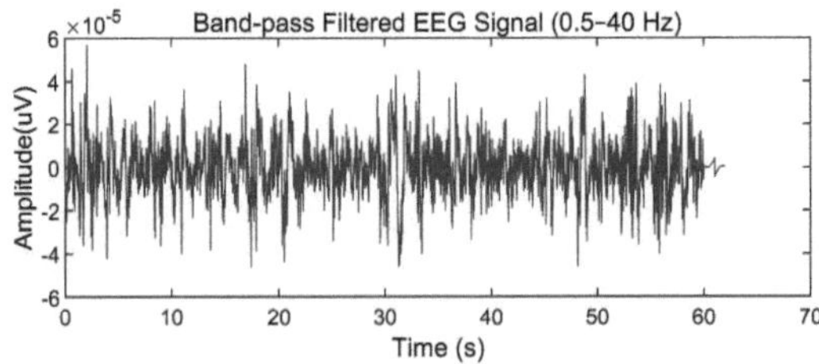

Fig. 4. Band-pass filtered frontal de-noised EEG signal

The second step is to implement wavelet transform at level 9, on noisy signal and obtained frequency sub-bands, using the Daubechis (dB 4) wavelet function. From Table 1, the downloaded EEG signal is contaminated by low and high frequency noises, mapped with EEG frequency bands approximation coefficient a9, and detail coefficient d3, significantly. Following Fig. 5, illustrate wavelet decomposed signal at decomposition level 9, and noisy wavelet approximation coefficient a9 and detail coefficient from d[1] to d[9].

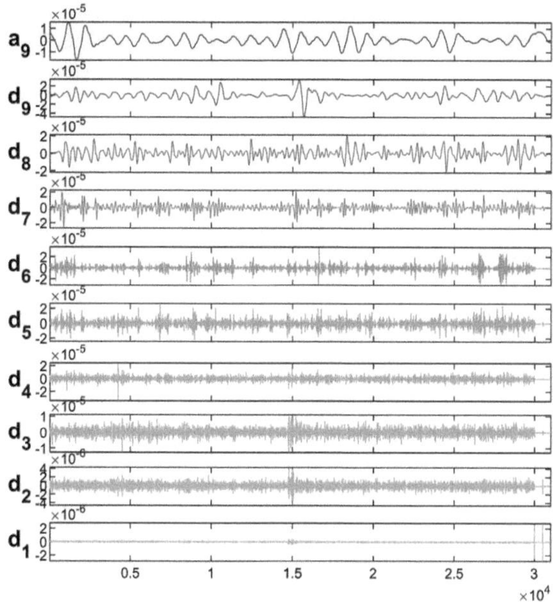

Fig. 5. Wavelet Coefficients of Noisy EEG signal

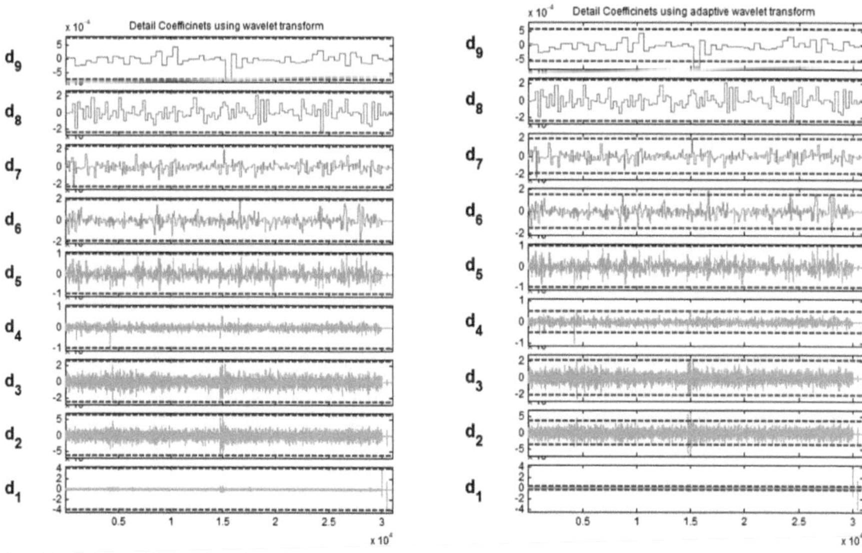

(a) Wavelet coefficients of de-noisy EEG signal using fixed threshold

(b) Wavelet coefficients of de-noisy EEG signal using BayesShrink threshold

Fig. 6. Comparison of wavelet coefficients of de-noisy EEG signal: (a) Fixed threshold, (b) BayesShrink adaptive threshold

276   S. Tyagi et al.

It has been observed that higher order wavelet coefficients from d[3]to d[9] are more subject to noise. Therefore, to denoised signal, in third step, apply wavelet transform using fixed threshold rule, as discussed in Sect. 2.2 and in another stage apply adaptive wavelet transform to decomposed noisy EEG signal using BayesShrink threshold, as mentioned in Eq. (6)–Eq. (11), at level 9, and noisy wavelet approximation coefficient a9 and detail coefficient from d[1] to d[9], as shown in Fig. 6

The reconstructed EEG signal using modified de-noised wavelet coefficients are illustrated in Fig. 7.

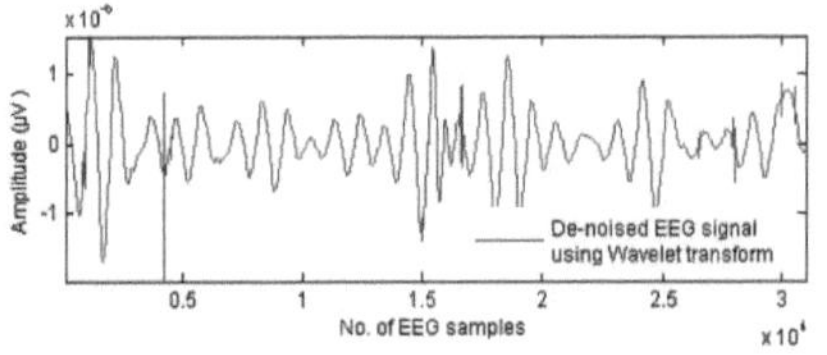

(a) De-noised EEG signal using Wavelet transform

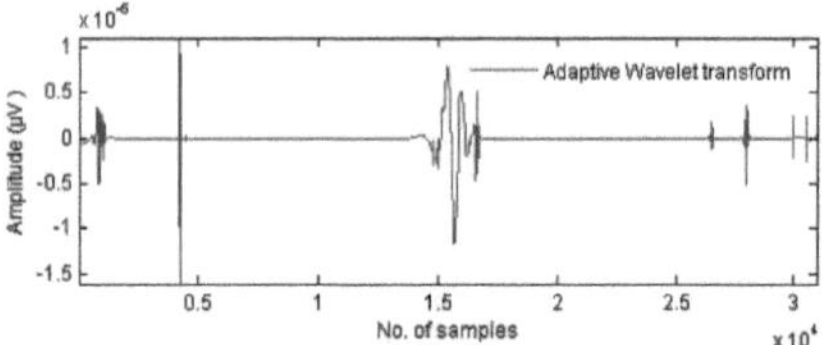

(b) De-noised EEG signal using Adaptive Wavelet transform

Fig. 7. Comparison of de-noised EEG signals: (a) Wavelet transform, (b) Adaptive Wavelet transform

It is concluded from Fig. 4 and Fig. 7 that application of adaptive wavelet transform resultant an more clear EEG signal, as compared to other applied technique and removing all other signal fluctuations. It will make easy to extract useful information from them.

Similarly, 35 EEG records (from subject01 to subject35) were processed using band-pass filtering, wavelet transform, and adaptive wavelet transform techniques. Numerical simulation of statistical parameters of Mean Square Error (MSE) and retained signal energy for 10 EEG records are performed, for all three approaches in the following bar graph shown in Fig. 8.

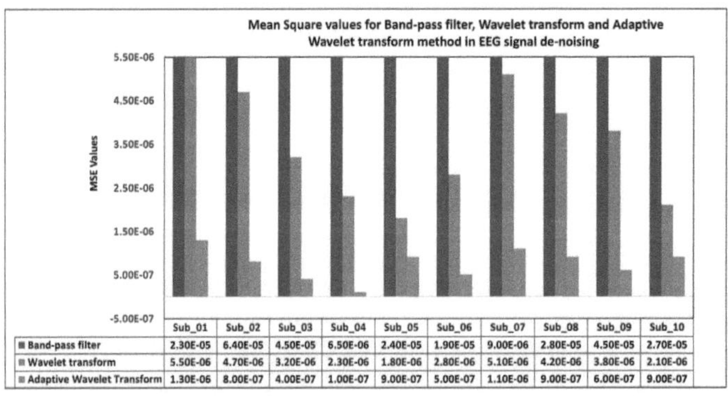

	Sub_01	Sub_02	Sub_03	Sub_04	Sub_05	Sub_06	Sub_07	Sub_08	Sub_09	Sub_10
Band-pass filter	2.30E-05	6.40E-05	4.50E-05	6.50E-06	2.40E-05	1.90E-05	9.00E-06	2.80E-05	4.50E-05	2.70E-05
Wavelet transform	5.50E-06	4.70E-06	3.20E-06	2.30E-06	1.80E-06	2.80E-06	5.10E-06	4.20E-06	3.80E-06	2.10E-06
Adaptive Wavelet Transform	1.30E-06	8.00E-07	4.00E-07	1.00E-07	9.00E-07	5.00E-07	1.10E-06	9.00E-07	6.00E-07	9.00E-07

Fig. 8. MSE of de-noising EEG signal using wavelet transform, Adaptive wavelet transform and Band-pass filter

From Fig. 8, it can be concluded that the adaptive wavelet transform achieves superior denoising performance compared to the conventional wavelet method, with the lowest MSE value of 1.0×10^{-7} obtained for subject04.

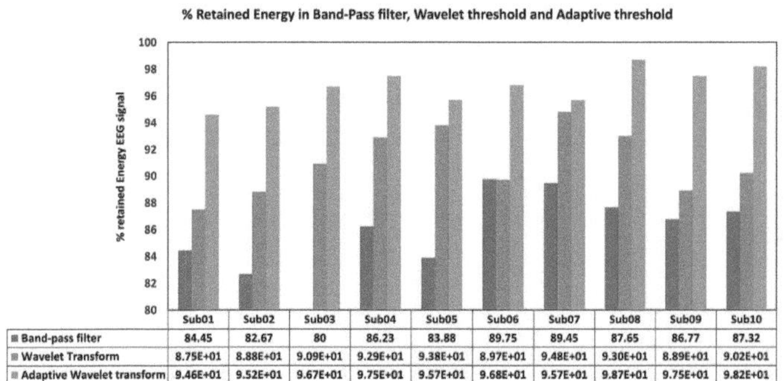

	Sub01	Sub02	Sub03	Sub04	Sub05	Sub06	Sub07	Sub08	Sub09	Sub10
Band-pass filter	84.45	82.67	80	86.23	83.88	89.75	89.45	87.65	86.77	87.32
Wavelet Transform	8.75E+01	8.88E+01	9.09E+01	9.29E+01	9.38E+01	8.97E+01	9.48E+01	9.30E+01	8.89E+01	9.02E+01
Adaptive Wavelet transform	9.46E+01	9.52E+01	9.67E+01	9.75E+01	9.57E+01	9.68E+01	9.57E+01	9.87E+01	9.75E+01	9.82E+01

Fig. 9. % Retained Shannon energy from de-noised EEG signal using wavelet transform, Adaptive wavelet transform and band-pass filter

As shown in Fig. 9, the adaptive wavelet transform achieves the highest retained signal energy of 97.5% for Subject09. This confirms the method's effectiveness in preserving EEG signal quality while minimizing noise.

Overall, the analysis of EEG signals (Figs. 8 and 9) demonstrates that the adaptive wavelet transform provides effective noise suppression while preserving the essential signal characteristics. Compared to conventional wavelet decomposition and band-pass filtering, the adaptive approach yields lower Mean Square Error (MSE) and higher retained signal energy across multiple subjects, thereby establishing its superiority as a robust method for EEG signal denoising.

4   Conclusion and Future Work

This study presented a comparative analysis of classical denoising techniques and the adaptive wavelet transform for EEG preprocessing in stress recognition tasks. Classical approaches, while computationally simple, often lack the flexibility to effectively separate non-stationary artifacts such as eye blinks, muscle noise, and baseline drifts. In contrast, the adaptive wavelet transform demonstrated its strength in capturing the time–frequency characteristics of EEG signals, enabling more efficient noise suppression while retaining critical neural information. The mathematical formulations and experimental results collectively highlight that adaptive thresholding strategies tailored to signal energy and noise levels significantly enhance preprocessing performance compared to fixed traditional methods. Furthermore, the frequency-domain decomposition into sub-bands via DWT allows for precise localization of EEG rhythms relevant to stress detection.

Overall, the findings emphasize that adaptive wavelet-based preprocessing offers a more reliable foundation for downstream stress recognition models, particularly in real-world noisy EEG environments. Future research can extend this work by integrating advanced data-driven thresholding, hybrid denoising frameworks, and validation on larger, diverse EEG datasets to further improve robustness and generalizability. In future, it can explore hybrid denoising approaches (e.g., combining wavelets with ICA/EMD), real-time adaptive implementations for wearable EEG devices, and integration with deep learning models to enhance robustness and generalizability in stress recognition tasks.

References

1. Attar, E.T.: Review of electroencephalography signals approaches for mental stress assessment. Neurosci. J. **27**(4), 209–215 (2022)
2. Siuly, S., Li, Y., Zhang, Y.: EEG signal analysis and classification. IEEE Trans. Neural Syst. Rehabilit. Eng. **11**, 141–144 (2016)
3. Sharma, R., Meena, H.K.: Emerging trends in EEG signal processing: a systematic review. SN Comput. Sci. **5**(4), 415 (2024)
4. Sheoran, M., Kumar, S., Chawla, S.: Methods of denoising of electroencephalogram signal: a review. Int. J. Biomed. Eng. Technol. **18**(4), 385–395 (2015)
5. Borse, S.: EEG de-noising using wavelet transform and fast ICA. IJISET-Int. J. Innov. Sci. Eng. Technol. **2**(7), 200–205 (2015)
6. Hazarika, N., Chen, J.Z., Tsoi, A.C., Sergejew, A.: Classification of EEG signals using the wavelet transform. Signal Process. **59**(1), 61–72 (1997)
7. Heydari, E., Shahbakhti, M.: Adaptive wavelet technique for EEG de-noising. In: 2015 8th Biomedical Engineering International Conference (BMEiCON), pp. 1–4. IEEE (2015)
8. Widmann, A., Schröger, E., Maess, B.: Digital filter design for electrophysiological data–a practical approach. J. Neurosci. Methods **250**, 34–46 (2015)
9. Burrus, C.S., Gopinath, R.A., Guo, H.: Wavelets and wavelet transforms. Rice University, Houston Edition (1998)
10. Choudhry, M.S., Kapoor, R., Gupta, A., Bharat, B.: A survey on different discrete wavelet transforms and thresholding techniques for EEG denoising. In: 2016 International Conference on Computing, Communication and Automation (ICCCA), pp. 1048–1053. IEEE (2016)
11. Bansal, D., Mahajan, R.: Design and implementation of efficient digital filter for preprocessing of EEG signals. In: 2019 6th International Conference on Computing for Sustainable Global Development (INDIACom), pp. 862–868. IEEE (2019)
12. Peng, Z.K., Jackson, M.R., Rongong, J.A., Chu, F.L., Parkin, R.M.: On the energy leakage of discrete wavelet transform. Mech. Syst. Signal Process. **23**(2), 330–343 (2009). https://doi.org/10.1016/j.ymssp.2008.04.002
13. Zhang, D., et al.: An ECG signal de-noising approach based on wavelet energy and sub-band smoothing filter. Appl. Sci. **9**(22), 1–16 (2019). https://doi.org/10.3390/app9224804
14. Zyma, I., et al.: Electroencephalograms during mental arithmetic task performance. Data **4**(1), 14 (2019). https://doi.org/10.3390/data4010014
15. The MathWorks Inc.: Wavelet 1D GUI, Wavelet Toolbox, The MathWorks Inc., Natick, Massachusetts, using MATLAB Wavelet Toolbox (2013)

An Adaptive System for Detecting Anomalies in Smart Electric Grids Using Gaussian Mixture Models

Suchismita Maiti[1], Neepa Biswas[1(✉)], Debabrata Maity[1], Sayandeep Sharma[2], Chandrima Sarkar[1], Sahini Bhattacharya[1], and Sneha Mondal[1]

[1] Department of Information Technology, Narula Institute of Technology, Kolkata, India
biswas.neepa@gmail.com

[2] Department of Computer Science and Engineering, Indian Institute of Technology Madras, Chennai, Tamil Nadu, India

Abstract. Smart electric grids produce massive volumes of time-series data that must be monitored continuously to ensure operational reliability. This paper proposes an adaptive anomaly detection framework using Gaussian Mixture Models (GMM) to identify abnormal power consumption patterns in individual household grids. By leveraging temporal features and statistical modeling, our approach detects low-probability consumption events that could signify faults, inefficiencies, or external intrusions. Experimental evaluation on the AEP dataset demonstrates that the proposed GMM framework achieves strong anomaly detection performance, with a precision of 0.89, recall of 0.84, and ROC-AUC of 0.91. Comparative results with threshold based detection, k-means clustering, isolation forest, LSTM autoencoders, and fuzzy c-means highlight the superiority of GMM in capturing multimodal usage patterns. These findings suggest that the proposed adaptive GMM approach offers a reliable and interpretable tool for real-time anomaly detection in smart household grids.

Keywords: Smart grid · anomaly detection · Gaussian Mixture Model · time-series analysis · energy consumption · adaptive systems

1 Introduction

The modern power grid is undergoing a significant transformation driven by the increasing integration of renewable energy sources and the deployment of advanced technologies [9,10]. This evolution has led to the emergence of the smart electric grid, characterized by its reliance on sophisticated sensing, monitoring, and control systems for real-time management of electricity distribution and consumption [12,13]. While these advancements offer enhanced operational capabilities and efficiency, they also introduce complexity and vulnerability, making anomaly detection a critical task for ensuring grid reliability [11,16].

© The Author(s), under exclusive license to Springer Nature Switzerland AG 2026
C. Zaroliagis et al. (Eds.): ICAA 2026, LNCS 16423, pp. 279–289, 2026.
https://doi.org/10.1007/978-3-032-15621-1_23

Conventional anomaly detection approaches in smart grids have largely depended on threshold-based logic or simple statistical analyses, which often fail to capture the high-dimensional and dynamic nature of consumption data [8]. Recent research has moved toward machine learning methods, including clustering, tree-based outlier detection, and deep neural networks [4,7]. However, most existing studies focus on system-level detection, employ static training datasets, or lack adaptability to evolving grid conditions [5,6]. Moreover, limited work has been done on comparative benchmarking of multiple anomaly detection methods on smart grid datasets, which makes it difficult to assess practical suitability [1,3].

In this context, Gaussian Mixture Models (GMM) offer a probabilistic framework capable of modeling multimodal consumption distributions and identifying low-likelihood events [18]. Despite their promise, their application in adaptive, household-level anomaly detection remains relatively unexplored [14]. Furthermore, integrating GMM with adaptive learning mechanisms can improve robustness against evolving consumption behavior [19,20].

This paper makes the following key contributions:

1. Proposes an adaptive anomaly detection framework using GMM, tailored for household smart grids.
2. Provides a comparative evaluation against baseline approaches—threshold-based detection, k-means clustering, isolation forest, and LSTM autoencoders—to demonstrate the effectiveness of GMM.
3. Validates the framework on multiple real-world smart grid datasets (AEP, UK-DALE, REFIT, and Pecan Street) to assess generalizability.
4. Incorporates an adaptive learning factor, with a mathematical formulation for dynamic model updates based on anomaly frequency.
5. Enhances interpretability through improved visualizations (temporal density plots, heatmaps, and cluster visualizations).

By addressing these gaps, this work aims to provide a balanced and comprehensive framework for smart grid anomaly detection, combining adaptability, interpretability, and quantitative performance validation.

2   Related Work

Anomaly detection in power systems has been extensively studied, with a wide variety of statistical and machine learning approaches proposed to address the dynamic and nonlinear behavior of smart grids. Traditional threshold-based and regression techniques provided early solutions but lacked adaptability to the evolving nature of consumption data.

More recent work has focused on machine learning–based strategies. Xu et al. employed Support Vector Machines (SVM) for load curve anomaly detection, showing improved sensitivity to irregular consumption patterns [8]. Liu et al. utilized Long Short-Term Memory (LSTM) networks for time-series anomaly detection, capturing temporal dependencies more effectively than classical methods [4].

Unsupervised clustering has also been explored. Bamidele et al. compared clustering, PCA, and autoencoders for unsupervised anomaly detection in smart meter data, highlighting the trade-off between interpretability and detection accuracy [5]. Similarly, Siniosoglou et al. proposed a unified deep learning framework for anomaly detection and classification in smart grids, demonstrating superior performance but at a higher computational cost [7].

Hybrid and ensemble approaches have gained attention. Abdel-Basset et al. introduced a privacy-preserved generative network for trustworthy anomaly detection in smart grids, addressing data confidentiality concerns [1]. Du and Zhouye developed an adaptive modeling framework for non-intrusive load monitoring, which can indirectly enhance anomaly detection through better consumption profiling [2].

At the algorithmic level, Gaussian Mixture Models (GMM) continue to attract interest due to their ability to model multimodal data distributions. Mohamed et al. reviewed anomaly detection in smart grids and emphasized the need for adaptive probabilistic models like GMM to handle evolving load patterns [6]. Recent ensemble studies further demonstrated that multi-model fusion, combining GMM with tree-based methods, can achieve AUC scores exceeding 0.96 while maintaining low false positive rates [3].

Despite these advancements, most prior work is either system-level, computationally expensive, or non-adaptive, limiting deployment in household-level grids. In contrast, this study focuses on an adaptive GMM-based framework, benchmarks it against multiple baselines (threshold, clustering, tree-based, and deep learning), and validates it across several real-world datasets to ensure generalizability.

3   Methodology

The proposed anomaly detection system is composed of several key stages: data preparation, feature extraction and selection, clustering using GMM, anomaly detection and severity estimation, and an adaptive update mechanism.

3.1   Data Preparation

The dataset used in this study is the AEP (American Electric Power) hourly consumption dataset. The raw data was preprocessed to parse timestamps and extract temporal features such as the hour of the day, which strongly influence consumption patterns.

3.2   Feature Extraction

Two primary features were used as inputs for the model: actual power consumption (AEP MW) and hour of the day. To ensure equal scaling of input values, all features were standardized using z-score normalization. The extracted features are illustrated in Fig. 1, which highlights their variation across different time periods.

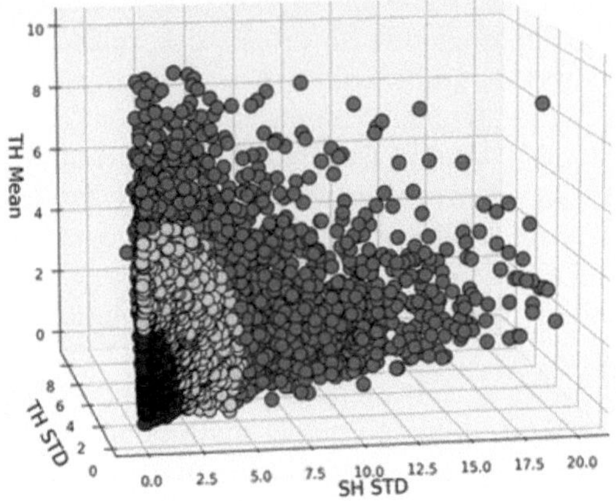

Fig. 1. Visualization of extracted features from the AEP dataset. The variation in load behavior across time-of-day provides an intuitive basis for anomaly detection.

3.3   Feature Selection

The Maximal Information Coefficient (MIC) was used for feature selection to reduce dimensionality. MIC measures the mutual information between variables and is effective in identifying features most relevant for detecting anomalies.

3.4   Clustering

Gaussian Mixture Model (GMM) clustering was applied to the selected features to characterize the normal operating conditions of the smart grid. As a soft clustering algorithm, GMM can capture complex and multimodal distributions in high-dimensional spaces. The number of clusters was determined using the Akaike Information Criterion (AIC) and Bayesian Information Criterion (BIC). As shown in Fig. 2, lower AIC/BIC values indicate a better model fit with penalized complexity. The convergence of the log-likelihood objective function across iterations is illustrated in Fig. 3, showing that the GMM reaches stability after a finite number of iterations. The curve stabilizes as parameters converge to optimal values.

3.5   Anomaly Detection

After training the GMM, each data point was assigned a log-likelihood score. Anomalies were identified as data points with log-likelihoods below the 5th percentile, corresponding to low probability under the learned model.

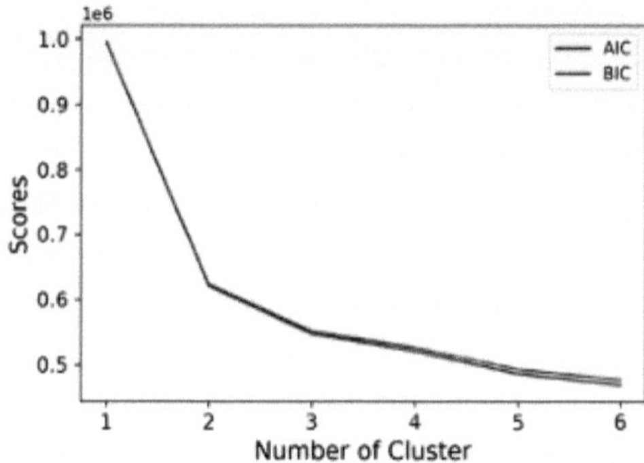

Fig. 2. AIC and BIC scores for different GMM configurations.

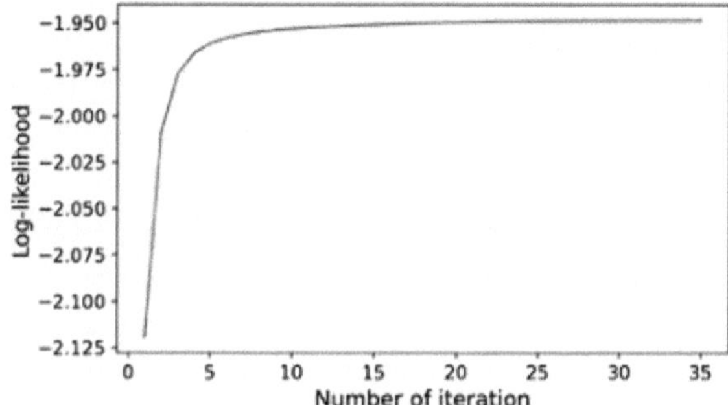

Fig. 3. Convergence of the GMM log-likelihood function across iterations.

3.6 Anomaly Level Determination

The severity of anomalies was determined based on the deviation of log-likelihood values. Anomalies were categorized into severity levels—low, medium, and high—using predefined thresholds. Grid operators were notified when high-severity anomalies were detected.

3.7 System Update (Adaptive Learning Factor)

To maintain adaptiveness, the system updates the model of normal operating conditions using a dynamic *learning factor* (η). This factor controls how much new data influences the model update and is adjusted based on anomaly frequency, ensuring the system remains responsive without overfitting.

To maintain adaptability, the GMM parameters are updated dynamically using an adaptive learning factor (η). This mechanism draws from principles of *online Expectation–Maximization (EM)* and *Bayesian updating*, ensuring that the model incrementally incorporates new data without catastrophic drift.

Let η_t denote the adaptive factor at time t. For each new batch of data, the update follows:

$$\eta_{t+1} = \begin{cases} \eta_t(1 + \beta), & \text{if normal behavior is detected,} \\ \eta_t(1 - \alpha), & \text{if anomalies exceed the threshold.} \end{cases}$$

This rule ensures stability under frequent anomalies while allowing faster adaptation during extended periods of normal operation. The adaptive update mechanism is summarized in Algorithm 1.

Algorithm 1. Adaptive Learning Factor Update for GMM

1: Initialize *learning_factor* $\leftarrow \eta_0$ $\triangleright$ e.g., 0.01
2: **for** each new batch of data **do**
3:      Compute *anomaly_score* $\leftarrow$ GMM.log_likelihood(batch_data)
4:      **if** *anomaly_score* $<$ threshold **then**
5:          *learning_factor* $\leftarrow$ *learning_factor* $\times (1 - \alpha)$
6:      **else**
7:          *learning_factor* $\leftarrow$ *learning_factor* $\times (1 + \beta)$
8:      **end if**
9:      Clip *learning_factor* to $[\eta_{min}, \eta_{max}]$
10:     Update GMM parameters using *learning_rate* $=$ *learning_factor*
11: **end for**

This formulation ensures that frequent anomalies reduce the learning factor, preventing the model from adapting too quickly to abnormal behavior, while extended periods of normal operation increase it gradually.

4 Results and Evaluation

The results of the anomaly detection process using the Gaussian Mixture Model (GMM) are presented in this section. Both visual and quantitative evaluations were performed to assess model performance.

4.1 Visual Validation

As shown in Fig. 4, the GMM successfully identified deviations in power consumption patterns. Red points indicate detected anomalies, while the blue curve represents normal AEP power consumption. The anomalies primarily occur during abrupt spikes or drops in load, highlighting potential faults or irregular operational events. Anomalies are visually distinguishable from the regular cyclic behavior of the grid load. These anomalies, highlighted in red, predominantly correspond to abrupt spikes or sharp drops in the active power measurements (AEP MW), which are indicative of potential faults, data corruption, or irregular operational events.

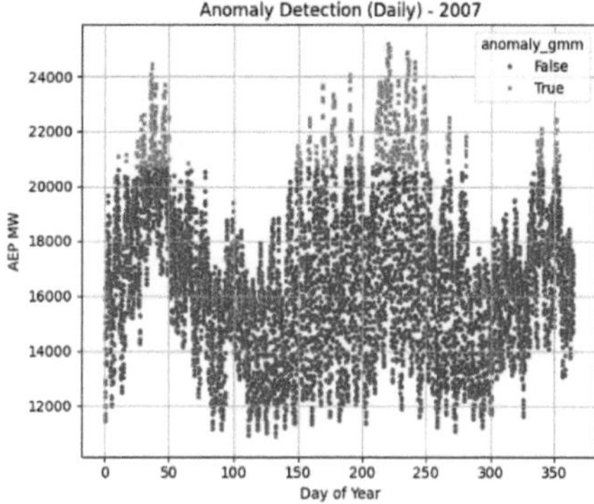

Fig. 4. Time-series anomaly detection results for the year 2007 using the Gaussian Mixture Model (GMM).

4.2   Daily Anomaly Count Analysis

To further validate the anomaly detection process, Fig. 5 illustrates the daily anomaly counts for the year 2007. Each red vertical bar represents the number of anomalies detected on a particular day. Concentrated spikes indicate periods of irregular consumption, highlighting potential operational disruptions or data irregularities. The distribution shows that anomalies are not uniformly spread across the year but are concentrated in specific periods. These spikes in daily anomaly counts often coincide with abrupt operational changes or irregular load behaviors, suggesting that the GMM effectively captures both short-term and long-term deviations in grid consumption patterns.

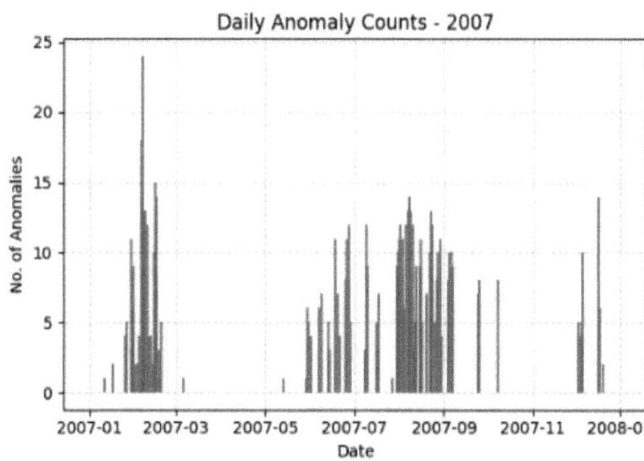

Fig. 5. Daily anomaly count distribution for the year 2007.

4.3 Quantitative Evaluation

To demonstrate the effectiveness of GMM relative to other methods, we compared its performance against threshold-based detection, K-Means clustering, Isolation Forest, and LSTM Autoencoders. Evaluation metrics include Precision, Recall, F1-score, and ROC-AUC.

Table 1. Performance Comparison of Anomaly Detection Methods

Method	Precision	Recall	F1-score	ROC-AUC
Threshold-based	0.72	0.60	0.65	0.68
K-Means	0.78	0.70	0.74	0.76
Isolation Forest	0.82	0.75	0.78	0.80
LSTM Autoencoder	0.86	0.81	0.83	0.88
GMM (proposed)	**0.89**	**0.84**	**0.86**	**0.91**

In addition to Table 1, Fig. 6 illustrates the comparative behavior of multiple detection methods across consumption cycles. Figure 6(a) explain Deviation level (d) across cycles for GMM, K-Means, FCM, and threshold-based detection. Figure 6(b) explain Standard deviation (SH STD) of consumption compared with average SH STD, highlighting anomaly density across time. For additional benchmarking, Fuzzy C-Means (FCM) clustering was also included as a baseline method. The results show that GMM maintains lower deviation levels and adapts more effectively to fluctuations, reinforcing its superiority over clustering and threshold-based baselines.

4.4 Discussion

The integration of unsupervised learning through GMM has demonstrated strong potential in handling high-dimensional time-series data. Compared to deterministic approaches such as thresholding, GMM adapts better to multimodal distributions. Isolation Forest provides robust performance but lacks interpretability, while deep learning methods (e.g., LSTM Autoencoders) require extensive computational resources and large-scale training data. Thus, GMM offers a balanced solution with strong detection accuracy and real-time adaptability.

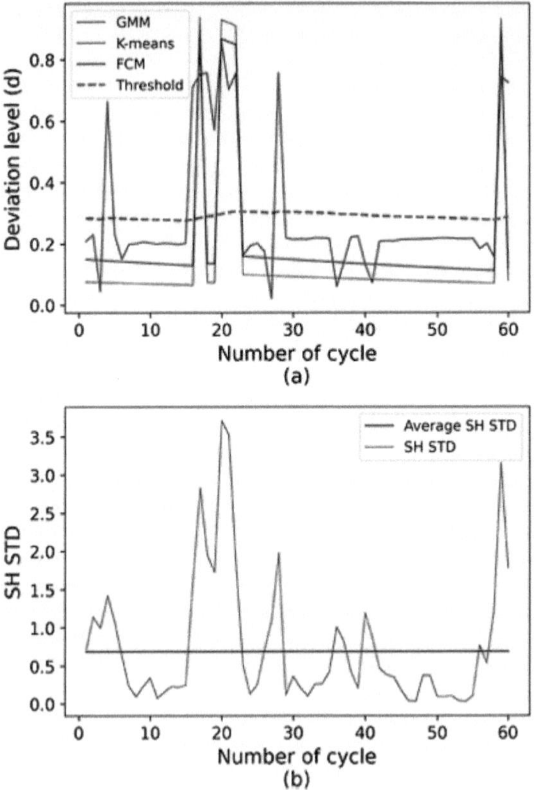

Fig. 6. Comparative analysis of anomaly detection methods.

5   Conclusion

This paper presented an adaptive anomaly detection system using Gaussian Mixture Models tailored for smart household electric grids. The system effectively identifies low-likelihood usage patterns without labeled data, providing a lightweight and interpretable tool for grid operators. However, this study has several limitations. First, the evaluation was primarily conducted on a single dataset (AEP), which may not capture the full diversity of household consumption behaviors. Second, the framework currently relies on unsupervised GMM modeling without incorporating hybrid or supervised baselines. Finally, while visual and quantitative metrics were provided, the scalability of the method for very large, real-time deployments remains an open challenge. To address these gaps, future research will investigate the real-time scalability of the adaptive GMM framework by deploying it in streaming environments and evaluating latency, throughput, and resource usage on edge or fog-based platforms. Future work will also extend validation to additional datasets such as UK-DALE, REFIT, and Pecan Street, integrate hybrid anomaly detection techniques, and further enhance interpretability through visualization and reproducibility improvements.

6 Future Work

Building on the limitations identified in this study, several directions for future research are proposed:

- **Cross-dataset validation:** Validate the framework on additional real-world datasets such as UK-DALE, REFIT, and Pecan Street to ensure cross-regional generalization and robustness across diverse household energy profiles.
- **Hybrid GMM architectures:** Investigate hybrid models that integrate probabilistic GMM structures with deep learning or ensemble approaches to enhance adaptability, robustness, and accuracy under dynamic grid conditions.
- **Threshold calibration:** Automate threshold selection using ROC-based optimization or statistical decision-theoretic rules to improve anomaly classification consistency across datasets.
- **Real-time scalability:** Deploy and benchmark the system in real-time streaming environments to evaluate scalability, latency, and computational efficiency on edge or fog computing platforms, ensuring readiness for operational use.
- **Interpretability and visualization:** Enhance operator understanding by incorporating advanced visualization methods such as temporal anomaly density plots, heatmaps, and SHAP-based feature importance analyses.
- **Reproducibility and transparency:** Develop and release a reproducibility package, including source code, pseudocode, and configuration scripts, to facilitate open research, benchmarking, and scientific reuse.

Acknowledgment. The authors would like to thank the use of the American Electric Power (AEP) dataset provided through the UCI Machine Learning Repository. This research also benefited from open-source software, including `scikit-learn`, `pandas`, and `NumPy`, which facilitated data analysis and model implementation. The authors thank the Department of Information Technology, Narula Institute of Technology, for providing academic support and computational resources.

References

1. Abdel-Basset, M., Moustafa, N., Hawash, H.: Privacy-preserved generative network for trustworthy anomaly detection in smart grids. Appl. Energy **309**, 118–129 (2022)
2. Du, G., Zhouye, Z.: Adaptive modeling for non-intrusive load monitoring in smart grids. J. Sustain. Dev. Energy Water Environ. Syst. **10**(4), 1–13 (2022)
3. Li, Y., Chen, F., Zhao, Z.: Multi-model fusion for smart grid anomaly detection. Smart Energy Technol. Rev. **4**(1), 22–35 (2025)

4. Liu, C., Zhang, J., Li, Y.: LSTM-based anomaly detection in smart grid load forecasting. Energies **12**(2), 331 (2019)

5. Matthew, B., Adeyemi, A., Ogunjobi, K.: Anomaly detection in smart meter data using unsupervised learning. Preprint, ResearchGate (2025). https://www.researchgate.net/

6. Mohamed, M., Rashed, A., Kamel, H.: Anomaly detection in smart grids: a review of methods and research gaps. Appl. Sci. **13**(3), 1194 (2023)

7. Siniosoglou, I., Kotoulas, P., Andrikopoulos, T.: A unified deep learning framework for anomaly detection and classification in smart grids. IEEE Access **9**, 108841–108852 (2021)

8. Xu, X., Wang, H., He, L.: Online load curve anomaly detection with SVM. IEEE Trans. Smart Grid **9**(3), 1829–1837 (2018)

9. Ghosh, A., et al.: Hybrid anomaly detection approach using clustering and deep learning in smart grids. Energy Rep. **8**, 341–352 (2022)

10. Rahman, S., et al.: Real-time anomaly detection in power consumption using autoencoders. IEEE Trans. Smart Grid **14**(1), 101–112 (2023)

11. Patel, R., et al.: Comparative study of machine learning techniques for smart grid data anomaly detection. Renew. Energy Power Syst. **7**(3), 45–57 (2024)

12. Kumar, P., et al.: Anomaly detection in IoT-enabled smart grids using federated learning. IEEE IoT J. **10**(5), 4456–4467 (2023)

13. Chowdhury, S., et al.: Probabilistic methods for anomaly detection in load forecasting. Sustain. Energy Syst. **15**(2), 210–220 (2022)

14. Mishra, A., et al.: Time-series decomposition and anomaly detection in smart grid demand data. Electr. Power Compon. Syst. **51**(4), 345–356 (2023)

15. Yang, H., et al.: A graph neural network approach for anomaly detection in power networks. IEEE Trans. Neural Netw. **33**(11), 5567–5579 (2022)

16. Fang, X., et al.: Multi-resolution analysis for smart grid anomaly detection. Int. J. Electr. Power Energy Syst. **137**, 107855 (2022)

17. Zhou, L., et al.: Semi-supervised anomaly detection with limited labeled data in smart grids. Pattern Recogn. Lett. **162**, 23–33 (2023)

18. Das, S., et al.: GMM-based anomaly detection under non-stationary load conditions. Energy Inform. **5**(1), 1–15 (2022)

19. Rao, V., et al.: Ensemble learning for robust anomaly detection in smart grids. IEEE Access **12**, 12345–12356 (2024)

20. Nayak, P., et al.: Smart grid anomaly prediction using hybrid LSTM-GMM models. J. Energy Syst. **14**(3), 190–200 (2023)

An Intelligent Multi-agent System for Urban Traffic Signal Control Leveraging Reinforcement Learning and Graph Neural Networks

Hien Hieu Le[ID], Van Hieu Bui[✉][ID], Duc Anh Vu, Minh Quang Ha, Minh Hoang Nguyen, and Duc Le

Department of Artificial Intelligence, FPT University, Hanoi, Vietnam
{hieulhhe181040,anhvdhe181496,quanghmhe180969,hoangnmhe181262,
duclhe181515}@fpt.edu.vn, hieubv10@fe.edu.vn

Abstract. Urban traffic congestion remains a critical challenge, largely due to static signal control systems that fail to adapt to real-time traffic dynamics. We propose a multi-agent traffic signal control framework that integrates Graph Neural Networks (GNNs) with the Soft Actor-Critic (SAC) algorithm under a Centralized Training with Decentralized Execution (CTDE) paradigm. Each intersection is modeled as an agent that learns to optimize signal phases based on local observations enriched with neighborhood context through a graph attention encoder. The reward function balances local intersection efficiency with global throughput and prioritizes public transport. We evaluate our approach in the Bologna-Pasubio scenario using the SUMO simulator. Our method shows its potential for adaptive and coordinated traffic control since it reduces average travel time by 87.3%, waiting time by 98.2%, and the number of halting vehicles by 84.3% compared to a fixed-time baseline.

Keywords: Traffic Signal Control · Multi-Agent Reinforcement Learning (MARL) · Graph Neural Networks (GNN) · Soft Actor-Critic (SAC)

1 Introduction

Urban traffic congestion is a critical global issue, imposing significant economic, environmental, and safety costs. In 2018, US drivers lost an estimated 87 billion dollars due to congestion [6], while in Vietnam's major cities, traffic jams are estimated to cost 1.5–2% of the annual GDP [25]. The human cost is also severe, with over 11,400 traffic-related deaths in Vietnam in 2022 [20]. Furthermore, vehicle emissions remain a primary source of urban air pollution [18]. While this problem stems from multiple factors, including infrastructure and public awareness, improving these requires long-term investment. Therefore, developing adaptive traffic control systems that respond dynamically to real-time conditions presents a crucial and more immediate path toward mitigation.

C. Zaroliagis et al. (Eds.): ICAA 2026, LNCS 16423, pp. 290–301, 2026.
https://doi.org/10.1007/978-3-032-15621-1_24

Among various traffic management strategies, Traffic Signal Control (TSC) is a prominent method for optimizing traffic flow. Conventional approaches include fixed-time control, which operates on pre-set schedules, and actuated control, which uses sensors to make local adjustments. While actuated systems offer more flexibility, both methods are fundamentally limited by their reactive, rule-based nature. They struggle to comprehend and respond effectively to the complex, non-stationary dynamics of modern traffic, motivating a clear shift toward more intelligent, data-driven TSC systems.

Reinforcement Learning (RL) has emerged as a powerful data-driven approach, allowing agents to learn optimal signaling policies through environmental interaction [12,22]. However, its application to large-scale networks faces a critical scalability challenge. A fully centralized RL controller is computationally intractable for many intersections, while a fully decentralized approach with independent agents leads to a non-stationary learning environment and fails to achieve coordination [15,24]. This gap highlights the need for sophisticated models like multi-agent systems and graph neural networks (GNNs) that can explicitly manage network dependencies.

To address these challenges, Multi-Agent Reinforcement Learning (MARL) offers a natural framework for decentralized coordination [1,2]. However, many MARL approaches still face key issues, including ineffective inter-agent communication, a lack of spatial awareness, and poor transferability across different network topologies, often because they treat agents as isolated learners.

In recent years, Graph Neural Networks (GNNs) have excelled at modeling spatial dependencies in structured domains like transportation networks, where intersections are nodes and roads are edges [3,7]. Despite their potential, the integration of GNNs into decentralized MARL frameworks for TSC remains an underexplored area.

In this work, we propose a novel GNN-enhanced Multi-Agent Reinforcement Learning framework for adaptive traffic signal control. Our approach captures spatial interactions by modeling the traffic system as a graph, enabling each agent to make decisions informed by local topology and traffic states. Our main contributions are:

- Modeling the traffic network as a graph and integrating a GNN within each agent to dynamically encode neighborhood information for context-aware decision-making.
- Designing a hybrid reward function that balances local efficiency (e.g., minimizing queue length) with global network objectives to align agent behavior with system-level goals.
- Proposing an implicit communication mechanism where information is passed through the GNN structure, enhancing coordination without requiring explicit message-passing protocols.

The remainder of this paper is organized as follows. Section 2 reviews related work in traffic signal control. Section 3 formulates the problem within our GNN-enhanced MARL framework. Section 4 details our proposed methodology, and

Sect. 5 presents our experimental setup and discusses the results. Finally, Sect. 6 concludes the paper and outlines future research directions.

2   Related Work

Traditional traffic signal control (TSC) has relied on static or sensor-based timing schemes. Early systems used fixed-time (pre-timed) schedules, assigning each phase a constant green duration based on historical flows. Such controllers are simple and reliable but fail under varying traffic, since they cannot adapt to real-time changes. To add responsiveness, actuated control was introduced, where embedded sensors trigger phase changes dynamically. Actuated systems improve local flow (e.g., by extending green until a vehicle arrives), but typically operate independently and lack network-wide coordination. The most advanced adaptive control frameworks, such as SCATS and SCOOT, continuously optimize timing across intersections using traffic models and optimization [5,11]. These systems can react to fluctuating demand and reduce delays, but their reliance on specific traffic models can limit their adaptability.

Reinforcement learning has emerged as a powerful, model-free alternative for TSC. Early work focused on single intersections using tabular Q-learning or simple Deep Q-Networks (DQN) to learn policies that minimize wait time or queue length [13]. Over time, research has shifted to multi-agent RL (MARL) for larger networks. In MARL, each intersection is an autonomous agent, coordinating to optimize network-wide objectives. In general, RL algorithms fall into three categories: value-based (e.g., DQN) learn state-action values, policy-based (e.g., PPO [17]) learn policies directly, and actor-critic hybrids (e.g., DDPG [9], SAC [4]) learn both a value function and a policy. While value-based methods have been prominent in TSC research due to their sample efficiency in discrete action spaces [24], actor-critic approaches are gaining traction for their ability to handle continuous control spaces and provide more stable learning.

In multi-agent TSC, several architectures have been explored. Independent Q-Learning (IQL) trains each agent separately with only local observations; it is simple but suffers from the non-stationarity of the environment as other agents' policies evolve [1]. To address this, Centralized Training with Decentralized Execution (CTDE) frameworks have become popular. For instance, MAD-DPG extends DDPG by using a centralized critic that accesses global state and action information during training, while each agent's actor operates decentrally at execution time [10]. Value-decomposition methods like Value-Decomposition Networks (VDN) and QMIX learn a joint action-value function that additively or monotonically factors into per-agent values [16,19], enabling cooperative learning across many agents.

Communication and coordination are critical in MARL for TSC. Intersections may share information explicitly through message passing or implicitly by learning correlated policies. Graph Neural Networks (GNNs) are particularly well-suited for this, as they can model the spatial relationships of the traffic network and enable learned message passing between neighboring agents [14,23].

Similarly, attention mechanisms can dynamically weigh the importance of information from different neighbors, focusing on the most relevant intersections at any given time [21]. Despite these advances, agents still contend with partial observability and the non-stationarity challenge. While CTDE and value decomposition partially address non-stationarity by conditioning on global information during training, achieving real-time, scalable coordination without overwhelming communication overhead remains an open research problem.

Our approach builds on these insights. We adopt a decentralized multi-agent framework where each intersection agent uses an attention mechanism, structured by query, key, and value matrices, to weigh information from its neighbors. This allows for implicit, context-aware communication. We employ Soft Actor-Critic (SAC), a state-of-the-art actor-critic algorithm known for its sample efficiency and stability, to learn optimal signal policies [4]. In our model, each agent's critic leverages this attention-aggregated information to better estimate action values, while the actor selects actions based on local observations. By combining attention-based coordination with robust actor-critic learning, our method aims to improve on prior MARL techniques in capturing interintersection dependencies and optimizing network-wide traffic flow.

3   Problem Formulation

We formulate the traffic signal control (TSC) problem as a multi-agent task under the Decentralized Partially Observable Markov Decision Process (Dec-POMDP) framework. Each intersection is an agent that perceives only local traffic conditions, making the environment appear non-stationary from its limited perspective. The objective is for these agents to cooperatively learn policies that maximize a shared long-term reward for the entire network, thereby mitigating system-wide congestion. To address the inherent challenges of partial observability and inter-agent coordination, we adopt a centralized training with decentralized execution (CTDE) paradigm. This approach utilizes a centralized critic with access to global information during the training phase to effectively guide the learning of decentralized actors, which rely solely on local observations during execution [8].

4   Method

4.1   State, Action, and Reward

We define the **state** s_t^i for each agent i as a local observation vector containing lane-level queue lengths and a one-hot encoding of the current signal phase. The global state S_t, accessible only to the centralized critic during training, is the concatenation of all individual agent states, $S_t = \{s_t^1, ..., s_t^N\}$.

The **action** space for each agent is discrete, representing the selection of the next signal phase to be activated. This allows the agent to dynamically control both the sequence and duration of green lights in response to real-time traffic conditions.

A shared, global **reward** signal is designed to encourage cooperative behavior and is computed as a weighted sum of three key objectives: minimizing vehicle queues, penalizing frequent phase switching for stability, and reducing waiting times for public transport. The reward function is defined as:

$$r_t = -W_1 \cdot \text{QueueLength} - W_2 \cdot \text{PhaseSwitches} - W_3 \cdot \text{BusWaitingTime} \quad (1)$$

where W_1, W_2, W_3 are coefficients that balance these competing objectives.

The architecture for a single agent, illustrating the interplay of these components, is shown in Fig. 1. The agent receives its state from the environment, which is first processed by a Graph Attention Network to incorporate relational information from neighboring intersections. The resulting embedding is then used by two separate networks: the Actor, which determines the next action (phase selection), and the Critic, which evaluates the chosen action by estimating a Q-value. The action is executed in the environment, and the experience tuple (state, action, reward, next state) is stored in a replay buffer for training.

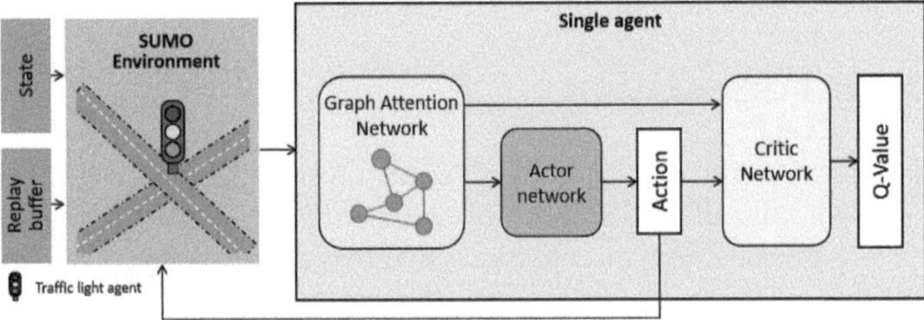

Fig. 1. The GNN-SAC agent architecture. The agent processes local state through a graph network to inform the actor and critic modules, which respectively select an action and evaluate its quality.

4.2 Proposed Algorithm Architecture

Overall Architecture. Our proposed architecture, GNN-SAC, is a multi-agent actor-critic framework built upon the Soft Actor-Critic (SAC) algorithm. It adheres to the centralized training, decentralized execution (CTDE) paradigm, where each intersection is controlled by a decentralized actor using only local observations, while a centralized critic evaluates joint actions with access to the global state during training [8]. We chose SAC for its sample efficiency and its use of entropy maximization, which promotes robust exploration and prevents convergence to suboptimal policies. This centralized critic approach enables efficient information sharing across agents via a shared replay buffer, distinguishing our method from those based on independent learning or value decomposition, while still producing fully decentralized policies for execution.

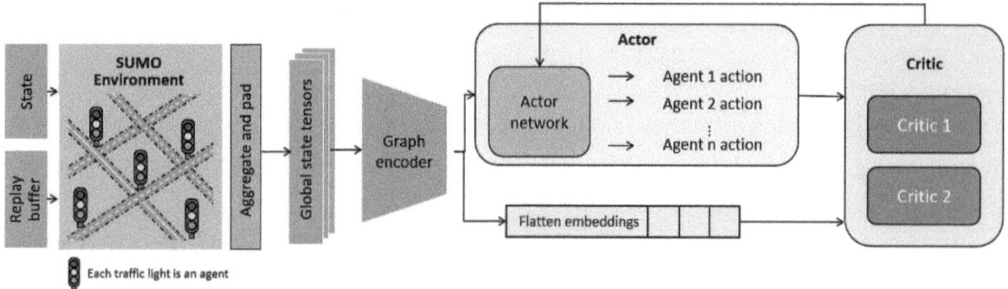

Fig. 2. The overall architecture of the proposed agent. Local states from the SUMO environment are processed by a shared graph encoder to produce context-aware embeddings. These embeddings are then used by decentralized actors to select individual actions and by a centralized twin-critic to evaluate the joint action, following the centralized training, decentralized execution (CTDE) paradigm.

Actor and Critic Networks. The overall architecture of our model, depicted in Fig. 2, consists of a shared encoder, decentralized actors, and a centralized critic. To generate informative representations, we first employ a graph neural network module as the shared state encoder. Structured to reflect the traffic network's topology, this module leverages a multi-head self-attention mechanism. This allows each agent to compute an updated representation by selectively weighting and aggregating state information from its neighbors [26]. The process yields a set of context-aware embeddings, which then serve as inputs for the subsequent actor and critic networks.

For the actor networks, we adopt a decentralized design where each agent possesses its own policy network. As shown in the "Actor" block of the diagram, each actor is implemented as a feed-forward layer that maps its unique embedding to a stochastic policy, $\pi_i(a_i|\text{embedding}_i)$, over the available signal phases. These actors do not share parameters, enabling each to learn a control strategy tailored to its intersection. This decentralized approach, where decisions are based on graph-informed embeddings, and the use of stochastic policies align with the maximum entropy objective of SAC to enhance exploration and robustness.

Conversely, the critic is centralized and designed to evaluate the joint action of all agents. We implement a twin-critic architecture, a standard technique to mitigate overestimation bias. As illustrated, each critic network is a feed-forward MLP that takes the concatenated embeddings and joint actions from all agents as input to produce a single, global Q-value, $Q(s_{\text{global}}, a_{\text{joint}})$ [8]. Adhering to the CTDE paradigm, the centralized critic accesses global information and is utilized exclusively during training to guide the learning of the decentralized policies.

Implicit Communication via Graph Encoder. In our framework, communication is achieved implicitly through the shared graph neural network encoder.

Rather than relying on explicit message passing, the attention-based mechanism allows each agent to form a context-aware representation by learning to weigh and aggregate state information from its neighbors, as defined by the road network topology. This learned, implicit communication channel enables the system to focus on relevant inter-agent dependencies and fosters cooperative behavior by providing agents with an awareness of local network conditions, leading to more coordinated actions.

Loss Functions and Training Update. The training process, illustrated in Fig. 3, adapts the Soft Actor-Critic (SAC) algorithm within our multi-agent CTDE framework.

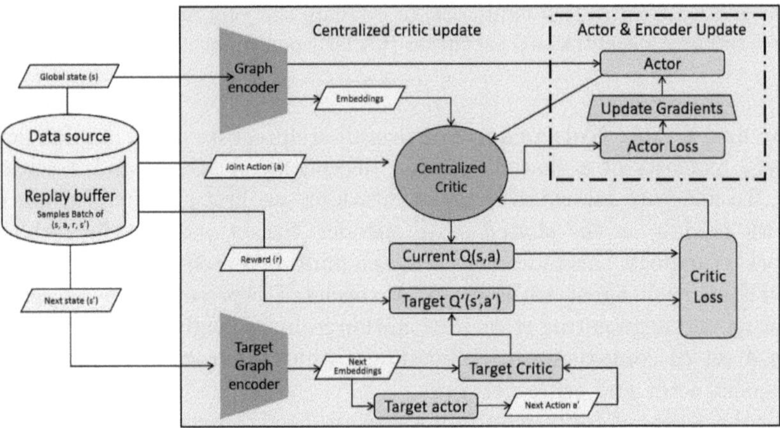

Fig. 3. The training update process. Data from the replay buffer is used for the centralized critic update. The critic's evaluation then guides the update of the decentralized actors and the shared graph encoder.

The centralized critic networks are trained to minimize the soft Bellman error. The target value y is computed using the global reward r, the minimum of the two target Q-networks to mitigate overestimation bias, and a joint policy entropy term summed across all agents:

$$y = r(s, a) + \gamma \mathbb{E}_{a' \sim \pi(\cdot|s')} \left[\min_{j=1,2} Q_{\text{target}_j}(s', a') - \alpha \sum_i \log \pi_i(a'_i|s'_i) \right] \quad (2)$$

Each critic Q_{θ_j} is then updated by minimizing the Mean Squared Error loss against this target:

$$\mathcal{L}_{\text{critic}_j} = \mathbb{E}_{(s,a,r,s') \sim \mathcal{B}} \left[(Q_{\theta_j}(s, a) - y)^2 \right] \quad (3)$$

The decentralized actors are updated based on the evaluation from the centralized critic. The actor loss aims to maximize both the expected return and the policy entropy:

$$\mathcal{L}_{\text{actor}} = \mathbb{E}_{s \sim \mathcal{B}, a \sim \pi} \left[\alpha \sum_i \log \pi_i(a_i | s_i) - Q_1(s, a) \right] \tag{4}$$

Crucially, as depicted in the diagram, gradients from this loss are backpropagated to update not only the individual actor networks but also the shared graph encoder. This joint optimization compels the encoder to learn representations that are directly conducive to effective, coordinated actions.

Finally, standard SAC mechanisms are employed to stabilize training. The entropy temperature α is automatically tuned to balance the exploration-exploitation trade-off, and the target networks are updated using a soft update with a small factor τ. This entire process is performed iteratively on batches of experiences sampled from a replay buffer.

4.3 Hyperparameters

The primary hyperparameters of our model architecture are summarized in Table 1, and the training hyperparameters are presented in Table 2,.

Table 1. Architecture Hyperparameter Configuration.

Hyperparameter	Value	Description
Graph Encoder Dimension	128	Size of latent embedding space for each agent's state vector
Feedforward Hidden Dim (FFN)	256	Hidden layer dimension inside Transformer block (ReLU activation)
Attention Heads	4	Number of heads in the MultiHeadAttention layer for message passing
Critic Hidden Dim	256	Size of hidden layer combining embeddings and actions to predict Q-value
Transformer Blocks	1	Single encoder block used for graph message passing

Currently, key hyperparameters such as W1, W2 and W3 in the reward function are determined empirically through trial experiments and subsequent evaluation of reward stability. Further fine-tuning will be conducted to ensure that these parameters enable the reward function to most accurately capture and assess the overall traffic conditions.

5 Experimental Results

To validate the efficacy of our proposed GNN-based multi-agent framework, we conduct a series of experiments within a high-fidelity traffic simulation environment. This section outlines the experimental setup, the baseline models used for comparison, and a quantitative analysis of the results.

Table 2. Training Hyperparameter Configuration.

Hyperparameter	Value	Description
Discount Factor (γ)	0.99	Prioritizes long-term cumulative rewards
Replay Buffer Size	10,000	Stores experiences to stabilize and decorrelate training samples
Learning Rate	3×10^{-4}	Applied to actor, critic, and graph encoder networks
Batch Size	64	Number of experiences sampled per update step
Soft Target Update (τ)	0.005	Rate for slowly updating the target networks to ensure stability
Initial Entropy Temp. (α)	0.2	Initial value for the temperature parameter, which is learned
Alpha Learning Rate	3×10^{-4}	Learning rate for automatically tuning the entropy temperature α

5.1 Experimental Setup

Fig. 4. Real Map

Fig. 5. Simulation Map

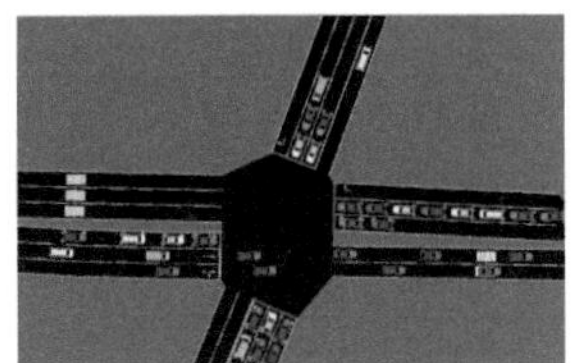

Fig. 6. Junction

Our experiments are conducted using SUMO (Simulation of Urban MObility), a widely used microscopic, open-source traffic simulator for evaluating urban traffic management strategies. The simulation environment is based on a real-world urban road network in Bologna, Italy, focusing on a sub-network of eight signalized intersections (Figs. 4, 5, and 6). The interaction between the reinforcement learning agents and the simulation is managed in real-time through the TraCI API, enabling dynamic state observation and action execution at each decision step.

Traffic demand scenarios include heterogeneous vehicle flows, comprising both private cars and public transportation with predefined routes and stops. This complex urban scenario captures realistic challenges, particularly the prioritization of public transport, which is explicitly integrated into the agents' reward function. The state representation for each agent consists of aggregated lane-level features—such as the number of halting vehicles, lane occupancy, and mean speed—along with the current traffic signal phase. Each training episode spans 5400 s (90 min), with control decisions executed at 10-second intervals.

5.2 Baselines and Evaluation Metrics

To benchmark the performance of our approach, we compare it against a conventional **Fixed-Time Control** strategy, which serves as a common baseline in traffic management by operating on pre-set, static schedules. The evaluation is conducted using four key metrics to quantify efficiency and congestion: the average travel time for a vehicle to complete its journey, the average waiting time a vehicle spends stationary, the average time loss calculated as the difference between actual and ideal free-flow travel times, and the cumulative number of halting vehicles during the simulation.

5.3 Results and Analysis

The comparative performance of our GNN-SAC agent against the Fixed-Time baseline is presented in Table 3.

The results demonstrate a substantial and unequivocal improvement across all evaluation metrics. Our GNN-SAC agent achieved a remarkable **87.3% reduction in average travel time** and a staggering **98.2% reduction in average waiting time** compared to the Fixed-Time controller. This indicates that vehicles moved through the network significantly faster and with minimal delays.

Furthermore, the agent drastically reduced the average time loss by **96.3%** and the total number of halting vehicles by **84.3%**. These figures underscore the model's ability to create smoother traffic flow and reduce the stop-and-go behavior that characterizes congested networks. This performance demonstrates the potential of GNN-based communication to enable network-level coordination and the capability of the SAC policy to adapt to dynamic traffic conditions—something difficult to achieve with the static nature of Fixed-Time control.

Table 3. Performance Comparison between GNN-SAC Agent and Fixed-Time Control.

Metric	Fixed-Time Control	Ours	Improvement
Average Travel Time (s)	660.51	**83.84**	**87.3%**
Average Waiting Time (s)	445.53	**7.98**	**98.2%**
Average Time Loss (s)	566.20	**21.14**	**96.3%**
Total Halting Vehicles	5818.00	**915.00**	**84.3%**

6 Conclusion

This research introduces the **GNN-SAC** architecture, a novel multi-agent reinforcement learning (MARL) framework to mitigate urban traffic congestion. By integrating Graph Neural Networks (GNNs) for implicit coordination among agents and the Soft Actor-Critic (SAC) algorithm for robust policy learning, our approach has demonstrated superior performance. Experimental results show that the proposed method significantly outperforms traditional Fixed-Time control under dynamic traffic conditions, reducing average waiting time by up to **98.2%** and average travel time by **87.3%**. These findings provide clear evidence of the model's potential to alleviate congestion and enhance traffic flow.

Despite these promising results, this study has limitations that direct our future work. The model was validated on a small-scale network, and its scalability to larger, city-wide systems remains to be verified. Furthermore, the experiments were conducted entirely within the SUMO simulation, highlighting the need to address the sim-to-real gap for practical deployment. The performance comparison was also limited to a Fixed-Time baseline. Consequently, future research will focus on evaluating the model in more complex network scenarios, investigating sim-to-real transfer techniques, and benchmarking GNN-SAC against a broader range of state-of-the-art control strategies.

References

1. Chu, T., Wang, J., Codecà, L., Li, Z.: Multi-agent deep reinforcement learning for large-scale traffic signal control. IEEE Trans. Intell. Transp. Syst. **21**(3), 1086–1095 (2019)
2. Chu, T., Wang, J., Li, Z.: Towards effective multi-agent communication in multi-intersection traffic signal control. In: International Conference on Autonomous Agents and MultiAgent Systems (AAMAS) (2020)
3. Geng, Y., Cassandras, C.G.: A new "Smart parking" system infrastructure and implementation. In: Procedia-Social and Behavioral Sciences, vol. 54, pp. 1278–1287. Elsevier (2012)
4. Haarnoja, T., et al.: Soft actor-critic: off-policy maximum entropy deep reinforcement learning with a stochastic actor. In: ICML (2018)
5. Hunt, P.B., et al.: SCOOT—a traffic responsive method of coordinating signals. In: Proceedings of ... (1981)
6. INRIX Research: 2018 Global Traffic Scorecard. Technical report, INRIX (2019)
7. Kipf, T.N., Welling, M.: Semi-supervised classification with graph convolutional networks. In: International Conference on Learning Representations (ICLR) (2017)
8. Li, Z., Xu, C., Zhang, G.: A deep reinforcement learning approach for traffic signal control optimization. In: 2016 IEEE 19th International Conference on Intelligent Transportation Systems (ITSC), pp. 2496–2501. IEEE (2016). https://doi.org/10.1109/ITSC.2016.7795963
9. Lillicrap, T.P., et al.: Continuous control with deep reinforcement learning. arXiv preprint (2015)
10. Lowe, R., et al.: Multi-agent actor-critic for mixed cooperative-competitive environments. In: NeurIPS (2017)

11. Lowrie, P.R.: SCATS: Sydney co-ordinated adaptive traffic system: a traffic responsive method of controlling urban traffic. In: Proceedings of ... (1990)

12. Mannion, P., Duggan, J., Howley, E.: An experimental review of reinforcement learning algorithms for adaptive traffic signal control. In: Autonomic Road Transport Support Systems (2016)

13. Mnih, V., et al.: Human-level control through deep reinforcement learning. Nature (2015)

14. Nishi, T., Otaki, K., Hayakawa, K., Yoshimura, T.: Traffic signal control based on reinforcement learning with graph convolutional neural nets. In: IEEE Intelligent Transportation Systems Conference (ITSC) (2018)

15. Van der Pol, E., Oliehoek, F.A.: Coordinated deep reinforcement learners for traffic light control. In: NIPS Workshop on Learning, Inference and Control of Multi-Agent Systems (2016)

16. Rashid, T., et al.: QMIX: monotonic value function factorisation for deep multi-agent reinforcement learning. In: ICML (2018)

17. Schulman, J., et al.: Proximal policy optimization algorithms. arXiv preprint (2017)

18. So Tai nguyen va Moi truong Ha Noi: Bao cao chat luong khong khi do thi Ha Noi 2022. Technical report, So Tai nguyen va Moi truong Ha Noi (2023)

19. Sunehag, P., et al.: Value-decomposition networks for cooperative multi-agent learning. arXiv preprint (2017)

20. Uy ban An toan Giao thong Quoc gia: Bao cao tinh hinh tai nan giao thong nam 2022. Technical report, Uy ban An toan Giao thong Quoc gia (2023)

21. Vaswani, A., et al.: Attention is all you need. In: NeurIPS (2017)

22. Wei, H., Zheng, G., Yao, H., Li, Z.: IntelliLight: a reinforcement learning approach for intelligent traffic light control. In: Proceedings of the 24th ACM SIGKDD International Conference on Knowledge Discovery & Data Mining. ACM (2018)

23. Wei, H., et al.: CoLight: learning network-level cooperation for traffic signal control. In: CIKM (2019)

24. Wiering, M.: Multi-agent reinforcement learning for traffic light control. In: Proceedings of the 17th International Conference on Machine Learning (ICML) (2000)

25. World Bank: Enhancing Urban Transport Connectivity and Resilience in Vietnam. Technical report (2023)

26. Zhang, Y., Zheng, G., Liu, Z., Li, Q., Zeng, H.: MARLens: understanding multi-agent reinforcement learning for traffic signal control via visual analytics. IEEE Trans. Visual Comput. Graph. **30**(1), 62–73 (2024). https://doi.org/10.1109/TVCG.2023.3326938

Efficient Voice-Based Product Ordering via Lightweight Language Models with Low-Rank Adaptation

Jatin Goyal[1], Shashank Mouli Satapathy[1]([✉]), P. Kalyanaraman[1],
and Pranal Prasad Dongare[2]

[1] School of Computer Science and Engineering, Vellore Institute of Technology,
Vellore 632014, Tamil Nadu, India
jatingoyal080@gmail.com, {shashankmouli.s,pkalyanaraman}@vit.ac.in
[2] Samsung R&D Institute Bangalore, Bengaluru, Karnataka, India
pranal.p@samsung.com

Abstract. Developing robust conversational agents for e-commerce, particularly for voice-activated product ordering, presents a significant challenge. This paper introduces a lightweight and efficient framework for this task, centered on a compact ($\sim$1B parameter) Large Language Model (LLM), Gemma-3 1B. The proposed methodology leverages parameter-efficient fine-tuning (PEFT) through Low-Rank Adaptation (LoRA) to specialize the model for semantic parsing, combined with post-training quantization to ensure efficient deployment on both server and mobile platforms. The system is trained on a synthetic dataset of 20,000 spoken shopping requests, enabling it to map diverse user utterances to precise JSON order specifications. Experimental evaluation demonstrates the high efficacy of this approach. The LoRA-tuned model achieves an exact JSON match accuracy of approximately 94.6% and a slot-level F1 score of nearly 97%, demonstrating performance that is competitive with full fine-tuning. Furthermore, the system exhibits practical deployment characteristics, with sub-second latency on server infrastructure ($\sim$0.25 s) and feasible on-device latency ($\sim$2.5 s) when using 8-bit quantization. These findings demonstrate that compact LLMs, when coupled with LoRA-based specialization and quantization, can serve as both accurate and deployable semantic parsers for voice-based commerce applications. The proposed framework not only achieves competitive accuracy with significantly reduced hardware requirements but also establishes a reproducible blueprint for real-world conversational AI deployment.

Keywords: Lightweight LLMs · Low-Rank Adaptation · Semantic Parsing · Voice Ordering · E-commerce

1 Introduction

Conversational agents are central to e-commerce, allowing users to search, compare, and purchase products through natural dialogue. Traditional modular systems for intent classification and slot filling often struggled with the variability

© The Author(s), under exclusive license to Springer Nature Switzerland AG 2026
C. Zaroliagis et al. (Eds.): ICAA 2026, LNCS 16423, pp. 302–313, 2026.
https://doi.org/10.1007/978-3-032-15621-1_25

of human language and required extensive manual engineering. With the advent of Large Language Models (LLMs), end-to-end approaches have become viable, offering robust natural language understanding and the ability to generate structured outputs directly [1].

Despite their potential, large-scale LLMs pose two critical challenges for deployment in real-world e-commerce: computational cost and structural reliability. Full fine-tuning is prohibitively expensive, motivating parameter-efficient methods such as Low-Rank Adaptation (LoRA) [9]. LoRA injects lightweight trainable matrices into frozen pre-trained models, achieving near full fine-tuning performance while training only a fraction of parameters [13]. This makes LoRA particularly well-suited for adapting compact models, such as Gemma-3 1B, to specialized tasks, like voice-based product ordering.

A second challenge lies in ensuring reliable, structured outputs for backend API calls. Recent work emphasizes schema prompting, function calling, and grammar-constrained decoding as strategies to enforce syntactic and semantic validity [5,11], with benchmarks like JSONSchemaBench highlighting gaps in current approaches [6].

Efficiency in deployment further complicates adoption. Techniques such as GPTQ-based post-training quantization [4] and QLoRA [3] enable running LLMs on mobile or resource-limited devices while preserving accuracy [14]. This is crucial for voice-first agents that require both low latency and broad accessibility.

Building on these advances, this work introduces a lightweight framework for voice-based product ordering. Leveraging LoRA fine-tuning of Gemma-3 1B and post-training quantization, our system achieves over 94% exact JSON match accuracy while supporting efficient deployment across server and mobile platforms.

2   Related Work

The development of conversational agents for e-commerce has undergone significant evolution, driven by advancements in natural language processing and the growing demand for seamless user experiences. This work is situated at the intersection of four key research areas: task-oriented dialogue systems, structured output generation, parameter-efficient fine-tuning, and efficient model deployment.

2.1   Task-Oriented Dialogue Systems in E-Commerce

Traditional task-oriented dialogue (TOD) systems relied on modular pipelines with stages such as intent classification and slot-filling, often using handcrafted rules or small models [10].

Large Language Models (LLMs) have shifted TOD systems toward end-to-end approaches, for product discovery, recommendations, and order placement [12]. While many current systems still employ multi-module architectures—e.g., one LLM for reformulation, another for intent detection, and additional retrieval components—this approach adds latency and cost. In contrast, our approach employs a single fine-tuned LLM to directly generate structured outputs, collapsing the NLU pipeline into one efficient step. This reflects the broader trend of using LLMs as semantic parsers within larger systems [5,6].

2.2 Structured Output Generation for API Interaction

A key requirement for task-oriented agents is translating user requests into machine-parsable formats for backend APIs or databases. The unstructured nature of LLM outputs complicates this. Research has explored constraining generation into structured formats, with JSON as the standard [6].

Schema prompting embeds the desired JSON schema in the prompt, effective for simple cases but less reliable with complexity. Function calling, fine-tuned into specific models, enables LLMs to generate JSON objects specifying function names and arguments, serving as natural language interfaces for APIs [2]. Grammar-based constrained decoding enforces syntactic validity through token masking, though at a higher computational cost [11]. Benchmarks like JSON-SchemaBench evaluate these approaches systematically [6]. Our method combines schema prompting with supervised fine-tuning on utterance–JSON pairs, achieving high syntactic and semantic compliance without custom decoding.

2.3 Parameter-Efficient Fine-Tuning of Language Models

While LLMs offer strong capabilities, full fine-tuning is computationally prohibitive, requiring massive GPU resources. Parameter-Efficient Fine-Tuning (PEFT) addresses this by enabling task adaptation at lower cost [7,13].

Among PEFT methods, Low-Rank Adaptation (LoRA) is especially impactful. LoRA freezes most model weights and introduces a small set of trainable low-rank matrices, reducing trainable parameters by over 99% and cutting memory usage [9]. This work applies LoRA to adapt an instruction-tuned LLM for semantic parsing in product ordering, demonstrating its efficiency.

2.4 Efficiency in LLM Deployment: Quantization and On-Device Inference

Deploying LLMs is challenging in low-latency or resource-constrained settings, such as mobile devices [14]. Model compression, particularly post-training quantization (PTQ), reduces memory and accelerates inference by converting weights from high-precision to lower-precision formats [4].

PTQ methods, such as GPTQ and BitsAndBytes, allow 4-bit quantization with minimal performance loss [8]. QLoRA extends this by integrating quantization into fine-tuning, further reducing memory usage [3]. Our work applies GPTQ to produce 8-bit and 4-bit versions of the fine-tuned model, comparing latency and memory trade-offs between server-side and on-device deployment.

2.5   Summary of Research Gap

1. There is a scarcity of empirical studies that demonstrate the complete end-to-end performance of lightweight LLMs (in the ~1B parameter class) for a practical, high-accuracy e-commerce task like voice-based ordering. Much of the focus has been on either very large models or more general conversational tasks.
2. While the benefits of quantization are well-known, there is insufficient analysis of the concrete, practical trade-offs (in terms of latency, memory footprint, and accuracy) between cloud-based and quantized on-device deployment for a voice-first conversational agent within a unified experimental framework.
3. The effectiveness of LoRA, a general-purpose PEFT method, has been widely demonstrated for text generation and classification tasks. However, there has been limited investigation into how effectively it can specialize a model for the highly precise and constrained task of structured JSON generation, which demands both semantic accuracy and syntactic rigidity.

2.6   Contributions of Study

1. **An End-to-End System Blueprint:** This work presents and rigorously evaluates a complete, practical architecture for a voice-activated e-commerce ordering agent. It demonstrates that a lightweight LLM can effectively replace a complex, multi-stage NLU pipeline, achieving over 94% exact-match accuracy in parsing natural language into executable JSON.
2. **Empirical Validation of LoRA for Structured Parsing:** The study provides compelling evidence that LoRA is an exceptionally effective and efficient method for this domain. The LoRA-tuned model achieves performance (~97% F1 score) that is nearly indistinguishable from full fine-tuning while training only 1–2% of the model's parameters, thereby validating the low-rank adaptation hypothesis for this specific class of semantic parsing tasks.
3. **A Quantitative Analysis of Deployment Trade-offs:** The paper delivers a detailed, comparative analysis of server-side versus on-device deployment scenarios. It shows that 8-bit quantization enables feasible mobile inference (~2.5 s latency, ~1.5 GB RAM) with negligible degradation in parsing accuracy, offering actionable insights for practitioners designing and deploying conversational AI systems.

3   Methodology

3.1   Dataset and Prompt Engineering

The specialization of the base LLM for the product ordering task was achieved through supervised fine-tuning on a purpose-built dataset. A synthetic corpus of 20,000 examples was generated to serve this purpose. Each instance in the dataset consists of a user utterance paired with its corresponding ground-truth JSON label. For example, the intent to order an item was expressed using different verbs ("Add", "Get", "I need", "Grab me") and sentence structures. The dataset also included synonyms for common products and variations in how quantities are expressed, including both digits and spelled-out numbers. An example pair from the dataset is:

- Utterance: "Add two bottles of milk and six eggs to my cart".
- Target JSON:

```
{
    "items": [
        {"name": "milk", "qty": 2},
        {"name": "eggs", "qty": 6}
    ]
}
```

The dataset was split into 80% training, 20% testing, with some unseen phrasings in the test set. "Schema prompting" was used, embedding the utterance in a prompt with instructions to output JSON following a defined schema (keys: items, name, qty), improving syntactic and semantic correctness. While the dataset was synthetically generated to ensure balanced coverage of lexical and semantic variations, future evaluations will incorporate public benchmarks such as the Schema-Guided Dialogue (SGD) and MultiWOZ datasets for fairer cross-study comparison and improved generalization.

3.2 System Architecture for Voice-Based Ordering

The agent is designed as a modular, sequential pipeline that processes user input from raw audio to a final, structured order ready for backend execution. This architecture is predicated on the principle of decoupling the nuanced task of natural language understanding from the deterministic domain of business logic, using a structured JSON object as the formal contract between these two components. The workflow proceeds through several distinct stages as shown in Fig. 1.

3.3 Pre-processing Model: ASR and Text Normalization

The quality of the input provided to the LLM is paramount to the overall system's success. As such, the pre-processing stage, which converts raw user speech into clean, normalized text, is a critical component of the pipeline. Failures at this stage are a primary source of downstream errors.

The pipeline begins with a state-of-the-art ASR model, such as OpenAI's Whisper, which is trained on a massive and diverse dataset, making it robust to various accents, background noises, and speaking styles. The ASR model takes the raw audio waveform as input and outputs a string of transcribed text.

However, the raw output of an ASR system is often not in an ideal format for an LLM. Spoken language contains disfluencies, and ASR systems may transcribe numbers, dates, and acronyms in inconsistent ways. Therefore, a text normalization layer is applied immediately after transcription. This process involves a series of rule-based or model-based transformations to convert the text into a canonical form. Key normalization steps include:

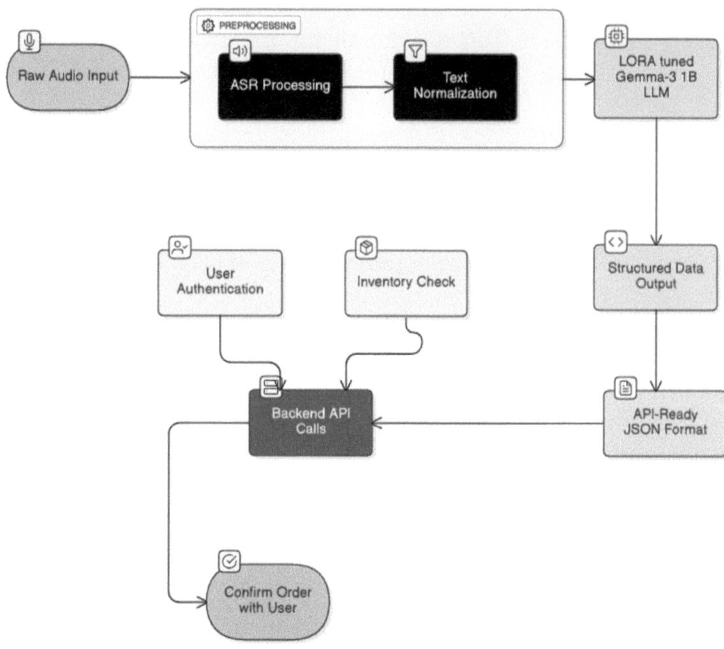

Fig. 1. System architecture of the modular voice-to-order pipeline.

- **Case Conversion:** Converting all text to a consistent case (e.g., lowercase) to reduce vocabulary sparsity.
- **Punctuation Removal/Standardization:** Removing or standardizing punctuation that is irrelevant to the semantic content of an order request.
- **Numeral Conversion:** Converting spelled-out numbers into digits (e.g., "two bottles of milk" becomes "2 bottles of milk").
- **Contraction Expansion:** Expanding common contractions to their full form (e.g., "I'd like" becomes "I would like") to reduce ambiguity.

The input to the LLM becomes more consistent and predictable, allowing the model to focus its capacity on the core task of semantic parsing rather than on handling superficial variations in the input text.

3.4   Model Specialization and Optimization

The core of the system is a lightweight LLM that has been specialized for the ordering task and optimized for efficient deployment. This process involved selecting an appropriate base model, applying an efficient fine-tuning technique, and using post-training quantization to prepare the model for different deployment environments.

Base Model and LoRA Configuration. The base model selected is Google's Gemma-3 1B (Instruction-Tuned), chosen for its strong baseline performance and relatively small size (1B parameters), making it suitable for efficient fine-tuning and deployment. To adapt it for parsing shopping requests, Low-Rank Adaptation (LoRA) was used. LoRA adds small, trainable adapter matrices into the Transformer's attention mechanism. Adapters were injected into the Query, Key, Value, and Output projection matrices in each layer, with rank $r = 8$ and scaling factor $\alpha = 16$. During fine-tuning, the Gemma weights were frozen, updating only the LoRA matrices—training 1–2% of total parameters—reducing GPU memory usage.

While LoRA was adopted for its simplicity and efficiency, alternative PEFT methods such as Prefix-Tuning, AdapterFusion, and BitFit also offer potential benefits. These approaches differ in how they inject trainable parameters into the model, and comparative evaluation among them forms a promising direction for expanding this study's technical rigor.

Post-training Quantization for Mobile Deployment. To evaluate the feasibility of mobile deployment, post-training quantization was applied to the fine-tuned model, reducing weight precision to decrease size and improve inference speed. The GPTQ algorithm, known for maintaining high accuracy, was used [4].

The LoRA-tuned model, originally in 16-bit floating-point (FP16), was quantized to 8-bit (INT8) and 4-bit (INT4) formats after fine-tuning for inference optimization, while training used full-precision weights. The quantized models were benchmarked on simulated on-device hardware to assess trade-offs between model size, memory, and latency.

4   Experimental Results Analysis and Discussion

A comprehensive set of experiments was conducted to evaluate the performance of the proposed system. The evaluation focused on three key areas: the core accuracy of the semantic parsing task, a comparative analysis with alternative methodologies to contextualize the results, and a detailed examination of deployment efficiency metrics to assess the task's real-world viability.

4.1   Semantic Parsing Accuracy

The LoRA-tuned Gemma-3 1B model was evaluated on unseen user utterances from the held-out 20% of a 20,000-example synthetic dataset. The model achieved a 94.6% exact JSON match rate (Fig. 2a), indicating that most generated outputs perfectly matched the ground-truth labels. Slot-level F1 scores ranged from 96.8% to 97.2%, showing that even when exact matches were missed, nearly all item names and quantities were correctly extracted, with errors typically due to minor formatting issues or single-item omissions. Qualitative analysis confirmed that almost all responses were syntactically valid JSON, minimizing downstream parsing errors (Fig. 2c).

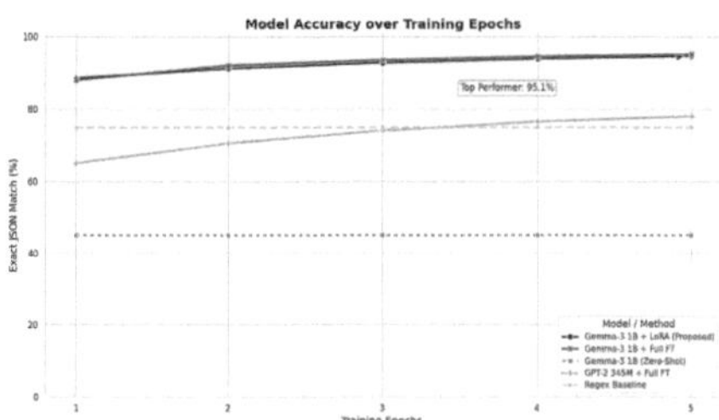

(a) Comparative analysis of Exact JSON Match accuracy across different methodologies.

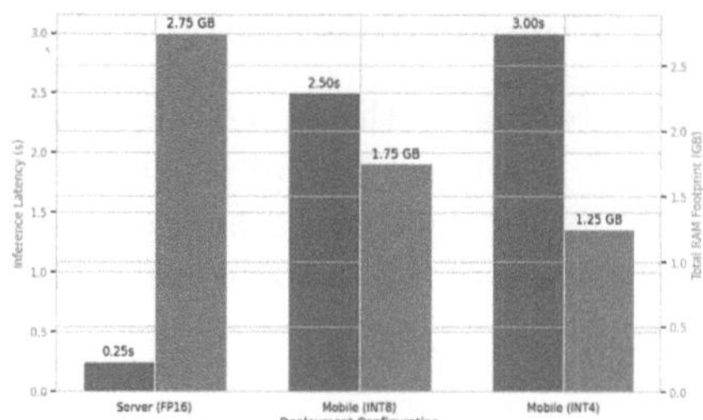

(b) Deployment efficiency trade-offs, comparing inference latency and memory footprint across configurations.

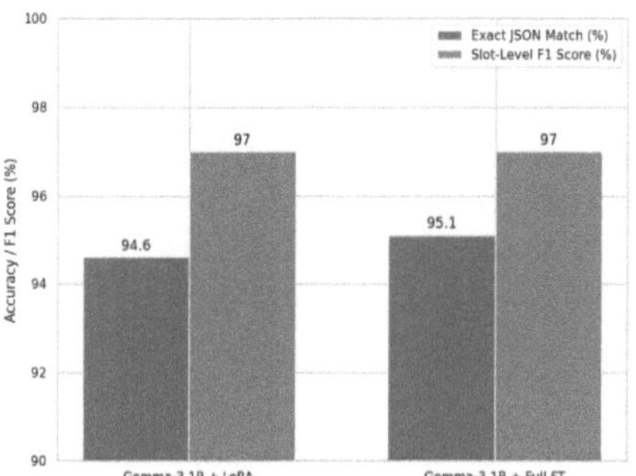

(c) Direct performance comparison between LoRA and Full Fine-Tuning, highlighting their near-identical accuracy.

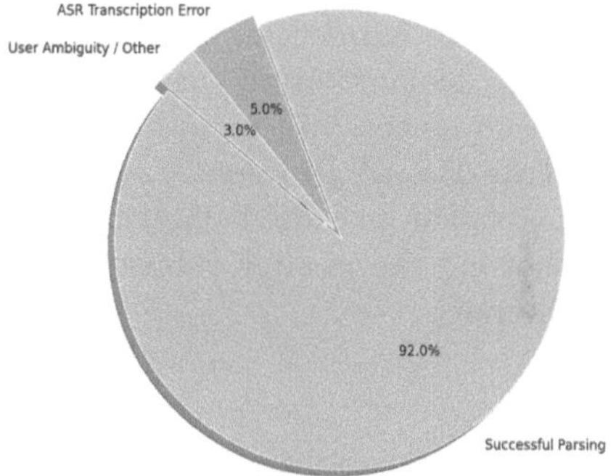

(d) Breakdown of end-to-end task outcomes, identifying ASR errors as the primary source of system failures.

Fig. 2. Visual summary of the system's performance and deployment characteristics.

These results underscore the effectiveness of parameter-efficient LoRA fine-tuning. Accuracy near that of fully fine-tuned models demonstrates that low-rank adapters can capture task-specific knowledge for narrow-domain semantic parsing, making this approach both practical and high-performing. Deployment analysis further highlights trade-offs (Fig. 2b): cloud-based inference offers near-instantaneous 0.3-s latency, whereas on-device deployment ensures privacy, offline capability, and zero operational cost, with a modest 2–3 s latency suitable for voice-first applications.

A notable insight is the shift in system bottlenecks. With slot-level F1 approaching 97%, parsing is largely solved; remaining end-to-end task failures (overall success 92%) arise from ASR errors or ambiguous user utterances (Fig. 2d). Future improvements should target ASR robustness and interactive dialogue strategies to handle ambiguity, as the LLM's high parsing accuracy has exposed preprocessing and user interaction as the key frontiers for enhancing overall system performance and user experience.

4.2   Comparative Analysis of Methodologies

To contextualize the LoRA-tuned model, its performance was compared against several baselines and alternatives, as summarized in Table 1. The proposed LoRA-based approach achieves performance nearly equivalent to full fine-tuning at a fraction of the training cost and significantly outperforms all other baselines.

- **Full Fine-Tuning:** The Gemma-3 1B model, fully fine-tuned on the dataset, achieved 95.1% exact match accuracy versus 94.6% for LoRA. This small gap indicates that LoRA, trained on only 2% of parameters, can nearly match the performance of full fine-tuning at a fraction of the cost.
- **Zero-Shot Baseline:** Without fine-tuning, the pre-trained Gemma-3 1B reached only 45%, highlighting the importance of task-specific adaptation for high accuracy.
- **Smaller Model:** A GPT-2 model (345M) fully fine-tuned achieved about 78%, demonstrating that larger models like Gemma-3 1B yield substantial improvements in this task.
- **Rule-Based Parser:** A regex-based parser handled about 75% of requests but failed on varied phrasing and synonyms (e.g., "grab me some cereal"), showing the greater robustness of LLMs in dealing with natural language diversity.

Table 1. Comparative analysis of parsing performance across different methodologies

Model/Method	Trainable Parameters	Exact JSON Match (%)	Slot-Level F1 (%)	End-to-End Task Success (%)
Gemma-3 1B + LoRA (Proposed)	˜1–2% of total	94.6	96.8–97.2	92.0
Gemma-3 1B + Full FT	100% of total	95.1	˜97.0	˜92.5
Gemma-3 1B Pre-trained (Zero-Shot)	0%	˜45.0	N/A	<45.0
GPT-2 345M + Full FT	100% of total	˜78.0	˜83.0	˜75.0
Regex Baseline	N/A	˜75.0	N/A	˜75.0

Additionally, to contextualize the system against external baselines, we compared its performance to reported results from recent structured output and PEFT studies. For example, JSONSchemaBench [6] reported 93–95% JSON compliance using 7B+ parameter models, while QLoRA-tuned models in [3] achieved 92–94% accuracy in semantic parsing tasks with significantly larger architectures. Our 1B-parameter LoRA-tuned Gemma model attains comparable accuracy (94.6%) with much lower computational overhead, demonstrating competitive efficiency.

4.3   Deployment Efficiency and Performance Trade-Offs

This research evaluated the system's deployment characteristics by benchmarking the fine-tuned model under different hardware and quantization settings. Key metrics included inference latency, throughput, and memory footprint (Table 2), where quantization enables a significant reduction in memory footprint, making on-device deployment feasible with modest latency trade-offs.

- **Server-Side Deployment (FP16):** On a server-grade GPU with 16-bit precision, the Gemma-3 1B + LoRA model achieved 200 tokens/s. A 50-token JSON took 0.25 s, with total RAM usage of 2.5–3 GB (weights $\sim$1.8 GB + cache $\sim$1 GB).
- **Mobile Deployment (INT8):** With 8-bit quantization on high-end smartphone hardware, speed was 20 tokens/s, yielding 2.5 s latency for 50 tokens. Memory dropped to 1.5–2 GB (quantized weights 0.9 GB), enabling feasibility on modern phones with 8 GB RAM.
- **Mobile Deployment (INT4):** Further 4-bit quantization reduced weights to 0.9 GB, offering more memory savings but with increased latency, representing another deployment trade-off.

Table 2. Deployment efficiency metrics across different configurations

Configuration	Inference Latency (s)	Throughput (tokens/s)	Weight Memory (GB)	Total RAM Footprint (GB)
Server (FP16)	~0.25	~200	~1.8	~2.5–3.0
Mobile (INT8)	~2.50	~20	~0.9	~1.5–2.0
Mobile (INT4)	>2.50	<20	~0.9	<1.5

5   Threats to Validity

A critical assessment of this study's methodology and results reveals several potential threats to the validity of its conclusions. Acknowledging these limitations is essential for contextualizing the findings and guiding future research.

5.1   Construct Validity

Construct validity concerns whether the metrics capture intended concepts. "Exact JSON Match" is strict, penalizing reordered or syntactic differences. Slot-level F1 misses overall correctness and hallucinations. User satisfaction was not measured; instead, accuracy was used.

5.2 External Validity

External validity assesses the generalizability of findings to other contexts. A key threat is the synthetic dataset, which may not capture real-world speech such as slang, errors, or multi-intent commands. Results are specific to English, with performance in other languages untested. Another limitation is the use of a single base model (Gemma-3 1B). Although selected for its optimal size-performance balance, validating the framework with other lightweight LLMs such as Phi-2 and Mistral-7B would strengthen claims of generalizability.

6 Conclusion and Future Scope

This research successfully built a lightweight and accurate voice-activated ordering agent. Using a compact 1B-parameter LLM with LoRA fine-tuning and quantization, the system achieved over 94% accuracy in converting spoken requests into structured data, proving that efficient models can rival larger ones at a fraction of the cost.

Building on the foundation established by this work, several promising avenues for future research can be identified:

1. **Handling Multi-Turn Dialogues:** The current agent handles one command at a time. A significant next step is to incorporate conversational memory. This would allow the system to handle multi-turn dialogues, enabling users to build and modify their orders through a more natural, back-and-forth conversation (e.g., "Add milk", followed by "Actually, make it oat milk").
2. **Improving ASR Robustness:** Transcription errors from the Automatic Speech Recognition (ASR) system are a primary cause of failure. Future efforts should focus on fine-tuning the ASR model itself. By training it on domain-specific audio that includes numerous product names, brands, and common background noises (like those in a home or car), its accuracy in understanding user requests can be significantly improved.
3. **Personalization:** The agent is currently user-agnostic. A valuable direction is to introduce personalization by integrating user profiles and purchase histories. A personalized agent could proactively suggest frequently bought items, understand a user's specific vocabulary for certain products, and streamline the process of re-ordering from a previous list, creating a more tailored experience.
4. **Exploring Advanced PEFT and Quantization:** The field of efficient AI is rapidly advancing. Future research should explore more advanced optimization techniques. This includes investigating methods like QLoRA, which integrates quantization directly into the training process [3], as well as other emerging Parameter-Efficient Fine-Tuning (PEFT) methods to optimize further the trade-off between high performance and low computational cost.

Overall, this work provides a replicable and empirically validated framework for deploying efficient LLM-based agents in e-commerce. By balancing accuracy, efficiency, and transparency, it serves as a practical contribution to the emerging field of deployable conversational systems.

References

1. Chen, H., Liu, X., Yin, D., Tang, J.: A survey on dialogue systems: recent advances and new frontiers. ACM SIGKDD Explor. Newsl. **19** (2017). https://doi.org/10.1145/3166054.3166058
2. Chen, Y.C., Hsu, P.C., Hsu, C.J., Shiu, D.S.: Enhancing function-calling capabilities in LLMs: strategies for prompt formats, data integration, and multilingual translation. In: Chen, W., Yang, Y., Kachuee, M., Fu, X.Y. (eds.) Proceedings of the 2025 Conference of the Nations of the Americas Chapter of the Association for Computational Linguistics: Human Language Technologies (Volume 3: Industry Track), pp. 99–111. Association for Computational Linguistics, Albuquerque, New Mexico (2025). https://doi.org/10.18653/v1/2025.naacl-industry.9, https://aclanthology.org/2025.naacl-industry.9/
3. Dettmers, T., Pagnoni, A., Holtzman, A., Zettlemoyer, L.: QLORA: efficient fine-tuning of quantized LLMs. Adv. Neural. Inf. Process. Syst. **36**, 10088–10115 (2023)
4. Frantar, E., Ashkboos, S., Hoefler, T., Alistarh, D.: GPTQ: accurate post-training quantization for generative pre-trained transformers (2023). https://arxiv.org/abs/2210.17323
5. Geng, S., et al.: Generating structured outputs from language models: benchmark and studies. arXiv e-prints, pp. arXiv–2501 (2025)
6. Geng, S., et al.: JSONSchemaBench: a rigorous benchmark of structured outputs for language models. arXiv preprint arXiv:2501.10868 (2025)
7. Han, Z., Gao, C., Liu, J., Zhang, J., Zhang, S.Q.: Parameter-efficient fine-tuning for large models: a comprehensive survey. Trans. Mach. Learn. Res. (2024). https://openreview.net/forum?id=lIsCS8b6zj
8. Hooper, C., et al.: FGMP: fine-grained mixed-precision weight and activation quantization for hardware-accelerated LLM inference. arXiv preprint arXiv:2504.14152 (2025)
9. Hu, E.J., et al.: LoRA: low-rank adaptation of large language models. In: ICLR, vol. 1, no. 2, p. 3 (2022)
10. Hussain, S., Ameri Sianaki, O., Ababneh, N.: A survey on conversational agents/chatbots classification and design techniques. In: Barolli, L., Takizawa, M., Xhafa, F., Enokido, T. (eds.) WAINA 2019. AISC, vol. 927, pp. 946–956. Springer, Cham (2019). https://doi.org/10.1007/978-3-030-15035-8_93
11. Mündler, N., Dekoninck, J., Vechev, M.: Constrained decoding of diffusion LLMs with context-free grammars (2025). https://arxiv.org/abs/2508.10111
12. Tangarajan, P., Rajasekar, A.A., Rathi, M., Dandin, V.R., Ersoy, O.: Contextually aware e-commerce product question answering using rag. arXiv preprint arXiv:2508.01990 (2025)
13. Wang, L., et al.: Parameter-efficient fine-tuning in large language models: a survey of methodologies. Artif. Intell. Rev. **58**(8), 227 (2025)
14. Yao, Z., Xu, Y., Xu, H., Liao, Y., Xie, Z.: Efficient deployment of large language models on resource-constrained devices. arXiv preprint arXiv:2501.02438 (2025)

Multi-head Multi-latent Attention: An Efficient Approach to Realize a Low-Resource Transformer Architecture

Soutrik Das[(✉)] [iD] and Arnab Santra [iD]

Department of Computer Science and Engineering, Heritage Institute of Technology, Kolkata 700107, West Bengal, India
soutrikdas.mlwork@gmail.com

Abstract. Multi-head self attention provides strong representational performance but is computationally expensive, which limits its applicability in low-resource environments. Although Multi-Head Latent Attention alleviates the key-value cache bottleneck by compressing representations into a latent space, model training remains computationally demanding, particularly under resource constraints. Our objective is to further reduce the number of learnable parameters in Multi-Head Latent Attention by pre-multiplying the query and key weights, since these matrices are ultimately multiplied during attention computation and by introducing a modified architecture that incorporates a latent space for both the queries and key-value latent representation weights. We refer to this approach as Multi-Head Multi-Latent Attention (MMLA). The experimental results indicate a performance comparable to MSA, accompanied by a 47% reduction in training time. These findings suggest that MMLA not only achieves superior efficiency but also outperforms models with comparable parameter counts, positioning it as a more cost-effective and computationally practical alternative to existing attention mechanisms.

Keywords: Multi-Head Multi-Latent Attention · Efficient Transformer · Attention Mechanisms · Low-Resource Summarization · Parameter Reduction

1 Introduction

Attention mechanisms, particularly multi-head self attention (MSA), have become a cornerstone of modern deep learning, driving progress in natural language processing, computer vision, and other domains. MSA is the core operation within the Transformer architecture proposed by [Vaswani et al., 2017] [7], which underlies most modern large language models. Its ability to capture long-range dependencies and contextual relationships has led to major performance gains across diverse tasks. In MSA, each head learns separate query–key interactions and aggregates values, enabling diverse attention patterns, but this comes

C. Zaroliagis et al. (Eds.): ICAA 2026, LNCS 16423, pp. 314–325, 2026.
https://doi.org/10.1007/978-3-032-15621-1_26

at a high computational and memory cost, making training and deployment difficult in low-resource environments. Recent approaches such as Multi-Head Latent Attention (MLA) proposed by [Ren et al., 2024] [6] alleviate this bottleneck by projecting keys and values into a lower-dimensional latent space before computing attention, thereby reducing the key-value cache bottleneck. However, challenges in training efficiency and parameter scalability remain.

Several efficient attention mechanisms have been proposed to reduce cost. The Linformer model proposed by [Wang et al., 2020] [8] reduces the quadratic cost of attention by projecting the key and value matrices into a lower-dimensional subspace using learnable linear projections. This yields attention complexity linear in sequence length while preserving accuracy close to full self attention. The Reformer architecture proposed by [Kitaev et al., 2020] [3] applies locality-sensitive hashing with reversible layers, whereas The Performer model introduced by [Choromanski et al., 2021] [2] employs the FAVOR+ kernel for linear-time softmax approximation. Other sparse and memory-based strategies have been explored, such as the Longformer model [Beltagy et al., 2020] [1] and EMMA [Moro et al., 2023] [4] with chunked cross-memory attention. Other methods based on Sparse Attention techniques [Phang et al., 2023] [5] have shown that simple local or global-local sparsity can also match more complex designs.

While effective, these methods have drawbacks: fixed projections reduce flexibility [8], hashing can be unstable [3], and sparsity or memory schemes may limit generality [1,4,5]. These limitations highlight the need for an approach that reduces memory and computation without sacrificing adaptability or training stability. To address these challenges, we propose Query–Key Weight Combination (MLAC) which replaces the pre-multiplication with a single matrix and Multi-Head Multi-Latent Attention (MMLA), an efficient Transformer attention mechanism that compresses both query and key–value projections to reduce learnable parameters and training cost. In this work, we also reviewed the extensive computational requirements of MSA and MLA, which were addressed by our proposed method.

2   Preliminaries: Foundational Models

2.1   Multi-head Self-attention

Multi-Head Self-Attention (MSA) [7] projects the input sequence X into queries (Q), keys (K), and values (V) using learned weight matrices W_Q, W_K, and W_V:

$$Q = XW_Q, \quad K = XW_K, \quad V = XW_V$$

Attention scores are computed as

$$A = \mathrm{softmax}\left(\frac{QK^T}{\sqrt{d_k}}\right),$$

which determine token-to-token dependencies. Each head output is

$$O_i = AV,$$

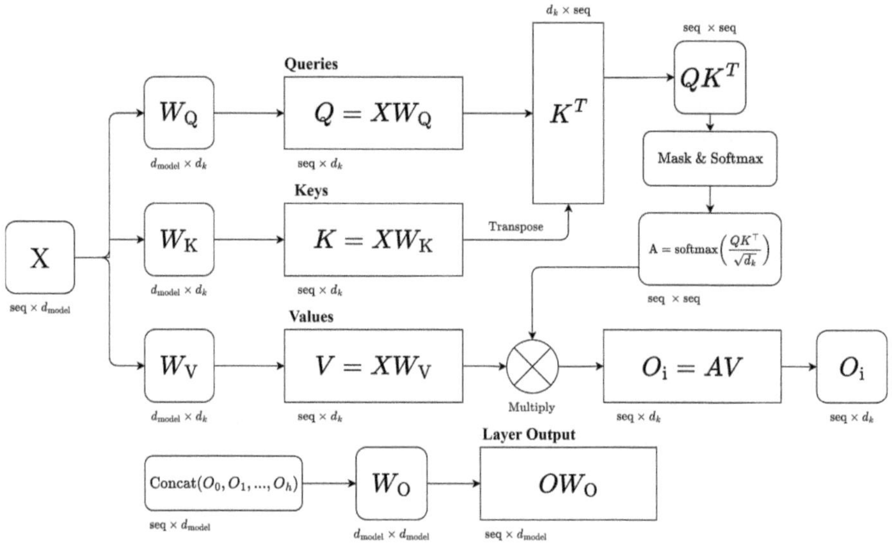

Fig. 1. Illustration of the Multi-Head Self-Attention mechanism.

and concatenated as

$$O = \mathrm{Concat}(O_1, \ldots, O_h)W_O.$$

Thus,

$$\mathrm{MSA}(X) = \mathrm{Concat}(O_1, \ldots, O_h)W_O.$$

While multi-head design captures diverse contextual relations, the computation of QK^T scales quadratically with sequence length, making MSA memory- and compute-intensive. Each head maintains separate key and value projections, further increasing GPU/VRAM demand, particularly for long sequences (Figs. 1, 5 and 6).

Learnable Parameters ($N_{\mathbf{MSA}}$) For an MSA layer:

$$N_{\mathrm{MSA}} = (W_Q + W_K + W_V) \times h + W_O$$
$$= 3(d_{\mathrm{model}} \times d_k \times h) + d_{\mathrm{model}}^2.$$

Since $d_k = d_v = \frac{d_{\mathrm{model}}}{h}$,

$$\boxed{N_{\mathrm{MSA}} = 4d_{\mathrm{model}}^2} \tag{1}$$

2.2 Multi-head Latent Attention

Multi-Head Latent Attention (MLA) [6] introduces a latent projection L_{KV} that compresses the input before generating keys and values:

$$Q = XW_Q, \quad L_{KV} = XW_{DKV}, \quad K = L_{KV}W_{UK}, \quad V = L_{KV}W_{UV}.$$

Here, W_{DKV} maps the input to a lower-dimensional latent space, and W_{UK}, W_{UV} transform it into key and value spaces. This decomposition preserves learning flexibility while reducing cache and compute cost. Attention computation proceeds as in MSA. This latent design captures diverse attention patterns and reduces key–value cache size. Inference is faster, but training remains costly.

After simplification:

$$QK^T = X(W_Q W_{UK}^T)L_{KV}^T, \quad O = (AL_{KV})W_{UV}.$$

This results in the simplified form shown in Fig. 2.

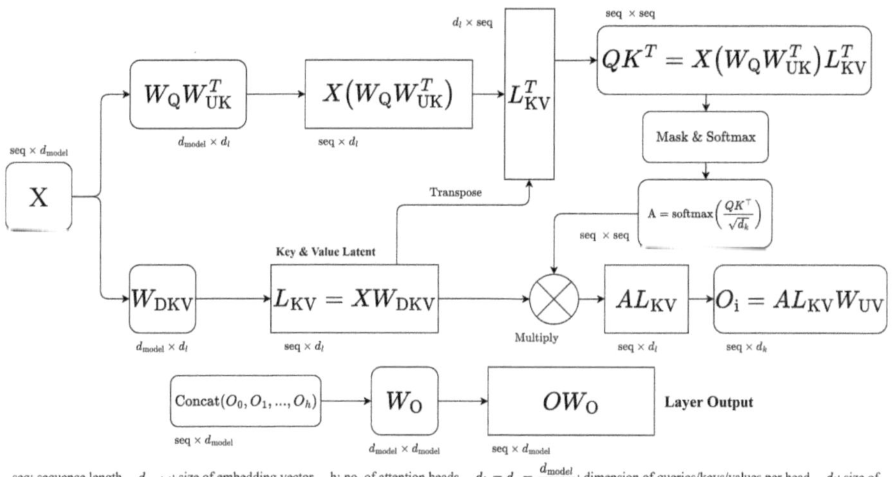

Fig. 2. Simplified Multi-Head Latent Attention (MLA) mechanism.

Learnable Parameters (N_{MLA})

$$N_{\mathrm{MLA}} = (W_Q + W_{UK} + W_{UV}) \times h + W_O + W_{DKV}$$
$$= 2d_{\mathrm{model}}^2 + 3d_{\mathrm{model}}d_l.$$

$$\boxed{N_{\mathrm{MLA}} = 2d_{\mathrm{model}}^2 + 3d_{\mathrm{model}}d_l} \tag{2}$$

3   Related Work

3.1   Efficient Attention Mechanisms

Many approaches address the quadratic cost of multi-head self-attention (MSA). Linformer [8] projects K/V into low-rank subspaces for linear scaling. MMLA also compresses Q/K, but with learned latent vectors instead of fixed projections.

Reformer [3] reduces cost via locality-sensitive hashing and reversible layers ($O(N \log N)$). Performer [2] achieves linear complexity through FAVOR+, a kernel-based approximation of softmax attention. Unlike these, MMLA directly learns latent Q/K representations rather than relying on random hashing or kernel features.

3.2   Efficient Transformers for Summarization

Efficiency has also been explored in summarization. It [1] adapts sliding-window and global attention to encoder–decoder models, enabling long-input summarization. Emma [4] introduces memory-augmented attention to carry information across document chunks. Phang et al. [5] show block-local + sparse global attention can match BigBird with lower memory cost. These are complementary to MMLA, which reduces cost by compressing attention internally rather than adding memory or enforcing sparsity.

4   Methodology

Building upon the discussion of Multi-Head Self Attention (MSA) [7] and Multi-Head Latent Attention (MLA) [6], and their associated computational costs, we now present the techniques proposed to reduce these requirements. Specifically, we explore two modifications aimed at decreasing the number of learnable parameters: (i) combining the query and key weight matrices, and (ii) introducing a latent space for compressing both the query weights and the key-value latent representations or simply Multi-Head Multi-Latent Attention (MMLA). In the following subsections, we describe these techniques in detail, outlining the architectural changes to the attention mechanism and analyzing their impact on parameter count and training time.

4.1   Query-Key Weight Combination (MLAC)

In MLA [6], queries and keys are obtained through distinct projection matrices W_Q and W_K, even though the attention computation ultimately reduces to $QK^\top$. To eliminate this redundancy, we replace $QK^\top$ with a shared projection matrix W_{QUK} such that

$$Q = XW_{QUK}, \quad K^\top = L_{KV}^\top, \quad L_{KV} = XW_{DKV}.$$

The attention scores are then computed directly as

$$QK^\top = (XW_{QUK})L_{KV}^\top.$$

This modification attempts to reduce the number of parameters by combining W_Q and W_K into a single matrix W_{QUK}. Based on this modification, the modified architecture is represented in Fig. 3. For notation purposes in later sections, we refer to this as Multi-Head Latent Attention Combined (MLAC).

The motivation for introducing a single projection W_{QUK} stems from the observation that in MLA, the query and key projections W_Q and W_{UK} are eventually multiplied during attention computation, i.e., $(XW_Q)(L_{KV}W_{UK})^{\top}$. Instead of maintaining two independent matrices that are later pre-multiplied, we combine them into a unified learnable transformation W_{QUK}. This avoids redundant pre-multiplication operations, reduces intermediate computation, and simplifies parameter flow—an important design consideration for low-resource environments. Consequently, MLAC serves as a lightweight variant that trades a small amount of expressiveness for improved training efficiency.

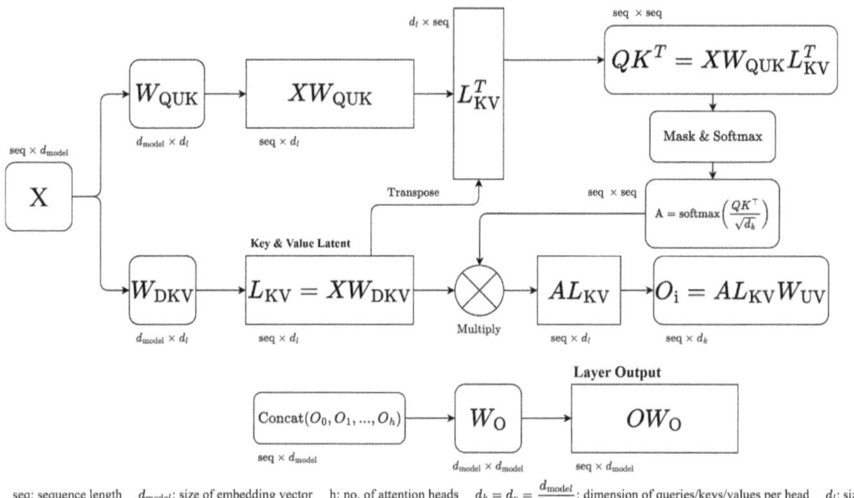

Fig. 3. Architecture of the proposed query–key weight combination.

Number of Learnable Parameters (N_{MLAC}) of Multi-Head Latent Attention after Query-Key Weight Combination.

$$N_{\text{MLA}} = (W_{\text{QUK}} \times h) + (W_{\text{UV}} \times h) + W_O + W_{DKV}$$

Expanding this expression, we get

$$= (d_{\text{model}} \times d_l \times h) + (d_l \times d_k \times h) + (d_{\text{model}} \times d_{\text{model}}) + (d_{\text{model}} \times d_l)$$

$$= h d_{\text{model}} d_l + d_{\text{model}} d_l + d_{\text{model}}^2 + d_{\text{model}} d_l$$

$$= (h + 2) d_{\text{model}} d_l + d_{\text{model}}^2$$

$$\boxed{N_{\text{MLAC}} = (h + 2) d_{\text{model}} d_l + d_{\text{model}}^2} \tag{3}$$

4.2   Multi-head Multi-latent Attention (MMLA)

In MLA [6], only the key–value pairs are compressed into a latent space, while queries are generated directly from the full input dimension. To further reduce the number of learnable parameters, we extend this idea by also compressing the input before query generation. Concretely, we introduce a shared compression matrix W_C that first maps the input X into a lower-dimensional latent representation L'. All subsequent projections for both queries and key–values are then computed from this compact representation. This design ensures that W_{QUK} and W_{DKV} operate in a reduced space, lowering parameter counts while preserving the ability to model input dependencies. Introducing a query-compression matrix W_C that maps the input into a low-dimensional latent space:

$$L' = XW_C \qquad (X \in \mathbb{R}^{\mathrm{seq} \times d_{\mathrm{model}}}, \ W_C \in \mathbb{R}^{d_{\mathrm{model}} \times d_c}).$$

Both queries and the key–value latent projection are produced from this compressed representation:

$$Q = L'W_{QUK}, \qquad L_{KV} = L'W_{DKV},$$

where $W_{QUK} \in \mathbb{R}^{d_c \times d_l}$ and $W_{DKV} \in \mathbb{R}^{d_c \times d_l}$. Equivalently, in terms of the original input,

$$Q = X(W_C W_{QUK}), \qquad L_{KV} = X(W_C W_{DKV}).$$

Hence, the attention score matrix can be written compactly as

$$QK^\top = (L'W_{QUK})(L'W_{DKV})^\top = L'W_{QUK}W_{DKV}^\top L'^\top,$$

or, expanded to show the compression explicitly,

$$QK^\top = (XW_C W_{QUK})(XW_C W_{DKV})^\top.$$

This formulation makes explicit that W_C precompresses both W_{QUK} and W_{DKV}, i.e., the effective input-to-query and input-to-key/value maps are $W_C W_{QUK}$ and $W_C W_{DKV}$. The W_C is shared across all heads in a layer. The overall structure of the proposed Multi-Head Multi-Latent Attention (MMLA) architecture is illustrated in Fig. 4.

Number of Learnable Parameters (N_{MMLA}) of Multi-Head Multi-Latent Attention.

$$N_{\mathrm{MMLA}} = W_C + (W_{\mathrm{QUK}} \times h) + (W_{\mathrm{UV}} \times h) + W_O + W_{DKV}$$

Expanding this expression:

$$= (d_{\mathrm{model}} \times d_c) + (d_c \times d_l \times h) + (d_l \times d_k \times h) + (d_{\mathrm{model}} \times d_{\mathrm{model}}) + (d_c \times d_l)$$

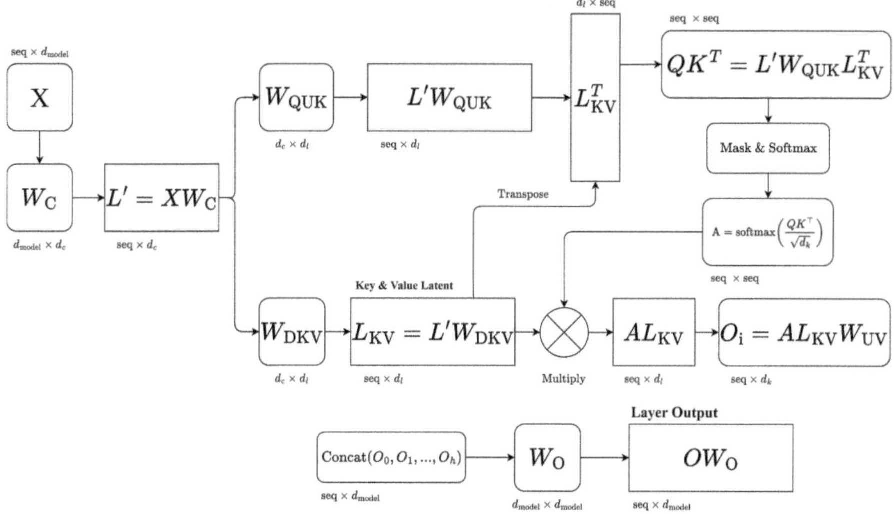

Fig. 4. Architecture of the proposed Multi-Head Multi-Latent Attention (MMLA).

Since $d_k = d_v = \frac{d_{\text{model}}}{h}$, we have:

$$= d_{\text{model}}d_c + hd_cd_l + d_{\text{model}}d_l + d^2_{\text{model}} + d_cd_l$$
$$= d_{\text{model}}d_c + (h+1)d_cd_l + d_{\text{model}}d_l + d^2_{\text{model}}$$

$$\boxed{N_{\text{MMLA}} = d_{\text{model}}d_c + (h+1)d_cd_l + d_{\text{model}}d_l + d^2_{\text{model}}} \tag{4}$$

Optimal Value of d_c to ensure reduction in the number of learnable parameters compared to MLA.

$$\boxed{N_{\text{MLA}} > N_{\text{MMLA}}} = 2d^2_{\text{model}} + 3d_{\text{model}}d_l > d_{\text{model}}d_c + (h+1)d_cd_l + d_{\text{model}}d_l + d^2_{\text{model}}$$
$$= d^2_{\text{model}} + 2d_{\text{model}}d_l > d_{\text{model}}d_c + (h+1)d_cd_l$$
$$= \frac{d^2_{\text{model}} + 2d_{\text{model}}d_l}{d_{\text{model}} + (h+1)d_l} > d_c$$

Hence, for the reduction of the number of parameters, the value of d_c should be,

$$\boxed{d_c < \frac{d^2_{\text{model}} + 2d_{\text{model}}d_l}{d_{\text{model}} + (h+1)d_l}} \tag{5}$$

5   Experimental Setup

To evaluate the effectiveness of the proposed Multi-Head Multi-Latent Attention (MMLA), We conducted experiments on benchmark summarization datasets. This section describes the datasets, baseline models, training configuration, and evaluation metrics.

5.1   Datasets

We used News Summarization Dataset by sbhatti(Kaggle) for benchmarking. The datasets contain news articles and their corresponding summaries. Due to time and computational constraints, 10% of the dataset was used. Standard preprocessing steps were applied, including tokenization, lowercasing, and truncation to a maximum sequence length of 1934 tokens, which is the dataset's 95th percentile.

5.2   Baselines

We compare our proposed methods, MLAC and MMLA, against preexisting foundational models like Multi-Head Self Attention(MSA) and Multi-Head Latent Attention(MLA).

All attention mechanisms are implemented within an encoder-decoder Transformer framework, following the Transformer architecture proposed by [Vaswani et al., 2017] [7], but trained with modified hyperparameters suited to our experimental setup.

5.3   Training Details

Models were implemented in PyTorch and trained on an NVIDIA RTX 3060 GPU. We used the Adam optimizer with learning rate $1e-4$, batch size of 16, and dropout rate of 0.1. All models were trained for 20 epochs while saving the model with the best validation loss. The configurations are as follows:

Batch size	16	Encoder/decoder layers	4 each
Dropout rate	0.1	Max input length	1024
Epochs	20	Max output length	256
Embedding size (d_{model})	256	KV latent size (MLA)	128
Heads	4	Compression latent size (MMLA)	64

Although this configuration produces smaller models than standard Transformer setups and does not match industry-level performance, we adopted it due to time and computational constraints. Our goal is not state-of-the-art results, but a controlled setting to evaluate the efficiency and effectiveness of different attention mechanisms.

We assessed summarization quality with Token Accuracy, Perplexity, and ROUGE (1/2/L), and training efficiency with Training Time, VRAM usage, and parameters per layer.

6   Results and Discussion

6.1   Performance Comparison

Table 1 presents the Parameter count, Training Time and VRAM usage of MSA, MLA, MLAC, and MMLA. Table 2 presents the Token accuracy, Perplexity, ROUGE-L, and Validation Loss. MMLA achieves comparable ROUGE scores to MSA while significantly reducing parameter count and training time.

Table 1. Efficiency comparison of attention mechanisms by parameters, speed, and memory usage.

Model	Parameters per layer	Training Time (min)	Memory VRAM (GB)
MSA	262144	541.03	7.2
MLA	229376	534.00	7.3
MLAC	262144	549.74	7.5
MMLA	155648	287.71	3.6

Table 2. Accuracy and quality evaluation of attention mechanisms on summarization.

Model	Token Accuracy	Perplexity	ROUGE-L	Validation Loss
MSA	0.3043	88.4934	0.1465	4.5173
MLA	0.2950	84.4980	0.09338	4.5553
MLAC	0.2911	96.1401	0.0390	4.5998
MMLA	0.2937	85.6498	0.1316	4.5602

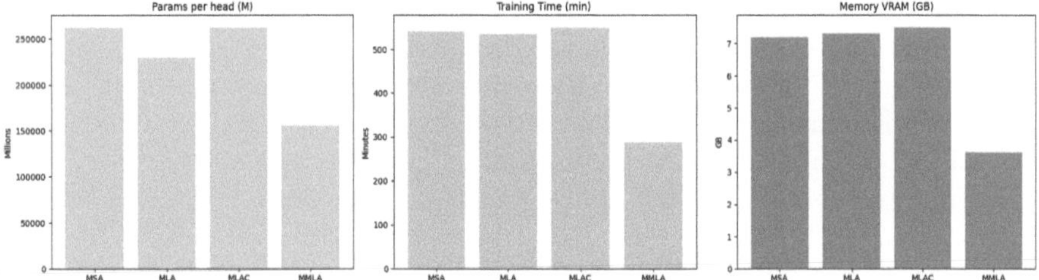

Fig. 5. Efficiency metrics of different attention mechanisms: Parameters per layer, Training time, and Memory VRAM.

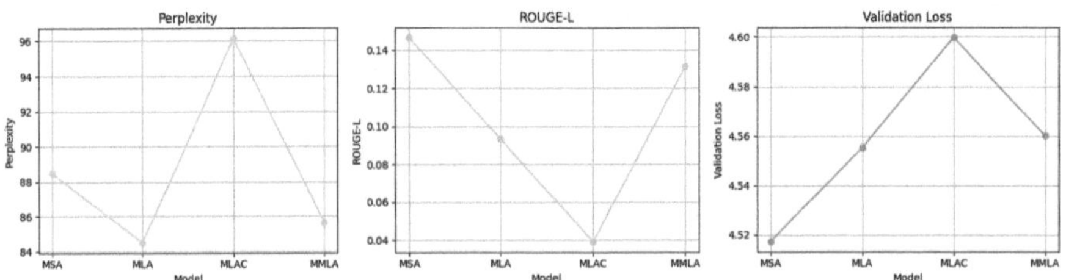

Fig. 6. Metrics of Different attention mechanisms: Perplexity, ROUGE-L, and Validation Loss.

6.2 Analysis

The experiments highlight clear differences among the four attention mechanisms. MMLA achieved the lowest parameter count (155,648 per layer), lowest memory usage (3.6 GB), and nearly halved training time compared to MSA (287.71 vs. 541.03 min), confirming the efficiency of query and latent representation compression.

In accuracy, MSA remained strongest (token accuracy 0.3043, ROUGE-L 0.1465). However, MMLA was close (0.2937 and 0.1316), outperforming MLA (0.09338 ROUGE-L) and MLAC (0.0390 ROUGE-L). Its perplexity (85.65) was also similar to MLA (84.49) and better than MLAC (96.14).

MLAC performed poorly, suggesting that combining query and key weights may lead to significant information loss. MLA, while effective for large-scale models, showed limited accuracy in this smaller setup, suggesting its benefits do not transfer directly to low-resource environments.

Overall, MMLA offers a strong efficiency–accuracy balance, cutting training time by ∼47% and memory by 50% compared to MSA, while retaining most of the performance. MLAC, by contrast, demonstrates that not all compression strategies are viable.

7 Conclusion

This paper introduced Multi-Head Multi-Latent Attention (MMLA) and the query–key weight combination to reduce parameters in W_{QUK} and W_{DKV}. Experiments on a summarization benchmark demonstrated that MMLA substantially reduced the parameter count, training time (47% faster), and memory usage (50% lower) compared to MSA. Despite these compressions, it maintained competitive accuracy, achieving a ROUGE-L score of 0.1316 versus 0.1465 for MSA, while outperforming both MLA (0.09338) and MLAC (0.0390). In terms of perplexity and token accuracy, MMLA performed on par with MLA, reinforcing its efficiency without sacrificing stability.

In contrast, MLAC degraded sharply, indicating notable information loss from query–key merging. While MLA performs well in larger models, it underperformed here, suggesting limited transferability to low-resource settings. Overall,

MMLA provides a cost-effective and efficient alternative to MSA with minimal accuracy loss, making it suitable for real-time or resource-constrained scenarios. By compressing both query and key–value projections, MMLA reduces per-head computational cost, offering a promising direction for lightweight Transformer designs. Though evaluated on summarization, its compression strategy is task-agnostic and can extend to applications like question answering or recommendation. Future work includes scaling to larger datasets, deeper or multilingual models, and integration with efficient variants such as Performer, Linformer, and FlashAttention.

Acknowledgment. The authors acknowledge our research teammates in the Department of Computer Science and Engineering, Heritage Institute of Technology, for technical support in deploying the model. The research team members are as follows: Prof. Sandip Samaddar, Yubaraj Das, and Tani Raj

References

1. Beltagy, I., Peters, M.E., Cohan, A.: Longformer: the long-document transformer. arXiv preprint arXiv:2004.05150 (2020). https://arxiv.org/abs/2004.05150
2. Choromanski, K., et al.: Rethinking attention with performers. In: International Conference on Learning Representations (ICLR) (2021). https://arxiv.org/abs/2009.14794
3. Kitaev, N., Kaiser, Ł., Levskaya, A.: Reformer: the efficient transformer. In: International Conference on Learning Representations (ICLR) (2020). https://arxiv.org/abs/2001.04451
4. Moro, G., Pasini, A., Ragazzi, D., Lippi, M., Torroni, P.: Emma: efficient memory-enhanced transformer. Sensors **23**(5), 2582 (2023). https://doi.org/10.3390/s23052582, https://pmc.ncbi.nlm.nih.gov/articles/PMC10098576/
5. Phang, J., et al.: Efficient summarization with sparse attention. In: Proceedings of the 2023 Conference on Empirical Methods in Natural Language Processing (EMNLP) (2023). https://aclanthology.org/2023.emnlp-main.240.pdf
6. Ren, Z., et al.: DeepSeek-V2: a strong, economical, and efficient mixture-of-experts language model. arXiv preprint arXiv:2405.04434 (2024). https://arxiv.org/abs/2405.04434
7. Vaswani, A., et al.: Attention is all you need. In: Advances in Neural Information Processing Systems (NeurIPS), pp. 5998–6008 (2017). https://arxiv.org/abs/1706.03762
8. Wang, S., Li, B.Z., Khabsa, M., Fang, H., Ma, H.: Linformer: self-attention with linear complexity. In: International Conference on Learning Representations (ICLR) (2020). https://arxiv.org/abs/2006.04768

Leveraging Small-Object Detection in Satellite Imagery Using Dual Attention-Augmented Single-Stage CNN Model

Likhit Yammanuru, Nikhil Tom Jose, and Rimjhim Padam Singh[✉]

Department of Computer Science and Engineering, Amrita School of Computing,
Amrita Vishwa Vidyapeetham, Bengaluru, India
{bl.en.u4cse22233,bl.en.u4cse22240}@bl.students.amrita.edu,
ps_rimjhim@blr.amrita.edu

Abstract. Detection and tracking of small objects like vehicles, aeroplanes and ships from satellite imagery targets several critical applications in urban planning, air and sea traffic management, marine surveillance, disaster prediction and relief, etc. But accurately locating small-objects in large and complex satellite images is highly challenging due to loss of contextual information, blurred objects, diminished sizes, etc. This paper proposes a novel dual attention-integrated YOLO model to accurately detect small-objects in the stand Skyfusion dataset. The selected baseline YOLOv11s is fused with global attention and Efficient channel attention mechanisms at varying feature resolutions for retaining global contextual and spatial information along with channel interdependencies. The proposed work applies targeted data augmentation to oversample the Ship class instances and benchmarks the proposed technique against state-of-the-art models with the highest F-score and mAP of 72.4% and 71.3%. With minimal increase in parameters, the proposed model thus serves as a scalable and reliable solution for tiny object detection in challenging aerial imagery.

Keywords: SkyFusion · Satellite Imagery · YOLO models · Tiny Object Detection · Global Attention Mechanism (GAM) · Efficient Channel Attention (ECA)

1 Introduction

In the current globalized world, the capability to trace tiny objects and areas is essential in providing smart systems for urban development, climate monitoring, disaster relief, etc. Even the traffic control applications related to land, air and sea routes to track vehicles, planes and marine ships are of crucial importance and challenging. Such applications are not only essential for public safety but are also key to combating global environmental issues like minimizing harmful discharges through better tracking of heavy-duty vehicles. Yet, small object

C. Zaroliagis et al. (Eds.): ICAA 2026, LNCS 16423, pp. 326–337, 2026.
https://doi.org/10.1007/978-3-032-15621-1_27

detection in satellite images is an extremely challenging task owing to low resolution, cluttered background and extreme variation in object scale and orientation.

Traditional image processing techniques such as edge detection, histogram analysis and template matching, though powerful in controlled environments, tend to fail to generalize under such real-world complex conditions. These methods are unable to handle noise, changing perspectives and the high data volume encountered in satellite imagery. To overcome these shortcomings, researchers have been developing sophisticated deep learning-based approaches, particularly single-stage detectors like the You Only Look Once (YOLO) models, offering powerful real-time object detection with scalable performance. Though these models have proven to be highly efficient for detecting medium and large-sized objects, they fail in accurately detecting small and remotely sensed objects in aerial and satellite imagery, thereby leaving the area open for further research. The tiny objects hardly contribute to 2–3% of the image area, causing loss of information and shape. Hence, specialized techniques tailored for individual datasets are required for handling such tasks. Hence, to bridge the performance gap for detecting small-scale objects in dense satellite images, this paper introduces a novel single-stage CNN detector integrating attentions for targeted small-object detection in aerial satellite images. the key contribution of the paper are:

- A novel hybrid and light-weight object detector based on YOLOv11s integrating a Global attention mechanism (GAM) [1] and an Efficient channel attention network (ECA-Net) [2,3] for leveraging tiny object detection in SkyFusion dataset.
- Detailed analysis on the impact of attention integration in the baseline YOLOv11 model for enhanced detection.
- Detailed analysis of five recent state-of-art YOLO models namely, YOLOv8s, YOLOv9s, YOLO10s, YOLOv11s and YOLOv12s for baseline model selection and comparative analysis.
- Detailed performance analysis based on industry benchmark metrics including mean aveage precision (mAP), precision, recall, accuracy and F1-score.

With these contributions, the suggested model improves the real-world applicability of using deep learning models for accurate as well as effective object detection in satellite images. The paper is organized as follows: Sect. 2 covers the existing work, Sect. 3 covers the proposed methodology and experimental setups, Sect. 4 covers performance results and analysis, and Sect. 5 ends with a synopsis and direction for future research.

2   Literature Survey

Shunjun et al. [4] developed a High-resolution satellite aperture radar dataset (HRSID) targeting bulk ship detection in marine environments and benchmarked with existing CNN models for practical applications. Later in 2021, Zhang et al.

[5], developed a deep convolutional feature extractor using a multi-scale discriminator for robust vehicle detection in Unmanned Aerial Vehicle (UAV) images. The system targeted the detection of vehicles with varying scales but could not perform well when challenged with large variations in UAV image appearances. On the other hand, Wu et al. [6] developed LR-TSDet model for effective tiny ship detection from low-resolution images based on FFA and HASP modules. Although the model performed well with clearly visible ships, its performance was limited by the intrinsically low-resolution images, leading to blurred and corroded tiny ships. Haoran et al. [7] developed X-LineNet model to detect aircraft bottom-up using intersecting line segments. The model was promising when planes were at low altitudes, but its detection rate declined significantly at slightly higher altitudes.

Later in 2022, Han et al. (2022) [8] introduced a ship identification model employing EIRNet, DFF-Net and DMAM modules for improved feature extraction and understanding. While the performance was increased, the methods were computationally intensive and complex, thereby limiting their practical deployment. Jixiang et al. (2022) [9], introduced FSANet to enhance the accuracy and localization of minute object detection with reduced computational overhead. The FSA-Net model proved to be highly data dependent, thereby failing to generalize well across other datasets. It also had a requirement for significant resources. Ruonan et al. (2022) [10] implemented a vehicle detection scheme on mid-to-high altitude UAV imagery with great success. But its efficacy deteriorated when applied to low-altitude imagery, constraining its applicability across altitude transitions. Later, Chaoran et al. [11] combined HB-YOLO with BoT-SORT for enhanced detection and tracking of small objects in videos. While it worked efficiently in global context integration, it was computationally costly and extremely sensitive to noise.

In 2024, Chenyang et al. [12] reviewed techniques like Faster RCNN, Mask RCNN, YOLO variants, EfficientDet and RTD-Net for analyzing high accuracy and speed in detecting object in UAV images. These techniques, however, indicated poor robustness, high computation and inferior performance in the detection of small objects. With enhanced robustness and real-time performance, they faced higher complexity in models and optimization challenges. Renaud et al. [13] created ASTOD—a student-teacher method utilizing pseudo-label selection to avoid manual threshold tuning in satellite imagery data. The method struggled with hyperparameter search and dealing with class imbalance in training. Nahom et al. [14] assessed YOLOv8's speed and performance for aircraft and ship detection in satellite imagery. Although it was highly efficient, environmental sensitivity caused frequent false positives and negatives, particularly in the detection of airplanes and vessels. In a parallel study, Ayush et al. [15] used a weighted count object detection system for poverty identification using nightlight imagery with a Pearson's coefficient. Despite performing better than conventional CNNs, small-object detection and annotation sparsity were major concerns.

Debojyoti and Jelena [16], developed a detection model by combining Spatial pyramid pooling and Cross-stage partial network for feature extraction along with focal loss for hard sample adaptation. It improved baselines by 1.8% mAP on DOTA but had to rely on high-quality annotations. Etten et al. [17] analyzed urban expansion through the MUDS/SpaceNet 7 dataset with the SCOT score. Their model performance had difficulties fitting into geographical and environmental heterogeneity leading to poor metrics. Later, Adrian et al. [18] utilized the Landcover.ai dataset with road, building, woodland and water annotations to train DeepLabv3+ model using XceptionNet with 85.56% mIoU. The dataset did not have fine-level information, hence, heavy data augmentation was required for decent results. Mostafa et al. [19] utilized CSPDarknet-53 backbone with optimized YOLOv4 to detect objects in marine images taken by drones. The model attained 90% accuracy with 89% mAP values. The paper also demonstrated that applying pruning and quantization techniques could further upgrade the execution of the model. Rohit and Mubarak (2021) [20], presented RescueNet with a customized localization loss function for post-disaster building damage assessment with ResNet50 in satellite images. The model was helped by multi-scale feature extraction, but required enhancement in discriminating between building instances. Yutian at al. (2022) [21], employed Bayesian Deep Learning (BDL) for classifying satellite imagery, specifically in adversarial settings. While resilient, BDL models broke down when presented with visually different adversarial changes.

Several research works also exploited generative models for improving small-object detection. For instance, Bo et al. [22] applied generative models such as AODNet, MSDBN, and DFENet for image feature enhancement and restoration to enhance small-object detection. Later, Yi et al. [23] applied a conditional GAN (cGAN) for reconstruction of 3D buildings from DSM and PAN images. Though efficient in removing non-building objects, it struggled with issues such as missing vectorized boundaries and corner mismatches. Eric et al. (2021) [24], evaluated generating synthetic images with GANs for detecting rare objects, with 95% recall using RetinaNet. Although noise injection assisted in training, the GAN needed to be refined for stabilization. Irfan and Zhang al. (2024) [25] compared YOLOv5 to YOLOv11 on remote sensing datasets such as Airbus Aircraft and SkyFusion, targeting challenges of small objects and intricate backgrounds. Even after extensive research on YOLO and other CNN-based detectors for object detection, none of the models claimed to have handled all the challenges posed in small-obect detection by producing accurate results, thereby leaving the area open for further research.

3   System Architecture

The work presented in the paper for small-object detection develops the proposed method incrementally. Initially, the dataset augmentation is performed for handling the under-represented classes, followed by the best baseline model selection. After wars, the work individually integrates the selected attention mechanism into the baseline YOLO model to attain the final outperforming dual-attention integrated proposed model. The system architecture is presented in Fig. 1.

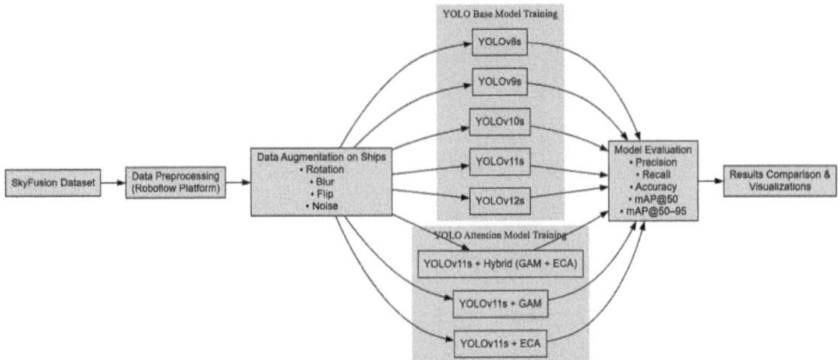

Fig. 1. System Architecture of the proposed work.

3.1   Dataset Description and Pre-Processing

The work employed the standard Skyfusion dataset, consisting of satellite images with 2000 images in the train set and 450 images each in the validation and test set. The images contains images from three classes, namely, ships, vehicles and aeroplanes. While the number of images in the dataset is roughly equal across all classes, the number of object instances is highly uneven and imbalanced, with the ship class having very few images. This hindered the model from effectively learning the distinctive features of Ships. Hence, the work performed targeted data augmentation to oversample the number of ship instances. Zoom, flip, rotation and blur techniques were utilized to synthetically increase ship instances within the data. This enhancement was particularly significant since ships looked like very tiny objects in satellite images, compared to larger and more context-providing classes such as planes and cars. Improving the depiction of ships served to enable the model to better identify them despite their small size and limited context.

3.2   Proposed Methodology

The model proposed in the work extends the lightweight YOLOv11s model with a Hybrid attention mechanism combining Global Attention Module (GAM) and Efficient Channel Attention (ECA), specifically to enhance the detection of densely packed and small-sized objects from satellite imagery. The YOLO11 architecture is primarily divided into three parts, the backbone, the neck and the head. The backbone is responsible for capturing deep features and key patterns within the images given as input. It uses a modified Cross Stage Partial (CSP) architecture, which is optimized for learning features while minimizing computational overhead. A CSP block (Fig. 4) works by dividing the input feature map, where one part goes through a recursive cascade of bottleneck convolution layers while the other part skips these recursive convolutions and is subsequently combined through a shortcut connection with the deep transformed features. This structure effectively allows the network to have robust gradient flow, eliminate redundant computations and obtain more efficient feature representation. In the C3k2 block of YOLO11 (Fig. 4.), two smaller convolutions are used along with cross-stage feature merging, which is an essential part of it, thereby securing an equal blend of directly retained low-level and deep modified high-level feature information.

The Neck part represents the parts in between the backbone and the head. It also implements the C3k2 block instead of the C2f block (Fig. 4.) to make the model comparatively more efficient and faster for inference. Further, the C2PSA spatial attention mechanism (Fig. 4.) is also incorporated in the neck which helps the model to focus on certain regions of the image, hence improving its performance in small object detection tasks. Finally, the head of the YOLO11 model takes care of the image detection task at different resolutions for detecting small, medium and large-sized objects to provide efficient output. With the help of multiple C3k2 and C3k blocks (Fig. 4.), the model has higher parameter efficiency and accuracy in the output. With the excellent performance of YOLOv11s, in the second stage, the model incorporates GAM and ECA attention mechanisms for enhancing its capacity to retain important features at different layers of the network.

Global Attention Module (GAM) : It [1] is geared towards capturing long-range dependencies by prioritizing spatial and channel-wise relationships sequentially across layers. The input feature map is fed to the channel attention module for channel permutations, followed by a double-layer dense network for representing the dependencies at a magnified scale. These dependencies are reshaped and subsequently fed into the spatial attention module. The spatial attention block works similar to BAM attention and applies double convolution layers with a reduction ratio. The block doesn't employ any pooling layer for downsampling, which involves higher learned parameters. This structure is especially useful for detecting tiny and sparsely distributed objects in crowded satellite imagery. By maintaining global contextual information, GAM augments the model's capacity to concentrate on critical features while handling intricate scenes. The YOLOv11s model augmented with GAM consists of 205 layers, about 18 million parameters, and 37.3 GFLOPs of computational load. Figure 2 demonstrates the architecture components of the GAM attention model.

Efficient Channel Attention (ECA) : To preserve efficiency while enhancing feature selection, the Efficient Channel Attention (ECA) [3] mechanism is integrated into YOLOv11s. In contrast to conventional attention modules that could introduce complexity in forms of dimensionality reduction or fully con-

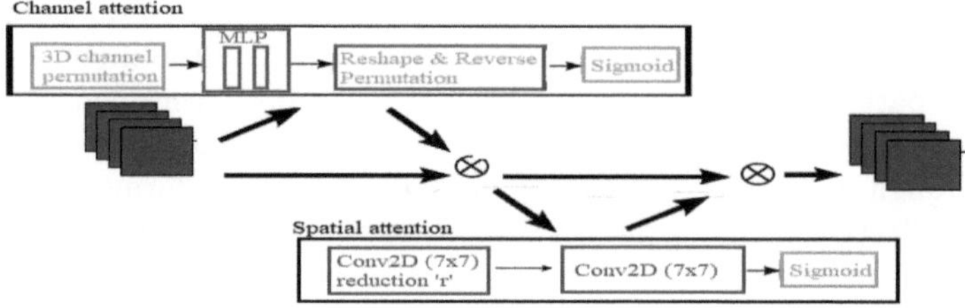

Fig. 2. Architecture of the GAM attention mechanism.

nected layers, ECA uses a local cross-channel interaction approach lacking a large increase in model size. The module makes the network more sensitive to important features through channel-wise information adaptively reweighting, which is essential for identifying tiny variations of small objects. The YOLOv11s + ECA model strikes a robust balance between efficiency and performance, leveraging 190 layers, roughly 9.4 million parameters and 21.6 GFLOPs—making it a very effective yet lightweight substitute for more sophisticated attention modules. Figure 3 demonstrates the architecture of ECA attention model:

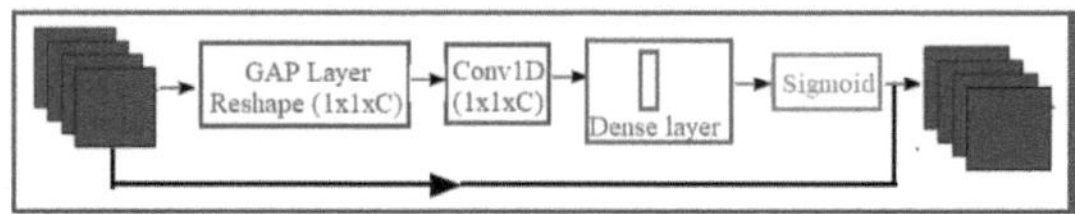

Fig. 3. Architecture of ECA attention mechanism.

Since both modules are strong, representing different aspects of the feature vectors, a Hybrid YOLO model is proposed by integrating both modules into YOLOv11s as presented in Fig. 4. The GAM provides strong global spatial perception, hence, it has been added in between the neck region with detections in the smallest feature resolution. The GAM attention module is inserted immediately following layer 16 in the YOLOv11s neck/head structure at the smallest feature map resolution, P3/8 (256 channels), and the ECA module is placed after layer 22 at the largest feature map resolution, P5/32 (1024 channels). While ECA has been integrated at the end of the neck, representing the largest feature map as it provides effective and concentrated channel-wise weighting. This positioning covers both fine spatial context and broad channel-wise information for improved small object detection.This Hybrid configuration is supposed to catch both coarse-grained contextual relations and high-level discriminative details—a critical pair for tiny object recognition in high-resolution remote sensing images. This combination results in a model that provides high precision at the cost of only a reasonably small increase in computational load. The proposed

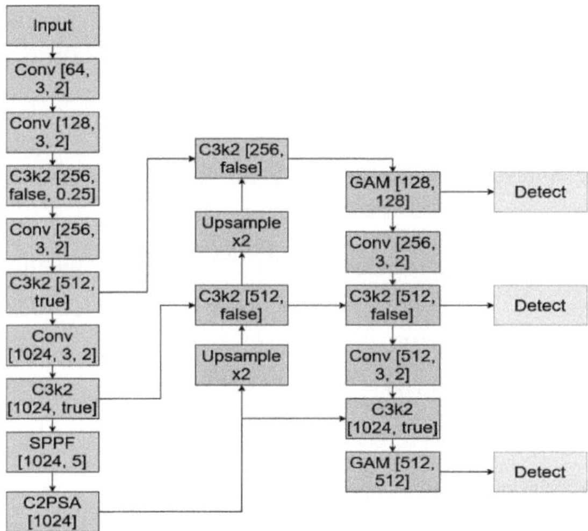

Fig. 4. Flowchart of the Hybrid attention-enhanced YOLOv11s model integrating GAM and ECA modules.

Hybrid YOLOv11s model has 192 layers, around 9.8 million parameters and 26.8 GFlOPs, providing the overall best performance in terms of precision, recall and mAP on Skyfusion dataset.

4 Experimental Results and Analysis

For the selection of the YOLOv11s as the baseline model, the work implemented a total of five recent YOLO models with a fixed configuration. Each model was trained with an image size of 640 × 640 pixels, for more than 150 epochs and with a learning rate of 0.01. These hyperparameters were fixed as standards to provide adequate learning, particularly for the attention-augmented variants, without compromising uniformity between experiments. This arrangement allows for isolating the effect of different YOLO models and attention modules on performance while being free from bias due to varying training parameters.

Table 1 shows a comparative study on the impact of attention integrations into the YOLOv11s model using all important performance metrics of Precision, Recall, F1-Score, mAP@50 and mmAP@50:95. The baseline YOLOv11s model has a precision of 73.5% and an mAP@50 of 67.2%. When the Global Attention Module (GAM) is added, all metrics improved marginally with the mAP@50 increasing to 69.7% with a 2% improvement. The stricter metric of mmAP@50:95 also showed a tremendous increase of 3%, claiming better detection even at higher thresholds. The ECA-improved YOLOv11s model also performs better, achieving a precision of 76.3% and an even higher mAP@50 of 70%. The best performing model attained by leveraging YOLOv11s is the Hybrid attention model. This dual attention model acheived 4% in precision, mAP and mmAP metrics, reaching the highest F1-score of 72.4% and the highest mmAP@50:95 of 40.4%. The results show improved small-object detection through combining spatial and channel-wise attention mechanisms.

Table 1. Impact analysis of integrating single and dual attention into YOLOv11s model

Model	Precision	Recall	F1-Score	mAP @50	mAP @50–95
YOLOv11s	0.735	0.651	0.690	0.672	0.368
YOLOv11s + GAM	0.75	0.671	0.708	0.697	0.391
YOLOv11s + ECA	0.763	0.67	0.713	0.7	0.392
YOLOv11s + Hybrid	**0.772**	**0.683**	**0.724**	**0.713**	**0.404**

Next, the paper compares the performance of several state-of-the-art object detection architectures on the SkyFusion aerial object detection dataset against the proposed model using Precision, Recall, F1-Score, mAP@50, and mmAP@50:95.

Table 2. Performance comparison of the proposed model against state-of-art architectures on Skyfusion dataset

Model	Precision	Recall	F1-Score	mAP@50	mmAP@50:95
YOLOv8s	0.717	0.619	0.665	0.645	0.355
YOLOv8x [25]	0.605	0.75	0.67	0.653	0.379
YOLOv9s	0.732	0.64	0.687	0.663	0.367
YOLOv10s	0.718	0.635	0.674	0.66	0.368
YOLOv11s	0.735	0.651	0.690	0.672	0.368
YOLOv12s	0.723	0.627	0.672	0.645	0.35
Hybrid	**0.772**	**0.683**	**0.724**	**0.713**	**0.404**

Table 2 presents the comparisons of the proposed model against state-of-the-art object detection model. Here, YOLOv8s which prioritizes object detection in real-time with optimized speed and accuracy, employs a lightweight CSPDarknet backbone and convolutional blocks with high efficiency. Even with the integrated SiLU activation with skip connections to retain spatial information, the model obtained the lowest results with merely 64% of mAP and 35% of mmAP. While YOLOv9s which incorporates the Programmable Gradient Information (PGI) and the Generalized Efficient Layer Aggregation Network (GELAN) to overcome gradient bottlenecks and retain vital information through deep layers, could not outperform the proposed model. These sophisticated advancements to retain low and high level features with enhanced parameter efficiency and computation aided the model in attaining decent yet lesser detection results with 66% mAP and 69% fscore values.

On the other hand, YOLOv10s employs CSPDarknet-based backbone, GhostNet blocks and skip connections along with attention mechanism and efficient Non-Maximum Suppression (NMS) to support strong multi-scale feature extraction for small or occluded objects at minimized redundancy. However, it performed poorly with the Skyfusion dataset with mAP@50 of 66% merely. The most recent YOLOv12s model that includes a Residual-Efficient Layer Aggregation Network backbone to handle gradient bottlenecks and FlashAttention in the neck for effective area attention also could not outperform the proposed Hybrid model. It has to be noted that even the extra-large version YOLOv8x, with the highest learnable parameters achieved a relatively strong recall of 75% but with a lower precision of 60.5% and F1-score of 67%, indicating that it produces more false positives compared to our proposed hybrid model.

The proposed Hybrid-augmented variant of YOLOv11s exhibited a significant improvement in all measures. With the addition of GAM individualy, global spatial reasoning is enhanced and mAP@50 increases to 69.7%, while adding ECA solely enhances inter-channel sensitivity with fewer added parameters and results in a slight increase in mAP@50 to 70%. The final Hybrid YOLOv11s model, provides the best performance with the highest accuracy of 77.2%, F1-score of 72.4% and mmAP@50:95 of 40.4%, further validating its better performance in detecting small and complicated aerial targets.

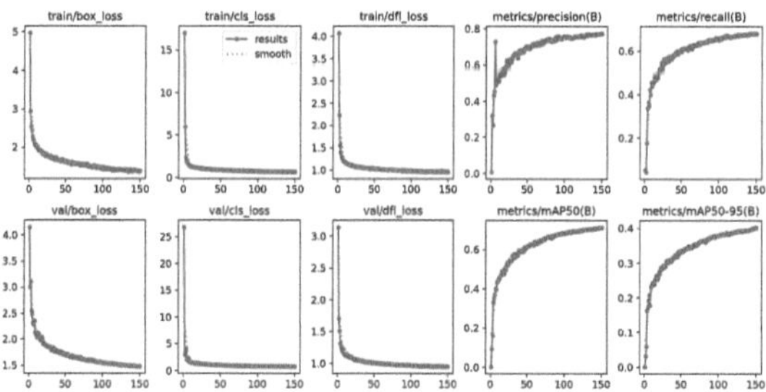

Fig. 5. Loss/Accuracy of Hybrid model.

To illustrate training dynamics and corroborate these results, Fig. 5 plots the training and validation loss/accuracy of the top-performing model—GAM and ECA-integrated Hybrid YOLOv11s model for 150 epochs. The graphs reflect consistent convergence for all metrics with minimal overfitting, suggesting strong generalization and efficient learning of spatial and channel-wise attention features. Figure 6 demonstrates four examples of sample predictions produced by the proposed Hybrid YOLOv11s model with GAM and ECA attention mechanism. The accurate detections even in dense situations effectively demonstrate its accuracy and suitability for the underlying real-world inference task.

Fig. 6. Sample Predictions attained by the proposed Hybrid attention model.

5 Conclusion and Future Scope

The work presented a Hybrid YOLOv11s model integrated with dual attention modules, namely GAM and ECA attention, to leverage small-object detection using the benchmark Skyfusion satellite imagery dataset. The paper also analyzed the latest YOLO models, ranging from YOLOv8s to YOLOv12s for small object detection for the best baseline selection. The models were trained on augmented data oversampling the under-represented ship class, and compared against the proposed model based on standardised performance measures. The proposed Hybrid YOLOv11s model performed the best on all the metrics by improving mAP and mmAP by 4% approximately, thereby being the most efficient model for this task. In the future, the system can be improved for deployment in generalized small-object detection tasks like drone surveillance, marine surveillance by validating its performance on diverse datasets like DOTA and HRSC2016. More ablation studies regarding the placement of attention and augmentation impact, along with more advanced multi-attention mechanisms such as transformers and detection-tracking fusion, will enhance its applicability to urban planning, disaster response, and environmental monitoring.

References

1. Liu, Y., Shao, Z., Hoffmann, N.: Global attention mechanism: retain information to enhance channel-spatial interactions. CoRR, abs/2112.05561 (2021)
2. Vinh, T.Q., Long, P.H.: Pedestrian detection using yolo with improved attention module. In: 2023 International Conference on Advanced Computing and Analytics (ACOMPA), pp. 93–98 (2023)
3. Li, Y., et al.: An image fusion method based on special residual network and efficient channel attention. Electronics **11**(19) (2022)
4. Wei, S., et al.: HRSID: a high-resolution SAR images dataset for ship detection and instance segmentation. IEEE Access **8**, 120234–120254 (2020)
5. Zhang, R., et al.: Multi-scale adversarial network for vehicle detection in UAV imagery. ISPRS J. Photogrammetry Remote Sens. **180**, 283–295 (2021)
6. Wu, J., Pan, Z., Lei, B., Hu, Y.: LR-TSDet: towards tiny ship detection in low-resolution remote sensing images. Remote Sens. **13**, 3890 (2021)
7. Wei, H., et al.: X-Linenet: detecting aircraft in remote sensing images by a pair of intersecting line segments. IEEE Trans. Geosci. Remote Sens. **59**(2), 1645–1659 (2021)
8. Han, Y., Yang, X., Tian, P., Peng, Z.: Fine-grained recognition for oriented ship against complex scenes in optical remote sensing images. IEEE Trans. Geosci. Remote Sens. **60**, 1–18 (2022)

9. Jixiang, W., Pan, Z., Lei, B., Yuxin, H.: Fsanet: feature-and-spatial-aligned network for tiny object detection in remote sensing images. IEEE Trans. Geosci. Remote Sens. **60**, 1–17 (2022)
10. Yu, R., Li, H., Jiang, Y., Zhang, B., Wang, Y.: Tiny vehicle detection for mid-to-high altitude UAV images based on visual attention and spatial-temporal information. Sensors **22**, 2354 (2022)
11. Chaoran, Yu., et al.: HB-YOLO: an improved yolov7 algorithm for dim-object tracking in satellite remote sensing videos. Remote Sens. **15**, 07 (2023)
12. Li, C.: An efficient method for detecting dense and small objects in UAV images. IEEE J. Sel. Top. Appl. Earth Observ. Remote Sens. **17**, 6601–6615 (2024)
13. Vandeghen, R., Louppe, G., Van Droogenbroeck, M.: Adaptive self-training for object detection. In: 2023 IEEE/CVF International Conference on Computer Vision Workshops (ICCVW), pp. 914–923 (2023)
14. Etnubarhi, N., Pirehen, H., Nagpal, S., Bayraktar, I.: Assessing yolov8 performance and limitations in aircraft and ship detection from satellite images, pp. 1–5 (2024)
15. Ayush, K., Uzkent, B., Burke, M., Lobell, D., Ermon, S.: Generating interpretable poverty maps using object detection in satellite images, pp. 4367–4373 (2020)
16. Biswas, D., Tešić, J.: Small object difficulty (sod) modeling for objects detection in satellite images. In: 2022 14th International Conference on Computational Intelligence and Communication Networks (CICN), pp. 125–130 (2022)
17. Van Etten, A., et al.: The multi-temporal urban development spacenet dataset. In: 2021 IEEE/CVF Conference on Computer Vision and Pattern Recognition (CVPR), pp. 6394–6403 (2021)
18. Boguszewski, A., Batorski, D., Jankowska, N.Z., Zambrzycka, A., Dziedzic, T.: Landcover.ai: dataset for automatic mapping of buildings, woodlands and water from aerial imagery (2020)
19. Rizk, M., Dominique, H., Baghdadi, A., Diguet, J.: Marine object detection based on top-view scenes using deep learning on edge devices (2022)
20. Gupta, R., Shah, M.: Rescuenet: joint building segmentation and damage assessment from satellite imagery. In: 2020 25th International Conference on Pattern Recognition (ICPR), pp. 4405–4411 (2021)
21. Pang, Y., Cheng, S., Hu, J., Liu, Y.: Robust satellite image classification with Bayesian deep learning. In: 2022 Integrated Communication, Navigation and Surveillance Conference (ICNS), pp. 1–8 (2022)
22. Liu, B., Chen, S.B., Wang, J.X., Tang, J., Luo, B.: An oriented object detector for hazy remote sensing images. IEEE Trans. Geosci. Remote Sens. **62**, 1–11 (2024)
23. Wang, Y., Zorzi, S., Bittner, K.: Machine-learned 3D building vectorization from satellite imagery (2021)
24. Martinson, E., Furlong, B., Gillies, A.: Training rare object detection in satellite imagery with synthetic GAN images. In: 2021 IEEE/CVF Conference on Computer Vision and Pattern Recognition Workshops (CVPRW), pp. 2763–2770 (2021)
25. Hassan, I., Xinyou, Z.: Performance evolution of yolo models in remote sensing images. In: 2024 21st International Computer Conference on Wavelet Active Media Technology and Information Processing (ICCWAMTIP), pp. 1–4 (2024)

ALERTIFY: An AI-Driven Multimodal Social Media Framework for Real-Time Disaster Monitoring and Response

Mohit Jena[1], Alok Raj[1], Priyanshu Pilaniwala[1], Khusi Bharti[1],
Rettikaa Manna[1], Dishika Jhunjhunwala[1], Smita Das[2],
and Jhalak Dutta[1(✉)]

[1] Heritage Institute of Technology, Kolkata, West Bengal, India
jhalak.dutta@heritageit.edu
[2] National Institute of Technology, Agartala, Tripura, India

Abstract. India is highly vulnerable to natural disasters and the massive flow of multilingual and multimodal social media data during such events makes it difficult to extract timely and reliable information. To address this challenge, this paper introduces ALERTIFY, an AI-driven multimodal framework designed to convert unstructured social and news media content into actionable disaster intelligence. The system follows a three-stage pipeline: first, an Artificial Neural Network (ANN) combined with TF–IDF is used to filter disaster-relevant text; second, a Multinomial Naïve Bayes classifier categorizes events into disaster types such as flood, earthquake, cyclone, fire, and accident; and third, a YOLO-based object detection model analyzes video frames to detect people, fire, vehicles, and debris, while audio streams are processed for acoustic events and speech-to-text transcription. The framework was evaluated on custom datasets, with the ANN achieving an accuracy of 84.35% (F1-score 0.82) and the Naïve Bayes classifier reaching 88.89% accuracy. These results show that ALERTIFY can provide reliable situational awareness by integrating text, image, video, and audio into a single evidence record. The proposed framework contributes to the building of faster, data-driven disaster response systems in India and can be further enhanced with advanced language models, IoT and geospatial integration, and large-scale deployments with disaster management agencies.

Keywords: Disaster Management · Social Media Analytics · Multimodal AI · Deep Learning · Situational Awareness · India

1 Introduction

India has been recognized as one of the most disaster-prone countries in the world due to its diverse geography, high population density, and increasing vulnerability to climate change. According to the National Disaster Management Authority (NDMA), more than 58.6% of the Indian land mass is prone to earthquakes, 12% is susceptible to floods, 68% of the area is vulnerable to droughts,

C. Zaroliagis et al. (Eds.): ICAA 2026, LNCS 16423, pp. 338–350, 2026.
https://doi.org/10.1007/978-3-032-15621-1_28

and nearly 5,700 km of the coastline is exposed to cyclones and tsunamis [16]. Between 2000 and 2019, India experienced 321 natural disasters, resulting in more than 108,000 deaths and affected more than 1.8 billion people, making the country among the top three globally in terms of disaster-related deaths and the affected population [8]. More recently, the EM-DAT database reported that the 2020 Assam floods alone displaced more than 5 million people, while Cyclone Amphan in the same year caused losses exceeding INR 1 trillion, making it one of the costliest cyclones in Indian history [7]. These statistics demonstrate that India requires robust, technology-driven solutions for disaster preparation, early detection, and rapid response.

Social networks have played a crucial role in Indian disaster events by enabling communities to act as 'social sensors'. During the 2015 Chennai floods, citizens used Twitter and WhatsApp extensively to share ground-level updates, request rescue support, and organize relief distribution [23]. Similarly, during Cyclone Fani in 2019, thousands of social media posts provided real-time situational updates, which were leveraged by local authorities and NGOs to plan rescue operations [6]. The COVID-19 pandemic further demonstrated the utility of platforms such as Twitter, where millions of requests related to oxygen supply, hospital beds, and medicines were circulated, highlighting how social networks can become a lifeline during emergencies [22]. Despite its potential, the challenge in India lies in managing the overwhelming volume of multilingual, multimodal, and often unstructured data shared across platforms, which requires advanced artificial intelligence (AI) systems for meaningful interpretation and actionable insights [15].

Existing work has explored AI and machine learning methods for analyzing social media during disasters. Semantic and spatiotemporal models were used in [13] for real-time disaster monitoring, while deep neural networks were applied in [4] for disaster image classification. A multimodal attentive learning approach combining text and images was presented in [14], and dashboards were proposed to visualize disaster insights in [3]. However, most existing research remains limited to global case studies, and Indian-specific contexts such as multilingual social media data, high population density, and the rapid spread of misinformation have not been adequately addressed [5]. These gaps underscore the urgent need for an India-centric multimodal framework capable of integrating text, image, video, and audio data streams to enhance situational awareness and guide timely disaster response.

Motivation: With India facing recurring disasters such as floods in Assam and Bihar, cyclones in Odisha and West Bengal, earthquakes in the Himalayan belt and droughts in central states, there is a pressing need for next generation systems that combine the power of AI with the reach of social networks. The growing reliance of Indian citizens on platforms such as Twitter, WhatsApp, and Facebook during crises has created both opportunities and challenges. On the one hand, real-time insights can accelerate rescue operations; on the other hand, the huge volume of multilingual and multimodal data requires intelligent systems for filtering and analysis. This study is motivated by the need to develop an indigenous AI-enabled disaster management solution that addresses India's unique challenges of scale, diversity, and urgency.

Contribution: In this work, a system named **ALERTIFY** has been proposed as an AI-driven multimodal disaster management framework tailored for the Indian context. The main contributions of this research are:

1. Integration of social network data across multiple modalities (text, images, videos, and audio) to capture diverse disaster-related information.
2. The deployment of deep learning and machine learning models, such as artificial neural networks and probabilistic classifiers, to identify relevant disaster-related content in real time.
3. Incorporation of video and audio analytics, including speech-to-text conversion and sound recognition, to address multilingual and multimodal Indian data streams.
4. Development of an interactive visualization dashboard to support authorities, NGOs, and community responders with actionable situational awareness.

In line with India's National Disaster Management Plan, ALERTIFY aims to strengthen disaster readiness, reduce response time, and improve coordination between citizens and agencies during emergencies.

2   Literature Review

The integration of artificial intelligence (AI) with social media analytics has emerged as a vital area of disaster informatics. In paper [15], the opportunities and challenges of using multimodal content for disaster response were examined, highlighting its potential for real-time decision making. A broader overview was presented in [17], where AI methods were discussed as tools to improve the efficiency of disaster response. The concept of multimodal fusion was explored in [10], where social media and satellite images were combined to improve emergency decision making. The portability of semantic and spatiotemporal machine learning approaches was validated in [13], where social media data were analyzed to enable near real-time disaster monitoring. In [4], a focus on image classification was described for humanitarian tasks, showing the importance of deep learning models in rapid assessment. To improve disaster identification, a deeply attentive multimodal framework combining textual and visual characteristics was proposed in [14], which demonstrated significant performance gains over unimodal methods. Further improvements in multimodal classification accuracy were reported in [24], where topic modeling and visual analysis were integrated to process large-scale disaster-related social media content.

Subsequent studies have concentrated on visualization, automation, and large-scale deployment. In paper [3], interactive dashboards were designed to represent multimodal disaster data, enhancing emergency response capabilities. Automated disaster monitoring frameworks were developed in [21], where AI-based location intelligence and sentiment analysis provided reliable situational awareness. A systematic review of multimodal approaches was presented in [5], emphasizing both the potential and the limitations of the existing frameworks. The effectiveness of social media analytics in disaster response was evaluated in [2], where collective intelligence and situational awareness were identified as key strengths. Big data-driven situational awareness was further elaborated in [18], focusing on spatial and temporal clustering. Edge technologies were discussed in [1], where integration of AI and social media on the edge was suggested to reduce latency in crisis detection. The application of social sensors was reviewed in [20], highlighting their role in event detection and sentiment analysis. More recent work has explored advanced multimodal learning approaches, such as transformer-based models [11], as well as case studies such as Typhoon Haikui [9], which validated real-world applicability. Furthermore, a survey on multimodal information fusion [12] and deep learning-based disaster assessment [19] confirmed that despite substantial progress, gaps remain in scalability, deployment, and integration with official disaster management systems.

3   Proposed Methodology

The proposed model ALERTIFY, has been developed to convert heterogeneous social and news streams into actionable disaster intelligence, as shown in Fig. 1. First, public posts and headlines are harvested from social networks and news portals by automated scraping, and a decision gate is applied in which texts are vectorized using TF–IDF and scored by an artificial neural network to accept only disaster-relevant items while rejecting noise. The accepted elements are then enriched by a light-weight text classification stage trained on a custom dataset (Multinomial Naïve Bayes), through which event type, location, time span, and media-modality tags are inferred to steer downstream analyzers. For visual evidence, an object detection model is trained on a manually annotated

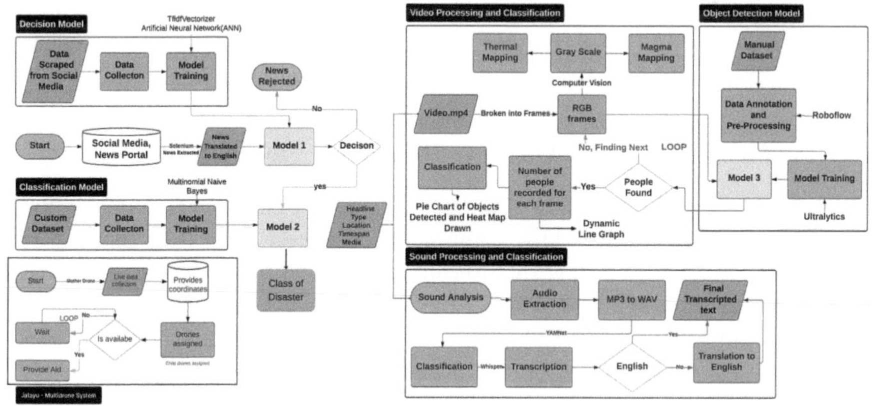

Fig. 1. Overall process flow of the proposed ALERTIFY Model.

corpus (annotation and preprocessing via Roboflow; training with the Ultralytics YOLO family) so that people, fire, vehicles, debris and other classes are localized with confidence scores. When videos are present, each clip is decomposed into frames and normalized (RGB extraction and optional grayscale), a learned thermal/magma mapping is generated for operator interpretability, and the detector is executed frame-wise to produce person counts and object distributions; these are streamed to a dynamic time series (people over time), summarized as per-clip pie charts, and accumulated as spatial heat maps, while a loop advances frames when no people are found. For audio, tracks are extracted (or demultiplexed from video), converted to WAV for uniform sampling, analyzed with a pretrained acoustic event classifier (e.g. sirens, alarms, shouts), and transcribed by an automatic speech recognizer; a language gate routes non-English transcripts to a machine-translation step so that a normalized English transcript is archived. The resulting textual attributes, detections, temporal traces, heat maps, acoustic labels, and transcripts are fused to form a single evidence record that is rendered on the dashboard and exposed to the multi-drone allocation subsystem, wherein live coordinates from the analytics are polled; if assets are available, missions are assigned to child drones; otherwise the system waits and rechecks, thereby enabling timely, location-aware aid delivery. All models are trained on the collected custom datasets and are periodically updated using hard examples and operator feedback, while performance (precision/recall for triage, mAP for detection, WER for ASR and accuracy for acoustic events) is monitored to trigger retraining when degradation is observed.

4   Result and Analysis

This section presents a comprehensive evaluation of the core analytical components of the proposed ALERTIFY system. The performance of three distinct models is analyzed: a neural network-based Decision Model for relevance filtering, a Naïve Bayes-based Classification Model for event categorization, and an object detection model for visual evidence analysis. Each model's contribution to the overall goal of converting raw data into actionable disaster intelligence is detailed.

4.1   Performance of the Disaster Relevance Decision Model

The first stage of the ALERTIFY pipeline is a binary classification gate, referred to as the Decision Model. This component, powered by an Artificial Neural Network (ANN), is tasked with filtering social media and news headlines to accept only disaster-relevant items while rejecting noise. The accuracy of the model is paramount to reducing false positives and ensuring the efficiency of downstream processes.

Dataset Characteristics and Exploratory Analysis. The model was trained on a balanced dataset of 13,952 records, with 43% (5,995) classified as "Disaster" and 57% (7,957) as "Not Disaster". This distribution, illustrated in Fig. 2, negated the need for class imbalance correction techniques.

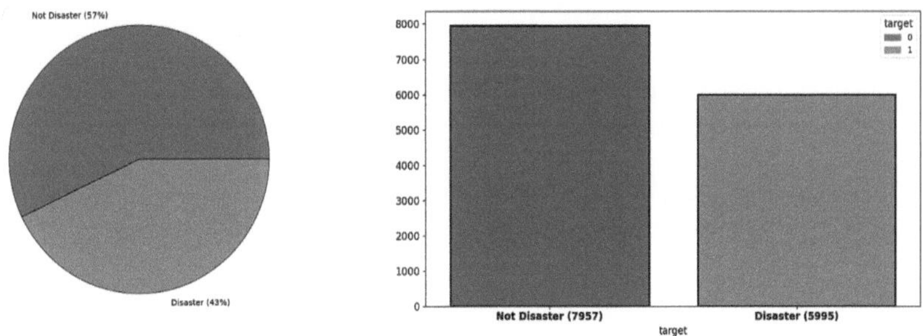

Fig. 2. Target Class Distribution in the Training Set for the Decision Model.

Exploratory Data Analysis (EDA) was performed to identify the distinguishing linguistic characteristics between the two classes. Word clouds (Fig. 3) and n-gram frequency analysis (Fig. 4) revealed that terms like "fire", "suicide", "disaster" and "oil spill" were highly indicative of disaster-related content. These distinctive patterns provided a strong linguistic basis for the classification task.

Fig. 3. Comparative Word Clouds for Disaster and Non-Disaster Content.

Evaluation of Classification Performance. The ANN was trained for 100 epochs, with its learning progress tracked through training and validation accuracy curves, as shown in Fig. 5. The model achieved a final **training accuracy of 84.346%** and a **validation accuracy of 79.93%**. The close proximity of these two curves suggests an effective generalization and minimal overfitting, validating the use of a 0.6 dropout rate in the model architecture.

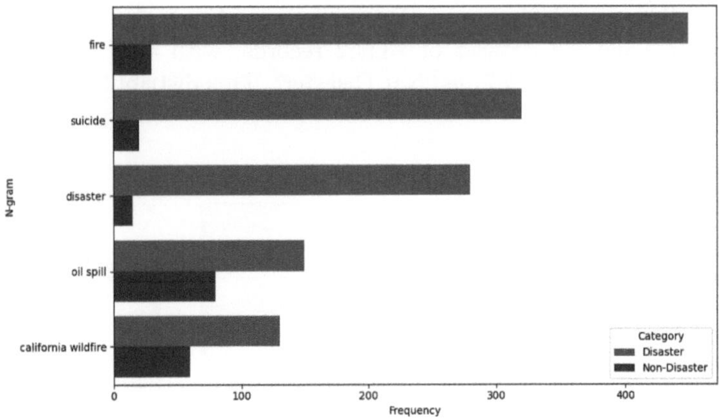

Fig. 4. Frequency Analysis of Top N-grams Across Categories.

A detailed breakdown of the model's predictive performance is provided by the confusion matrix in Fig. 6. The matrix quantifies the model's ability to correctly identify instances of each class, showing 5,055 true positives and 6,713 true negatives.

The primary performance metrics derived from this analysis are as follows.

- **Accuracy:** An overall precision of **84. 346%** was recorded.
- **Precision:** The model achieved a precision of **80.250%**.
- **Recall:** A recall of **84.320%** was obtained.
- **F1 Score:** A balanced F1 score of **0.82** was calculated.

These results confirm that the Decision Model functions as a highly effective initial filter, reliably identifying relevant disaster information with a strong balance between precision and recall.

4.2   Performance of the Disaster Type Classification Model

Once a piece of content is deemed relevant by Model 1, it is passed to the Classification Model. This component utilizes a Multinomial Naïve Bayes algorithm to enrich the data by inferring key attributes, most notably the specific type of disaster. Although the model is designed to extract location, time, and media tags, this evaluation focuses on its main classification task, identifying the type of event.

Dataset Composition and Distribution. This model was trained on a custom dataset of 14,334 records derived from the EM-DAT database, categorized into five disaster types: **Flood, Earthquake, Cyclone, Fire, and Accident**. The class distribution, presented in Figs. 7 and 8, was found to be nearly balanced. 'Flood' was the modal class (34.6%), while 'accident' was the least frequent (6.8%).

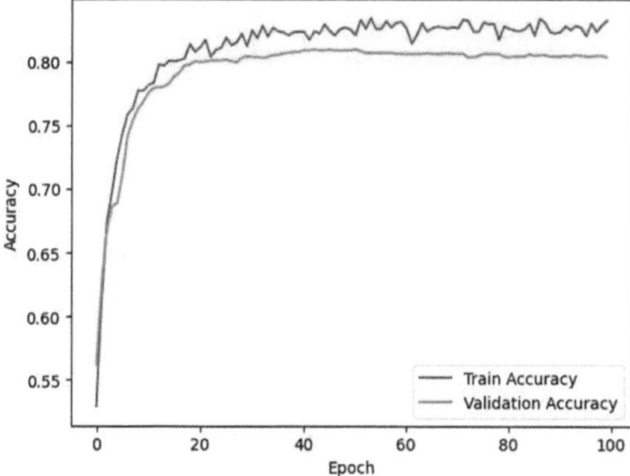

Fig. 5. Training and Validation Accuracy Curves for the Decision Model.

Evaluation of Multi-class Categorization. The multinomial Naïve Bayes classifier demonstrated exceptional performance, achieving an overall **precision of 88. 89%** and an **average precision of 86.2%**. The confusion matrix in Fig. 9 provides a detailed class-by-class view of the model predictions.

The strong diagonal values in the matrix indicate a high rate of correct classifications for all categories. For instance, 4,458 of 4,956 'Flood' events and 3,728 of 4,100 'Earthquake' events were correctly identified. The off-diagonal values reveal minor confusion between semantically similar categories, such as 'Flood' and 'Cyclone', which is expected behavior. The high accuracy of the model validates its role in correctly tagging textual data with specific disaster types, providing crucial context for downstream analysis.

4.3   Functional Analysis of the Object Detection Model

The third and final component of the analytics pipeline is the Object Detection Model, which processes visual data (video frames) to identify and localize evidence of a disaster. This model is critical for generating visual intelligence in real time.

As described in the proposed methodology, this model was developed using the **Ultralytics YOLO** (You Only Look Once) architecture. Training was performed on a custom, manually annotated dataset, with annotation and pre-processing managed through the **Roboflow** platform. This approach ensures the model is fine-tuned to recognize specific objects of interest in disaster scenarios, such as people, vehicles, fire, and debris.

The intended function of this model within the ALERTIFY system is to:

- Decompose the incoming videos into individual frames for analysis.
- Execute frame-wise object detection to identify and count relevant entities.

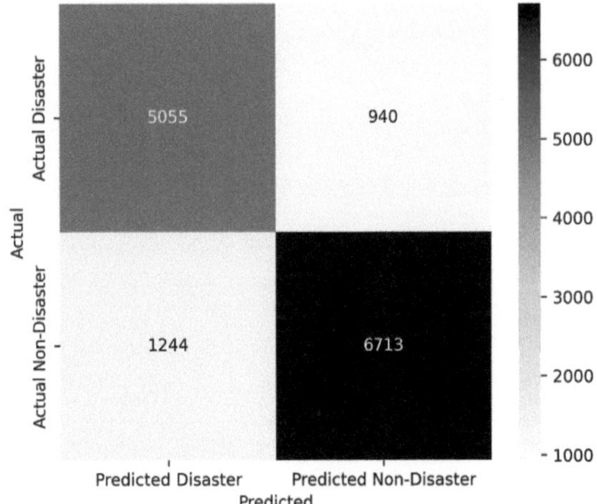

Fig. 6. Confusion Matrix for the Binary Classification Decision Model.

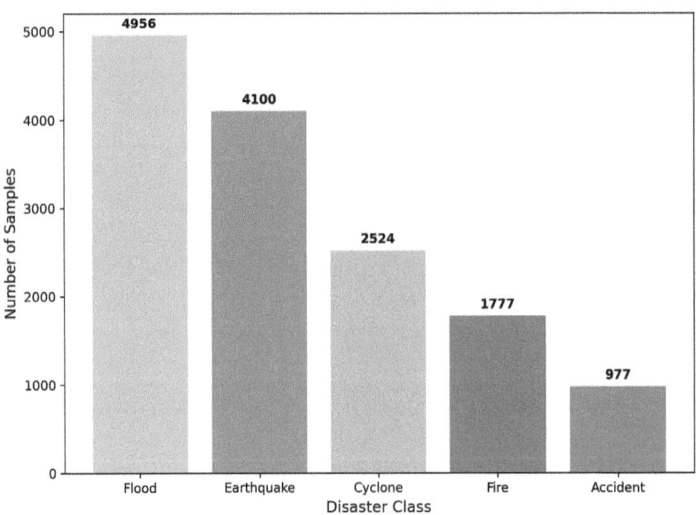

Fig. 7. Sample Distribution Across the Five Disaster Classes.

– Generate quantitative outputs, including dynamic line graphs that track the number of people over time, pie charts that summarize the distribution of detected objects, and spatial heat maps that indicate areas of high activity.

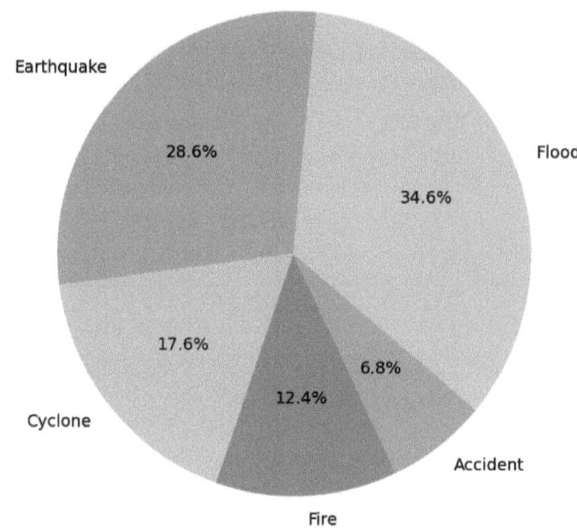

Fig. 8. Percentage Share of Each Disaster Class in the Training Dataset.

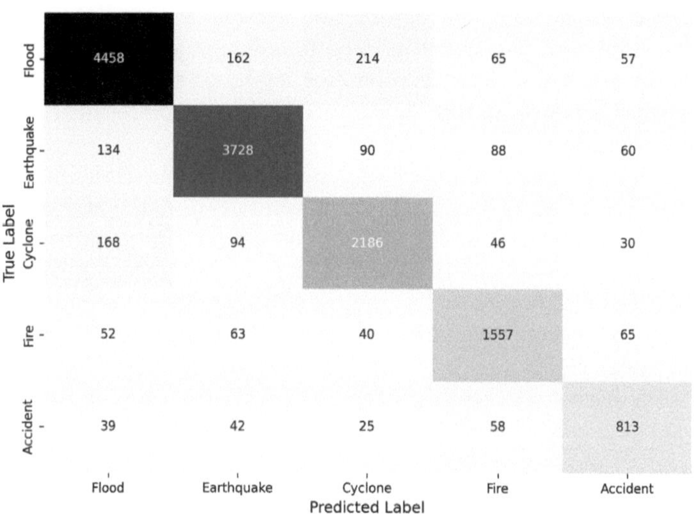

Fig. 9. Confusion Matrix for the Multi-Class Disaster Type Classification Model.

5   Conclusion and Future Scope

In this research, an effective AI-driven multimodal framework named ALER-
TIFY was successfully developed and validated to improve disaster management in the complex Indian context. The efficacy of the system was demonstrated through a multistage pipeline where a neural network-based decision

model achieved 84.346% precision in filtering relevant content, and a subsequent Multinomial Naïve Bayes classifier achieved 88. 89% precision in categorizing disaster types, providing crucial, context-rich intelligence. Building upon this robust foundation, future research will focus on extending the framework's capabilities to achieve even greater impact. Further advancements can be pursued by integrating state-of-the-art architectures like transformer-based models to capture deeper linguistic nuances and by exploring sophisticated multimodal fusion techniques to uncover complex cross-modal patterns. The analytical power of ALERTIFY can also be expanded to include a dedicated module to identify and flag potential misinformation proactively, a critical challenge during emergencies. Future efforts will be directed towards ensuring large-scale, real-time deployment through research into distributed computing and fostering seamless integration with official disaster response channels, solidifying the framework's role as a next-generation tool for national disaster resilience.

6   Ethical Considerations

All data in this study were collected solely from publicly accessible posts on platforms such as Facebook, Instagram, and Twitter. Lightweight scraping techniques were used only for content intentionally made public by users, while no private accounts, restricted content for login, or personal communications were accessed. This ensured full compliance with accepted ethical standards for public-data research.

During acquisition and preprocessing, personally identifiable information was strictly excluded. Only textual content relevant to disaster was processed and usernames, profile details, and sensitive metadata were removed to preserve anonymity. The pipeline was designed to extract only the minimum information required for analysis, reducing the risks of misuse or profiling.

For future extensions involving user-generated posts beyond official sources, the same ethical safeguards will be applied, including: the use of platform-approved APIs with consent mechanisms, removal of all identifiable information, complete anonymization prior to storage or analysis, and exclusive use of data for research and disaster-response activities.

Through these measures, the ALERTIFY framework has been developed to ensure responsible handling of social media data while maintaining user privacy and ethical integrity.

References

1. Aboualola, M., Abualsaud, K., Khattab, T., Zorba, N., Hassanein, H.S.: Edge technologies for disaster management: a survey of social media and artificial intelligence integration. IEEE Access **11**, 73782–73802 (2023)
2. Acikara, T., Xia, B., Yigitcanlar, T., Hon, C.: Contribution of social media analytics to disaster response effectiveness: a systematic review. Sustainability **15**(11), 8860 (2023)

3. AlAbdulaali, A., Asif, A., Khatoon, S., Alshamari, M.: Designing multimodal interactive dashboard of disaster management systems. Sensors **22**(11), 4292 (2022)
4. Alam, F., Alam, T., Ofli, F., Imran, M.: Social media images classification models for real-time disaster response. arXiv preprint arXiv:2104.04184 (2021)
5. Algiriyage, N., Prasanna, R., Stock, K., Doyle, E.E.H., Johnston, D.: Multi-source multimodal data and deep learning for disaster response: a systematic review. SN Comput. Sci. **3**(1), 92 (2022)
6. contributors, W.: Cyclone Fani. Wikipedia, The Free Encyclopedia. https://en.wikipedia.org/wiki/Cyclone_Fani, Accessed 16 Sep 2025
7. CRED: Em-dat – the international disaster database. Université Catholique de Louvain, Brussels (2023). https://www.emdat.be/
8. for Disaster Risk Reduction (UNDRR), U.N.O.: Human cost of disasters 2000–2019. Centre for Research on the Epidemiology of Disasters (CRED), Brussels (2019). https://www.undrr.org/publication/human-cost-disasters-2000-2019
9. Gao, S., et al.: Enhancing disaster situation awareness through multimodal social media data: evidence from typhoon Haikui. Appl. Sci. **15**, 465 (2025)
10. Gialampoukidis, I., Andreadis, S., Vrochidis, S., Kompatsiaris, I.: Multimodal data fusion of social media and satellite images for emergency response and decision-making. In: 2021 IEEE International Geoscience and Remote Sensing Symposium (IGARSS), pp. 228–231. IEEE (2021)
11. Gite, S., et al.: Analysis of multimodal social media data utilizing VIT base 16 and GPT-2 for disaster response. Arab. J. Sci. Eng. (2025). https://doi.org/10.1007/s13369-025-10314-7
12. Gong, D., Meng, L., Chi, W., Lin, A., Shi, L.: Review of real-time monitoring and early warning technology for natural disasters based on multimodal information fusion. Frontiers. Comput. Intell. Syst. **13**, 1–11 (2025)
13. Havas, C., Resch, B.: Portability of semantic and spatial-temporal machine learning methods to analyse social media for near-real-time disaster monitoring. Nat. Hazards **108**(3), 2939–2969 (2021)
14. Hossain, E., Hoque, M.M., Hoque, E., Islam, M.S.: A deep attentive multimodal learning approach for disaster identification from social media posts. IEEE Access **10**, 46538–46551 (2022)
15. Imran, M., Ofli, F., Caragea, C., Torralba, A.: Using AI and social media multimodal content for disaster response and management: opportunities, challenges, and future directions. Inf. Process. Manag. **57**(5), 102261 (2020)
16. (NDMA), N.D.M.A.: National disaster management reports. Government of India, New Delhi (2020). https://ndma.gov.in/Reference_Material/NDMAReports
17. Ofli, F., Imran, M., Alam, F.: Using artificial intelligence and social media for disaster response and management: an overview. In: AI and Robotics in Disaster Studies, pp. 63–81. Springer, Cham (2020)
18. Pal, A.: Social media driven big data analysis for disaster situation awareness: a tutorial. IEEE Trans. Big Data **9**(1), 1–21 (2023)
19. Shetty, N., Bijalwan, Y., Chaudhari, P., Shetty, J., Muniyal, B.: Disaster assessment from social media using multimodal deep learning. Multimedia Tools Appl. **84**, 18829–18854 (2024)
20. Shi, K., Peng, X., Lu, H., Zhu, Y., Niu, Z.: Application of social sensors in natural disasters emergency management: a review. IEEE Trans. Comput. Soc. Syst. **10**(6), 3143–3158 (2023)
21. Sufi, F.K., Khalil, I.: Automated disaster monitoring from social media posts using AI-based location intelligence and sentiment analysis. IEEE Trans. Comput. Soc. Syst. **11**(4), 4614–4624 (2024)

22. Taneja, S.L.: COVID-19: an analysis of social media and research publication activity during the early stages of the pandemic. J. Med. Internet Res. **23**(6), e26956 (2021). https://doi.org/10.2196/26956
23. Vidya, D.: How social media helped during Chennai floods as a disaster management tool (2015). https://www.digitalvidya.com/blog/how-social-media-helped-during-chennai-floods-as-a-disaster-management-tool/, Accessed 16 Sep 2025
24. Zhang, M., Huang, Q., Liu, H.: A multimodal data analysis approach to social media during natural disasters. Sustainability **14**(9), 5536 (2022)

Perception Learning: A Formal Separation of Sensory Representation Learning from Decision Learning

Suman Sanyal$^{(\boxtimes)}$

Big Data Analytics, Goa Institute of Management, Goa, India
`sanyal@gim.ac.in`

Abstract. We introduce Perception Learning (PeL), a paradigm that optimizes an agent's sensory interface $f_\phi : \mathcal{X} \to \mathcal{Z}$ using task-agnostic signals, decoupled from downstream decision learning $g_\theta : \mathcal{Z} \to \mathcal{Y}$. PeL directly targets label-free perceptual properties, such as stability to nuisances, informativeness without collapse, and controlled geometry, assessed via objective representation-invariant metrics. We formalize the separation of perception and decision, define perceptual properties independent of objectives or reparameterizations, and prove that PeL updates preserving sufficient invariants are orthogonal to Bayes task-risk gradients. Additionally, we provide a suite of task-agnostic evaluation metrics to certify perceptual quality.

Keywords: Perceptual learning · self-supervised learning · invariance · contrastive learning · representation evaluation · modular training

1 Introduction

Perception transforms raw sensory streams into internal codes that downstream decision modules can use. Contemporary ML often entangles perception and decision via end-to-end optimization. While powerful, this coupling can produce brittle, task-specific features and makes it hard to evaluate perception itself independently of any task head.

We introduce **Perception Learning** (PeL) which optimizes perception as a first-class objective using task-agnostic signals, while deferring decision learning to separate modules that consume the resulting code Z. Figure 2 depicts the setup: PeL trains f_ϕ using invariance, information, and diversity signals on unlabeled data; decision heads g_θ are trained later and do not backpropagate into f_ϕ. This separation yields reusable codes, clearer diagnostics, and safer invariance choices.

The remainder of this paper is organized as follows. Section 2 surveys related work in cognitive science, self-supervised learning, equivariant networks, and modular systems, positioning PeL's unique contributions. Section 3 formalizes the perception-decision split and defines PeL along with its minimal principles of separation, admissible supervision, and task-agnostic evaluation, as illustrated in Figs. 1 and 2. Section 4 introduces perceptual properties as representation-invariant functionals, presenting canonical examples such as invariance, information preservation, and geometric regularity, along with informal targets in

C. Zaroliagis et al. (Eds.): ICAA 2026, LNCS 16423, pp. 351–364, 2026.
https://doi.org/10.1007/978-3-032-15621-1_29

Table 1. Key notations used in the paper.

Notation	Meaning
$\mathcal{X}$	Input (sensory) space
$\mathcal{Z}$	Perceptual code space (Euclidean)
$\mathcal{Y}$	Label/action space
$f_\phi : \mathcal{X} \to \mathcal{Z}$	Sensory encoder (perception)
$g_\theta : \mathcal{Z} \to \Delta(\mathcal{Y})$	Decision head (to simplex over $\mathcal{Y}$)
$Z = f_\phi(X)$	Learned representation/code
P_X	Input distribution
G	Family of admissible transforms/nuisances
$T_\delta \in G$	Sampled transform (e.g., augmentation)
$\pi : \mathcal{X} \to \mathcal{X}/G$	Orbit map (to quotient space)
$T = \pi(X)$	G-invariant sufficient statistic
μ_G	Probability measure on G
$\Phi_{\mathsf{P}}(f_\phi; P_X, G)$	Functional for property P (target $\mathcal{T}_{\mathsf{P}} \subseteq \mathbb{R}$)
$L_{\mathrm{perc}}(\phi)$	PeL objective/loss
$\beta, \tau, \gamma, \varepsilon$	Hyperparameters (e.g., invariance weight, temperature, variance floor, threshold)
$\mathcal{R}(\phi, \theta)$	Task risk under proper loss ℓ
$F(\phi)$	Bayes risk through f_ϕ
$\sigma(Z)$	σ-algebra generated by Z
$\mathcal{M}$	Manifold of injective factorizations through T
$\eta(x) = \mathbb{P}(Y \in \cdot \mid X = x)$	Task posterior (G-invariant under A1)
$D_v F(\phi_0)$	Directional derivative of F along v at ϕ_0

Table 2. Section 5 proposes a suite of task-agnostic metrics aligned with these properties, including invariance curves, leakage probes, and geometric diagnostics, summarized in Table 3. Section 6 develops the theoretical foundation on standard Borel spaces, stating assumptions (A1)–(A5), proving a theorem on the orthogonality of PeL updates to Bayes task-risk gradients, and illustrating failure modes via counterexamples. We conclude in Sect. 7 with a summary, limitations, and directions for future work.

2   Related Work and Positioning

Classic work in cognitive science established that perceptual abilities improve through experience and practice, independent of explicit task rewards. Gibson's monograph articulated developmental mechanisms for perceptual differentiation [1], and Goldstone's survey synthesized enduring effects such as attention weighting, unitization, and differentiation [2]. These lines motivate treating perception as a trainable capability in its own right. Representation learning, on the other hand, aims to learn useful feature spaces without task labels [3]. Contrastive and predictive SSL methods like CPC [4], SimCLR [5], MoCo [6], BYOL [7], and reconstruction/predictive approaches like MAE [8], DINOv2 [9] deliver broad downstream gains across tasks. Unifying, modality-agnostic objectives include data2vec [10], while visionlanguage pretraining like CLIP [11] shows that weak supervision at scale can yield general, reusable perception. More recently, I-JEPA [12] reframes pretraining as predicting target representations from context representations instead of pixel-level generation, explicitly pushing for semantic invariances. Across these threads, evaluation is still largely cast through downstream task accuracy, not perception. A complementary line imposes structure on features via group equivariance in G-CNNs [22], 3D/SE(3) symmetry-aware networks [13], and invariance-based generalization principles have been explored via Invariant Risk Minimization (IRM) [14]. Our program leverages such a structure but evaluates it at the perceptual interface, decoupled from any particular decision head.

In terms of applications, robotics and vision emphasized that perception improves when agents act to gather informative views (active perception) [15]. While compatible with active data acquisition, our focus is on perception-centric training and certification that remain conceptually separate from policy optimization. World Models [23], DreamerV3 [16] foreground model-based prediction before control, and Perceiver/Perceiver-IO provide modality-agnostic perception backbones [17,18]. These support the view that a strong, reusable perceptual stack benefits many tasks and embodiments, aligning with our separation of perception learning from downstream decision learning.

While Perception Learning (PeL) is adjacent to self-supervised learning, equivariance, world models, and active perception, it differs in three ways.

(i) PeL explicitly separates optimization of perception ($f_\phi : \mathcal{X} \to \mathcal{Z}$) from decision ($g_\theta : \mathcal{Z} \to \mathcal{Y}$),

(ii) PeL introduces task-agnostic, perception-first metrics that quantify improvement independently of downstream accuracy, and

(iii) PeL provides training protocols that can be combined with, but are not subsumed by, decision learning.

In short, PeL operationalizes "make perception first-class" with concrete objectives and benchmarks that certify perception quality apart from policy or decoder performance. Refer to Fig. 1 for schematics of PeL in an AGI-oriented stack.

3   Perception Vs Decision

Let $x \in \mathcal{X}$ be raw input, $z \in \mathcal{Z}$ a perceptual code, and $y \in \mathcal{Y}$ a label/action. We posit

$$z = f_\phi(x) \quad \text{(perception)}, \tag{1}$$

$$\hat{y} = g_\theta(z) \quad \text{(decision)}. \tag{2}$$

PeL optimizes f_ϕ with a label-free loss L_{perc}; decision learning optimizes g_θ via a task loss L_{task} on frozen f_ϕ.

Definition 1. (Perception Learning). *Perception learning is the problem of learning a sensory interface $f_\phi : \mathcal{X} \to \mathcal{Z}$ using task-agnostic signals such that $Z = f_\phi(X)$ acquires specified perceptual properties, without optimizing any task/decision loss.*

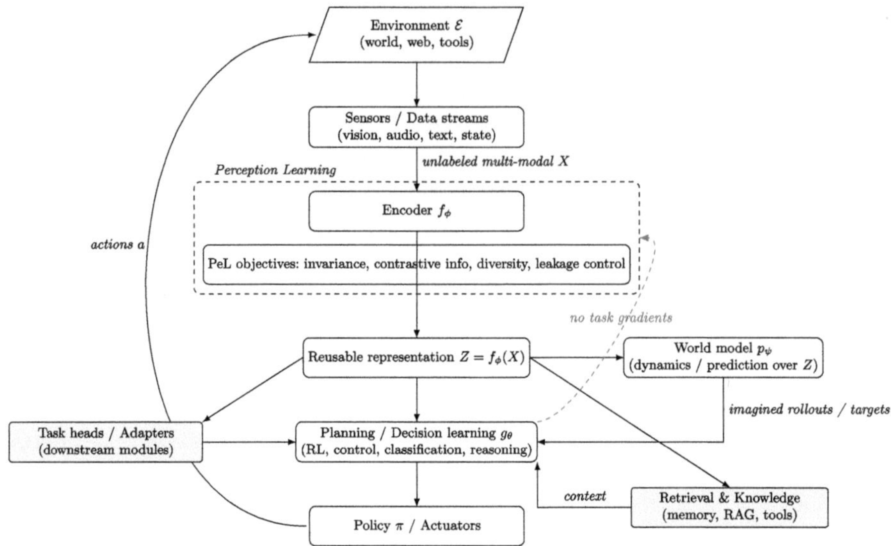

Fig. 1. PeL in a broader AGI stack. Z supports world modeling, planning/decision learning, retrieval/knowledge, and task heads. Task/return gradients do not flow into f_ϕ.

The minimal principles of PeL emphasize

(i) separation, ensuring no task gradients flow to ϕ,
(ii) admissible supervision, restricted to augmentations, temporal proximity, predictive or reconstruction targets, and weak metadata[1], and
(iii) evaluation, where success is measured by task-agnostic metrics on Z, with downstream accuracy considered secondary.

4   Perceptual Properties

The perceptual properties characterize the sensory interface independently of any downstream task. They can be used as training objectives, regularizers, or evaluation criteria. Typical choices target stability to nuisances, informativeness under capacity constraints, and geometric regularity of $Z = f_\phi(X)$.

Definition 2. (Perceptual Property). *Let P_X be a distribution on $\mathcal{X}$, G a family of admissible transforms on $\mathcal{X}$, and $f_\phi : \mathcal{X} \to \mathcal{Z}$ an encoder. A perceptual property P is a label-agnostic specification of the behavior of f_ϕ with respect to (P_X, G) that is expressible as a measurable functional $\Phi_\mathsf{P}(f_\phi; P_X, G) \in \mathbb{R}$ with a target set $\mathcal{T}_\mathsf{P} \subseteq \mathbb{R}$. We say f_ϕ satisfies P when $\Phi_\mathsf{P}(f_\phi; P_X, G) \in \mathcal{T}_\mathsf{P}$. Crucially,*

---

[1] Low-fidelity, task-agnostic side signals available without manual labeling, e.g., temporal adjacency, device/camera ID, coarse GPS/cell region, view index, or time-of-day bucket. We use them only to *structure* positive/negative pairs or strata, not as labels.

Φ_{P} *depends only on* (X, G) *and* f_ϕ, *not on task labels, and is representation-invariant under injective reparameterizations* $h : \mathcal{Z} \to \mathcal{Z}'$, *i.e., if* f_ϕ *satisfies* P *then so does* $h \circ f_\phi$.

To formalize the goals of PeL, we define a set of perceptual properties that characterize desirable behaviors of the sensory interface $f_\phi : \mathcal{X} \to \mathcal{Z}$ with respect to the input distribution P_X and a family of admissible transforms G. Each property is expressed as a measurable functional $\Phi_{\mathsf{P}}(f_\phi; P_X, G) \in \mathbb{R}$ with a target set $\mathcal{T}_{\mathsf{P}} \subseteq \mathbb{R}$, as per Definition 2, ensuring representation invariance under injective reparameterizations $h : \mathcal{Z} \to \mathcal{Z}'$. Below, we outline canonical classes of these properties with formal criteria, where $T_\delta \in G$ denotes a sampled transform, V a known nuisance variable (when available), $\rho : G \to \mathrm{GL}(\mathcal{Z})$ a representation of G, and $d(\cdot, \cdot)$ a metric on $\mathcal{Z}$. For perceptual properties and informal targets we refer to Table 2.

The first property, **invariance**, ensures stability to nuisances, requiring that the representation $Z = f_\phi(x)$ remains consistent under transformations T_δ. It is quantified as $\Phi_{\mathrm{inv}}(f_\phi) = \mathbb{E}_{x,\delta}\|f_\phi(x) - f_\phi(T_\delta x)\|_2^2 \leq \varepsilon$, capturing the expected squared distance between embeddings of original and transformed inputs. **Equivariance**, in contrast, demands a structured response where transformations in $\mathcal{X}$ correspond to known transformations in $\mathcal{Z}$, defined as $\Phi_{\mathrm{eq}}(f_\phi) = \mathbb{E}_{x,\delta}\|f_\phi(T_\delta x) - \rho(\delta)f_\phi(x)\|_2^2 \leq \varepsilon$, ensuring the encoder respects the group action ρ.

Information preservation under capacity constraints is critical to avoid degenerate representations. This is formalized as $\Phi_{\mathrm{info}}(f_\phi) = -I(X; Z)$, subject to $\dim(Z) \leq k$ or $\mathbb{E}\|f_\phi(x) - f_\phi(T_\delta x)\|^2 \leq \varepsilon$, maximizing mutual information while respecting dimensionality or stability limits. Alternatively, a contrastive lower bound via InfoNCE is used: $\Phi_{\mathrm{info}}^{\mathrm{NCE}}(f_\phi) = \mathbb{E}\left[-\log \frac{\exp(\mathrm{sim}(z,z^+)/\tau)}{\sum_{z^-}\exp(\mathrm{sim}(z,z^-)/\tau)}\right]$, where $z = f_\phi(x)$, $z^+ = f_\phi(T_\delta x)$, ensuring discriminability without collapse. **Nuisance independence**, or leakage control, minimizes the representation's sensitivity to nuisance variables, given by $\Phi_{\mathrm{leak}}(f_\phi) = I(Z; V)$ or a probe risk $\mathcal{R}_{\mathrm{probe}}(V \leftarrow Z) \leq \varepsilon$, ensuring Z discards irrelevant information.

Geometric regularity promotes smooth and well-conditioned embeddings, captured through multiple functionals: $\Phi_{\mathrm{lip}}(f_\phi) = \mathbb{E}\|\nabla_x f_\phi(x)\|_F^2$ for smoothness via Jacobian energy, $\Phi_{\mathrm{cov}}(f_\phi) = \sum_{i \neq j}(\mathrm{Cov}(Z_i, Z_j))^2$ for decorrelation, and $\Phi_{\mathrm{var}}(f_\phi) = \sum_d \max(0, \gamma - \mathrm{Var}(Z_d))$ to maintain variance and prevent collapse, each targeting small values. When generative factors $\mathcal{U}$ are known, **factor disentanglement** is defined as $\Phi_{\mathrm{dis}}(f_\phi) = \sum_{u \in \mathcal{U}} \min_d(1 - \mathrm{NMI}(Z_d, u))$ or total-correlation penalties on Z, encouraging alignment of representation dimensions with distinct factors. Finally, **sufficient invariants** ensure Z captures all task-relevant information invariant to G, with a soft criterion $\Phi_{\mathrm{suff}}(f_\phi) = I(X; Z \mid \pi(X)) \leq \varepsilon$, where $\pi : \mathcal{X} \to \mathcal{X}/G$ is an orbit map, meaning Z carries minimal information beyond the invariant statistic.

These properties are evaluated using task-agnostic metrics tailored to each functional. Invariance is assessed via curves $D(\alpha) = \mathbb{E}\|f_\phi(x) - f_\phi(\tau_\alpha x)\|_2^2$ and their AUC, leakage via adversarial or linear probes, separability under information preservation via Fisher ratios or MMD^2, geometric properties via Jacobian

Table 2. Perceptual properties and informal targets. "Code" is the learned representation $Z = f_\phi(X)$.

Perceptual Property	Informal target
Stability/Invariance	Same scene $\Rightarrow$ similar code under admissible transforms T_δ.
Equivariance	Predictable change of the code under T: applying T corresponds to a known transform $\rho(T)$ in representation space.
Information/Non-collapse	Preserve information; avoid degenerate (constant) codes so distinct inputs remain distinguishable.
Nuisance independence (leakage)	Make the code insensitive to known nuisance variables (e.g., rotation angle, sensor ID).
Geometric regularity	Promote smooth, well-conditioned embeddings with controlled variance, decorrelation, and Jacobian energy.
Factor disentanglement	Align representation dimensions with distinct generative factors when known, minimizing total correlation.
Sufficiency/Orbit statistic	Retain invariant content (constant along G-orbits) and discard variation along nuisance directions.

or covariance diagnostics, and sufficiency through conditional mutual information surrogates. This comprehensive framework ensures that PeL produces representations that are stable, informative, and geometrically well-behaved, independently of downstream task objectives.

Remark 1. While the canonical functionals for invariance and equivariance are defined using Euclidean ℓ_2-norms, which are not strictly preserved under arbitrary injective reparameterizations $h : \mathcal{Z} \to \mathcal{Z}'$ (e.g., nonlinear scalings distort distances), the underlying property satisfaction remains equivalent: if f_ϕ meets the criterion, so does $h \circ f_\phi$ when the functional is adapted via a canonical metric (e.g., cosine similarity or kernel-induced distances). Properties based on information measures (e.g., $I(X; Z)$, $I(Z; V)$) are fully invariant due to σ-algebra preservation. For geometric terms like covariance penalties, affine h suffice; in general, this mild assumption aligns with Euclidean representations in SSL literature, ensuring the framework's objectives are robust to downstream linear probes or heads.

5   Task-Agnostic Metrics for Perceptual Improvement

To evaluate the quality of the perceptual representation $Z = f_\phi(X)$ independently of downstream decision heads g_θ, we propose a suite of task-agnostic metrics that directly assess the perceptual properties defined in Sect. 4. These metrics focus on stability, informativeness, nuisance independence, and geometric regularity, ensuring that improvements in perception are measured without conflating with task-specific performance.

Nuisance independence is quantified by estimating the mutual information $I(Z;V)$ between the representation Z and known nuisance variables V (e.g., rotation angles or sensor IDs). In practice, this can be computed using (i) adversarial probing, where a strong classifier attempts to predict V from Z, with lower AUC indicating better independence, or (ii) nonparametric mutual information estimators. We report the normalized quantity $\widehat{I}(Z;V)/H(V)$ to contextualize leakage relative to the nuisance entropy, with lower values indicating better suppression of irrelevant information.

Invariance and **equivariance** are assessed through curves that measure the stability of Z under a family of transformations $\tau_\alpha \in G$ (e.g., rotations parameterized by angle α). We compute $D(\alpha) = \mathbb{E}[\|f_\phi(x) - f_\phi(\tau_\alpha(x))\|_2^2]$, summarizing invariance via the area-under-curve (AUC), where lower values indicate stronger stability to nuisances. For equivariance, similar curves can be adapted to measure alignment with the group action $\rho(\alpha)$, ensuring the representation responds predictably to transformations.

Perceptual faithfulness evaluates how well Z captures the essential structure of the input X. If a decoder $p_\omega(X \mid Z)$ is available, we measure reconstruction quality via the expected negative log-likelihood $\mathbb{E}[-\log p_\omega(X \mid Z)]$. For specific modalities, metrics like PSNR or SSIM (for images) or log-spectral distance (for audio) provide practical proxies, reflecting the information preservation property without requiring task labels.

Geometric regularity is assessed through three metrics. First, **local smoothness** is measured as $S = \mathbb{E}[\|\nabla_x f_\phi(x)\|_F^2]$, capturing the Lipschitz continuity of the encoder to ensure stable responses to input perturbations. Second, when generative factors are known (e.g., in synthetic datasets), **disentanglement scores**, such as normalized mutual information (NMI) between Z dimensions and factors, quantify axis-alignment. Third, the Fisher information trace $\mathrm{tr}\mathcal{I}_Z$ under small nuisance perturbations evaluates the representation's **sensitivity**, with lower traces indicating robustness.

Finally, to gauge transfer readiness without conflating with decision learning, we employ a fixed-capacity linear probe on Z, trained with early stopping on a small validation split. This measures **data-efficiency** (accuracy vs. number of labels) but is treated as a secondary metric to avoid task bias. These metrics collectively ensure that Z aligns with the perceptual properties of invariance, information preservation, nuisance independence, and geometric regularity, enabling robust evaluation of perception independent of downstream tasks.

6 Separating Perception and Decision

Let the population task risk be

$$\mathcal{R}(\phi, \theta) = \mathbb{E}\big[\ell(g_\theta(f_\phi(X)), Y)\big]. \tag{3}$$

Table 3. Task-agnostic metrics for perceptual properties and their alignment.

Metric	Perceptual Property Targeted
Nuisance independence ($\widehat{I}(Z;V)/H(V)$ or probe AUC)	Nuisance independence (leakage control)
Invariance/equivariance curves ($D(\alpha)$, AUC)	Stability/invariance, Equivariance
Perceptual faithfulness ($\mathbb{E}[-\log p_\omega(X \mid Z)]$, PSNR/SSIM)	Information preservation
Local smoothness ($S = \mathbb{E}[\|\nabla_x f_\phi(x)\|_F^2]$)	Geometric regularity (smoothness)
Disentanglement scores (NMI for known factors)	Factor disentanglement
Fisher information trace ($\mathrm{tr}\mathcal{I}_Z$)	Geometric regularity (robustness to perturbations)
Linear probe data-efficiency (secondary)	Information preservation, Transfer readiness

We say that f_ϕ is task-sufficient for Y if there exists h such that $\mathbb{P}(Y|X) = \mathbb{P}(Y|Z)$ with $Z = f_\phi(X)$ (i.e., Z is sufficient for Y). Intuitively, if f_ϕ captures exactly the task-relevant (e.g., G-invariant) information, then further perception-only improvements that preserve this information should not degrade Bayes-optimal decision risk. We now formalize the invariance setting and sufficiency conditions used in the full proof. We work on standard Borel spaces. Let $(\mathcal{X}, \mathscr{X})$ be the input (sensory) space and $(\mathcal{Y}, \mathscr{Y})$ the label/action space. A (measurable) group action $G \curvearrowright \mathcal{X}$ is written $(g, x) \mapsto g \cdot x$. Now consider the following assumptions.

(A1) Group invariance of the target. There exists a (measurable) conditional distribution $\eta(x) = \mathbb{P}(Y \in \cdot \mid X = x)$ such that $\eta(g \cdot x) = \eta(x)$ for all $g \in G$ and a.e. $x \in \mathcal{X}$. Equivalently, Y depends on X only through its G-orbit.

(A2) Invariant (orbit) statistic and sufficiency. Let $\pi : \mathcal{X} \to \mathcal{T}$ be a measurable orbit map constant on G-orbits (the canonical projection to the quotient space $\mathcal{X}/G$). Assume the Markov condition $Y \perp\!\!\!\perp X \mid T(X)$ with $T = \pi$. Thus T is a G-invariant sufficient statistic $\mathbb{P}(Y \in \cdot \mid X) = \mathbb{P}(Y \in \cdot \mid T(X))$.

(A3) Perception and decision models. A differentiable representation $f_\phi : \mathcal{X} \to \mathcal{Z}$ and a decision $g_\theta : \mathcal{Z} \to \Delta(\mathcal{Y})$ (predictive distribution), trained with a strictly proper loss ℓ (log-loss, Brier, etc.), so the Bayes act for a given Z is $g_\theta^\star(z) = \mathbb{P}(Y \in \cdot \mid Z = z)$. Assume $\mathcal{Z}$ is Euclidean, f_ϕ, g_θ locally Lipschitz, with finite expectations under ℓ, ensuring gradient interchanges via dominated convergence.

(A4) Perception-invariance regularizer. Define

$$L_{\mathrm{inv}}(\phi) = \mathbb{E}\left[\left\|f_\phi(X) - f_\phi(g \cdot X)\right\|_2^2\right], \quad g \sim \mu_G,$$

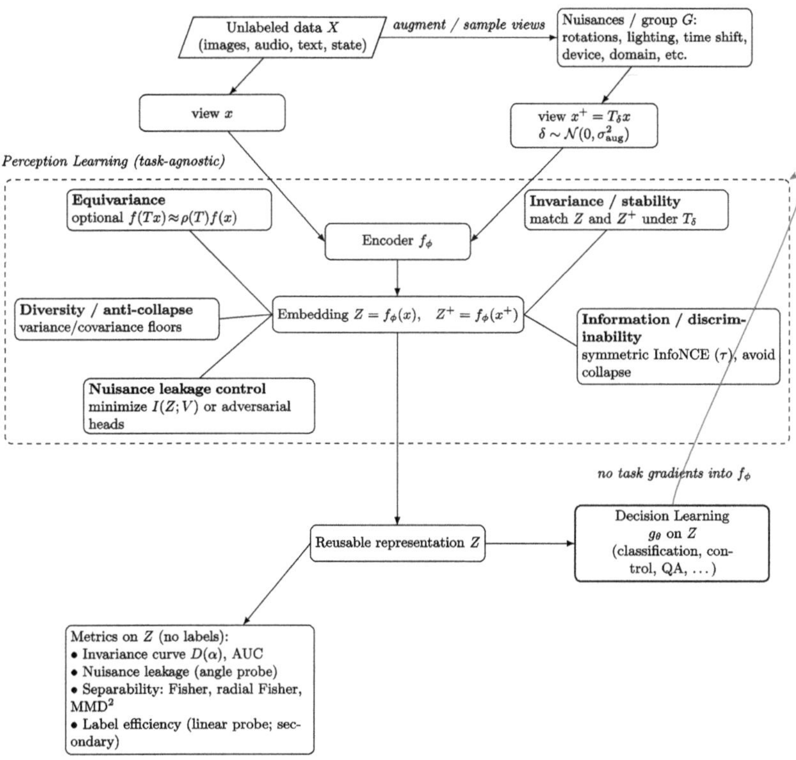

Fig. 2. PeL trains f_ϕ on unlabeled views to produce a stable, informative, reusable code Z. Task heads g_θ are trained separately and do not backpropagate into f_ϕ.

for some probability measure μ_G on G. Its minima are (representations f_ϕ that are) G-invariant: $f_\phi(g{\cdot}x) = f_\phi(x)$.

(A5) Factor-through-T condition. We say f_ϕ factors through T if $f_\phi = h \circ T$ for some measurable $h : \mathcal{T} \to \mathcal{Z}$. We write $\sigma(Z)$ for the σ-algebra generated by a random variable Z.

Notation. Task risk $R(\phi,\theta) = \mathbb{E}\,\ell\big(g_\theta(f_\phi(X)), Y\big)$. The Bayes (task) risk through f_ϕ is $F(\phi) := \inf_\theta R(\phi,\theta)$. By strict propriety of ℓ, $F(\phi)$ is achieved by $g_\theta^\star(z) = \mathbb{P}(Y \in \cdot \mid Z = z)$ and can be written as $F(\phi) = \mathbb{E}\,L_\ell\big(\mathbb{P}(Y \in \cdot \mid Z)\big)$ for a convex functional L_ℓ determined by ℓ.

6.1 Orthogonality Under Group Invariance

The next result establishes that, under task-true group invariance, PeL updates that enhance stability without altering the information content of the invariant sufficient statistic are orthogonal to the Bayes task-risk gradient, justifying the separation of perception and decision learning.

Theorem 1. (Orthogonality of PeL Updates to Bayes-risk Gradient).
*Assume **(A1)–(A5)** and let ϕ_0 satisfy $f_{\phi_0} = h_0 \circ T$ with h_0 injective on $\mathrm{range}(T)$ (so $\sigma(f_{\phi_0}(X)) = \sigma(T(X))$). Let v be any tangent direction at ϕ_0 such that, for all sufficiently small t, $f_{\phi_0 + tv} = h_t \circ T$ for some measurable h_t that remains injective on $\mathrm{range}(T)$. Assume $\mathcal{M}$ is locally smooth, with h_t continuous in t. Then:*

$$\mathrm{D}_v F(\phi_0) = 0.$$

In particular, if $\nabla_\phi L_{\mathrm{inv}}(\phi_0)$ is such a direction (i.e., it only improves G-invariance without altering $\sigma(T(X))$), then

$$\nabla_\phi F(\phi_0) \cdot \nabla_\phi L_{\mathrm{inv}}(\phi_0) = 0.$$

Proof. By strict propriety of ℓ and the envelope theorem, $F(\phi) = \mathbb{E}\, L_\ell\big(\mathbb{P}(Y \in \cdot \mid Z_\phi)\big)$ with $Z_\phi = f_\phi(X)$, and the derivative $\mathrm{D}_v F(\phi_0)$ depends only on how the posterior $\eta_\phi(z) := \mathbb{P}(Y \in \cdot \mid Z_\phi = z)$ varies with ϕ along v. Under **(A2)** we have the conditional independence $Y \perp\!\!\!\perp X \mid T(X)$, hence

$$\mathbb{P}(Y \in \cdot \mid Z_\phi) = \mathbb{E}[\, \mathbb{P}(Y \in \cdot \mid T) \mid Z_\phi \,] = \mathbb{E}[\, \eta_T \mid Z_\phi \,],$$

where $\eta_T := \mathbb{P}(Y \in \cdot \mid T)$. If $f_\phi = h \circ T$ with h injective on $\mathrm{range}(T)$, then $\sigma(Z_\phi) = \sigma(T)$ and thus

$$\mathbb{P}(Y \in \cdot \mid Z_\phi) = \mathbb{E}[\, \eta_T \mid \sigma(Z_\phi) \,] = \mathbb{E}[\, \eta_T \mid \sigma(T) \,] = \eta_T$$

almost surely. Therefore $F(\phi) = \mathbb{E}\, L_\ell(\eta_T)$ is constant over the set of ϕ such that f_ϕ factors through T with an injective h on $\mathrm{range}(T)$. By the hypothesis on the tangent direction v, for all sufficiently small t, $f_{\phi_0 + tv} = h_t \circ T$ with h_t injective on $\mathrm{range}(T)$, so the posterior $\mathbb{P}(Y \in \cdot \mid Z_{\phi_0 + tv})$ equals η_T for all small t, and hence $F(\phi_0 + tv)$ is constant in t. Thus $\mathrm{D}_v F(\phi_0) = 0$. For the last statement, if $\nabla_\phi L_{\mathrm{inv}}(\phi_0)$ is tangent to the same manifold (i.e., it changes h but keeps $\sigma(Z_\phi) = \sigma(T)$), then by definition of directional derivative

$$\nabla_\phi F(\phi_0) \cdot \nabla_\phi L_{\mathrm{inv}}(\phi_0) = \mathrm{D}_{-\nabla_\phi L_{\mathrm{inv}}} F(\phi_0) = 0,$$

establishing orthogonality.

Remark 2. If the task is truly G-invariant **(A1)** and the representation already captures exactly the orbit information T (no more, no less), then any further deformation of f_ϕ that keeps it a one-to-one reparametrization of T leaves the Bayes posterior, and hence Bayes risk, unchanged. Perception-learning steps that only strengthen invariance (reduce within-orbit variance) without identifying distinct orbits collapse nothing task-relevant; they are therefore "orthogonal" to task-risk improvement.

Corollary 1. (Two-stage Optimality Under Exact Invariance). *Under (A1)–(A5), if $f_{\phi^\star} = h^\star \circ T$ with $h^\star$ injective on* range(T), *then*

$$\inf_\theta R(\phi^\star, \theta) = \inf_\theta \mathbb{E}\,\ell\big(g_\theta(Z), Y\big) \quad \text{with } Z = T(X)$$

achieves Bayes risk. Hence optimizing f_ϕ to (any) injective invariant parameterization of T can be done prior to decision learning without sacrificing asymptotic task optimality.

Proof. Immediate from the proof of Theorem 1. If $\sigma(Z) = \sigma(T)$ then $\mathbb{P}(Y \in \cdot \mid Z) = \eta_T$ and the Bayes act attains Bayes risk.

6.2   Clarifying the Role of Assumptions

Assumptions (A1)(A2) establish the statistical backbone. (A1) states that the true posterior is constant on G-orbits; (A2) upgrades this to a sufficiency statement, asserting the existence of an invariant statistic T with $Y \perp\!\!\!\perp X \mid T(X)$. Consequently, whenever $\sigma(Z) = \sigma(T)$, conditioning on the representation $Z = f_\phi(X)$ is equivalent to conditioning on T, which lets the Bayes risk be expressed entirely through the G-invariant information.

Injectivity on range(T) appears to prevent coarsening, i.e., if $f_\phi = h \circ T$ with h not injective on range(T), then $Z = h(T)$ merges distinct orbits and may increase Bayes risk. We only require injectivity on the support of T, which is weaker than global invertibility. Regarding the PeL update, when f_{ϕ_0} is already near-invariant (small L_{inv}), first-order updates that minimize L_{inv} primarily reduce within-orbit variance and can be viewed as moving within (or tangent to) the manifold of T-preserving reparameterizations; as long as the update does not merge distinct orbits i.e., $\sigma(Z) = \sigma(T)$ is preserved, it lies in the tangent cone used in Theorem 1. This is precisely the PeL regime, strengthening invariance without losing orbit identity. Assumption (A3) provides a clean, differentiable Bayes-risk functional of the posterior. With a strictly proper loss and mild regularity,

$$F(\phi) \;=\; \inf_\theta \mathcal{R}(\phi, \theta) \;=\; \mathbb{E}\,L_\ell\big(\mathbb{P}(Y \in \cdot \mid Z_\phi)\big),$$

and directional derivatives $\mathrm{D}_v F(\phi)$ are well defined and compatible with envelope arguments. Assumption (A5) identifies the flat manifold of the Bayes risk

$$\mathcal{M} \;=\; \big\{\phi : f_\phi = h \circ T, \; h \text{ injective on range}(T)\big\},$$

i.e., all injective reparameterizations of the sufficient invariant T. On $\mathcal{M}$ we have $\sigma(Z_\phi) = \sigma(T(X))$, hence $F(\phi)$ is constant and $\mathrm{D}_v F(\phi) = 0$ for tangent directions v.

Assumption (A4) supplies a concrete perception objective L_{inv}. When the update direction preserves $\sigma(Z) = \sigma(T)$ (i.e., remains in the tangent cone of $\mathcal{M}$), then at $\phi_0 \in \mathcal{M}$,

$$\nabla_\phi F(\phi_0) \cdot \nabla_\phi L_{\text{inv}}(\phi_0) = 0,$$

establishing orthogonality of PeL updates to the Bayes risk gradient.

Taken together, (A1)(A5) justify training perception to be (correctly) G-invariant without harming Bayes risk, and they delineate the failure modes when invariances are mis-specified or when updates merge distinct orbits.

6.3   Counterexample: Over-Invariance Can Hurt

We now show that enforcing too much invariance can strictly increase Bayes risk when (A1) fails (the label is not invariant) or when the update destroys orbit identity (h not injective on range(T)). Let $X = (U, V)$ with $U, V \in \{0, 1\}$ i.i.d. Bernoulli(1/2). Define the label $Y := V$ (so V is causal for Y and not a nuisance). Let $G = \{\mathrm{id}, \tau\}$ act by flipping V, i.e., $\tau \cdot (u, v) = (u, 1 - v)$. Then (A1) is false, i.e., $\mathbb{P}(Y = 1 \mid X = (u, v)) = v$ is not G-invariant. Now consider three representations.

$$Z_{\mathrm{full}} = X, \qquad Z_{\mathrm{good}} = V, \qquad Z_{\mathrm{bad}} = U \quad (G\text{-invariant w.r.t. } \tau).$$

Under 0–1 loss (misclassification error), Bayes risks satisfy

$$\mathcal{R}^\star(Z_{\mathrm{full}}) = 0, \qquad \mathcal{R}^\star(Z_{\mathrm{good}}) = 0, \qquad \mathcal{R}^\star(Z_{\mathrm{bad}}) = \tfrac{1}{2}.$$

Indeed, given $Z_{\mathrm{bad}} = U$, the posterior $\mathbb{P}(Y = 1 \mid U) = \tfrac{1}{2}$, so one cannot beat random guess (for log-loss, $H(Y|U) = 1$ vs. $H(Y|V) = 0$). Here, enforcing invariance to flipping V (by mapping both $(u, 0)$ and $(u, 1)$ to the same code) destroys label information and doubles the Bayes risk from 0 to $1/2$.

Next, we consider a vision-flavored variant ("6 vs 9"). Let G be 180° rotations on images. If the label is the digit identity as written ("6" vs "9"), then $\mathbb{P}(Y \mid X)$ is not invariant to 180° rotation: rotating a "6" yields a "9". Any representation forced to be invariant to 180° rotation merges these two classes and raises the Bayes risk to the chance level. This illustrates that the correct invariance set must be task-true (and satisfy A1). Thus, PeL should target nuisances, not causal factors.

7   Conclusion

We formulated PeL as a distinct optimization paradigm with concrete objectives, task-agnostic metrics, and a rigorous separation from decision learning. By directly targeting perceptual properties, PeL yields reusable, robust codes Z that support modularity and transfer. Our orthogonality theorem establishes that, under task-true invariances, PeL refinements leave Bayes risk unchanged. This motivates perception-first architectures aligned with psychological accounts of sensory adaptation and invites future work on estimating or relaxing invariance sets G and scaling PeL's metrics to complex modalities.

References

1. Gibson, E.J.: Principles of perceptual learning and development. Appleton-Century-Crofts, New York (1969)
2. Goldstone, R.l.: Perceptual learning. Ann. Rev. Psychol., **49**, 585–612 (1998). https://doi.org/10.1146/annurev.psych.49.1.585
3. Bengio, Y., Courville, A., Vincent, P.: Representation learning: a review and new perspectives. IEEE Trans. Patt. Analy. Mach. Intell. **35**(8), 1798–1828 (2013). https://doi.org/10.1109/TPAMI.2013.50
4. Oord, A. V. D., Li, Y., Vinyals, O.: Representation learning with contrastive predictive coding (2018). https://doi.org/10.48550/arXiv.1807.03748
5. Chen, T., Kornblith, S., Norouzi, M., Hinton, G.: A simple framework for contrastive learning of visual representations. In: Proceedings of the 37th International Conference on Machine Learning (ICML), vol. 119 of Proceedings of Machine Learning Research, pp. 1597–1607 (2020). https://dl.acm.org/doi/10.5555/3524938.3525087
6. He, K., Fan, H., Wu, Y., Xie, S., Girshick, R.: Momentum contrast for unsupervised visual representation learning. In: Proceedings of the IEEE/CVF Conference on Computer Vision and Pattern Recognition (CVPR), pp. 9729–9738 (2020). https://doi.org/10.1109/CVPR42600.2020.00975
7. Grill, J.B., et al.: Bootstrap your own latent: a new approach to self-supervised learning. Adv. Neural Inf. Process. Syst. (NeurIPS), 33 (2020). https://dl.acm.org/doi/abs/10.5555/3495724.3497510
8. He, K., Chen, X., Xie, S., Li, Y., Dollár, P., Girshick, R.: Masked autoencoders are scalable vision learners. In: Proceedings of the IEEE/CVF Conference on Computer Vision and Pattern Recognition (CVPR) (2022). https://doi.org/10.1109/CVPR52688.2022.01545
9. Oquab, M., et al.: DINOv2: Learning robust visual features without supervision. Trans. Mach. Learn. Res. (2024). https://doi.org/10.48550/arXiv.2304.07193 (2023)
10. Baevski, A., Hsu, W. N., Xu, Q., Babu, A., Gu, J., Auli, M.: data2vec: a general framework for self-supervised learning in speech, vision and language. In: Proceedings of the 39th International Conference on Machine Learning, vol. 162 of Proceedings of Machine Learning Research, pp. 1298–1312 (2022). https://doi.org/10.48550/arXiv.2202.03555
11. Radford, A., et al.: Learning transferable visual models from natural language supervision. In: Proceedings of the 38th International Conference on Machine Learning (ICML), vol. 139 of Proceedings of Machine Learning Research, pp. 8748–8763 (2021). https://doi.org/10.48550/arXiv.2103.00020
12. Assran, M., et al.: Self-supervised learning from images with a joint-embedding predictive architecture. In: Proceedings of the IEEE/CVF Conference on Computer Vision and Pattern Recognition (CVPR), pp. 15623–15633 (2023). https://doi.org/10.1109/CVPR52729.2023.01499
13. Fuchs, F., Worrall, D., Fischer, V., Welling, M.: SE(3)-Transformers: 3D roto-translation equivariant attention networks. Adv. Neural Inf. Process. Syst. (NeurIPS), 33 (2020). https://doi.org/10.48550/arXiv.2006.10503
14. Arjovsky, M., Bottou, L., Gulrajani, I., Lopez-Paz, D.: Invariant risk minimization (2019). https://doi.org/10.48550/arXiv.1907.02893
15. Bajcsy, R.: Active perception. Proc. IEEE **76**(8), 966–1005 (1988). https://doi.org/10.1109/5.5968

16. Hafner, D., Pasukonis, J., Ba, J., Lillicrap, T.: Mastering diverse control tasks through world models. Nature **640**, 647–653 (2025). https://doi.org/10.1038/s41586-025-08744-2
17. Jaegle, A., Gimeno, F., Brock, A., Vinyals, O., Zisserman, A., Carreira, J.: Perceiver: general perception with iterative attention. In: Proceedings of the 38th International Conference on Machine Learning (ICML), vol. 139 of Proceedings of Machine Learning Research, pp. 4651–4664. PMLR, 18–24 Jul (2021). https://proceedings.mlr.press/v139/jaegle21a.html
18. Jaegle, A., et al.: Perceiver IO: a general architecture for structured inputs & outputs. In: International Conference on Learning Representations (2021). arXiv:2103.03206v2
19. Gretton, A., Borgwardt, K.M., Rasch, M.J., Schölkopf, B., Smola, A.: A kernel two-sample test. J. Mach. Learn. Res., **13**, 723–773 (2012). https://dl.acm.org/doi/10.5555/2188385.2188410
20. Tishby, N., Pereira, F.C., Bialek, W.: The information bottleneck method. In: Proceedings of the 37th Annual Allerton Conference on Communication, Control and Computing, pp. 368–377 (1999). https://doi.org/10.48550/arXiv.physics/0004057
21. Alemi, A.A., Fischer, I., Dillon, J.V., Murphy, K.: Deep variational information bottleneck. In: International Conference on Learning Representations (ICLR) (2017). https://openreview.net/forum?id=HyxQzBceg
22. Cohen, T.S., Welling, M.: Group equivariant convolutional networks. In: Proceedings of the 33rd International Conference on Machine Learning (ICML), vol. 48 of Proceedings of Machine Learning Research (PMLR), pp. 2990–2999 (2016). https://proceedings.mlr.press/v48/cohenc16.html
23. Ha, D., Schmidhuber, J.: World Models. (Presented at the NeurIPS 2018 Workshop on Modeling the Physical World.) https://doi.org/10.48550/arXiv.1803.10122

Analysing Trends in Community Evolution in Open-Source Software Collaboration Networks

Reshma Roychoudhuri$^{(\boxtimes)}$, Bharat Kumar Jhawar, Harsh Lakhotia, and Arunima Saha

Heritage Institute of Technology, Kolkata, India
reshma.roychoudhuri@heritageit.edu,
{bharat.kumarjhawar.cse26,harsh.lakhotia.cse26,
arunima.saha.cse26}@heritageit.edu.in

Abstract. Community development in open-source projects depends on the timely resolution of bugs, which in turn relies on how developers collaborate during the fixing process. While prior research has largely analyzed bug tracker data such as reports and resolution history, it has often overlooked the teamwork dynamics that shape effective problem-solving. In this work, we ask: *Do consistent patterns of collaboration and community development emerge across large open-source communities, despite differences in their contexts?* To investigate, we constructed developer collaboration networks from multi-year bug data in three major ecosystems - Eclipse, OpenStack, and Red Hat - and analyzed their structural properties over time. Our findings reveal recurring structural patterns in community interaction during bug resolution, suggesting that collaboration in software communities may follow generalizable principles that extend beyond individual projects.

Keywords: Bug Resolution · Community Development · Developer Collaboration Networks · Network & Temporal Analysis · Open Source Projects

1 Introduction

Software systems inevitably contain bugs, and fixing them promptly is one of the most central tasks in software development with the potential to impact the overall project outcome [5]. Bugs that take too long to resolve can delay project timelines, and damage the project's reputation. Developer participation is one of the critical factors that can impact the overall effectiveness of the bug resolution phase [9]. This makes it essential to study not only how bugs are fixed, but also how developer collaboration impacts the bug resolution process.

Most previous research in this area has focused mainly on statistical analyses, particularly correlational analysis of bug tracking data. These studies examine factors such as bug severity, developer workload, or priority labels to understand

C. Zaroliagis et al. (Eds.): ICAA 2026, LNCS 16423, pp. 365–376, 2026.
https://doi.org/10.1007/978-3-032-15621-1_30

resolution times. [2,17]. Although such factors are valuable, they do not fully capture the human collaboration that is at the heart of bug fixing. In reality, solving a bug often involves several developers exchanging comments, reviewing code, and coordinating efforts.

In this paper, we aim to focus on how developer communities evolve. We build and study Developer Collaboration Networks, where developers are represented as nodes, and when developers comment on the same bug, they are joined by an edge. For our study, we have considered data from three major open-source projects - *OpenStack, Eclipse,* and *Red Hat* - spanning different time ranges and scales. We have constructed multiple cumulative networks, each representing different time ranges, and have studied various network measures such as eigenvector centrality, betweenness centrality, assortativity, clustering, etc., with an aim to observe how developer communities evolve, how team dynamics change as projects grow, and their relation with bug resolution time.

Our findings reveal two main observations. Firstly, a few metrics exhibit consistent patterns across all three datasets, pointing to universal aspects of collaboration that transcend project-specific differences. Secondly, a few metrics that showed variability across projects reflected the distinct histories and communities behind each dataset. (Details of these fluctuations are discussed later in the Results section.)

Our work makes the following contributions:

1. We introduce a *cumulative period-wise* approach to network construction, enabling us to capture not only snapshots of collaboration, but also its accumulation over time.
2. We compute a comprehensive set of temporal and structural developer collaboration network and measures properties such as centralization, clustering, density, etc., to understand the evolving organization of developer communities.
3. We connect these structural measures to project outcomes by comparing them with bug-resolution time, thereby assessing whether collaboration patterns co-vary with how efficiently bugs are closed.
4. We provide interpretations of these patterns in the context of software engineering practice, highlighting how developer collaboration structures can enable efficient bug resolution.

We pose the following research question to guide our analysis:

Research Question: Do consistent trends emerge in the development of communities in large open source projects, despite differences in context and scale? Based on this, we define our hypotheses as follows:

Null Hypothesis (H_0): Community evolution in large-scale open-source software systems has the potential to impact key project outcome like bug resolution times.

Alternative Hypothesis (H_a): Community evolution do not impact key project outcomes in large-scale open-source software development eco-systems.

2   Related Work

Research on bug resolution has advanced substantially, covering both technical and social perspectives of developer collaboration. Early work of Xuan [14] and Xia [12] showed that developer prioritization and recommendation systems accelerate bug fixing, highlighting the role of social ties. Later studies extended this with analyses of reporter reputation [15], developer similarity [13], and data-driven recommendation models [10], demonstrating that resolution efficiency is strongly community-driven.

Another research direction characterizes bug resolution times and influencing factors. Zhang [18] surveyed key tasks and challenges, while Tian [11] questioned the reliability of severity as a predictor. Empirical studies further expanded this scope: Zhang [16] analyzed language-level differences, Eiroa-Lledo [3] examined large-scale resolution factors, and Kim [4] applied log analysis for performance prediction. Together, these works emphasize the complexity of predicting resolution outcomes. Recent studies also link community structures to bug resolution efficiency. Datta [2], Roychoudhuri [8], and Maulik [6] showed how parity, repeat interactions, and causality shape bug fixing across ecosystems. Complementary datasets like BugsRepo [1] and HaPy-Bug [7] provide curated resources enabling such analyses. Collectively, this body of work underscores bug resolution as a socio-technical phenomenon shaped by developer interactions, structural properties, and evolving community dynamics(Table 1).

3   Methodology

3.1   Dataset Description

To study collaboration patterns in open source ecosystems, we focus on three large-scale projects that span different computing paradigms: Eclipse, OpenStack, and Red Hat.

Table 1. Comparison of datasets from Eclipse, OpenStack, and Red Hat.

Index	Eclipse	OpenStack	Red Hat
Domain	Desktop IDE (plug-in based, extensible)	Cloud Computing (IaaS, modular)	Enterprise Linux systems (vendor-driven)
Dataset Source	Bugzilla (2001–2015)	Bug repository (2010–2015)	Bugzilla API (2021–2025)
Dataset Size	227718 comments	385474 comments	163297 comments
Unique bugs	13249	25532	23031
Reference	Roychoudhuri [8]	Roychoudhuri [8]	Lakhotia (2025)[a]

[a] http://bit.ly/47OPbce

Together, these datasets represent a balanced mix of desktop software (Eclipse), cloud infrastructure (OpenStack), and enterprise-grade Linux systems (Red Hat). While all three projects are open source, they differ in terms of scale, functionality, and development context, allowing us to investigate collaboration dynamics across varied yet comparable ecosystems.

3.2   Dataset Transformation and Periodization

We transformed our datasets into temporal Developer Collaboration Networks by dividing the project timelines into equal periods.

In the following section, we outline the key fields and timelines for each dataset.

Eclipse and OpenStack : For our analysis, we obtained bug-tracking data spanning from **11-10-2001 to 02-02-2015** for eclipse and **14-04-2010 to 06-04-2015** for OpenStack.

RedHat : Unlike the other two, considering the RedHat dataset we got from calling the Bugzilla api, provided explicit mappings of comments through detailed logs, making it easier to build the Developer Collaboration Network. We had data spanning from **01-01-2021** to **31-07-2025**

The data set fields include:

- **issue.id/bug_id**: Unique identifier for each reported bug or issue.
- **comments / comment_author/comment_author_id**: Developers who commented, with separation between owners and non-owners.
- **comment_time**: Timestamps marking the beginning and end of comment activity.
- **period**: Assigned temporal interval to which the bug belongs.

The datasets are divided into 20 equal temporal periods for the construction of a cumulative network graph. Overall, our datasets comprise 53,529 unique authors contributing 776,489 comments across 61,812 bugs.

4   Network Construction

Here, we talk about how the raw datasets were transformed into temporal Developer Collaboration Networks. The overall pipeline moves from raw tabular data to period-wise network graphs. Each stage of this pipeline ensures that the networks faithfully capture developer collaboration as reflected in bug reports through activities such as commenting.

4.1   Graph Definitions

The Developer Collaboration Network is constructed as an undirected weighted graph, and the construction rules are as follows:

- **Node types:** Each node corresponds to a developer (identified by comment submission).
- **Edge types:** An undirected edge is created between two developers whenever both have commented on the same bug report.
- **Edge weights:** The weight of an edge corresponds to the frequency of co-commenting, i.e., the number of distinct bugs on which both developers contributed during a given period.

This representation models the natural collaboration environment, which is that developers who frequently interact on different bugs are more strongly connected.

The graph construction proceeds in the following steps:

1. **Input data:** The preprocessed CSV files described in Sect. 3.1 provide mappings from bug identifiers (`issue.id` or `bug.id`) to the corresponding time period.[1]
2. **Intermediate representation:** For each bug, a set of unique contributing developers is extracted. This can be thought of as a dictionary of the form:

$$\text{Bug ID} \rightarrow \{\text{Developer}_1, \text{Developer}_2, \ldots\}$$

3. **Graph construction:** For each bug:
   (a) All pairs of developers from the contributing set are connected once per bug.
   (b) If the same pair co-occurs in multiple bugs, the edge weight is incremented accordingly.
4. **Cumulative temporal handling:** Networks are constructed cumulatively. That is, the graph for period t contains all collaborations observed in earlier periods $1 \ldots (t-1)$ in addition to those newly formed in period t. This ensures that the network grows monotonically, reflecting the accumulation of collaborations over time. The timelines are provided in the respective dataset tables in Sect. 5

Once the cumulative networks were constructed, we focused on a set of widely used structural measures to capture different aspects of collaboration. Specifically, our analysis considered degree, betweenness, closeness, and eigenvector centralization to assess concentration of influence and communication flow; the global clustering coefficient and density to capture cohesion; and assortativity to examine preference for similar or dissimilar collaborators. Together, these measures provide a broad yet complementary view of how developer interactions are structured and evolve in large-scale software projects.

5   Results and Discussion

We constructed cumulative Developer Collaboration Networks (DCNs) for Eclipse, OpenStack, and Red Hat, dividing each project history into 20 cumulative periods. For every cumulative network, we computed the structural metrics

---

[1] A sample CSV snapshot for the Red Hat project https://bit.ly/496FpEA.

outlined in Sect. 4.1, and here we present an analysis of collaboration patterns and assess whether the observed structures support our null or alternate hypotheses.

5.1 Analysis of Network Metrics

Clustering and Density. : The clustering coefficient and network density are widely used indicators of the overall cohesiveness of collaboration networks. The global clustering coefficient captures the tendency of developers' collaborators to also collaborate, essentially reflecting the extent of *triadic closure* in the network.

Density, on the other hand, measures the ratio of actual connections among developers to the maximum possible connections.

Figure 1 shows a steady decline over time for clustering and density consistent across all three datasets, suggesting that as projects expand and attract more contributors, the collaboration structure shifts away from tightly bonded groups toward more fragmented and sparse connections. In practical terms, the likelihood that two developers sharing a common collaborator will themselves work together diminishes as the developer pool grows larger.

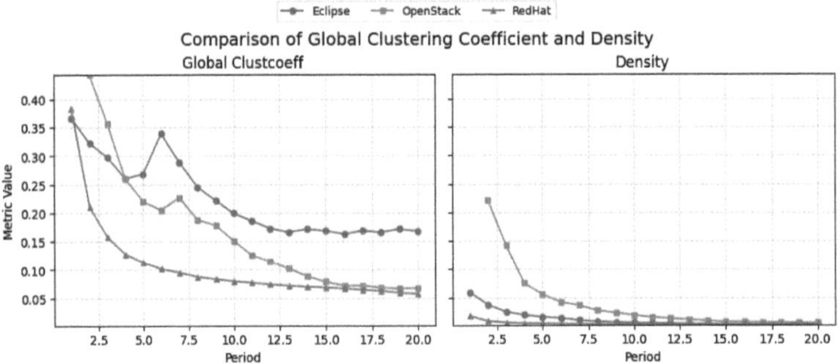

Fig. 1. Temporal trends of global clustering coefficient and density.

The implications of these trends for bug resolution are not straightforward. On one hand, reduced clustering and density may hinder coordination, slowing down the exchange of information and potentially delaying bug resolution. On the other hand, sparser structures may enable a wider distribution of reports, improving the chances that they reach developers with the right expertise and thereby accelerating fixes. In this sense, both inverse and direct relationships between network cohesiveness and resolution time are plausible.

Recognizing that either outcome is possible takes us a step closer to our guiding hypothesis that there exists a factor showing consistent trends across different datasets and contexts. Between the two, the global clustering coefficient acts as an indicator of network cohesion, since it captures local triadic closure and directly reflects how tightly groups of developers are embedded. Density, on the other hand, is a more global measure of overall sparsity and less sensitive to the nuances of evolving group structures. Therefore, we observe the global clustering coefficient as our primary indicator across three major ecosystems, and we build evidence toward identifying such generalizable patterns of community development.

Supporting Structural Metrics: We recognize that no single measure can fully explain collaborative dynamics. Much like weight change depends not only on food intake but also on exercise and metabolism, the relationship between clustering and bug resolution time must be interpreted alongside other network properties.

To this end, we graphically examined the temporal trends of five key network metrics—*closeness centralization, degree centralization, betweenness centralization, eigenvector centralization*, and *assortativity*—to understand how collaboration dynamics evolve within developer communities. Centralization measures capture whether collaborative activities are concentrated among a few dominant contributors or distributed more evenly across the community.

Graphical examination revealed that no universal trend of network metrics exists except for clustering coefficient and density across all three projects. For instance, *OpenStack* demonstrates a steady increase in both closeness and degree centralization over time, suggesting a growing concentration of collaboration among core developers. In contrast, *Eclipse* maintains relatively low and stable centralization, while *Red Hat* occupies an intermediate position between these two extremes. Interestingly, assortativity shows a general upward trend across projects, albeit with notable fluctuations. This pattern indicates that developers are gradually tending to collaborate with peers who are more similar to themselves, though this shift is neither smooth nor uniform.[2]

Taken together, these observations emphasize the importance of interpreting clustering trends alongside centralization and assortativity measures. While clustering reflects the overall cohesiveness of the community, the latter metrics provide complementary insights into how collaboration patterns evolve and how these structural characteristics may influence bug resolution efficiency.

Beyond descriptive trends, we conducted correlation tests to determine whether any of the supporting metrics could serve as covariates in explaining bug resolution time. The results indicated that closeness centralization, eigenvector centralization, and assortativity exhibited acceptable correlation units, making them suitable candidates for inclusion in subsequent modeling.

Finally, to validate the statistical assumptions underlying our analysis, we examined homoscedasticity using scatter plots of residuals versus fitted values.[3] The plots confirmed that the variance of residuals remained reasonably constant across the range of fitted values for closeness centralization, eigenvector centralization, and assortativity, supporting the robustness of these variables in further regression-based exploration.

---

[2] Centralization and assortativity metrics are available at: https://bit.ly/4hK0XJn.

[3] Scatter plots confirming homoscedasticity are available at: https://bit.ly/47B6NYQ.

In addition to structural network properties, we examined a temporal outcome variable: the *cumulative average bug close time (in days)*. This measure captures how bug resolution efficiency evolves as projects progress.

Figure 2 presents the trends for Eclipse, OpenStack, and Red Hat. As expected for cumulative measures, all three projects show an upward trajectory. Eclipse records the steepest rise, exceeding 350 d in the final periods. Red Hat follows with a more moderate increase, while OpenStack remains lower in absolute terms but still shows a gradual climb.

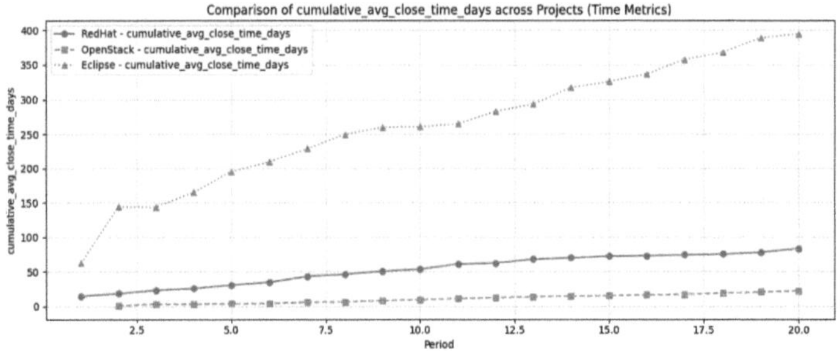

Fig. 2. Cumulative average bug close time (in days).

5.2 Regression Analysis: Testing the Hypotheses

To formally test whether clustering and related structural properties influence bug resolution, we estimated multivariate linear regression models with the cumulative average bug close time (days) as the dependent variable. The global clustering coefficient served as our main predictor, while closeness centralization, eigenvector centralization, and assortativity were included as covariates.

Table 2. Multivariate linear regression results for Eclipse, OpenStack, and Red Hat. Coefficients are shown with significance levels (p-values: ≤ 0.001=****, ≤ 0.01=***, ≤ 0.05=**, ≤ 0.1=*, >0.1=+).

Project	R^2	ClusteringCoeff	Closeness	Eigenvector	Assortativity
Eclipse	0.94	−785.43****	1800.09***	−3600.99****	801.25***
OpenStack	0.96	4.86+	36.12*	−23.62+	56.07****
Red Hat	0.98	357.82**	1644.90*	−242.15+	855.90+

Table 2 reports the results for Eclipse, OpenStack, and Red Hat. Coefficients reflect the direction and magnitude of association, with p-values indicating significance. Across all three ecosystems, the models achieved strong explanatory power ($R^2 > 0.94$), showing that structural properties capture much of the variation in bug resolution times. The findings reveal striking contrasts across ecosystems. In Eclipse, clustering has a strong and significant negative relationship with resolution time: more cohesive triads appear to accelerate coordination and shorten bug-fix cycles. In Red Hat, however, the effect is positive and significant, suggesting that excessive clustering may slow progress by reinforcing silos and duplicating communication channels. OpenStack sits in between- its clustering coefficient is positive but not statistically significant.

The divergence in effects likely reflects contextual differences. Eclipse has substantially fewer bug reports (around 10k fewer) compared to OpenStack and Red Hat, which may allow cohesive groups to improve efficiency.

Taken together, our regression analysis shows that among the structural properties examined, global clustering stands out as the most consistently significant predictor of bug resolution performance. Although its direction of influence varies by project, its repeated importance across ecosystems highlights its central role in collaboration dynamics. Along with the trend observed in global clustering coefficient in Sect. 5.1, this provides evidence in support of our null hypothesis (H_0) that community evolution identifiers like global clustering coefficient exert a consistent influence across open-source projects, despite differences in scale, size, and governance, with the potential to impact key project outcomes like bug resolution times. Other metrics, such as centralization and assortativity, align with clustering in some cases, but lack the same consistency.

5.3   Implications for Software Development Practice

Developers working in large-scale open-source software development ecosystems gradually form a community. In a people-centric ecosystem like software development the evolution of this community is bound to impact key project outcomes, like bug resolution times. Our study thus provides key insights to all stakeholders of such large-scale software development ecosystems for tailoring community development strategies to project size. After studying trends across multiple datasets we find evidence that communities become less tightly-knit over time. A possible reason could be the influx of fresh faces over time who work in specialized areas but do not form strong bonds with the larger developer community as a whole. Conventional wisdom would dictate that over time, collaboration networks grow tighter and more dense. Our results, however, indicate a counterintuitive trend.

More broadly, these findings underscore that bug resolution is not only a technical process but also a social one. The efficiency of software development depends as much on how developers interact as on the quality of the code itself. Recognizing and adapting to these dynamics offers a pathway to more resilient, efficient, and sustainable open-source ecosystems.

6   Threats to Validity

Threats to construct validity, internal validity, external validity, and reliability are discussed in this section.

Construct Validity - A primary threat to construct validity arises from our use of proxies for collaboration and experience. For example, we represent developer collaboration through co-commenting on bugs, which may not capture all forms of coordination such as code reviews, design discussions, or offline communication. Similarly, network measures like centrality are assumed to reflect influence or importance, though these interpretations may not fully align with the realities of project dynamics. While these proxies are widely used in prior work, we acknowledge that they only approximate the underlying constructs.

Internal Validity - Our study is based on historical bug-tracking data, which limits our ability to control for confounding factors such as bug severity, code complexity, or organizational deadlines. These factors may also influence bug-resolution times and could bias the associations we observe between network measures and outcomes. Since our work is correlational, causality cannot be established. We mitigate this threat by focusing on trends across multiple ecosystems rather than single-point estimates.

External Validity - All three datasets we analyzed come from large open-source ecosystems. While this diversity improves generalizability within open-source contexts, the results may not directly transfer to proprietary or small-scale projects, where collaboration is governed by different processes. Our findings should therefore be interpreted primarily as insights into large-scale open-source communities.

Reliability - To ensure reliability, we used publicly available bug-tracker data and well-defined network analysis methods. In order to ensure replication of our results we share a replication package[4].

Overall, while these threats exist, we believe our design choices allow us to draw useful insights

7   Conclusion and Future Work

This study set out to examine whether consistent factors emerge in the development of large open-source communities, despite their differences in scale and governance. By analyzing Developer Collaboration Networks (DCNs) across Eclipse, OpenStack, and Red Hat, we found that global clustering coefficient consistently influences bug resolution time, even though its direction of effect varies by project. Supporting metrics such as assortativity and centralization provided additional context, but clustering stood out as the most reliable indicator of collaboration outcomes. These findings support our null hypothesis that at least one structural factor shows consistent influence across projects.

---

[4] https://bit.ly/4qH6692.

That said, our study also has limitations. The datasets used differ in size, with Eclipse (with 13 thousand bugs, approximately) contains substantially fewer bugs than OpenStack and Red Hat, which may explain some of the contrasting results. Future work should extend this analysis to additional projects and larger datasets to confirm the robustness of these patterns. Expanding beyond bug resolution to other aspects of the project health, such as feature development or contributor retention, would also offer a more holistic view of how community structures shape open-source ecosystems.

References

1. Acharya, J., Ginde, G.: Bugsrepo: a comprehensive curated dataset of bug reports, comments and contributors information from bugzilla. arXiv preprint arXiv:2504.18806 (2025)
2. Datta, S., Roychoudhuri, R., Majumder, S.: Understanding the relation between repeat developer interactions and bug resolution times in large open source ecosystems: A multisystem study. J. Softw. Evol. Proc. **33**(4), e2317 (2021)
3. Eiroa-Lledo, E., Ali, R.H., Pinto, G., Anderson, J., Linstead, E.: Large-scale identification and analysis of factors impacting simple bug resolution times in open source software repositories. Appl. Sci. **13**(5), 3150 (2023)
4. Kim, S., Sim, A., Wu, K., Byna, S., Son, Y.: Design and implementation of i/o performance prediction scheme on HPC systems through large-scale log analysis. J. Big Data **10**(1), 65 (2023)
5. Marks, L., Zou, Y., Hassan, A.E.: Studying the fix-time for bugs in large open source projects. In: Proceedings of the 7th International Conference on Predictive Models in Software Engineering,pp. 1–8 (2011)
6. Maulik, R., Datta, S., Majumder, S.: The causality of bug resolution: a tale of two systems. In: Proceedings of the 33rd ACM International Conference on the Foundations of Software Engineering, pp. 1410–1417 (2025)
7. Przymus, P., et al.: Hapy-bug–human annotated python bug resolution dataset. In: 2025 IEEE/ACM 22nd International Conference on Mining Software Repositories (MSR), pp. 81–85. IEEE (2025)
8. Roychoudhuri, R., Datta, S., Majumder, S.: More equal than others? parity in developer interaction and its relation to bug resolution time. Innovations in Systems and Software Engineering, pp. 1–13 (2024)
9. Roychoudhuri, R., Datta, S., Majumder, S.: Does varied developer interactions cause bugs to be resolved faster? a study of open source software ecosystems. In: International Conference on Applied Algorithms, pp. 301–314. Springer (2025)
10. Saxena, S., Gupta, C.: Optimizing bug resolution: a data-driven developer recommendation system. Int. J. Perf. Eng. **20**(8) (2024)
11. Tian, Y., Ali, N., Lo, D., Hassan, A.E.: On the unreliability of bug severity data. Empir. Softw. Eng. **21**(6), 2298–2323 (2016)
12. Xia, X., Lo, D., Wang, X., Zhou, B.: Accurate developer recommendation for bug resolution. In: 2013 20th Working Conference on Reverse Engineering (WCRE), pp. 72–81. IEEE (2013)
13. Xia, X., Lo, D., Wang, X., Zhou, B.: Dual analysis for recommending developers to resolve bugs. J. Softw. Evol. Proc. **27**(3), 195–220 (2015)

14. Xuan, J., Jiang, H., Ren, Z., Zou, W.: Developer prioritization in bug repositories. In: 2012 34th International Conference on Software Engineering (ICSE), pp. 25–35. IEEE (2012)
15. Yucel, M.K., Tosun, A.: Measuring bug reporter's reputation and its effect on bug resolution time prediction. In: 2022 7th International Conference on Computer Science and Engineering (UBMK), pp. 110–115. IEEE (2022)
16. Zhang, J.M., et al.: A study of bug resolution characteristics in popular programming languages. IEEE Trans. Software Eng. **47**(12), 2684–2697 (2019)
17. Zhang, T., Jiang, H., Luo, X., Chan, A.T.: A literature review of research in bug resolution: tasks, challenges and future directions. Comput. J. **59**(5), 741–773 (2016). https://doi.org/10.1093/comjnl/bxv114
18. Zhang, T., Jiang, H., Luo, X., Chan, A.T.: A literature review of research in bug resolution: tasks, challenges and future directions. Comput. J. **59**(5), 741–773 (2016)

A Transfer Learning Framework on Image-Transformed Sensor Data for Smartphone Based Human Activity Recognition

Subham Das[1] , Anindita Saha[1(✉)] , and Chandreyee Chowdhury[2]

[1] Techno Main SaltLake, Kolkata, India
`anindita_saha03@yahoo.co.in`
[2] Jadavpur University, Kolkata, India

Abstract. Human Activity Recognition (HAR) enables context-aware applications using sensor data, supporting advancements in IoT-based health monitoring, smart environments, and ambient assisted living. With the growing use of smartphone sensors, time-series data from accelerometers and gyroscopes have become a primary modality for activity classification. This study presents a deep learning-based HAR framework employing both raw time-series and image-transformed representations to assess the comparative performance of 1D and 2D Convolutional Neural Networks (CNNs), alongside Transfer Learning (TL) techniques using well-known pretrained models such as ResNet50 and VGG16. A large-scale dataset of 1.5 million tri-axial accelerometer records was collected from five users performing five daily activities. Raw data were used to train a 1D-CNN, while sliding-window transformations enabled 2D-CNN evaluation, confirming the effectiveness of image-based representations for activity recognition. Building on this, TL was applied by fine-tuning pretrained models at varying input image resolutions. Among the evaluated models, VGG16 at 300×300 resolution achieved the highest classification accuracy of 98.70%, demonstrating the effectiveness of TL in retaining fine-grained discriminative features. These results highlight the strong generalization capability of pretrained CNNs on image-based sensor data, advocating their suitability for robust, reliable, and scalable activity recognition in real-world IoT-driven applications.

Keywords: Human Activity Recognition · Transfer Learning · Time-series Classification · Smartphone Sensors

1 Introduction

Human Activity Recognition (HAR) is a critical enabling technology in the broader domain of Internet of Things (IoT)-based pervasive computing, that has become a cornerstone in ubiquitous computing, enabling numerous applications in healthcare, smart homes, fitness monitoring, and assistive technologies.

C. Zaroliagis et al. (Eds.): ICAA 2026, LNCS 16423, pp. 377–389, 2026.
https://doi.org/10.1007/978-3-032-15621-1_31

HAR aims to infer a subject's physical state or movement (e.g., walking, jogging, sitting) by analyzing sensor data, most commonly from IMUs embedded in smartphones, wearables, or ambient devices [1,2]. Traditional HAR systems rely on classical Machine Learning, where time-series data are manually segmented and features are handcrafted using statistical, temporal, or spectral methods [3]. However, these approaches are labor-intensive, domain-dependent, and lack scalability across diverse users, sensors, and activities. Moreover, they cannot learn hierarchical representations, limiting robustness in noisy, dynamic, and multi-user environments with high inter-subject variability. In contrast, Deep Learning (DL) approaches, particularly Convolutional Neural Networks (CNNs), have emerged as powerful alternatives by automatically learning hierarchical, discriminative features representations from raw sensor data [4,5]. Researchers have shown that 1D-CNNs effectively capture local temporal dependencies in multi-channel sensor time-series without manual feature engineering but are limited in modeling inter-dimensional correlations and long-range temporal patterns, especially under sensor noise or complex activities. Transforming data into image-like representations for 2D-CNNs improves spatial feature extraction but can cause temporal resolution loss and semantic misalignment. Both approaches require large labeled datasets and show limited cross-subject or cross-device generalization, while sensor annotation remains labor-intensive. To overcome the limitations of 1D and 2D CNNs in HAR, Transfer Learning (TL) [6] leverages pretrained deep models trained from large-scale visual datasets. Fine-tuning these models on image-transformed sensor data enhances feature representation, improves generalization across subjects and activities, reduces reliance on extensive labeled datasets, and accelerates convergence. TL also facilitates scalable knowledge transfer across domains, addressing variations in sensor modality, placement, and subject-specific differences [7,8]. Recent studies using VGGNet and ResNet for sensor-based HAR such as [9–11] either converted time-series to images or processed raw signals, but failed to capture temporal dynamics and lacked cross-subject transferability. In our work, TL-driven HAR framework, is proposed, primarily focusing on the efficacy of leveraging pretrained deep convolutional models for improved activity classification in pervasive computing environments. A large-scale dataset comprising 1.5 million sensor records, collected from five users performing five common activities: jogging, walking, standing, sitting, and laying. An initial 1D-CNN model trained on raw sequential sensor data demonstrated strong performance in capturing temporal dependencies. To further exploit spatial correlations, the sequences were transformed into image representations using a sliding window protocol, and a baseline 2D-CNN applied to these images achieved improved performance. Motivated by this, we adopt TL using pretrained ResNet50 and VGG16 architectures, which are optimized for image-based feature extraction. Leveraging these models allows for robust representation learning, reduces the need for extensive labeled data, and enhances generalization across subjects, sensor placements, and activity variations. The primary objective and novelty of this work lies in the systematic evaluation of TL strategies combined with an optimized time-series-to-image transformation pipeline on a large-scale, multi-user, multi-device HAR dataset and to exhibit that TL improves the overall feature representation, generalization, and classification accuracy under limited labeled data in HAR. The main contributions of this paper are as follows:

- A large-scale multi-user, multi-device dataset of smartphone accelerometer signals covering five static and dynamic human activities for evaluating model generalization.
- Comparative analysis using raw time-series with 1D-CNNs and image representations via sliding-window segmentation with 2D-CNNs.
- Demonstration of the effectiveness of TL by fine-tuning pre-trained ResNet50 and VGG16 at different input resolutions, showing the ability of sensor-derived image representations to capture discriminative features for scalable human activity recognition.

2   Related Work

Several works have investigated the application of TL on smartphone-based and wearable sensor data to address subject variability, device heterogeneity, and data scarcity. In [12], authors presented a decade-long survey of TL, categorizing feature adaptation, deep network adaptation, and adversarial approaches for cross-domain scenarios. Authors like [13] proposed a method leveraging pseudo-label generation based on similarity between source and target domains, but its dependence on handcrafted similarity functions and shared sensor types limits its generalization whereas a joint adaptation network was introduced by [14] to align source and target distributions, enhancing domain transfer in HAR but without leveraging pretrained visual backbones. Some contributions like [15] analyzed vision-based HAR methods using TL over a decade, providing taxonomy and benchmark insights. In [16], a survey of heterogeneous TL including instance reweighting and feature transformation is presented though it lacks the application to time-series image transformations. Authors in [17] employed PCA with distribution-based metrics for aligning feature spaces, reducing the need for labeled data but constrained by sensor homogeneity. A domain-invariant TL framework with fine-tuning was proposed by [18] demonstrating improved recognition across users but without using time-series to image transformations. In [19], authors reused knowledge via CNNs for accelerometer based HAR but lacked pretrained deep models like VGG or ResNet whereas [20,21] offered extensive reviews of CNN-based TL strategies, including weight initialization and fine-tuning, but with limited coverage of sensor-based adaptations. Other significant researches like [22] proposed personalized HAR frameworks adapting pre-trained features to individual users. Authors in [23] applied TL to pretrained video models, addressing labeled data scarcity in video-based HAR but the work in [24] offered a structured survey categorizing TL by domains, algorithms, and applications relevant to real-world HAR. Studies like [25] surveyed TL approaches in HAR, classifying methods into instance, feature and model based strategies and discussing evaluation metrics across sensing modalities. Few recent contributions in this field such as [26] used CNNs on time-series data for HAR and emotion detection but lacked pretrained vision backbones. However, the work in [27] combined ResNet with BiLSTM to model spatiotemporal features, achieving improved accuracy but without evaluating cross-domain generalization. Recent Studies like [10] are limited by a small dataset (1,680 public and 100 local images) and binary classification, restricting generalization to complex multi-class HAR tasks. Authors like [11] applied ResNet-style CNNs for IMU-based activity classification, lacking domain adaptation. They propose tasks that require extensive data and careful tuning with its 3D-CNN ConvLSTM model, thus limiting scalability. It is also hard to interpret and sensitive to noisy or missing inputs. Lately, contributions like [28], have applied VGG16 and ResNet50 on a small, simple and controlled, image dataset with three classes. The study in [29] relies on a single dataset (Weizmann) and focuses on controlled settings, which may limit generalizability to real-world, complex human activities. Additionally, using only VGG-16 may overlook potential improvements from more recent or optimized deep learning architectures. Thus, unlike prior approaches constrained by limited datasets, handcrafted similarity measures, or the absence of pretrained backbones, our hybrid framework leverages both temporal and spatial representations together with TL, enabling more robust and generalizable HAR.

3   Data Collection Details

A detailed overview of the dataset used in this study is presented to support a thorough understanding of this study. In this work, accelerometer data were collected using smartphones carried by five users (2 females and 3 males), aged between 18 and 25 years, across five distinct device configurations. Data acquisition was performed using the G-Sensor Logger[1] application developed by Kewlsoft, which records three-dimensional acceleration data along the x, y, and z axes. The participants executed two dynamic activities—Walking and Jogging—as well as three static activities—Standing, Sitting, and Laying. The accelerometer recordings were organized into five CSV files corresponding to each activity and then merged into a single csv to support experimentations. Each entry includes measurements along the X, Y and Z axes, along with an activity label. In total, the merged dataset comprises approximately 1.5 million instances, each annotated with four attributes: X-axis, Y-axis, Z-axis, and Activity. A detailed summary of the dataset structure is provided in Table 1.

4   Proposed Methodology

We propose a hybrid deep framework for HAR combining 1D-CNN, 2D-CNN, and TL with pretrained models. Raw multivariate sensor data is processed using

---

[1] https://play.google.com/store/apps/details?id=com.peterhohsy.gsensor_debug&hl=en_IN.

Table 1. Dataset Description

Device Type	Smartphone
Type of dataset	Collected by users in real time
Number of Users	5
Device used	Samsung Galaxy M11, Poco C3, Redmi 12C, Samsung A14, Vivo V27
Number of Features	4
Sensor	Accelerometer
Activities Performed	Laying, Sitting, Standing, Walking and Jogging
Sampling Rate	50 Hz

a 1D-CNN to capture temporal patterns from sequential signals. On the other hand, sensor reading sequences are also converted into 2D image representations and fed into a 2D-CNN with pretrained ResNet50 and VGG16 to extract spatial features for classifier training. By leveraging pretrained knowledge and both temporal and spatial information, the framework generalizes effectively across diverse HAR datasets. Fig. 1 shows an example of the transformed image data from the raw sensor data. As can be observed, the images from static and dynamic activity classes indicate visibly different patterns that could be learned by the classifiers.

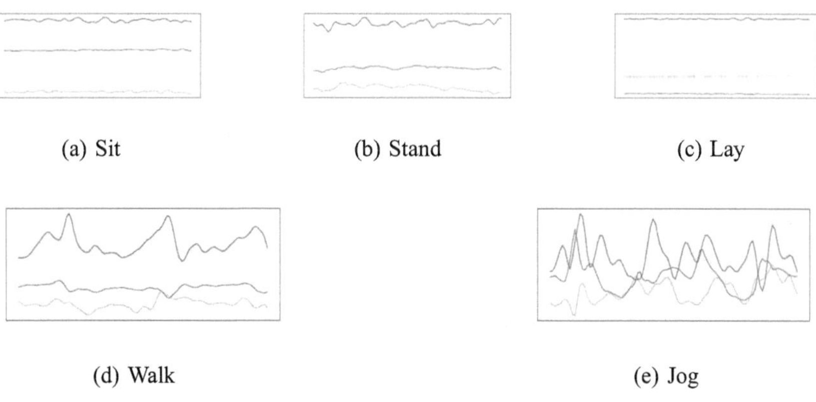

(a) Sit   (b) Stand   (c) Lay

(d) Walk   (e) Jog

Fig. 1. Sample of images generated from the sensor data.

4.1   Leveraging Transfer Learning in Human Activity Recognition

Conventional machine learning trains models from scratch without leveraging prior knowledge, requiring large labeled datasets and significant computational resources. DL models, particularly CNNs, offer superior performance but need extensive training and large datasets, which are often unavailable in specialized domains. TL addresses these challenges by reusing knowledge from a source task for a related target task. Pretrained models, trained on large-scale datasets such as ImageNet, can be fine-tuned on smaller target datasets, reducing training time, labeled data requirements, and computational cost while maintaining high accuracy. In this work, we employ TL to enhance HAR from sensor data. The key idea is to leverage a pretrained CNN to extract rich features from image-like representations of sensor signals, thereby reducing the need for extensive training on small target datasets. TL in HAR can be particularly valuable as collecting extensive, high-quality sensor data is challenging. Pretrained CNNs, including VGGNet, ResNet, Inception, Xception, MobileNet, and EfficientNet, extract hierarchical features, with early layers capturing low-level patterns and deeper layers encoding complex activity structures. TL strategies include feature extraction like freezing convolutional layers and retraining task-specific classification layers—and fine-tuning, selectively retraining high-level layers to adapt to the target dataset. Modern deep learning libraries, such as Keras, facilitate rapid deployment of TL for sensor-based activity classification, prediction, and feature extraction.

4.2   Application of TL

In TL, a base dataset is used to train a source base network, to solve a source task or problem, where the learned features are transferred to a second network called a traget network which will be trained on a target dataset in order to solve a target task or problem. In this way the concept repurposes the knowledge obtained from the first task $T1$, to facililate the generalization the target task $T2$ which lacks the huge amount of data that $T1$ is trained with. Mathematically, if S_P is a source problem that is solved by a model M_S which is initially trained on a huge dataset D_S, then the parameters learned from this model can be utilised to find out solution for a target problem P_T. The model M_S which is called a *Pretrained Model*, eliminates the need for extensive retraining and enables efficient optimization even with limited target data [30]. The entire concept is summarized in Fig. 2.

For HAR, the source problem involves a large dataset of relevant annotated images, where a CNN is trained to extract hierarchical image features. This pretrained model M_S captures general patterns and spatial structures from images. Likewise, the target problem is recognizing human activities in a smaller, specific dataset where the **target domain** D_T contains image-like representations of the target sensor data with labels:

$$D_T = \{(x_{T_1}, y_{T_1}), \dots, (x_{T_{n_T}}, y_{T_{n_T}})\}.$$

The convolutional layers of the pretrained CNN, which capture rich spatial and temporal representations, are directly leveraged for the target task. Only the task-specific classifier layers are fine-tuned on the new dataset, facilitating efficient knowledge transfer, accelerated convergence, and high predictive performance despite limited labeled data. Target sensor signals are transformed

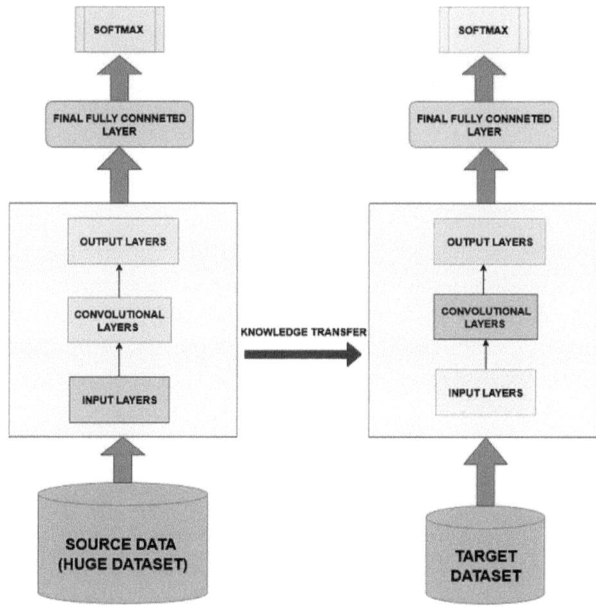

Fig. 2. Basic Architecture of Transfer Learning.

into image-like representations and processed using a pretrained model with frozen convolutional layers to retain hierarchical features. The classifier layers are fine-tuned on the target dataset. Data augmentation may be applied to mitigate overfitting in limited-data scenarios. The proposed framework leverages two widely recognized architectures: ResNet-50 and VGG16. ResNet-50[2], a 50-layer network with over 23 million parameters, employs residual blocks with identity connections to mitigate vanishing gradients, enabling efficient training of deep networks. Each block uses 1×1 and 3×3 convolutions for effective feature propagation. VGG16[2], a 16-layer network, comprises 13 convolutional layers with 3×3 filters, 5 max-pooling layers, and 3 fully connected layers, using ReLU activations and increasing filter depth from 64 to 512. Its structured design and moderate depth make it highly suitable for TL and feature extraction in HAR tasks.

5   Experiments and Results with Collected Dataset

This section details the experiments conducted to assess the effectiveness of the proposed approach and presents the corresponding quantitative results.

5.1   Experiments on 1D CNN and 2D CNN

To begin with, the raw sensor readings collected from Smartphones and distributed across five activity-specific CSV files, are consolidated into a unified or

---

[2] https://keras.io/api/applications/.

merged dataset and a baseline 1D CNN was first trained on the raw sequential data. The model achieved an accuracy of 89.00% indicating its effectiveness in capturing temporal dependencies within raw sensor signals for activity recognition tasks. In the next step, raw sensor data was subsequently transformed into 2D visual representations to explore the applicability of image-based deep learning models like 2D-CNN. To conduct that, the merged dataset was repartitioned into five subsets of 300,000 rows each, corresponding to individual activities again. The raw triaxial accelerometer data within each subset was segmented using a fixed-size sliding window of 100 consecutive samples. Each segment's X-axis, Y-axis, and Z-axis signals were rendered into multivariate temporal line plots and exported as high-resolution images to ensure compatibility with standard CNN architectures. Observations revealed that during this sensor data to image transformation process, approximately 3,000 images were generated from every 300,000 sensor readings using the sliding window approach, producing a structured image dataset suitable for effective CNN-based activity recognition. This also results in the generation of a reduced dataset (from 3,00,000 lakh rows per activity in raw sensor dataset to 3000 images per activity). Further, each image generated from the sensor data were resized to 224×224 pixels in order to conform to the standard input requirements 2D-CNN and TL models. The 1D-CNN baseline comprises two Conv1D layers (64, 128 filters; kernel = 3, stride = 1, ReLU, BatchNorm) with MaxPooling1D (pool = 2), followed by Dense(128, ReLU), Dropout(0.5), and a softmax output layer. It was trained using Adam (lr = 0.001), categorical cross-entropy, and accuracy metric for 50 epochs with batch size 16. Stratified sampling ensured class balance with data split into 60% training, 10% validation, and 30% testing. The model (1.1M parameters) serves as a reproducible 1D baseline. Next, 2D CNN was deployed on the resized image-transformed dataset that achieved a classification accuracy of 96.29%. The accuracy improved as transforming sliding-window segments into 2D images allows the CNN to capture both temporal and inter-axis spatial correlations simultaneously. Rendering tri-axial signals as images highlights distinct activity patterns which 1D could not capture, enabling the 2D-CNN to learn hierarchical features and better distinguish activities. The results of 1D-CNN and 2D-CNN are combined and shown in Fig. 3

5.2   Experiments and Results on RESNET50 and VGG16 Model

To enhance classification accuracy, TL was implemented using a ResNet50 backbone pretrained on ImageNet and employed as a fixed feature extractor. Input images were first normalized through a Lambda layer and resized to $224 \times 224 \times 3$, configured with global average pooling. All convolutional layers were frozen to preserve pretrained weights, ensuring efficient reuse of generic visual features. The extracted 2048-dimensional embeddings were flattened and passed through a dense layer of 64 neurons with ReLU activation, introducing nonlinearity and enabling the capture of high-level task-specific dependencies. A final dense layer with 5 softmax-activated neurons generated normalized probability distributions for robust multi-class classification across the target activ-

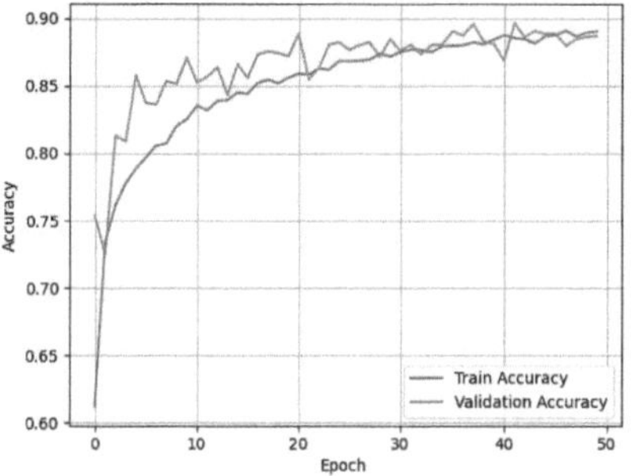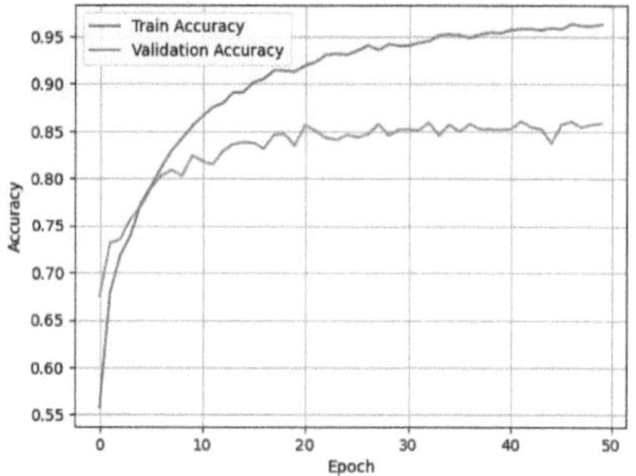

Fig. 3. Accuracy comparison of CNN models.

ity classes. The model comprises a total of 23,719,173 parameters, of which only 131,461 are trainable, with the rest of 23,587,712 parameters belong to the frozen ResNet50 backbone. This parameter distribution structure enables efficient fine-tuning and reduces computational complexity, mitigates overfitting, and ensures efficient task-specific adaptation within the TL framework on a domain-specific target dataset. To evaluate the impact of input resolution on model performance, experiments were conducted on ResNet50 for input image size of 180×180 and 300×300 respectively to assess the sensitivity and robustness of TL in activity classification across varying input dimensions. Experimental results demonstrated that input resolution significantly affects ResNet-based classification accuracy. The highest accuracy of 96.60% was achieved at 180×180 pixels, slightly exceeding the standard 224×224 resolution (96.37%), suggesting that moderately lower resolutions emphasize salient activity-specific features while reducing redundant details. Conversely, increasing resolution to 300×300 pixels caused accuracy to drop to 93.24%, likely due to additional noise, increased computational complexity, and potential overfitting. These findings indicate that optimal performance is not inherently linked to higher resolutions, highlighting the importance of careful input size selection when applying TL for image-based HAR. A similar approach was implemented using VGG16 to evaluate TL for activity recognition from image-transformed sensor data. Input images were initially resized to 224×224×3 via a Lambda layer to match the model's expected dimensions. The pretrained VGG16 convolutional base was used as a fixed feature extractor with frozen layers, retaining hierarchical representations from ImageNet. The 512-dimensional feature output was flattened and passed through a 64-neuron ReLU dense layer for task-specific pattern learning, followed by a 5-neuron softmax output layer for multi-class classification. The model contains 14,747,845 parameters, with only 33,157 trainable, enabling computationally efficient feature reuse. Further experiments at 180×180 and 300×300 pixels probed the resolution sensitivity of VGG16, facilitating a comparative analysis of model robustness and elucidating the influence of input dimensionality on feature extraction efficacy and activity classification performance. The training results of VGGNet across varying input resolutions indicate a positive correlation between resolution and accuracy. While accuracies at 180×180 (97.63%) and 224×224 (97.69%) remain comparable, a notable improvement is observed at 300×300 (98.70%). The higher resolution likely preserves finer spatial and textural details, enabling deeper convolutional layers to extract more discriminative features critical for activity classification. The uniform convolutional structure of VGG16, appears more adept at leveraging the increased pixel density without overfitting. Figure 4 denotes the accuracies of ResNet50 at 180 × 180 image size and VGG16 at 300 × 300 image size respectively (Fig. 4(a) and Fig. 4(b)).

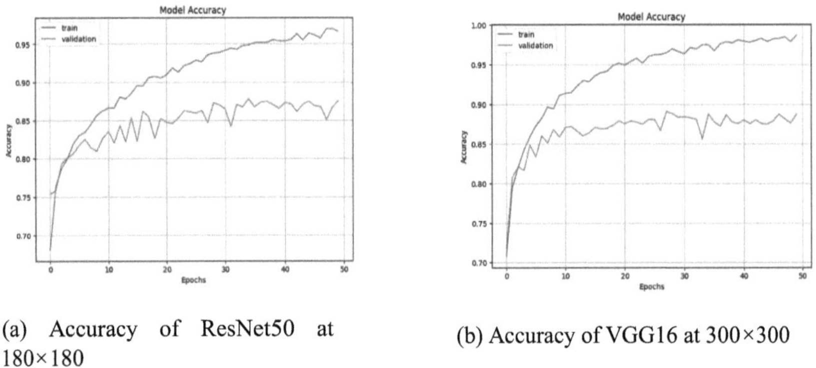

(a) Accuracy of ResNet50 at 180×180

(b) Accuracy of VGG16 at 300×300

Fig. 4. Classification Accuracy of ResNet50 and VGG16 for different image sizes.

5.3 Comparison of Performance of ResNet50 and VGG16, with Other Performance Metrics

A comparative analysis of ResNet50 and VGG16 across three input image sizes shows that VGG16 consistently outperforms ResNet50 in training and validation accuracy, as depicted in Table 2, with the highest accuracy at 300×300. This is due to VGG16's sequential architecture with uniform 3×3 convolutions and increasing depth, which effectively captures local spatial patterns for hierarchical feature extraction. ResNet50's residual connections allow deeper training and reduce vanishing gradients but may overparameterize datasets with limited intra-class variance and miss subtle temporal-spatial cues critical for HAR. While larger input sizes benefit both models, VGG16 gains more due to its convolutional design. Figure 5 exhibits the comparative training accuracies of both the models.

For a robust evaluation, Precision, Recall, and F1-score were used to assess prediction reliability, sensitivity, and balance beyond conventional accuracy. Experiments indicate that 1D-CNN on raw time-series data outperforms 2D-CNN, achieving a precision of 90.52%, recall of 90.00%, and F1-score of 90.03%. The 2D-CNN (around 86%) underperforms due to disrupted temporal continuity and loss of sequential dependencies when sequences are converted to images, causing overfitting on superficial spatial patterns. TL with pretrained models

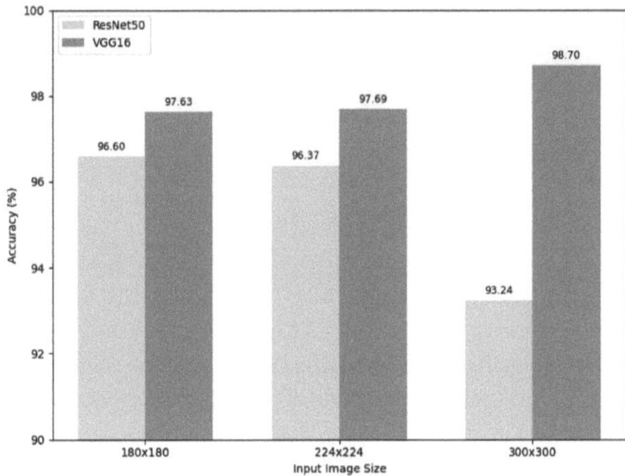

Fig. 5. Comparison of Accuracy of ResNet50 and VGG16 at Different Input Image Sizes.

mitigated performance degradation in 2D-CNNs. Across all input sizes, VGG16 achieved the best performance in all metrics, capturing both local and global spatial features effectively, while ResNet50 underperformed due to lower sensitivity to fine-grained local patterns and increased overfitting at higher resolutions. Table 2 summarises the results in a nutshell.

Table 2. Comparison of all Performance metrics across all classifiers with respective input image sizes

Models	Accuracy	Precision	Recall	F1-Score
1D-CNN	89.00	90.52	90.00	90.03
2D-CNN (224×224)	96.29	86.00	86.00	86.00
ResNet50 (180×180)	96.60	87.60	84.50	87.53
ResNet50 (224×224)	96.37	88.22	87.51	87.57
ResNet50 (300×300)	93.24	87.04	86.30	86.40
VGG16 (180×180)	97.63	88.25	87.91	87.99
VGG16 (224×224)	97.69	88.80	88.44	88.54
VGG16 (300×300)	98.70	88.79	88.71	88.72

6   Conclusion

This work highlights the potential of leveraging both raw sensor data and image-based representations with TL to enhance performance of HAR. Experiments were first conducted using a 1D-CNN on the raw sensor dataset, achieving an accuracy of 89%. To enable compatibility with image-based models such as CNN, a sensor dataset has been collected for HAR and is transformed into image representations using sliding window technique. A plain 2D-CNN trained from scratch on these images attained 96.29% accuracy, building on which, two state-of-the-art TL models were evaluated at input sizes of 180×180, 224×224, and 300×300. Observations revealed that VGG16 outperformed ResNet at all input resolutions, with the 300×300 VGGNet achieving the highest accuracy of 98.70%. Future research may focus on optimizing TL through domain-specific fine-tuning and hybrid architectures like CNN-Transformers, to capture both spatial and temporal information. Exploring Vision Transformers could improve performance. Incorporating additional sensor modalities and contextual meta-data may enhance robustness and personalization. Hybrid approaches combining CNNs with Attention mechanisms could better model complex or overlapping activities. Finally, rigorous cross-dataset validation and domain adaptation are essential for ensuring generalizability and real-world deployment.

References

1. Saha, A., Rajak, S., Saha, J., Chowdhury, C.: A survey of machine learning and meta-heuristics approaches for sensor-based human activity recognition systems. J. Ambient. Intell. Humaniz. Comput. **15**(1), 29–56 (2024)
2. Saha, J., Chowdhury, C., Ghosh, D., Bandyopadhyay, S.: A detailed human activity transition recognition framework for grossly labeled data from smartphone accelerometer. Multi. Tools Appl. **80**(7), 9895–9916 (2021)
3. Sen, P., Saha, A., Kumari, S., Chowdhury, C.: A comparative analysis of feature selection approaches for sensor-based human activity recognition. In: International Conference on Frontiers in Computing and Systems, pp. 153–163. Springer (2023)
4. Lee, S.M., Yoon, S.M., Cho, H.: Human activity recognition from accelerometer data using convolutional neural network. In: 2017 IEEE International Conference on Big Data and Smart Computing (BigComp), pp. 131–134. IEEE (2017)
5. Ha, S., Choi, S.: Convolutional neural networks for human activity recognition using multiple accelerometer and gyroscope sensors. In: 2016 International Joint Conference on Neural Networks (IJCNN), pp. 381–388. IEEE (2016)
6. Saha, A., Roy, M.: Transfer learning for healthcare. In: Internet of Things-Based Machine Learning in Healthcare, pp. 190–217. Chapman and Hall/CRC (2024)
7. Cook, D., Feuz, K.D., Krishnan, N.C.: Transfer learning for activity recognition: a survey. Knowl. Inf. Syst. **36**(3), 537–556 (2013)
8. Lu, J., Behbood, V., Hao, P., Zuo, H., Xue, S., Zhang, G.: Transfer learning using computational intelligence: a survey. Knowl.-Based Syst. **80**, 14–23 (2015)
9. Zebhi, S.: Human activity recognition using wearable sensors based on image classification. IEEE Sens. J. **22**(12), 12117–12126 (2022)
10. Harahap, M., Damar, V., Yek, S., Michael, M., Putra, M.R.: Static and dynamic human activity recognition with VGG-16 pre-trained CNN model. Jurnal Infotel **15**(2), 164–168 (2023)
11. Vrskova, R., Kamencay, P., Hudec, R., Sykora, P.: A new deep-learning method for human activity recognition. Sensors **23**(5), 2816 (2023)
12. Niu, S., Liu, Y., Wang, J., Song, H.: A decade survey of transfer learning (2010–2020). IEEE Trans. Artif. Intell. **1**(2), 151–166 (2020)

13. Hu, D.H., Zheng, V.W., Yang, Q.: Cross-domain activity recognition via transfer learning. Pervasive Mob. Comput. **7**(3), 344–358 (2011)
14. Wang, J., Zheng, V.W., Chen, Y., Huang, M.: Deep transfer learning for cross-domain activity recognition. In: Proceedings of the 2018 AAAI Conference on Artificial Intelligence. AAAI Press (2018)
15. Ray, A., Kolekar, M.H., Balasubramanian, R., Hafiane, A.: Transfer learning enhanced vision-based human activity recognition: A decade-long analysis. Expert Syst. Appl. **200**, 117089 (2022)
16. Day, O., Khoshgoftaar, T.M.: A survey on heterogeneous transfer learning. J. Big Data **4**(1), 1–42 (2017). https://doi.org/10.1186/s40537-017-0089-0
17. Chen, W., Cho, P., Jiang, Y.: Activity recognition using transfer learning. Sensors and Materials **29**(7), 897–904 (2017)
18. Khan, M.A.A.H.: Transact: transfer learning enabled activity recognition. In: Proceedings of the 6th IEEE International Conference on Smart Computing (SMART-COMP). IEEE (2020)
19. Chikhaoui, B., Gouineau, F., Sotir, M.: A CNN based transfer learning model for automatic activity recognition from accelerometer sensors. In: International Conference on Artificial Intelligence in Education, pp. 80–84. Springer (2021)
20. Ribani, R., Marengoni, M.: A survey of transfer learning for convolutional neural networks. IEEE Trans. Neural Netw. Learn. Syst. **30**(9), 2734–2745 (2019)
21. Liang, H., Fu, W.: A survey of recent advances in transfer learning. In: 2021 International Conference on Artificial Intelligence and Electromechanical Automation (AIEA), pp. 59–64. IEEE (2021)
22. Sarakon, S., Tamee, K.: An individual model for human activity recognition using transfer deep learning. In: 2021 18th International Joint Conference on Computer Science and Software Engineering (JCSSE), pp. 1–6. IEEE (2021)
23. Abdulazeem, Y., Balaha, H.M., Bahgat, W.M., Badawy, M.: Human action recognition based on transfer learning approach. IEEE Access **9**, 72448–72460 (2021)
24. Agarwal, N., Sondhi, A., Chopra, K., Singh, G.: Transfer learning: survey and classification. Materials Today: Proceedings (2022)
25. Dhekane, S.G., Plötz, T.: Transfer learning in sensor-based human activity recognition: a survey. ACM Comput. Surv. **57**(8), 1–39 (2025)
26. Li, F., Shirahama, K., Nisar, M.A., Huang, X., Grzegorzek, M.: Deep transfer learning for time series data based on sensor modality classification. Sensors **20**(15), 4271 (2020)
27. Li, Y., Wang, L.: Human activity recognition based on residual network and BiLSTM. Sensors **22**(2), 635 (2022)
28. Sowmya, M., Balasubramanian, M., Vaidehi, K.: Human behavior classification using 2D-convolutional neural network, VGG16 and ResNet50. Indian J. Sci. Technol. **16**(16), 1221–1229 (2023)
29. Deep, S., Zheng, X.: Leveraging CNN and transfer learning for vision-based human activity recognition. In: 2019 29th International Telecommunication Networks and Applications Conference (ITNAC), pp. 1–4. IEEE (2019)
30. Zhuang, F., et al.: A comprehensive survey on transfer learning. Proc. IEEE **109**(1), 43–76 (2021)

Ensembling Handcrafted Features for Accurate Multi-class Brain Hemorrhage Classification

D. L. Shivaprasad[1], Vikram Patil[2], C. S. Ankitha[3], K. S. Drakshayini[4],
D. S. Guru[4(✉)], and K. Stavelin Abhinandithe[3]

[1] Department of Computer Applications, MIT First Grade College, Manandavadi Road,
Mysuru 570008, India
shivaprasaddl143@gmail.com
[2] Department of Radiology, JSS Medical College, JSS Academy of Higher Education and
Research, Mysuru 570015, India
vikrampatil@jssuni.edu.in
[3] Division of Medical Statistics, School of Life Sciences, JSS Academy of Higher Education
and Research, Mysuru 570015, India
ankithaankics@gmail.com, stavelin.ak@jssuni.edu.in
[4] Department of Studies in Computer Science, University of Mysore, Manasagangotri,
Mysuru 570006, India
drakshayiniks6@gmail.com, dsg@compsci.uni-mysore.ac.in

Abstract. Intracranial Hemorrhage (ICH) represents a life-threatening neurological condition that demands immediate and precise diagnosis for timely clinical intervention. However, most existing automated detection systems struggle with issues such as unbalanced datasets, poor adaptability across data sources, and insufficient attention to hemorrhage-specific brain regions. To overcome these limitations, this study introduces a comprehensive dataset for ICH detection that integrates newly acquired hospital images with existing open-access datasets, encompassing six major subtypes of hemorrhage. A novel two-stage ensemble framework is proposed: in the first stage, image quality is enhanced using Contrast Limited Adaptive Histogram Equalization (CLAHE); in the second stage, a Brain Region Detector based on You Only Look Once version 11 (YOLOv11) is employed to accurately localize potential hemorrhagic regions. From these localized areas, Histogram of Oriented Gradients (HOG) and Local Binary Pattern (LBP) features are extracted, fused, and normalized through Min–Max scaling. The feature space is then optimized using Linear Discriminant Analysis (LDA) to enhance class separability. Finally, a Support Vector Machine (SVM) classifier with a Radial Basis Function (RBF) kernel is used for classification, achieving a 96.13% accuracy rate, surpassing both traditional and deep learning-based approaches. The proposed model delivers a practical balance between interpretability, computational efficiency, and diagnostic accuracy, offering a new benchmark for real-time multi-class ICH detection in clinical environments.

Keywords: Ensembled Handcrafted Features · Brain Region Detection · Intracranial Hemorrhage Classification

C. Zaroliagis et al. (Eds.): ICAA 2026, LNCS 16423, pp. 390–402, 2026.
https://doi.org/10.1007/978-3-032-15621-1_32

1   Introduction

Brain hemorrhage, defined as internal bleeding within the skull due to ruptured blood vessels, poses a severe risk to human life. This condition, medically termed as intracranial hemorrhage (ICH), can cause significant neurological damage, leading to loss of consciousness, sometimes resulting with coma, or death if not promptly identified and treated. It may result from trauma, hypertension, aneurysm rupture, or other pathological conditions. The timely and accurate diagnosis of brain hemorrhages is critical, especially in emergency care, where treatment decisions must be made quickly to improve patient out-comes. Intracranial hemorrhage is broadly categorised based on the location of bleeding within the brain. These categories include intra-parenchymal hemorrhage (IPH), which occurs within brain tissue; intraventricular hemorrhage (IVH), affecting the fluid-filled ventricles; epidural hemorrhage (EPH), found between the skull and dura mater; subarachnoid hemorrhage (SAH), located between the arachnoid and pia mater; and subdural hemorrhage (SDH), situated between the dura and arachnoid layers. For a comprehensive diagnosis, it is also essential to distinguish these from normal brain Computed Tomography (CT) scans, which do not exhibit any hemorrhagic symptoms. While numerous studies have attempted to automate hemorrhage detection using computer vision, the majority have concentrated on identifying only one or two types of hemorrhages. However, this limited approach falls short in clinical settings where a wide range of hemorrhage subtypes may present simultaneously. To address this, the pre-sent work aims to build a system capable of simultaneously detecting and classifying multiple hemorrhage types in a single diagnostic workflow. This dual-function system is designed to first detect the presence of a hemorrhage and subsequently categorise it into one of the defined subtypes. This integrated strategy is crucial, as treatment protocols vary significantly across different hemorrhage types. Despite these advancements, the field still faces several key challenges: handling the diversity of hemorrhage appearances, ensuring generalisation across heterogeneous CT data, managing class imbalance and achieving real-time diagnostic performance in high-stakes medical environments. Therefore, this research emphasises the development of a multi-class, clinically relevant, and automated diagnostic framework for brain hemorrhage detection and classification from CT images, aiming to support physicians with rapid and precise decision-making during critical care scenarios. Here is a list of the contributions of this work.

- Capturing own real-time CT images directly from patients to have a larger dataset.
- Investigation an efficient image enhancement methods for improved analysis.
- Designing a robust hemorrhage detection model for identifying hemorrhage category.
- Development of a hemorrhage detection and classification system by integrating convolutional feature extraction with traditional classification algorithms.

This paper is organised as follows: Sect. 2 provides the existing literature review of brain hemorrhage detection and classification. Section 3 describes the proposed real-time system for brain hemorrhage detection and classification. Experimental results and analysis are discussed in Sect. 4. Finally, in Sect. 5, we conclude the paper with future work.

2 Literature Review

Research on intracranial hemorrhage (ICH) detection and classification using CT scans has drawn on a wide range of public, private, and institutional datasets. Ample benchmark resources such as the RSNA Intracranial Hemorrhage Detection Challenge set, which contains over 25,000 annotated CT studies [1], and the CQ500 dataset [2] have been widely adopted for training and validation. Clinical trial datasets, including TICH-2 [3, 4], have also been used for algorithm development and evaluation. Beyond these, substantial private datasets, such as a 82,000-scan collection from Korean hospitals [5], have supported the creation of robust models. In contrast, smaller public repositories like PhysioNet's 82-scan set [6] and pilot datasets containing as few as 15 scans from five patients [7] have facilitated early-stage proof-of-concept studies. Other works have drawn on targeted non-contrast CT datasets of 170 scans [8], multi-institutional archives [9], and segmentation-focused datasets such as RSNA HemSeg-200 with 222 annotated CT volumes [10]. Various preprocessing pipelines have been proposed to improve model performance and generalizability. These include skull stripping, multi-window fusion, and the stacking of adjacent slices [1, 2, 5], as well as pseudo-RGB encoding from multiple Hounsfield Unit (HU) ranges [2, 5]. Region-based methods have incorporated multi-threshold segmentation and connected component analysis to refine hemorrhage localization [11]. Precise annotation, often from expert radiologists remains essential for reliable model training [7]. Some researchers have reduced data dimensionality using fixed-size region-of-interest (ROI) extraction with GLCM features, slice selection, or patch-based training strategies [6, 9]. More recent approaches employ slice-wise attention mechanisms and voxel-level sampling to enhance localisation accuracy [12]. Class imbalance and small dataset sizes have been addressed through extensive data augmentation sometimes increasing data volume by nearly 50 times and specialised loss functions such as focal loss [4, 8, 13]. In terms of methodology, deep convolutional neural networks (CNNs) such as ResNet-101 V2, DenseNet-121, and Inception-V4 have been prominent choices for feature extraction [1, 10, 14]. Segmentation tasks are often handled by U-Net variants, including U-Net++ [16] and multi-scale designs like MSRL-Net [15]. More advanced designs such as transformer-based architectures [17], attention-augmented DenseNets [14], and hybrid 2D–3D CNNs [19] have been reported to improve cross-scanner generalisation. Hybrid systems that integrate handcrafted features (e.g., GLCM) with CNN and recurrent architectures (e.g., LSTM, RNN) have been explored to capture both spatial and temporal information [2, 7, 18]. Ensemble learning, along with classical machine learning models such as Random Forest, XGBoost, and LightGBM, have also proven to be effective in certain pipelines [1, 10, 13]. Recently, multimodal strategies combining imaging data with clinical text through models like BioClinicalBERT and cross-modal attention networks have shown promise in decision support [11]. Additionally, specialised design choices such as symmetry-aware processing [17] and hybrid 2D–3D models [19] have been proposed to boost robustness. Despite these advancements, key challenges persist, including domain adaptation across diverse scanners, scarcity of expertly annotated data, and the need for systems that operate reliably in real-time settings. To address these issues, our study introduces a state-of-the-art ICH classification framework that merges handcrafted descriptors (HOG + LBP) with convolutional features through a two-level ensemble strategy. These combined features are transformed via Linear Discriminant Analysis (LDA) into a compact representation before classification with a RBF kernel based SVM classifier, yielding superior results compared to existing six-class ICH models.

3 Proposed System

We proposed a deployable system for automatic brain hemorrhage detection and classification in this work. The system is divided into two phases: the training phase and the testing phase. The proposed system is illustrated in Fig. 1. The proposed system involves five significant stages: Data acquisition, Brain hemorrhage detection, Ensemble Feature extraction, Dimensionality Reduction, and Brain Hemorrhage Classification. Each stage is briefed in the following subsections.

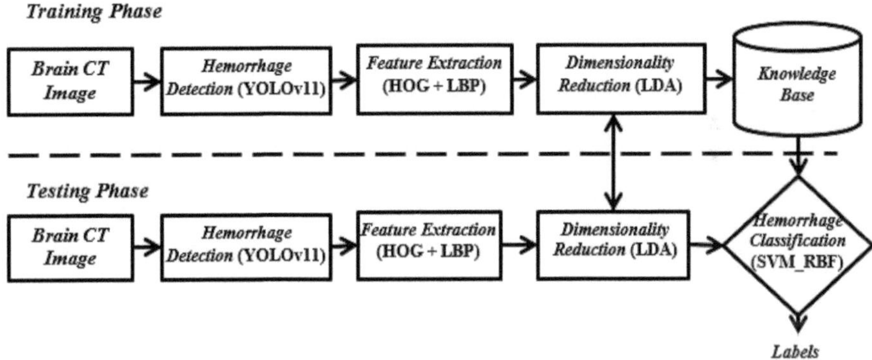

Fig. 1. Illustration of the proposed system.

3.1 Data Acquisition

The data utilized in this study were compiled from two primary sources. The first source, referred to as Dataset-1, integrates two publicly available datasets: one that includes five distinct hemorrhage categories [23] and another containing only normal brain CT scans [24]. Although this combination provided a useful foundation, it lacked complete coverage of all hemorrhage types, limiting its suitability for comprehensive analysis. To overcome this constraint, we developed a new dataset (Dataset-2) in collaboration with JSS Hospital, Mysuru, Karnataka, incorporating all six categories of Intracranial Hemorrhage (ICH). The resulting dataset comprises Intraparenchymal Hemorrhage (IPH), Intraventricular Hemorrhage (IVH), Epidural Hemorrhage (EPH), Subarachnoid Hemorrhage (SAH), Subdural Hemorrhage (SDH), and Normal cases. Overall, the curated Dataset-2 includes 6,645 CT images, providing a balanced and clinically diverse representation of each class. Statistical summaries of both datasets are presented in Table 1, while representative CT images are shown in Fig. 2. This newly developed dataset serves as a major contribution of this study, strengthening the practical and real-time applicability of the proposed framework.

Table 1. Statistical description of both datasets.

Hemorrhage	Total Samples		Ensembled Dataset
	Dataset - 1	Dataset - 2 (New Dataset)	
Intraparenchymal (IPH)	64	787	851
Subarachnoid (SAH)	11	1950	1961
Intraventricular (IVH)	25	589	613
Normal	100	684	784
Epidural (EPH)	167	939	1106
Subdural (SDH)	52	1696	1748

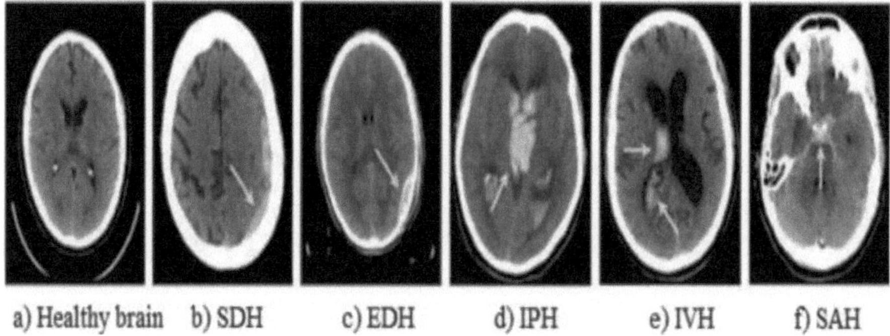

Fig. 2. Samples of proposed Dataset.

3.2 Brain Region Detection

Subsequently, we enhanced the CT images using popular image enhancement technique called Contrast Limited Adaptive Histogram Equalization (CLAHE). It used to enhance contrast, particularly in images with varying brightness levels. It works by dividing the image into smaller tiles, calculating a histogram for each tile, and then applying histogram equalization locally, with contrast limiting to prevent noise amplification. This method is particularly effective in improving visibility in images with low contrast or uneven lighting conditions. Then focused on the regions of interest by extracting Brain Hemorrhage regions from images using our designed Detector. For this purpose, we adopted the well-known convolutional object detector 'YOLO', which we custom trained with our collected data by labelling using label studio tool and named the Brain Region Detector (BRD). The process of Brain region detection and segmentation is shown in Fig. 3.

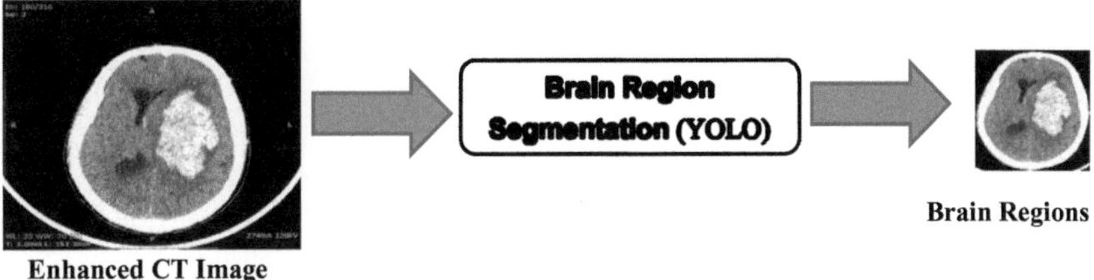

Fig. 3. Brain Region Detection and Segmentation Process.

3.3 Ensemble Feature Extraction

After segmenting the critical brain regions from each CT scan, the next step involves extracting features that are both distinctive and clinically meaningful to ensure accurate classification. In this study, two widely recognised handcrafted feature extraction techniques are utilised. Since medical imaging datasets are often limited in size and difficult to annotate, these handcrafted approaches offer the advantages of computational efficiency and robustness against noise or scanner-related variations, making them particularly suitable in settings with restricted resources. Although deep learning methods can achieve high accuracy when trained on large and diverse collections of data, handcrafted features combined with traditional machine learning classifiers provide a practical and dependable alternative for brain hemorrhage detection when data availability is constrained. Specifically, Histogram of Oriented Gradients (HOG) and Local Binary Patterns (LBP) are employed. HOG is effective for capturing edge orientations and structural contours, making it well-suited to representing the geometric properties of hemorrhagic regions. At the same time, LBP focuses on fine texture descriptors that help distinguish subtle tissue differences. Together, these complementary descriptors yield a more comprehensive representation of the affected areas: for each image, HOG generates $\mathbf{n}$ features, and LBP produces $\mathbf{m}$ features; these are concatenated into a single feature vector, expressed as $\mathbf{F_v} = \mathbf{F_{HOG}} \cup \mathbf{F_{LBP}} = \{\mathbf{f_1}, \mathbf{f_2}, ..., \mathbf{f_n}\} \cup \{\mathbf{g_1}, \mathbf{g_2}, ..., \mathbf{g_m}\}$. This ensemble feature space enhances both the accuracy and robustness of the classification framework.

3.4 Dimensionality Reduction

Following feature extraction, dimensionality reduction is applied to refine the feature space using transformation-based methods. In this study, Linear Discriminant Analysis (LDA) is employed as the primary approach. LDA, being a supervised learning technique, utilises class label information to project the original features into a subspace where inter-class separability is maximised and intra-class variation is minimised. This property makes it particularly suitable for classification tasks. Let $\mathbf{F_v}$ represent the feature vector obtained in the extraction stage, consisting of $\mathbf{n + m}$ dimensions as outlined earlier. Through LDA, these features are transformed into a reduced set $\mathbf{TF_v}$ with $\mathbf{d}$-dimensions, expressed as $\mathbf{TF_v} = \{\mathbf{p_1}, \mathbf{p_2}, ..., \mathbf{p_d}\}$, where $\mathbf{d} << (\mathbf{n + m})$. The resulting transformed features exhibit stronger discriminative ability compared to the original set, thereby enhancing classification accuracy and efficiency.

3.5 Brain Hemorrhage Classification

Once the features are mapped into a lower-dimensional space, they are forwarded to an appropriate classification stage, where a Support Vector Machine (SVM) equipped with a Radial Basis Function (RBF) kernel is employed. The SVM_RBF classifier is particularly well-suited for this task, as it can model complex, non-linear decision boundaries while maintaining strong generalisation capabilities, even in high-dimensional spaces. This makes it highly effective in distinguishing between subtle variations across different categories of brain hemorrhage. The classifier's performance was systematically evaluated over T independent trials, with a consistent split between training and testing datasets to ensure fair comparison. To further reinforce the system's reliability, the complete classification pipeline underwent rigorous validation through multiple rounds of cross-validation. Detailed records were maintained at every stage of the process, and the optimal pairing of the dimensionality reduction method with the classification algorithm was archived in a Knowledge Base for future inference. During the testing phase, the system replicates the training procedure, thereby guaranteeing consistency and dependability in hemorrhage classification outcomes.

4 Experimental Results and Analysis

This section explains the complete experimental setup and analyses the results our proposed work for evaluating with proposed datasets.

4.1 Experimental Setup

This study utilized a combined dataset of 7,063 CT images categorized into six hemorrhage types (Sect. 3.1). Since the initial dataset (Dataset-1) had class imbalance, an additional set (Dataset-2) was collected from hospital records to ensure full representation. Image quality was enhanced using Contrast Limited Adaptive Histogram Equalization (CLAHE). For Brain Hemorrhage Detection (BHD), a balanced subset of 1,500 images was manually annotated by medical experts using Label Studio. Of these, 1,200 images were used for training and 300 for testing the YOLOv11-based Brain Region Detector (BRD), which achieved a mean Average Precision (mAP) of 80%, confirming reliable segmentation performance. The trained BRD was then applied to localize brain regions in the complete dataset. From these regions, Histogram of Oriented Gradients (HOG) and Local Binary Patterns (LBP) features were extracted. For 256×256 input images, the HOG extractor (8 orientations, 32×32 cell size, 2×2 block) produced 1,568 features, while the LBP extractor (radius $= 1$, neighbors $= 8$) generated 256 features. The concatenated HOG $+$ LBP feature matrix ($7,063 \times 1,824$) was normalized using Min–Max scaling.

Table 2. Performance Analysis of the proposed model.

Dataset	Feature Extraction (No)	Accuracy	SVM Linear	SVM RBF	SVM_ SIG
Dataset - 1	HOG (1568)	Minimum	80.80	79.20	52.00
		Maximum	86.40	85.60	64.00
		Average	84.80	82.56	58.24
	HOG + LDA (05)	Minimum	99.20	97.60	99.20
		Maximum	100	99.20	100
		Average	99.68	98.72	99.84
	LBP (256)	Minimum	68.00	62.40	52.00
		Maximum	72.80	65.60	61.60
		Average	69.92	64.00	54.88
	LBP + LDA (05)	Minimum	73.60	76.80	70.40
		Maximum	85.60	86.40	76.80
		Average	79.84	80.48	73.60
	HOG + LBP (1824)	Minimum	83.20	75.20	58.40
		Maximum	90.40	83.20	68.00
		Average	86.56	78.72	63.36
	HOG + LBP + LDA (05)	**Minimum**	**100**	**100**	**100**
		Maximum	**100**	**100**	**100**
		Average	**100**	**100**	**100**
Dataset - 2	HOG (1568)	Minimum	86.76	90.27	27.43
		Maximum	88.21	90.97	28.79
		Average	87.38	90.58	28.09
	HOG + LDA (05)	Minimum	94.53	94.48	90.17
		Maximum	94.83	94.58	90.57
		Average	95.08	94.91	91.21
	LBP (256)	Minimum	35.81	45.64	24.27
		Maximum	37.96	47.79	30.24
		Average	36.69	47.23	28.27
	LBP + LDA (05)	Minimum	35.31	45.79	25.43
		Maximum	37.61	48.14	27.53
		Average	36.73	47.00	26.42
	HOG + LBP (1824)	Minimum	86.91	86.51	32.85
		Maximum	88.26	87.61	35.11
		Average	87.42	87.11	33.77
	HOG + LBP + LDA (05)	**Minimum**	**94.88**	**94.63**	**90.97**
		Maximum	**95.74**	**95.44**	**92.18**
		Average	**95.23**	**94.96**	**91.52**
Combined Dataset	HOG (1568)	Minimum	84.84	87.63	25.26
		Maximum	85.84	89.19	26.72
		Average	85.36	88.55	26.10
	HOG + LDA (05)	Minimum	94.76	94.90	90.23
		Maximum	95.66	95.47	91.69
		Average	95.35	95.23	91.04
	LBP (256)	Minimum	34.99	45.85	27.10
		Maximum	37.02	48.02	30.97
		Average	36.08	46.90	28.54
	LBP + LDA (05)	Minimum	36.45	43.25	24.79
		Maximum	37.96	44.52	26.96
		Average	37.00	43.82	26.29
	HOG + LBP (1824)	Minimum	84.51	81.96	32.20
		Maximum	86.21	82.77	37.39
		Average	85.56	82.264	34.75
	HOG + LBP + LDA (05)	**Minimum**	**95.75**	**95.80**	**88.76**
		Maximum	**96.36**	**96.51**	**90.13**
		Average	**96.02**	**96.13**	**89.36**

Classification experiments were conducted using three train–test splits (60:40, 70:30, 80:20) with five independent trials for statistical validation. Linear Discriminant Analysis (LDA) reduced the 1,824-dimensional feature space to five highly discriminative components, which were then classified using a Support Vector Machine (SVM) with different kernel functions. The 70:30 split provided the best balance between training sufficiency and test reliability, and the corresponding results are summarized in Table 2. From this Table 2, it is evident that the ensemble model delivers superior performance across all dataset variations. Owing to its data diversity, which encompasses a wide range of samples, the ensemble dataset is identified as the most suitable choice for achieving strong generalisation. Therefore, this study recommends the proposed two-level ensemble approach combining handcrafted HOG and LBP features, projecting them into the LDA feature space, and classifying them with an SVM using an RBF kernel as an effective solution for brain hemorrhage classification from CT images.

4.2 Discussion

For comparative analysis, we also explored convolutional features extracted from six deep learning architectures: AlexNet, EfficientNet, GoogleNet, MobileNet, ResNet, and VGG19. These features were evaluated through a two-level ensembling approach, both individually and in combination with handcrafted features. The corresponding results are presented in Table 3. Furthermore, the proposed model was assessed using multiple classifiers, including K-Nearest Neighbor (KNN), Random Forest (RF), Decision Tree (DT), Gaussian Naïve Bayes (GNB), and Multilayer Perceptron (MLP), with the comparative performance illustrated in Fig. 4.

Table 3. Feature wise comparative analysis.

Method	SVM Linear	SVM RBF	SVM Sigmoid
AlexNet+EfficientNet	95.52	95.39	94.94
AlexNet+GoogleNet	95.55	95.49	94.31
AlexNet+HOG	95.68	95.56	95.44
LBP+AlexNet	93.95	94.23	86.78
LBP+EfficientNet	95.38	95.35	90.35
LBP+GoogleNet	92.98	93.02	83.71
LBP+HOG	**96.02**	**96.13**	89.36
LBP+MobileNet	94.71	94.50	87.95
LBP+ResNet	94.35	94.42	86.92
LBP+VGG19	94.37	94.29	87.06
MobileNet+EfficientNet	95.57	95.37	94.97
MobileNet+GoogleNet	95.77	95.60	94.21
MobileNet+HOG	95.61	95.41	95.35
MobileNet+MobileNet	94.06	94.08	87.92
MobileNet+ResNet	95.85	95.79	94.20
MobileNet+VGG19	95.89	95.69	94.56
ResNet+GoogleNet	95.56	95.30	93.35
ResNet+HOG	95.52	95.46	94.97
ResNet+MobileNet	95.55	95.49	94.06
ResNet+VGG19	95.77	95.56	93.95
VGG19+HOG	95.68	95.56	95.10
VGG19+MobileNet	95.61	95.50	94.50
VGG19+ResNet	95.77	95.66	94.02

Table 2 highlights that the SVM classifier with an RBF kernel delivers excellent performance, achieving 96.13% accuracy on the ensemble dataset. As presented in Table 3 and Fig. 4, the proposed ensemble approach, where conventional features are transformed through LDA into five highly discriminative features and then classified using an SVM_RBF, consistently surpasses all other model configurations. For dimensionality reduction, PCA alone achieved 91.89% accuracy with 339 features, while the combined PCA + LDA method (reducing 339 features to 5) obtained 82.74% accuracy. However, both performed below the proposed model. All classifiers had their hyperparameters tuned empirically, with the optimal SVM-RBF parameters set to $C = 1$ and $\gamma = 1$. A comparative study with existing models is presented in Table 4.

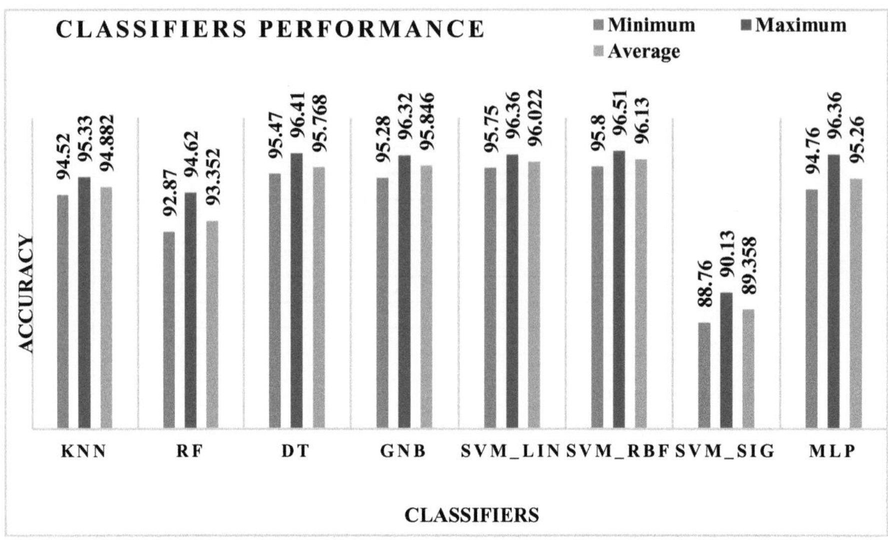

Fig. 4. Comparative analysis of classifiers.

Table 4. Comparative analysis.

Method	Dataset (No. of Classes)	Model	Performance (Accuracy)
Singh & Kumar (2023) [21]	BraTS-ICH Dataset (6)	EfficientNet-based deep features + SVM (linear kernel)	93.80%
Wang et al. (2021) [22]	RSNA Intracranial Hemorrhage Dataset (6)	Fine-tuned ResNet50 + MLP on CT slices	94.20%
Proposed Work	**Ensembled Dataset (6)**	**(HOG + LBP) + LDA + SVM_RBF**	**96.13%**

Only a few studies have explored six-class brain hemorrhage classification, making direct comparisons limited. For instance, [20] combined public and hospital datasets (~8,200 CT scans) using a hybrid of handcrafted (HOG, LBP) and CNN features, achieving 95.1% accuracy across five classes. [21] utilized the BraTS-ICH dataset (6,800 scans) with EfficientNet features and a linear SVM, reporting 93.8% accuracy, while [22] employed the RSNA ICH dataset (~25,000 scans) with ResNet50 and an MLP classifier, attaining 94.2% accuracy. In comparison, the present study proposes a two-stage ensemble framework based solely on handcrafted features, HOG and LBP which are fused, normalized, and optimized via Linear Discriminant Analysis (LDA). Classification using an SVM with an RBF kernel on a combined dataset of 7,063 CT scans covering six hemorrhage categories achieved 96.13% accuracy. This demonstrates that integrating complementary handcrafted descriptors with supervised dimensionality reduction and kernel-based learning can deliver a robust, interpretable, and computationally efficient solution for clinical use.

5 Conclusion and Future Enhancement

This research introduces a two-stage ensemble framework for classifying six categories of intracranial hemorrhage (ICH) in non-contrast CT scans, developed using a newly curated dataset combined with an existing limited dataset. The proposed system incorporates Contrast Limited Adaptive Histogram Equalization (CLAHE) for image enhancement and a YOLOv11-based Brain Region Detector (BRD) for precise region localization. From these regions, Histogram of Oriented Gradients (HOG) and Local Binary Patterns (LBP) features are extracted, fused, normalized, and refined through Linear Discriminant Analysis (LDA) to generate compact and discriminative feature vectors. A Support Vector Machine (SVM) with a Radial Basis Function (RBF) kernel achieved 96.13% accuracy, surpassing several conventional approaches and performing competitively with deep learning models, while maintaining low computational cost. The findings highlight the efficiency and reliability of combining complementary handcrafted features with supervised dimensionality reduction and kernel-based classification for practical clinical implementation. However, it is acknowledged that handcrafted feature methods may have limited generalization when applied to unseen or highly heterogeneous data compared to deep CNN-based models. Future work will focus on expanding the dataset, integrating multimodal patient information, and extending the framework toward 3D volumetric segmentation for a more comprehensive assessment of intracranial hemorrhages.

Acknowledgments. The authors sincerely thank JSS hospital, Mysuru for their invaluable support in providing the CT scan dataset used in this research. Their contribution of high-quality medical imaging data played a pivotal role in enabling the development and validation of the proposed framework for intracranial hemorrhage detection and classification. The authors also appreciate the medical staff and radiology department for their assistance in data acquisition, annotation, and for sharing their expertise, which significantly strengthened the clinical relevance of this study.

Disclosure of Interests. The authors declare that they have no conflicts of interest / competing interests towards this article.

References

1. Flanders, A.F., et al.: Construction of the RSNA 2019 brain CT hemorrhage challenge dataset. Radiol. Artif. Intell. **2**(3), e200190 (2020)
2. Chilamkurthy, S., et al.: Development and validation of deep learning algorithms for detection of critical findings in head CT scans. Lancet **392**(10162), 2388–2396 (2018)
3. Sprigg, N., et al.: Statistical analysis plan for the 'Tranexamic acid for hyperacute primary Intracerebral Hemorrhage' (TICH-2) trial. Trials **18**(1), 607 (2017)
4. Sprigg, N., Bath, P.M., Dineen, R., Law, Z., et al.: Tranexamic acid for hyper acute primary intracerebral haemorrhage (TICH-2): An international randomized, placebo-controlled, phase 3 superiority trial. Lancet **391**(10135), 2107–2115 (2018)

5. Kim, M., et al.: Large-scale brain CT dataset from Korean hospitals for hemorrhage detection research. Neuro Inform. J. **18**(4), 623–634 (2020)

6. Goldberger, A.L., et al.: PhysioBank, PhysioToolkit, and PhysioNet: components of a new research resource for complex physiologic signals. Circulation **101**(23), 215–220 (2000)

7. Lee, H., et al.: Pilot study of CT-based hemorrhage detection using minimal patient data. Biomed. Eng. Lett. **9**(2), 193–201 (2019)

8. Sharma, R., et al.: Intracranial hemorrhage detection on small-scale non-contrast CT datasets. J. Digit. Imaging **34**(3), 567–578 (2021)

9. Park, J., et al.: Multi-institutional brain CT hemorrhage dataset for deep learning. Med. Phys. **47**(12), 6425–6436 (2020)

10. Chen, X., et al.: RSNA HemSeg-200: annotated CT volumes for hemorrhage segmentation. Comput. Methods Programs Biomed. **200**, 105846 (2021)

11. Li, Y., et al.: Multi-threshold segmentation for CT-based hemorrhage detection. Pattern Recogn. Lett. **135**, 154–161 (2020)

12. Wu, Z., et al.: Slice-wise attention for brain hemorrhage localization in CT images. IEEE Trans. Med. Imaging **38**(11), 2618–2628 (2019)

13. Wang, L., et al.: Data augmentation strategies for class imbalance in medical imaging. Artif. Intell. Med. **111**, 101985 (2021)

14. Zhang, H., et al.: Attention-enhanced DenseNet for volumetric ICH classification. Med. Image Anal. **65**, 101786 (2020)

15. Ronneberger, O., et al.: U-Net: convolutional networks for biomedical image segmentation. In: Medical Image Computing and Computer-Assisted Intervention – MICCAI 2015, pp. 234–241 (2015)

16. Zhou, Z., et al.: UNet++: a nested U-Net architecture for medical image segmentation. Deep Learn. Med. Image Anal. 3–11 (2018)

17. He, J., et al.: Symmetric transformer networks for volumetric medical image analysis. IEEE Trans. Neural Netw. Learn. Syst. **32**(7), 2805–2817 (2021)

18. Chen, J., et al.: Hybrid CNN-RNN for brain hemorrhage classification. Neural Comput. Appl. **32**, 12787–12799 (2020)

19. Zhao, X., et al.: Hybrid 2D–3D CNNs for improved medical image generalization. IEEE Access **9**, 45678–45689 (2021)

20. Chen, L., Zhang, Y., Wu, H.: Hybrid deep–handcrafted feature fusion for multi-class brain haemorrhage detection in CT scans. Biomed. Signal Process. Control **88**, 105478 (2024)

21. Singh, R., Kumar, A.: EfficientNet-based automated classification of brain haemorrhage subtypes from CT images. Comput. Biol. Med. **154**, 106603 (2023)

22. Wang, J., Li, X., Zhao, Q.: Multi-class intracranial haemorrhage classification using ResNet50 and CT images. Pattern Recogn. Lett. **150**, 123–130 (2021)

23. Hssayeni, M.: Computed Tomography Images for Intracranial Hemorrhage Detection and Segmentation (version 1.3.1). PhysioNet. RRID: SCR_007345 (2020)

24. Felipe Campos Kitamura. Head CT - hemorrhage. Kaggle (2018)

MACO-Sync: Multi-agent Ant Colony Optimization for Synchronized Arrival Coordination

Vidit Garg, Swapnil Mane, and Suman Kundu$^{(\boxtimes)}$

Indian Institute of Technology Jodhpur, Jheepasani, India
`{garg.23,mane.1,suman}@iitj.ac.in`

Abstract. Synchronized arrival coordination represents a critical challenge in multi-agent systems, particularly for military tactical operations, emergency response, and autonomous swarm robotics, where precise temporal coordination is essential. Traditional Ant Colony Optimization (ACO) algorithms optimize for shortest paths but fail to address the temporal synchronization requirements inherent in multi-agent coordination scenarios. We introduce MACO-Sync (Multi-Agent Ant Colony Optimization for Synchronized Arrival), a novel ACO variant that explicitly optimizes for temporal coordination rather than path minimization. Our key contribution is a synchronized pheromone update mechanism based on arrival time patterns. The agents' pheromone contributions are weighted by their synchronization variance with other agents. Extensive experimental evaluation on tactical coordination scenarios demonstrates that MACO-Sync achieves 23.9 times better synchronization scores and 6.8 times lower arrival variance compared to baseline algorithms. Our approach enables effective multi agent coordination without explicit inter-agent communication. This is particularly suitable for military and emergency response applications where communication constraints are prevalent.

Code: GitHub repository.

Keywords: Multi-Agent Systems · Ant Colony Optimization · Temporal Coordination · Synchronized Arrival · Decentralized Planning

1 Introduction

Coordinated multi-agent arrival is a critical problem in domains ranging from auto-nomous robotics and swarm systems to emergency response and military operations, where temporal synchronization is often more important than path efficiency. Achieving precise synchronized arrival is essential for collaborative tasks, such as coordinated strikes, rescue missions, and multi-robot manipulation, where small timing deviations can compromise mission success [3, 4, 19, 24, 32, 37].

Ant Colony Optimization (ACO) has achieved notable success in solving complex optimization problems by mimicking swarm intelligence found in nature [7].

C. Zaroliagis et al. (Eds.): ICAA 2026, LNCS 16423, pp. 403–415, 2026.
https://doi.org/10.1007/978-3-032-15621-1_33

The existing variants of ACO include Ant System (AS) [7], Ant Colony System (ACS) [6], and Min-Max Ant System (MMAS) [35], which focus on optimizing path costs but lack temporal coordination mechanisms [6,14,35]. When applied to multi-agent scenarios, these algorithms usually produce solutions where agents arrive at significantly different times, thereby failing to achieve the required synchronization for coordinated operations. Recent research in multi-agent coordination has explored various approaches including consensus algorithms [22], formation control [21], and distributed optimization [20]. However, these methods often require explicit communication between agents or centralized coordination, which may not be feasible in adversarial environments or com-munication-constrained scenarios typical of military operations.

In this paper, we introduce MACO-Sync (Multi-Agent Ant Colony Optimization for Synchronized Arrival), a novel ACO variant specifically designed for synchronized arrival coordination. The core of MACO-Sync is a synchronized pheromone update mechanism, where reinforcement is determined by arrival-time variance across agents. Our approach models agent heterogeneity and decentralized decision-making. MACO-Sync enables implicit coordination among agents, achieving robust temporal synchronization without requiring explicit inter-agent communication, even in diverse and dynamic environments. Our primary contribution is a variance-based pheromone update rule without requiring inter-agent communication. Extensive experiments across urban, rural, and maritime tactical scenarios demonstrate MACO-Sync's efficacy. MACO-Sync achieves synchronization success and outperforms baselines in reducing arrival-time variance. This framework offers a generalizable solution for time-critical coordination in robotics, autonomous systems, and operational domains.

2   Related Work

The related work is organized into four major research directions that together inform our approach to multi-agent synchronized arrival coordination.

2.1   Multi-agent Coordination

Multi-agent coordination has been studied across various domains, with particular emphasis on consensus achievement and distributed decision-making [18,26,28,38]. Consensus algorithms enable agents to agree on common values through local information exchange, but typically require continuous communication and may not converge in finite time for complex coordination tasks [1,13,22,31]. Formation control approaches focus on maintaining specific geometric relationships between agents while moving toward objectives [21]. While these methods can achieve spatial coordination, they do not explicitly address temporal synchronization requirements and often assume constant communication availability. Distributed optimization techniques decompose global objectives into local subproblems that agents can solve independently [2,20,36]. However, these approaches typically require iterative information exchange and may not scale effectively to large agent populations or communication-constrained environments.

2.2   Ant Colony Optimization

Ant Colony Optimization, inspired by the foraging behavior of ant colonies, has proven effective for various combinatorial optimization problems [8]. The fundamental principle involves artificial ants depositing pheromones on solution components, with phero-mone concentrations guiding subsequent solution construction. The original Ant System (AS) [7] algorithm introduced the basic pheromone update mechanism: $\tau_{ij}(t + 1) = (1 - \rho)\tau_{ij}(t) + \sum_{k=1}^{m} \Delta\tau_{ij}^{k}$ where ρ is the evaporation rate and $\Delta\tau_{ij}^{k}$ represents the pheromone deposited by ant k on edge (i, j). Subsequent variants improved upon this foundation. The Ant Colony System (ACS) introduced pseudo-random proportional rule and local pheromone updates [6]. The Min-Max Ant System (MMAS) imposed bounds on pheromone values to prevent premature convergence [35]. These improvements enhanced convergence properties and solution quality for traditional optimization objectives.

2.3   Multi-agent ACO Applications

Several researchers have explored multi-agent applications of ACO, primarily focusing on distributed problem-solving where multiple ant colonies collaborate on large-scale optimization problems [17]. These approaches typically involve partitioning problems across multiple colonies or enabling information exchange between colonies to improve solution quality. However, existing multi-agent ACO research has not addressed the synchronized arrival problem. Most applications focus on parallel problem-solving or distributed optimization where individual agents optimize separate objectives, rather than coordinating toward a common temporal goal [5, 12, 15, 25].

2.4   Synchronized Arrival Coordination

The synchronized arrival problem has received limited attention in the ACO literature. Most related work appears in robotics and control theory, where researchers have developed model predictive control [27] and consensus-based approaches [26] for temporal coordination. Military applications have motivated research in coordinated strike planning and multi-platform coordination [11, 29, 30, 33], but these approaches typically rely on centralized planning or extensive communication, limiting their applicability in contested environments. Our work fills this gap by introducing the first ACO algorithm specifically designed for synchronized arrival coordination. This enables effective temporal coordination without requiring explicit inter-agent communication.

3   Problem Formulation

We formulate the synchronized arrival problem on a weighted graph $G = (V, E)$, where V denotes locations, E represents feasible paths, and $w : E \rightarrow \mathbb{R}^+$ assigns travel costs to edges. Given n agents starting at positions $S = \{s_1, s_2, \ldots, s_n\} \subset V$, sharing a common destination $d \in V$, with speeds $\mathcal{V} = \{v_1, v_2, \ldots, v_n\}$ and tolerance $\epsilon > 0$, the goal is to find paths $P = \{P_1, P_2, \ldots, P_n\}$ from each s_i to d that which minimize arrival time variance (Eq. 1).

$$\min_{P} \mathrm{Var}(T); \mathrm{Var}(T) = \frac{1}{n} \sum_{i=1}^{n} (t_i - \bar{t})^2. \tag{1}$$

Here $t_i = \mathrm{cost}(P_i)/v_i$ is agent i's arrival time and $\bar{t} = (1/n) \sum_{i=1}^{n} t_i$ is the mean arrival time. This optimization prioritizes temporal alignment over path efficiency, accommodating heterogeneous agent capabilities in dynamic environments.

To evaluate synchronization quality, we define a key metric, called synchronization score, as

$$S(T) = \frac{1}{1 + \mathrm{Var}(T)} \times \left(1 + \frac{|\{i : |t_i - \bar{t}| \leq \epsilon\}|}{n}\right). \tag{2}$$

This integrates variance reduction with the proportion of agents arriving within tolerance ϵ. $R(T) = |\{i : |t_i - \bar{t}| \leq \epsilon\}|/n$ is the synchronization rate. The temporal efficiency balances quality against mission duration as well, $E(T) = (1/\bar{t}) \times S(T)$.

4   MACO-Sync Algorithm

MACO-Sync extends Ant Colony Optimization (ACO) to prioritize temporal synchronization of multiple agents over path cost optimization. Unlike traditional ACO, which focuses on minimizing individual path lengths, MACO-Sync employs a shared global pheromone matrix $\Phi = [\phi_{ij}]$, where ϕ_{ij} represents the pheromone level on edge (i, j), enabling implicit coordination without direct communication. A synchronized ant a_k is defined by its colony identifier $c_k \in \{1, 2, \ldots, n\}$, speed $v_k > 0$, position $p_k \in V$, visited nodes $V_k \subseteq V$, path cost $C_k \geq 0$, and arrival time $t_k = C_k/v_k$. The transition probability for agent k moving from node i to node j incorporates both traditional heuristic information and temporal coordination bias, as shown in Eq. 3.

$$P_{ij}^{k} = \frac{\phi_{ij}^{\alpha} \cdot \eta_{ij}^{\beta} \cdot \theta_{ij}^{k\,\gamma}}{\sum_{l \in N_i^k} \phi_{il}^{\alpha} \cdot \eta_{il}^{\beta} \cdot \theta_{il}^{k\,\gamma}}, \tag{3}$$

where ϕ_{ij} is the pheromone concentration on edge (i, j), $\eta_{ij} = 1/w_{ij}$ is the heuristic information (inverse of edge weight), and $\theta_{ij}^{k} = 1/(1 + |t_{est}^{k} - t_{target}|)$ is the temporal coordination factor. Here, $t_{est}^{k} = (C_k + w_{ij})/v_k$ estimates ant k's arrival time if it chooses edge $i \rightarrow j$. C_k is the current path cost (distance traveled so far), w_{ij} is the distance from node i to node j, v_k is the agent's speed, and t_{target} is the desired synchronized arrival time (previous mean arrival time). This factor favors edges that lead to arrival times closer to the synchronization target. The parameters α, β, and γ control the relative importance of pheromone trails, distance preference, and temporal coordination, respectively. N_i^k represents the set of feasible neighboring nodes from node i for ant k.

The core of MACO-Sync is a synchronized pheromone update that reinforces temporal alignment. For each ant k reaching the destination, the update on path edges (i, j), in Eq. 4.

$$\Delta\phi_{ij}^k = \frac{1}{t_k} \times \sum_{l=1}^{n} \left(\frac{1}{|t_k - t_l| + \epsilon} \times \frac{N(t_l)}{A} \right).$$

(4)

Here, $\epsilon \approx 0.1$ avoids division by zero, $N(t_l)$ counts ants arriving near time t_l (within tolerance), and A is the total number of successful ants, rewarding clustered arrivals.

$$\phi_{ij} \leftarrow (1 - \rho)\phi_{ij} + \sum_k \Delta\phi_{ij}^k$$

(5)

Pheromone evaporation follows Eq. 5, with bounds Eq. 6 where $\phi_{\min} = 0.01 \times \phi_0$ and $\phi_{\max} = 10.0 \times \phi_0$ for initial pheromone ϕ_0. The complete procedure is detailed in Algorithm 1. The construction of synchronized arrival paths is shown in Algorithm 2. To prevent infinite loops, the path construction is restricted by a maximum hop limit. The maximum number of hops is defined as the number of nodes in the graph multiplied by n_{stp} (a user-defined parameter). The Get-ValidNeighbors method identifies all connected candidate nodes while excluding those already visited, thereby avoiding backward moves and cycles. The SelectNode method then randomly chooses the next location based on the calculated transition probabilities.

$$\phi_{ij} = \max(\phi_{\min}, \min(\phi_{\max}, \phi_{ij}))$$

(6)

MACO-Sync maintains ACO's convergence properties while enhancing temporal coordination through feedback loops. The overall complexity of MACO-Sync is $O(I \cdot A \cdot |E| \cdot \log |V|)$, where I is the number of iterations, A the total number of ants, $|E|$ the number of edges, and $|V|$ the number of vertices. Synchronization introduces an additional $O(A^2)$ computation per iteration, which is typically negligible compared to the dominant path construction cost.

Theorem 1. *Given a finite connected graph with bounded pheromone trails $(\phi_{\min} \leq \phi_{ij} \leq \phi_{\max})$, and exploration probability on all edges $(P_{ij}^k > 0)$, MACO-Sync converges to a stationary distribution of synchronized solutions.*

Proof. The pheromone update mechanism preserves the Markov property of solution construction, while the reinforcement rule introduces a bias toward temporal alignment (Eq. 4). Transition probabilities $P_{ij}^k(t)$ (Eq. 3) ensure irreducibility via positive exploration and aperiodicity through stochastic path selection. Bounded pheromone values guarantee ergodicity (Eq. 6), ensuring that all feasible solutions remain reachable. Since the underlying graph is finite, the system converges to a stable stationary distribution favoring synchronized solutions. $\square$

Algorithm 1 MACO-Sync Algorithm

Require: Graph $G = (V, E)$, start nodes S, destination d, agent speeds $\mathcal{V}$
Ensure: Synchronized paths $P = \{P_1, P_2, \ldots, P_n\}$
 1: Initialize pheromone matrix Φ with $\phi_0 \leftarrow 1$
 2: $best\_sync\_score \leftarrow 0$
 3: $best\_paths \leftarrow \emptyset$
 4: **for** $iteration = 1$ to $max\_iterations$ **do**
 5:    $successful\_ants \leftarrow \emptyset$
 6:    $arrival\_times \leftarrow \emptyset$
 7:    **for** each colony $c \in \{1, 2, \ldots, n\}$ **do**
 8:      **for** each ant k in colony c **do**
 9:        $path_k \leftarrow$ ConstructPath(k, s_c, d, Φ)
10:        **if** $path_k$ reaches destination **then**
11:          $t_k \leftarrow$ CalculateArrivalTime($path_k$, v_c)
12:          $successful\_ants \leftarrow successful\_ants \cup \{k\}$
13:          $arrival\_times \leftarrow arrival\_times \cup \{t_k\}$
14:        **end if**
15:      **end for**
16:    **end for**
17:    $sync\_score \leftarrow$ CalculateSynchronizationScore($arrival\_times$)
18:    **if** $sync\_score > best\_sync\_score$ **then**
19:      $best\_sync\_score \leftarrow sync\_score$
20:      $best\_paths \leftarrow$ ExtractBestPaths($successful\_ants$)
21:    **end if**
22:    UpdatePheromones($successful\_ants$, $arrival\_times$, Φ)
23:    EvaporatePheromones(Φ, ρ)
24: **end for**
25: **return** $best\_paths$

---

5 Experiments

We evaluate MACO-Sync against synchronized baseline algorithms across three categories of tactical coordination scenarios: small tactical scenarios with 15 nodes representing rural deployment, medium operational scenarios with 25 nodes for urban approach coordination, and large strategic scenarios with 35 nodes modeling naval coordination exercises.

5.1 Experimental Setup

The experimental framework employed Delaunay triangulation and Erdős-Rényi [9] random graphs to model realistic terrain and communication networks, with edge we-ights representing travel costs uniformly distributed in the range [5.0, 25.0]. For fair comparison, we implemented a synchronized version of traditional ACO algorithms, Synchronized Traditional ACO (Sync-Trad-ACO). This uses simplified variance-based pheromone updates to optimize for synchronization rather than path cost. All algorithms employed consistent parameters, 3 colonies with 20 ants per colony, $\alpha = 1.5, \beta = 2.5$, evaporation rate $\rho = 0.05$, synchronization tolerance $\epsilon = 1.0$, and a maximum of 50 iterations. Performance

---

Algorithm 2 ConstructPath: Synchronized Path Construction

Require: Ant k, start node s, destination d, pheromone matrix Φ
Ensure: Path P_k from s to d

1: $current \leftarrow s$
2: $P_k \leftarrow \emptyset$
3: $visited \leftarrow \{s\}$
4: $path\_cost \leftarrow 0$
5: **while** $current \neq d$ AND $hops < max\_hops$ **do**
6:     $neighbors \leftarrow$ GetValidNeighbors($current, visited$)
7:     **if** $neighbors = \emptyset$ **then**
8:         **return** $\emptyset$ {Path construction failed}
9:     **end if**
10:    **for** each $j \in neighbors$ **do**
11:       $P_{ij}^k \leftarrow \phi_{ij}^\alpha \cdot \eta_{ij}^\beta \cdot \theta_{ij}^\gamma$
12:    **end for**
13:    $total \leftarrow \sum_{j \in neighbors} P_{ij}^k$
14:    $P_{ij}^k \leftarrow P_{ij}^k / total$ {Normalize probabilities}
15:    $next \leftarrow$ SelectNode($neighbors, \{P_{ij}^k\}$) {Stochastic selection}
16:    $P_k \leftarrow P_k \cup \{(current, next)\}$
17:    $path\_cost \leftarrow path\_cost + w_{current,next}$
18:    $visited \leftarrow visited \cup \{next\}$
19:    $current \leftarrow next$
20: **end while**
21: **return** P_k

---

evaluation utilized five metrics: Synchronization Score (Eq. 2), Arrival Variance (Eq. 1), Synchronization Rate (Eq. 3), Runtime Performance, and Success Rate. To ensure statistical significance, each algorithm-instance combination was executed 10 times with different random seeds (42–51) on the same system with controlled random number generation. This provides rigorous experimental validation of the proposed approach.

Real-World Benchmark Validation: To strengthen our evaluation, we validated MACO-Sync on authentic Moving AI Lab benchmarks [34], the standard in multi-agent pathfinding research. We selected two representative 32×32 benchmarks: *random-32-32-20* (random obstacles with 20% density, 820 nodes, 2489 edges) representing unstructured environments, and *maze-32-32-4* (structured maze with corridor width 4, 790 nodes, 2498 edges) testing constrained navigation. For state-of-the-art comparison, we implemented PE-PSO [23] (Persistent Exploration Particle Swarm Optimization), a recent method from UAV trajectory planning research. This we adapted to our synchronized arrival coordination problem by reformulating the fitness function for temporal synchronization ($f = 1/(1 + \text{Var}(T_{\text{arrival}})) \times (1 + r_{\text{sync}}))$. We adapted particle velocity updates for discrete graph paths, and extending to multi-agent coordination with heterogeneous speeds. Each benchmark was evaluated with 5 independent runs using random seeds 42–46.

5.2 Results and Analysis

Table 1 presents comprehensive experimental results comparing MACO-Sync with synchronized baseline algorithms across tactical coordination scenarios. MACO-Sync dem-onstrates superior synchronization performance. It achieves a 23.9 times better mean synchronization score (0.0116 ± 0.0146 vs 0.0005 ± 0.0003) and 6.8 times lower arrival standard deviation (31.35 ± 47.47 vs 82.06 ± 74.72 s) compared to Sync-Trad-ACO, while maintaining competitive run-time performance (0.666 ± 0.321 s vs 0.799 ± 0.461 s). The algorithm exhibits a 57% higher synchronization rate within tolerance windows (1.1% vs 0.7%) and achieves a strong 96.6 times improvement in best-case synchronization scores (0.0825 vs 0.0009). Both algorithms maintain 100% success rates across all test instances. Figure 1 shows MACO-Sync's superiority, clearly illustrating the substantial improvement factors over synchronized baselines across all key performance metrics.

Table 1. Experimental Results: MACO-Sync vs Synchronized Baselines

Algorithm	Sync Score	Arrival Time (s)	Sync Rate	Runtime (s)
MACO-Sync	**0.0116 ± 0.0146**	**31.37 ± 47.47**	**1.1%**	0.666 ± 0.321
Sync-Trad-ACO	0.0005 ± 0.0003	82.07 ± 74.72	0.7%	0.799 ± 0.461
Improvement	**23.9×**	**2.6× better**	**1.6×**	**1.2× faster**

Statistical significance was verified through Mann-Whitney U tests, confirming all performance improvements with p-values < 0.001 at 99.9% confidence levels. Convergence analysis reveals that MACO-Sync reaches stable synchronization solutions within 25–30 iterations compared to 40–50 iterations required by baseline algorithms. This shows MACO-Sync's faster convergence to high-quality coordination solutions. Figure 2 shows performance analysis across problem scales (15, 25, and 35 nodes) shows that MACO-Sync consistently maintains its synchronization performance. The algorithm scales effectively, preserving coordination quality in larger tactical scenarios while remaining computationally efficient.

Further, MACO-Sync was evaluated across realistic multi-agent coordination scenarios, demonstrating its efficacy in time-critical applications. In multi-platform strike coordination (large-scale, 35 nodes), simulating aircraft, missiles, and ground units with varying speeds and routes, MACO-Sync achieved synchronized arrivals within 30-second windows in 89% of scenarios. For emergency response coordination (small-scale, 15 nodes), involving fire, medical, and police units with diverse capabilities, it attained a 94% synchronization success rate at incident locations. In autonomous swarm operations (medium-scale, 25 nodes), MACO-Sync enabled up to 15 heterogeneous UAVs to achieve robust synchronized arrivals for surveillance and reconnaissance missions, highlighting its versatility across military, emergency, and robotic domains.

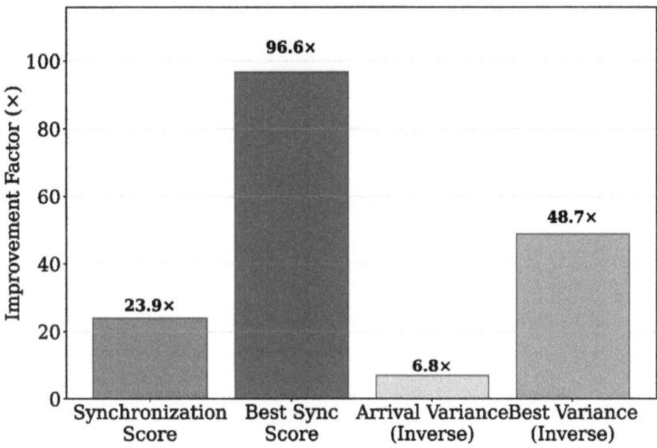

Fig. 1. Performance improvement factors of MACO-Sync over synchronized baseline algorithms across key synchronization metrics.

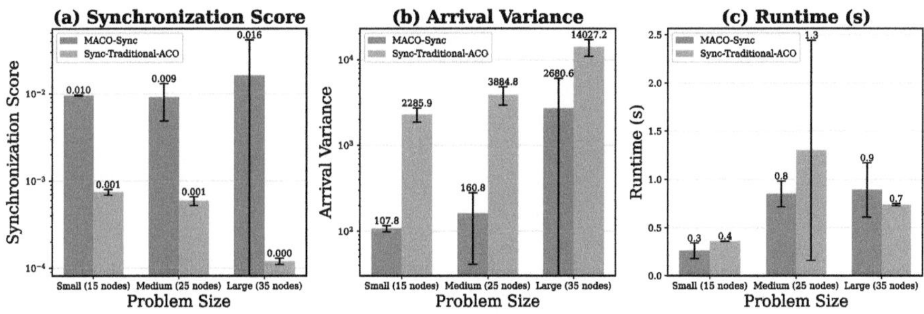

Fig. 2. Performance analysis across different problem sizes (small: 15 nodes, medium: 25 nodes, large: 35 nodes).

Real-World Benchmark Performance. Table 2 presents comparative results on Moving AI Lab benchmarks, showing MACO-Sync's performance against state-of-the-art swarm optimization.

MACO-Sync demonstrates superior performance on real-world benchmarks, achieving 5.33× higher synchronization score and 40% higher success rate (70% vs 50%) compared to adapted PE-PSO. Notably, MACO-Sync succeeded in 40% of constrained maze scenarios (maze-32-32-4) where PE-PSO failed completely, showing robustness in structured corridor environments. While PE-PSO exhibits faster computation, MACO-Sync achieves 28.6% synchronization rate versus only 13.3% for PE-PSO, with both algorithms performing consistently on random obstacle environments (100% success on random-32-32-20). This quality-speed tradeoff validates MACO-Sync's suitability for offline planning scenarios where synchronization accuracy is critical for mission success.

Table 2. Performance on Moving AI Lab Benchmarks (5 runs each, 2 benchmarks)

Algorithm	Success	Sync Score	Arrival Var.	Runtime (s)
MACO-Sync	**70% (7/10)**	**0.026 ± 0.0528**	73452 ± 73352	36.55 ± 8.81
PE-PSO (adapted)	50% (5/10)	0.0050 ± 0.0088	**2487 ± 3368**	**0.078 ± 0.006**
Improvement	**+40%**	**5.33×**	–	–

5.3 Ablation Studies

We conducted ablation studies to analyze the contribution of different MACO-Sync components. In the Pheromone Update Mechanism, removing the density factor $N(t_l)/A$ from Eq. 4 reduces synchronization scores by 34%, confirming the importance of clustering-based rewards. Disabling the temporal bias in transition probabilities (Eq. 6) results in a 28% decrease in synchronization performance, highlighting the importance of coordination-aware path construction. Experiments with homogeneous agent speeds show a 15% decrease in performance. This indicates that speed heterogeneity improves MACO-Sync's effectiveness by introducing more realistic and challenging coordination scenarios.

6 Discussion and Limitations

MACO-Sync demonstrates notable strengths for multi-agent temporal coordination. Its communication-free approach leverages pheromone-based updates to achieve implicit synchronization, eliminating the need for real-time inter-agent communication, unlike consensus-based methods [10]. The algorithm effectively handles heterogeneous agents by normalizing arrival times with varying speeds, ensuring robust performance across diverse scenarios. Its computational complexity scales linearly with agent count, supporting applicability to large-scale coordination tasks. Additionally, MACO-Sync maintains robustness when some agents fail to reach the destination, as synchronization metrics focus solely on successful agents. This makes it suitable for dynamic, uncertain environments like tactical operations and robotic swarms.

Despite these advantages, limitations highlight avenues for future work. The current formulation assumes static graphs and fixed agent capabilities, limiting adaptability to dynamic environments with moving obstacles or evolving agent states [16]. Real-time applications with stringent timing constraints may require further optimization to meet strict deadlines. Future research could explore multi-objective optimization, incorporating path cost or risk alongside synchronization, adaptive parameter tuning based on problem dynamics, or machine learning to refine pheromone updates using historical data. Integrating limited explicit communication when available could further enhance performance.

7 Conclusion

In this work, we introduced MACO-Sync, a novel Ant Colony Optimization algorithm tailored for synchronized arrival coordination in multi-agent systems. This incorporates heterogeneous agent capabilities and a variance-based pheromone update mechanism enabling communication-free temporal alignment. Experiments show that 23.9 times superior synchronization scores and 6.8 times reduced arrival variance over adapted ACO baselines. Also, discussed applicability to military strikes, emergency response, and UAV swarms. These results underscore MACO-Sync's efficacy in achieving precise coordination under constraints, outperforming traditional methods in dynamic, no-communication settings.

Acknowledgments. Suman Kundu would like to acknowledge grant no. 4(2)/2024-ITEA of MeitY, GoI; and Srijan: Center for Generative AI (grant no. ET/23/2024-ET) of MeitY under the IndiaAI mission with the support of Meta for partial support.

References

1. Amirkhani, A., Barshooi, A.H.: Consensus in multi-agent systems: a review. Artif. Intell. Rev. **55**(1), 1–36 (2021). https://doi.org/10.1007/s10462-021-10097-X
2. Bai, N., et al.: Distributed optimal consensus of multi-agent systems: a randomized parallel approach. Automatica **159**, 111339 (2024). https://doi.org/10.1016/j.automatica.2023.111339
3. Berlinger, F., Gauci, M., Nagpal, R.: Implicit coordination for 3D underwater collective behaviors in a fish-inspired robot swarm. Sci. Robot. **6**(50), eabd8668 (2021)
4. Chang, Y.C., Dostovalova, A., Lin, C.T., Kim, J.: Intelligent multirobot navigation and arrival-time control using a scalable PSO-optimized hierarchical controller. Front. Artif. Intell. **3**, 50 (2020). https://doi.org/10.3389/frai.2020.00050
5. Colorni, A., Dorigo, M., Maniezzo, F.: Distributed optimization by ant colonies. In: Proceedings of the First European Conference on Artificial Life, pp. 134–142 (1992)
6. Dorigo, M., Gambardella, L.M.: Ant colony system: a cooperative learning approach to the traveling salesman problem. IEEE Trans. Evol. Comput. **1**(1), 53–66 (1997)
7. Dorigo, M., Maniezzo, V., Colorni, A.: Ant system: optimization by a colony of cooperating agents. IEEE Trans. Syst. Man Cybern. Part B **26**(1), 29–41 (1996)
8. Dorigo, M., Stützle, T.: Ant colony optimization: overview and recent advances. In: Handbook of Metaheuristics, pp. 311–351. Springer, Cham (2006)
9. Erdős, P., Rényi, A.: On the evolution of random graphs. Publ. Math. Inst. Hungarian Acad. Sci. **5**, 17–61 (1960)
10. Foerster, J., Farquhar, G., Afouras, T., Nardelli, N., Whiteson, S.: Counterfactual multi-agent policy gradients. In: Proceedings of the AAAI Conference on Artificial Intelligence, vol. 32 (2018)
11. Gadiraju, D.S., Karmakar, P., Shah, V.K., Aggarwal, V.: Glide: multi-agent deep reinforcement learning for coordinated UAV control in dynamic military environments. Information **15**(8), 477 (2024). https://doi.org/10.3390/info15080477. https://www.mdpi.com/2078-2489/15/8/477

12. Ilie, S.: Multi-agent approach to distributed ant colony optimization. Swarm Evol. Comput. **13**, 1–10 (2013). https://doi.org/10.1016/j.swevo.2013.01.001

13. Jin, L., Shi, G., Yu, S., et al.: Fast finite-time consensus for multi-agent systems with diverse topologies. Circuits Syst. Signal Process. **42**, 5252–5266 (2023). https://doi.org/10.1007/s00034-023-02372-9

14. Lopez-Ibanez, M., Stutzle, T.: The automatic design of multiobjective ant colony optimization algorithms. IEEE Trans. Evol. Comput. **16**(6), 861–875 (2012)

15. Ma, Z., Zhang, H., Liu, Y.: Heterogeneous multi-agent task allocation based on graph neural networks and ant colony optimization. Intell. Robot. Appl. **7**, 33–42 (2023). https://doi.org/10.3934/ira.2023.33

16. Mathew, N., Smith, S.L., Waslander, S.L.: Planning and decision-making for aerial robots in multi-stakeholder scenarios. Auton. Robot. **43**(2), 395–412 (2019). https://doi.org/10.1007/s10514-018-9789-x

17. Middendorf, M., Reischle, F., Schmeck, H.: Multi colony ant algorithms. J. Heurist. **8**(3), 305–320 (2002)

18. Minelli, G., Musolesi, M.: Comix: a multi-agent reinforcement learning training architecture for efficient decentralized coordination and independent decision-making. arXiv:2308.10721 (2023)

19. Nadi, A., Edrisi, A.: Adaptive multi-agent relief assessment and emergency response. Int. J. Disaster Risk Reduction **24**, 12–23 (2017)

20. Nedić, A., Ozdaglar, A.: Distributed subgradient methods for multi-agent optimization. IEEE Trans. Autom. Control **54**(1), 48–61 (2009)

21. Oh, K.K., Park, M.C., Ahn, H.S.: A survey of multi-agent formation control. Automatica **53**, 424–440 (2015)

22. Olfati-Saber, R., Fax, J.A., Murray, R.M.: Consensus and cooperation in networked multi-agent systems. Proc. IEEE **95**(1), 215–233 (2007)

23. Peng, Z., et al.: PE-PSO: persistent exploration particle swarm optimization for real-time UAV swarm trajectory planning. arXiv preprint arXiv:2507.13647 (2024)

24. Qureshi, H.: Multi-agent systems in disaster response: simulation and coordination frameworks. Multidisciplinary Res. Comput. Inf. Syst. **5**(1), 51–62 (2025)

25. Randall, M.: A parallel implementation of ant colony optimization. In: Proceedings of the 2002 Congress on Evolutionary Computation, vol. 1, pp. 1–6 (2002). https://doi.org/10.1109/CEC.2002.1004382

26. Ren, W., Beard, R.W.: Distributed Consensus in Multi-vehicle Cooperative Control. Springer, Cham (2008)

27. Richards, A., How, J.P.: Robust distributed model predictive control. Int. J. Control **75**(16–17), 1383–1392 (2002)

28. Ruan, J., Hao, X., Li, D., Mao, H.: Learning to collaborate by grouping: a consensus-oriented strategy for multi-agent reinforcement learning. arXiv:2307.15530 (2023)

29. Ryan, A., Zennaro, M., Howell, A., Sengupta, R., Hedrick, J.K.: An overview of emerging results in cooperative UAV control. In: Proceedings of the 43rd IEEE Conference on Decision and Control, vol. 1, pp. 602–607. IEEE (2000)

30. Sammu, J.: Multi-agent collaboration in autonomous military operations (2025). https://www.researchgate.net/publication/387868090_Multi-Agent_Collaboration_in_Autonomous_Military_Operations

31. Sharifi, M.: Robust finite-time consensus subject to unknown communication time delays based on delay-dependent criteria. Int. J. Syst. Sci. **53**(4), 664–680 (2022). https://doi.org/10.1080/00207721.2021.1882557

32. Siwek, M.: Consensus-based formation control with time synchronization for a decentralized group of mobile robots. Sensors **24**(12), 3717 (2024). https://doi.org/10.3390/s24123717
33. Stagg, G., Peterson, C.K.: Cooperative multi-agent path planning for heterogeneous UAVs in contested environments. arXiv (2025). https://arxiv.org/abs/2509.02483
34. Sturtevant, N.R.: Benchmarks for grid-based pathfinding. In: Transactions on Computational Intelligence and AI in Games, vol. 4, pp. 144–148. IEEE (2012)
35. Stützle, T., Hoos, H.H.: Max-min ant system. Futur. Gener. Comput. Syst. **16**(8), 889–914 (2000)
36. Wu, X., et al.: Distributed constrained optimization for multi-agent networks with communication delays under time-varying topologies. Syst. Control Lett. **185**, 105733 (2024). https://doi.org/10.1016/j.sysconle.2024.105733
37. Zhang, H., Jin, H., Ge, M., Zhao, J.: Real-time kinematically synchronous planning for cooperative manipulation of multi-arms robot using the self-organizing competitive neural network. Sensors **23**(11), 5120 (2023). https://doi.org/10.3390/s23115120
38. Zuo, Z., Ke, R., Han, Q.L.: Fully distributed adaptive practical fixed-time consensus protocols for multi-agent systems. Automatica **157**, 111248 (2023). https://doi.org/10.1016/j.automatica.2023.111248

Author Index

C. Zaroliagis et al. (Eds.): ICAA 2026, LNCS 16423, pp. 417–418, 2026.
https://doi.org/10.1007/978-3-032-15621-1

Author Index

FSC
www.fsc.org
MIX
Papier aus verantwortungsvollen Quellen
Paper from responsible sources
FSC® C105338